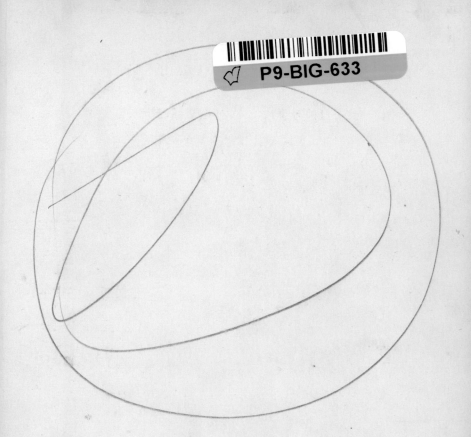
P9-BIG-633

A HISTORY OF
MARRIAGE AND THE FAMILY

TEXT-BOOK SERIES

EDITED BY PAUL MONROE, PH.D.

TEXT-BOOK IN THE HISTORY OF EDUCATION.
By PAUL MONROE, PH.D., Professor of History of Education, Teachers College, Columbia University.

SOURCE BOOK IN THE HISTORY OF EDUCATION.
FOR THE GREEK AND ROMAN PERIOD
By PAUL MONROE, PH.D.

PRINCIPLES OF SECONDARY EDUCATION.
By PAUL MONROE, PH.D.

TEXT-BOOK IN THE PRINCIPLES OF EDUCATION.
By ERNEST R. HENDERSON, PH.D., Professor of Education and Philosophy, Adelphi College.

DEMOCRACY AND EDUCATION. An INTRODUCTION TO THE PHILOSOPHY OF EDUCATION.
By JOHN DEWEY, PH.D., Professor of Philosophy, Columbia University.

STATE AND COUNTY SCHOOL ADMINISTRATION.
SOURCE BOOK
By ELLWOOD P. CUBBERLEY, PH.D., Professor of Education, Stanford University, and EDWARD C. ELLIOTT, PH.D., Professor of Education, University of Wisconsin.

STATE AND COUNTY EDUCATIONAL REORGANIZATION.
By ELLWOOD P. CUBBERLEY, PH.D.

THE PRINCIPLES OF SCIENCE TEACHING.
By GEORGE R. TWISS, B.Sc., Professor of the Principles and Practice of Education, Ohio State University.

THE PRUSSIAN ELEMENTARY SCHOOLS.
By THOMAS ALEXANDER, PH.D., Professor of Elementary Education, George Peabody College for Teachers.

HOW TO MEASURE IN EDUCATION.
By WILLIAM A. MCCALL, PH.D., Assistant Professor of Education, Teachers College, Columbia University.

A HISTORY OF MARRIAGE AND THE FAMILY, REV. ED.
By WILLYSTINE GOODSELL, PH.D., Associate Professor of Education, Teachers College, Columbia University.

THE HISTORY OF THE EDUCATION OF WOMEN.
By WILLYSTINE GOODSELL, PH.D.

STATISTICAL METHOD.
By TRUMAN L. KELLEY, PH.D., Professor of Education, Stanford University.

FOUNDATIONS OF EDUCATIONAL SOCIOLOGY, REV. ED.
By CHARLES C. PETERS, PH.D., Professor of Education in Ohio Wesleyan University.

SOURCE BOOK IN THE PHILOSOPHY OF EDUCATION, REV. ED.
By WILLIAM H. KILPATRICK, PH.D., Professor of Education, Teachers College, Columbia University.

A History of
Marriage and the Family

BY

WILLYSTINE GOODSELL, Ph.D.

ASSOCIATE PROFESSOR OF EDUCATION, TEACHERS COLLEGE
COLUMBIA UNIVERSITY

REVISED EDITION

HQ
503
G65
1934

NEW YORK
THE MACMILLAN COMPANY
1934

MARIN JUNIOR COLLEGE
LIBRARY

Revised Edition Copyrighted, 1934,

By WILLYSTINE GOODSELL

All rights reserved — no part of this book may be
reproduced in any form without permission in writing
from the publisher, except by a reviewer who wishes
to quote brief passages in connection with a review
written for inclusion in magazine or newspaper.

Printed in the United States of America.
Set up and electrotyped. Published May, 1934.

First edition copyrighted, 1915,
By Willystine Goodsell
First edition published December, 1915.

7484

PREFACE

Since the opening of the twentieth century the interest of anthropologists, historians and sociologists has been increasingly focused upon the family as the basic institution of society. In consequence more ample light has been shed upon marriage and family customs in primitive societies, in by-gone ages and at the present time. Such enrichment of knowledge about the family makes imperative the revision of this historical study, published eighteen years ago, if it is to serve as a reliable textbook for college students.

The chapter on *The Primitive Family* has been largely revised; and substantial revisions and additions have been made in other chapters, particularly in those treating of *The Patriarchal Family among the Hebrews and Romans, The Influence of Early Christianity upon Marriage, The Mediæval Family, The Family during the Renaissance and Reformation* and *The Family in the American Colonies.* The chapter on *The Nineteenth Century Family in England and America* has been divided into two chapters treating separately the important changes in domestic relations laws and family practices in England and America up to recent times, with the addition of much new material. Finally the last two chapters of the earlier work have been eliminated and have been replaced by a chapter on *The Problems of the Twentieth Century Family*, which outlines the current maladjustments of marriage and the family to present social conditions and briefly discusses new ideas and tendencies that may point the way to more stable and satisfying family relationships in the future. A final chapter gives a sketch of the various forms of governmental and social aid that are being rendered the contemporary family in the interest of its stability and happiness.

WILLYSTINE GOODSELL

TABLE OF CONTENTS

CHAPTER I

THE PRIMITIVE FAMILY

CHAPTER II

THE PATRIARCHAL FAMILY: THE HEBREW TYPE

CHAPTER III

THE PATRIARCHAL FAMILY: THE GREEK TYPE

CHAPTER V

THE INFLUENCE OF CHRISTIANITY UPON MARRIAGE AND THE FAMILY IN THE ROMAN EMPIRE

CHAPTER VI

THE FAMILY IN THE MIDDLE AGES

CHAPTER VII

THE FAMILY DURING THE RENAISSANCE

CHAPTER VIII

THE ENGLISH FAMILY IN THE SEVENTEENTH AND EIGHTEENTH CENTURIES

CHAPTER IX

THE FAMILY IN THE AMERICAN COLONIES

CHAPTER X

THE ENGLISH FAMILY IN THE NINETEENTH AND TWENTIETH CENTURIES

CHAPTER XIII

SOCIAL AID IN FAMILY CONSERVATION

INTRODUCTION

To the student of social evolution it is a striking fact that until a generation ago the family institution had escaped critical and objective study save at the hands of anthropologists and a very few daring social writers who sought to reveal existing injustices and evils in the marriage relation. In the long course of social history well-nigh every other institution of society — the Church, government, education, the economic system — has been subjected at crucial times to a barrage of criticism and to vigorous demands for reform. But the family has remained virtually immune, alike from the attacks of discerning critics and from changes espoused by zealous reformers, until well into the nineteenth century.

Only when a revolution had taken place in the economic system, followed by a revolution in political theory, both of which reacted powerfully upon the home and its members, did the ancient institution of the family show signs of change. When machine industry had drawn women and even children into the factories to contribute to the family income, the first blows were struck at the monarchical power of the father, and ground for the long road leading to the freedom of wives and children began to be broken. When the theories of human liberty and equality were first preached in France and then transferred to the struggling English colonies across the Atlantic, few men thought of applying these doctrines to women and children. Yet the principles of democracy were destined to prove a continuously vitalizing ferment in the human mind, the applications of which are not yet clearly seen.

When men became politically free and an equalizing of intellectual opportunities was furnished them through popular education, then came the turn of daughters and wives. Endowed with leisure as the gift of machine industry, the majority of women had time for intellectual development for the first time in cultural history. Then commenced the establishment of higher schools and colleges for women, first in America, somewhat later in England; and with the advanced education of women began their individualization. More clearly than ever before women began to perceive the restrictions laid upon their activities and personal development, especially after marriage. With this perception went a broadening appreciation of the varied interests and opportunities open to the educated woman in a dynamic and diversified world. Marriage and family life, as conceived in the nineteenth century, appeared to some individualized women as a trap baited with certain emotional satisfactions; and restless discontent with old-fashioned marriage became increasingly general. Such an outcome of the higher education of women could hardly have been avoided. Only by the firm refusal of sound education to daughters could wives have been contentedly held to the restricted interests and loyalties of nineteenth century family life.

Thus the industrial revolution, the wide extension of democratic principles and the intellectual education of women, in transforming society have transformed the family. From an institution taken for granted, whose stability was never remotely questioned, it has become, perhaps, the most unsettled of all social organizations. Far from being taken for granted, the family is at present studied, analyzed, diagnosed and prescribed for by social investigators with an interest and concern in sharp contrast to the matter-of-fact indifference of preceding periods.

Moreover the puissant *tabu* which Christian culture has laid upon all objective investigation and discussion of sex relations has been rapidly breaking down under the impact of scientific knowledge and method. During the twentieth century the spread of the scientific attitude of mind has proceeded apace and is largely responsible for the increased willingness of intel-

ligent people to view sex, marriage and family life with a degree
of frankness and impartial detachment unheard of a generation
ago. Obviously such a change in the popular mind was an
essential preliminary to any serious study of the historical
development and contemporary maladjustment of the family,
in institutions of higher education. At present more and more
universities and colleges are acquainting students with the
basic facts concerning family evolution and contemporary
difficulties in family adaptation; and there is ample reason to
believe that American youth just reaching maturity will approach these problems with better-informed minds and greater
intellectual honesty than did their Victorian parents and
grand-parents.

At a time when the family, with whose interests those of
every human being are more or less entwined, is clearly out of
joint, a detached and impartial study of this basic institution
should prove timely and helpful to all students, but perhaps
especially to trained social workers and investigators, to teachers, to economists and sociologists and to directors and assistants in nursery schools. Such a study should reveal the
supreme importance, in the past, of the family as the nursery
and school of the young and as the soil in which the germs of
a spiritual and enduring love between the sexes were brought
to fruition. The great services of the family in training children to adjust themselves to society and to carry on the culture
of their age; its contributions to the regulation of crude sex
impulse; to the development of public law out of private or
family law; and to the maintenance of industry and religion
should be made plain. Contemporary customs and ideas concerning sex, marriage, the position of women and family relationships may be illuminated by such study; and students
may be led to develop that "historical sense" respecting the
family — its genesis and development — which seems indispensable in any intelligent attempt to bring about beneficent
changes in marriage and family life.

Although the family is passing through an era of crucial

social change, it seems not unreasonable to believe that it will eventually emerge an altered but likewise a strengthened and humanized institution, far better adapted to promote the happiness and to secure the unfettered personal development of its members than ever it was in former times. In the past the family secured unity and strength through the power of the father and at the expense of mothers and children; in the future such unity as it has must rest upon the affection and spontaneous loyalty of the free individuals who compose it.

A HISTORY OF
MARRIAGE AND THE FAMILY

A HISTORY OF MARRIAGE
AND THE FAMILY

CHAPTER I

THE PRIMITIVE FAMILY

Definition of Terms. — At the outset of this work it becomes necessary to define the significance attached to the terms "primitive" and "family," since these have developed more than one meaning in the current usage of social writers. The word "primitive" may have reference (1) to an absolutely original state of society, or (2) it may be applied to such savage or barbarian groups as exist at the present time. In this work the term will be commonly used in the second sense. Likewise the term "family" may refer to the social unit of Western nations, comprising usually father, mother and offspring; or it may be applied, as it frequently is by anthropologists, to a much larger group tracing descent to some real or mythical ancestor and organized into clans or living in village communities. Examples of such so-called "families" are furnished by the "gens" of the Greeks and Romans and the clan of the American Indians. Even today the village communities among the Slavs are kinship groups and hence "families" in this sense of the term. In these villages several households of relatives live under one roof and work together in organized fashion on the farm, which is common property. Likewise all the group possessions are held in common. In the present study, however, the term "family" will be commonly employed in its more familiar usage to indicate the basic family of two generations — parents and children. Frequent reference, however, will be made to the clan, gens and village kinship group, called by a German writer the *Grossefamilie* (Great family).

Available Material for the Study of the Primitive Family. — If the term "primitive" is defined strictly to mean the *original* human family, the difficulties in the way of the student are very real. It is well-nigh impossible to collect reliable evidence concerning the earliest forms of family life, since that evidence is largely lacking. Such descriptive material as we have refers to the marriage customs of peoples who have already proceeded some distance along the path of civilization. This material includes (1) references to uncivilized peoples in ancient writings, *e.g.*, in Herodotus and Strabo; (2) travelers' accounts of family organization among present-day savages; (3) the reports of trained investigators concerning marriage and the family among primitive groups selected for special study; (4) analogies drawn from the life of the higher animals, especially the man-like apes. It is hardly necessary to point out that all of these sources of knowledge, except the accounts of men of scientific training, should be used with caution. Ancient writers and modern travelers may easily fail either to observe fully and exactly or to interpret accurately such family customs and sex relations as they do observe. Hence it is quite possible for social writers, using much the same material, to form widely variant theories on many questions concerning the family as an institution. This is illustrated by the conflicting views of sociologists with respect to the original form of marriage and family life.

THE SIGNIFICANCE AND ORIGIN OF MARRIAGE

Meaning of the Term " Marriage." — It is probable that most anthropologists and social writers are in agreement concerning the biological meaning of marriage. The word has reference to a union of the male and female which does not cease with the act of procreation but persists after the birth of offspring until the young are capable of supplying their own essential needs. If this view be accepted, it becomes clear at once that marriage exists among birds and some of the higher animals. Indeed, birds furnish an excellent example of parental care and affection. Together the male and female share the work of nest-building; and later, while the mother sits on the eggs, the father furnishes food and protection. After the young are hatched, both share the tasks of food getting and of teaching the fledglings to care for themselves. Apparently monogamic marriage, ending only with life, is not uncommon among birds. This is by no means the case with the higher mammals, however. Among these animals the female assumes most of the care and protection of her offspring and is even called upon at times to defend them against the attacks of the father. But the evidence of travelers shows that among the manlike apes — the orang-utan, the gorilla and the chimpanzee — the male regularly builds a nest in a forked tree for the pregnant female and remains on guard to defend her. He also assists in the care of the young and constitutes himself their defender. Such facts make it impossible to restrict marriage, in the sense in which it is defined above, solely to human beings.

The Probable Origin of Marriage. — The previous discussion has perhaps shed some light on the question of the origin of marriage. It seems clear enough that the sexual instinct of itself could not have brought about permanent relationships between male and female. So fluctuating a desire could hardly have constituted a firm basis for family life among animals and among the cave-men, who were our original ancestors. Let it be remembered that aboriginal man in all probability had no glimmering conception of that ideal love which today binds men and women together in the strongest of human ties. Nor was the female's need of protection a lasting bond of union; for the female savage, like the female ape, is nearly as strong and capable of self-defense as the male. The source of marriage, then, must probably be looked for in the utter helplessness of the new-born offspring and the need of both mother and young for protection and food during a varying period. Natural selection doubtless operated to kill off those stocks in which the male refused this protection and care, and to "select" those for survival in which it was rendered. *Thus it appears that marriage has its source in the family, rather than the family in marriage.*[1] The full significance of this fact does not dawn upon us until we recall the marked decline of the birth rate among most modern nations and reflect that the very root of the permanent union of the sexes is found in those parental duties that today are often repudiated with more or less deliberation and wisdom.

CONFLICTING THEORIES OF THE ORIGINAL FORM OF THE FAMILY

The Theory of Promiscuity. — At the outset we should consider a theory of sex relationships that negates the original existence of marriage and the family. This view was presented in 1861 by Bachofen, a Swiss writer, in his book called *Mutterrecht* (Mother-right). In this famous work Bachofen takes the ground that aboriginal men lived in hordes like other gregarious animals and that complete promiscuity in sex relations prevailed. Children were the charges of the group as a whole. Under such a régime of unrestricted sexual intercourse fatherhood could not be determined; consequently descent was reckoned through females, who, in the course of time, became thereby influential and even powerful. This was the period of the "matriarchate" when women were the ruling forces of primitive society. After long ages there developed a form of family life based on "father love" with something of the characteristics of the present monogamous marriage. Bachofen's theory of original sex communism has been widely accepted by enthusiastic followers, and has been held in modified form by social writers of considerable prominence. The Scotchman McLennan, in his well-known work *Primitive Marriage*, and the American Morgan, in his book on

[1] See Westermarck, *The History of Human Marriage*, p. 22; and Fiske, *The Meaning of Infancy*, Riverside Educational Monographs, pp. 29, 30.

Ancient Society, both maintain that in the beginning of human history sexual intercourse was quite unrestricted and sexual unions were transitory. Each writer then develops his own theory of the stages by which more permanent sex relationships and a crude family organization have developed. The evidence to which these writers point to support their theory is as follows: (1) A few ancient authors and some modern travelers have described savages, low in the scale of civilization, as being quite promiscuous in sex relations; (2) certain savage groups at the present day have curious customs which are alleged to be survivals from a period of complete promiscuity. Such practices as "wife lending," and group marriage as it exists among certain Australian tribes today, are illustrations of these customs. Also the practice in some tribes of giving a bride over to the priest or medicine-man to be deflowered before entering her husband's home is cited by some writers as evidence of original promiscuity in sex relations. Westermarck, in his valuable work on *Human Marriage*, and Lowie, in his *Primitive Society*,[1] have sifted this evidence very carefully and conclude (1) that no case of a people living in unrestricted sexual communism can be found today; (2) that the customs which point to promiscuity admit of different and more satisfactory explanations. For example, "wife lending," as found among many savage peoples, is probably traceable to their exaggerated ideas of the duty of hospitality; and the deflowering of brides by the priest or chieftain might reasonably be regarded as conferring honor upon the marriage. Lowie finds that "group marriage," as it exists among the Dieri, the Chukchi and a few other tribes, is limited by custom and is not destructive of the individual family. The more the matter is investigated, the more questionable it becomes that primitive groups generally lived in a condition of absolute promiscuity, although great laxity in marital relations undoubtedly prevailed among them.

[1] Pp. 50–56.

The Theory of the Patriarchal Family. — In the same year that saw the publication of Bachofen's work (1861) there appeared a book by a well-known English writer, Sir Henry Maine, which set forth a wholly different theory of original sex relationships and family organization. In this work (*Ancient Law*) the author elaborated his reasons for believing that the earliest form of family life, the germ from which all later forms have developed, was the patriarchal family as exemplified in ancient Rome. The characteristics of this type of family organization are, first, its inclusiveness. All those related by descent through common male ancestors, all persons received into the family by the ceremony of adoption, and even all slaves and servants were regarded as members of the *familia*. A second characteristic of the patriarchal family is the almost absolute authority exercised by the oldest male parent as the priest of the family in its worship of ancestors. By virtue of this supremacy he was sole administrator of the family property, and held the power of life and death over his wife, children and slaves, with few limitations. Nor did this despotic authority cease with the marriage of his sons, but was extended over their wives and children as well as themselves. A third distinguishing mark of this type of family organization is *agnation*, or the kinship system which traces relationship through males only. In the view of Sir Henry Maine the system of agnation existing among certain peoples at present, combined with the authority exercised by male heads of families over women and minor children in many parts of the world today, point to a period when the patriarchal family was the universal and original type.

The weakness of this theory of the original family lies in the fact that the author has failed to take note of a mass of evidence concerning savage peoples which contradicts it at several points. Very briefly this evidence goes to show that (1) the *maternal* kinship system, which traces relationship through mothers only, is even more widely prevalent among primitive peoples than the paternal system, and traces of it may be found even among the ancient Hebrews who had developed the patriarchal family in Old Testament times; (2) the organization of the patriarchal family and its clearly defined kinship system are based upon ideas far in advance of the capacities of the primitive mind; (3) although the father among savage groups frequently exercises despotic control by reason of superior strength, this control is thrown off by his sons as soon as they are able to shift for themselves. A power grounded in brute force is hardly to be identified with the patriarchal authority of the Roman father, based as it was upon ancestor worship and exercised under more highly advanced conditions of social and industrial life than ever existed among primitive peoples. The conclusion reached by most contemporary social writers is that the patriarchal family, far from being the original social unit, is a comparatively recent development in the long history of family organization.

The Theory of Original Pair Marriage. — There remains to be considered the view of a small number of social investigators. This theory holds that the original form of sexual union was pair marriage — the union of one man and one woman for a period more or less transitory. The researches of Tylor, Starcke, Westermarck and others all tend to support this view, which, however, is by no means conclusively established. The arguments in its favor may be briefly summarized. First, pair marriage is occasionally found among beasts of prey, while among the manlike apes it is the more usual form. This simple family, consisting of parents and offspring, seems to be the outcome of animal experience in the intense struggle for food. It is probable that a small group can more readily obtain sustenance, where supplies are not abundant, than a numerous herd. Moreover, coöperation in food getting would be far more likely to occur within a group bound together by familiar association and by the needs of helpless young than in an irresponsible horde. That such coöperation does exist among animal families has been abundantly demonstrated. Secondly, the feeling of jealousy seems too strongly rooted in the natures of men and beasts alike to make the theory of absolute promiscuity at all probable. Such a passion would tend to produce a modified form of monogamic family, even though such unions were probably transitory in character. Thirdly, polygyny and polyandry, forms of marriage held by some writers to precede monogamy, seem to be the outcome of a more advanced social and industrial organization than primitive man could have developed. For example, there is a close connection between polygyny and the division of society into classes based on wealth or military prestige. Plurality of wives very generally adds to the prestige of the leading men in savage or barbarous tribes. Furthermore, for the majority of mankind pair marriage must, perforce, have been the only form of union at all possible, owing to the fact that in most countries the male and female birth rate is nearly equal. Finally, Westermarck attempts to show that in cases where pair marriage does not now prevail there are evidences that it once did exist and has been superseded by a laxer form of marriage.

Westermarck's theory that pair marriage was the original and probably universal form has been vigorously attacked by Briffault [1] in recent years. This widely read writer holds that in the so-called "nascent family" monogamy was uncommon and polygyny was general. It was only when economic production was transferred to men, upon the development of higher agriculture, that monogamy arose and came to prevail. Briffault holds that when women, the earliest and most important producers, lost their economic power, their sexual value as wives and mothers alone remained. Monogamy then became the established form of marriage in advanced countries because a man wished to be certain of the paternity of the children to whom he bequeathed his property. Moreover, Briffault argues that the occurrence of monogamous marriage has been greatly exaggerated. He

[1] *The Mothers* (1927), Vol. II, pp. 254–257.

points out that not a few of Westermarck's examples of monogamy among tribes have been proved errors. Indeed he goes so far as to state that eight out of ten of Westermarck's citations of monogamic tribes in South America have been contradicted.[1] However true these criticisms may be, they do not dispose of the ineluctable facts pointed out by Lowie [2] that monogamy must have been the general rule in practice, because the numerical ratio of the sexes is nearly equal; and, further, that the custom of matrilocal residence in many tribes, together with the prevalence of a high bride price, would tend rigidly to limit polygyny.

Relation between Family Organization and the Food Supply. — Perhaps the most obvious deduction from these conflicting views is that no one theory has been satisfactorily established. The life of aboriginal man is shrouded in an obscurity hard to penetrate. It is probable that no one type of sexual union ever prevailed over the whole earth. Rather is it reasonable to believe that the struggle for existence, reduced to its lowest terms in the struggle for food, largely determined what form of marital relationship or family life should prevail in any one locality. The close connection between family organization and the food supply seems fairly well established. The German writer Grosse, in a valuable study,[3] has carefully traced the forms probably assumed by the family in the hunting, pastoral and agricultural stages of civilization. In his theory the evidence goes to show that in the lowest groups which live mainly upon the produce of the hunt, eked out by seeds, fruits and shellfish, the struggle for a livelihood is severe and a modified form of the monogamic family is the prevailing type, as best suited to the conditions. When the pastoral stage is reached by certain peoples, private property in domesticated animals and rude implements has become a widespread institution and has marked effects

[1] *Op. cit.*, pp. 285–286.   [2] *Primitive Society*, pp. 40–42.
[3] *Die Formen der Familie und die Formen der Wirtschaft* (The Forms of the Family and the Forms of Industry).

upon the family. For with the development of the institution of property wives come to be regarded as valuable assets, since they carry on crude agricultural work and perform all the productive household labor. Family organization is monogamic or polygynic, according to the wealth of the male head. If his possessions are few, monogamy is a necessity; if he has wealth in lands and cattle, he is able to purchase numerous wives who furnish him with useful offspring and add to his possessions.

In Grosse's view the agricultural stage slowly succeeds the pastoral when the population has so increased in numbers that grazing lands furnish insufficient food for the needs of men and cattle. Part of these lands is gradually cultivated with greater care and intensiveness and the returns in a steady food supply amply repay the labors of the agriculturist. The land, now coming to be regarded as the most valuable source of wealth, is held and cultivated in common as the property of the group, who divide its produce among households or individuals. Now it is no longer the simple family that constitutes the social unit, but the "Sippe" or clan which owns the land. Among many agricultural peoples the common land descends in the clan through maternal ancestors only. The reason for this probably lies in the fact that women were the first tillers of the soil, the inventors of agriculture; and many savage tribes, as the Iroquois, Wyandottes and Hurons in North America, recognize their rights in the land they have cultivated. The family within the clan may be monogamic or polygamic in form. This depends as before upon the ability of the male to purchase wives, since women are still looked upon as property. The households frequently contain several generations of related families and are ruled by a head who is usually, although not always, the oldest male relative. Even today in the Slav villages of Eastern Europe the household head apportions the work of tilling the common lands and disposes of the produce and the income with the consent of the adult members of the household.

The final stage of development recognized by Grosse is that of the higher agriculturists. At this stage industry and division of labor have so advanced that only one section of the community is devoted to agricultural pursuits. Other groups pursue a variety of industries, of which crude manufacturing is most important. Among these peoples two forms of family organization may be distinguished: (1) the patriarchal family, now fully developed as in ancient Rome, China and Japan; (2) the *Sonderfamilie*, or monogamic family of two generations — parents and children — prevailing in the Western world at the present time. The patriarchal family no doubt existed in germ within the clan, as the Slav households above described clearly show. With the breakdown of clan organization and control, however, full power over the family (including all those related by descent through males from a common ancestor) fell into the hands of the oldest male head. The modern simple family of Western Europe and America, Grosse believes to be a later offshoot from the patriarchal family, due to an advance in economic life. As a variety of industrial pursuits developed with advance in civilization, the household was no longer held together by coöperative labor upon the family lands. Hence it was possible for the younger members of the family to break away and earn their living independently in a chosen field of industry.

Certain conclusions may be drawn from this brief summary of Grosse's theory. (1) It should be remembered that all peoples have not passed in regular order through the several stages mentioned by Grosse. Many tribes, as the Central Australians, the Bushmans and the Fuegians, have remained in the condition of the lower or upper hunters, while the races of Western Europe outside the Latin countries have, apparently, never developed the patriarchal family in its complete form. (2) Although it appears true that a relation exists between the industrial conditions of a group and its family organization, this fact should not be pushed too far. The family has a psychical as well as an industrial basis.

MARIN JUNIOR COLLEGE LIBRARY

Feelings of responsibility and rudimentary affection for dependent offspring *created* the family, and these feelings, beyond question, have operated in part to maintain it and determine its form. Even when the power of the clan among certain peoples became supreme, the simple family was held together by the bonds of mutual dependence, custom and, at least in some instances, of real affection. A further point is emphasized by Lowie. "Cultural diffusion," or the introduction into one tribe of customs established among a neighboring people, has played an important part in determining forms of marriage and family organization among not a few primitive tribes.[1]

KINSHIP SYSTEMS

Very early in the history of primitive peoples there appeared a form of social organization based upon kinship other than that of the simple family. Society was divided into groups tracing descent to a real or imagined common ancestor; and from these crude divisions bound by the blood tie there developed the clan, exercising control of a political, moral and economic sort over its members. There has been much controversy among anthropologists concerning the causes which led to the kinship group and the matter remains still unsettled. Two types of kinship organization have prevailed at one time or another among different peoples all over the earth: (1) the metronymic (mother-name) system; (2) the patronymic (father-name) system.

The Metronymic or Maternal System. *Causes of Its Development.* — In the metronymic group kinship is traced through the mother only, the father's relationship to his offspring being sometimes entirely ignored, as among the Malay people. Various explanations have been brought forward to account for this widespread custom. McLennan[2]

---

[1] *Primitive Society*, pp. 195-198.
[2] Cf. "Primitive Marriage," in *Studies in Ancient History* (1886), pp. 87, 91-93.

sees in it a proof of his theory that originally sexual relations were quite unrestricted. Thus he argues that the custom of tracing descent through mothers was rendered necessary since it was impossible to determine the father of a child in an age of sexual license. Westermarck and others, however, maintain that this theory is by no means satisfactorily proven. There are tribes living under the maternal system among whom lax sexual relations are almost unknown : whereas there are patronymic kinship groups whose marital customs reveal the utmost laxity and licentiousness. Doubtless the widespread tendency in primitive society to trace descent through females only may be in part accounted for by the close association of mother and child before birth and during the latter's years of infancy and dependence. Polygyny, also, must have had its influence, since under this form of family life separate huts were built by the father for his various wives and their children. This custom would tend, of necessity, to withdraw the children from their father's influence and to strengthen the ties which bound them to their mother.

Unquestionably one of the most important causative influences in the development of the maternal kinship system was the custom of matrilocal residence, whereby a man after marriage went to live with his wife's people. In those instances in which a man could not pay the full bride-price for a wife he very generally lived in the village of his wife's kin, often in his wife's home, and "worked out" the bride-price by doing prescribed forms of labor and furnishing food to his wife's family. The custom is widespread, being found among the Malay tribes, the peoples of New Guinea and Sumatra, certain of the Pacific Islanders, the Iroquois and Pueblo tribes of America, the Hottentots and Zulus of Africa and many other groups. Perhaps it has attained its extreme development among the Pueblos. In this tribe kinship and property descend through women, who also own the house and household goods. The family consists of the maternal grandmother, mother, maternal aunts, the unmarried brothers and all the children of the adult women. In any quarrel the husband has to reckon with his wife's relatives, who do not scruple to expel him from the house. Naturally, therefore, the husband regards his tenure in his wife's abode as insecure and looks upon the household of his mother as his true home. Here he was brought up under the guidance of his maternal uncles, who act as the masters of the house, exact obedience from children and probably have more authority over their sisters' offspring than the father himself. Under such a system of property ownership by women, matrilocal residence would be a natural outcome; and the custom of tracing descent and inheriting property through mothers would also be the natural consequence.

In his able book, *The Mothers*, Briffault has developed a theory of the maternal constitution of the original family — the "nascent human family." He holds that the "biological family is a manifestation of the maternal instincts of the female." Woman was the maker of the home and the home-dweller. The restless, roving instincts of the male were less urgent in the female and were repressed by the demands of her maternal functions. In support of his theory Briffault cites a mass of evidence to the effect that in the original family matrilineal descent and matrilocal residence, now very general, must once have been universal. Men married outside the clan and went to live with their wife's kin. Only in this way could the feminine constitution of the family have been preserved. This matriarchal organization of the family Briffault calls "The Motherhood." But he is far from holding that a matriarchy existed in primitive society in the sense in which that term is commonly employed to mean the dominance of women over men. Thus he writes:

"The maternal biological group subserves the maternal instincts and is governed by those instincts, but that functional fact does not impose a dominance over the male . . . in the primitive human group, the motherhood . . . implied, as in the animal group, a preponderance of the female as compared with her position of economic dependence in the patriarchal group; but it was not a dominance imposed upon the male, or one which, before the development of personal property, conflicted with any of his interests or instincts." [1]

It need hardly be said that Briffault's theory of the "Motherhood" has proved both challenging and interesting. Yet, in attempting to judge of its validity, certain points should be kept in mind. In the first place the method of arguing from certain general customs in contemporary primitive society as to the constitution of the *original* human family of long-past ages seems hazardous and unreliable. Secondly, Briffault appears to ignore a mass of evidence opposed to his theory of the maternal organization of the primitive family. For example, peoples very low in the scale of civilization, such as some Australian tribes, the Fuegians, the Veddahs of Ceylon and the African Bushmans have no maternal family organization. Finally, the bewildering variety of family customs among primitive peoples at present, due to an equal variety of natural and cultural causes, should make the student of the primitive family reflect carefully before accepting any theory that reduces the original family to one universal type. The maternal kinship system and matrilocal residence are found among many widely separated peoples, but they are by no means universal customs.

The Patronymic or Paternal System. *Causes of Its Development.* — As the name implies, the patronymic group traces kinship through males who are the dominant sex. Where this system is found, rank and property likewise descend through the father as a general custom. It would be a mistake to assume that the paternal kinship system regularly succeeded the maternal. At the present time there are very primitive groups in which descent is traced through the father, who determines the clan or totem group of his children. This is true of the Fuegians of South America, the Todas of India and of some Australian and Melanesian tribes. Among these

[1] *Op. cit.*, Vol. I, p. 434.

rude peoples there exists little evidence of a prior maternal system. One important cause of patronymic social organization may be found in economic conditions. In cases where the group had come to depend largely on the produce of the hunt and where agriculture was hardly developed, or was meager in returns, an enormous value would be placed upon the activities of the male as the chief food provider. Moreover, as population increased, the struggle for food became relatively more intense and led to warfare over hunting and fishing grounds. In such a struggle for bare subsistence, the fighting qualities and superior physical strength of the men were of the utmost value to the group. It naturally followed that males gained rapidly in power and prestige at the expense of the females and tended more and more to pass their name and property on to their offspring.

Another cause for the rise of the paternal kinship group lies in the relatively late discovery, among many savage tribes, of the function of the father in generation. The part played by the mother in the conception and birth of offspring is obvious enough; but an advance in intelligence was necessary before the male function was understood. With the spread of this knowledge, however, there developed a tendency among certain tribes to emphasize and even exaggerate the physiological tie between father and child. Westermarck notes that among Australian tribes the belief is prevalent that the child owes its being to the male parent only. He quotes from Howitt the remark of an Australian native : "The man gives the child to the woman to take care of for him, and he can do what he likes with his own child." Where this notion prevailed, it must have been a potent influence in the development of paternal social organization.

Ethnologists are agreed that the development of private property and the taking over by men of the chief functions of production have been powerful influences in the development and extension of father power and a paternal organization of peoples. Briffault holds that in those tribes where the change from a maternal to a patriarchal organization of the family is going forward at present a potent causal factor is contact with Europeans. As evidence he cites the North American Indians (who, he believes, have adopted paternal descent during the period of European occupation), the Massim of New Guinea and the tribes of Sumatra most exposed to European influence.[1]

EXOGAMY AND ENDOGAMY

Explanation of Terms. — Among very many savage groups there exists a strong aversion to the marriage of near kin. This aversion, however, expresses itself in a wide variety of forms. The horror of cohabitation between parents and children is well-nigh universal. Yet a few early peoples, as the ancient Peruvians and Egyptians, approve brother-and-sister marriages within the family of king or chieftain on the theory that no other members of the group are worthy to mate with the ruler's kin. On the other hand, by far the majority of tribes not only condemn sexual relations between close blood relatives but forbid marriages between members of the same clan or totem group. As these clans may be metronymic or patronymic, this restriction, of course, would prevent marriage between maternal or paternal relatives as the case might be, even to the most remote degrees of kinship, but would make it possible for a man to marry a near relative of another clan on the ground that no kinship tie exists between them. The case of Abraham, who espoused his half sister Sarah (his father's daughter by another wife than his mother), is a well-known instance of this apparent inconsistency. Probably in these early days the Hebrews still traced kinship through mothers, and thus Sarah was not in the same kinship group as her half-brother Abraham. Malinowski states that among the Trobriand Islanders "cross-cousin" marriage, or the union of a man's son with his sister's daughter, is regarded as the most suitable form of marriage.[2]

[1] *The Mothers*, Vol. I, pp. 335–336.
[2] *The Sexual Life of Savages in North-Western Melanesia*, p. 95.

The prohibition of marriage within the clan, with its consequent fixed custom of extra-clan marriage, is called *exogamy*. The custom of marriage within the clan is called *endogamy*. It should be noted that where exogamy prevails, the custom relates to *intra-clan* not *intra-tribal* marriage. Exogamy as applied to tribes is virtually non-existent.

Causes for Rise of Exogamy. — Numerous explanations have been offered by anthropologists to account for the existence of exogamy. McLennan, in the work on *Primitive Marriage*, already cited, holds that it was the outgrowth of a widespread custom of female infanticide which forced primitive groups to prey upon each other for wives. In time the practice of seeking a wife outside the clan or tribe would gain all the tremendous sanction of custom. Westermarck, however, has pointed out some serious flaws in this theory. (1) Female infanticide has, apparently, never been a universal custom and is sometimes not found among very primitive peoples, *e.g.*, the Yahgans of Tierra del Fuego. (2) Even if female infanticide were general enough to force men to seek wives outside the group, that would not prevent men within the clan from marrying such females as were permitted to live and grow up. The theory, then, does not account for the widespread *prohibition of marriage within the clan or totem group* that is so characteristic of exogamy. Westermarck's own explanation of the rise of exogamy [1] is that the custom is the expression of an innate aversion, on the part of people closely associated from childhood, to sexual intercourse with each other. This aversion, he believes, is rooted in an instinct which has survived because it has proved useful. Those races are most vigorous which do not "breed in and in." Westermarck freely concedes that the instinct does not show itself in a distaste for sexual intercourse *between relatives;* for ignorance of relationship has not infrequently led to sexual love between near kin. He holds rather that the instinct expresses itself in indifference or aversion to

[1] Cf. *Human Marriage*, Chs. XIV, XV,

cohabitation with household associates. Tylor, on the other hand, finds the origin of exogamy in the desire of savage groups to cement friendly relations with each other through intermarriage.[1]

Effects on the Family. — Whatever may be the true explanation of exogamy, however, its effects upon family life have, on the whole, been beneficent. Not only has it operated quite generally to prevent sexual intercourse between kindred living under the same roof, but it has brought new blood into the clan, thus maintaining its vigor. The whole question of the evil effects of inbreeding is under discussion by biologists and anthropologists at the present time, and cannot be regarded as fully settled. Yet it is well to remember that the most "in and in bred" people of whom we have any knowledge, the Veddahs of Ceylon, are described as short of stature, vacant in expression, and so infertile that the race is rapidly becoming extinct.

Affection and Freedom of Choice in Primitive Marriage. — Reference has been made to wife capture and wife purchase as modes of obtaining mates which were widely prevalent among savages. But what can be said of mutual choice and affection in primitive marriage? It seems clear enough that wife purchase could not have been the original custom of securing wives; for this implies a higher degree of social and economic development than was reached by primitive peoples among whom the property sense is rudimentary. On the contrary, there is some evidence to show that in the lowest groups a considerable degree of freedom of choice is allowed to the woman. Westermarck has collected some valuable material which indicates that, at the beginning of human history, marriage was grounded in the mutual attraction and consent of the parties.[2] With rare exceptions the male among the rudest peoples appears as the wooer. The female, less dominated by sexual passion, must be courted; and thus she

---

[1] *The Matriarchal Family System in the Nineteenth Century* (1896).
[2] *Human Marriage*, Chs. VII–XIII.

plays a prominent rôle in sexual selection. Nor is this fact surprising. Darwin,[1] Groos[2] and others have shown that courtship, in one form or another, very generally prevails in the animal kingdom. Male birds and animals alike not only fight fiercely with rivals of their own sex for their mates, but follow these conflicts up with attempts to charm the female onlookers in various ways. Why should not primitive man have employed the same tactics? In a state of nature where each individual man or woman was his own food provider, the female, as previously stated, was very nearly the equal of the male in strength and self-reliance, and was by no means so dependent upon his prowess in war and skill in the hunt as she later became. Hence she could, and probably did, choose among her suitors. It may be objected that the sale of girls as wives is a common practice among primitive groups; but it should be remembered that, although purchase marriage is and has been a general custom among savages, most of these peoples are far from living under primordial conditions. The Australians, Bushmans, Hottentots and Gold Coast Negroes, who frequently arrange for the sale of infants in marriage shortly after their birth, are by no means in an absolutely primitive social condition.

Even among savages who contract for the marriage of their children with complete indifference to their wishes, the engaged couple sometimes break the contract, when they reach maturity, and the girl elopes with another suitor. Elopements used to be common among the Dacotah Indians and are stated to be the rule among the Kurnai of Australia. A few North American Indian tribes were surprisingly generous in permitting freedom of choice in marriage to their girls. Among the Creeks the consent of the woman was regularly obtained by courtship; and no Pueblo girl was forced to marry a suitor against her will. The rude Maoris of New Zealand have a proverb which runs: "As a kahawai (a fish) selects the hook which pleases it best out of a great number,

[1] *Descent of Man*, Ch. VIII.   [2] *The Play of Animals*, pp. 257–271.

so also a woman chooses one man out of many." [1] Other instances are furnished by the Dyaks of Borneo, among whom the women are apparently given entire liberty in the choice of a husband, and the peoples of Samoa.

Thus, marriages grounded upon mutual liking are not quite so rare in savage groups as certain anthropologists would have us think. Indeed, there is some reason to believe, as Howard [2] has suggested, that marriage began in free choice, passed through the stage of contract and purchase arranged by family or clan, and with the decay of the kinship group and paternal power, became, very slowly, once more an individual matter as in modern times.

Forms of Marriage. — The different forms of marriage and family organization which have prevailed among savage peoples are three in number, *monogamy,* [3] *polygamy* and *polyandry.* Of these three monogamy, or the union of one man and one woman for a varying period of time, has been the persistent type. The controlling reason for the prevalence of monogamy is a biological rather than a social or psychological one. It lies in the fact already mentioned that among most peoples the sexes are nearly equal in numbers where the natural ratio is not artificially disturbed. It cannot be expected that primitive man would be aware of the physical, moral and social advantages of monogamic marriages, much less be governed by such considerations.

Polygyny, or that form of marriage in which one man has two or more wives at the same time, has been a widespread type. Unquestionably the causes leading to polygynous marriage are economic and social as well as personal. Obviously enough a plurality of wives satisfies the sex impulses of the savage more completely than monogamy. But such marriage also adds to his wealth and social standing and thus gives him a distinct advantage over the monogamist. Not only has he

---

[1] Quoted by Westermarck, *op. cit.,* p. 217.
[2] *A History of Matrimonial Institutions,* Vol. I, p. 202.
[3] More correctly *monandry,* a transitory form of monogamic union.

amassed the property to pay the bride-price for several wives, which enhances his prestige, but these women work for him and add to his wealth. Likewise, they bear him children who are a potential source of wealth as workers and who increase the size and influence of his family in the clan.

A third form of marriage existent among primitive peoples is *polyandry*, or the union of one woman with several husbands. This practice is confined at the present time to a very few groups, notably to the Todas of India and the inhabitants of portions of Ceylon and Thibet. Among the leading causes of polyandry is the numerical disproportion between the sexes. In certain rugged and relatively barren countries male births largely outnumber the female for reasons not yet well understood, but quite possibly connected with the food supply. There is some evidence to the effect that scanty nourishment tends to an excess of male births. Nature may thus protect groups living in barren areas by limiting their reproductive capacity. Again, as Westermarck has pointed out, there seems to be a close connection between endogamy, or marriage within the group, and the practice of polyandry. Polyandrous peoples are almost without exception also endogamous. Such a custom apparently tends to increase the proportion of male births, and thus it may well be a factor in the development of polyandrous marriages. Female infanticide has often been pointed out as a powerful cause of polyandry, but the evidence does not wholly support this theory. The Todas and the Eskimos, who are two of the leading polyandrous peoples, have until recent times practiced female infanticide, if we are to believe the reports of travelers who have lived among them. On the other hand, the Tibetans, another polyandrous people, do not commonly practice female infanticide, although there is a paucity of women among them. It seems probable, then, that polyandry is closely bound up with a marked excess of males in any community.

Despite the attempts of certain social writers to show that at the beginning of human society polyandry was a widely prevalent form of marriage, the theory has little to support it. On the contrary, as we have seen, there is some reason to believe that monogamy was the original form of marriage. Furthermore, among the many primitive peoples practicing polygyny at the present time the majority of the men are monogamous for lack of sufficient females to serve as wives. Thus in Turkey, where polygyny flourished until a new social and political régime was established after the World War, about 90 per cent of the men were monogamous by force of circumstances.

MODES OF OBTAINING WIVES

Among primitive peoples a variety of methods of securing wives has prevailed in the past and most of these are customary at present. The most common methods are (1) marriage by purchase, (2) marriage by service, (3) marriage by consent, (4) marriage by capture. Although the last named plays a large part in writings on the family of twenty-five years or more ago, it is probably the least prevalent method of obtaining wives. No doubt women were captured in war and were forced to become the wives of their captors. Lowie states that the war-like Plains Indians of America often captured the women of hostile tribes and married them; and wrestling matches for wives sometimes occur among the Eskimos of the West Coast of Hudson Bay.[1] But there appears to be no well-established instance of a primitive tribe with whom wife capture has been the regular and habitual method of securing wives. No people could afford to sanction brute force as the recognized means of getting mates. Such a tribe, if it existed, would be involved in constant warfare within or outside its own community.

The most widespread method of obtaining wives among primitive tribes at present is purchase marriage. Although this is a very ancient custom, it probably was not an original form of securing a mate. Only when valuable property had

[1] *Primitive Society*, p. 23.

accumulated within a tribe and a wife's labor in producing goods had definite value would purchase marriage be likely to develop. Among certain tribes, as the Khirgiz of Siberia, the bride-price is so high — over 80 head of cattle — that the father of a boy will begin to collect the amount as soon as his son is betrothed at ten years of age. Probably the almost universal custom of purchase marriage should not be regarded as a degradation of the woman according to primitive standards. Her purchase in marriage does not involve the right to re-sell her as a mere chattel. Moreover, the gifts brought by the girl in marriage sometimes equal the bride-price, as among the Turks, the Yakuts and the Malays of Malacca. In such instances, the transaction cannot strictly be called a sale. Moreover, as Lowie has pointed out, there are tribes, as the Hidatsa of North Dakota and the Crow Indians, among whom purchase marriage was the most honorable form and was reserved for those desirable girls who had never previously been married.

Marriage by service has developed among certain peoples as a method of paying for a wife with labor when the purchase price was difficult to amass. Briffault regards this as the original mode of acquiring a wife. The custom is found in Sumatra, among the Pueblos and many other tribes, and is often associated with matrilocal residence. If a man must render stipulated services for his wife, especially in providing food for her relatives, it would be natural for him to reside with his wife's family, at least until the purchase price was "worked out." Among the Hupa and Hidatsa tribes in North America, where patrilocal residence is customary, a man often lives temporarily with his wife's kin until the bride-price is paid, when he takes his wife to his own village.

Marriage by mutual consent appears to be a far less common practice than purchase marriage, yet it is not as rare as has generally been assumed. Mead found it among the Samoans and Malinowski among the Trobriand Islanders; and in certain North American tribes, as the Crow Indians, it is not uncommon. Westermarck has amassed an imposing body of evidence to show that this method of acquiring a wife is scattered among tribes all over the earth.[1]

THE POSITION OF WOMEN IN PRIMITIVE SOCIETY

Obviously enough the bodily structure and functions of the female put her at a tremendous disadvantage in a primitive society based upon brute strength in warfare and upon skill in trapping game. To her was assigned by nature the work of motherhood, which entails not only severe physical strain, but also the responsibility for the nurture of helpless children. These tasks bound primitive woman to her home and its immediate environs. Upon her first devolved the heavy drudgery of agriculture, which she carried on with such rude implements as the digging stick and hoe invented by herself. While she labored in the fields, she often carried her youngest child strapped to her back. Under such a handicap she supplied the family with edible roots, grains and fruits to eke out the supplies of animal food furnished by the father. Such tasks must have told heavily upon the strength and energy of women in primitive societies. Yet there is little doubt that in this early period they were much more nearly the equal of the males in physical strength, as well as in the skill required in the daily hand-to-mouth struggle for food, than at present.

The Relative Status of Father and Mother under the Maternal System. — An important group of social writers have held the theory that the position of the father in the metronymic group was distinctly inferior to that of the mother, who was the ruling power in the household. As evidence they point to the Malay peoples, among whom it is customary for the man after marriage to visit his wife's abode only occasionally. His real home continues to be among his own people whom he assists in cultivating the family lands. The offspring of his marriage are the property of the mother's kindred and are cared for and controlled largely by their

[1] *The History of Human Marriage* (1922), Vol. I, Chs. VII–XIII.

maternal uncle, who is regarded as their nearest male relative. But this instance is far from typical. Where the maternal system prevails, it is a general, although by no means a universal, custom for the husband to make his home among the kindred of his wife; and it is probable that in such instances his position in the household is a somewhat subordinate one. He must prove himself a good hunter and a generous provider of animal food for his wife's family. Otherwise he may be ignominiously dismissed from the household. Such was the practice among the Pueblos and the Iroquois tribes of America. But these customs are not evidence that women under the maternal system had sufficient power and influence to establish a matriarchate or rule of women. Quite often the household head was the woman's elder brother, the uncle of her children. Moreover, even among the Iroquois, the chief political offices were held by males, although women nominated the chiefs of the Council of the League of Five Nations and played an important part in ceremonial matters.[1] Among the Wyandottes, women even held positions in the council.[2] Also it should be noted that the maternal system is frequently found among peoples who have adopted the custom of removing the wife from her own kindred to the hut of the husband. In such cases, although kinship is traced through the mother, property and rank sometimes descend through the father, who is the unquestioned head of his household. Such is the custom among the Fijians and many other groups of the Pacific Islanders as well as among the West Australians. These rude societies illustrate an interesting combination of the maternal and the paternal systems that may possibly represent a transition from one to the other.

Concerning the whole vexed question of woman's status under the metronymic system the following conclusions seem fairly well established.

[1] Goldenweiser, *Early Civilization*, pp. 73–81.
[2] Powell, *Wyandotte Government*, First Annual Report of Bureau of Ethnology, Vol. XXV, pp. 76 ff.

(1) In those instances where the husband lived and served among his wife's kindred the position of the woman was *relatively* high. She was protected by her male relatives from unjust divorce, from abuse and from gross overwork.

(2) On the other hand, it should be remembered that the maternal kinship system does not imply that women were in supreme control of the household nor even that they held a determining voice in the management of the affairs of the kinship group or clan. This view of female supremacy or of a matriarchate has been maintained by Bachofen and in a modified form by Briffault in recent times, but it has not been satisfactorily established. On the contrary, the evidence goes to show that, even when name, rank and property descended through the mother, she was not the controlling force in the household. Rather was it the woman's oldest brother or maternal uncle who had the deciding voice in all important matters and who determined the training and arranged the marriages of his nephews. The customs controlling the relationship of nephews to the maternal uncle are called the *avunculate*. The mother's brother assumes a varying degree of responsibility and control of his sister's sons, often teaching them tribal lore and ceremonies. Lowie states that the avunculate in its extreme form is found among the coast tribes of British Columbia, where the nephew lives with his maternal uncle, works for him and even marries his daughter and inherits his property.[1]

Diverse Theories of Primitive Woman's Status. — The position of woman in primitive society has provoked more sharp and contrasting differences of opinion than most other questions concerning early civilization. The theories regarding her status range from the view that primitive woman was subjected to all the brutal treatment she could bear and continue to survive and reproduce, to the theory of Briffault that woman held a predominant position in aboriginal society by virtue of her maternal instincts, around which the

[1] Lowie, *op. cit.*, p. 82.

family was organized.[1] From these varying opinions one important fact emerges which should be held in mind in judging all controversial questions concerning the primitive family, namely, that the utmost variety of customs may be found in the tribal societies of the present, thus making free generalization more often than not incorrect and misleading. Woman's position among primitive peoples shows the same bewildering variety as do other phases of savage life. Malinowski reports that among the Trobriand Islanders the status of women approximates that of men;[2] and Mead paints similar conditions among the Samoans, where women are relatively free and unoppressed.[3] Many savage societies throw a heavier burden of work upon women than falls to the lot of men, but this condition should not be interpreted to mean that women's position is degraded. As Lowie has shown, onerous labor is no criterion of status. In the Andaman Islands and among the Veddahs of Ceylon women have the heavier burden of work and yet are on a plane of equality with men. Women do little work among the Todas of India, but their position is distinctly inferior. In certain tribes of South Africa and South America, although women plant and harvest crops, they are in a very subordinate position. Probably, as Hobhouse maintains, the status of women is lower among the pastoral tribes than among agriculturists, yet even this generalization is subject to striking exceptions. Clearly the economic factor is only one among many determinants of the position of women in savage society. As Lowie points out, cultural diffusion has played an important rôle in determining women's status. Evidence exists that tribes have not rarely borrowed social customs from each other, including practices with regard to the treatment of women.[4]

---

[1] *The Mothers*, Vol. I, pp. 200, 251.
[2] *The Sexual Life of Savages in North-Western Melanesia*, pp. 1–5, 30–34.
[3] *Coming of Age in Samoa*, passim.
[4] For this entire question see Lowie, *op. cit.*, pp. 187–195.

The complicated question of the position of primitive woman cannot be left without reference to those physiological functions of women which have exercised a powerful influence upon the minds of men and have unquestionably been factors in determining women's tribal status. Among most primitive tribes there exists a fear and dread of menstrual blood, a belief that a menstruating woman is a potent source of evil. From this conviction spring those *tabus* found in a number of tribes which require that during her menstrual period a woman shall retire to an isolated hut until she ceases to be a menace to her people. Some *tabus* are concerned with forbidding a menstruating woman from going near fishing waters or hunting grounds or from approaching any man. Similarly, primitive men show dread of childbirth, as a phenomenon which endows women with vast powers for working harm. Occasionally the prevalent feeling about women's creative function, in its bodily manifestations, takes the form of awe more than dread and fear. Some tribes believe that women have supernatural powers for good as well as evil and are potent workers of magic. Priestesses are numerous among African tribes, and in Dahomey they pass through a three-year initiation. Among American Indians, also, "medicine women" endowed with magic powers are often found; and during the annual Corn Feast, Iroquois women exercise tremendous authority. Among the Zuñi, the college of priests is composed of men but at their head is a woman, the Priestess of Fertility. Here is clear evidence of the intimate connection believed by some tribes to exist between woman's function as mother and her power over the fertility of the soil.[1] This awe and reverence for the creative functions of women no doubt has contributed to the elevation of their status in certain tribes, as among the Pueblos, the Iroquois and the barbaric Teutons of the first Christian Century.

[1] For this whole question see Briffault, *op. cit.*, Vol. I, pp. 359, 516–557.

DIVORCE AMONG PRIMITIVE PEOPLE

Freedom of Divorce. — Nothing appears more striking to the student of the primitive family than the instability of marriage. In many instances the most flimsy pretexts are sufficient to bring about a divorce which is usually accomplished without any formalities whatever. Marriage is commonly regarded as a private contract and as such may be dissolved at the will of both parties or of only one. Such facility of divorce of course implies that the affections are not very deeply involved in marriage. In many savage groups incompatibility of temper, the aging of the wife and hence her depreciation in value as a worker, petty quarrels and other causes equally slight are regarded as constituting grounds for divorce.

The greatest variety with respect to freedom of divorce may be discovered among savage tribes. Some rude peoples permit the utmost liberty to both husband and wife. Thus among the Point Barrow Eskimo, the negroes of the Gold Coast of Africa and certain tribes of Asia and America, the marriage bond is easily broken at the whim of either party. But this is not always the case. There are tribes as, *e.g.*, the Karo-Karo of Sumatra, who permit divorce *only by mutual consent*. In West Victoria (Australia) a man can divorce his wife only after the consent of the chiefs of her family and of his own has been obtained. The wife herself has little or no liberty of divorce although she may complain of mistreatment to the chief who, if he sees fit, may send the husband away for a brief period as a punishment.[1] On the Slave coast of Africa a wife who is grossly abused may leave her husband without repaying the "head money" if she can prove her case before the headmen of the village.[2] In such instances where the tribal chiefs or a family council control all divorces it seems clear that marriage is regarded as a public concern,

[1] Howard, *History of Matrimonial Institutions*, Vol. I, p. 229.
[2] Ellis, *The Ewe Speaking Peoples of the Slave Coast*, Ch. X.

affecting the clan or gens, rather than as a purely private affair. As Lowie has pointed out, the actual frequency of divorce among primitive peoples should not be confounded with its possibility in theory. A man who has paid a high price for his wife's person and services will think twice before divorcing her. Then, too, children tend to limit divorce in savage society as in our own. Among the Crow Indians and the Greenland Eskimos, marriage becomes more stable after the birth of offspring.[1]

Wife purchase, as might be inferred, has operated to curtail the liberty of divorce accorded to the woman. In a majority of savage tribes, where the custom of purchase marriage prevails, the sole right of divorce lies with the male. Such is the case among the Aleutian Islanders, the Dacotahs and Abipones in America and among many African tribes. Even here, however, custom has tended to mitigate the unjust treatment of the wife. In some groups the husband who casts off his wife without cause must forfeit the purchase money paid down for her. Even in cases where the dissatisfied husband may claim a return of the purchase price, after unjustly divorcing his wife, he has to fear the vengeance of the woman's relatives, who may promptly declare a blood feud. It should further be noted that in a number of tribes which restrict the right of divorce to the male the causes for divorce are clearly laid down. Adultery on the wife's part, or the loss of virginity on the part of a betrothed girl, are very generally recognized as just occasions for repudiation of the guilty partner. Childlessness is another cause which has obtained wide recognition, not only among primitive peoples, but among the ancient Hebrews and Romans. Laziness, desertion and incompatibility of temper serve as grounds for divorce in the custom of some tribes.

Curiously enough a few of the rudest people of whom we have any knowledge do not permit divorce under any circumstances. Such are the Veddahs of Ceylon and the Papuans

[1] Lowie, *op. cit.*, p. 69.

of the Island of New Guinea among whom death alone may serve to unloose the bond of marriage.

Disposal of Wife and Children after Divorce. — But, although marriage is easily dissolved and frequently of short duration among primitive peoples, their customs in regard to the disposal of the repudiated wife and her children show a considerable degree of sound sense and regard for justice. No woman, except in case of gross misconduct, is turned adrift in the world after her divorce. Usually she returns to her own people, who provide for her until she marries again, as she frequently does. The children are divided between the parents according to various customary rules. Sometimes the mother takes the female children and the father the male. Again, where the maternal kinship system prevails, the children quite often follow the mother, just as in cases where the group is patronymic they remain with the father, since they belong to his kindred. Again, if the children of a divorced wife are very young, it is usual to leave them under the care of the mother. In certain tribes custom requires that if the divorced woman is the guilty party, she pay a fixed sum to her husband for every child she takes away with her.

Property Arrangements. — No less reasonable are primitive customs regarding the disposal of property after divorce. Very generally the party in fault is discriminated against. The wife discarded because of adultery or barrenness must repay the purchase price or obtain it from her kindred. In addition she must sacrifice all gifts bestowed on her at her marriage and all property accumulated afterwards. Likewise the husband who divorces his wife without due cause usually forfeits the price paid for her and in some cases, though by no means in all, he must hand over the children to the mother. In a few instances the man and woman receive the property owned by each at the time of marriage and divide any property accumulated afterwards. Westermarck cites the case of the Manipuris among whom custom requires that the wife divorced without just cause shall take "all the personal property of her husband, except one drinking-cup and the cloth round his loins." [1]

Tendency toward Group Regulation of Divorce. — From the above discussion it appears that divorce is not restricted to civilized nations but is a custom as old as marriage. Indifference, personal dislike or incompatibility play their part in determining divorce among primitive races as among modern. Very early, also, custom serves more or less to regulate these separations and to determine the disposal of wife, children and property. Even among some of the least civilized peoples may be observed the rudimentary tendency to bring divorce under the control of the group as in modern times.

SERVICES RENDERED BY THE PRIMITIVE FAMILY TO CIVILIZATION

Social Services. — In the rude ages that mark the beginning of human history the family, as we have seen, appears to be the earliest, because the most natural organization of society. Before the recognition of kinship bonds had developed the clan, and long before clans had become amalgamated into tribes, the natural family of two generations was probably in existence. The dependent offspring of sexual unions, which otherwise might well have been merely temporary, served as a bond uniting the male and female in a common service of protection and nurture. In the family, then, as the matrix of organized society, were nourished those altruistic virtues which, when carried beyond the boundaries of the family and the kinship group, were to prove the greatest unifying force in society. When savage man extended the instincts of sympathy, fellow-feeling and coöperation to all those united to him by the blood bond and later to all members of the tribe, the foundations of justice, law and progress were securely laid.

But the primitive family doubtless performed another social service of no small importance. Long before the medicine-man, the shaman or the tribal elders had taken the

[1] Westermarck, *op. cit.*, p. 531.

group customs into their peculiar charge, the family must have been the custodian of such crude human experience as seemed most worth preserving. From father to son, from mother to daughter, were passed on the small but precious hoards of knowledge painfully wrested from nature. Thus the family in its simple or its group form, as the only social organization, exercised a variety of functions now widely distributed. The home was the center of such crude industry as then existed. It was in addition the sole training school of the young in the virtues most prized by the savage, as well as in the arts of warfare, the hunt and agriculture.

The Primitive Family as an Industrial Unit. — The earliest human groups doubtless had no economy, *i.e.*, no practical adjustment of means to ends. The lowest peoples of whom anthropologists have knowledge, the Veddahs of Ceylon, the Bushmans of South Africa, the Negritos of the Philippines and certain Australian tribes, are even now engaged in a daily, almost hand-to-hand struggle with nature to obtain a bare livelihood. Such a struggle for existence reveals no attempt to adapt present means, in respect to food supply and clothing, to future needs. The first genuine economy was practiced not by primitive groups, but by savage peoples a little higher in civilization, and is closely bound up with the life of the household. Indeed it is well to remember that our word "economy" is derived from a Greek term signifying the practical administration of *household* affairs. In the family was developed the original division of labor upon the basis of sex differences. To the restless male with his greater physical strength and relative freedom from the care of offspring fell the task of supplying the family with animal food in the intervals of warfare. His were the more stimulating duties of hunting and fighting. Upon the female, forced to be more stationary by the demands of motherhood, devolved less exciting and more irksome burdens. She must provide a constant supply of vegetable food at the same time that she bore and reared her offspring. From the beginning of human history mankind have been more dependent upon plant food than has been generally recognized. Game was often scarce and uncertain and primitive groups thus found their most reliable source of subsistence in roots, seeds and fruits. To the woman, the home-maker, fell the task of collecting nature's products in the region around the home, while the man roamed far, alone or with others, in search of game. It is probable, then, that woman was the most reliable food provider among primitive peoples.[1]

The old saw that "necessity is the mother of invention" is well illustrated in the crude industries of primitive women. A long forward stride was made by civilization when woman, no longer content to gather the meager products of an uncultivated soil, conceived the idea of planting seeds to secure a richer harvest. First with her hands she scraped the soil and dropped her seeds. The need for a more satisfactory implement led her to invent a rude digging stick. From this bent stick, in response to a daily challenge upon her inventiveness, woman evolved the hoe and later a crude forerunner of the plow, which she herself dragged over the soil in default of domesticated animals. To woman's ingenuity may be traced the first primitive mill for grinding seeds, where one stone is made to move over another. The metate and muller, likewise used for grinding grain, was her invention. It was the primitive housewife who discovered that from steatite (soapstone) could be made a cooking pot which would stand the heat of the fire without cracking. In the pursuit of her multifarious tasks she was forced to be inventive; and the crude spindle, the weaving frame with its heddle, the scraper, the stone knife, the adz and other rude stone implements, witness to her success. Such achievements constitute an honorable record for primitive womankind. There are writers, however, who maintain that women's inventiveness never advanced very far. They point out that the domestication of cattle and their use in drawing the plow, important improve-

---

[1] See Bücher, Karl, *Industrial Evolution*, Ch. II.

7484

ments in the plow itself and above all the progress from crude stone implements to more serviceable metal tools were all the work of man when his attention could profitably be diverted from war to industry. These facts should not, however, blind us to the truth that in the invention of the *first* agricultural and household implements woman was the pioneer.[1]

With respect to variety of pursuits the primitive housewife seems clearly in the lead over her husband, although there is at present the most varied usage with respect to the labors commonly performed by one sex or the other. In some tribes men dress skins and make pottery, pursuits which are often carried on by women. Among the Hopi men do all the spinning and weaving, whereas among the neighboring Navahos women alone perform these tasks. In some tribes labor is equally distributed between the sexes. In others by far the greater burden of the work is borne by the woman, whose husband is little more than a parasite. In general it may be said that the man fights, hunts, fishes, tends cattle, makes nets and weapons and sits around the camp-fire for hours or even days at a time. In contrast to this industrial program the occupations of the wife and mother seem varied indeed and the demands upon her versatility persistent and exacting. Before the invention of the plow, in addition to her labors as an agriculturist, she must go out and find the game her husband had carelessly thrown down and cut it up into food portions, after stripping off the hide to be converted into leather by simple processes she had herself discovered. She was more often than not the tailor, the shoemaker, the food preparer, the potter and the basket-maker of the family. Frequently she was even the builder of the hut or tepee, after men had placed the original props in place. And these labors were hers in addition to her cares as a mother. Truly the home among more advanced savage tribes was a hive of industry centering about the wife and mother. Her life stands out in striking contrast to that of the idle "lady" of

[1] See Mason, Oliver T., *Woman's Share in Primitive Culture*, passim.

modern times — a type developed among civilized nations. Primitive woman was a producer of the utmost economic importance — not merely a consumer, like her luxurious sister in the wealthy class of Europe and America.

One further point should be noticed in connection with primitive industry. It can hardly be questioned that the chief pursuits of the male — war and group fishing and hunting — demanded powers of coöperation and organization not exacted in nearly the same degree of the female by her more individualistic tasks. These demands developed in man a stronger sense of social solidarity and social obligation than was possible to the woman, confined as she was largely to the home with its personal interests. Through the long course of social history, this division of labor has operated to develop in man a larger social and political interest and a greater capacity for organized effort than the home-staying woman has hitherto possessed. The feminine virtues and accomplishments most valued by men in all ages have been precisely those individualistic ones developed by the home-staying wife and mother — devotion to husband and children, unselfish service, docility, meekness and industry. Therefore it is not strange that women as a whole have a more restricted social interest and vision than men. But, despite this fact, one of the most striking and hopeful features of our modern age is the ability shown by contemporary women to organize and coöperate in behalf of important social ends, now that they have received full citizenship rights and the sphere of their activities and interests is no longer bounded by the home.

The Family as the Earliest Educational Institution. *Status of Children in the Primitive Household: Parental Affection.* — The status of children in primitive tribes is generally determined less by fixed custom than by the caprice of the parent. In the lowest groups the power of the father over his children is absolutely unlimited, extending to the taking of life or sale into slavery. Among the Eẉe-speaking people of the Gold Coast the terms for father mean " he who maintains," " he who owns." Falkner in his *Description of Patagonia* states of the savage inhabitants of that land that, although parental love seems highly developed among them, the men not infrequently sell wives or children for Spanish brandy. And this is by no means an isolated case. In the words of Herbert Spencer: " The status of a primitive man's child is like that of a bear's cub. There is neither moral obligation nor moral restraint; but there exists the unchecked power to foster, to desert, to destroy, as love or anger moves."[1]

Such being the status of children in the lowest savage groups, we are not surprised to learn that infanticide was freely practiced whenever circumstances seemed to warrant it. The motives actuating parents who destroyed their new-born children were doubtless chiefly economic. Would the food supply of the family suffice for a new member? Or, if the group were migratory, always on the search for fresh hunting or fishing grounds, could the infant be easily transported? If there were already a child in arms and one or two toddlers besides, the death sentence of the newcomer would probably be pronounced and promptly executed. Doubtless, too, other motives were at work, such as the unwillingness of an overworked mother to assume the added burden of rearing an infant, or the deformity or weakness of the child. Under stress of famine or war or a scanty food supply the Bushmans, the Fuegians, the Fijians, the Central African and other tribes are said by anthropological writers to destroy infants with little hesitation. Margaret Mead reports that female infanticide is often resorted to by tribes in the interior of New Guinea. However, it should be remembered that this method of disposing of surplus mouths to feed is not confined to savages. Among the impoverished masses of India and China down to modern times infanticide, especially of female babies, has been common; and history records cases of infanticide among the so-called " Christian " barbarians of Western Europe up to the eleventh century.

[1] *Principles of Sociology*, Vol. I, p. 747.

But if the harsh conditions of life impel some savage peoples to get rid of unwanted offspring, this fact is far from giving a correct picture of the relation of parents and children in primitive families. An impressive body of evidence has been amassed by ethnologists which shows that warm and even tender affection for children and a due regard for their future welfare is by no means rare in savage society. Among the Pueblos children are held in high regard and are carefully trained in the myths and customs of their people. This holds true of many Indian tribes, of the Eskimos, of certain African and Melanesian peoples. Malinowski stresses the warm affection shown by fathers among the Trobriand Islanders for their children, even though the child belongs to the mother's kin. The father is the close companion of his children, nurturing them when babies and sharing in their activities. To the Trobriand child the word "father" recalls a host of happy experiences of early childhood.[1] Mead reports that among the Manus of the Admiralty Islands the mother is given a year to coddle and nurse her baby, after which she must go to work in the mangrove swamp while the father, who "takes a violent proprietary interest in the new baby," tends to preëmpt the child and take it from the mother. Descent and property inheritance being paternal, he regards the child as his own and under the protection of the spirits of his family.[2] Every day he plays with his children and helps to train them in those skills which a Manus child must master if he is to exist in an environment full of pitfalls for the unwary.

Ignorance of the Physiology of Generation. — In many primitive tribes knowledge of the equal contribution of father and mother to the generation of offspring is wholly unknown. Quite generally paternity is regarded not as a physiological relation but as a social one; whereas the physiological bond between mother and child is unmistakable. This ignorance springs from the fact that primitive peoples often see no direct

[1] *The Sexual Life of Savages in North-Western Melanesia*, p. 6.
[2] *Growing Up in New Guinea*, p. 65.

connection between sexual intercourse and the birth of offspring, and attribute pregnancy to eating certain foods, passing certain haunted spots or being impregnated by the moon
or an animal spirit.   The Maori of New Zealand have a saying
that "the moon is the real husband of all women," as well as
the cause of menstruation.   Briffault has brought together
some interesting facts reported by ethnologists concerning the
widespread belief of savage tribes in impregnation through
eating.   The women of Sumatra who do not wish to conceive
are careful not to eat a particular kind of cocoanut, while
Greenland women avoid a certain fish.   Kwakiutl Indian girls
prevent pregnancy by refraining from chewing the gum of the
white pine.[1]   Malinowski relates that among the Trobriand
Island peoples the belief prevails that there is no bond of
physical union whatever between father and child.   It is solely
the mother who builds up her child's body, who feeds it while
it remains within her and nourishes it with her milk after it is
born.[2]

The Custom of Couvade. — A curious custom has grown up
among a limited number of tribes, *e.g.*, certain Brazilian groups,
the Caribs of Guiana and a few Pacific Islanders, whereby the
father takes to his bed during the time his wife is giving birth
to a child.   Indeed cases are described where the father remains in his hammock for some time after the birth, refrains
from eating certain foods likely to harm the infant and is carefully tended by his wife, who is still weak from her ordeal.
Various explanations have been offered of this quaint practice
but no one has received general acceptance.   Tylor explains
it as marking the transition from descent through the mother
to descent through the father.   The father by "lying in"
attempts to minimize the importance of the mother and emphasize the importance of the father's relationship to his child.
Tylor's theory has been criticized on the ground that he assigns
one universal cause to a social custom which admits of several

[1] *The Mothers*, Vol. II, pp. 448–454, 583–586.
[2] *Op. cit.*, pp. 4, 5.

explanations. Tozzer appears to think that the custom of couvade may grow out of the belief held by some savages, as the Ainu, that, as the mother gives the child a body, the father gives it a spirit. Because of the close spiritual union between father and offspring the father must refrain from any actions liable to injure the child.[1]

Pregnancy and Birth Tabus: Purification Rites. — Quite generally the awe or horror felt by many primitive peoples for menstrual blood is extended to pregnancy and childbirth. A pregnant woman must conform to certain rigid *tabus* designed to protect the community, for she is regarded as physically abnormal and at least a potential source of evil to those who approach her. Therefore it is not uncommon for an expectant mother to live in a special hut apart from her family and to refrain from eating certain foods held to be harmful to the unborn child. Tozzer cites the case of the Northwest Amazons who forbid a pregnant woman to eat the flesh of the capibara lest her children have teeth like a rodent's. Likewise she must not eat the flesh of the spotted paca or the infant will be spotted at birth. Among the Yukaghir, a Siberian tribe, a pregnant woman must raise her feet high as she walks and push stones out of her path, thus symbolizing the removal of all obstructions at childbirth. Tozzer also states that certain tribes open all locks on doors or boxes at time of confinement and untie all knots on the clothing of a woman in labor.[2]

After giving birth to a child women are generally considered to be unclean and they cannot return to life in the household and community without some purifying rite. It is interesting to note that this primitive idea has been surprisingly long-lived, being found among the ancient Hebrews and among the mediæval and modern Christians of the West. Witness the ritual of the "churching of women" after childbirth still included in the prayer-books of the Anglican and Episcopal churches, even if rarely observed. The tribes of the African

[1] *Social Origins and Social Continuities*, p. 93.
[2] *Op. cit.*, pp. 89–90.

Slave Coast employ priests and priestesses to perform purifying sacrifices after the birth of a child to prevent malicious spirits from working harm and to cleanse both mother and child from uncleanness. Not rarely a period of quarantine is required of both mother and child; and the umbilical cord, once cut, is disposed of in customary ways designed to ward off harm. Occasionally a tribe, as the Omaha Indians, makes a ceremonial announcement of the birth of a child to the tribal membership. Among the Omahas this rite took place on the eighth day after birth and consisted of a supplication to the spirits that rule the earth, the air and the heavens for the safety and well-being of the infant.[1]

The Nurture of Infants. — When the parents in primitive society are agreed that their offspring shall live, what care do they bestow upon the new-born child? The accounts of travelers reveal a wide variety of customs in respect to the nurture of children. Some tribes show a commendable desire to start the infant aright on that path of custom which is regarded as safe and honorable. Occasionally, as we have seen, an expectant mother modifies her food for the sake of her unborn child. Thus, among the Kafirs, she refrains from eating the flesh of the buck lest her child be ugly, and the under lip of the pig lest the lower lip of her baby be too large.[2] In the Banks Islands of the Pacific both parents eat only such food as would not cause the illness of a new-born child. Such food tabus are not always relaxed until a considerable time after the birth of offspring. For example, the Eskimo mother must refrain from eating raw meat a whole year and during this period is expected to put a little of her food into a skin bag after each meal. Although none of this stored-up nourishment is given to the child, the custom is called "laying up food for the infant" and is probably designed to ward off a possible future famine from its life. Quite often parental concern for offspring does not stop with food tabus.

[1] Cf. Tozzer, *op. cit.*, p. 93.
[2] Kidd, *Savage Childhood: A Study of Kafir Children*, p. 8.

Charms are plentifully used to drive off the ever-present evil spirits who might work injury to the helpless child. A Kafir woman smokes her infant over a fire of scented wood to ward off lurking demons; while the father causes his boy child to inhale the smoke of a vulture feather to make him brave.[1] It is interesting to note that the custom of hanging charms about the necks of infants is as ancient as primitive society. The savage Kafir, the Gold Coast negro, the ancient Roman and some modern peoples are all alike in maintaining this superstitious custom.

Unfortunately charms and food tabus do not prevent an enormous infant mortality among savages. A priest laboring among the primitive groups in Lower California relates that he baptized in succession seven children of one mother and buried them all "before one of them had reached its third year. . . ." Another writer cites the cases of four women among the Yakuts: one bore nine children and raised one; another also had nine and lost them all; another bore eight, all of whom died; another brought up two of the ten infants born to her. Commenting on these facts, Todd writes: "Probably these figures could be matched almost at random among savage and barbarous peoples, but it has always proved extremely difficult to collect child-mortality statistics among them, largely on account of their feeble memorial powers in this particular."[2]

It is not difficult to account for the appalling mortality-rate among savages. Ignorant as they are of the merest essentials of proper child nurture, primitive parents cheerfully violate every principle of infant hygiene. The advantages of cleanliness, fresh air and suitable food are ignored at every turn. Yakut babies are permitted to lie in damp, unventilated rooms, neglected for hours at a time; Thlinkeet infants are kept in a condition of filth which produces sores that scar their bodies for life; and Igorot children fare little better. Some tribes look askance at bathing; and the young suffer accordingly. Then,

[1] Kidd, *op. cit.*, pp. 18–19.
[2] *The Primitive Family as an Educational Agency*, p. 123.

too, the food given to children is often quite beyond their powers of digestion. We are told that Bushwomen from the birth of their children "feed them with roots and meat which they chew for them. They are taught to chew tobacco when very young, and have scarcely any human protection or attention whatever." Unfortunately primitive peoples have little knowledge of the virtues of cow's milk as an infant diet; for even in tribes where cattle are domesticated and milk can be easily procured it is quite often not given to babies. Savage mothers, to be sure, suckle their children much longer than do mothers in civilized societies, the suckling in many instances not ceasing until the child is four years old. But this custom makes it very difficult for the child when weaned to digest the coarse food eaten by adults.[1]

Home Training and Education. — If the infant is vigorous enough to withstand the effects of his oft-mistaken nurture and grows to self-reliant childhood, his training and education may begin. This falls naturally into two divisions: (1) the social and moral and (2) the practical. Of course the amount of moral training given in the primitive home depends largely upon the degree in which group customs have become fixed and authoritative. Where a tribe has well-defined notions concerning sex relations, treatment of women, attitude toward parents, food tabus, methods of warding off evil spirits, etc., the family has the important task of starting the education of the unformed child in the group way of thinking and acting in these respects. But it must not be supposed that any conscious ethical aim is present in the minds of the parents. So far as they pay any attention to the moral education of their children, this takes the form of training them in certain habits by an appeal to unthinking imitation. Discipline in savage households is generally lenient. The child is usually neither scolded nor whipped unless the parent falls into one of those sudden fits of uncontrollable passion to which primitive peoples are subject. In such cases punishment may be swift and cruel.

[1] Todd, *op. cit.*, p. 120.

Among more advanced groups, as the Pueblos of North America, a high value is consciously set upon obedience of elders and observance of moral customs. This obedience, however, is not secured by corporal punishment, but by the use of weird tales told by the older men over the evening fire, tales carefully designed to arouse superstitious fear in the shuddering boys and girls.

The part played by the mother in the moral training of her children varies with her status in the household and the group. Among tribes such as the Kafirs and the Fiji Islanders, where women are little more than beasts of burden, held in scorn and contempt, the influence of the mother must be slight indeed, at least upon her male children after the stage of infancy. Sex antagonism and sex tabus are highly developed among some primitive peoples and have worked havoc with the mother's control of her children. Webster [1] tells us that, during their initiation into full tribal membership, Hottentot youths are encouraged by their fathers and the older men publicly to flout and deride their own mothers; and in certain New Guinea tribes boys are deliberately taught to beat them as a mark of manliness. Then, too, in those tribes where the sexes remain rigidly separated, little boys are taken at two or three years of age from the mother and brought up in the "Men's House." Such club-houses are common in the Pacific Islands and even among the Southwestern tribes of the United States. On the other hand, among the more civilized Iroquois and Wyandottes, where women were the heads of households and had no little economic and political power, the influence of the mother in shaping the character of her children must have been important and lasting.

At puberty the moral education of the boys is taken out of the hands of the parents and given over to the older men of the tribe. Indeed there is good reason to believe that the initiation rites, so common in savage groups, constitute by far the most important part of the moral training of the youth. By means

[1] *Primitive Secret Societies*, p. 24.

of fasting, ordeals, dramatic representations, songs and dances, together with some explanation by way of interpretation, the tribal elders seek to impress indelibly upon the boy's excited mind the moral ideas, myths and customs of his people. The chief interest of these puberty rites for the student of the family lies in the fact that some of the ceremonies are definitely designed to prepare the boy for marriage. Also the boy learns at this time the totem groups or classes into which he may marry and those which he must carefully avoid when taking a wife. He is made by the elders to understand that he must consider the interests of the group in choosing a mate, and select a woman likely to bear children. After the long ordeals are over the youths are regarded as men and are permitted considerable sexual license before they marry.[1]

In some tribes, as puberty approaches, the girls are kept in close seclusion in huts or cages and required to fast rigidly. The light of the sun and bathing are tabu. During or after this period they may receive instruction from adult female relations in such sexual customs and household skills as it is essential for them to know.[2]

The *practical education* of boys and girls in primitive families, like their moral training, is gained quite often by blind imitation of their elders accompanied by little or no instruction. In this respect, however, marked differences exist among savage peoples. For example, the Lower Californians, the Seminoles and certain tribes of New Guinea and the Caroline Islands, pay little attention to the training of the young, while the Apache Indians, the Blackfeet, the Pueblos and the islanders in Torres Straits take much pains to train their children in practical duties. When the children grow old enough to share in the tasks of the household, they assist the mother in bringing wood and water, hunting for shellfish, lizards, edible weeds,

---

[1] See Webster, *op. cit.*, p. 43, who cites Toplin's *The Native Tribes of South Australia and Helms, New South Wales.*

[2] Frazer, *The Golden Bough*, Vol. III, pp. 204–233; Crawley, *The Mystic Rose*, pp. 215–221, 294–314.

roots, etc. Very early in their lives sex division of labor becomes marked. The boys learn by imitation of their father to make the weapons, traps and nets used in warfare, hunting and fishing; while the girls imitate the work of their mothers in cooking, weaving, skin-dressing, pottery-making and the grinding tasks of crude agriculture. Mead describes the careful training given to children among the Manus of New Guinea in adapting themselves to the dangers of life on land and sea. Even small children become masters of those fields of skill called "understanding the fire," "understanding the house" (on piles), "understanding the sea" and "understanding the canoe." Scant sympathy is shown the child who is clumsy in acquiring this knowledge, so essential to life, but every fresh gain in skill is applauded by the parents. Yet the *social* training of the young, apart from sex tabus and respect for property, is almost wholly neglected by the Manus, whose children are often disobedient, impertinent, neglectful of the convenience of their parents and given to gross obscenity of language.[1]

In some tribes, as the Eskimos, the Sioux and the Dacotah Indians, the value of directing the early play activities of children seems to have been more or less consciously felt by the parents. Thus the Eskimo boy is given a tiny bow and arrows and is encouraged to shoot at a reindeer fœtus set up for him. The Dacotah girl has a little work-bag containing an awl and some sinew; and while her mother makes moccasins she watches and imitates her.[2] Describing his boyhood among the Sioux Indians Dr. Eastman says: "Our sports were molded by the life and customs of our people; indeed we practiced only what we expected to do when grown. Our games were feats with the bow and arrow, foot and pony races, wrestling, swimming and imitation of the customs and habits of our fathers. We had sham fights with mud balls and willow wands; we played lacrosse, made war upon bees, shot winter arrows (which were only used in that season) and coasted upon the

[1] *Growing Up in New Guinea*, pp. 33, 34.
[2] Todd, *op. cit.*, p. 164.

ribs of animals and buffalo robes."[1] So far as the parents
directed this training, as they certainly did in the more advanced tribes, the home may rightly be called a school of
apprenticeship.

SELECTED READINGS

Sources

Boas, Franz. "The Central Eskimo," in *Report of the American Bureau of
Ethnology*, VI, 516–526.

Codrington, R. H. *The Melanesians*, Oxford, Clarendon Press, 1905,
Chs. II, IV.

Danks, Rev. B. "Marriage Customs of the New Britain Group," in
Journal of the Anthropological Institute, Vol. XVIII, 1889.

Eastman, C. A. *Indian Boyhood*, Little, 1902.

Ellis, A. B. *The Tshi-speaking Peoples of the Gold Coast*, Chapman,
1887, Chs. XVII, XX.

——. *The Ewe-speaking Peoples of the Slave Coast*, Chapman, 1890,
Chs. X, XVI.

——. *The Yoruba-speaking Peoples of the Slave Coast*, Chapman,
1894.

Kidd, Dudley. *Savage Childhood: A Study of Kafir Children*, London,
1906.

Malinowski, Bronislaw. *The Sexual Life of Savages in North-Western
Melanesia*, Horace Liveright, 1929.

McGee, W. J. "The Seri Indians," in *Report of American Bureau of
Ethnology*, Washington Government Printing Office, 1881–1932,
Vol. XVII, Part I, pp. 269–287.

Mead, Margaret. *Growing Up in New Guinea*, N. Y., William Morrow
and Co., 1930.

——. *Coming of Age in Samoa*, N. Y., William Morrow and Co.,
1927.

Murdock. "The Point Barrow Eskimo," in *Report of the American
Bureau of Ethnology*, Washington Government Printing Office,
1881–1932, Vol. IX, pp. 410–423.

Powell. "Wyandotte Government," in *Smithsonian Miscellaneous
Collections*, 1879–1880, Vol. XXV, pp. 76 ff.

Rivers, W. H. R. *The Todas*, Macmillan, 1906, Chs. XIV, XXII.

[1] *Indian Boyhood*, p. 64.

Spencer, Baldwin, and Gillen, F. J. *The Native Tribes of Central Australia*, Macmillan, 1899, Chs. II, VII, XVII, and pp. 406–407, 469–471.

——. *The Northern Tribes of Central Australia*, Macmillan, pp. 27–49, 70–74, 133–142, 606–618.

Stevenson, Matilda Coxe. "The Zuñi Indians," in *Report of the American Bureau of Ethnology*, Washington Government Printing Office, 1881–1932, Vol. XXIII, 1901–1902, pp. 94–107, 290–305, 349–354.

Thomas, W. I. *Source Book for Social Origins*, R. G. Badger, 1909.

SECONDARY REFERENCES

Bachofen, J. J. *Mutterrecht*, Basel, B. Schwabe, 1897.

Bosanquet, Helen. *The Family*, Macmillan, 1906, Ch. I.

Briffault, Robert. *The Mothers*, 3 Vols., Macmillan, 1927.

Bücher, Karl. *Industrial Evolution*, Holt, 1912, pp. 25–43.

Chamberlain, A. F. *The Child and Childhood in Folk-Thought*, Macmillan, 1896, Chs. VII, XIII, XIV.

Frazer, J. G. *The Golden Bough*, Macmillan, 1915, Vol. III, pp. 204–233.

Goldenweiser, Alexander A. *Early Civilization*, Knopf, 1922.

Grosse, Ernst. *Die Formen der Familie und die Formen der Wirtschaft*, Mohr, 1896, Chs. II–IX.

Hartland, E. S. *Primitive Paternity*, Holt, 1909–1910, Vol. II, Ch. I.

Hobhouse, L. T. *Morals in Evolution*, Holt, 1915, Vol. I, Ch. VI.

Howard, G. E. *History of Matrimonial Institutions*, University of Chicago Press, 1904, Vol. I.

Lowie, Robert H. *Primitive Society*, N. Y., Boni and Liveright, 1920.

McLennan, J. F. *Studies in Ancient History, Primitive Marriage*, Macmillan, 1886, pp. 87 ff., Chs. V–VIII.

Mason, O. T. *Woman's Share in Primitive Culture*, Appleton, 1910.

Morgan, Lewis H. "Houses and House-Life of the American Aborigines," Washington, 1881, Chs. III–VI. In *U. S. Geographical and Geological Survey of the Rocky Mountain Region* (Powell). *Contribution to North American Ethnology*, Vol. IV.

——. *Ancient Society*, Kerr, 1907, Part II, Chs. I, II–V, VIII.

Parsons, Elsie Clews. *The Family*, Putnam, 1906.

Spencer, F. C. *The Education of the Pueblo Child*, Columbia University Press, 1899, pp. 45–56 and Ch. IV.

Sumner, W. G. *Folkways: A Study of the Sociological Importance of Usages, Manners, Customs, Mores and Morals*, Ginn, 1907, pp. 343–476.

Todd, A. J. *The Primitive Family as an Educational Agency*, Putnam, 1913, pp. 96 ff.

Tylor, E. B. "The Matriarchal Family System," in *The Nineteenth Century*, July, 1896, Vol. XL, p. 81.

——. *Anthropology*, Appleton, 1909, Ch. XVI.

Webster, H. *Primitive Secret Societies*, Macmillan, 1908, Chs. I–V.

Westermarck, E. A. *The History of Human Marriage*, 5th ed., 3 Vols., Macmillan, 1921, Chs. I–VIII, XIV–XXIII.

CHAPTER II

THE PATRIARCHAL FAMILY: THE HEBREW TYPE

Sources of Knowledge of the Patriarchal Hebrew Family. — The most fruitful sources of information concerning the Hebrew family are found (1) in the Old Testament, especially in the Pentateuch and the Book of Ruth, and (2) in the Talmud, an ancient work consisting of the commentaries of the sages and rabbis of Israel on the Mosaic law. These commentaries on the oral law are said to go back to the period of Simon the Just, who lived at the beginning of the third century B.C. From this time to the close of the second century A.D. an unbroken succession of Jewish rabbis and judges had interpreted and reinterpreted the law of Moses as given on Mt. Sinai. About 200 A.D. the Mosaic law with its various commentaries and interpretations was codified by Rabbi Jehuda the Nasi, and this code formed the Mishna, one of the important divisions of the Talmud. The Mishna, in turn, served as the basis of a later body of commentaries called the Gemara; and these two treatises together constitute the Talmud, the authoritative exposition of the moral law for all Israel. This entire body of oral and written law was codified by Maimonides in 1180 and again by Joseph Karo of Adrianople in 1554. The latter code, best known as the Shulhan Arukh, is, with some changes, an authoritative exposition of Jewish sacred law at the present time. The treatises of the Talmud devoted to marriage and divorce are (1) Kiddushin (on betrothal); (2) Kethuboth (on dower or marriage settlements); (3) Yebamoth (on prohibited marriages and levirate); (4) Sota (on the women suspected of adultery); (5) Gittin (on divorce). In addition to these treatises there are numerous references to the duties of parents and children scattered through other books of the Talmud.

Stages of Hebrew Civilization. — Like most Semitic peoples, the Hebrews have passed from the stage of nomadic, pastoral life to the agricultural stage in which land tends to supplant cattle in property value. The legends of the Old Testament patriarchs picture them as shepherds dwelling in tents and moving from place to place in search of better pasture for their flocks and herds. Such was the life of Abraham and Lot in the Bible story. But in course of time the traditions change — the tent of the nomad gives way to the fixed abode of the dwellers in village communities; and the villages, in turn, expand into prosperous towns and cities. Flocks and herds no longer occupy the foreground, but make place for vineyards, olive gardens, orchards and cornfields. Little by little the strong tribal feeling of the Israelites becomes weaker and yields in some measure to the neighborhood tie furnished by the common interest in agricultural lands. Obviously a large tribe cannot cultivate vast arable tracts in common. Hence agriculture has commonly had the effect of breaking up the tribe into smaller groups forming village communities. These are probably the "families" or "houses" so frequently referred to in the Old Testament (see I Samuel xx, 29 ; Judges xviii, 1–2). They consisted of several households united by actual kinship or by the artificial relationship furnished by adoption into the "family." In the words of Sir Henry Maine: "The community is a community of kinsmen, but though the common ancestry is probably to a great extent real, the tradition has become weak enough to admit of considerable artificiality being introduced into the association . . . through the adoption of strangers from the outside." [1] Within the village community or "great" family, the basic family, consisting of parents, children and often grandparents and grandchildren, remains intact and has its own homestead. The heads of these households constitute the village council of elders or "fathers."

[1] *Early History of Institutions*, pp. 80, 81.

During this early period individual ownership is restricted to cattle and movables; pastures and cultivated land are held in common and portioned out to the homesteads. But by the time of King David (c. 1055–1015 B.C.) villages are expanding into cities; and in the age of Solomon, his successor, there is evidence that individual ownership of land as well as movable property is becoming more general. Commerce and industry have developed; a navy for trade with Ophir and Tarshish has been organized; and merchantmen are rising into prominence (cf. I Kings x). In the days of Ahab, King of Israel (c. 875–853 B.C.), private ownership of land is clearly established, as is shown by the attempt of Ahab to get possession of the vineyard of Naboth (I Kings xxi). Yet when tribal control was almost completely superseded by that of the family, the men of Judah were always careful to preserve the tradition of their particular "families" or "houses" within the tribes of the sons of Jacob.

With the advance of the Hebrews in civilization went a progressive softening of the early rigorous laws and customs. This had its effect upon the provision of the rabbis with respect to marriage, divorce and the rights of the man as head of the household. Little by little more consideration was shown to women and some limitations were put upon the power of the husband and father over his wives and children.

ORGANIZATION OF THE HEBREW FAMILY

The Family as Patriarchal in Type. — In the earliest times of the Old Testament narrative the Hebrew family was patriarchal in type, although it furnishes no such perfect example of this form of family organization as is afforded by ancient Rome. It is probable that the domestication of cattle and the pastoral and nomadic life which followed have had much to do with the development of the patriarchal type of family. The owner of large flocks and herds must wander in search of fresh pasture lands. He needs a numerous following to assist in tending the sheep and cattle. Thus the tendency is for a group, bound by ties of blood, to wander away from the tribe, and find its common interest in the care and protection of the herds.   Such an isolated pastoral life is usually attended by two important results : (1) the owner of the flocks seeks to subordinate all the group to his control; (2) paternal relationship is made prominent and important rather than maternal kinship.   Certainly, in patriarchal times, the Hebrews very generally traced kinship through males (Numbers i, 22 ; iii, 15–20), although evidence is not lacking that this patronymic system had supplanted an earlier maternal kinship system.[1]   Vestiges of this more primitive method of reckoning relationship are found in Genesis (Ch. xxxvi) where the "generations of Esau" are traced through his wives, and in the Book of Ruth where Leah and Rachel are referred to as the women who "did build the house of Israel" (Ruth iv, 2).

With the development of the paternal kinship system among the ancient Hebrews went a steady increase in the power of the head of the family — the patriarch — over wives, children, slaves and the *ger* or stranger within his gates.   All these, together with the daughters-in-law of the patriarch, were almost absolutely under his authority.   It would be a mistake to regard any Israelitish woman of Biblical times as a free agent.   She was all her life under male control — that of her father, older brother, husband or father-in-law.   Only the widowed mother, who frequently dwelt under her son's roof after the death of her husband, held an independent position in the household.   The male head of the family had been trained in respect and obedience to his mother, whereas his wives and concubines were regarded, at least in early times, as his property.   Even in the Talmud women are frequently grouped with slaves and children.[2]   Yet the affection of the husband for his wife, the influence of the wife's family and the

[1] See Fenton, *Early Hebrew Life* (1880), pp. 2 ff.
[2] See Bennett, "The Hebrew Family," in Hastings's *Dict. of the Bible*, Vol. I, pp. 846–849.

force of public opinion must in course of time have assisted in raising the status of the married woman above that of a mere chattel. Moreover, nowhere do we read that the patriarch held the power of life and death over his wives save in the one case of adultery (Genesis xxxviii, 24).

Like their mothers, Hebrew children in early times were almost completely under the authority of the father. That this control extended to life and death in the rude days of the patriarchs is made plain by Abraham's attempt to sacrifice his son Isaac as a burnt offering. Yet very early the Israelites were forbidden by Mosaic law to burn their children upon the altars of Moloch (Leviticus xviii, 21). In but two other respects was the power of the patriarchal father restricted : he might not make his daughter a prostitute (Leviticus xix, 29), nor might he sell her to a stranger (foreigner). Within these limits he had full authority and might marry his children as he saw fit or even sell them as slaves to a fellow-countryman (Exodus xxi, 7–9). The utmost respect and reverence toward parents, coupled with the most scrupulous obedience, were exacted of all Hebrew children. The Mosaic law required that the child who smote or cursed his father should be put to death (Exodus xxi, 15, 17) ; and the stubborn or gluttonous son was condemned to be stoned by his fellow-Israelites after the father and mother had testified against him before the elders (Deuteronomy xxi, 18–21). Apparently the father did not himself carry out the awful punishment prescribed by the law of Moses ; hence it is probable that the power of life and death was not so completely in his hands as in those of the Roman father.

The Israelitish household likewise included slaves and sometimes strangers sojourning in Israel who placed themselves under the protection of the patriarch. So long as they remained, these individuals were substantially members of the family, *i.e.*, they were under the control of its head. As for the Hebrew slave his path seems not to have been a thorny one. Instances are not lacking where a female slave became her master's concubine (Genesis xxx, 1–14) and a male slave his owner's son-in-law or even his heir (Genesis xv, 3). By the law of Israel the *purchased* slave must be set free within seven years; hence the relation of the home-born slave to his master must have been more firm and intimate than that of the slave born outside the family.

The Hebrew Family as a Religious Organization. — In addition to its other functions the Israelitish family was a religious organization of great strength and unity. At the head of the family the patriarch served as priest in the various ceremonials connected with the feasts and fasts of the Jewish religion. These elaborate religious observances were intimately connected with the home [1] and served to bind its members in religious unity. The detailed regulations of the Mosaic law concerning ritual cleanness, the strict observance of the Sabbath and the Passover, must have had the effect of making family life a continuous round of ceremonial observances. It is quite possible that at the dawn of Hebrew civilization the people were ancestor-worshipers. The Teraphim, or images, referred to in Genesis (Ch. xxxi, 19, 30–34) and held in high veneration, are regarded by some writers as symbols of family ancestors. Furthermore the family burial place was a sacred spot to every son of Israel as to the Greeks and Romans, among whom ancestor-worship was thoroughly established. Thus it may well have been true that, before the Hebrew tribes were welded into a strong nation with a national religion, each family practiced religious rites of its own, connected with the worship of ancestors. But before the dawn of Hebrew history such family cults had yielded place to the tribal and national worship of the one true God of Israel — Jahweh.

Inheritance of Property among the Ancient Israelites. — In early times the stability and unity of the Hebrew family were further secured by the preservation of landed property within the family. Even in patriarchal days the sons inherited cattle and movable property from the father; and it was

[1] The Passover is essentially a family rite.

specially decreed that the first-born son should have a double portion (Deuteronomy xxi, 15–18). At first daughters seem to have had no share in the inheritance. Later the Biblical narrative relates that the daughters of Zelophehad protested to Moses against the extinction of their father's name in Israel because he had no son. Then "the Lord spake unto Moses saying, The daughters of Zelophehad speak right; thou shalt surely give them a possession of an inheritance among their father's brethren: . . . And thou shalt speak unto the children of Israel saying, If a man die and have no son, then ye shall cause his inheritance to pass unto his daughter." Further instructions were given to Moses that in default of children, male or female, the estate should pass to the brothers or uncles of the deceased man and if none were living then the lands should be given to the next of kin (Numbers xxvii, 1–11). This "next of kin," or Goël, seems to have been a prominent figure in the Hebrew patriarchal family. Upon him devolved such important duties as the care of the widow and orphaned children of his deceased relative, the management of the property of the minor heirs, and the avenging of his kinsman's injury or death upon his enemies.

The Levirate. — Such was the desire of the Hebrew to preserve his name and estates within the tribes of Israel that a curious practice developed in primitive times and persisted long after the dawn of the Christian era. This was the custom of *levirate* whereby the brother of a man who died childless was expected to marry the dead man's widow and "raise up seed" unto his brother "that his name be not put out of Israel." The first-born child of this union became the heir of the departed Israelite and was generally regarded as his son (Deuteronomy xxv, 5, 6). Such a primitive custom, existing in modified form among certain savage groups today, was bound to meet with some opposition on the part of the brother thus used as an instrument; and even in patriarchal times a way was opened up for his escape from the distasteful duty. It was provided (Deuteronomy xxv, 7–10) that if a

man were averse to meet this obligation of raising up "unto
his brother a name in Israel" he should so declare himself in
the presence of the Hebrew elders and his brother's widow.
The repudiated woman was then privileged to loosen the shoe
of her dead husband's brother and to spit in his face with the
words : "So shall it be done unto that man that will not build
up his brother's house." This crude ceremony was called
chalitza. As civilization advanced and the aversion to levirate
marriage waxed stronger among the Jews, *chalitza* was frequently resorted to as a means of escape from an irksome obligation. The custom of levirate seems in direct opposition to
the Mosaic law expressed in Leviticus (Ch. xviii, 16 ; xx, 21),
which forbids marriage with a brother's wife. However, the
explanation of the apparent conflict is probably that the law
of levirate in Deuteronomy applied only to a special case —
that of the childless man whose name and family were threatened with extinction after his death. Thus it seems closely
connected with the ancient agrarian law of Israel which was
designed to retain all property intact within the tribe and
family. The custom of levirate may also serve as a curious
and interesting survival of the primitive tendency to look upon
women as property who may be handed over with children and
slaves to the next of kin. Be this as it may, the practice appears by no means to have died out in the time of Christ (see
Matthew xxii, 25 ff.) ; but the decisions of the rabbis during
the Middle Ages were, on the whole, in favor of abandoning it.
The ceremony of *chalitza*, however, persisted into modern times,
even though it had long since become meaningless through the
decay of levirate marriage. At the Rabbinical Conference
held in Philadelphia in 1869, it was considered advisable formally to declare the custom obsolete in the following words :
"The precept of levirate marriage, and eventually of Chalitza,
has lost to us all meaning, import and binding force." [1]

The Hebrew Family as Polygynous in Form. — Unlike the
patriarchal family as it existed among the Greeks and Romans,

---

[1] Mielziner, *The Jewish Law of Marriage and Divorce*, p. 58.

the Hebrew family was polygynous. The marriage of one man with several wives was general among the patriarchs and kings of Israel (see Judges viii, 30; II Samuel v, 13; I Kings xi, 1–3). Moreover, the practice was expressly recognized in Mosaic law (Deuteronomy xxi, 15) although some attempt was made to limit the number of wives one man might possess (Deuteronomy xvii, 17). Female slaves were quite frequently the concubines of their masters, and the law of Moses sought in some degree to protect their interests, especially by the provision that they be not sold to foreigners (Exodus xxi, 7; Deuteronomy xxi, 10–14). In early times, slave girls were sometimes voluntarily handed over by Hebrew wives to their husbands to serve as concubines. Sarah, Leah and Rachel all gave their personal slaves to their husbands as concubines and claimed the offspring of the union as their own. This custom has been found among other early societies, notably among the Spartan Greeks. Apparently the lawful wives of Hebrews did not have great advantages over concubines. Probably the children of wives inherited a larger share of their father's property than did the offspring of concubines (Genesis xxi, 10). Probably also a wife was treated with somewhat more respect and consideration than was accorded a concubine. This would depend largely upon her husband's favor, as well as upon the power and prestige of her own family. There can be small doubt that the custom of polygyny brought disharmony and division into the households of Israel, especially during the centuries following the age of the patriarchs, when advancing civilization brought refinement of sentiments and ideals. Probably the practice resulted in the division of the household into small groups each consisting of the mother and her offspring. Certainly in early patriarchal times each wife had her own abode. Thus Isaac brought his bride Rebekah "unto his mother Sarah's tent" (Genesis xxiv, 67); and Jacob's several wives and concubines had separate tents (Genesis xxxi, 33).

But widespread as was the practice of polygyny among the

Israelites it was doubtless restricted in several ways. As we have seen, the numerical proportion of male and female births among most peoples is nearly equal, although at maturity the females commonly outnumber the males because of the more dangerous pursuits, especially warfare, in which men engage. This fact alone must have made monogamy a necessity for the majority of the adult Jewish population. Then, too, the provision requiring that every man secure to his betrothed before marriage a dower to be paid in case of his death or divorce no doubt prevented many a plural marriage. Furthermore, enlightened public opinion gradually became increasingly hostile toward polygynous marriage. There is an implied protest against it in the later prophetical writings, notably in Hosea (ii, 19–23), where monogamous marriage is used as a symbol of the union of Jehovah with Israel, and in Isaiah where idolatry and polygyny are conceived as counterparts (lvii, 3–8). Again, the prophet Malachi, writing in the fifth century B.C., extolled absolute conjugal fidelity (Malachi ii, 14, 15). Yet beyond question polygynous marriage was permitted by the rabbis for many centuries during the Christian era. Writing in the second century after Christ, Justin Martyr states that Jewish law permitted a man to have four or five wives.[1] This statement is borne out by a similar declaration in Josephus.[2] It is probable, however, that polygyny gradually died out among the Hebrews in the Middle Ages and had become practically extinct before it was formally prohibited. This prohibition was pronounced at the famous rabbinical Synod of Worms in the beginning of the eleventh century by Rabbi Gershom ben Jehuda; and thus Jewish law was brought into harmony with the existing practice of monogamy. The persistence of polygyny among the Jews for a thousand years after they were scattered among European peoples at least nominally monogamic is a striking fact.

[1] *Trypho*, p. 134.   Quoted in Bennett, "The Hebrew Family," in *Dict. of the Bible*, Vol. I, p. 848.

[2] *Antiquities of the Jews*, Bk. XVII, Ch. I, § 3.

MARRIAGE LAWS AND CUSTOMS

Respect in Which Marriage Was Held. — For several reasons marriage was held in high esteem among the people of Israel. Doubtless in rude pastoral times economic and social causes were at the basis of this esteem.   Large families were a blessing to the patriarchs, since the boys could render valuable assistance in tending the flocks, tilling the fields and guarding the homestead of their father.   The girls, though less esteemed, were yet of value for domestic service and for the price they brought as wives or concubines.   Then, too, marriage was regarded as a family affair rather than a personal one; indeed, the generation of offspring was the supreme motive of every union, to the end that a man's "house" or family might not die out in Israel.   The present conception of marriage as the completion of the personal life and happiness of the man and woman concerned would have been incomprehensible to the Hebrews of old as to all ancient peoples.   Later, in the age of the Messianic prophecies, marriage gained an added sanctity from the precious possibility that the fruit of the union might be the promised Messiah of the Jews, its long-desired savior from oppression.   It is probable also that the more reflective of the Hebrews recognized the value of early marriages in restricting sexual license.   In the Babylonian Talmud Rabbi Huna states: "Whoever is twenty years old and has not taken a wife his days are all polluted with sin. . . .   All his days are defiled with sinful thoughts."   And Rabbi Chisda, commenting on the same theme of early marriage, further states: "If I was better able to learn than my companion, it has this explanation, for I married at my sixteenth year.   And if I had married at my fourteenth, I should have said to Satan: A dart in thine eyes." [1]   All these reasons, together with a highly developed parental instinct, combined to secure for marriage, especially when blessed with children, an honorable place in Hebrew life.

[1] Wünsche, *Der babylonische Talmud* (ed. 1878), *Tractat Kidduschin*, Vol. III, pp. 87, 88.

Conditions Necessary to a Valid Marriage. — The Mosaic law and the later commentaries upon it laid down certain conditions which must be complied with if a marriage were to be valid. These conditions were concerned with (1) prohibited marriages, (2) the legal age of the parties and (3) their consent to the marriages.

Prohibited Marriages. — In the Books of Leviticus and Deuteronomy prohibitions are declared against marriages within certain degrees of relationship. A man may not marry his half-sister, his daughter-in-law, his aunt, his uncle's or his brother's widow, or his wife's sister *during the lifetime of the wife* (Leviticus xviii, 18; xx). The rabbis later extended these prohibitions to ascending and descending lines of whatever degree of relationship, although they permitted marriage between cousins and between step-brothers and sisters. By later Talmudic law the above prohibitions were enlarged to include the following: (1) A man might not marry his divorced wife who had remarried and become a widow, or been again divorced. It has been suggested that this regulation was designed to prevent a current practice of exchanging wives.[1] (2) A man was not permitted to remarry a wife divorced for barrenness or bad reputation. The desire of the Hebrews for offspring led them frequently to dissolve an unfruitful marriage as not having accomplished its true function. In such a case it was held that the union should not be renewed. (3) A man who had committed adultery with another man's wife or who was under suspicion of so doing was forbidden to marry the woman after she had been divorced. Such a prohibition seems designed as a penalty exacted for this supreme marital offense. The children of the foregoing prohibited unions were regarded by all Hebrews as bastards or "mamzers" and were forever sternly denied the privilege of marrying Jewish women or men of legitimate birth.

The Element of Consent. — Quite early in Hebrew history the law required that the consent of the parties to a marriage

[1] See Mielziner, *The Jewish Law of Marriage and Divorce*, p. 42, footnote.

be a condition of its validity. Furthermore it was stipulated that this consent should not be forced. Probably the woman was favored in this regard, since the law declared that if her consent were compelled, the marriage was *ipso facto* null and void. If, on the contrary, the consent of the male were forced, no such consequence followed, since he could at once free himself by divorce. Neither idiots nor the insane were regarded by the Jews as capable of contracting a valid marriage since the union depended upon intelligent consent. Curiously enough, also, the consent of parents to a marriage was not a legal requirement if the parties were of age; yet respect for parents was so thoroughly ingrained in Jewish children that marriages against their will must have been very rare.

Legal Age for Marriage. — By Talmudic law the legal age for contracting marriage was fixed at puberty — the completed twelfth year in females and the completed thirteenth in the case of males. Marriage under that age was void. Nevertheless the father was permitted to contract for the marriage of his daughter before she had attained puberty; but if on reaching legal age, the girl refused to carry out the contract, it became null and void. In this regard Talmudic law seems distinctly in advance of the marriage laws of Greece and Rome; yet this advantage may be more apparent than real. Few young girls or boys brought up in the spirit of respectful awe and submission toward parents, so thoroughly inculcated in Hebrew homes, would ever attempt defiance of parental wishes. Moreover, girls, at least, soon learned that marriage meant security and assured social position. In the half-barbarous ages of the patriarchs, and for a long period thereafter, the condition of the unmarried woman without a male protector must have been forlorn indeed. Having no independent existence, either legally or from an economic standpoint, her lot was bound to be a cruel one if she lacked father, brother or husband to protect and support her. For in ancient society *families*, not individuals, were in a far truer sense than today the units of society. Outside some family the individual was virtually an outcast. This condition gave rise to the custom of contracting very young girls in marriage — a custom that flourished during the Jewish persecutions of the Middle Ages. Yet not all rabbis approved of this practice and at least one well-known Talmudic authority protested against it as early as the third Christian century: "It is a moral wrong," he urges, "that a father should contract a marriage in behalf of his daughter before she has attained the age of consent." [1]

Legal Formalities in Contracting Marriage. — Apparently the law of Moses made little distinction between betrothal and marriage (see Deuteronomy xx, 7; xxii, 23, 24). The betrothed woman was practically a wife. According to Epstein, Jewish marriage was originally "a cash transaction — the money for the bride paid and the bride delivered." [2] Betrothal and marriage were one. But after the Babylonian Captivity, when the law of the rabbis developed as an extension of the primitive Mosaic law, betrothal and nuptials were established as two distinct ceremonies.

Betrothal. — As among most ancient peoples, the ceremony of betrothal was the actual beginning of marriage, although the union was not consummated until later. Consequently the girl who proved faithless to her betrothed was treated as an adulteress, and received the cruel punishment meted out to that offender among the Israelites. Betrothal was a solemn contract of marriage involving certain customary formalities. Either of two rites might be chosen since both were perfectly legal: (1) Kaseph (money); (2) Kiddushin (a written instrument). According to the first the man gave to the woman a coin of small value with the words, "Be thou wedded (or consecrated) to me." Even the Peruta, a copper piece of the lowest denomination, was frequently used. This

---

[1] Mieliziner, *op. cit.*, p. 83.
[2] Epstein, L. M. *Jewish Marriage Contract; a Study of the Status of the Woman in Jewish Law*, p. 12.

little ceremony is of interest since it appears to have been the last vestige among the Jews of marriage by outright purchase — once a common practice. In patriarchal times Abraham's servant gave rich "gifts" to Rebekah's mother and brother that he might win the damsel for his master's son Isaac (Genesis xxiv, 51–53); and Jacob, who was an exile without property to exchange for a wife, was obliged to serve his uncle Laban fourteen years for Rachel (Genesis xxix, 16–30). Again Hamor, prince of the Hivites, sought to win Jacob's daughter Dinah to be his son's wife by offering "never so much dowry and gift" (Genesis xxxiv, 12). Clearly, in these rude days, and for ages after, women were regarded, quite frankly, as having a property value. But by the time of the Roman rule in the first century, B.C., the crude act of purchase had become a mere symbol. Indeed, certain writers maintain that the custom of betrothal by *Kaseph* did not originate before the age of King Herod (reigned 40–4 B.C.) and was probably borrowed from a similar marriage form in use among the Romans (*coëmptio*). Under Roman influence, also, a ring came to be used instead of the coin during the Middle Ages. In betrothal by Kiddushin the groom gave to his bride a written document which probably read "I, so-and-so, do hereby betroth thee, so-and-so, according to the law of Moses and Israel." [1] In both ceremonies of betrothal the presence of two qualified witnesses was essential. After this simple rite, a benediction upon the young couple was pronounced, in which references were made to Jehovah's sanctification of marriage and to the Talmudic law that the marriage must not be consummated until after nuptials. This benediction might be pronounced by a rabbi, invited to be present, or by the male relative of the bride who gave her in marriage.

Nuptials. — In later Biblical times quite commonly a year intervened between betrothal and the nuptial rites which concluded the marriage, yet had no legal significance at first.

[1] Epstein, *op. cit.*, p. 11.

In course of time, however, popular opinion came to hold that the bride is not really a wife until after nuptials. This belief tended to weaken the bond of betrothal and strengthen that of nuptials, which became a real legal factor in the marriage, with important financial consequences. If a betrothed woman died before nuptials, her father (not her betrothed) inherited her possessions. On the other hand, the obligations of the husband to furnish sustenance, shelter, ransom and burial no longer applied to his betrothed.[1] Essentially, nuptials consisted in the conduct of the bride in gay procession surrounded by her friends and greeted by songs, to her husband's home. By this act she was brought under his marital control; and with the commencement of their life together the marriage was held to be consummated. The wedding procession was followed by a banquet after which friends of the bride led her to the nuptial chamber. By Talmudic law simple religious rites, such as the recital of benedictions, accompanied the wedding festivities. The presence of a rabbi at nuptials was not a legal requirement, however, and the benedictions might be pronounced by the bridegroom himself or by any of the ten witnesses demanded by the law. Thus it will be seen that both betrothal and nuptials were regarded by the Hebrews as largely *private* matters, in which neither civil nor religious authorities were required to take part. Indeed a marriage was recognized as *legally valid* without any religious rites whatever, although, since these were held to add solemnity to the contract, their omission was probably rare. Apparently the custom of requiring the presence of a rabbi at nuptials was not thoroughly established until late in the Middle Ages. It is noteworthy that this private character of Hebrew marriage is common to the rites of nearly all ancient peoples. Only very gradually does private contract marriage yield to the complete control of religion and later of the state.

The Ketubah or Marriage Deed. — Although most rabbis

[1] Epstein, *op. cit.*, p. 14.

ascribe far greater antiquity to the *Shetar Kiddushin*, or simple declaration of marriage given to the bride at betrothal, than to the *Ketubah*, or marriage deed, Epstein holds that originally the two were one instrument. Later the Ketubah developed from a mere deed of marriage into a "memorandum of guarantees."[1] This change took place about a century before the Christian era when Simeon ben Shetah, President of the Sanhedrin[2] in Jerusalem, promulgated the law of the marriage deed as a memorandum of the rights and obligations of the parties to the marriage. The contents of the Ketubah were made out by the husband. First appeared the marriage clause, in earliest times uttered by the father, but later, in accordance with Talmudic law, pronounced by the husband: "Behold thou art consecrated (or betrothed) unto me according to the law of Moses and Israel." This formula is used even to this day by orthodox Jews. Next appeared a declaration that the *mohar*, or purchase price, had been paid and received. In early times this was paid in cash to the father, later to the bride herself and later still, by the law of Simeon ben Shetah, it became a mere promise to pay a fixed sum to the wife in case of her divorce or her husband's death. This sum was a minimum of 200 zuzim, or 50 shekels, in the case of a virgin but only half that sum in the case of a widow. The mohar clause of the Ketubah reads: "And I shall give thee the mohar of thy virginity, two hundred silver zuzim, Biblically due thee." Because of the greater value attached to a virgin, it was customary to establish the virginity of the bride before mohar was paid. In addition to the mohar the husband often made gifts to the bride which were called *mattan* and later were fused with the mohar.

The third clause of the Ketubah enumerated the dowry received by the husband with his bride. Even in ancient times it was customary for Jewish fathers to give their

---

[1] Epstein, *op. cit.*, p. 11.

[2] The supreme council of the Jewish people consisting of seventy-one priests, scribes and elders.

daughters a marriage dowry.   Sarah, Rachel and Leah, in the Biblical narrative, all received slaves as part of their dowry. In early Jewish custom the dowry represented a daughter's share of her father's property and took the form of gifts to the bride at her wedding which were regarded as *her private possession*.   The husband did not even enjoy the usufruct of the dowry in Old Testament times.   But in the early centuries of the Christian era there were issued a series of rabbinical laws limiting a wife's control of her private estate (called *mulug*). Not only was she forbidden to sell it, but the income of the property was given over to her husband.   Epstein quotes a mishna (or rabbinical ruling) of Christian times as revealing the "pitiful poverty of a married woman": "A woman and a slave are bad opponents : whoever injures them is liable for damage, but they are not liable for injury to others."   And he adds a saying from the Talmud : "How can a woman have anything; whatever is hers belongs to her husband." [1]   However, a husband could not sell his wife's mulug without her consent ; and if he died first, she would regain her dowry, mohar and mattan, and such other property as belonged to her.   It is interesting to note how similar are the rabbinical laws, depriving a married woman of all control of her property and enjoyment of its income, to the laws that prevailed in ancient Rome and in Western Europe almost to modern times.   It would seem as if men in former ages clearly realized that control of the purse-strings spells power ; and that, conversely, depriving a married woman of financial independence results in her subjugation.

In the fourth clause of the Ketubah the law of succession to property *in case that no issue were living* was laid down.   Early Jewish law decreed that a husband had no right of succession to his wife's property.   But in later times the rabbis showed a disposition to modify this practice in favor of the husband until he was made "an heir of the first order" after the nuptial ceremonies were performed.   And this remained the final

[1] *Op. cit.*, p. 112,

Jewish law. On the other hand, a widow with no issue had no claim on her husband's estate. If she had children, she was supported by her husband's heirs. The inheritance clause was followed by one laying down the conditions of divorce. These will be considered later. There followed the sixth clause of the Ketubah prescribing fines for mistreatment of the wife and for her expulsion from the home. The later rabbinic Ketubah no longer contained this general mistreatment clause but instead a statute providing against specific kinds of mistreatment. Last in the older Ketubah was a clause laying limitations upon polygamy and fines for their infringement. The rabbis of the Christian era strongly advised that no man should marry more than four wives "so that he can be with each wife at least once a month." Conjugal intercourse with his wives was a husband's duty, no matter how many wives he had, and failure to perform his sexual obligations constituted ground for divorce on his wife's part. Indeed, so important did the rabbis regard the sexual duty of marriage that willful neglect of it subjected both husband and wife to a fine. The wife's neglect, however, was regarded as the more serious offense, entailing a larger fine which was deducted weekly from the financial provisions of her Ketubah until it was canceled.

In the later rabbinic Ketubah there appeared certain clauses not contained in the earlier instrument. Among these were a promise to give the wife food, clothing, medicine, ransom in case of capture, burial and marital satisfaction. The husband's duty to support his wife arose from the generally accepted belief that "he owns her as he owns his slave." [1] As in modern times the amount and kind of maintenance was determined by the husband's means and social status. A further clause of the rabbinic Ketubah obligated the husband to pay his wife's debts. Next came an order to support the wife and unmarried daughters out of the estate after the husband's death. Finally was added a clause placing a lien on the husband's property for fulfillment of all the terms of the

[1] Epstein, *op. cit.*, p. 149.

Ketubah. It is clear that these later provisions of the marriage deed were designed to protect the interests of the wife who had been reduced to a condition of complete financial dependence.[1] Not until late in the Middle Ages was any attempt made to modify Jewish law relating to the wife's property, and even then the action was taken only by the rabbis of France and Northern Italy. These rabbis adjudged that the dowry of a childless wife dying in the first year of marriage should be returned to her father or his heirs.

DIVORCE AMONG THE HEBREWS

Rights of the Husband. — From the days of the patriarchs until the Christian era no restrictions were placed upon the right of a Hebrew to divorce his wife. The Mosaic law (Deuteronomy xxiv, 1, 2) states that if a wife find no favor in her husband's eyes because of "some uncleanness in her : then let him write her a bill of divorcement and give it in her hand, and send her out of his house." But long before the birth of Christ the later prophets had expressed their strong disapproval of divorce, and Malachi (450 B.C.) declared in no uncertain tones that Jehovah looked upon the custom with hatred (Malachi ii, 14, 16). About the time of Christ the opposed rabbinical schools of Shammai and Hillel disagreed concerning the meaning of the Biblical expression "some uncleanness." The School of Hillel interpreted the term to mean anything displeasing to the husband and thus countenanced the current practice which gave to the husband unlimited freedom of divorce. On the contrary the School of Shammai understood the words to mean serious moral fault or actual unchastity, and would thus have sharply curtailed the husband's privileges. However, the customary interpretation of Hillel prevailed for many centuries.[2] As is well known, Christ disagreed with the views

[1] For the above account of the Ketubah the author is indebted to Dr. Epstein's book *Jewish Marriage Contract* . . ., published by the Jewish Theological Seminary of America in 1927.

[2] Mielziner, *The Jewish Law of Marriage and Divorce*, p. 106.

of his age and recognized no right of divorce save for the cause of adultery (Matthew v, 32), but His teachings seem to have had no effect upon Hebrew custom in this respect. In the early centuries of the Christian era the moral sense of the rabbis clearly revolted against the custom of unrestricted divorce. Rabbi Yohanan (199–279 A.D.) boldly declared that "He that putteth her (his wife) away is hated of God." By this time also enlightened public opinion tended to regard with disapproval the divorce of the wife save for certain definite moral offenses such as adultery, flagrant disregard of moral decency, refusal to cohabit for a year or more, change of religion, refusal to carry out the ritual law in household management and insulting the husband or his father in his presence. Physical disability, such as leprosy and barrenness, was likewise regarded as just ground for the divorce of the wife. Early in the eleventh century, however, at the Sanhedrin of Mayence, Rabbi Gershom ben Yehudah declared: "To assimilate the right of the woman to the right of the man, it is ordained that even as the man does not put away his wife except of his own free will, so shall the woman not be put away except by her own consent." [1] Presumably this ordinance did not affect the right of the husband in cases of adultery or grave moral delinquency.

Privileges of the Wife. — In the days of the patriarchs the Hebrew wife had no rights of divorce whatever save in the one case cited in Exodus xxi, 7–11. Here it is provided that the bondwoman, raised by her master to the status of a wife (or concubine), shall go free if her husband fails to provide for her. She shall receive no money, but her husband is bound to give her a bill of divorcement. Some writers maintain that this provision was the germ out of which grew the wife's right to demand divorce for certain causes, a right which they claim was very early extended to free wives in Israel. No clear evidence of such a privilege exists, however, before the period of the Roman occupation of Palestine (after 65 B.C.). Under

[1] Amram, *The Jewish Law of Divorce*, p. 52.

the influence of Roman law and custom, the practice of the divorce of the husband by the wife gradually became general. However, the wife must use the indirect method of requesting the husband to write her a *get* or bill of divorcement, which, in case of his refusal, must have made it difficult for her to win freedom.[1] The causes recognized by rabbinical law were (1) physical impotence if admitted by the husband, (2) change of religion, (3) extreme dissoluteness, (4) refusal to support, (5) continued ill-treatment, (6) commission of a crime followed by escape from the country, (7) affliction with a loathsome disease or pursuit of a disgusting trade, both acquired after marriage. It is interesting to note that most of these causes are recognized by many states in America today as constituting just grounds for divorce. Likewise it is noteworthy that adultery on the part of the husband was not regarded in rabbinical law as a serious offense against the wife giving her the right of divorce. Until comparatively recent times Western nations likewise held this position, a position having its foundation in the double standard of morals which condones as venial in the man an act regarded as beyond forgiveness in the woman.

Status of the Divorced Woman. — The social position of a divorced wife was vastly more independent than that of her unmarried or married sisters. She was for the first time in her life entirely in "her own power" (*sui juris*). Not only was she freed from the control of husband and father, but, in a *legal* sense, she was no longer a member of her father's family, since in families of the patriarchal type, this membership fundamentally consisted in being under the power of the male head. If a divorced woman were innocent of any grave fault, she lost nothing in social standing by her divorce and she gained the priceless privilege of marrying in accordance with her own desires. Moreover, the return of her dowry was an inalienable right of the divorced wife if she were innocent of wrong. In cases where the wife was convicted of moral offenses or breach of the law of ritual cleanness in household management, she

[1] Amram, *op. cit.*, pp. 63–77.

lost all right to the dowry. And be it remembered that "immorality" in a wife was not restricted in ancient times to adultery, but included such relatively trivial offenses as going abroad bareheaded with her hair loose, spinning in the streets, flirting with strange men or scolding so noisily as to disturb the neighbors. Women who refused to cohabit or who deserted their husbands also lost all claim to the Kethubah.[1]

Control of Divorce by the Courts. — In early times divorce, like marriage, was purely a private concern with which neither law nor rabbis interfered. It consisted simply in the husband's handing the wife a "Get" or Bill of Divorce containing the words "Be thou divorced (or separated) from me." At a later period, however, the rabbis, looking to the protection of the woman, prescribed, in minute detail, the formalities to be gone through with in writing and handing over the bill of divorce. These regulations were probably designed to afford an angry husband time for reflection and reconsideration. The court further encroached upon the earlier private character of divorce by *enforcing separation upon husband or wife* in cases where the marriage was opposed to rabbinical law, *e.g.*, where the wife was found guilty of adultery, where either party was afflicted with a loathsome and incurable disease, or where the marriage was childless. In the latter case the essential purpose of marriage was held to have been unfulfilled and therefore the union was dissolved by the rabbis with or without the consent of the parties. It is evident that the control of divorce, as well as of marriage among the Hebrews, was more and more taken over by the religious authorities; and this has been the history of the marriage institution among our forefathers in Western Europe until a comparatively recent period, when divorce cases have been relegated to the secular courts.

Custody and Support of Children of Divorced Parents.— In ancient times the offspring of any Israelitish marriage belonged to the father and remained with him as his property after the wife's divorce. But with the advance of civilization

[1] Amram, *op. cit.*, p. 123.

more just ideas prevailed concerning the mother's rights in her children.　During the early Christian era the rabbis rather tended to favor the woman in their judgments on this question, probably because of the boundless rights of divorce possessed by the husband.　The law came to demand that the divorced mother of a suckling child be provided for by the husband until the child was weaned.　Toward the close of the third century A.D. certain rabbis of Palestine and Babylon took the ground that a divorced mother could keep her son with her until his sixth year and her daughter permanently.　The husband was liable for his son's support during the time that he remained with the mother and was also liable for the support of his daughter until her marriage.　Furthermore, if the mother for any reason declined to keep the children, the father was bound to do so.　In the event of the father's death the children became "wards of the congregation."　An impartial survey of these Talmudic regulations shows how far the Hebrews had traveled in the direction of equity with respect to women since those primitive ages when a woman was regarded as the property of father or husband.　Although she was still a minor before the law and under the control of some male authority, she was coming to be regarded as nevertheless an individual possessed of certain positive rights.

JEWISH HOME LIFE AND TRAINING

The Economy of the Hebrew Household. — After the pastoral age among the Hebrews there ensued, as we have seen, a period when agriculture was the dominant pursuit.　In these patriarchal days the land was held in common, and certain portions were given out to individual homesteads for cultivation.　As the generations passed, however, communal ownership gave place to private, and great estates came into the possession of single families.　Within each separate household division of labor, as in primitive times, was upon a sex basis.　The man pursued agriculture or trade and fulfilled such political and religious duties as devolved upon him as a citizen and head of a family. In his home were carried on various productive industries all under the direction of the Hebrew housewife. Indeed the households of Israel were well-nigh self-sustaining in Old Testament times. That beautiful chapter in Proverbs (xxxi, 10–31) which extols the virtues of a good wife sketches in clear outlines the numerous activities of a Jewish woman. Apparently she sometimes purchased the fields and planted the vineyards in which she raised the raw products to be manufactured in the household. She spun and wove the wool and flax that later she fashioned into garments for her entire family. She embroidered tapestries and made clothing of silken stuffs. Also the Biblical narrative tells us that she sold "fine linen" and "girdles" of her own making to the merchant. From her stores she gave out daily to her servants the supplies of food necessary for the family and kept careful oversight of their work when she did not herself prepare the food for the table. Her children were the objects of her special care; and as they grew up they did not fail to "call her blessed." Even the poor and needy at her gates were the recipients of her thoughtful bounty.

To her other duties the Hebrew woman added the solemn obligation of preparing all food used by the family in strict accordance with the ritual law. She must never serve as food the flesh of animals which do not cleave the hoof and chew the cud, such being regarded as ritually unclean. Moreover all clean animals must be slaughtered according to the elaborate prescriptions of Talmudic law; and the flesh of these animals must be rejected if certain specified defects or taints were discovered in the organs. The vessels and utensils used in the Feast of the Passover must be carefully cleansed without water and put away for use at the return of the sacred festival. The housewife, furthermore, must separate "the first of her dough" for the priest if she would bring a blessing on her house and avoid misfortune. Then, too, she must follow exactly all the minute and detailed regulations of the Talmud concerning the right observance of the Sabbath. As we have seen, failure to comply with any of these elaborate ritual laws constituted valid ground for divorcing the wife.

The tracts of the Talmud treating of the Sabbath shed a flood of light on the employments of the Hebrew housewife. These regulations make it clear that bleaching linen thread in ovens prepared for the purpose and the making of ink and dyes for woolen cloths were domestic industries. Olives and grapes were crushed in "press-pits," and dates were put up in the home for sale in the market. The Talmudic tracts also mention a wide variety of household implements and utensils such as spindles, shuttles, mortars, skimmers, kneading-troughs, pottery and hand-mills.[1] Most Hebrew families owned hand-mills which were usually worked by slaves, or, in poorer homes, by two women of the family. From all this it is clear that the housewife in Israel was a valuable economic factor. In the words of Solomon: ". . . her price is above rubies for she looketh well to the ways of her household and eateth not the bread of idleness."

The Jewish Home as a Training School of the Young. — The preceding discussions have, perhaps, made it clear that the Jewish household was a closely knit social, religious and economic organization ruled by a patriarchal head in whom centered powers at first almost unlimited. But the Hebrew home had other highly important functions to perform which were regarded as of the utmost value to the families and tribes of Israel. The household was the only educational institution for the masses of the people until the time of Christ, and the parents were the chief teachers. The relation of Hebrew parents and children was such as we should expect to find in a family of the patriarchal type. In the hands of the father reposed great power with respect to the training of his children and the direction of their lives, even after they had married in accordance with his desires. Great respect and reverence

---

[1] Cf. *Babylonian Talmud* (trans. by Michael Rodkinson), Vol. I, pp. 23, 24, 27–28, 41, 55; Vol. II, Ch. XVIII.

toward parents, coupled with exact and unquestioning obedience, were demanded of all Hebrew children from their babyhood; and even at the present time the affectionate consideration of Jewish children for their aged parents is often in pleasing contrast to the attitude of the children of other races.

But the powers of the father in Israel carried with them certain serious responsibilities. Upon him rested the duty of bringing up his offspring in the fear of Jehovah and in the knowledge of His law. It was expected that he "command his children and his household after him, and they shall keep the way of the Lord, to do justice and judgment" (Genesis xviii, 19). By the law of Moses every Hebrew male child must be circumcised on the eighth day of his life and thus set apart to Jehovah (Genesis xvii, 10). Then, too, the first-born son must be redeemed by the payment of five shekels to a *cohen* or descendant of Aaron. In the Babylonian Talmud it is written: "Our Rabbis have taught: The father is obliged to circumcise his son, to redeem him, to teach him the Books of Moses (Torah), to marry him and to have him taught a trade. According to many he must also let him learn to swim." [1] But the father did not carry this responsibility alone. He was assisted by the Hebrew mother who took an active part in the child's training until he was five years of age. At his mother's knee the boy learned brief prayers and passages from the Books of Moses. As soon as he could speak he was taught to say: "The law which Moses commanded us is the heritage of the congregation of Jacob." His mother also taught him to utter the inspiring words: "Hear, O Israel, the Eternal our God is one God." After his fifth birthday the boy came more directly under the care of his father, who instructed him in the Torah (Mosaic law), and such portions of the Talmud as it was essential for every good Israelite to know. Furthermore, every father owed it to his son to teach him a trade as a means of livelihood. In the Babylonian Talmud Rabbi Jehuda is

[1] Wünsche, *Der babylonische Talmud*, p. 90.

credited with the saying : "Whoever does not permit his son to learn a trade it amounts to the same as if he had taught him robbery." [1]   That it was customary for the ancient Hebrews to employ "artisan masters " for the instruction of their sons seems evident from the prohibition in the Talmud forbidding such teachers to be engaged on the Sabbath.

Every son of Israel thus carefully trained was expected to fulfill certain obligations laid down in the Talmud where it is written : "In what does the fear and reverence which the son owes to his father consist ?   The fear (or awe) shows itself in this that the son does not stand or sit in his father's place in the congregation, does not speak in opposition to him and also does not take upon himself judgment against him (in any controversy).   Reverence consists in this, that the son give his father food and drink, clothe and shelter him and lead him in and out.   Some one has asked : Out of whose means (shall this be done)?   According to Rabbi Jehuda, out of the son's means, according to Rabbi Nathan bar Oschaja, out of the father's means." [2]

It was Rabbi Joshua ben Gamla to whom the honor is due of having instituted schools apart from the homes in every town and village of Palestine.   This great work was undertaken about the time of Christ and aroused profound interest throughout the nation.   An ordinance was made providing that the inhabitants of every town must establish a school which male children at the ages of six or seven should be compelled to attend.   The chief subject-matter in the new schools continued to be the Mosaic law and the two portions of the Talmud called the Mishna and the Gemara.   Probably the Greek language was also studied, since intercourse between Greeks and Hebrews had been greatly stimulated by trade and travel.   Advanced students likewise paid some attention to the sciences of geometry and astronomy.

[1] Wünsche, *Der babylonische Talmud*, p. 87.
[2] *Ibid.*, p. 97.

Hitherto nothing has been said of the education of girls. Yet their intellectual training was not wholly neglected. Certain passages in the Talmud seem to point to private instruction of girls in the Jewish religion and ritual. Indeed this training would appear to be imperative if Hebrew women were to conduct their households in accordance with ritual law. Occasionally, also, a Jewish girl was taught a foreign language, usually Greek.[1] There can be little doubt, however, that the education of girls was above all things designed to fit them for their special sphere — the management of a household — and was therefore almost wholly domestic. Young women of every rank in life were taught cooking, spinning, weaving and fashioning of garments. Such religious and moral training as they received through participation in family worship and study of the sacred writings served to make them better mothers, capable of giving wise assistance to their husbands in their responsible task of bringing up their children in the fear of Jehovah.

The Hebrew family, then, was a school of great moral and social value. Representing as it did a strongly knit organization, with well-defined social, religious, economic and educational functions, the Jewish household affords a contrast little less than startling to our modern individualistic homes which have long relegated many of these duties to such specialized social agencies as the school, the church and various clubs and organizations for children.

SELECTED READINGS

SOURCES

Babylonian Talmud, English trans. by Michael Rodkinson, "Tracts on the Sabbath," Macmillan, Vols. I, II.

Bible. Books of Genesis, Deuteronomy, Leviticus, Numbers, Judges, Ruth.

Wünsche, Aug. *Der babylonische Talmud*, Ebend, 1886, Vol. II, pp. 82–97.

[1] Spiers, *Education in the Talmud.*

SECONDARY WORKS

Amram, D. W.   *The Jewish Law of Divorce*, Greenstone, 1896.

Barton, Geo. A.   *A Sketch of Semitic Origins*, Philadelphia, 1896, New York, 1902, Ch. II.

Bennett, W. H.   "The Hebrew Family," in Hastings's *Dictionary of the Bible*, Scribner, 1909, I, 846–850.

Edersheim, A.   *Sketches of Jewish Social Life in the Days of Christ*, London, Religious Tract Society, 1876, Chs. VI–VIII.

Ellis, A. B.   "Marriage and Kinship among the Ancient Israelites," *Popular Science Monthly*, January, 1893, XLII, 325–337.

Epstein, L. M.   *Jewish Marriage Contract; a Study of the Status of the Woman in Jewish Law*, New York, Jewish Theological Seminary of America, 1927.

Fenton, John.   *Early Hebrew Life*, London, Trübner and Co., 1880, pp. 1–45, 53–65.

Gide, P.   *Étude sur la condition privée de la femme*, Paris, Durand et Pedone-Lauriel, 1867, pp. 58–66.

Hobhouse, L. J.   *Morals in Evolution*, Holt, 1915, pp. 200–203.

Jewish Encyclopedia, Articles on "Marriage," the "Family," "Woman," "Divorce," Funk, 1925.

Kayserling, M.   *Die judischen Frauen in der Geschichte, Literatur und Kunst*, Leipzig, Brockhaus, 1879, pp. 119–133.

Mielziner, Dr. M.   *The Jewish Law of Marriage and Divorce*, Bloch, 1901.

Morgan, L. H.   *Ancient Society*, Kerr, 1907, pp. 366 ff.

Patterson, W. P.   *Hebrew Marriage*, in Hastings's *Dictionary of the Bible*, Scribner, 1909, Vol. III, 262–277.

Schuster, E. J.   *The Wife in Ancient and Modern Times*, London, Williams and Norgate, 1911, Ch. I.

Spiers, Rev. B.   *The School System of the Talmud*, London, Stock, 1898.

CHAPTER III

THE PATRIARCHAL FAMILY: THE GREEK TYPE

Relation of the Athenian Family to the Gens and Tribe. —
In the time of the lawgiver Solon (c. 600 B.C.) the Athenian
Greeks were divided into four tribes. Each tribe was organized into three phratries, or religious brotherhoods, and
these in turn were divided into thirty *gentes* or "great families"
tracing descent to some common ancestor. This being was
quite generally believed to be of divine origin or one of the
renowned heroes of Greek antiquity. The gens or "great
family" had important functions to perform. Upon it devolved the responsibility of investigating the legitimacy of
every new-born child within its midst. In the case of male
children this legitimacy, as well as the child's descent from pure
Athenian ancestry on both sides, must be established before the
name of the boy could be entered upon the register of the gens
as a future citizen-member. In no period of Greek history
do we find property held in common by the gens as was the case
among the early Hebrews. The institution of private property
seems established even in Homeric times, although the gens
could prevent the alienation of lands from the kinship group.
To this end, if the head of a family died leaving no sons, his
daughter, if he had one, was forced by her kinsmen in the gens
to marry the nearest male relative of her father. In some
instances this custom forced the uncle of an heiress, himself
already married, to divorce his wife in order to marry his niece
and thus become the head of the family in the place of his
deceased brother.

The Greek Family as Patriarchal in Form. — The Greek
family, like that of the Hebrews, was patriarchal in type; that

is, all power was centered in the father as the governing head. Indeed the word for "father" in the Hebrew, Greek and Roman tongues signified, fundamentally, not paternal relationship, but authority, dignity and power.   Yet there was clearly a difference between the source of patriarchal authority in the case of the Hebrews and of the Greeks.   In the former instance the father was an absolute monarch in his own right, patterning his government after that of an all-powerful Jehovah.   The Greek father, on the contrary, derived his authority from the fact that he was the trustee of the family estates and power and priest of the domestic worship of ancestors.   The family, then, not the patriarch, was the unit of power in Greece, and the father's authority was derivative, not inherent.

The Kinship System of the Greeks. — Although the Greeks in the historic period traced kinship exclusively through males, certain evidences may be found in their literature of an earlier custom of reckoning relationship through mothers.   However, the few instances in the Homeric poems which may point to an earlier practice of tracing descent through females almost exclusively refer to gods or foreigners.   The Greeks as a people had beyond doubt adopted the paternal system of tracing kinship and even tended to exaggerate the physiological rôle of the father in conception.   This fact is clearly brought out in the drama of Æschylus called the *Eumenides* (Furies) where the mother's share in the generation of offspring is stoutly denied.   Apollo, addressing the gods who are sitting in judgment upon Orestes for the murder of his mother, utters these remarkable words :

> ". . . The mother's power
> Produces not the offspring, ill called hers.
> No, 'tis the father, that to her commits
> The infant plant ; she but the nutrient soil
> That gives the stranger growth, if fav'ring Heaven
> Denies it not to flourish : this I urge
> In proof, a father may assert that name
> Without a mother's aid ; an instance sits
> Minerva, daughter of Olympian Jove ;

Not the slow produce of nine darkling months,
But formed at once in all her perfect bloom ;
Such from no pregnant goddess ever sprung." [1]

The Greek Family as a Religious Organization. — The
authority possessed by the Greek father as head of the family
probably had one important source in economic causes. Not
only was the man the protector of the family in times of warfare, but when he turned his attention to the domestication of
cattle and to agriculture his economic effectiveness became
relatively greater than that of the woman and his power was
accordingly increased. But the authority of the Greek
patriarch was further enormously enhanced by the institution
of ancestor-worship which made of every Hellenic family a
closely knit religious organization bound together by the worship of the family gods around the family altar. Indeed
certain writers maintain that the true bond of the Greek family
as of the Roman "was the religion of the sacred fire and of dead
ancestors. This caused the family to form a single body both
in this life and in the next." [2] In the central court of the
Greek home stood the altar of *Zeus Herkeios*, protector of the
family circle. Here the father, as priest of his household,
offered sacrifices in behalf of his family. Opening into the
court was a reception-room, the *andron*, in which was usually
placed the hearth, the true center of domestic life in Greece.
Around this family hearth occurred many of the solemn
religious ceremonials that were believed to secure the welfare
of the home. The origin of the sacred hearth-fire, always
carefully tended, dates far back into the earliest life of the
Aryan races. "Agni," says the Indian Rig Vega, "must be
invoked before all other gods." In a field, not far from the
Greek house, stood the tomb of the family ancestors. Here,
on certain days, the household gathered to offer a funeral meal
of cakes and wine or to burn the flesh of an animal as a sacrifice
to the spirits of the dead. These offerings made, the living

[1] *Op. cit.*, Morley's Univ. Library (trans. by Robert Potter), p. 240.
[2] De Coulanges, *The Ancient City*, pp. 51, 52.

members of the family called upon the shades of the departed, now revered as gods, to bring fruitfulness to their fields and happiness to their home. The family spirits were believed to be divine and joyous only so long as funeral repasts were offered them by the living members of the family. Deprived of these offerings, the household gods were transformed into malignant demons, dangerous to the peace and prosperity of the home. Because of this ever present need of propitiation of ancestral spirits, it followed that every family must seek to perpetuate itself without break; therefore it was of supreme importance that there be male descendants to offer sacrifices at the tomb of the ancestors.

Membership in the Greek family was based, not merely upon ties of blood relationship, but upon (1) sharing in the worship of the family gods, and (2) coming under the power of the family head. A son, once emancipated by the father from his control, no longer shared in the family worship. Therefore he became *ipso facto* an outsider. Likewise a daughter, when married, was received by solemn ceremonial into the family circle of her husband and invoked his domestic gods instead of those of her girlhood home of which she was no longer a member. On the other hand, a youth of another kin adopted by appropriate ceremonies into any Greek family became a real member of it, since he shared in the cult of its household gods. De Coulanges has pointed out that one of the meanings of the Greek word "family" is "that which is near the hearth." And Plato has referred to kinship as "the community of the same domestic gods." [1] Since men alone could carry on the ancestral worship, relationship and descent were reckoned through males only — the kinship system known as *agnation*. Hence adopted sons might be agnates, while daughters by blood and their offspring were not.

The Powers of the Greek Father. — As among the Hebrews so among the Greeks large governing powers were centered in the father as head of the family. Indeed it might truly be

[1] *The Laws* (Jowett trans.), Bk. V, 729.

said that ancient law had its source in the family and was chiefly concerned with family relationships, powers and duties. True to the patriarchal type, the Greek family included parents, children and slaves unified into a society in little by the authority of the male head. Before the time of Solon the father had the right to sell both his son and daughter. Probably, however, the sale was not of the person of the child, but only of his labor, as he still remained under the father's authority. With the gradual refining of customs and ideas that accompanied the advance of Greek civilization, the sale of offspring fell into disrepute. By a law of Solon a father was forbidden to sell his daughter and this act may have extended to his son also. However, a Greek father always possessed the right to accept a child at birth or to reject and condemn it to exposure. Like the Hebrew, he had the further right to bestow both son and daughter in marriage. But, unlike the Jewish custom, there was no law in Greece requiring the consent of the children to the marriage contract. Finally, the father's powers included the right to emancipate his son, *i.e.*, exclude him from the family and release him from paternal authority. Probably, in early times, the authority of the Greek patriarch continued to be exercised over the son as long as the father lived. But by the time of Solon the son, on reaching a certain age, was freed from paternal control.

The Status of the Greek Wife. — As head of the household, the powers of the husband over the wife were no less clearly defined than those exercised over the children. Since the family must not die out, a Greek husband might repudiate his wife for barrenness, which of course defeated the true purpose of the marriage. After Homeric times the dowry brought by an Athenian wife belonged absolutely to her husband during his lifetime. If the wife were employed in some gainful occupation, as frequently happened among the poorer class, the fruits of her work were the unquestioned property of her husband. The person of the wife was, furthermore, completely under her husband's control; and, if the family were of good social standing, she could not leave her home without his permission. Indeed, the position of a Greek wife within the family circle must have been little above that of her own children.   Women were regarded by all Ionian Greeks as a distinctly inferior order of beings to men and were guarded within the home with almost Oriental strictness.   "The male," says Aristotle, "is by nature fitter for command than the female, just as the elder and full-grown is superior to the younger and more immature." [1] Among the Spartan Greeks, on the contrary, the position of the wife seems to have been much higher than in Athens.   The wife was given the significant title of "mistress" by her husband; and, although she was expected to be the homekeeper, she was granted liberty to go abroad.   Unmarried Spartan girls were permitted a large amount of freedom and were criticized by men of the other Greek states for their pert forwardness.   In the period of Homeric folk-lore, also, women seem to have been strikingly free from the narrow restrictions of a later age.   Youths and maidens met with some freedom in the house of the girl's father, and even danced together in the vintage festivals.   Apparently their relations as depicted in the *Iliad* and the *Odyssey* were frank and natural.   The lovely Helen freely entertained Paris, the faithless guest of her husband Menelaus.   Andromache left the palace of Priam and hastened to the Secan gates to watch the progress of the battle raging between Greeks and Trojans.   The princess Nausicaa rode with her maids to the riverside to wash the family clothing. And when Odysseus, cast up from the sea, naked and forlorn, besought her aid, the princess, deserted by her attendants, bravely stood her ground and heard his tale of manifold woes. Then to the house of her father she directed his steps.   All this betokens a freer life than was ever led by a well-born Ionian Greek woman in historic times.

Doubtless the influence of the Orient was obscurely responsible for the limitations put upon the liberty of the women of Athens, Thebes and other Ionian city-states.   Under

[1] *Politics* (Jowett trans.), Bk. I, 12; 1239 b.

tutelage all their lives as minors, having no legal status, ill-educated and treated as moral and intellectual inferiors, Ionian wives were poorly fitted to be in any sense the companions of their husbands. Although they were admitted to the family worship round the sacred fire, their presence at the sacrifices was not necessary as in Rome, and hence no offerings were made at their tombs after death. Even when widowed, the Ionian woman was not free, but came under the guardianship of some man appointed by her husband. Needless to say, being herself under perpetual tutelage, she was not at any time the legal custodian of her children, who, like herself, passed under the control of an appointed guardian. The lives of well-born Athenian women were incredibly narrow and were aptly summed up by the Greek poet Menander in the pithy saying : "The life of a respectable woman is bounded by the street door." Only foreign-born women like Aspasia and certain gifted courtesans were free to move about and received the benefits of education.

Property Rights and Inheritance. — In earliest antiquity, as we have seen, the Greeks had developed the institution of private property. Even in Homeric times there was no community of property, but the family estates were held by the patriarch and passed on to his eldest son. With the development of ancestor-worship, custom and law forbade that the family house and lands be alienated since they were the abiding place of the domestic gods. When a new family hearth was established, the god took up his abode near the sacred fire and remained there as long as the household endured. Thus the family, grouped around the altar, was fixed to the soil. Even the free space which the law required to be left around each house was a sacred inclosure, for the altar fire of one god must not be mingled with that of another. It was a legend of the Greeks that the sacred fire taught men to build houses. "The walls are raised around the hearth to isolate and defend it." [1] Likewise the field which contained the tomb of departed ances-

[1] De Coulanges, *The Ancient City*, pp. 81–82.

tors was regarded as sacred ground. Hence, until the time of
Solon, no Athenian Greek might sell his burial field; and, although Solon removed the prohibition, he punished the sale
by a heavy fine and loss of the rights of citizenship.[1]

As the eldest son had the responsibility of continuing the
domestic religion he alone inherited the family estates. In no
case could a daughter inherit since she ceased to be a member
of the family at her marriage. If an Athenian Greek died
leaving a son and daughter, the son as the sole heir must provide a dowry for his sister and arrange for her marriage. As
we have seen, if the deceased left only a daughter, his nearest
male relative must marry the girl even if he divorced a wife
to do so. By such drastic measures the Athenians prevented
the alienation or dismemberment of family property. Apparently another scheme was sometimes resorted to in order that
estates might remain intact. A father who had no son might
contract his daughter in marriage to some man with the express
stipulation that the first male child of the union be given to him
as his son. This suggests the similar custom of levirate among
the Hebrews. The restriction of inheritance to males did not
exist in Sparta, however, and women there might freely inherit
lands and personal property. Aristotle tells us that nearly
two fifths of the whole country was held by the women; "this is
owing to the number of heiresses, and to the large dowries which
are customary." [2]   In Athens, however, where the "privilege
of elder" existed with respect to house and lands, the movable
property only was equally divided among the sons after the
father's death. The younger sons, as they married, left home
to found new households and light sacred fires of their own.

MARRIAGE AMONG THE ANCIENT GREEKS

The Greek View of Marriage. — As in all societies of the
patriarchal type, marriage was held in high esteem in Greece
and was looked upon as a sacred ceremony. By means of such

[1] De Coulanges, *The Ancient City*, p. 90, citing *Diogenes Laertius*, I, 55.
[2] Aristotle, *Politics*, Bk. II, 9; 1270 a.

union the family was perpetuated, the inheritance of property provided for and the worship of ancestral spirits continued. Therefore celibacy was regarded as a serious offense — a crime against the household gods. So strong was this feeling in Athens that a law was enacted enjoining the first magistrate of the city to see to it that no family became extinct. And in Sparta Plutarch tells us that the man who did not marry lost certain rights and was not treated by younger men with that respect so scrupulously accorded by Spartan youths to their elders.[1] Clearly in Greece as in Palestine marriage was regarded as a contract entered into for *family ends* and as such was arranged for by parents with small attention to the preferences of their children. Doubtless some of these unions ended happily; but the very general absence of sentiment in the customary preliminaries, together with the ignorance of the betrothed pair of each other and the prominence of financial considerations, must have told rather heavily against the prospects of married happiness for the man and maiden thus contracted.

Preliminaries of Marriage. — In Homeric times marriage was a crude affair. "Gifts," usually of cattle, were made to the bride's father and the maiden was shortly after handed over to the groom with simple ceremonies and a wedding feast. Sometimes the bride-price was not paid all at once, but in installments. Instances are not uncommon in folk-lore where a bride was given to some hero in return for valuable services rendered the maiden's father. Thus Perseus was rewarded by the gift of Andromeda as his wife after he had saved her from the dragon. Usually, however, the woman was the prize of the suitor who bore the richest "gifts." No dowry was needed by a woman in the Homeric age in order to attract a husband; but before the time of Solon the custom of setting aside a sum of money and personal property for each daughter's dowry had become thoroughly established in the families of well-to-do and poor alike. In his life of Solon, Plutarch tells us that the

[1] *Life of Lycurgus*, Bohn's Classical Library, Vol. I, p. 81.

lawgiver introduced an act limiting the amount of the bride's dowry. This restriction, however, probably referred to the clothes and ornaments she might bring in marriage. In any case the obligatory provision of the dowry must have been a burden upon many fathers; and this accounts for the rather frequent exposure of female infants among the Greeks. In accordance with the practice of most ancient peoples, the ceremonies of marriage consisted of (1) betrothal, (2) nuptials.

Betrothal. — Betrothal was a contract of marriage concluded between the parents or the appointed guardians, with no attempt to secure the formal consent of the girl or the youth. This consent was taken for granted and the presence of the parties most interested was not even necessary at the betrothal. Financial arrangements played a prominent part in the formalities. The bride's dowry was agreed upon and securities given for its payment as well as for its return in case of her divorce without just cause. Sometimes special arrangements were made for community of goods between man and wife after marriage. No religious rites accompanied this business-like contract, which was essentially a legal act.

Nuptials. — It was regarded by all the Greeks as highly important that the final marriage ceremonies should occur on an auspicious day. The time of the full moon was regarded as favorable, the period of the waning moon as unfavorable. In the *Politics* [1] Aristotle mentions winter as the usual and most suitable time for marriages, although he gives no reason for the preference. At the approach of the nuptial day, the bride, often a mere girl of fourteen or fifteen, performed certain acts pathetically symbolic of her farewell to girlhood and her acceptance of the duties of a married woman. Thus she dedicated her maiden girdle, her doll and other toys of childhood and sometimes a lock of her hair to the virgin goddess Artemis or to some local divinity. On the

[1] *Politics*, Bk. VII, 16; 1335 b.

chosen wedding day rather elaborate ceremonies took place which were sanctioned alike by custom and religion. Early in the morning bride and groom each bathed in the water of a sacred stream or spring brought to their homes by members of the family. In Athens the fountain Callirrhoë was used for the bridal bath; in Thebes water was brought from the Ismenos, a sacred spring. As daylight waned the groom, dressed in festal attire and crowned with a wreath, went to the home of the bride, where were gathered the family friends invited to attend the ceremony. As each guest entered the house he was given a cake made of pounded sesame seeds mixed with honey. The eating of this ancient prototype of the modern wedding-cake was an essential part of the nuptial ceremony, and was never omitted. When the guests were all assembled, the bride's father offered sacrifices to the gods of marriage — Zeus, Hera and Artemis. Great care was taken to remove the gall of the victim that no bitterness might enter the married life of the young pair. The sacrifice performed, the father handed over his young daughter to her husband with a sacramental formula which freed her from his control and from the worship of his family gods. With the utterance of these solemn words, the bride ceased to be a *legal* member of her father's family and entered into the family of her husband under whose authority she passed. It is noteworthy that these religious ceremonies were entirely private. The father himself served as priest and no other representatives of religion were necessary. Marriage was essentially an inter-family affair in which neither state nor national religion interfered.

After the transfer of the bride to her husband a marriage banquet followed, at which women were graciously allowed to be present, although it was customary for them to sit at tables separate from the men and to remain partially veiled. As evening approached the mother performed her part in the marriage ceremonies by handing over her young daughter to the groom. Shy and shrinking in the midst of this unwonted publicity, the girl was lifted into the bridal chariot, drawn by mules, which was then quickly surrounded by the wedding guests. Led by flute players and torch-bearers, the procession made its way through the streets to the home of the groom, the marchers singing the nuptial hymn to Hymenæus. Some writers assert that the bride's mother followed the chariot bearing torches. It is possible, however, that she merely lighted the nuptial torch which was then borne by a family servant at the head of the gay procession. Arrived at her husband's home, the portals of which were decorated with garlands, the bride feigned reluctance and, after a mock struggle, was carried over the threshold in the arms of the groom. This symbolic act probably marked the fact that the wife had as yet no assured rights in her husband's home, the abode of his household gods, and therefore she must be introduced by force. However, the ceremony may be a relic of a primitive practice of wife capture. After the entrance of bride and groom the final ceremonies took place with impressive simplicity. The bridal pair, dressed in white and crowned with garlands, drew near to the family hearth, the shrine of the domestic gods, which the young wife sprinkled with lustral water. Then she approached her hand to the sacred fire, after which certain prayers were repeated commending her to the favor of the gods of her new hearth and home. Finally the husband and wife ate together a cake of sesame seeds to symbolize their communion with each other and with the domestic divinities. By these acts, the wife was received into the family worship of her husband. She was then led into the *thalamos*,[1] at the door of which a chorus of maidens sang the epithalamium or bridal hymn. By a law of Solon it was prescribed that the bride should eat a quince — the symbol of fruitfulness — before entering the wedding chamber. Sometimes a pestle for crushing grains was hung at the door of the room to remind the young wife of the household tasks which would be hers.

[1] Bridal chamber.

In Sparta the marriage ceremonies were much more crude and simple. Here, after the preliminary arrangements between parents had been made, the groom forcibly carried off the bride to his own house. In his *Life of Lycurgus* [1] Plutarch relates that, after the bride had been thus rudely brought to her new home, a bridesmaid "received her, cut her hair close to her head, dressed her in a man's cloak and shoes, and placed her upon a couch in a dark chamber alone." Here the bridegroom found her when he returned from dining as usual at the barracks. By Spartan custom, so restricted was the social intercourse between husband and wife that many a man, visiting his wife only at night and then by stealth, had not seen her face in daylight until months had passed after the marriage.

Relations of Husband and Wife. — Since the preliminaries of marriage were arranged by the parents, no doubt it often happened that the bride and groom saw each other for the first time on the wedding-day. Such ignorance of each other's temperament and character must have been a serious handicap to happy marriages. The situation was rendered still more difficult by the shyness and immaturity of the bride whose early secluded life apart from men, remote from all developing social influences save those of her own family and a few friends, ill fitted her to become the companion of a husband whose personality had been developed by careful training and broad social experience. The docility of a typical girl-bride is well portrayed in the *Economics* of Xenophon where the husband Ischomachus is described as introducing his wife to her household duties. To the attempts of her husband to explain the partnership involved in marriage the girl replies: "But how can I assist you? what is my ability? Nay everything depends on you. My business, my mother told me, was to be sober-minded." [2] Apparently, however,

---

[1] Bohn ed., p. 81.
[2] The *Works of Xenophon* (trans. by H. C. Dakyns, 1897), Vol. III, Part I, p. 228.

Greek wives were not invariably sober-minded, even though
we are informed by Aristophanes that a married woman commonly shrank back and blushed if she were by chance seen
at a window by a man.   However this may be, adultery on the
part of Ionian women seems not to have been an altogether
rare occurrence;   and even intercourse with slaves was not
unknown.   These lapses from virtue appear to the student
of social life as mute evidences of the truth we are just beginning to comprehend, that purity in its truest sense cannot be
secured by ignorance and seclusion.   In those instances where
the marriage of his son was resorted to by an anxious Greek
father as a means of bringing to an end the youth's flagrant
debaucheries, the bride must have been looked upon by her
unwilling husband as a penalty to be endured rather than as
a wife to be cherished. Custom, however, exacted that,
whatever his feelings, the husband should carefully abstain
from indecent language in his wife's presence and from any
act which might lower his dignity or detract from the respect
in which his wife was bound to hold him.

   Although the Greek wife was allowed somewhat more
liberty than the unmarried girl, yet she was closely confined to
the *gynæconitis*, or women's apartments, and was certainly
not expected to leave the house without her husband's permission.   When she did go upon the streets she was carefully
veiled and invariably attended by a slave assigned to her by
her husband for that purpose.   While the man spent most
of his day abroad, in the market-place discussing public
questions, or in the state gymnasium outside the city, the
woman remained at home directing the work of her slaves or
whiling away the hours as best she might.   Although husband
and wife commonly took their meals together, the arrival
of her lord with male friends meant the prompt withdrawal
of the wife to the women's apartments. No Greek woman
who had the least regard for her good name would think of
attending a banquet given by her husband to his friends or
even of being present when her husband brought a single

guest to share his meal. Thus the lives of man and wife flowed on in widely separate channels; and as he developed in mental power and increased the range of his interests and activities the woman, with her narrow outlook on life, limited wholly to personal and household concerns, must have appealed to him less and less as a companion. It must often have followed that a marriage which began in indifference, not infrequently ended in cold estrangement, if not in positive aversion. In their conception of women and of the whole marital relation the Greeks showed a blindness, even a stupidity, which is in striking contrast to the intellectual brilliancy they brought to bear upon other phases of life. Plato saw the evil in the marriage system of his day and suggested that more kindly relations might be established between husband and wife if the young people were given more frequent opportunities of seeing each other.[1] But the practice of isolating women was too firmly established in the Ionian states to be modified, even at a much later period.

Euripides, last of the great tragedians of Greece, reveals clearly in his drama the general attitude of his day toward women. In the drama of *Hippolytus* he puts these words into the mouth of the hero:

> " How great a pest
> Is woman this one circumstance displays:
> The very father who begot and nurtured,
> A plenteous dower advancing, sends her forth,
> That of such loathed incumbrance he may rid
> His mansions: but the helpless youth who takes
> This noxious image to his bed, exults
> While he caparisons a worthless image,
> In gorgeous ornaments and tissued vests
> Squandering his substance. . . ."[2]

In the *Medea*, however, Euripides, often sympathetic with the woes of women, reverses the shield and presents to us the woman's side. The wretched queen exclaims:

[1] Plato, *The Laws* (Jowett trans.), Bk. VIII, 841.
[2] Euripides, *Hippolytus*, Morley's Universal Library, pp. 290–291.

" Of all things upon earth that bleed and grow,
    A herb most bruised is woman.   We must pay
Our store of gold, hoarded for that one day,
To buy us some man's love; and lo, they bring
A master of our flesh !   There comes the sting
Of the whole shame.   And then the jeopardy,
For good or ill, what shall that master be;
Reject she cannot; and if he but stays
His suit, 'tis shame on all that woman's days.
So thrown amid new laws, and new places, why,
'Tis magic she must have, or prophecy —
Home never taught her that — how best to guide
Toward peace this thing that sleepeth at her side.
And she who, labouring long, shall find some way
Whereby her lord may bear with her, nor fray
His yoke too fiercely, blesséd is the breath
That woman draws !   Else, let her pray for death.
Her lord, if he be wearied of the face
Within doors, gets him forth; some merrier place
Will ease his heart; but she waits on, her whole
Vision enchainéd on a singel soul." [1]

Concubinage and Prostitution among the Greeks. —

Although the family in the historic age of Greece was, on
the whole, monogamous, yet, from the earliest antiquity,
concubinage had existed.   In the age of the Homeric epics
the distinction between wife and concubine consisted in this :
the wife was honorably purchased of her father and was
married with customary ceremonies; while the concubine
was the prize of war and was in effect the chattel of her captor.
Numerous references in both the *Iliad* and the *Odyssey* make
it clear enough that concubinage was a common practice in
times of war.   In the Trojan epic the virgin Chryseis, daughter
of the priest of Apollo, is given to Agamemnon as his concubine; and when a pestilence, sent by the god, to avenge
this sacrilege ravages the Greek camp and Agamemnon is
forced to accept a ransom for the maid he exclaims :

". . . 'Twas my choice
    To keep her with me, for I prize her more
    Than Clytemnestra, bride of my young years,

[1] Euripides, *Medea* (trans. by Gilbert Murray), p. 15.

And deem her not less nobly graced than she,
In form and feature, mind and pleasing arts."[1]

And again he protests in bitter indignation:

"This maiden I release not till old age
Shall overtake her in my Argive home,
Far from her native country, where her hand
Shall throw the shuttle and shall dress my couch."[2]

The last lines make plain the position of concubines within the Homeric family: frequently of noble birth, they were employed like slaves in personal, if not menial, services for their lord and captor. It was for the sake of his concubine Breseis, unjustly taken from him, that Achilles sulked so long within his tent. Again, the murder of Agamemnon by his false wife Clytemnestra was defended by her on the ground that her lord had brought the princess Cassandra from fallen Troy to serve as his concubine within the palace.

But concubinage was apparently not confined to rude Homeric times. In the *Oration Against Neæra*, ascribed to Demosthenes, the orator makes a statement which sheds a flood of light upon the modified monogamy of the Greek family: " Mistresses we keep for pleasure, concubines for daily attendance upon our person, wives to bear us legitimate children; and be our faithful housekeepers."[3] It is probable, then, that when concubines were kept by a Greek householder these women were usually selected from among the household slaves. Certain it is that their children were never regarded as true members of the family, since they could not share in the worship of the domestic gods. Therefore such offspring had no rights of succession to any part of the family patrimony.

The Hetairæ. — The integrity of Greek family life was further threatened by another custom. In most of the cities

---

[1] *Iliad* (trans. by Bryant), Bk. I, ll. 146–150.
[2] *Ibid.*, ll. 38–41.
[3] Demosthenes, *Orations*, Bohn's Classical Library, Vol. V, p. 272.

of Greece, notably in Corinth and Athens, there existed a class of young women called hetairæ, who were trained from childhood to a life of immorality. Some of these unfortunates were the exposed children of families respected in the community, who had fallen into the hands of unscrupulous persons and were ruthlessly exploited. Among this class were certain young women of foreign birth, distinguished not only for their beauty but for their wit and intellectual attainments. Such were Aspasia, a brilliant lecturer on philosophy in Athens and the mistress and subsequently the wife of Pericles,[1] Lamia, daughter of a citizen of Athens, Phryne and Laïs of Corinth. A famous hetaira of Arcadian birth was at one time a pupil of Plato and another attended the discourses of the philosopher Epicurus.[2] Although these were probably exceptional cases, yet most of the hetairæ were well educated, well informed on public affairs and socially gifted.

In addition to this select group, who were accessible only to the wealthy or the socially prominent, there were the common prostitutes·living in houses licensed by the state.

It is a curious fact that the Athenian Greeks so generally neglected the education of their respectable women, who thus proved in many instances dull and naïve in the company of their cultivated husbands, while they freely granted to dissolute women the intellectual training so conspicuously lacking in their own wives. In consequence Greek men, including statesmen and scholars, eagerly sought the more stimulating society of these attractive hetairæ. Nor was such action on the part of married men harshly condemned by public opinion.

DIVORCE IN ANCIENT GREECE

Rights of the Husband. — In the *Iliad* and the *Odyssey* there is not a single mention of divorce; therefore we are justified in believing that such separations were not an es-

[1] Authorities disagree on the question of the marriage of Pericles and Aspasia; but it is certain that his son by the famous courtesan was made legitimate by a special act of the people.   [2] Becker, *Charicles*, p. 248.

tablished custom in primitive times. But in the historic period of Greece divorce was far from unusual. As with the Hebrews, so with the Greeks, larger rights of divorce were conceded to the husband than to the wife. A Greek might simply dismiss his wife in the presence of witnesses if he found her unattractive or uncongenial. Although such separations were probably not uncommon, yet they were not wholly un-restricted, both because public opinion did not approve them, and also because in such a case the husband must return his repudiated wife's dowry to her father or guardian. In two instances the husband was very generally considered to be justified in divorcing his wife: (1) in case of barrenness, (2) in case of adultery. As respects the first cause, the Greeks held that the fundamental purpose of marriage — the gener-ation of offspring to perpetuate the worship of ancestors — had not been realized and therefore a fruitless union ought to be dissolved. For this reason childless women sometimes procured exposed infants, whom they passed off as their own, in order to escape the odium attached to barrenness.[1] Adul-tery on the part of a wife was visited with severity by Greek law and custom. If surprised in the act, the man might be put to death by the outraged husband; and there is reason to believe that the same fate was meted out to the woman also. If the husband took time for reflection, however, he was not permitted to kill his offending wife, but might inflict corporal punishment upon her and keep her in close confinement within the house. In case the affair became public, the wife was made infamous and by law was denied all right to par-ticipate in the national religious rites and sacrifices or even to enter the temples. The adulteress who attempted to attend the public sacrifices might "suffer any maltreatment short of death with impunity." Moreover, in cases where the wife's adultery became known, the law commanded the annulment of the marriage.[2] The Spartan Greeks often

[1] Becker, *Charicles*, p. 497.
[2] *Ibid.*, p. 497.

boasted that adultery was far less common with them than among the Ionian Greeks; indeed they declared that the evil did not exist among them. But this is only to say that sex relations were much freer among the Spartans than the Athenians. If a Spartan had no children or had become old, he might and frequently did encourage his wife to have intercourse with some younger and more vigorous man in order to raise up children to continue his name. Plutarch tells us that Lycurgus "permitted men to associate worthy persons with them in the task of begetting children, and taught them to ridicule those who insisted on the exclusive possession of their wives." [1] The reason for this apparent laxness is clearly stated: "Lycurgus did not view children as belonging to their parents, but above all to the state"; and a military state was naturally concerned to obtain a goodly number of future citizens born of sound stock.

Rights of the Wife. — As may be supposed, the Greek woman had few rights in the matter of divorce. Adultery on the part of her husband, even continual and open resort to the houses of hetairæ, gave the neglected wife no ground for separation in any Greek state. Only if the husband's debaucheries resulted in the gross neglect of his family, or in genuine cruelty, was his wife justified in seeking a divorce. But, even then, the undertaking was very difficult. She must submit a written complaint in person before the chief archon of the city; and it was quite possible for a suspicious husband to prevent this by forcibly confining his wife to the house. [2] Even if the woman obtained a divorce, she must return to her old home, perhaps as an unwelcome member, and must submit once more to the authority of father or brother. Yet Greek husbands and wives not rarely resorted to separations by mutual consent, even though the wife thereby lost the small degree of freedom accorded the married woman.

[1] *Life of Lycurgus*, Bohn Library, Vol. I, p. 82.
[2] Cf. Gulick, *The Life of the Ancient Greeks*, p. 125.

Divorce, like marriage, was looked upon by the Greeks as a private and family matter not under the authority of religion or of the state, save in the single case of the wife's adultery, when the law intervened to dissolve the marriage if the husband failed to do so.

THE GREEK HOUSEHOLD AS AN ECONOMIC INSTITUTION

Slavery. — It is impossible to consider the economic functions of the Greek household without recognition of the institution of slavery which was closely interwoven with all forms of home industry. The origin of slavery among the Greeks is buried in antiquity; certainly it was a well-nigh universal institution in Homeric times. In those early days of war and rapine, slaves were obtained by conquest and by open piracy; but in the historic period slaves were most frequently barbarians purchased in the market-towns of the Black Sea and Asia Minor. This class was further recruited from among exposed children, large numbers of whom were rescued to be brought up as professional dancers and flute-players. In the heroic age, when life was simple and patriarchal, the condition of the slaves was probably little inferior to that of other members of the household. Since they came under the power of the family head, they were regarded as part of the family, and were treated with a kind friendliness which at times is sharply contrasted with their treatment in the historic age. Quite frequently, in these early times, slaves were intrusted with responsible posts of superintendence on the farm and in the household and lived on a familiar footing with their masters, even eating at the same table and sharing in their pleasures. Such conditions had largely disappeared in the fifth century B.C., although they tended to persist in remote pastoral sections such as Arcadia. Since slaves were not persons in the eyes of the law, they could not contract legal marriages. Yet unions were formed between slaves, with the consent of their masters, and slave-families

were established. The members, however, might at any time
be separated by sale or otherwise, at the will of the owner.
Upon the slaves, of course, devolved all the heavier and more
distasteful labors of the household, such as farm work, cattle
and sheep tending and grinding grain in the rude hand-mills
of early times.

The Household as an Industrial Center. — In the Homeric
age the home was still the nucleus of most of the industries
of the community. On the lands of the chiefs and their followers were produced nearly all the necessities required by
the patriarchal family. Each well-to-do household had its
own cattle, sheep and goats, its farm and grazing lands, its
mill, its implements for converting raw materials into food
and clothing. The distaff and spindle were in daily use and
weaving was highly developed, although the loom was still
primitive in form. So much we learn from the patient labors
of Penelope in the *Odyssey*. Homer's epics show nothing
of the contempt for hand labor so widespread among the
Greeks in historic times. Even the gods are represented as
workers: Hephæstos labors at the forge; Athena spins and
weaves. The nobly born are not ashamed to work as carpenters or to make the various implements needed in household
industry. Yet, although the family in the heroic age was
largely self-supporting, certain industries had even then been
organized into crafts which were carried on outside the home.
Such were the trades of carpenters, masons, smiths and
workers in precious metals.

By the fifth century, however, the household had, in many
instances, ceased to be an economic unit. Only on the country
estates of the rich, where large numbers of slaves were employed, do we find grain threshed and ground, grapes and olives
pressed into wine and oil, bread and cakes baked in the family
ovens, and all the processes concerned with making woolen and
linen cloth and fashioning it into garments carried on by the
members of the household. In Athens tanning of leather had
become a distinct trade pursued by law outside the city

because of its unpleasant smell. Shoemaking, hat manufacturing, pottery making, metal-working in iron, bronze
and gold had become separate crafts doing a thriving business in special streets named for these trades. All these facts
concerning extra-domestic industries may be drawn from the
illustrations on Greek vases. No longer did each household
grind its own grain. Instead large public mills did most of
this work, at least in the cities, and sold the flour to public
bakers. The bakehouses contained enormous earthen ovens
for baking loaves of the standard weight and size fixed by the
city's market commissioners. The Athenians prided themselves on the quality of the bread and sweetened fancy cakes
prepared by these public bakers. The comedies of Aristophanes convey the impression that bread was rarely baked
at home, but was quite commonly bought of women venders
who set up their stalls in the market-place.[1] Then, too,
certain processes connected with the making of clothing had
likewise been taken over by craftsmen. Except on large
country estates, the fleeces of sheep were commonly cleansed
and dyed by professional fullers and dyers who had practiced
these crafts for generations. Tailoring establishments existed
in all the more important Greek cities where cloth was cut,
fitted and even made up into garments for those of the
wealthier classes who chose to have this labor performed
outside their homes. There is reason to believe that linen
goods, at least, were not even woven on household looms, but
almost exclusively by the tailors in these cloth factories.[2]
Division of labor in some industries seems to have been almost
as minute as it is today. For example, certain establishments
manufactured only women's garments, others only men's.
In the manufacture of household furniture we find one group
of workers making beds, another chairs, another chests for
clothing, and still another bronze doors and gates, mirrors
and even hairpins of metal. The making of pottery for

[1] Cf. Becker, *Charicles*, p. 289.
[2] See Gulick, *The Life of the Ancient Greeks*, p. 229.

domestic use, once no doubt the province of Greek women, as it still is of the women in primitive tribes, had become a thriving extra-household industry. Athens was especially famed among the cities of Greece for the beauty and durability of its pottery, no doubt because of the beds of clay in Attica which were peculiarly adapted to such uses.

Thus conditions were at work in Greece in the fifth century B.C. to withdraw from the household a goodly number of the industries which had for centuries been exclusively carried on within its walls. Yet it would be a serious mistake to regard the well-to-do Greek woman of the age of Pericles as a "lady" in our modern economic sense; *i.e.*, as chiefly a consumer of the goods produced by the working-classes. Most Greek women spun and wove the woolen if not the linen garments worn by the slaves as well as the free women of the household, besides doing some of the family cooking. In the homes of the wealthy, it is true, the women probably directed these labors more than they shared in them; but, with a numerous family of slaves, such direction must have consumed much time. In addition, the women of Greece were experts in the art of embroidering. This is made plain by the various vase paintings which depict them at work and reproduce the exquisite designs they embroidered on the borders of chitons and other garments. In several Greek states corporations of women wove and decorated the festive robes thrown over the statues of their patron gods and goddesses. We are told that the maidens of Athens were required every four years to weave a peplos for the statue of Pallas Athene in the Parthenon to be used at the return of the great Panathenaic festival. Into these garments were woven the portraits of the nation's great men so that they served, like the tapestries of the Middle Ages, as a chronicle of the heroes of the city-state.

Xenophon, the Greek historian and soldier of the fifth century B.C., has bequeathed to future ages a delightful picture of the household pursuits of the Greek wife and the careful economy of the average Greek home as it existed in his own day. The discourse is in the form of a dialogue between Ischomachus, a young Greek husband, and Socrates, who, according to his wont, is in search of knowledge. Ischomachus relates, with pardonable pride, that he has trained his girl-wife in her household duties entirely by himself, since she was less than fifteen years of age at her marriage and "had spent the preceding part of her life under the strictest restraint, in order that she might see as little, hear as little and ask as few questions as possible." The young husband describes to the delighted Socrates the instruction he gave to his bride in the management of what he is pleased to call, with rather unusual generosity, their "common household." He explains the primitive division of labor which assigns to males the production of the necessaries of life out of doors and to females the rearing of children, the care of supplies and the manufacture of raw materials — pursuits which can best be carried on under shelter. Very ingeniously Ischomachus presents the time-worn argument that "the gods . . . have plainly adapted the nature of the woman for work and duties within doors, and that of the man for works and duties without doors." With much patient detail he relates how he introduced his wife to her specific tasks and responsibilities. She must take charge of and keep strict account of all supplies; take care that garments were made for all who needed them from the raw wool brought into the house; and see to it that the dried provisions were fit for eating. Upon her fell the burden of nursing the sick slaves until their recovery. She it was also who must train the unskilled slave girl to be an expert spinner. She must learn what were the best places in the house for storing wine and corn, and for putting away couch coverings, vases, household vessels, implements and utensils for spinning, cooking, kneading bread, etc. Finally she was to "consider herself the guardian of the laws established in the house, and inspect the household furniture whenever she thought proper . . .; to signify her approbation if everything was in good condition, as the senate signifies its approval of the horses and horse-soldiers; to praise and honor the deserving like a queen, according to her means, and to rebuke and disgrace any one that required such treatment." By these wise instructions the young wife of Ischomachus was clearly informed of her functions in life — to be the director of the household slaves and guardian of the household supplies, and "to produce offspring, that the race may not become extinct." Nowhere in literature is there a more sane and temperate exposition of the age-old masculine theory of the duties of womankind; nowhere is there a more complete failure to recognize this woman as an *individual* with personal tastes and capacities worthy of consideration and development.

HOME NURTURE AND EDUCATION

Birth and Early Training. — If Plato is to be believed, the Greek home played an important rôle in the early training of children. "Education and admonition," he writes, "commence in the first years of childhood and last to the very end of life." [1] At the birth of a Greek child the joyful event was announced by symbols fastened to the door of the house. If the newcomer were a boy, an olive wreath was used to signify the public honors and preferment that might be his. But if the infant were a girl, a piece of wool was attached to the door as a symbol of the household industries to which most of her life would be devoted. On the fifth, or as some writers assert on the seventh day after birth, the ceremony of *Amphidromia* occurred. At this family festival the nurse, or some female relative, carried the new-born infant around the sacred hearth of the home. The ceremony was clearly intended to introduce the child into family membership which, as we have seen, included the spirits of departed ancestors. At this time, the father, as the supreme family head, probably made formal declaration that he accepted the responsibility of rearing the

[1] Plato, *Protagoras*, in Monroe, *Source Book in the History of Education*, p. 31.

child. Otherwise the infant was ruthlessly exposed. Exposure was sanctioned by law, but was probably not so frequent as some writers would have us think. More commonly this fate was reserved for girls and for illegitimate children, although boys were sometimes exposed by poor parents to escape the burden of rearing them, and by well-to-do parents to avoid too minute a division of the family property. A letter has come down to us from the year 1 B.C., in which a certain Greek named Hilarion writes to his wife Alis from Alexandria as follows: "If — good luck to you — you bear offspring, if it be a male, let it live, if it is a female, expose it." [1] The laconic quality of this statement is matched by its utter failure to recognize any right of the mother in the child she had borne. On the tenth day after birth there occurred a more imposing ceremony consisting of solemn sacrifice at the family altar followed by a banquet. To this festival relatives and friends were invited, and the new-born infant was named. Usually this little ceremony was performed by the father, and at its close presents were showered upon parents and child by the guests and even by the family slaves.

After formal acceptance into family membership the Greek child of well-to-do parents was nurtured chiefly by slaves. Few mothers of the wealthier classes suckled their own children: except in Sparta, wet-nurses were very generally employed for this purpose. Apparently the first nurse was not always a slave, for Plutarch informs us that Spartan mothers, famed for their skill and good sense, were sometimes hired by Athenians to suckle and train their infants. Thus the wetnurse of Alcibiades was a Spartan woman. Boys and girls remained under the care of nurses and mothers until the sixth or seventh year and were brought up in close association. We know that they had much the same playthings as modern children; for frequent references are made in Greek literature to rattles, go-carts, dolls of painted

[1] Milligan, *Greek Papyri*, p. 81.

clay, hoops and tops.   Aristophanes in his comedy of *The Clouds* refers to a cockchafer fastened by a thread as a popular toy.[1]

In the matter of discipline, the child was by no means neglected.   The Greek parents of the more favored classes sought carefully to maintain their dignity in the presence of children and insisted upon prompt obedience.   Personal chastisement with sandal or slipper was the approved form of punishment, although Greek nurses and mothers, like those of later times, did not hesitate to make frequent dark references to popular bogeys as a means of frightening children into docile behavior.   Slave nurses had a rich fund of myths and tales of heroes which they were fond of relating to their charges.   Because of the profound influence exercised by these stories upon the child's moral nature, Plato emphasizes the care with which they should be selected.   He even goes so far as to eliminate the Homeric poems from the educative material given to children on the ground that they portray the gods in immoral and undignified situations.   "Then the first thing," he urges, "will be to have a censorship of the writers of fiction and let the censors receive any tale of fiction which is good and reject the bad ; and we will desire mothers and nurses to tell their children the authorized ones only.   Let them fashion the mind with these tales, even more fondly than they form the body with their hands ; and most of those which are now in use must be discarded." [2]   According to Plato the training of children in harmony with approved moral standards was vigorously carried on in the Greek home.   In the *Protagoras* he describes this training : "Mother and nurse and father and tutor are quarreling about the improvement of the child as soon as ever he is able to understand them ; he cannot say or do anything without their setting forth to him that this is just and that is unjust ; this is honorable, that is dishonorable ; this is holy, that is unholy ; do this and abstain from that.   And if he obeys, well

---

[1] Cf. Klein, Anita E., *Child Life in Greek Art* (1932).
[2] *Republic* (Jowett trans.), Bk. II, p. 59.

and good; if not, he is straightened by threats and blows, like a piece of warped wood." [1]

At seven years of age the lives of sisters and brothers in Greek families began to diverge. Under the charge of his pedagogue, the boy was sent to palæstra and music school and later to the public gymnasium to receive that carefully planned education, terminating for the favored youth only with his legal majority, which was designed to fit him for full citizenship. All his education from this time forward was carried on outside the family; there is no mention by Greek writers of any regular home instruction after the boy had attained school age. While her brother's education was thus proceeding, the Greek girl was leading a highly restricted life, rarely leaving her home, and receiving no definite instruction save in spinning, weaving, embroidering and probably cooking if her family were not well-to-do.

It would appear, then, that in Greece, as in the modern countries of Europe and America, the educative influence of the home was chiefly confined to the early years of the boy's life; and that his musical, literary, moral and physical education was handed over to institutions such as the music school and gymnasium, followed by the organized military training of the ephebic period. That the family exercised a valuable influence in shaping the moral and religious nature of both boys and girls can hardly be doubted. Yet it appears equally certain that the inferior position of the Greek mother, her lack of knowledge of the world and of life — a knowledge commonly gained either through direct experience or through the medium of literature — must have served to lessen enormously the degree and the value of her influence over her children. The moral guidance of an ignorant, inexperienced, imperfectly trained mother can hardly be more than narrowly conventional save in very rare instances. The egregious blunder of intelligent Greek men in almost totally neglecting the intellectual and social education of their women of good repute must have

[1] Monroe, *Source Book*, p. 31.

been paid for in the relative ineffectiveness of the wives and mothers.

THEORIES OF GREEK PHILOSOPHERS CONCERNING THE FAMILY

Any discussion of the Greek family would be manifestly incomplete without some reference to the views of the great philosophers of Greece on this subject. Both Plato and Aristotle, viewing the whole question of the family and the training of offspring from the high standpoint of the needs of society, would empower the State to interfere in the making of marriages and in determining the fitness of the offspring of these unions to live. In the *Republic* Plato sets forth radical views with respect to the regulation of marriages by the State. Men and women of the "guardian" or ruling class are to choose their mates by lot at great nuptial festivals appointed and directed by the State. Plato advocated that the guardians of the State juggle these lots in such a way as to bring together the more vigorous and intellectual men and women and thus determine, as he thought, the character of their offspring. Thus he says : The "best of either sex should be united with the best as often, and the inferior with the inferior as seldom, as possible ; and . . . they should rear the offspring of the one sort of union, but not of the other, if the flock is to be maintained in first-rate condition." [1] Parents are to separate after the birth of children and the offspring, if permitted to live, are to be promptly sent to state nurseries, there to be reared by public nurses properly trained for their duties. The bereft parents, Plato holds (and be it noted that this idealist was unmarried), will console themselves by developing warm parental feeling for all children born at about the same period as their own child ! To the proper state officials Plato commits the whole matter of determining which of the new-born infants shall be reared and which shall be exposed as weaklings, likely to grow into undesirable citizens.

[1] *Republic* (Jowett trans.), Bk. V, p. 153.

All children born of unions not recognized by the state are to be exposed.[1] It will be seen that Plato, the world's first eugenist, fearlessly adopts the ground that marriage as well as the procreation and rearing of offspring are, above all else, matters which profoundly concern the State.

As regards the early education of children, no writer of ancient times has written more suggestively than Plato. He clearly recognized the impressionability of young minds and the lasting character of early ideas and habits. Hence his careful censorship of literature and music and his belief that children from their earliest infancy should be surrounded with beautiful forms, in art and architecture, in literature and in conduct.

But beyond question Plato's most radical theory was the view that women have the same natures, the same gifts and capacities as men, only in a lesser degree. Therefore he holds that they should receive the same education and be admitted to the same spheres of work and of public service. "And so, my friend," he writes, "in the administration of a State neither a woman as a woman, nor a man as a man has any special function, but the gifts of nature are equally diffused in both sexes; all the pursuits of men are the pursuits of women also, and in all of them a woman is only a weaker man." [2] It is surprising to learn that Plato forestalled, by twenty-three centuries, the views that are rapidly gaining headway in the modern world. That his voice was merely "lifted in the wilderness" to the unheeding multitude of his own age needs hardly to be stated. The Greeks were very far indeed from accepting, much less carrying out, the theories of their great idealist.

Aristotle, being less speculative and more scientific than Plato, reckons with conditions as they exist and thus is more conservative. We find no recommendation in this philosopher's writings that the family be undermined nor destroyed. Nevertheless he believes in state intervention in marriage,

[1] *Republic* (Jowett trans.), Bk. V, p. 154.
[2] *Ibid.*, Bk. II, p. 148.

for he suggests that "the *legislator* ought to take care that
the bodies of children are as perfect as possible"; therefore
"his first attention ought to be given to matrimony; at which
time and in what situation it is proper that citizens should
engage in the nuptial contract."[1] Apparently he would have
the State determine the marriageable age for men and women.
He deplores too early marriages as productive of "very small
and ill-framed children"; and would have the "succession
of children" fall within the time when their parents have
attained bodily perfection. Legislators must see to it that
pregnant women get sufficient exercise by commanding them
"once every day to repair to the worship of the gods who are
supposed to preside over matrimony." Like Plato, Aristotle
does not rise above the views of his age regarding child exposure. Thus he writes: "As to the exposure and rearing
of children, let there be a law that no deformed child shall
live. . . ."[2] Here pagan disregard for the value of the
individual human life is allied with a wholesome concern for
the well-being of the city-state.

While their philosophers thus discussed and wrote, the established Greek practices with respect to marriage and family
life went on practically unchanged. It is true that Greek
comedians toward the close of the fifth century represent
women as seeking a larger measure of freedom and influence,[3]
but there is little evidence that their strivings ever resulted
in a fuller and more satisfying life.

SELECTED READINGS

Sources

Aristophanes. *Lysistrata.*
——. *Ecclesiazucæ.*
Aristotle. *Nichomachean Ethics* (Jowett trans.), Bk. VIII, Ch. XII.

[1] *Politics*, Bk. IV, Ch. 16.
[2] *Op. cit.*, Bk. IV, Ch. 16.
[3] See the *Comedies of Aristophanes* — the *Lysistrata* and the *Ecclesiazucæ*,
Bohn Classical Library (London, 1853), Vol. II.

Aristotle. *Politics* (Jowett trans.), Bk. I, pp. 5, 22–26, 52–53, 238–243.

Demosthenes. *Oration against Neæra*, Bohn Classical Library, 1889, Vol. V.

Euripides. *Medea* (Gilbert Murray trans.), London, G. Allen, 1906.

——. *Hippolytus*, Morley's Universal Library, 1911.

Milligan, George, trans. and ed. *Selections from Greek Papyri*, Cambridge University Press, 1910, pp. 1–4, 8–11, 41, 81, 85, 104.

Monroe, Paul. *Source Book of the History of Education for the Greek and Roman Period*, N. Y., Macmillan, 1921; Xenophon's *Economics*, pp. 37–50; Plato, *Republic*, pp. 173–179; Plato, *The Laws*, pp. 243–244.

Plato. *Republic* (Jowett trans.), 3rd ed., Clarendon Press, 1888, Bk. V, pp. 455–467.

——. *The Laws*, Loeb Classical Library, 1926, pp. 294–295, 312–313.

Plutarch. *Lives*, Bohn Classical Library, 1908, Vol. I, pp. 80–83, 147–148, 150.

SECONDARY WORKS

Becker, W. A. *Charicles; or Illustrations of the Private Life of the Ancient Greeks*, trans. by Rev. Frederick Metcalfe, N. Y. and London, Longmans, Green, and Co., 1899, Excursus to Scene I, pp. 217–227, 236, Excursus to Scene II, pp. 241–250, Excursus to Scene III, pp. 251–271, Excursus to Scene XII, pp. 462–498.

Blümner, Hugo. *Home Life of the Ancient Greeks*, trans. from the German by Alice Zimmern, London, Cassell and Co., Ltd., 1893, pp. 129–183, 202–208.

Bücher, Karl. *Industrial Evolution*, trans. from the 3rd German ed. by S. Morley Wickett, N. Y., Holt, pp. 95–97.

Davis, Wm. S. *A Day in Old Rome*, N. Y. and Boston, Allyn and Bacon, 1925, pp. 45–54, 65–74.

Decharme, Paul. *Euripides and the Spirit of His Dramas*, trans. by Jas. Loeb, N. Y. and London, Macmillan, 1906, pp. 93–112.

Dickinson, G. Lowes. *The Greek View of Life*, 6th ed., N. Y., Doubleday, Page, 1909, pp. 71–80, 154–167.

Donaldson, Sir James. *Woman, Her Position and Influence in Ancient Greece and Rome*, N. Y. and London, Longmans, Green, and Co., 1907, Chs. I–III.

Fustel de Coulanges. *Ancient City*, trans. by Willard Small, Boston, Lothrop, Lee and Shepard Co., 1920, pp. 41–71.

Guhl, E. K., and Kroner, W. D.   *Life of the Greeks and Romans*, trans. from 3rd German ed., pp. 75–85, New York, D. Appleton and Co., 1875.

Gulick, Chas. B.   *Life of the Ancient Greeks*, N. Y., D. Appleton and Co., 1902, Chs. VI, IX.

——. *Modern Traits in Old Greek Life*, N. Y., Longmans, Green, and Co., 1927, pp. 14–77.

Linton, E. Lynn.   "Womanhood in Old Greece" in *Fortnightly Review*, Vol. XLVII, January and May, 1887, pp. 105–123, 715–731.

Mahaffy, John P.   *Social Life in Greece from Homer to Menander*, London, Macmillan, 1913, pp. 146–153, 224–227.

Murray, Gilbert.   *The Rise of Greek Epic*, Oxford, Clarendon Press, 1907, 16–22, 124–126, 150–153.

Peck, H. T., ed.   *Harper's Dictionary of Classical Literature and Antiquities*, Harper, 1898, articles on "Adulterium," "Amphidromia," "Divortium," "Matrimonium."

Putnam, Mrs. Emily J.   *The Lady*, N. Y., Sturgis and Walton Co., Ch. I, 1910.

Robinson, Cyril E.   *The Days of Alkibiades*, N. Y., Longmans, Green, and Co., 1916, pp. 176–202.

St. John, Jas. A.   *The History of the Manners and Customs of Ancient Greece*, London, R. Bentley, 1842, Vol. I, 107–164, 369–401; II, pp. 1–28, 75–125.

Schuster, E. J.   *The Wife in Ancient and Modern Times*, London, Williams and Norgate, 1911, Chs. II, IV.

CHAPTER IV

THE PATRIARCHAL FAMILY: THE ROMAN TYPE

Periods in the History of the Roman Family. — The history of the family in ancient Rome, unlike that of Greece, is markedly progressive in character. This makes it necessary to divide Roman family history into two periods widely divergent in ideals and customs. The earlier period begins with the dawn of Roman legend and extends approximately to the close of the Punic wars (753–202 B.C.). During this period the prevalent ideals of marriage and family life are stern, simple and wholesome, although harsh and rigid. The later period covers the centuries from the end of the Punic wars (202 B.C.) to the fourth century A.D. when Christian influence begins very gradually to modify pagan marriage and family customs.

THE ROMAN FAMILY IN THE EARLY PERIOD (753–202 B.C.)

Its Patriarchal Character. — Prior to the time when the Romans began that ruthless career of conquest, which resulted in transforming all their social institutions, the family presented the most complete example known to history of the patriarchal type. The early Roman family, consisting of wife, children, sometimes grandchildren and slaves, was a religious, legal and economic unit. Its integrity was preserved through the centuries because in its oldest male head were vested all religious rights, as priest of the family ancestor-worship, all legal rights, as the only "person" recognized by law, and all economic rights as the sole owner of the family property, both real and movable. Unlike the custom in Greece, the power of the family head over all adult male members was permanent, enduring throughout the lifetime of the patriarch.   The Roman jurist Gaius,[1] in his *Institutes of Roman Law*, makes the following statement concerning the complete subordination of the members of a Roman family to its ruling head: " It should be noted that nothing can be granted in the way of justice to those under power; *i.e.*, to slaves, children and wives.   For it is reasonable to conclude that, since these persons can own no property, they are incompetent to claim anything in point of law." [2]   But this vast power, reposed in the *pater*, was, after all, delegated power as was the case in Greece. Not as an absolute monarch did the Roman patriarch exercise this authority, but as the representative of the family in its cult of ancestors.   He alone knew the traditional ceremonials by which ancestral spirits could be appeased and transformed from malign into beneficent forces; and he alone as household priest could pass on this important knowledge to his eldest son.

In its strongly unified aspect the Roman family institution most vividly contrasts with the modern, which is composed of individuals with approximately equal rights before the law and with a disposition to assert those rights in ways likely to weaken the unity of family life.   The prevalence of divorce and of family desertion, as well as the increase in the numbers of young people breaking home ties to " start out for themselves," or throwing off parental authority as soon as they become self-supporting, are but so many indications of a spirit of individualism in the modern household quite unknown in the family of ancient times.   Indeed, in those simple days, there was no place for the individual outside the family institution — to be a free-lance, not owing obedience to a family head, was to be a social outcast.   In progress of time, however, as Roman society developed, and customs changed with the change of ideas, the family in Rome became more indi-

[1] Flourished 138–161 A.D.

[2] *Op. cit.*, II, 96; quoted by Couch, "Woman in Early Roman Law," *Harvard Law Rev.*, Vol. VIII, p. 43

vidualistic until, in late Imperial times, it resembled in more than one respect the American family of the present age.

The *Patria Potestas*. — The power of the father (*patria potestas*) was expressly recognized in the Laws of the Twelve Tables,[1] and extended to life and death. Sir Henry Maine has said of the relations of son to father that " in all the relations created by Private Law, the son lived under a domestic despotism which, considering the severity it retained to the last, and the number of centuries through which it endured, constitutes one of the strangest problems in legal history." [2] The *pater familias* might scourge his children, sell them into slavery, banish them from the country or put them to death. In one respect only was his authority as the legal judge and executioner of his children at all limited. In case a child had committed any grave offense, the patriarch must summon a council of the adult male members of his *gens* or " great family " and confer with them before passing sentence on his son which would condemn him to slavery or death. If he differed from the views of the majority, however, he was apparently free to carry out his own judgment. Although the Laws of the Twelve Tables expressly recognized the father's right to sell his offspring, there seems to be no instance in history of the exercise of this power. By the quaint ceremony of *emancipation*, which consisted in a fictitious sale formally carried out three times, the son was set free from the *patria potestas*, and thus ceased to be a member of the family. But, since sons were highly valued by the father as the maintainers of the family religion, this ceremony was comparatively rare. On the other hand, adoption was widely practiced among the Romans as among the Greeks. Where no son was born to the family head, a youth was adopted with proper ceremonial into the family membership and was taught the cult of the sacred hearth fire and of the domestic gods (Lares). A

---

[1] Compiled about 450 B.C.
[2] *Ancient Law* (ed. 1894), pp. 137–138.

Roman father chose a wife for his son and gave his daughter in marriage with scant regard for their wishes; and he could divorce his children with or against their wills.[1] Even after his marriage a son remained under the *potestas* of his father and the grandchildren likewise came under the authority of the patriarch at their birth. No male under power, even if he were a public official, could control his property or his earnings nor could he make a will as long as his father lived. Thus the Roman family was a state *in parvo*, consisting of wife, children, grandchildren and slaves, all ruled by an absolute head. Such was its character until the early years of the Empire.

Manus: The Status of the Roman Matron. — The power of the Roman husband over his wife was called *manus*. In the rude centuries of the kingdom and the early Roman Republic, women seem to have had few, if any, legal rights. As we have seen, a woman could not control property and hence was not regarded as a "person" before the law. At her marriage her husband acquired her *dos* or dowry, of which he had the entire management and profits. The wife merely passed from the *potestas* of her father to that of her husband, who sat as judge over her if she were accused of serious offenses. It is true that the husband must summon a tribunal of his own and his wife's male relatives to consider her case before he was permitted to pass judgment. But the matter once discussed in this family council, the husband might himself condemn his wife to death for a capital offense committed by her. If he discovered her in adultery, he might put her to death at once with no obligation to call a council of relatives. A Roman husband had also the power of personal chastisement and correction of his wife. Moreover, it is probable that in cases where the wife had committed offenses entailing fines upon her husband, who was legally liable for her actions, he might sell her labor, if not her person, in order to indemnify himself for the expense he had incurred.[2] Likewise he could surrender

[1] *Ancient Law* (ed. 1894), p. 141.   [2] Cf. Becker, *Gallus*, p. 156.

his wife to a plaintiff who brought suit for any civil offense
she had committed, thus relieving himself of liability for her
action.[1] Cato the Censor, that stern old Roman of the early
type, in a fragment called *De dote*, writes thus of the husband's
power: "The husband is the judge of his wife. If she has
committed a fault, he punishes her; if she has drunk wine,
he condemns her; if she has been guilty of adultery, he kills
her." [2]

By custom and law a Roman woman was kept under perpetual tutelage. When her father died, she came under the
authority of a guardian appointed by him. After marriage
she became *in a legal sense* the daughter of her husband and
included in his *patria potestas*. "All her property became
absolutely his, and she was retained in tutelage after his death
to the guardian whom he had appointed by will." [3]

Yet, in spite of all these restrictions upon her freedom, it
remains true that the Roman matron, in early times, was
thoroughly respected and held a place of dignity and honor
within the family and the State. She was unquestioned mistress of the household, as the man was master. After she was
lifted over the threshold of her husband's home at her marriage,
she calmly faced him with the ancient formula: "Where thou
art Caius I am Caia (*Ubi tu Caius, ego Caia*); *i.e.*, "Where
thou art lord, I am lady." And these were no idle words.
The Roman matron was not confined to the women's apartments like her Greek sister. Instead she took up her abode
in the *atrium*, the central room of the family life. Here she
sat, spinning and weaving, and directing the labors of her
household. Within the apartment, in early times, stood the
bridal bed (*lectum genialis* or *adversus*), the outward and visi-
ble sign of honorable married life. Marked respect was
accorded the Roman wife as the guardian of the family honor,

[1] Bryce, James, "Marriage and Divorce under Roman and English Law," in
Studies in History and Jurisprudence, p. 790.

[2] See Cato's *Quæ Extant*, ed. by H. Jordan (Leipsic, 1860), p. 68.

[3] Maine, *op. cit.*, p. 155.

and the partner of her husband in the education of their children. In all the ceremonies of family worship she officiated at the altar as priestess beside her husband. She might even walk abroad with considerable freedom. Custom alone restricted her movements in this regard, not the command of her husband. When she did appear upon the narrow streets robed in the *stola maternalis*, men were expected to make way for her as a mark of their respect for a matron of Rome. Apparently, also, if one may judge from the early pictorial work which has come down to us, Roman wives joined their husbands at table, perhaps even at banquets. Since women had no legal status, they probably could not appear in a court of law as complainant or defendant. Yet Becker holds that in very early times women might give evidence in court and might even appear to make complaint for another, until the abuse of the privilege led to its withdrawal by edict.[1] This right must have been very rarely used in ancient times, however, and seems in direct contradiction to legal opinion and precedent, which denied women individuality before the law.

Thus the Roman wife and mother was at once honored and subordinated; she was thoroughly respected and yet granted almost no legal rights. To quote Bryce: " One can hardly imagine a more absolute subjection to one person of another person who was nevertheless not only free but respected and influential, as we know that the wife in old Rome was." [2]

Property Rights in the Ancient Family. — In prehistoric times, prior to the reforms of Servius Tullius, landed property was quite probably held by the *gens*. But long before the Laws of the Twelve Tables were framed property had become individual to the extent that it was held and administered by the family head for the benefit of its members. At the death of the *pater familias* his possessions were equally divided among the members of his family who were under his power (*in potestate*). Thus the widow and the unmarried daughters

[1] *Gallus*, p. 153.
[2] *Op. cit.*, p. 790.

received equal shares with the sons. Primogeniture seems to have been unknown among the Romans; yet some writers [1] have assumed that it existed in order to account for the fact that estates long remained undivided within a family. A more probable explanation is that the estates were commonly held together in two ways: (1) by agreement of the heirs, (2) by provisions in the testament of the deceased father. A married daughter lost all right to inheritance and such was the law as late as the age of Justinian (sixth century A.D.). If the decedent left no immediate heirs, his property was divided among his nearest agnates, *i.e.*, relations descended from a not remote ancestor through the male line. If no agnates were living, the inheritance passed to the members of the deceased man's gens, *i.e.*, those claiming common descent from some long dead and perhaps mythical ancestor. As in Greece the gens controlled the estates of a member in two ways: (1) lands could not be alienated from the gens; (2) orphaned daughters who had inherited property could not marry without the consent of the gens nor could they alienate their share of the family lands by sale or otherwise. Guardians or "tutors" were appointed for a woman from the gens of her father at his death. In early times these tutors kept a rigid oversight and control of the property of an heiress, and arranged for her marriage with great care.

Marriage in Ancient Rome. *Matrimonium Justum and non Justum.* — Only when the parties to a marriage were of equal social rank could that form of marriage which conferred upon the man the civil rights of *patria potestas* and *manus* be entered upon. This form of marriage, entailing full rights to the husband and children, was called *matrimonium justum*. In earliest times it could not be contracted between a patrician and a plebeian; but this restriction was removed by law in 445 B.C. Another form of marriage existing in ancient Rome was called *matrimonium non justum* and was contracted with a man or woman of inferior social rank. This form did

[1] Cf. De Coulanges, *The Ancient City*, pp. 94 ff.

not carry with it the rights of *manus* and *patria potestas* although it was legally and morally binding. Children of such marriages could not become full Roman citizens. *Matrimonium justum* could be performed either with *manus* or without it. In the former case the wife passed under her husband's power; in the latter she remained under the power of her own father. In earliest times by far the larger number of marriages were performed *cum mano*, thus placing the wife in the position of a daughter to her husband and making her an integral member of his family. Like all ancient peoples the Romans looked upon marriage as a sacred and important act and stamped celibacy with public disapproval, since it was disadvantageous alike to the State, which needed supporters, and to the family, which needed sons to continue its domestic worship.

The Ceremonies of Espousals and Marriage. — Unlike the Greeks the early Romans did not regard the betrothal ceremony as legally binding on the parties. Before espousals or betrothal took place, the parents carefully selected a mate for daughter or son and arranged the amount of the *dos* or dowry brought by the bride to her husband. Either party to the engagement could withdraw from it and such withdrawal did not constitute ground for legal action although it met with popular disapproval. In early days, however, unchastity on the part of an engaged girl was probably regarded as adultery, and so punished. The betrothal ceremony among Roman patricians in later Imperial times was often a brilliant affair which took place in the *atrium* of the girl's home amid a large gathering of relations and friends. The young suitor of the girl and her father exchanged formulas as follows: The suitor says: "Do you promise to give your daughter to me to be my wedded wife?" The father replies: "The gods bring luck! I betroth her." Whereupon the suitor replies similarly: "The gods bring luck!" By these words the girl was made a spouse or betrothed maiden. Her betrothed then presented her with gifts and a ring to be worn on the third finger of the left hand. This little ceremony was followed by the congratulations of friends and a social hour during which wine and refreshments were served.[1]

Marriage Rites. — Let us suppose that two people of equal social condition have agreed to contract *matrimonium justum* with *manus*. What were the ceremonies connected with such marriage? First, there must be the formal *consensus*, or consent of the parties, which was the first and essential step in any valid marriage. However, be it noted that this consent was that of the *parents*, not of the young persons most concerned, whose consent was largely taken for granted. Then, in order that the woman might be brought under the power of her husband, any one of three formalities might be followed : (1) *confarreatio*, (2) *coëmptio*, (3) *usus*. The first was a solemn religious ceremony, most commonly employed by the patrician class in Rome. The rites of *confarreatio* were performed at the home of the bridegroom in the evening after the bride had been carried in brilliant procession (*deductio*), lighted by torches, from her father's house and had been lifted over the threshold of her new home. At this point the bride, turning to her husband, uttered the significant words already quoted, "Where thou art Caius I am Caia," thus reminding him of her honorable position as mistress of his household. The ceremony of *confarreatio* followed. This essentially consisted in the eating by the bride and groom of a sacred cake, made of the ancient Roman "far."[2] The simple rite was performed in the presence of the Pontifex Maximus,[3] the Flamen Dialis[4] and ten other witnesses. It was followed by the joining together of the hands of the young couple, probably by the chief priest. Following this ceremony the auspices were carefully taken and a sheep was sacrificed upon the family altar. The skin of the slain sheep was then stretched

---

[1] See Davis, Wm. S., *A Day in Old Rome* (1925), pp. 65–66.
[2] Far was a grain like spelt.
[3] Chief of the college of priests or pontiffs.
[4] Priest of Jupiter.

over two seats on which the bride and groom seated themselves, thus signifying that they were united by one bond despite their different duties within the family. After a gay banquet shared by the bridal couple and the assembled guests, the pronubæ [1] led the bride to the marriage-bed which had been placed in the atrium on the day of the wedding. Standing before the door of the bridal chamber they sang ancient hymns and songs in honor of marriage which would doubtless sound coarse and even indecent to modern ears. These marriage songs were likewise common in Greece and among all Aryan peoples.

Marriage with *manus* was also effected by the ceremony of "coëmptio." Here, again, the formal consent of the two parties constituted the essential step in marriage. The rite called coëmptio followed this consent and included many of the ceremonies of confarreatio — viz., the procession by torchlight, the lifting of the bride over the threshold of her husband's house, the salutation "Where thou art Caius, I am Caia," the taking of auspices and the joining of hands. But instead of the religious rite which consisted in eating the sacred cake, a symbolical sale of the woman to the man took place. A coin of small value was generally used and the sale was purely symbolic of the fact that the woman was brought under the *manus* or hand of her husband. That this quaint ceremony was the last relic of purchase marriage is highly probable although not an established fact.

In one other way might the woman be brought under her husband's power, and that was by the ancient custom of *usus*. When a woman had given her consent and had lived in the marriage relation with her husband for one year, during which time she had not remained three days absent from his home, she automatically came under his power and became an integral part of his family, thus losing membership in her own.

[1] These were young Roman matrons, only once married, who served as attendants to the bride.

This marriage custom was very general during the early centuries of Roman history, although it was largely confined to the plebeian class. Since it was lacking in all religious sanction or ceremonial dignity, it was never popular among the Roman patricians until a much later period.

Concubinage. — The monogamic character of marriage was far more strictly preserved by the early Romans than by the Greeks. As among most peoples of antiquity, concubinage existed as a recognized institution; but it was carefully regulated by the State. Concubinage was of two kinds: (1) the legalized union called *matrimonium non justum*, where a citizen lived with a woman of inferior social rank with whom he could not by law contract *matrimonium justum;* (2) the kind not sanctioned by public opinion or law where a man lived with one or more mistresses. In the first case the relation was formally recognized by law and custom, although the offspring of the union were not members of their father's family and thus could not inherit his property. But the second relation was as thoroughly condemned by the wholesome public opinion of the early Roman Republic as it is in the Western world today. Hence concubinage was comparatively rare before the period of the Punic wars.

Divorce. — That the right of divorcing his wife belonged to the Roman husband in very early times cannot be doubted, since it is expressly recognized in the Laws of the Twelve Tables. But during the first centuries of the Republic this privilege was carefully restricted and apparently was rarely used. Indeed marriage with *confarreatio* could be dissolved with great difficulty if at all and only after a ceremony of *diffarreatio* or breaking of the marriage bonds, to which all those present at the earlier ceremony of union were invited. The causes justifying the divorce of the wife were the preparation of poisons, adultery and wine-drinking, which last was always severely condemned and punished among the early Romans. One writer adds to this list the offense of counterfeiting the keys intrusted to the wife as *domina* or house

mistress.[1]   Yet, even when one of these acts had been clearly
committed, the husband was compelled to call a council of
his own and his wife's male relatives and lay the matter
before them ere he could pronounce the customary words of
separation.   Only in the case of the wife's adultery could the
husband dispense with the advice of the family council before
taking her life.   On this point Cato the Censor writes: "If
you were to catch your wife in adultery, you would kill her
with impunity without trial; but if she were to catch you,
she would not dare to lay a finger upon you, and indeed she
has no right." [2]   The formula of repudiation, as given in the
Twelve Tables, was: "*Tuas res tibi habeto.*" [3]   This was
sometimes followed by a command to leave the house (*foras
exi*).   Although the husband had sole rights of divorce in this
early period (save in the case of separation by mutual consent, which rarely occurred), yet if he exercised this right for
causes not recognized by law and custom, he brought upon
himself both public disapproval and the sharp reproof of the
Censor.   It is probable, therefore, that divorces were rare
occurrences.   Indeed Plutarch refers to the case of Spurius
Carvilius Ruga (230 B.C.) as the first instance of the repudiation of a wife at Rome.   This can hardly, however, be in
accordance with the facts.   Historians are inclined to believe
that Plutarch's statement should be interpreted to mean that
Sp. Carvilius was the first Roman to divorce his wife for
any but the three causes mentioned above.   It is well known
that the wife's repudiation in this historic case was due to the
fact that she had not borne a child.   She had failed in her
supreme duty, from the ancient point of view, of bearing a
son to her husband to maintain the family name and worship.   Yet, even then, public disapprobation of the act of
this Roman citizen was expressed in no uncertain tones.
Sp. Carvilius was compelled to forfeit half his property

[1] Cf. Lynton, *Fortnightly Review*, Vol. XLII, p. 43.
[2] Fragment, *De Dote*, in the *Quæ Extant* (Leipsic, 1860), p. 68.
[3] Take your property for yourself.

to the goddess Ceres and the other half to his divorced wife.[1]

It will be seen from the above account that divorce was largely a private matter in ancient Rome. Even when custom was violated in respect to divorce, the State intervened only by way of the rebuke of the Censor. Thus Rome is in agreement with the other nations of antiquity in regarding marriage and divorce as concerns of the family or of individuals interested.

The Early Roman Household as an Economic Unit. — Perhaps in no respect is the national spirit of the Greeks and Romans more strikingly contrasted than in their attitude toward industry. Prior to the Punic wars the Romans were a hard, stern, simple people with a high regard for manual labor; whereas the Greeks, as we have seen, held all pursuit of trade and industry which demanded actual manual work in genuine contempt. In the early days of the Republic, before Rome was launched upon her wars for conquest and expansion, the number of slaves in any household was small. As in Greece they were not only an essential part of the family,[2] but lived in somewhat friendly intimacy with its free members, despite the unlimited power of the master over their persons. In his life of Cato Major, Plutarch relates that the whole family ate in common in these primitive times, although the slaves probably sat on benches placed at the foot of the *lecti* or couches on which the rest of the family sat.[3] These household servants relieved the well-to-do Roman matron of the more burdensome and unpleasant forms of household labor and left her free to carry on her special pursuits of spinning and weaving which were held in high esteem.

In the early days of the kingdom almost every free Roman possessed a few jugera [4] of land which he frequently cultivated

[1] Cf. Colquhoun, *A Summary of the Roman Civil Law*, Vol. I, pp. 527–528.
[2] The Roman word *familia* was a term first applied to household slaves.
[3] The custom of reclining at meals belongs to a much later period.
[4] A *jugerum* was a little more than half an acre.

by himself, or with the assistance of a servant or two. Most
of the Romans of this period were farmers, who, clad in
woolen tunics, drove their crude bronze-shod plows over
the family acres. One of the highest ideals of their lives was
to become good plowmen; just as their ideal of womanhood was the chaste and industrious housewife spinning wool
far into the night. Such a man was Cincinnatus, called from
his plow to take command, as dictator, of the defeated
Roman forces in their war against the Sabines and Æquians.
The most eminent men of the early Republic were content
with the simple life of the farmer. Valerius Maximus [1] tells
us: "At that time there was little money; there were few
slaves, seven jugera of land, poverty in families, funerals paid
for by the state, and daughters without dowry; but illustrious
consulates, wonderful dictatorships, and countless triumphs
— such is the picture of these old times!" [2]

Probably these early Roman households were largely self-
supporting — the father furnishing the food supplies of grain,
green vegetables and *legumes*, and the raw wool and flax
which were prepared within the house by the matron and her
few family slaves. Division of labor other than that on a
sex basis had not gone far before the Punic wars. No slaves
skilled in cookery were found in the households, nor were
special bakers kept until after the wars in Asia.[3] All the
labors concerned with cooking and baking fell upon the
housewife. Even in early times, however, certain industries
had been carried outside the home. Roman women rarely
washed the family clothing at home, but sent all garments to
professional fullers to be cleansed in great tubs filled with alka-
line water. The later processes of cleansing garments are
pictured in the wall-paintings of a fuller's establishment in
Pompeii, which was unearthed years ago. Not only did these
men cleanse clothing, but apparently they cleaned and

[1] A Roman writer of the age of Tiberius Cæsar (14–37 A.D.).
[2] Quoted in Botsford, *A History of Rome*, pp. 92, 93.
[3] Cf. Becker, *Gallus*, p. 452.

dressed cloth sent to them fresh from the loom.[1] Very early, also, the crafts of the dyer, currier, coppersmith and goldsmith had developed into gilds called "colleges." Plutarch, in his life of Numa, the fabled successor of Romulus in the kingship, states that popular legend ascribed the founding of these primitive "colleges" of craftsmen to that king.

The Early Roman Home as a School. — For several centuries after the mythical founding of Rome (753 B.C.) the home was the only institution directly concerned with the education of youth. Within its revered precincts — sacred to Vesta, goddess of the hearth, to the Lares, spirits of ancestors, and to the Penates who blessed the family store — the child was nurtured in rigorous simplicity and trained in those hardy virtues and habits of industry and self-control which were of the utmost value to the family and the State. In spite of the narrowness of this training from our modern viewpoint, there was far more of true family life and spirit in the early Roman home than in the Greek. This was due to the higher and more dignified position of the Roman mother, who not only carefully instructed her children in their early years, but superintended them as long as they remained at home. In his life of the Gracchi, Plutarch has described the noble nature of the Roman matron Cornelia and the intelligent care she bestowed on the upbringing of her sons. So honored was this Roman mother that a statue was erected to her memory by the State.[2]

The numerous references made by early writers to the practice of child exposure make it clear enough that the Roman custom of putting an unwelcome child out of the way was similar to the Greek, although there is reason to believe that it was not as freely practiced. Nine days after the birth of a boy and eight days after that of a girl, the ceremony of *lustratio* took place, and was celebrated as a family festival. On this happy occasion the child was lifted from

---

[1] Cf. Becker, *Gallus*, p. 449.

[2] Plutarch, *Life of Tiberius and Caius Gracchus*, Bohn Library, Vol. I, p. 95.

the floor and named by its father, after which it received numerous small gifts from parents and friends, some of which were afterward worn suspended from its neck. The *bulla* was an amulet of gold worn at first only by children of patrician birth. It was no doubt hung about their baby necks as a protection against evil charms. After the family ceremony of *lustratio* the child's name was entered in the public registers of Rome which were carefully kept in order that the age and social station of any person might be readily established.

Unlike the Greeks, Roman parents did not commit their children to the care of slaves. Every Roman mother in ancient times nursed and reared her own offspring. In those stern and simple days education at the mother's knee was no idle expression. Great care was taken that the children should hear no evil speech and that the household attendants should be discreet in word and action. Boys were instructed first by the mother, later by the father in those family and civic virtues of frugality, self-control, gravity, piety, courage and loyalty to the State upon which the early Romans set such high value. To inculcate the national ideals of conduct the Roman mother told her boy tales of the bravery and devotion to the State of his honored ancestors, as well as legends of the nation's heroes. In a great cabinet in the *tablinum* [1] of every patrician home were placed images and waxen masks of dead ancestors, and children were very early trained to know and to honor the brave deeds of their forefathers. At a later day Cato the Elder wrote histories for his son, telling of the glorious achievements of illustrious Romans and the honored customs of the country. There was little or no intellectual education in this early time. Yet every boy was taken to the forum by his father and required to learn by heart the Laws of the Twelve Tables. By the stern regulations of this code he must guide both his public and private life.

[1] An alcove at one end of the atrium, serving as an office for the *pater familias*.

After his early moral education at the knee of his mother, the boy, at about six or seven years of age, became the constant companion of his father, who took his son about with him from place to place as his duties on the farm and in the military field or on the forum demanded. Thus the Roman boy was trained in the school of life to perform the tasks so soon to be laid upon him. He learned by actual practice to drive the oxen at the plow and to oversee the workmen on the farm. His drill in the Campus Martius made of him a hardy soldier. His visits to the forum, the law courts and later to the Senate, where he waited upon his father if he were a member, taught him legal procedure and acquainted him with public affairs. When a great Roman died, the boy was taken by his parents to hear the funeral oration in which the virtues of the dead were extolled. Plutarch's *Cato* and Varro's *Monnius* paint the simple, hardy training of this early time. Cato the Elder says that from his first years he was brought up to be frugal, industrious and unquestioningly obedient. His body grew hardy and strong, due to his strenuous work on the family farm in the Sabine region, where the soil was stony and infertile. Plutarch, in describing the education of the younger Cato, states that his father "was as careful not to utter an indecent word before his son as he would have been in the presence of the Vestal Virgins." [1]

The religious education of boys and girls was as carefully looked after as their moral and practical training. When quite young, they were taught to assist in all the sacrifices and rites of family worship in the capacity of *camilli* and *camillæ* (acolytes). It has been suggested that the reason why boys were permitted to wear the *toga prætexta* with the purple stripe, which was otherwise restricted to the use of magistrates and priests, was because of their active participation in the worship of the domestic gods.

When the boy had reached his sixteenth year, or thereabouts, he exchanged the *toga prætexta* for the *toga virilis*,

[1] *Life of Marcus Cato*, Bohn Classical Library, Vol. II, p. 119.

which symbolized his growth to manhood. The change was accompanied by a solemn ceremony held on the day called *Liberalia* — the sixteenth of March. Probably the day began with sacrifices to the Lares at the family altar on which the youth laid the insignia of his boyhood. Among these were his favorite toys and the *bulla* that he had worn around his neck since his naming day. It is probable that the toga of manhood was donned at home; but this little ceremony was immediately followed by a more imposing one in the forum. Surrounded by a brilliant train of friends and retainers, the patrician youth was led to the forum and afterwards to the Capitol, where public sacrifices were offered. After these ceremonies the boy was put on probation for a year, during which his conduct was carefully observed by public officials. Meanwhile his life became more free and public. He took prescribed exercises in the Campus Martius, frequented the tribunals and the forum and sought by these means to prepare himself for public life. Thus carefully did the ancient Romans introduce their youth to the duties of manhood; and their painstaking efforts contrast very advantageously with the happy-go-lucky methods of modern states. These domestic and public ceremonies, together with their direct contact with public affairs, must have made a deep impression upon the minds of adolescent Roman boys, who were thus made to feel the responsibility and dignity of the life of a true Roman citizen.

Not very much is said by Roman writers about the education of girls in this early period. It is certain, however, that they received a careful home training in their future duties as Roman housewives and mothers. They were taught especially to spin, weave and fashion garments; for upon women, in these ancient days, rested the entire responsibility of clothing the family. Also girls were at least occasionally sent to the *ludi*, or private elementary schools. The historian Livy relates that Virginia, the lovely daughter of a plebeian, was seized by order of Appius Claudius while on her way to one of these schools. Probably the *ludi* were attended almost wholly by girls of the middle class. Although it may never have been a general custom to send girls to school, it is probable that they were not left in complete ignorance as were the Greek maidens, but were given some instruction in reading and writing at home.[1]

THE ROMAN FAMILY FROM THE CLOSE OF THE PUNIC WARS TO THE LAST CENTURIES OF THE EMPIRE

Changes in the Status of Women. — In the hotly contested campaigns of the two Punic Wars,[2] Rome matched her mettle against Carthage, an ancient and powerful foe. She emerged completely victorious and vastly elated at the humiliation of her dreaded enemy. During the thirty and more years of actual warfare, a large proportion of all able-bodied Romans saw service in the field. This meant that husbands were away from home for years at a time and the management of their estates and households devolved upon their wives. Many women thus received a training in self-reliance and efficiency in responsible positions. It can hardly be doubted that this education was admirably calculated to develop in them vigorous personalities, accustomed to the exercise of power. Such women would submit with an ill grace to the restrictions upon their daily lives and interests imposed by the husband on his return from the wars. *Manus* would seem, no doubt, a tyranny.

Rome's imperialistic wars of the succeeding centuries, which extended her domain from Palestine to the Straits of Gibraltar and from North Africa to the Danube, had far-reaching effects upon family custom. First, wealth began to flow into Rome from the subject provinces, and to accumulate in influential families. Quite naturally fathers grew more and more reluctant that not only the rich dowry given to their daughters

[1] Fowler, *Social Life at Rome*, p. 178.
[2] The first war extended from 264–249 B.C.; the second from 219–202 B.C.

at marriage but all gifts and bequests made to them after marriage should pass into the absolute control and ownership of their husbands.   In consequence there gradually grew up, after the Second Punic War, the custom of marriage without *manus*.   Such a marriage left the wife in the *potestas* of her father, who was usually too much engaged with personal and public affairs to interfere with her actions.   In the event of her father's death, the married woman passed under the control of an appointed guardian or "tutor" who, in course of time, granted her a considerable degree of liberty.   Indeed Maine declares that the power of the guardian in the Imperial age tended to become a nullity.   Moreover, Roman lawyers showed great ingenuity in devising expedients which would enable women to evade the old restricting laws.   In time important results followed from the practice of marriage without *manus*, for women who brought large dowries and had independent means claimed from their husbands a freedom of opportunity and even an equality of right hitherto undreamed of.   So wealthy did certain Roman women become that two laws were passed in different periods which were designed to limit both their riches and their extravagance.   The Oppian Law (215 B.C.) restricted the value and kind of ornaments and apparel worn by women.   But so great was the opposition of the fair sex to this ordinance that it was repealed in the lifetime of the elder Cato (195 B.C.), despite his bitter opposition.   The *Lex Voconia* (169 B.C.) forbade any Roman owning property of 100,000 *asses* [1] in value to make a woman his heir.   The law, however, was evaded by the creation of trusts for the benefit of women.

A second effect of the almost continuous wars of the third and second centuries B.C. was a marked decrease in the male population of Rome due to death, enslavement or absence on duty.   As the men diminished in numbers, and as the authority of absent husbands passed to their wives, the social status

---

[1] A Roman *as* at this time was a copper coin worth about 7.9 mills in American money.

of women was steadily elevated. Their power, to be sure, was a delegated one, and was promptly withdrawn on the return of the family head from foreign campaigns, if he did return. But this did not in the least prevent its inevitable result — the growth within the women, thus raised to positions of responsibility and power, of a sense of their own personal worth and a sturdy desire for greater freedom, broader opportunity and influence. Indeed the elder Cato (d. 147 B.C.) bitterly complains that "all men rule over women, we Romans rule over all men, and our wives rule over us." [1] Thirdly, the conquest of Greece in 148 B.C. led to an influx of Greek scholars and teachers into Rome. Not only did the Roman men profit by this introduction of a higher culture into their midst, but apparently the women were gradually influenced by it. Roman matrons deliberately sought to become learned and clever. In the age of Cicero (106–43 B.C.) Clodia and Sempronia led the band of brilliant and often unscrupulous women who were not only versed in the learning of their time but were a power in politics. It was against such women that Juvenal in a later age launched his biting satire: "Let not the matron that shares your marriage bed possess a set style of eloquence, or hurl in well-rounded sentence the enthymeme [2] curtailed of its premiss; nor be acquainted with all histories. But let there be some things in books which she does not understand. . . . A husband should have the privilege of committing a solecism." [3]

Changes in Marriage and Family Customs. *Marriage and Property Rights.* — As we have seen, the practice of free marriage, *i.e.*, marriage without *manus*, grew up in Rome after the wars for conquest and became an established custom in the late years of the Republic. In Imperial times the sacred rites of *confarreatio* marriage, which brought the wife into the family of her husband and under his iron rule, had well-nigh disap-

---

[1] Plutarch's *Lives*, Bohn Library, Vol. II, p. 105.
[2] An incomplete argument; a syllogism with the minor premise lacking.
[3] Juvenal, *Satires* (trans. by Evans, 1890), Satire VI, pp. 55–56.

peared, save in the marriage of priests. So likewise had the ceremony of *coëmptio* and the custom of *usus* which also resulted in bringing the wife under marital power. Marriage came to rest wholly upon the formal consent of the parties to the union; hence the Roman maxim "Marriage is by consent only" (*Nuptiæ solo consensu contrahuntur*). The formal betrothal, which included an oral agreement concerning the *dos* or bride's dowry, was still customary. Also the wedding procession by torchlight and the marriage banquet in the home of the groom were popular customs. The former was chiefly important, however, as evidence of the union already contracted by free consent. Marriage in Rome, always a purely private matter, now required no religious rite, although it was customary for the auspices to be taken at weddings and for priests to be present. Since marriage no longer entailed *manus*, the wife remained a member of her own family and was almost independent of her husband, who had little or no legal power over her conduct. Although her *dos* was administered by her husband, who enjoyed its usufruct, the ultimate ownership rested nominally in the father, often actually in the wife. In case of the husband's insolvency the wife's *dos* could not be used to satisfy his creditors. Moreover it became a common practice for patrician fathers to endow their daughters at marriage with personal property designed for their sole use. As a result Roman women attained a position of "great personal and proprietary independence," and no doubt showed the same dominating qualities so conspicuous in Roman men. "Why do I not marry a rich wife?" asks a Roman writer. "Because I do not wish to be my wife's maid."

During the period of the Empire another kind of matrimonial property was introduced which was called the "gift for the sake of marriage" (*donatio propter nuptias*). It consisted in a portion of the husband's estate set apart for the bride in case of his death or her divorce without just cause, although remaining with the residue of his property under his own control. If the husband became insolvent, however, his wife's *donatio* could not go to the payment of his creditors. But the effects of "free marriage" were not wholly advantageous to the married woman. As the Roman wife of Imperial times was not a member of her husband's family she had only a limited right of succession to his property should he die intestate. Only after relatives as far as second cousins had obtained their share could the widow receive any consideration. Indeed, in the sixth century A.D., the Emperor Justinian so far extended the list of relations who could inherit in case of intestacy as practically to exclude the wife. Only if she were in actual need was provision made for the widow from her husband's estate. The laws of Hadrian and Marcus Aurelius, however, recognized the close relationship of mother and child by granting to them reciprocal rights of inheritance.[1]

The well-to-do Roman matron was thus, to all intents and purposes, a free agent controlling her own actions and to some extent her property. Before noting the abuses which crept into family life in the days of the Empire, it would be well to recognize explicitly the worthy ideal of marriage which prevailed during the late Republic. That the ideal was not realized in many instances does not impugn its high and honorable character. This conception of marriage made the wife the equal of her husband and recognized her right to the full and free development of her powers as an individual having responsibilities and privileges. A famous jurist has defined free Roman marriage as "a partnership in the whole of life, a sharing of rights both sacred and secular. . . ."[2] It is interesting to note that this pagan ideal of marriage is accepted in large measure by modern nations. It cannot be too emphatically pointed out that the evils characteristic of sex relations and family life in the Roman Empire were signs of the general social and moral degeneracy of the times, rather than the direct outcome of the increased liberty ac-

[1] Cf. Bryce, "Marriage and Divorce under Roman and English Law," in *Studies in History and Jurisprudence*, pp. 790-798.

[2] Quoted by Bryce, *op. cit.*, p. 798.

corded to women. Moreover, writers have tended to exaggerate the extent of the immorality of the Imperial period, and especially the deterioration in family ideals. The devoted married life of Pliny and his noble wife Calpurnia is evidence that Roman society as a whole was not infected by the decadence so glaringly apparent among many of the wealthy and influential class. It is probable that the earlier conception of marriage, narrow and yet wholesome in some respects, still lived on in individual families of the middle class as well as among those of higher social rank. Fortunately a lengthy inscription on the tomb of a Roman matron who died about 8 B.C. has come down to us. It was the tribute of Q. Lucretius Vespilla to his wife Turia and reads as follows: "You were a faithful wife to me and an obedient one; you were kind and gracious, sociable and friendly: you were assiduous at your spinning (*lanificia*): you followed the religious rites of your family and your state, and admitted no foreign cults or degraded magic (*superstitio*): you did not dress conspicuously, nor seek to make a display in your household arrangements. Your duty to our whole household was exemplary: you tended my mother as carefully as if she had been your own. You had innumerable other excellencies in common with all other worthy matrons, but these I have mentioned were peculiarly yours." [1] Similar eulogies of Roman wives have likewise been copied from the ancient tombstones.[2]

Decline of the Patria Potestas. — The decline of the patriarchal power of the husband over the wife was followed by a similar weakening of the *patria potestas*. The decay of father power showed itself first in legal changes, giving a son somewhat more control of property. Augustus Cæsar conferred upon a son under power (*filius familias*) the right to dispose by will of whatever he had acquired in the active exercise of his profession as a soldier. The Emperor Hadrian extended

---

[1] Paraphrased by Fowler from the mutilated original, in his *Social Life at Rome*, pp. 166–167.

[2] See Friedländer, *Roman Life and Manners*, Vol. I, pp. 264–266.

this privilege to sons honorably discharged from military service. Later the son *in potestate* was permitted to dispose by will of all that had come to him directly or indirectly in connection with his military service. The doctrine of a "natural law" based on justice, in accordance with which legal principles must be patterned, was gaining strong hold upon Roman conceptions of law in the first centuries of the Empire. This accounts for the marked tendency of the Emperors to restrict the rights of a father over his son. Parents were still permitted to expose their infants, but no father was allowed, in the capacity of household judge and executioner, to put his son to death. In the reign of Alexander Severus (191–211 A.D.) the father's power over the person of his son was limited to moderate chastisement; for serious offenses the son must be turned over to the ordinary legal tribunals for trial. Also the father's right of sale was restricted to young children and even then could be exercised only when he was unable because of extreme poverty to support them. Yet the *pater familias* was still regarded as the rightful owner of all the earnings and acquisitions of his children outside of those obtained through military service.

Growth of Celibacy. — During the later Republic as well as in Imperial times, the marked decline of the marriage rate was a cause of great concern to statesmen. It is probable that this social phenomenon was partly due to the increased wealth and prestige of women. Roman men resented the independence shown by wives whose possessions exceeded their own, and who showed in consequence a tendency to dominate. Of these women Plutarch writes: "Men who marry wives that are much their superiors in riches often become, before they are aware of it, not the husbands of their wives, but the slaves of their marriage portion." [1] Then, too, some Romans did not take more kindly to learned women than did their poet Juvenal; nor were they disposed to bring into their homes as helpmeets ambitious wives who might and some-

[1] *Plutarch on Education; The Education of Boys,* ed. by W. H. Super, p. 82.

times did use their influence over men to direct the course of politics, and thus possibly to involve their husbands in serious difficulties. Of the political activity of women in Imperial Rome, a modern historian writes: "On the walls of Pompeii female admirers posted up their election placards in support of their favorite candidates."[1] Here and there married women exercised a powerful indirect influence in governmental affairs under the first Emperors — and that not always for good.

But the cleverness and dominating character of these newly emancipated Roman matrons can account only in part for the enormous increase of celibacy during the last centuries of the Republic and the first of the Empire. The tendency was fundamentally due to the steady deterioration of the ancient family ideals; and this, in turn, was part of the widespread decline of moral standards following upon Rome's wars for dominion. The vast influx of wealth flowing from pillage and tribute laid upon the conquered provinces, and the spread of slavery through conquest combined to produce, on the one hand, a leisure class bred in luxury and idleness, and on the other, a steadily increasing group of landless men whose small farms had been bought up or seized by wealthy Romans to enlarge their country estates. Small landowners tended to disappear and to give place to a troublesome proletariat, incapable to a large degree of self-support, since at this time most labor was in the hands of slaves. Such conditions do not furnish favorable soil for the growth of healthy ideals of civic or of family life. In the senatorial class men and women alike were infected with the dry rot of selfishness and a frenzied pleasure-seeking; in consequence they looked upon the earlier almost religious conceptions of family duties and responsibilities as troublesome and outgrown. When marriages were contracted, the motives were often mercenary or concerned with mere personal gratification. Rarely, in the senatorial class, was marriage any longer regarded as a solemn obliga-

[1] Dill, *Roman Society from Nero to Marcus Aurelius*, p. 81.

tion to the State and to the domestic gods. Concubinage and prostitution grew by leaps and bounds as men sought to satisfy their passions without assuming the cares of married life. In time the vices of the men, darkly painted by Juvenal in his second *Satire*, infected the women and produced the Messalinas, the Julias and the Poppæas of the early Empire. These women, reared in an atmosphere of extreme moral laxness and political intrigue, are described as "the cruellest and most wanton women of antiquity."

So serious did the evils of celibacy become that as early as 131 B.C. Metellus Macedonicus, the Censor, publicly urged Roman men to marry for the sake of maintaining the vigor of the State. In his oft-quoted speech he caustically remarks : "If we could do without wives we should be rid of that nuisance; but since nature has decreed that we can neither live comfortably with them nor live at all without them, we must e'en look rather to our permanent interests than to a passing pleasure." [1] But the speeches of public men had little effect in increasing the marriage rate. Julius Cæsar, in his brief period of power, sought to encourage marriage by rewards. Likewise in the year 18 B.C. Augustus Cæsar proposed a law encouraging marriage and imposing disabilities on the unmarried. The law was carried with difficulty through the Senate but was rejected by the Comitia or popular assemblies of Rome. However, in 3 B.C. Augustus succeeded in getting the law passed. This was the famous Lex Julia, or Julian law. In 9 A.D. another statute called Papia Poppæa was passed containing further regulations concerning marriage. In its final form the Lex Julia et Papia Poppæa provided that unmarried persons between the ages of 20 and 50, in the case of women, and of 25 and 60, in the case of men, were disabled from receiving legacies or inheriting estates unless they married within 100 days. The penalty could be evaded by an engagement to marry if carried out within two years. Prop-

---

[1] Quoted by Fowler, *Social Life at Rome*, p. 150, from Livy, Epistle 59.

erty thus sacrificed reverted to the State.[1]   These laws, however, seem to have had little effect, since Tacitus in his *Annals*
writes : "It was next proposed to relax the Papia Poppæa
law which Augustus in his old age had passed — for yet further
enforcing the penalties on celibacy and for enriching the exchequer.   And yet marriages and rearing of children did not
become more frequent, so powerful were the attractions of a
childless state." [2]

Childlessness. — As suggested above, the spread of celibacy
was not the only social evil of the age.   Even where marriages
were contracted in the higher social ranks there was often
little disposition on the part of either husband or wife to rear
a family.   When a child was conceived by an unwilling
mother, abortion was freely practiced or infanticide was
promptly resorted to after its birth.   These practices constituted part of those social abuses in Imperial Rome against
which Christianity sternly set its face.   They illustrate the
general pagan tendency to regard human life as not valuable
in itself, and therefore to be taken if circumstances seem to
require it.

In time childlessness became so general in the wealthier
classes that the adoption of an heir to the family estates became a widespread custom.   This adoption was secured by a
ceremony similar to that of *lustratio* by which the new-born
child was received into family membership.[3]   In consequence
poor men became shameless hangers-on and sycophants of the
rich in the hope of receiving fat bequests at their death, if not
of inheriting the entire estates (*familia*).   Of this custom,
Ammianus Marcellinus [4] writes in the fourth century A.D. :
"Some persons look on everything as worthless which is born
outside the walls of the capital save only the childless and the

---

[1] Cf. Muirhead, *Historical Introduction to the Private Law of Rome*, pp. 285–
286 ; and *Harper's Dictionary of Classical Literature and Antiquities*, article on
" Matrimonium."

[2] *Op. cit.*, trans. by Church and Brodribb, Vol. III, p. 25.

[3] See above, p. 129.

[4] A Roman historian who died about 390 A.D.

unmarried. Nor can it be conceived with what a variety of obsequious observance men without children are courted at Rome." [1] Legacy hunting seems to have been a favorite pursuit of worthless scoundrels. Pliny the Younger describes such an individual in one of his letters to Calvisius. "The fellow gets estates," he writes, "he gets legacies conferred upon him as if he really deserved them." In another letter Pliny relates how this same Regulus freed his son from his power in order to entitle the youth to an estate left him by his mother; for even in this period sons *sub potestate* could not inherit during the father's lifetime. After his son was set free Regulus "fawned upon the lad with a disgusting show of fond affection." Finally the son died and Pliny satirically describes the ostentatious grief of the legacy-hunting father who thus fell heir to the young man's fortune.

In order to penalize childlessness and encourage larger families the Lex Julia et Papia Poppæa, mentioned above, provided that childless pairs were disqualified from receiving more than one half of any legacy or estate bequeathed to them. However, men escaped the penalty if they had even a single adopted child. The law further provided that preference should be given to candidates for public office according to the number of their children. Apparently these legal provisions accomplished nothing in increasing the size of families. Despite the failure of the Augustan laws to increase marriage and decrease childlessness, it is interesting to note that the Fascist government of Mussolini enacted in June, 1929, a law designed to bring about an increase in the birth rate of Italy, even now a state suffering from overpopulation. The law provides that in government service, whether national, provincial or municipal, "other things being equal, married persons with children shall be preferred to those without children and married persons without children to unmarried persons." As further encouragement to marriage and fruitfulness the law provides that in the assignment of apartment houses, built with gov-

[1] Quoted by Davis, *The Influence of Wealth in Imperial Rome*, p. 298.

ernment aid, preference shall be given first to married persons
with children, next to those without children, before unmarried persons are served.   Since Italy, like other countries, has
suffered from a shortage of housing in the years succeeding
the World War, the privilege offered in the above law may well
have proved a stimulus to an increased birth rate.   Yet it is
doubtful whether matters of such intimate concern to individuals as marriage and the birth of offspring can ever be permanently and measurably influenced by legislation.   Mussolini might do well to study the history and outcome of the
Augustan laws.

Divorce under the Empire. — Although divorce was uncommon in the early period of Roman history, it had ceased
to be a rare occurrence in the second century B.C.   Since marriage rested solely on the consent of the parties, it followed
that each party agreed, tacitly or otherwise, to continue the
union only so long as the other desired it.   This meant, of
course, that marriage could be dissolved at pleasure.   Such
freedom requires a highly developed sense of moral responsibility in those exercising it ; and, as we have seen, the ethical
standards of the age were steadily deteriorating.   In such a
period of moral decadence every institution of society was
affected ; and perhaps marriage and family life suffered most
of all.   Plutarch's *Lives* are full of instances of the carelessness with which marriage was contracted and the ease with
which the loosely knit bonds were broken.   In his *Life of
Æmilius* [1] the writer gives us an admirable statement of the
attitude of many men of the time toward the question of
divorce.   Æmilius was asked why he had divorced his wife
Papiria and he replied, stretching out his shoe : "Is it not
beautiful?   Is it not new?   But none of you can tell where it
pinches me.   In fact some men divorce their wives for great
and manifest faults, yet the little but constant irritation which
proceeds from incompatible tempers and habits, though unnoticed by the world at large, does gradually produce between

[1] Lived in the second century B.C.

married people breaches which cannot be healed." Such a statement is illuminating; for it shows that the spirit of individualism was even then in conflict with the earlier civic and religious ideals that had led men to contract marriage for social and religious ends. And this new spirit, asserting as it did the right of the individual man to complete his own happiness through marriage and to dissolve the association when it no longer served his personal ends, was speedily communicated to the women. These Roman wives of the late Republic and the Empire were dominant types, as determined as their husbands to secure power and pleasure and "the fullness of life" as they conceived it. Such independent matrons were no whit more willing to bear the yoke of an irksome or unhappy marriage than were their husbands.

And so the practice of divorce spread rapidly, until in the Augustan age it had become a public scandal. This Emperor tried to restrict the practice by requiring the active party in the divorce to execute a *repudium*, or written statement renouncing the marriage, in the presence of seven witnesses, all full Roman citizens.[1] But the law seems to have had little or no effect in stemming the flood of divorces, although it was on the statute books for more than five centuries. The Christian Father Tertullian, living in the second and third centuries A.D., is credited with the epigram: "Divorce was now looked upon as one fruit of marriage." Men in public life were no more serious in their attitude toward marriage than were private citizens. Cæsar divorced Pompeia, his wife, on the merest suspicion of laxity of conduct; Cicero repudiated his wife, Terentia, in middle age to marry a young and wealthy girl of whose property he had been made guardian. This unsuitable marriage was unhappy from the outset and was soon dissolved. But the matrimonial affairs of Pompey best reveal the disregard of marital rights and responsibilities on the part of many influential Romans. Sulla, the famous Roman general and consul, was desirous to reward Pompey

[1] In the famous Lex Julia de Adulteriis, passed in 17 B.C.

for his services in war, and at the same time to win his support in the furtherance of his own (Sulla's) interests. Therefore he persuaded Pompey to divorce his wife Antistia, who was mourning the recent death of her father, and to marry Sulla's step-daughter Æmilia. Æmilia herself was not only married, but was an expectant mother. The shameful bargain was nevertheless accomplished, and it promptly brought tragedy in its wake; for the mother of Antistia committed suicide and Æmilia died in childbirth after her marriage to Pompey.[1]

As we have seen, marriages were frequently made at this time for purely political or economic reasons and were sometimes followed by divorce within a few days, when the specific end had been attained. Thus a Roman Quæstor[2] was deposed by the Emperor Tiberius for marrying a woman two days before the lots for offices were drawn and divorcing her the day after in order that he might appear as a married man and thus fulfill the state requirement for public officials. Seneca says of the women of his day that they counted their years not by consuls, but by their husbands; and Juvenal, always harsh in his judgment of women, charges some of them with divorcing their husbands before the marriage garlands had faded on the lintels. That such statements are exaggerations can hardly be doubted; but that they have a solid groundwork of fact seems equally true from the evidence at hand. Thus Quintus Lucretius Vespilla, Consul in 19 B.C., inscribes these words upon his wife's tombstone in 8 B.C.: "Seldom do marriages last till death undivorced; but ours continued happily for forty-one years."[3] It is well to bear in mind such cases as this, lest we fall into the error of believing that hasty divorce had penetrated all grades of society alike.

In a serious effort to curb the increase of marital infidelity, so conspicuous in his reign, the Emperor Augustus brought

---

[1] Plutarch's *Lives*, Bohn Library, Vol. II, pp. 203–204.
[2] Two quæstors were annually appointed to keep the treasury in the Temple of Saturn.
[3] Cf. Friedländer, *op. cit.*, Vol. I, p. 243.

about the enactment of the famous Julian law concerning adultery, the Lex Julia de Adulteriis, passed in 17 B.C. The law sought to penalize the offense of adultery in the wife by declaring that any husband who kept his wife after she had been found an adulteress was guilty of the crime called *lenocinium*. Sixty days were allowed husband or father to start legal action against the wife, after which period any interested person might prosecute. If the woman were found guilty, she was deprived of half her dowry and one third of her property and was banished to a desert island. Frequently offenders were sent to Seriphus in the Ægean Sea, an island used by Roman emperors as a place of banishment for State criminals. One of the unfortunate women to suffer the penalties of the new law was Julia, daughter of Augustus himself, who was guilty of such gross infidelities during her marriage to Tiberius Claudius Nero that her father divorced her himself and sent her to the lonely Island of Pandatoria off the coast of Campania. When Tiberius became emperor in 14 A.D., the treatment accorded Julia became so severe that she died of starvation.

In certain cases the Julian law permitted the father of an unfaithful wife to kill both the woman and her lover. But such exact conditions and nice distinctions were laid down by the law that it was probably not often resorted to by outraged fathers. Although the husband was not permitted to kill his wife if he surprised her in the act of adultery, he might kill the adulterer if he belonged to certain classes specified in the law. Not only was the husband permitted to retain one sixth of the dowry forfeited by his wife but he might also claim compensation from the guilty lover and hold him in restraint until he found sureties for payment. On the other hand, if the husband were guilty of adultery the Julian law condemned him to lose half his property, to restore the entire amount of his wife's dowry and to suffer banishment.[1]

[1] Cf. *Harper's Dictionary of Classical Literature and Antiquities*, article on " Adulterium."

Household Economy in the Imperial Period. — The vast changes introduced into Roman society as a result of the nation's aggressive wars and conquests made themselves felt no less radically in the economic life of the family than in its social and moral life.   Even in the time of Cicero, landed property on a large scale was regarded as the only source of wealth worthy a free Roman citizen of senatorial rank.   The rude, simple farming life of the early Romans had begun to disappear even in the days of Cato the Censor (232–147 B.C.). Trade and industrial pursuits, hitherto largely in the hands of free plebeians, tended more and more to be turned over to slaves, of whom vast numbers were brought to Rome as captives at the close of each campaign of conquest.   In Imperial times most of the trade and industry of Rome and the Latin cities were controlled by slaves or freedmen; the former supplying all the varied needs of the wealthy household, and the latter selling their wares in shops.   Every Roman of wealth and assured social standing attempted to maintain at least two households — a city home and a villa in the country.   Pliny the Younger describes with enthusiasm and in minute detail every feature of his charming villa at Laurentium, and in another letter sets forth the beauties of his Tuscan country home.[1]   As town and country houses grew more spacious and luxurious, the number of slaves required to manage them vastly increased.   Especially when great estates took the place of the old-time country farms a large staff of out-of-door laborers was required in addition to the house servants.   The slaves attached to the country villa were called *familia rustica;* those belonging to the city house were called *familia urbana.*

Division of Labor. — The wealthy households of Imperial Rome were characterized by division of labor so minute as in part to defeat its own end.   In the villas, besides the agricultural slaves proper who were employed in plowing, sowing, reaping and tending grape-vines and olive trees, there were

[1] *Letters* (Bosanquet ed.), Bk. II, Letter XVII; Bk. V, Letter VI.

also slaves trained as gardeners, poulterers, gamekeepers, tenders of bee-hives and fish-ponds. On the largest estates several thousand slaves were thus employed. Hence the villa of a wealthy Roman was not only a haven of rest and delight in days of leisure but it was also the source of supply of most of his daily wants; — a highly organized economic institution independent of most of the outside sources of industry and supply. Within the household, division of slave labor was even more minute. Here were staffs of expert handicraftsmen in almost every kind of work. One group of slaves was trained for dining-room service and was under the direction of a head called the *triclinarchus*.[1] Another group had charge of bedrooms and living rooms. In the kitchen was a staff of skilled slaves, including plain cooks, pastry cooks, bakers, etc.; for most wealthy households in Imperial times maintained large bakeries. Many families boasted their own tailors, spinners, weavers and hairdressers. Frequently physicians and surgeons were attached to the largest households. These men were usually slaves or freedmen, carefully trained by the master for their work of healing. Every great house had also its private architects, its secretaries and men of literary attainments, and its skilled musicians, jugglers and mimics to entertain the master and mistress and their guests. Occasionally even a philosopher was attached to the household to instruct the mistress in the theories of Stoics and Epicureans.

This lavish provision for slave labor rendered it quite unnecessary for the mistress of such a household to ply her earlier, honorable tasks of spinning and weaving or even to direct the work of her slaves, except when she so desired. Thus there appeared in Rome the pleasure-loving "lady," so well known in modern times, with little to do except beautify her person and attend the circus, theaters and banquets. The more intelligent and able of these women, however, ill satisfied with lives of empty enjoyment, sought to become forces in politics, writers of verse, literary critics and students of the sciences.

[1] From *triclinium*, the name for dining-room.

Plutarch says of Cornelia, wife of Crassus and later of Pompey, that she added the graces of music, geometry and literature to the charms of her beauty, and had even attended courses in philosophy. The changes in the mode of living of these Roman ladies were reflected in the *atrium*, once the center of the household activities, where its mistress spun and wove surrounded by her maids and children. The slaves were now removed to apartments in the rear; the family hearth was also banished to a more private spot; the household gods were tucked away in a special *sacrarium*, or sacred place; the family meals were no longer served near the hearth, but in various dining-rooms in different parts of the house. In course of time the *atrium* became little more than a reception room for guests. Yet the marriage bed, now a mere symbol, remained in its ancient place; and the images and waxen masks of famous dead with "relics of their valor" still reposed in a cabinet in the *tablinum*.

But, although women of wealth and social position had become mere consumers of the goods produced by slaves, the wives of the middle class and the poor still performed their household tasks as of old, feeding and clothing their families by their own efforts, assisted, perhaps, by a few slaves. Again the tombstones erected to the memory of their wives by men of simple birth bear eloquent testimony to the virtues of these industrious Roman matrons even in a decadent age. One such inscription reads: "Short, wanderer, is my message; halt and read it. The loathly stone covers a lovely woman. Claudia her parents called her: she loved her husband; bore him two sons; — She was of proper speech and noble gait, kept her house and spun. This is all. Go." [1]

The Roman Home in Its Educational Aspect. *Early Home Training.* — Such profound changes in family life and ideals as have been described above were necessarily reflected in the nurture and training of children. Far from being the sole teachers of their offspring, the Roman fathers and mothers of

[1] Cf. Friedländer, *op. cit.*, Vol. I, p. 265.

Imperial times showed much the same disposition to turn over their responsibilities to servants and teachers as do parents today. The literature of the first century A.D. abounds in bitter criticism or earnest exhortation of unworthy parents. Plutarch advises fathers "who wish to beget noble children not to associate with women of doubtful reputation, . . ." and not to be "unduly fond of wine" if they do not wish to see their sons drunkards also. Turning to the women he urges them to nurse and care for their own children rather than turn them over at birth to slaves. If nurses are employed, says Plutarch, they should be "Greek by birth and training," since it is "important to train and develop harmoniously from the beginning the disposition and character of children." Then follows a satirical account of the practice of his own time in respect to choice of nurses: "What is done at present by many men is in the highest degree absurd. They select from among their slaves some to work in the fields, some for service at sea and some to look after their merchandise. They pick out others to oversee their household affairs and still others to manage their finances. But if they happen to have a slave who is given to drink and gluttony, who is in fact good for nothing, to this fellow they assign the oversight of their boys." [1]

But the deficiencies of parents were unfortunately not confined to careless selection of nurses for their children. The lax conduct and improper language of parents in the presence of boys and girls of tender age, as well as their too luxurious nurture of their children, provoked sharp comments from the writers of the time. Thus Quintilian [2] exclaims: "Would that we ourselves did not corrupt the morals of our children! We enervate their very infancy with luxuries. . . . What luxury will he not covet in his manhood, who crawls about on purple! We form the palate of children before we form their pronunciation. They grow up in sedan chairs; if they touch the ground, they hang by the hands of attendants supporting them on each

[1] Plutarch, *op. cit.*, pp. 47–54.
[2] A famous teacher of grammar and rhetoric in Rome in the first century A.D.

side. We are delighted if they utter anything immodest. Expressions which would not be tolerated even from the effeminate youths of Alexandria we hear from them with a smile and a kiss. Nor is this wonderful; we have taught them; they have heard such language from ourselves. They see our mistresses, our male objects of affection; every dining-room rings with impure songs; things shameful to be told are objects of sight. From such practices springs habit, and afterward nature. The unfortunate children learn these vices before they know that they are vices; and hence, rendered effeminate and luxurious, they do not imbibe immorality from schools, but carry it themselves into schools." [1]

Education Shifted to the School. — Yet it can hardly be doubted that the stern moral training of an earlier age, with its sincere reverence for the purity of childhood, lived on in families untainted by wealth. Horace (65–8 B.C.) pays ardent tribute to his father's solicitude for his education : "And yet," he writes, "if the faults and defects of my nature are moderate ones, . . . if (that I may praise myself) my life is pure and innocent, and my friends love me, I owe it all to my father; he, though not rich, for his farm was a poor one, would not send me to the school of Flavius, to which the first youths of the town, the sons of the centurions, the great men there, used to go . . .; but he had the spirit to carry me, when a boy, to Rome, there to learn the liberal arts which any knight or senator would have his own sons taught. . . . He himself was ever present, a guardian incorruptible, at all my studies. Why say more? My modesty, that first grain of virtue, he preserved untainted, not only by an actual stain, but by the very rumor of it; . . ." [2] The reference suggests the change that had come over Roman education owing to Greek influence. Ever since the Punic Wars the grammar school and the rhetor-

---

[1] *Institutes of Oratory*, Bohn Library series, Ch. II.
[2] *Satires* of Horace, I, 6; in Monroe, *Source Book in the History of Education*, p. 397.

ical school for training orators and statesmen, both modeled after Greek institutions, had been gaining a foothold in Rome despite the opposition of a powerful conservative group. In Horace's time the long struggle was ended; Roman education was carried on largely outside the home and had become more and more literary and intellectual in character. As in the present age the home had shifted to the shoulders of the schoolmaster the burden of responsibility for shaping the youth intellectually and morally; and the schools were already demonstrating their insufficiency for the task without the coöperation of the home.

The Home Training of Girls. — In conclusion, brief mention should be made of the education of girls in Imperial Rome. After the early years of childhood under the care of a nurse, sometimes a Greek slave, the girl's instruction began. It is probable that only the daughters of the higher class received much intellectual training, and these girls were taught at home under the direction of tutors. Martial and Ovid make brief references to the nature of this education. Apparently it was literary in character like that of the boys, designed to give a thorough linguistic training as well as appreciation of the poets and prose writers of Greece and Rome.

When the girl had reached her thirteenth year, her parents began to seek out a husband for her. An unmarried girl at nineteen was distinctly an "old maid"; indeed at twenty a woman who had not become the mother of legitimate children was liable to incur the penalties laid down in the Lex Julia of Augustus.[1] Although the law required that the girl's consent to the union be secured, it was always assumed as given unless she openly refused it. In reality the parents' will was absolute in most instances; and their choice was governed by considerations of wealth and family convenience. Often girls were betrothed in their childhood, the arrangements being made in a businesslike way by professional intermediaries or "marriage-brokers." It is a significant fact in this connection that the

---

[1] See above, p. 141.

Latin language contains no words corresponding to "court" or "woo" in our English tongue.

After the wedding festivities were over, the girl-wife of the senatorial class tasted a freedom of life which must have been in pleasant contrast to the seclusion and constant surveillance of her girlhood days at home, where she was still under the *patria potestas*. As a married woman she was to all intents and purposes as free as her husband. To quote Friedländer: "In the microcosm of a great house, with its scattered properties, legions of slaves and retinues of clients and subjects, her will granted or withheld fortune or even life. . . . Whatever claims to admiration she might have, wit, talent or education, her position ensured her success." [1] She attended banquets, theaters, the circus and mingled freely with her peers in the social world of her time. Instances are on record of women who were promoted to consular rank by will of the Emperor. The privileges of such women were very great, and it is questionable whether men even of the grade of præfect [2] could take social precedence over them. Roman married women of senatorial rank were organized into a guild, the *conventus matronarum*, which was a sort of feminine senate. At times this body was consulted by certain of the emperors on minor questions of state.[3]

Comparison of the Roman Woman of the Empire with the Modern American Woman. — A review of family history in Rome brings into glaring relief the divergence between the customs of the early and the later period. The simple restricted home life of the Roman wife and mother of primitive times is separated by a wide gulf from the almost unlimited social and economic freedom of her sister of a later age. This matron of the Imperial period has far more in common with the emancipated American woman of the twentieth century than with her country woman of the early Roman Republic.

---

[1] *Op. cit.*, Vol. I, p. 240.
[2] A præfect was ruler of a Latin city.
[3] Friedländer, p. 240.

Just as the legal, economic, educational and personal rights of the Roman woman were restricted by the early law of the Republic, so were those of the American woman under the English common law. As the rights of Roman women were gradually extended after the Punic Wars, in an age when the wealth and culture of Rome were steadily increasing and the stern patriarchal ideas were dying out, so have the rights of American women been extended and their disabilities lessened, due to much the same causes. With wealth usually come leisure and opportunity for reflection; and these bring in their train an amelioration of ideas and of manners. But the parallel can be carried further. As in Rome women eagerly sought outlets for their trained capacities in social, intellectual and political activities, so likewise do American women in the present day. As the wives and mothers of Imperial Rome chafed against the physical burdens and the exacting demands upon time and strength of child-bearing and rearing, so likewise does a group of American women today, who strive for complete freedom to live their lives and develop their talents outside the limits of the home. The decline of marriage among the intellectual class in America parallels the more general decline in Imperial Rome; the increase of divorce in one country bears striking likeness to that of the other. But in one respect the parallel ceases. American women of today, educated to a realization of practical, social issues, show a far more dynamic interest in the social and economic problems of their age and in the betterment of the conditions of life for all classes than was ever revealed by the hard and brilliant women of the first centuries of the Roman Empire. Moreover social consciousness has attained a higher development in the modern world than in the ancient. This is revealed in educated groups at present by a spirit of self-criticism and a desire for a better and finer type of life that promises well for the future, and especially for the family as the basic social institution. The unrest and apparent disintegration of the modern family may well be the precursor of a type of family life more nearly adapted to the conditions of the twentieth century.

SELECTED READINGS

SOURCES

Arnaud, Germain. *La vie privée des Romains décrite par les auteurs latins*, Marseille, Librairie Classique Laffitte, 1899, Chs. I, V, VI.

Juvenal. *Satires*, trans. by Rev. Lewis Evans, London, G. Bell and Sons, 1901, II, VI, XIV.

Monroe, Paul. *Source Book of the History of Education for the Greek and Roman Period*, Macmillan, 1921, Tacitus, *Dialogues concerning Oratory*, pp. 361–363, Suetonius, *Life of Cæsar Augustus*, pp. 375–376, *Musonius on the Education of Women*, pp. 401–406, Juvenal, *Satire XIV*, pp. 419–420, *Laws of the Twelve Tables*, pp. 337–338, *Institutes of Quintilian*, pp. 451–459.

Pliny, the Younger. *The Letters of Caius Plinius Cæcillus Secundus*, trans. by Melmoth; Rev. F. C. T. Bosanquet, ed., London, G. Bell and Sons, 1900, Book I, Letters IX, XIV, Book II, Letters IV, XVII, XX, Book III, Letters I, XIV, XVI, XX, Book IV, Letters II, X, XIX, Book V, Letters VI, XVI, Book VI, Letter IV, Book VII, Letter V.

Plutarch. *Lives*, Bohn Classical Library, 1908, Vol. I, pp. 47–84, 56–57, 95, 196–197; Vol. II, pp. 105, 384–387, 430; Vol. III, pp. 203–204, 390–399.

Super, W. H., ed. *Plutarch on Education; The Education of Boys*, Syracuse, C. W. Bordeen, 1910, pp. 47–84.

SECONDARY WORKS

Becker, Wilhelm A. *Gallus; or Roman Scenes of the Time of Augustus*, pp. 151–187, 199–225, 231 ff., trans. by Rev. Frederick Metcalfe, N. Y. and London, Longmans, Green, and Co., 1898.

Bosanquet, Helen D. *The Family*, N. Y. and London, Macmillan, 1906, Ch. I.

Bryce, James. *Marriage and Divorce under Roman and English Law*, pp. 782–833. In *Studies in History and Jurisprudence*, Oxford, Clarendon Press, 1901; N. Y., Oxford University Press, Am. branch, 1905.

Couch, Herbert N. "Woman in Early Roman Law" in *Harvard Law Review*, VIII, pp. 39–50.

Davis, W. S.   *Influence of Wealth in Imperial Rome*, N. Y., Macmillan, 1913, Chs. IV, VII.

Dill, Samuel.   *Roman Society in the Last Century of the Western Empire*, 2nd rev., London, N. Y., Macmillan, 1899, pp. 130, 134, 163–164, 208.

Donaldson, Sir James.   *Woman; Her Position and Influence in Ancient Greece and Rome*, N. Y. and London, Longmans, Green, and Co., 1907.

Ferrero, Guglielmo.   *Ancient Rome and Modern America*, N. Y. and London, G. P. Putnam's Sons, 1914, Ch. III.

——.   "Woman and Marriage in Ancient Rome," in *Century*, 1911, Vol. 82, pp. 3–14.

Fowler, Wm. W.   *Social Life at Rome in the Age of Cicero*, N. Y., Macmillan, 1915, Chs. V, VII, VIII.

Friedländer, Ludwig.   *Roman Life and Manners under the Early Empire*, authorized trans. of the *Sittengeschichte Roms* by L. A. Magnus, 4 Vols., London, G. Roulledge and Sons, Ltd.; N. Y., E. P. Dutton, 1908–1913, Vol. I, Ch. V.

Guhl, E. K., and Koner, W. D.   *Life of the Greeks and Romans*, N. Y., D. Appleton and Co., 1875, trans. from 3rd German ed. by F. Hueffer, pp. 355–365, 371–375, 511–523.

Hastings, Jas., ed.   *Encyclopedia of Religion and Ethics*, 1908–1927, N. Y., Scribner's, Vol. V, pp. 746–749.

Inge, W. R.   *Society in Rome under the Cæsars*, N. Y., Scribner's, 1907, pp. 61–70, 159–162, 172–183, 245, 262.

Johnstone, Harold W.   *Private Life of the Romans*, Chicago, Scott, Foresman and Co., 1903, Chs. I, III–VIII.

Lacombe, P.   *La famille dans la société romaine; étude de moralité comparée*, Paris, Lecrosnier et Babe, 1889, Part II, Chs. II–V.

McClees, Helen.   *The Daily Life of the Greeks and Romans*, N. Y., The Gillis Press, 1924, pp. 19–39.

Maine, Sir Henry.   *Ancient Law*, Holt, 1894, pp. 123–268.

Morey, Wm. C.   *Outlines of Roman Law*, N. Y. and London, G. P. Putnam's Sons, 1884, pp. 5–7, 29–37, 239–249, 313–334.

Muirhead, Jas.   *Historical Introduction to the Private Law of Rome*, Edinburgh, A. & C. Black, 1886, pp. 24–36, 43–49, 64–69, 115–126, 345–348, 415–426.

Peck, H. T., ed., *Harper's Dictionary of Classical Literature and Antiquities*, Harper, 1898, articles on "Adulterium," "Connubium," "Divortium," "Dos, Amancipatio," "Familia," "Liberalia," "Lustratio," "Matrimonium," "Manus," "Voconia Lex."

Pellisson, Maurice. *Roman Life in Pliny's Time,* trans. from French by Maud Wilkinson, N. Y., Flood and Vincent, 1897, Chs. II–IV, pp. 131–135.

Preston, Harriet W., and Dodge, Louise. *Private Life of the Romans,* Boston and N. Y., Leach, Shewell, and Sanborn, 1894, Chs. I, IV.

Putnam, Emily. *The Lady,* N. Y., Sturgis and Walton Co., 1910, pp. 39–68.

Schuster, E. J. *The Wife in Ancient and Modern Times,* London, Williams and Norgate, 1911, Chs. V, VI.

Tucker, Thos. G. *Life in the Roman World of Nero and St. Paul,* N. Y., Macmillan, 1910, Chs. IX, X, XVI, XVII.

CHAPTER V

THE INFLUENCE OF CHRISTIANITY UPON MARRIAGE AND THE FAMILY IN THE ROMAN EMPIRE

1 A.D.–500 A.D.

Spread of Christianity in Italy. — Into the Roman Empire of Tiberius Cæsar was introduced a new religion, born, like all great religions, in the East. Its founder, Jesus Christ, the supreme spiritual leader among the Hebrews of Palestine, having been crucified by the Romans, left to his apostles the stupendous task of spreading his gospel not only among the Jews but throughout the world. In the early centuries of the Christian era St. Paul and later other disciples preached the doctrines of Christ in the capital city of Rome itself. But the new religion spread very slowly within the mainland of Italy, not only because of its emphasis on humility, purity and self-sacrificing love — virtues little prized by the dominating and pleasure-loving Romans — but because the Christians definitely placed the authority of religion above that of the State wherever the two were opposed. Believing in the spiritual reality of one God revealed through Christ, the followers of Christianity refused to offer sacrifices and do reverence to the spirits of departed Emperors who had been deified by the State. Moreover, Christian leaders preached the gospel of peace and discouraged their converts from recruiting the armies of Rome. These doctrines brought the new religion into conflict with the Imperial Government and led to those outbursts of persecution of Christians which stigmatized the reigns of Nero and subsequent Emperors. It was not until 311 A.D. that the Emperor Galerius held out the olive branch of peace to the Christians, now grown into a numerous and powerful group, difficult to suppress. Two years later his successor, the Emperor Constantine, gave formal recognition to Christianity as the official religion of the State.

The tardy spread of Christianity in Italy and the provinces during the first three centuries of the Christian era is accountable for the negligible influence of its teachings on Roman law and practice with respect to marriage and the family during that period. Until well into the fourth century Rome went on marrying and giving in marriage according to ancient custom, while the Christian Fathers were preaching and enforcing among their own followers doctrines regarding marriage, family relationships and divorce in direct opposition to Roman practice at many points. Side by side the two systems existed until Christianity at last climbed into a position of supremacy among the religions of the Empire in the second half of the fourth century, when its influence was clearly reflected in marriage laws and customs.

Views of the Church Fathers concerning Marriage. The Respective Merits of Virginity and Marriage. — There can be no reasonable doubt that the views of the early Christian Fathers concerning the marriage bond were profoundly influenced by the opinions of St. Paul who never married. The doctrines of this great leader are so familiar that only brief reference need be made to a few of the more influential of them. He writes: "Nevertheless, *to avoid fornication*, let every man have his own wife, and every woman have her own husband." [1] But he promptly follows this doubtful sanction by the words: "But I speak this by permission and not of commandment. . . . For I would that all men were even as I myself. . . . I say therefore to the unmarried and widows, It is good for them if they abide even as I. But if they cannot contain, let them marry; *for it is better to marry than to burn*." [2]

From these passages and many others similar in spirit it seems evident that St. Paul looked upon marriage as a substi-

[1] I Cor. vii, 2.   Italics mine.
[2] *Ibid.*, 7-9.

tute for a worse state — that of illicit sexual intercourse. Better is marriage than fornication; but, after all, the choice lies between two evils of greater and less degree. There is no hint in Paul's writings, nor does it clearly appear in the treatises of the *later* Church Fathers, that marriage is a spiritual as well as a physical union, and that the latter should be impossible without the former. It is true that the earlier Fathers have a worthier ideal of marriage than their successors. Thus Clement of Alexandria, who died in 220 A.D., declares that marriage "as a sacred image must be kept pure from those things which defile it." [1] Likewise Ignatius in his *Epistle to Polycarp* and Athenagoras in his *Plea for Christians* maintain the purity of the marriage state.[2] But the dominant note in the later patristic writings is a frank recognition of the physical basis of marriage, with a rather grudging acceptance of its necessity — an acceptance that becomes more and more reluctant as the spirit of asceticism gains headway within the Christian body. At the opening of the third century Tertullian in his *Letter to his Wife* writes: "We do not indeed forbid the union of man and woman, blest by God as the seminary of the human race, and devised for the replenishment of the earth and the furnishing of the world, and therefore permitted, yet singly." Later, however, in referring to Christ's saying that the man who looks upon a woman to lust after her hath committed fornication already in his heart, Tertullian comments: "But has he who has seen her with a view to marriage done so less or more?" In reply to the question of a critic whether he is not destroying even single marriage he boldly answers: "And not without reason (if I am); inasmuch as it, too, consists of that which is the essence of fornication." In the same treatise he asserts of a married woman: ". . . nor yet is the means through which she becomes a married woman any other than that through which withal (she becomes) an adulteress." [3]

---

[1] Cf. *Ante-Nicene Fathers*, Vol. II, pp. 377–379.
[2] *Ibid.*, Vol. I, p. 95; Vol. II, p. 147.
[3] *Ibid.*, Vol. XVIII, p. 14, *An Exhortation to Chastity.*

Obviously these pronouncements show scant appreciation of the uplifting and strengthening influence of a true marriage — of its power to quicken and deepen all worthy emotions. Thus it is that the reading of the marital views of the later Church Fathers is a distasteful task, from which the student willingly turns.

Yet it would be manifestly unfair to judge these writings, covering the period from the days of Tertullian to those of St. Jerome and St. Augustine, solely from the standpoint of the twentieth century. It should be remembered that the struggling company of early Christians, striving as they were to realize on earth the pure ethical teachings of their Master, found themselves in the midst of a corrupt and degenerate society, the leaders of which were in many instances shamelessly licentious. In the preceding chapter the great laxity with respect to sex relations and divorce that prevailed in Imperial Rome has been indicated. Although the gross immorality of Roman social life has possibly been exaggerated by well-meaning moralists, a sufficiently solid basis of fact remains to explain, if not to justify, the attitude of the leaders of the Christian Church toward all sexual relationships. To their minds, bent upon purification of conduct, as of inner motive and ideal, most of the shameful misdeeds of their age might be traced to the attraction of one sex for the other. Gormandizing, drinking, brutalizing games and exhibitions of all sorts, bad as they were in their immediate results, served the further vicious end of arousing animal passions which, in court circles at least, not infrequently sought outlet in unrestrained sexual license. Thus, in the final analysis, the love of the sexes appeared to the Church Fathers to be the root of many evils — if not of all.

But this does not wholly account for the scant approval of marriage accorded by the later Church Fathers. Very early in the history of the Church the idea of virginity, as a state of special purity pleasing to Christ, took root among Christians and received the sanction and encouragement of the Fathers.

If sexual love is responsible, not only for gross immorality, but also for a worldly absorption in the joys and cares of family life, instead of in the unseen world of the spirit, should it be placed on the same plane of holiness as the virgin state which demanded no such fealty to earthly things? One and all, the later Church Fathers answered this query in the negative. Yet they did not and could not openly condemn marriage, since it had received the sanction of Christ himself as well as the more reluctant recognition of St. Paul. Moreover, the Fathers themselves could hardly overlook the necessity for marriage from the standpoint of the renewal of the race. Also, if virgins were to be dedicated to the service of Christ, they must be the fruit of unions sanctified by the Church. Hence marriage is never explicitly condemned or forbidden by Christian teachers; but it is placed third and lowest in the scale of Christian purity. Highest and best is absolute virginity, and next lower is placed that incomplete and belated, yet acceptable celibacy that is voluntarily adopted after marriage or after the death of husband or wife.[1]

St. Jerome, preacher of the beauties of the monastic life, writing toward the close of the fourth century, leaves the reader in no doubt as to his position concerning the moral beauty of celibacy. In his famous letter *To Eustochium*, a young Roman girl who had dedicated her life to Christ in perpetual virginity, he admonishes her: "Do not court the company of married ladies or visit the houses of the high-born. . . . Learn in this respect a holy pride; know that you are better than they." And again: "To show that virginity is natural while wedlock only follows guilt, what is born of wedlock is virgin flesh, and it gives back in fruit what in root it has lost." In reply to his critics who had attacked his views of marriage St. Jerome declares: "I praise wedlock, I praise marriage, but it is because they give me virgins."[2] But it is in his well-

---

[1] Tertullian, *Exhortation to Chastity*, in *Ante-Nicene Fathers*, Vol. XVIII, p. 2.
[2] *Letters* of Jerome, in *A Select Library of the Nicene and Post Nicene Fathers*, ed. by Schaff and Wace, Vol. VI, pp. 28–30.

known treatise *Against Jovinian* that Jerome allows his growing antipathy to the married state to find full expression. Referring to the oft-quoted words of St. Paul, "It is better to marry than to burn," Jerome comments : "It is good to marry simply because it is bad to burn." And commenting further on the statement of the apostle that "Such (*i.e.*, married persons) shall have trouble in the flesh," he sarcastically exclaims : "We in our ignorance had supposed that in the flesh at least wedlock would have rejoicing. But if married persons are to have trouble in the flesh, *the only thing in which they seemed likely to have pleasure, what motive will be left to make women marry?* for, besides having trouble in spirit and in soul they will also have it even in the flesh." [1]

But St. Jerome was by no means alone in sounding the praise of virginity and in declaring the married state to be morally inferior to it. In his treatise *On Widows* St. Ambrose writes : "The apostle has not expressed his preference for marriage so unreservedly as to quench in men the aspiration after virginity; he commences with a recommendation of continence, and it is only subsequently that he stoops to mention the remedies for its opposite." Likewise St. Augustine's enthusiasm for the virgin life is repeatedly expressed in his *Letters*. Writing to the Lady Juliana, whose daughter had taken the vow of chastity, he says : "For she did not contract an earthly marriage that she might be, not for herself only, but also for you, spiritually enriched, in a higher degree than yourself, since you, even with this addition, are inferior to her, because you contracted the marriage of which she is the offspring." In another letter in praise of this same maiden Demetrius he exclaims : "May many handmaidens follow the example of their mistress; may those who are of humble rank imitate this high-born lady. . . ." [2]

Influence of Asceticism. — Teachings such as these, from

---

[1] *Library of Nicene and Post Nicene Fathers*, Vol. VI, p. 77; *Against Jovinian*, Vol. I, p. 13. Italics mine.

[2] *Ibid.*, Vol. I, pp. 504, 549–550.

Christian leaders in high places, bore their inevitable fruit. A blow was struck at the purity and honorable nature of the married state from which it had not recovered at the close of the Middle Ages. This is true despite the fact that early in its history the Church declared marriage to be a sacrament and had thoroughly established this doctrine by the middle of the twelfth century.[1] As asceticism spread over the Western world, the praise of celibacy became more insistent and the depreciation of marriage more positive. The early efforts of the Church to deny matrimony to the secular and regular clergy, who were held to be dedicated to a life of especial purity, steadily gained headway, even though they were not crowned with success until centuries later.[2] The attitude of monks and other Christian ascetics toward all women, even those of their own immediate family, was unwholesome and even prurient. Woman was viewed wholly from the physical standpoint of sex and was condemned because of the carnal pleasures and temptations she suggested. Commenting on the harmful effect of asceticism upon mediæval ideas of marriage, a modern historian writes: "History all too plainly shows that the benefits conferred by monasticism and the enforced celibacy of the secular clergy come far short of balancing the evils flowing from the conception of wedlock as a 'remedy for concupiscence.' The influence of the church did, indeed, tend to condemn the breach of conjugal fidelity by the husband as equally sinful with that of the wife; although this righteous principle has by no means always been observed in Christian legislation. On the other hand, celibacy bred a contempt for womanhood and assailed the integrity of the family."[3]

In view of the theories of Christian leaders outlined above it is not surprising to learn that cohabitation, even in marriage,

[1] The first *explicit* recognition of marriage as one of the seven sacraments of the Church is made in the *Sentences* of Peter the Lombard in 1164.

[2] A Roman council under Innocent I, 402 A.D., ordered bishops, priests and deacons to remain unmarried.

[3] Howard, *History of Matrimonial Institutions*, Vol. I, p. 331.

was held, at least by inference, to be an essentially impure act. At the fourth Council of Carthage, which sat in 398 A.D., it was enacted that "When the bridegroom and bride have received the benediction, let them remain the same night in a state of virginity out of reverence for the benediction." [1] This ruling of the Council was incorporated in canon law and the period of abstinence was extended to two or three nights. In his valuable work, *Folk Lore in the Old Testament*, Frazer states that the rule was later modified so that a husband might have intercourse with his wife on the first night of the marriage if he "paid a moderate fee for the privilege to the proper ecclesiastical authority." [2] As late as the seventh Christian century (668) we read in the Penitential of Archbishop Theodore of Canterbury [3] that married couples should abstain three nights from intercourse before receiving the Holy Communion. Furthermore a husband is enjoined to refrain from cohabitation for forty days before Easter and eight days at the Easter festival.

It is difficult to estimate the extent of the injury inflicted on the popular conception of marital intercourse by thus branding it as an impure and unholy act, depriving the participants, temporarily at least, of the comfort and inspiration of the sacrament. There can be little doubt that this attitude of the Church has been one factor in developing in the minds of certain pious folk, down to the present time, an idea that cohabitation is a vulgar and even bestial act which should rarely be indulged in and then only for the purpose of procreation of offspring. Perhaps there is no reform more deeply needed today than an education of men and women to an appreciation of the possibilities of beauty and spiritual quickening in marital intercourse growing out of mutual love and sympathy.

[1] Migne, *Patrologia Latina* (Paris, 1850), Vol. XXXIV, col. 201. Quoted in Pomerai, Ralph, *Marriage, Past, Present and Future, an Outline of the History and Development of Human Sexual Relationships* (London, 1930), p. 123.

[2] *Op. cit.*, Vol. I, p. 497.

[3] Haddan and Stubbs, *Councils and Ecclesiastical Documents*, Vol. III, p. 199.

Second Marriages: Continence in Marriage. — Very early the Christian Church took a firm stand against second marriages. In the well-known *Letter to His Wife* above referred to, Tertullian sets forth the doctrine of the Church in this regard. "How detrimental to faith, how obstructive to holiness, second marriages are, the discipline of the church and the prescription of the apostle declare, when he suffers not men twice married to preside [over a church], when he would not grant a widow admittance into the order unless she had been 'the wife of one man'; for it behooves God's altar to be set forth pure." St. Jerome, while granting a reluctant permission to any widow to re-marry, lest she fall into the sin of fornication, justifies his consent on the ground that "It is preferable that she should prostitute herself to one man rather than to many." [1] Second marriages were strongly discountenanced by the Christian Emperor Theodosius and his successors, and finally such unions entailed forfeiture of the dower or *donatio*, as the case might be, in favor of the children of the first marriage. [2]

Some of the patristic writings comment favorably upon continence within the marriage bond and the lives of Christian ascetics abound in tales of such renunciation. In his *History of European Morals* Lecky mentions half a dozen or more of such cases taken from the legends of the saints. [3] So much bitterness of spirit and alienation were naturally produced within families by these one-sided resolves to remain virgin after marriage that the more prudent of the Church leaders became alarmed; and it was later ordained that the abstinence of married pairs from sexual intercourse, in accordance with the prevalent ascetic ideal, should be only by mutual consent.

The Influence of Early Christianity upon the Status of Women. — In the Gospel story women occupy a prominent and honorable position. Mary and Martha, the sisters of

---

[1] Letter to Pammachius, *op. cit.*, p. 70.
[2] Muirhead, *Historical Introduction to the Private Law of Rome*, p. 388.
[3] *Op. cit.*, Vol. II, pp. 324–325.

Lazarus of Bethany, are counted among the closest friends of Christ. To the woman at the well of Samaria Jesus discoursed of profound truths. To Mary of Magdala, we are told He first appeared after His resurrection. Yet Christ advanced no new theories with respect to the nature, position and influence of womankind. He accepted the marriage state as it existed among the Jews with the proviso that this union could not be dissolved save for adultery only. Man and wife "are no more twain but one flesh." It remained for the apostle Paul to express the earliest authoritative opinions of Christian leaders in regard to the status of women. In I Corinthians he urges that a woman should cover her head or be shorn. "For a man indeed ought not to cover his head, forasmuch as he is the image and glory of God : but the woman is the glory of the man. For the man is not of the woman; but the woman of the man. Neither was the man created for the woman, but the woman for the man." [1] In such plain language St. Paul declares his belief in the essential inferiority of women. Again he writes : "Let your women keep silence in the churches : for it is not permitted them to speak; but they are commanded to be under obedience, as also saith the law" (I Corinthians xiv, 34). Obviously the Apostle speaks here as a firm believer in the patriarchal family idea so long upheld by his Hebrew countrymen. Women shall "adorn themselves in modest apparel, with shamefacedness and sobriety"; for not Adam but the woman was deceived by the serpent and therefore in transgression (I Timothy ii, 14). In this original sin of Eve all women have a share — all are tainted with the same offense, by which man fell and sin was brought into the world. Woman, then, shall be in subjection to her husband who yet shall give "honor to the wife as unto the weaker vessel." These and other similar statements faithfully set forth the attitude of St. Paul toward womankind. Furthermore they furnished the standards that determined the status of women under Christianity for many centuries.

[1] I Cor. xi, 7–9.

Yet, at the time the Apostle wrote these oft-quoted sayings, women in the imperial city of Rome, as we have seen in the preceding chapter, had advanced to a position of great social, economic and intellectual freedom. Unquestionably the influence of St. Paul had much to do with the spread of a reactionary tendency among Christians toward restricting the life of women very narrowly to the home and the church. To be sure, during the first years of the Christian era, women played an important rôle as teachers and prophetesses. But this activity was soon curtailed, until women could publicly work within the Church only as widows and deaconesses, if we except their splendid service as martyrs to the faith. From the first the Christian Church supported its own poor, including dependent widows and orphans. To assist in this work widows of at least sixty years of age were appointed by church officers to visit the sick, to aid poor women and to care for friendless orphans. Such women were carefully selected with respect to character and skill and their duties were clearly defined and restricted. Following out the exhortation of St. Paul, they were strictly forbidden to teach religious doctrine. In course of time the class of widows tended to give place to the order of deaconesses. Probably this change was due to the fact that "widowhood had fallen in the spiritual market and virginity had risen." [1] Be this as it may, by the middle of the third century the order of deaconesses had become well established. But let it not be supposed that these women held a position of freedom and responsibility within the Church; on the contrary, their work was almost as narrowly restricted as that of the widows. Tertullian in his treatise *On Baptism* states positively that no woman should ever administer that sacrament. He justifies his position by reference to St. Paul's well-known views: "For how credible would it seem that he who has not permitted a woman even *to learn* with overboldness, should give a female the power of teaching

---

[1] Donaldson, *Woman; Her Position and Influence in Ancient Greece and Rome and in Early Christianity*, p. 139.

and baptizing." "Let them be silent," he says, "and at home consult their own husbands."

So much for the position of women as active workers within the Church. What of the status of women in general — as daughters and wives and mothers? From the beginning of its history the early Church clearly recognized the *spiritual* equality of women and men. Both had been redeemed by the Savior of the world and their souls were alike precious in the sight of God. Thus Clement of Alexandria in his work on the daily conduct of the devout Christian declares: "The virtue of man and woman is the same. And those whose life is common have common graces and a common training." [1] Yet his contemporary Tertullian is frequently harsh in his denunciations of women and in his exhortations to them as the daughters of Eve to walk shamefacedly before men. In his Letter *On Female Dress* he breaks forth in bitter invective: "And do you not know that you are (each) an Eve? The sentence of God on this sex of your lives in this age: the guilt must of necessity live too. *You* are the devil's gateway: *you* are the unsealer of that (forbidden) tree: *you* are the first deserter of that divine law: *you* are she who persuaded him whom the devil was not valiant enough to attack. *You* destroyed so easily God's image, man. On account of *your* desert — that is, death — even the Son of God had to die. And do you think about adorning yourself over and above your tunics of skins?" [2] These two passages sound the dominant chord of most of the later patristic writings on women. As a dangerous seducer of man, as the prime cause of his fall from Eden, let woman seclude herself, dress in sober garments, veil her face and walk humbly in the world. By the age of Tertullian, if not earlier, married women were exhorted to remain in the seclusion of their homes, engaged in housewifely duties and in prayer.

The foregoing passages show that the status of the married

[1] "The Instructor," in *Ante-Nicene Fathers*, Vol. II, p. 211.
[2] *Ibid.*, Vol. XI, p. 305.

woman within the family became less free after the establishment of Christianity. The words of St. Paul concerning the subjection of the woman to her husband fell on fertile soil and bore fruit for many centuries. The wife tended once more to become in theory and practice, if not in Roman law, the obedient handmaiden of her husband who was lord of her person and her services.

THE REGULATION OF MARRIAGE BY THE EARLY CHRISTIAN CHURCH

Betrothal and Nuptials. — During the first three centuries the Church did not interfere with the betrothal and marriage customs then in vogue in the Empire. Indeed in his work *On Idolatry*, written in 200 A.D., Tertullian authorizes the attendance of Christians on the family rites — betrothal, marriage, *lustratio* and *liberalia* — of their pagan friends. Nearly two centuries later, however, the Emperor Theodosius issued a stern edict against these family rites as saturated with paganism. The early Church occupied itself with the task of working out an elaborate scheme of degrees of kinship within which marriage was prohibited. At the same time it attempted to enforce single marriages upon Christian clergy and laymen alike. In his scholarly work on *The History of Matrimonial Institutions*, Professor Howard writes: "It is a noteworthy fact that the early church accepted and sanctioned the existing temporal forms of marriage. Her energy was directed mainly to the task of enforcing her own rules relating to marriage disabilities, such as those arising in affinity or nearness of kin; to devising restraints upon the freedom of divorce and second marriage; and to administering matrimonial judicature." [1] The Church, then, sanctioned in the first place the Roman forms of betrothal and nuptials, just as, after the barbarian invasions, it recognized the customs that prevailed among the various tribes of the North. This means that for many cen-

[1] *Op. cit.*, Vol. I, p. 291.

turies Christian marriage, like pagan, rested upon the free consent of the contracting parties and *was not essentially a religious ceremony.*

At first the Church accepted the Roman idea of betrothal as an engagement — not a legal contract. Apparently veiling was part of the betrothal ceremony in Tertullian's time, at least among Christians, for he speaks of girls being brought veiled to betrothal "because they are united both in body and in spirit to the man by the kiss and the joining of right hands." It is interesting to note that in the time of Constantine the exchange of a kiss by the betrothed couple had come to have legal value. This probably reflects the influence of barbarian customs and ideas, which gradually permeated the Roman Empire under the later emperors, and caused Romans to attach far greater importance to the betrothal contract as the actual beginning of marriage than had been customary. So far did this tendency go that in 680–681 the Council of Constantinople in Trullo virtually assimilated betrothal to marriage by declaring that the man who married a betrothed woman during the lifetime of her betrothed was guilty of adultery.[1]

From the end of the fourth century on Roman customs were influenced by barbarian practice in another respect. It became rather common for the betrother of a girl to pay *arrha* or earnest money to the girl's father as a guarantee that he would pay the *donatio*, or dower named in the betrothal contract, to his wife in case of his death or her unjust divorce. This custom of paying *arrha* as an evidence of good faith was firmly intrenched in the Byzantine betrothal ceremony in the time of Justinian. The sum must be returned to the suitor if the betrothal contract was broken or if the girl died. Before the ninth century, however, the betrothal ring had taken the place of *arrha*, as a guarantee of the betrother's intention to fulfill the terms of the betrothal contract. The reply of Pope Nicholas I (858–867) to the Bulgarians, who consulted him about

[1] *Dictionary of Christian Antiquities*, Vol. I, p. 204.

Christian betrothal and marriage customs, contains these words: "... after the betrother hath betrothed to himself the betrothed *with earnest* by marking her finger with the ring of affiance, and the betrother hath handed over to her a dower satisfactory to both, with a writing containing such contract," then at a fitting time the betrothed pair "enter into the marriage bond." [1]

Although the Christian Church accepted current Roman marriage customs, it reserved the right to hallow the union by bestowing upon it the blessing of God.   Not that the early Christian leaders *required* that marriage be performed within the church, for apparently they did not.   Indeed, Christianity had no formal marriage ritual for centuries; nor did pagan usage prescribe any religious ceremony.   But the Church did urge upon its members the duty of seeking the blessing of the priest upon their nuptials; and this was probably a fairly well-established custom among Christians in the first century A.D.   In the fourth century Ambrose declares that "marriage should be sanctified by the priestly veil and by benediction . . ."; but this does not remotely imply that the marriage was not legal without this ceremony, or that it was not quite frequently contracted without it.   By the time of St. Augustine, however, and thereafter, it was probably customary for the newly married pair, after the nuptials had been privately celebrated, to attend the ordinary religious services within the church, partake together of the sacrament, and receive the benediction of the priest upon their married life.   In the letter cited above, written about 860 A.D. by Pope Nicholas to the Bulgarians, we read: "First of all they (*i.e.*, the bridal pair) are placed in the church with oblations, which they have to make to God by the hands of the priest and so at last they receive the benediction and heavenly veil." [2]   From this it is safe to conclude that by the ninth century, if not before, the custom of marriage within the church had been very

---

[1] *Dictionary of Christian Antiquities*, Vol. I, pp. 143–144.   Italics mine.
[2] Howard, *History of Matrimonial Institutions*, Vol. I, p. 295, note 6.

generally established in Rome. The reference in the quotation to the "heavenly veil" needs a word of explanation. Originally the veil was used by Christians in the betrothal ceremony and was worn by the betrothed maiden as well as by the newly married woman. Later, however, the ceremony of veiling seems to have been restricted to nuptials. In the Eastern Church crowning the bride with flowers or olive wreaths took the place of the veiling ceremony of the West.

Prohibited Degrees. — In the pagan empire the earlier restrictions upon the marriage of second cousins had disappeared and even first cousins married freely.[1] But under the Christian emperors this freedom was very largely curtailed. Theodosius I forbade the marriage of first cousins under pain of death by burning. The penalty was reduced at a later period; but the prohibition remained in force in the Western Church. The sons of Constantine went farther and expressly forbade marriage with a deceased wife's sister or a deceased husband's brother, and this prohibition was adopted by the Emperor Justinian. These early regulations mark the beginning of a long series of similar decrees issued by church councils during subsequent centuries. The prohibited relationships within which no Christian might marry were (1) consanguinity, (2) affinity, (3) spiritual affinity. Consanguinity, of course, refers to blood relationship. The Church at first prohibited marriage within the remotest degrees of blood kinship; but Pope Gregory I (590–604) limited the impediment to the seventh degree of relationship. The second prohibited relationship was that of "affinity." Relatives of a husband and his wife might not marry within the seventh degree of relationship. This prohibition derived from the saying of Christ with reference to husband and wife, "they twain shall be one flesh," which was interpreted by the Church Fathers to mean that the relatives of both husband and wife were brought into mysterious relationship by the marriage of the pair. The third prohibition of the Church related to

[1] Tacitus, *Annals*, Bk. XII, 6.

"spiritual affinity," *i.e.*, the relationship which was held to exist between godfathers and godmothers at the baptism of a child, and sponsors of both sexes at a child's confirmation. In 506 A.D. the Council of Agde proclaimed that any of the above forms of consanguinity or affinity constituted an impediment to marriage.

From the sixth century on for a thousand years no marriage could take place until it was first determined whether the couple were related within the prohibited degrees — a long and bewildering task, that often resulted in hopeless confusion. In the year 802 Charlemagne forbade the celebration of any marriage in his realm until "the bishops, priests and elders of the people" had diligently inquired into the consanguinity of the parties.[1] Out of this regulation grew the custom of publishing the banns in the churches, a custom made obligatory by Pope Innocent III in the thirteenth century. A modern historian comments on the contradictory theories of the Church respecting marriage as follows: "Reckless of mundane consequences, the Church while she treated marriage as a formless contract (*i.e.*, resting on the mere verbal consent of the parties) multiplied impediments which made the formation of a valid marriage a matter of chance." [2] So hedged about with difficulties became the whole matter that at the Lateran Council of 1214 Pope Innocent III relaxed the prohibition relating to "affinity" so that relatives of a husband and his wife might marry if outside the fourth degree of relationship.

ATTITUDE OF THE EARLY CHRISTIAN CHURCH TOWARD THE EVILS OF PAGAN FAMILY LIFE

Adultery. — From its earliest history the Christian Church proclaimed purity as the chief of all virtues and set its face like flint against the pollution of marriage which was so com-

---

[1] See *Encyclopædia Britannica*, article on "Marriage," 14th ed., Vol. XIV, pp. 951–952.

[2] Pollock and Maitland, *The History of English Law*, Vol. II, pp. 383 *et seq.*

mon in the pagan world. Over and over again the Church
Fathers declared the lifelong union of one man and one woman
to be the only form of sexual relation sanctioned by the
Church. Adultery was condemned in unmeasured terms and
the duty of faithfulness in marriage was enjoined upon the
man as upon the woman. St. Jerome expressly states that
among Christians what is not permitted to the woman is
equally prohibited to the man; [1] and St. Chrysostom writes
in similar vein. St. Augustine even goes so far as to maintain that adultery is more criminal in man than in woman.
Thus the teaching of the Christian Church on this point was
unequivocal and just; it maintained from the first the single
standard in morals. It is much to be regretted, however, that
the doctrine of the Church did not become the common sentiment of the great body of the Christians. Probably the double
standard of morality was no more consistently followed in the
pagan world than it has been among Christian nations almost
to the present time. Thus the ideal of the Church has failed
in large measure to be realized in the practice of its members.
It is interesting to note that the more noble minds in the pagan
world had recognized the injustice involved in exacting faithfulness of the wife while permitting constant infidelity to the
husband. The Emperor Antoninus Pius, on granting a Roman
husband a condemnation for adultery against his guilty wife,
added this condition : "Provided always it is established that
by your life you gave her an example of fidelity. It would be
unjust that a husband should exact a fidelity he does not himself keep." [2] Aristotle, among the Greeks, and Plutarch and
Seneca, among the Romans, had also urged the justice of reciprocal fidelity. But the principle remained in the realm of
pure theory, apparently held only by a noble few among the
pagans and rarely, if ever, legally enforced. The Christian
Church, however, in the first three centuries of its unsullied

[1] Letter LXXVII.
[2] Cf. Lecky, *History of European Morals*, Vol. II, p. 313, who quotes St.
Augustine.

purity and sincerity, *did* enforce the single moral standard upon its members, punishing guilty husband, as guilty wife, with exclusion from the Church and its sacraments.

Abortion, Infanticide and Child Exposure. — One of the greatest services rendered by Christianity to the advancement of morality consisted in the importance it attached to every human life and in the emphasis it laid on the gentler and more altruistic sentiments. Maintaining at all times the sanctity of human life, bought as it was with the blood of Christ, the leaders within the Christian Church harshly condemned the practices of abortion, infanticide and child exposure, then so general throughout the Roman Empire. Utility and personal comfort, rather than compassion, had determined the attitude of the pagan nations toward these practices. The motives leading mothers to destroy their unborn children or to kill them shortly after birth were various. Extreme poverty, or the malformation of the child, were the least unworthy; while vanity, the shrinking from pain and care, and even gross licentiousness served as motives with others. From the first, Christian teachers made no distinction in the degree of guilt between abortion and infanticide. Both were crimes, excluding the guilty parent from the saving grace of the sacraments until the final hour of life. In the teaching of the Church the unborn fetus, no less than the infant just brought into the world, was the temple of an immortal soul which would be condemned to everlasting punishment if ruthlessly cut off from life without the purifying rite of baptism. It can hardly be questioned that the doctrine of the Church concerning the damnation of the unbaptized constituted an important motive for its condemnation of child murder in all its forms.

While the best pagan thought had condemned infanticide, and pagan legislators had passed laws against it, neither public opinion nor law had done much to restrain the evil. Moreover, both popular sentiment and legal opinion in the pagan world were decidedly lenient in the matter of child exposure. Hence this evil assumed enormous proportions under the

Empire. Every year new-born children were brought by scores and hundreds to a column in Rome, where they were left to perish or to meet the fate of adoption by professional panders who brought them up as prostitutes or sold them into slavery. Against this evil the Church launched the thunders of its wrath and punishment no less vigorously than against infanticide. Severe penitential sentences were passed upon parents found guilty of child exposure. Furthermore, the Church earnestly sought to arouse in its members by exhortation an effective sense of the criminal nature of the act.

Legislation of Christian Emperors. — Not content with ecclesiastical measures, the Church used its powerful influence to secure legislation against infanticide, child exposure and the sale of infant children. As we have seen, pagan law condemned infanticide but was not in any degree successful in stamping out the practice. It remained for the Christian Emperor Valentinian, in 374 A.D., to declare infanticide a crime punishable by death, and to enforce the statute against it. The exposure of new-born infants proved a custom very difficult to uproot. In 331 A.D. Constantine had enacted a law designed to increase an exposed child's chances of adoption. The law provided that (1) a savior of a foundling might hold it as his property, whether he adopted it as his child or made of it a slave; and (2) the parent of the abandoned child could never reclaim it. Mr. Lecky has pointed out that this enactment, however well-intentioned, marks a backward step in legal procedure, since an earlier decision of the Emperor Trajan had declared that an exposed child could under no circumstances be made a slave. The law of Constantine, while enhancing an exposed infant's chances of life, "doomed it to an irrevocable servitude." [1] Nevertheless, the law was in force until the time of Justinian, when it was enacted that (1) a father lost all authority over the child he had exposed; (2) the child could not be deprived of its natural liberty by

[1] *History of European Morals*, Vol. II, p. 30.

the person who had rescued it. Unfortunately, this humane law applied only to the Eastern section of the Roman Empire, thus making it possible for exposed children to be enslaved throughout the West for many centuries thereafter.

Another unfortunate enactment of Constantine, passed during the disastrous civil wars that marked his reign, authorized parents in great destitution to sell their offspring. This sale of free children had been openly disapproved by previous pagan Emperors and had been expressly condemned by Diocletian, although it is probable that the custom had never been stamped out before the age of Constantine. Theodosius the Great attempted to mitigate the effects of Constantine's law by providing that children sold by their parents might become free after a limited period of service without repayment of the purchase price. Apparently, however, the law did not meet with popular approval, since it was repealed by Valentinian III, after whose reign no Christian Emperor seems to have made any attempt to restrict the inhuman sale of children. This is but one instance out of many where legislation in Christian Rome lagged far behind the teaching of the Church Fathers.

The Influence of Christianity on Roman Custom and Law with Respect to Divorce. *Legal Enactments of Christian Emperors.* — Just as the early Christians accepted the current pagan ideas concerning the private and secular character of marriage, so they did not go counter to the prevailing conceptions of the private and non-religious character of divorce. *So far as the law was concerned*, Christian Rome fully recognized the right of married persons to dissolve their marriage without invoking the aid of either Church or State. No suit for divorce was required nor was public registration of divorces demanded. Yet, with the spread of the Christian doctrine that marriage was a sanctified union there developed the idea that it should be indissoluble. This theory, however, was not universally accepted, even among the Christian Fathers, until the fifth century. Such tardy adherence to a dogma, which later was regarded as fundamental in canonical law, was due to the fact that the Fathers were themselves divided on the question of the permissibility of divorce and the causes recognized by the Church as just grounds for dissolving marriage. Their mental confusion on this question had its source in the fact that in the gospel of Mark (x, 11, 12) Christ is quoted as forbidding divorce for any cause whatever, whereas in Matthew (v, 32) He is declared to have prohibited the dissolution of marriage on any ground *"saving for the cause of fornication."* So various were the opinions of the Christian Fathers, due to the conflict in the Biblical writings, that no universal agreement on the matter was reached for four centuries.

In the second century Hermas [1] held that idolatry, apostasy and covetousness, together with fornication, were grounds for divorce. Origen, one of the great Fathers of the Eastern Church (185–254 A.D.), held that if a woman were guilty of a crime as serious as fornication she might be lawfully divorced for the offense as well as for other forms of sexual crime. As late as the fourth Christian century St. Jerome (340–420 A.D.) accepted the grounds mentioned by Hermas as just causes for divorce, and also he forbade the remarriage of a divorced wife, as was the Church custom. His contemporary, St. Chrysostom, however, held that only for the offense of adultery could a marriage be dissolved. St. Augustine, one of the most influential of the Western Fathers, vacillated in his views concerning the permissibility of divorce. In his earlier years he held that "unlawful lusts," other than sexual offenses committed by men and women, "which make the soul, by the ill-use of the body, go astray from the law of God " were legitimate grounds for divorce.[2] In his later life, however, he proclaimed marriage to be indissoluble. In taking this attitude he was

---

[1] A Christian hortatory writer, who wrote *The Shepherd of Hermas.* He is believed to have been the brother of Pius, Bishop of Rome.

[2] Quoted from St. Augustine's "De Sermo Dom. in Monte," Lib. I, c. XVI, by Ralph De Pomerai, in *Marriage, Past, Present, and Future*, p. 176.

doubtless influenced by the growing unanimity of Christian opinion with regard to the doctrine of indissolubility. In 314 A.D. the Council of Arles approved of the dogma in principle; and in 407 A.D. the Council of Carthage proclaimed the strict doctrine of the indissolubility of marriage for any cause.[1]

But whatever were the views of Church Councils, the practice of divorce was so deeply rooted among the Roman people that Christian Emperors made no attempt to prohibit it. Rather they confined their efforts to making divorce less desirable by increasing the pecuniary loss that fell upon the culpable party. So careful an authority as Muirhead has stated that the divorce legislation of Christian Emperors "forms a miserable chapter in the history of law." He adds that not one Emperor "who busied himself with the matter, undoing the work of his predecessors and substituting legislation of his own quite as complicated and futile, thought of interfering with the old principle that divorce ought to be as free as marriage and independent of the sanction or decree of a judicial tribunal." [2] The Emperors from Constantine to Justinian contented themselves with (1) increasing the penalties previously imposed on the guilty party to a divorce; (2) imposing pecuniary penalties on the active agent in a divorce secured on frivolous grounds. With reference to the first point, Christian legislation provided that the guilty husband should forfeit the entire dowry of his wife, instead of a fraction of it, and the guilty wife should lose the entire *donatio*, or marriage settlement of her husband. If there were offspring of the marriage, the ultimate ownership of this property reverted to them, the innocent party to the divorce enjoying only the usufruct. In case no dowry or *donatio* had been provided the culpable party forfeited one fourth of his or her property. With respect to the second point, the law declared that the person who obtained a divorce on frivolous grounds was guilty of misconduct and became liable to the pecuniary penalties described above.

---

[1] See De Pomerai, *op. cit.*, pp. 175–177.
[2] *Historical Introduction to the Private Law of Rome*, p. 356.

As late as the age of Justinian,[1] Christian Emperors permitted one-sided divorces without penalty in the following cases : (1) where one partner desired to dissolve the union in order to enter a monastic order ; (2) where the husband had been five years in foreign captivity ; (3) where there had never been prospect of offspring owing to physiological impediment. The last cause is interesting as evidence that Christian lawmakers were in accord with early Hebrew and pagan thought in regarding the essential purpose of marriage as the procreation of offspring.   Divorce for any of these three reasons was not penalized and was known as *divortium bona gratia* — divorce by good grace.   But legislation in early Christian times went even further and recognized the right of the partners to a marriage to dissolve it by mutual consent.   Such divorce was called *divortium communi consensu*.   It will be seen that considerable freedom of divorce without penalty was accorded in Rome long after Christianity had become the dominant religion of the Empire.   In consequence the writings of St. Jerome and other leaders within the Church abound in lamentations over the frequency of divorce.   St. Jerome states that he himself had seen a man in Rome living with his twenty-first wife who had had twenty-two husbands.   The Bishop of Amasia, writing about forty years before Justinian, declares that men changed their wives as easily as their garments, and that marriage beds were removed from the atrium as readily and frequently as market stalls.   Such extreme cases may have been exceptional ; yet they indicate the laxity of custom and law alike in the matter of divorce.

In the reign of Justinian that austere Christian Emperor made some attempt to curb the existing freedom of divorce. In one of his *Novellæ* [2] he enacted that in cases where the parties agreed to a divorce on insufficient grounds both should

---

[1] Roman Emperor, with his capital at Constantinople ; reigned 527–565.

[2] The *Novellæ* or Novels of Justinian were imperial statutes issued subsequent to the great *Code* of laws prepared under his direction and were designed to correct errors or repair omissions in this code.

be compelled to enter a monastery or convent and should forfeit two thirds of their property to their children. Otherwise the marriage should be null and void. This edict, however, caused profound popular dissatisfaction, since it was opposed to both the theory and the custom of the Roman people. Furthermore, experience proved that the requirement concerning the adoption of monastic life did not tend to elevate the tone of morals within convent or monastery.[1] In consequence, the obnoxious act was repealed by Justin the Second, nephew and successor of Justinian. In the Eastern Empire, therefore, freedom of divorce by mutual consent lasted until late in the ninth century when such divorce was pronounced invalid by Emperor Leo the Philosopher.[2]

The Views of the Christian Church concerning Divorce. — Hitherto we have considered chiefly the legislation of Christian Emperors with respect to divorce. But it cannot be doubted that the freedom in this regard conceded by Roman law was directly opposed to the teachings of the later Church Fathers and Councils alike. Although, as we have seen, the early Fathers were hesitant to declare themselves hostile to divorces on the grounds of adultery, apostasy and idolatry, they pronounced all other divorces to be grave offenses expiable only by long and severe penance. Thus the laxity of civil law in Christian Rome is in strong contrast to the inflexibility of the Church's doctrine. This dualism in ecclesiastical and civil legislation persisted far into the Middle Ages. While the Church had from early times threatened divorced persons with the awful penalty of excommunication, it was not until the twelfth century that the civil law was brought into entire conformity with canon law by prohibiting divorce for any cause whatever. Commenting on the stringency of the Church doctrine with respect to divorce, Lecky observes that its sweeping prohibition "was not originally imposed in Christian nations upon utilitarian grounds, but was based upon the sacramental

---

[1] Muirhead, *op. cit.*, p. 356.
[2] Cf. Bryce, James, *Studies in History and Jurisprudence*, p. 805.

character of marriage, upon the belief that marriage is the special symbol of the perpetual union of Christ with His Church, and upon a well-known passage in the Gospels." [1] It may be added that no utilitarian motive could have had the tremendous effect in restricting divorce that was accomplished by this mystical dogma of the Church, inculcated as it was with profound earnestness and enforced with threats of exclusion from the Christian body and in consequence from the membership of the saved.

Remarriage after Divorce. — Opposed as they were to second marriages, the Church Fathers denounced with special bitterness the marriage of a divorced woman during the lifetime of the other partner. In their eyes such marriages were little better than adultery. In one of his *Letters* St. Jerome, referring to a passage in Romans where a woman who had married during the lifetime of her husband is called an adulteress, declares : "A husband may be an adulterer, or a sodomite, he may be stained with every crime and may have been left by his wife because of his sins; yet he is still her husband, and, so long as he lives, she may not marry another." [2] This was the theory of the Church throughout the Middle Ages, although conditions from the sixth to the tenth century forced Churchmen to modify the doctrine.

The Influence of Christianity in Modifying Family Legislation in Rome. — The influence of Christianity on Roman laws concerning marriage and family relations was comparatively insignificant until after it had been recognized as a state religion by Constantine. From the fourth century on, however, the Christian Church exercised a powerful influence on domestic legislation. (1) Numerous laws were passed imposing disabilities with respect to marriage with heretics and apostates. Very early the Church discouraged and opposed "mixed marriages," *i.e.*, unions between Christians and unbelievers; and this opposition was reflected in Roman law

---

[1] *Op. cit.*, Vol. II, p. 353.
[2] Letter LV.

under Theodosius. (2) Christianity was also directly responsible for the repeal of those provisions of the *Lex Papia Poppæa*,[1] which imposed penalties on celibacy and childlessness and encouraged fruitful marriages. With the rapid spread of asceticism, celibacy became in the eyes of Churchmen a virtue rather than a social evil; hence these penalties were abolished by Constantine in 320 A.D. (3) To Christian influence may be traced the divorce legislation discussed in the previous section. (4) Second marriages, as we have seen, came to be discountenanced by Christian Emperors; and in the Theodosian Code such unions entailed forfeiture of the dower and *donatio* to the offspring of the first marriage if such existed. (5) The custom of granting a *donatio* or marriage settlement to the bride had grown up in the early centuries of the Empire and had been made the subject of legislation by Theodosius and Valentinian. But it remained for the Emperor Justinian in his famous Code carefully to define the procedure in regard to both *dos* and *donatio*. Whenever a dowry was furnished by the wife a *donatio* must be provided by the husband; and if one were increased during marriage, a corresponding increase must be made in the other. More important was the legal provision authorizing the wife to demand the transfer to herself of both the dowry and the *donatio* in case of her husband's insolvency. She was, however, under legal obligation to use these funds for the support of the family. In another respect also the legislation of Justinian was favorable to the wife, for it provided that after the death of her husband or her own divorce without just cause she might recover both her dowry and the *donatio*. Moreover, under certain conditions, the mother was given the right, so long denied to her, of legal guardianship over her children. How far the influence of the Christian Church was responsible for these last enactments is doubtful; they seem to be rather the direct outgrowth of the earlier pagan tendency to free women from economic and legal disabilities.

[1] Passed in the reign of Augustus Cæsar.

Decline of the *Patria Potestas.* — Long before the establishment of Christianity the decline in the power of the Roman husband and father over the members of his family had been marked and progressive. This decline went steadily forward in the later centuries when Christianity became supreme. In the words of Muirhead: "With the Christian Emperors the last traces disappeared of the old conception of the *familia* as an aggregate of persons and estate subject absolutely to the power and dominion of its head." [1] Husband and wife were made equal before the law, although Muirhead is inclined to believe that the wife was the more privileged as regards protection and indulgence. By the time of Justinian the *patria potestas* had been so stripped of its earlier rights that it was little more than a name. The exposure of new-born children was prohibited in the Code of Justinian under severe penalties. The killing of a grown-up child (except in the case of a daughter taken in adultery and slain with her partner) was definitely branded as murder and was punished as such. No father could sell his child as a slave except in case of extreme destitution and then only when the child was an infant. The ancient custom whereby a father was set up as judge of his wife and children and was endowed with powers of life and death over them had long since fallen into disuse. Under Justinian a father could no longer surrender his son to an injured party bringing suit and thus wash his hands of legal responsibility for his son's fines. To quote again from Muirhead: "All that remained of the *patria potestas* in Justinian's legislation is what is sanctioned in modern systems : the right of moderate chastisement for offenses, testamentary nomination of guardians, giving of the son in adoption, and withholding consent to the marriage of a child. The latter was subject to magisterial intervention if unreasonable." [2] The right of a father over the earnings of a son had been limited by Augustus, and this limitation was extended by Hadrian and later pagan rulers.

[1] *Historical Introduction to the Private Law of Rome*, p. 387.
[2] *Op. cit.*, p. 390.

The Christian Emperors had simply carried further a tendency already under full headway when they denied the father any right of ownership over his son's property except in case of (1) acquisitions made by the son with funds advanced by the father for his separate use, (2) bequests to the son. In one of the chapters of his *Novels* Justinian insured to a child, as his own in death as in life, all his property except the *peculium profecticium* or funds advanced by the father for his son's use. So far did legislation go in limiting a father's rights in the property of his son that in cases where the son died intestate his possessions passed to his father only by title of inheritance and in the absence of direct descendants.

From this brief study it would appear, then, that the amelioration of family laws in Christian Rome and the extension of the rights and privileges of the wife and mother were only a continuation of tendencies clearly present in the enactments of pagan emperors. But in matters of divorce, mixed marriages and second marriages, prohibited degrees and the removal of the penalties attached to celibacy, Christianity unquestionably introduced novel features into Roman legislation.

SELECTED READINGS

SOURCES

Ante Nicene Christian Library. N. Y., Christian Literature Co., 1890–1897.

Ignatius, *Epistle to Polycarp*, Vol. I, p. 85, 1896.

Clement of Alexandria, *Pedagogus or the Instructor*, Vol. II, pp. 211–293, 377–379.

Clement of Rome, *Homilies.*

Athenagoras, *Plea for Christians*, Vol. II, p. 147.

Tertullian, *Letter to His Wife*, Vol. XI (Vol. I of series of Tertullian's writings), Letter XI.

On Female Dress, Vol. XI, Letter XII.

An Exhortation to Chastity, Vol. XVIII, pp. 1–14.

On Monogamy, Vol. XVIII, p. 21.

Painter, Franklin V. *Great Pedagogical Essays; Plato to Spencer*, N. Y., American Book Co., 1905, " Apostolical Constitutions," pp. 150–154.

Schaff, Philip, ed. *A Select Library of the Nicene and Post Nicene Fathers,* Scribner, 1890–1908.

St. Augustine, *Letters,* Vol. I.
> Letter to Juliana, pp. 549–550.
> Letter CL to Proba and Juliana.
> *Confessions,* Vol. I, p. 206.

St. Jerome, *Letters,* Vol. VI.
> To Laeta, CVII, pp. 189–195.
> To Eustochium, XXII.
> To Pammachius, XLVIII.
> To Amandus, LV.

SECONDARY WORKS

Dealey, J. A. *The Family in its Sociological Aspects,* Houghton Mifflin, 1912, pp. 52–62.

Donaldson, James. *Woman: Her Position and Influence in Ancient Greece and Rome and among the Early Christians,* London, Longmans, Green, and Co., 1907, Bk. III, Chs. I, II.

Encyclopædia Britannica, 14th ed., Vol. XIV, pp. 951–952, article on "Marriage."

Hastings, Jas., ed. *Encyclopedia of Religion and Ethics,* N. Y., Scribner, 1908–1927, Vol. V, pp. 746–749, 1912.

Howard, George E. *History of Matrimonial Institutions,* 3 Vols., University of Chicago Press, Callaghan and Co., 1904, Vol. I, pp. 291–292, 324–332.

Jeaffreson, J. C. *Brides and Bridals,* Hurst, 1872, Vol. I.

Lecky, W. E. H. *History of European Morals,* N. Y., D. Appleton and Co., 1900, Vol. II, pp. 20–34, 316–327, 336–347, 350–358.

Maine, Sir Henry. *Ancient Law,* Holt, 1894, pp. 156–158.

Muirhead, Jas. *Historical Introduction to the Private Law of Rome,* London, A. and C. Black, Ltd., 1916, pp. 345–426.

Schmidt, Carl. *Social Results of Early Christianity,* London, Sir Isaac Pitman, 1907, Bk. II, Ch. III.

Smith, Wm., and Cheetham, A., eds. *Dictionary of Christian Antiquities,* 2 Vols., Boston, Little, Brown and Co., 1875–1880.
> Meyrick, article on "Marriage," Vol. II, pp. 1902 ff.
> Ludlow, articles on "Betrothal," Vol. I, p. 203, and "Benediction," Vol. I, p. 193.

Thwing, C. F. *The Family,* Boston, Lee and Shepard; N. Y., C. T. Dillingham, 1887, Ch. III.

CHAPTER VI

THE FAMILY IN THE MIDDLE AGES

The Barbarian Invasions. — From the closing years of the fourth century until well into the sixth, the barbarian hordes of the North overran the empire of the Cæsars, disrupting its unity and establishing themselves in the territories won by conquest. The Vandals seized the northern coasts of Africa ; the Visigoths made their home in Spain ; the Franks occupied the fertile lands of Gaul and annexed in course of time the domains of the fierce Burgundians and Alemanni on their eastern frontiers. Into Italy poured the East-Goths, only to be completely routed and driven out by the armies of Justinian in the sixth century. But Italy was not permanently freed from barbarian inroads. After the death of Justinian in 565, the savage Lombards invaded the country and established themselves in the region north of the Po River, a territory which has been called Lombardy from that time to the present. To the north and east of the Frankish dominions lay the territories of the Frisians, the Saxons, the Jutes and the Angles, peoples who were not far removed in civilization from the Iroquois Indians of America at the landing of the white men. Some time after the withdrawal of the Roman troops from Britain, at the opening of the fifth century, those islands were overrun by the Angles, Jutes and Saxons, who, after repeated incursions, succeeded in thoroughly routing the native Britons. When Augustine made his missionary visit to Britain in 597, he found the invaders firmly established in the conquered islands. Such, in brief, was the geographical arrangement of the barbarian tribes in Western Europe in the sixth century.

Sources of Our Knowledge of Family Customs among the Barbarians. — The most valuable source of our knowledge of the family life of the Germanic peoples in the first century of the Christian era is the *Germania* of the Roman historian Tacitus. In this account of the customs of the barbaric Teutons there is a brief description of their family life and their mode of contracting marriage. "The matrimonial bond," says Tacitus, "is . . . strict and severe among them; nor is there anything in their manners more commendable than this. Almost singly among the barbarians they content themselves with one wife; a very few of them excepted, who, not through incontinence, but because their alliance is solicited on account of their rank, practice polygamy." [1] A subsequent statement of Tacitus reveals some misunderstanding of Teutonic marriage customs. Thus he writes: "The wife does not bring a dower to her husband, but receives one from him. The parents and relations assemble, and pass their approbation on the presents — presents not adapted to please the female taste, or decorate the bride; but oxen, a caparisoned steed, a shield, spear and sword." There can be no doubt that these articles, which Tacitus mistook for presents, were really the purchase price of the bride, paid down by the rude suitor to the girl's father for the right to marry her and thus control her person.

In addition to the *Germania*, Cæsar's *Gallic War* furnishes the student with a few references to family conditions in Britain about 55 B.C. At this time the natives must have been in the lowest stages of barbarism, for Cæsar describes their family relations as follows: "Ten and twelve have wives common among them, especially brothers with brothers and parents with children; if any children are born they are considered as belonging to those men to whom the maid was first married." [2]

After the first four centuries of the Christian era, our most important sources of knowledge of Germanic marriage cus-

---

[1] *The Works of Tacitus* (Oxford trans., N. Y., 1884), p. 308.
[2] See Cheyney's *Readings in English History*, pp. 15, 16.

toms are the folk laws of the various Teutonic tribes. The earliest laws are those of the Ripuarian Franks of the fifth century. To the sixth century belong the Burgundian folklaws; to the seventh the Visigothic, to the eighth the Salic and Saxon laws, and to the ninth the Frisian. All these collections of customary law abound in references to family relations and marriage forms. Thus they constitute a valuable source of knowledge of Teutonic family customs from the fifth to the tenth century.

The Kinship Group and the Household among the Anglo-Saxon and Germanic Races. — It is necessary at the outset to distinguish between the great family or "kin" and the separate household as these existed among the Germanic tribes. Just as we find the "house" and the gens among the Hebrews, the Greeks and the Romans, so we find the "kin" among Teutonic peoples. The Saxons and Frisians of the continent called their kinship group the *sippe*, while the Anglo Saxons in Britain called it the *mægth*. In both cases it consisted of a group of kindred descended from the *grandchildren* of two common ancestors, the "kin" thus taking its rise not from the original pair, but from the third generation, — the children of their offspring. Although each *mægth* or *sippe* included only those united by blood or by formal adoption, any particular individual's "kin" was a union of both the paternal and maternal kinship groups. In this respect the *sippe* of the Germanic peoples is in striking contrast to the gens of the Romans. The Teutons traced kinship through both the father and the mother; hence the offspring of any marriage was a member of two kinship groups. The Romans, on the contrary, reckoned relationship from the common ancestor through males only (the system of agnation); therefore the gens included only those descended in the male line from the reputed founder of the family. It follows that the kinship groups of the Germans were intertwined in a network, while the Romans held each gens distinct and separate by ignoring kinship through women.

The great family or sib among Germanic races was the fundamental institution of private law. The tribe and later the
state depended upon the "kin" to keep the peace and punish
crimes within its membership. In consequence the sib had
large powers over each household as well as over the individuals
composing it. The "family" as a whole could protect a child
even from his father. Likewise the members acted as guardians of widows and children, taking charge of the estates of
orphans until they were of age. Even remote kinsmen, as
possible heirs, could prevent the sale or alienation of family
estates. It followed that the relations of husband to wife and
parents to children were strongly influenced by the fact that
each member of the household was bound by the general law
of the sib as well as by the more particular laws of the household. Both the kin of the father and that of the mother had
rights and obligations in the new household formed by marriage, although the paternal kin assumed the larger share of
both in the case of any individual. The wife remained in her
own sib after marriage. This meant that her kin made compensation in fines for offenses committed by her and bore the
"feud," *i.e.*, sought redress, in case of her gross mistreatment
or murder.

The Law of the Mægth or Sippe. *Membership in the
Family or Kin.* — By the law of the sib no child born out of
wedlock had any rights of inheritance, since he was not an
acknowledged member of his father's kin. He did, however,
have some rights of protection since, if he were slain, his
"price" or *wergild*, as the Anglo-Saxons called it, must be paid,
in part to the king and in part to the paternal kindred. Even
a legitimate child did not become a true member of the kin
until his father had formally acknowledged him. Infanticide
and child exposure were far from uncommon in the Middle Ages
up to the eleventh century, largely owing, no doubt, to the
harsh conditions of existence and the frequent famines that
visited a rude people who had little understanding of natural
laws. But the father's power of life and death over his off-

spring was limited by the law of the *sippe* to children who had not tasted food. If milk or honey had passed or even touched the child's lips the father must admit him into membership in the kin of both father and mother. Such membership secured to an individual the protection so urgently needed in the warlike period of the Middle Ages. If he were slain, the kin avenged his death or exacted of the slayers his *wergild*.[1] If, on the contrary, he killed a member of another family, the paternal kin, among the Anglo-Saxons, paid two thirds of the murdered man's *wergild* and the maternal kin one third. On the death of a father before the children had attained their majority, the father's kin assumed all rights of guardianship so far as property was concerned. Among the Anglo-Saxons, however, the actual control of the children was left with the mother. This is made clear by a law of Ine in the eighth century. "If a ceorl [2] and his wife have a child between them and the ceorl die, let the mother have her child and feed it; and let VI shillings be given her for its fostering, a cow in summer and an ox in winter; and let the kindred take care of the homestead until it be of age." [3] On coming of age, wards could sue their guardians within the kin for misuse or alienation of any portion of their property.

In addition to the rights and duties just mentioned, the sib assumed responsibility for the conduct of each individual member, especially of landless men. These men had less incentive to an industrious and law-abiding life than their more fortunate kindred, and in consequence were inclined to rove about and get into brawls with neighboring groups. Thus the first police authority among our Anglo-Saxon ancestors was vested in the family. Before the Norman Conquest, however, this responsibility had been handed over to the organized courts.

[1] A sum of money fixed by customary law as just compensation for the human life taken.

[2] A ceorl was a freeman.

[3] Young, "Anglo-Saxon Family Law," in Adams, *Essays in Anglo-Saxon Law*, p. 180.

With such powers of protection and control in the hands of the kin, membership in some family group was of the utmost importance to every individual during the early Middle Ages. His security from robbery, attack or injury of any kind, as well as his social position and influence, depended almost wholly on the power, numbers and wealth of his kindred. Although withdrawal from the kindred was permitted in specified instances there was little temptation for any one to forego the tremendous advantages which sprang from such membership.

The Law of the Household. — In addition to the law of the family group was the household law, regulating the relations of husband and wife, parents and children. This private law, like that of the sib, was almost wholly the product of custom, and, as the centuries advanced, it was more and more limited and curtailed by the growing power of public law. It may be noted that this has been the history of all family law from the days of the ancient Greeks and Romans to our own times, when important family relations are wholly regulated by public law. At present the ancient rights of the father over the persons and property of wife and children have shrunk to a mere shadow.

Powers of the Father. — The power of the father over his offspring among most of the barbarian tribes was in the nature of a protectorship, and was called in Anglo-Saxon *mund*. That the father's authority was not absolute has been suggested in the discussion of the law of the *mægth*. The kindred could intervene to protect the rights of any child who had once been acknowledged by his father. An Anglo-Saxon parent could not sell his child into slavery after it was seven years of age, and before that age only under pressure of necessity. On the continent, however, the Germanic tribes apparently did not so curtail the father's power to dispose of his offspring. One writer tells us that as late as the thirteenth century a German could sell both wife and child in time of famine.[1]

Despite the limitations set by the kin upon the father's power to kill or sell his offspring, his authority was more than ample

[1] Gummere, *Germanic Origins*, p. 154.

from our modern point of view. A father had the right to chastise his children freely, and this privilege must not infrequently have been abused. The laws of the Jutes permitted a man to beat his children with a heavy staff provided he broke no bones.

Until the eleventh century the Anglo-Saxon father might bestow his young daughter in marriage with no regard to her wishes. In the *Pœnitentiale* of the English Archbishop Theodore, written in the seventh century, it is stated that a girl up to sixteen or seventeen years of age is in the power of her parents; after that age parents may not marry her to any suitor against her will.[1] Probably the absolute right of a father to dispose of daughters in marriage was lost in England by the time of the Danish King Cnut, whose oft-quoted law runs as follows: "And let no one compel either woman or maiden to him whom she herself mislikes, nor for money sell her. . . ." Yet the father's power to send his daughter and probably his son to a monastery to be dedicated to the life of nun or monk was unquestioned. Such a step must often have brought great bitterness into the lives of helpless children, quite unfitted by nature for the monastic life. In England from the sixth until late in the twelfth century the church held a girl thus dedicated to be bound by her father's action even when, after reaching years of discretion, she sought release from the convent.[2] For many centuries the father was the legal representative of his children before the courts, making such restitution in fines as the law demanded for offenses committed by them and securing compensation for injuries done them. Finally the father had the right to administer the property received by his children from their maternal kindred; and with the right of administration went the right to use the fruits of that property, *i.e.*, the usufruct. Among the Anglo-Saxons, however, the father never was permitted to control his son's earnings.

---

[1] Young, *Anglo-Saxon Family Law*, p. 153. The *Pœnitentiale* may be found in Haddan and Stubbs, *Councils*, Vol. III, pp. 173–213.

[2] Thrupp, *The Anglo-Saxon Home*, pp. 113, 114.

The Partial Emancipation of Children at Majority. — Unlike the Roman custom, the folk laws of the Middle Ages all recognize the right of the son to greater freedom on his coming of age. The age at which a son attained his majority varied among the different Teutonic peoples, and likewise changed from time to time. In the period of Tacitus (first century A.D.) a son was freed from the father's authority when he was capable of bearing arms. Certainly the age at which the German youths were admitted to the body of freemen seems very early to the modern man. It was probably twelve or fifteen years. Among the Anglo-Saxons, who had no ceremony of "emancipation," the age of majority was at first ten years; but a law of Cnut, in the eleventh century, reads: "And we will that every freeman above twelve years make oath that he will neither be a thief nor cognizant of a theft." At the completion of his twelfth year, then, the Anglo-Saxon boy was made a freeman, responsible to the law in his own person. Later the age of majority was raised to fifteen years.

At the majority of his son a father's power over him was limited by household law and custom. Probably he could no longer freely chastise him nor prevent his marriage by forcible means, although his disapproval might and probably did prove sufficient in many instances. Also in the opinion of some historians the son, on coming of age, had the right of veto in all alienations of land by the father. This was an important privilege, since among many Germanic tribes the marriage of the son (usually at an early age) was accompanied by a division of the family property to enable the youth to set up a new home of his own. However, the father's control over the actions of his son did not wholly cease at the latter's majority, but continued, in a milder form, until the youth had married and established an independent household. Among the Anglo-Saxons, moreover, there is no evidence that the father had any legal rights over property bequeathed to his son when the latter had come of age.

Like the son the daughter attained majority at the completion of the twelfth year; but the freedom accorded to her was far less than that bestowed on the boy. The father still enjoyed the usufruct of his daughter's property, and the right to represent her in court. He likewise had full right to chastise and correct her by whatever means he saw fit to use. By the eleventh century, however, he had, theoretically at least, lost the right to dispose of her in marriage against her will. Even before this time Roman betrothal customs had begun to influence Saxon England. In consequence the free consent of the contracting parties came to be held as essential. It is true that parents still had the right to betroth their children as early as seven years of age. But if parent or offspring wished to terminate the contract when the child was ten years old this might be done without penalty. When the child was between ten and twelve, the breaking of the agreement entailed fines for the parent, and after the age of twelve years both parent and child were liable to fines for refusal to keep the marriage contract.

THE SINGLE WOMAN IN THE MIDDLE AGES

Apparently the single woman was a *rara avis* in the Middle Ages with the exception of the women in convents and in certain lay sisterhoods like that of the Beguines in the Netherlands, who took no irrevocable vows but devoted themselves to a religious life. One writer says of the single woman in mediæval times: "It is hardly too much to say that the early mediæval law never seems to have contemplated the existence of an unmarried woman of full age . . . her position is never the subject of statute law, as is that of widows; hence it seems probable that among the higher classes the independent 'femme sole' was, outside the convent, a negligible quantity."[1] However, as Sir Henry Maine has pointed out, canon law, which represented a fusion of barbarian folk law with the more

[1] Chapman and Wallis, *The Status of Women under English Law*, p. 2.

advanced jurisprudence of Rome, recognized the independence of the single woman to the extent of permitting her to own property, while fixing an inferior status upon the married woman. He adds that the law of western Europe is distinguished even to modern times by "the comparative freedom it allows to unmarried women and . . . the heavy disabilities it imposes on wives." This distinction, he adds, may be traced to the powerful influence of canon law which, in turn, was molded in this regard more by barbarian practice than by the civil law of Rome.

MARRIAGE CUSTOMS AND LAWS IN THE EARLY MIDDLE AGES

Wife Capture and Wife Purchase. — Before the Christian era the capture of wives was probably not uncommon among Germanic tribes. Traces of the custom may be found in certain old-time marriage practices in Wales. Howard relates that the Welsh bridegroom a century ago went on horseback accompanied by his friends to demand his bride. The bridal party, which was also mounted, refused to give up the girl, whereupon a mock fight ensued. Finally the bride was carried off by her nearest kinsman, while the bridegroom and his friends followed in hot pursuit. When horses and men were thoroughly fatigued, the suitor was allowed to overtake his lady and lead her away in triumph. Then followed the usual wedding festivities.[1] In the first Christian century, however, wife capture had generally been superseded by wife purchase, as the account of Tacitus makes clear. There is ample evidence in the early folk laws to show that women were openly bought in marriage up to the tenth century. Thus an Anglo-Saxon law of Æthelbert, dating about 600 A.D., runs as follows: "If one buys a maiden, let her be bought with the price, if it is a fair bargain; but if there is deceit, let him take her home again and get back the price he paid." [2] The com-

---

[1] *History of Matrimonial Institutions*, Vol. I, p. 173.
[2] Gummere, *Germanic Origins*, p. 152.

plete absence of affection or romantic interest from most of these old-time marriages is revealed in another law of Æthelbert, which states: "If a man carry off a freeman's wife, let him procure another with his own money, and deliver her to him." [1] Clearly any woman would do if she were strong and reasonably well favored. To avoid misunderstandings the Saxon laws of the early ninth century conveniently fixed the price of the woman sought in marriage at 300 shillings. In his work on German women Weinhold quotes a peasant saying of the present day to the effect that "It's not man that marries maid, but field marries field, — vineyard marries vineyard, — cattle marry cattle." [2] Here is indicated clearly enough a survival, among the German peasantry, of the custom of gross bargaining in connection with the taking of a wife. Indeed the expression "to buy a wife" was in common use in Germany throughout the Middle Ages, although the actual sale of the bride had probably ceased by the tenth or eleventh century.

Forms of Contracting Marriage: *Beweddung* and *Gifta*. — Among all the Teutonic peoples there were two stages in contracting marriage: (1) *Beweddung*, (2) *Gifta*. At first *beweddung* was a contract between the father and the suitor to give the girl to the man for certain stipulated valuables in cattle, arms or money. *Gifta* consisted in the "tradition" or handing over of the woman to her husband by the father. In the earliest times no doubt the bargain was concluded and the maid handed over at one and the same time. But as the centuries passed the interval between *beweddung* and *gifta* lengthened until, in the late Middle Ages, when *beweddung* had become betrothal and when this betrothal often took place in infancy, the interval was one of years. Certain other changes had likewise taken place in the *beweddung* or contract ceremony before the tenth century. (1) The bride price was no longer paid outright but had given place to *arrha*, a small sum of money given the father by the

---

[1] Thorpe, *Ancient Laws*, Vol. I, pp. 24, 25.
[2] *Deutsche Frauen*, Vol. I, p. 319.

suitor as a guarantee of payment of the full bride price at nuptials.   In the course of time the *arrha* was paid to the bride herself and, probably owing to Roman influence, came much later to take the form of a ring — the betrothal ring of modern times.   (2) Not only was *arrha*, in one form or another, paid to the bride, but in the period from the sixth to the ninth century the purchase money itself was gradually being transformed into provision for the wife from the husband's property in case he died before her.   Certainly from the tenth century onward *beweddung* was nothing but a formal contract or *wed* to pay the bride price to the wife in case of the husband's death. The contract was concluded by certain quaint ceremonies such as the exchange of straws between suitor and maid, or the breaking of a coin between them.   Later in the Middle Ages these forms had largely given place to "hand-fasting" or solemn clasping of hands before witnesses.   Whatever the binding ceremony, *beweddung* among all the Germanic races was the first step in marriage.   Hence the infidelity of the girl was counted as adultery and was punished as such.[1]

As stated above, the second act in marriage was *gifta* or giving of the bride to the groom by the father or guardian. In early times the father handed over his daughter to her husband together with certain objects, such as a sword, hat and mantle, which served as symbols of the power over the person of the woman thus transferred from the father to the husband.   Among certain Teutonic tribes the husband then very ungallantly trod upon his bride's foot as a mark of his newly acquired authority; but later this mode of asserting the dominance of the male was changed to the harmless delivery of a slipper or shoe to the bride.   These marriage practices show clearly enough that *gifta* or nuptials *was a purely private matter* until late in the Middle Ages.   Up to the tenth century the father gave the bride in marriage; after that time it became customary for the bride to select a

[1] See Howard, *History of Matrimonial Institutions*, Vol. I, pp. 258–272, for a full discussion of *beweddung*.

guardian, her father, some near relative, or even a friend, who gave her away. Such was a common custom in the thirteenth century despite the opposition of the Church. Quite frequently, also, the simple marriage ritual was recited by the chosen guardian, or independently by the bride and groom, who thus, to all intents and purposes, married themselves. Out of this "self-gifta" has grown the common-law marriage of England and America.[1]

The Morning-Gift. — In the centuries between the seventh and the tenth there had grown up the custom of bestowing upon the bride who had found favor in her husband's eyes a bridal gift on the morning after the marriage. After receiving this mark of her husband's approval the Anglo-Saxon bride at once rose from her couch and bound her flowing hair about her head to signify that she was now an accepted wife and that her husband no longer had the right to return her to her family as unsatisfactory. At first the morning-gift seems to have been of little value; but as time went on its value so increased that it overshadowed the bride price in importance. Before the tenth century the man was bound by law to provide for the morning-gift as well as the bride price in the marriage contract. Noblemen and princes included slaves, horses, church revenues and even large estates in the morning-gift to their brides. History tells us that the Princess Eadgyth, sister of the Anglo-Saxon King Athelstan, received from her husband, the Emperor Otto of Germany, the entire city of Magdeburg as her morning-gift.[2] Several interesting examples of these marriage contracts, dating from the tenth century, have come down to us.[3] In course of time the morning-gift merged completely into the bride price and became provision for the wife, to be handed over to her on the death of her husband.

---

[1] For a full discussion of *gifta* see Howard, *op. cit.*, Vol. I, pp. 272–286.

[2] Thrupp, *The Anglo-Saxon Home*, p. 61.

[3] See Young, *Anglo-Saxon Family Law*, pp. 171–172; Howard, *op. cit.*, Vol. I, p. 270.

Intervention of the Church in Marriage. — It must not be supposed that the Church was a silent and inactive party to such private and lay marriages as have been described above. After the conversion of the Germanic races to Christianity, during the period from the fifth to the eighth century, the Christian clergy exerted all their energy to enforce upon these barbaric peoples the canonical rules concerning the marriage of near and remote kin. Very wisely the Church did not at first combat the Germanic marriage forms, not even the sale of the bride. As it had previously accepted the forms in use in the Roman Empire, so it accepted the customs of the barbarians. From the fifth to the eleventh century, however, the Christian clergy strove to impress upon the minds of the rude Teutons the sacred character of marriage. To this end the Church exercised its influence to induce the contracting parties to seek the blessing of the priest upon their nuptials. In course of time it became customary for bride and groom to attend mass on the day following the marriage, although the practice was never universal during this early period. Moreover, the bride mass was in no sense an essential part of the marriage ceremony, which still consisted in the handing over of the bride to her husband by her father or chosen guardian, after her consent had been signified. Yet the solemn service of the mass, followed by the priestly benediction upon the newly wedded pair, came to be regarded by many as a fitting ceremony to sanctify a union already consummated. It is interesting to note, however, that until *after the tenth century* the bride mass contained no special marriage ritual other than the priestly blessing. In a Kentish betrothal contract of the tenth century it is expressly provided that "At the nuptials there shall be a mass priest by law, who shall, with God's blessing, bind their union to all prosperity." [1] In England the nuptial benediction was pronounced while bride and groom stood under a veil or "care-cloth," held at each corner by the groom's friends. This seems to have been an adaptation

[1] Young, *op. cit.*, p. 172.

of a similar Roman custom and is doubtless due to Roman influence, which, as we have seen, was strongly felt in southern England by the tenth century. To the same source is due the custom of crowning the bride with a wreath of myrtle or olive, as Christian brides were crowned in the Eastern Empire.

As the barbaric tribes advanced in civilization, the Church further extended its influence over the marriage rite. During the tenth century it became customary for *gifta* to take place *at the church door*, in the presence of the priest. It should be carefully noted that the essential act in marriage — the formal consent of the parties to live as man and wife — was still regarded as a lay and private matter, since it was not performed within the church, and since the chosen guardian, not the priest, gave the bride in marriage. Howard furnishes us with an interesting copy of the marriage service in use in York about the end of the twelfth century.[1] This shows conclusively that even at this late period the ceremony of marriage in England was commonly performed before the door of the church. Here the bride's dower was assigned ; here the priest asked : "Who giveth this woman to this man ?" And after the formal "tradition" of the bride by her father or guardian, the priest pronounced the benediction upon the married pair. Only then did the bridal party enter the church and participate in the bride mass, which was followed by a second blessing.

SOCIAL POSITION AND PROPERTY RIGHTS OF MARRIED WOMEN

Woman's Status in the Family. — Since a woman among the Germanic tribes did not enter her husband's family, but remained a member of her own kin, the bride's *mægth* or *sippe* was responsible for her offenses after she became a wife. Therefore it was customary for the woman's relatives to give security at her marriage to answer for her conduct during her married life. Also injuries against the woman were payable

[1] *Op. cit.*, Vol. I, pp. 303–304.

in fines to her family or kin, under whose protection she remained. In a Kentish betrothal of the tenth century one article reads : "If then, he desire to lead her [*i.e.*, the bride], out of the land into another thane's land, then it is right that her friends have there an agreement that no wrong shall be done her : and if she commit a fault, that they may be nearest in the *bot*, if she have not wherewith she may make *bot*." [1] As a matter of fact, however, the woman at marriage came pretty completely under the control of her husband, who had full authority to enforce her obedience by personal chastisement. Only in case of extreme cruelty resulting in bodily injury, or in case of unjust divorce, would the kindred feel bound to interfere. Although the ancient folk laws did not deprive women of legal protection, even making the *wergild* of women in some instances higher than that of men, yet women at this time were not "persons" in a legal sense. Father or brother or guardian answered for them in the courts and paid their fines. Such had long been the custom among the ancient Romans, and in all families of the patriarchal type. In the early centuries of the Middle Ages refractory wives might be sold by their husbands when bodily chastisement failed to accomplish its end. An idle, gadding woman was the especial aversion of the Anglo-Saxons, and she met with swift punishment from the male head of the family. In the quaint Gnomic verses found in the Exeter Book we read :

> "A damsel it beseems to be at her table;
> a rambling woman scatters words,
> she is oft charged with faults,
> a man thinks of her with contempt,
> oft smites her cheek."

And woe betide the woman who attempted to return upon her husband a few of the blows showered upon her. Among certain of the Teutonic peoples the woman who had struck her husband was compelled to ride on an ass through the

---

[1] Young, *op. cit.*, p. 172. *Bot* was a money payment in compensation for an injury inflicted on another.

streets, seated backwards, and holding the astonished animal's tail ! So firmly ingrained among the German tribes was the idea of the supremacy of the husband that the man who meekly accepted blows from his wife would probably some day see his neighbors gather and take the roof off his house, on the ground that he who could not protect himself from his wife did not deserve to be sheltered from wind and rain.[1]

Yet the position of the married woman, even in the rude period of the folk laws, was not as abject as it may seem. Although she was expected to obey her husband, it must sometimes have happened that the wife possessed the stronger personality of the two ; and in such instances it is idle to look to the laws to enforce the supremacy of the husband. By superior shrewdness, as well as by moral power, the woman no doubt enforced her will, then as now, in a score of matters affecting the daily life of the household. Nor did her position in the family rest entirely upon her strength of mind and character. Most of the barbarous races of the continent granted to women a certain degree of independence in their own sphere. Among the Danes, the wife had the custody of the household keys ; and when Cnut the Dane became King of England he extended that privilege to Anglo-Saxon wives, together with the right to have a store-room, chest and cupboard of their own. This was a privilege not to be despised ; for at this time if stolen goods were found in a man's house, his wife must suffer the penalty with him. The new law provided, however, that if the goods were not found in places which the wife controlled, and if she swore that she was ignorant of the theft, she escaped the cruel punishment or the heavy fines meted out to thieves. The lot of many a married woman must, also, have been made easier by the fact that her husband felt a certain respect for the capable wife who administered the complex affairs of homekeeping with efficiency and skill. Many a man doubtless learned

[1] Buckstaff, "Married Women's Property in Anglo-Saxon and Anglo-Norman Law," in *Annals of the American Academy*, Vol. IV, p. 238.

that by giving his wife freedom in the household he received from her better work and thus the whole family profited by the concession.

It is probable that the pagan religions of the Teutonic tribes played some part in improving the position of women. Tacitus tells us that the German barbarian believed that "there dwells in his women something holy and prophetic." Such reverence as attached to these women, through whom the gods were believed to speak, may have been extended in a measure to all women as possible possessors of the divine gift.

Influence of the Church on the Status of Women. — On the whole, the Christian clergy exercised their influence to improve the condition of married women and girls, and to mitigate the too harsh exercise of authority by the husband and father. Yet so careful a historian as Wright does not hesitate to declare that in their efforts to undermine the powerful authority of the patriarch the clergy were looking to their own interests by seeking to substitute the influence of the church for that of the family. Many women were doubtless drawn from their homes by priestly influence to be joined to Christ in spiritual marriage. During the last centuries of the Anglo-Saxon régime we are told that religious houses were filled with women who had left their husbands and with girls who refused to marry the men selected by their fathers.[1] However this may be, the Church rendered a service to civilization in stamping out the last vestiges of polygamy among the Anglo-Saxon peoples. Furthermore, it accomplished by its influence a gradual softening of manners and elevation of the women's position in the home. In the tenth and eleventh centuries the status, at least of Anglo-Saxon women, had vastly improved. This is shown by quaint prints of the period which represent the wife as no longer serving her lord at table, but as sitting in dignity at his side. It is significant, also, of an improvement in the social position of women of the highest class that in 856 King Ethelwulf crowned his wife

[1] Wright, *Womankind in All Ages of Western Europe*, p. 72.

Judith at their marriage. From that period queens were crowned in England and sat beside their husbands on occasions of state. Two centuries later, a woman had gained the priceless right to veto a marriage arranged by her father if it was thoroughly distasteful to her. To be sure she ran the risk not only of being beaten but of being sent to a convent for her obstinacy, especially if she were under age. But we may well believe that such penalties were not always inflicted by indignant fathers. For these mitigations of their lot women were largely indebted to the Christian clergy. Likewise the education bestowed upon the more intelligent girls of noble birth was owing to the influence of the Church. The literary tastes of King Alfred were awakened by his mother; and Alfred's own daughter Ethelfleda was highly educated for that time. In the eleventh century the queen of Edward the Confessor, last of the Saxon kings, was renowned for her learning and accomplishments. Referring to these facts, Thrupp declares: "The high education bestowed on women during the last era of Anglo-Saxon civilization, and the independent position they attained, tended to place them on an equality with the male sex; and combined with the chastity and sobriety which generally distinguished them, offered a sound foundation for the chivalrous respect and devotion of later times." [1] It should be remembered, however, that the historian refers here only to women of royal or noble birth. The position of women of the lower social classes was distinctly inferior to that of their more favored sisters.

Married Women's Property Rights. — Before the days of feudalism, married women, both on the continent and in England, enjoyed larger property rights than were granted them later under the feudal régime. The early folk laws make this clear enough. Among the continental tribes the wife's property consisted of (1) the bride price (after it became customary to give it to the bride instead of the father), (2) the morning-gift, (3) the *gerade*. As we have seen, the bride price

[1] *The Anglo-Saxon Home*, p. 74.

and the morning-gift later became fused into one provision for the bride which was agreed upon at the time of the marriage contract, or *beweddung*, and was confirmed at nuptials. The laws of the Ripuarians, the Frisians and the Westphalian Saxons stipulated that, if a wife bore a son, she should lose her morning-gift and instead be entitled to one-half the joint acquisitions of the family. Among the Germanic tribes a bride commonly received a gift of personal property [1] from her own family, no doubt to assist her in establishing a new household. This was reserved for her own use. In it was included the *gerade*, which consisted of house linen, furniture, ornaments, money, sometimes even the poultry tended by the bride before her marriage and the sheep her hands had shorn. This personal property of the wife descended strictly to her female heirs.

How far did married women among the Teutons control the property to which they were entitled? On this point there seems some difference of opinion among historical writers. Apparently, however, the *gerade* belonged to the wife without qualification; and if this were of generous proportions, a German wife might be economically independent, especially as her separate earnings were her own. To offset these advantages, however, it is probably true that in some tribes all the possessions of the wife except the *gerade*, viz., the morning-gift, and all property by bequest, was under the management of the husband during his lifetime. Law and custom differed among the various tribes with respect to the control granted a married woman over her property. But upon one point the Germanic peoples were practically a unit. With the exception of the Visigoths, who had come under Roman influence, all the Teutons excluded women from ownership of land.

Yet, although some restrictions with respect to the control of her property were put upon the German wife, very few were placed on a widow. At her husband's death a woman entered into possession of her morning-gift *for life* and also received

[1] Called *Aussteuer*.

any other personal property bequeathed or given to her. Among the Westphalian Saxons, as has been stated, the widow who had borne sons received, instead of the morning-gift, a full half of the family possessions. These she enjoyed for life, after which they passed to her husband's nearest heirs. In early times a widow among the Germans passed into the guardianship of her husband's kin and could return to the control of her own *sippe* only if a price were paid for her guardianship. But later this custom died out and the German widow before the days of feudalism seems to have enjoyed a considerable degree of independence.

Hitherto we have considered the property rights of married women and widows solely among the tribes of the Continent. What were the corresponding privileges among the Anglo-Saxons in England? The Anglo-Saxon wife had the *full ownership* of her morning-gift and could bequeath it as she saw fit, unless her husband in the contract had expressly limited her to a life use. Moreover, if the wife bore children, she was entitled by a law of Ethelbert (584–616 A.D.) to half the family property. If the husband had provided no morning-gift for his wife, Anglo-Saxon law gave her a right to " an undivided portion of her husband's property." This meant that the husband could not alienate his land without his wife's consent. Furthermore, there is evidence, in the form of wills and deeds, to show that from early in the ninth century until after the Norman Conquest, the Anglo-Saxon wife was co-possessor of the family property with her husband. A deed of gift of certain lands to the Church by Thurkill and Æthgift, his wife, states that the ownership is to be "as full and free as we two possess it, after the day of us." [1] No restriction seems to have been placed upon the right of an Anglo-Saxon woman to inherit land, as was the case on the continent. In this respect there was sex equality among the Anglo-Saxons. A father might divide his real estate equally among sons and daughters if he chose to do so.

[1] Buckstaff, *op. cit.*, p. 247.

Anglo-Saxon widows were at first under the guardianship of their nearest male kin. Such was the law in the sixth century. But by the reign of Ethelred in the tenth century, widows were for all practical purposes independent agents. Not only did they own their morning-gift and property by inheritance, but they had the full management of these, and at times appear in the records as alienating or bequeathing their possessions without the consent of their sons. After the death of the husband and father the wife and children frequently remained in the family homestead and held the estates together. In such cases the consent of the sons was necessary to the sale of landed property by the widow.

DIVORCE IN THE MIDDLE AGES

Folk Laws and Customs. — In the prehistoric period the right of repudiating the wife was probably the privilege of every husband in the various barbarian tribes. But it may well have been sparingly used for fear of the blood feud or of the fines which would infallibly have been exacted by the relatives of a woman unjustly repudiated. In the folk laws of the Burgundians divorce by mutual consent is sanctioned, doubtless owing to Roman influence. Gradually the folk laws of other tribes conceded this right to every married pair. These codes of customary law made a sharp distinction between the sin of adultery as committed by husband and wife. To be sure, a married man guilty of adultery might be slain if taken in the act; but his crime did not consist in unfaithfulness to his own wife, but in "violating the rights of another husband."[1] On the other hand, Tacitus relates that among the early Germans an adulterous woman was beaten through the village until she died because she had proved unfaithful to her own husband. On the whole the early folk laws show the influence of Christian teachings in a tendency to restrict the grounds on which a man may divorce his wife. Likewise in the monk Bede's *Ecclesias-*

[1] Howard, *History of Matrimonial Institutions*, Vol. II, p. 35.

tical History (731 A.D.), it is expressly stated that barrenness, gluttony, drunkenness, quarrelsomeness and gadding about were not sufficient reasons for divorcing a wife. The law of the Visigoths is surprisingly advanced, going so far as to restrict a man's right of divorce to the cause of adultery, while granting the woman a similar right if the husband has committed "two scandalous wrongs." It is significant, however, that unfaithfulness on the part of the husband was not held by the Visigoths to be one of these "scandalous wrongs." This fact shows that the Christian principle of the equal heinousness of adultery in man or wife had made little headway in changing either sentiment or customary law among the barbarians.

Influence of the Mediæval Church upon Divorce. — The influence exercised by the Church of the Middle Ages in the matter of divorce makes interesting history. At the outset it is necessary to distinguish clearly between the Church's advocacy of the principle that marriage is indissoluble and its actual practice when brought face to face with the conditions of a barbarous society. As early as the fifth century the Council of Carthage had declared the indissolubility of the marriage bond and the Roman Popes had repeatedly forbidden divorce with remarriage. Yet the doctrine proved difficult to uphold without compromise. In consequence we find the Council of Agde (505) threatening with excommunication, not the men who divorce their wives, but those who fail to establish the causes of their divorce before the provincial bishops prior to their remarriage. Likewise the *Pœnitentiales*,[1] both on the Continent and in England, permit divorce for several causes and even permit remarriage. Thus the *Pœnitentiale* of Archbishop Theodore [2] grants a husband the right to divorce a wife guilty of adultery and to marry again. Even the guilty wife may remarry after a penance of five years. Likewise a man deserted by his wife is permitted to take another wife if he

---

[1] These were private manuals written by bishops for the instruction of parish priests in their relations to the members of their churches.

[2] Archbishop of Canterbury about the middle of the seventh century.

obtain the bishop's consent; and a woman whose husband is imprisoned for crime may also remarry. Other grounds for divorce and remarriage recognized in Theodore's *Pœnitentiale* are the conversion of one spouse to Christianity while the other remains heathen, and the capture of husband or wife in time of war. Nowhere is the spirit of compromise, forced upon the Church by barbarous social conditions, more clearly shown than in its early sanction of divorce by mutual consent. Not only is this privilege granted in the English penitential, but in the subsequent Frankish manuals modeled after it.[1]

Such was the state of affairs up to the ninth century when Church Councils took an uncompromising attitude toward divorce, and the penitentials in current use were carefully revised so as to harmonize with the Christian principle of the indissolubility of marriage. Not until three hundred years later did the great masters of canon law, Gratian and Peter the Lombard, seek to reconcile the conflicting views of the Church Fathers, the Popes and the Councils, by codifying all the canons concerning marriage and divorce. These codes became authoritative for all Christian nations and thus are marks of the growing power of the Church in all matters of marriage and divorce. This authority, however, was of slow growth. As we have seen, the Church had met great practical difficulties in enforcing its views concerning divorce upon an unwilling public accustomed to regard such separation as a private matter. The Christian clergy found the only solution of this problem in the complete control of divorce by their own body. Very early they initiated the struggle to secure supreme authority in this field and to wrest jurisdiction from the civil powers, but their efforts did not meet with success until the tenth century when the Bishop's court had become the ordinary tribunal for divorce cases among the German peoples. Before long such was the case throughout Christendom.

But although the Church triumphed in upholding the doctrine of the indissolubility of marriage, as a matter of fact

[1] See Haddan and Stubbs, *Councils*, Vol. III, p. 199.

divorces of two sorts were granted by the Bishop's court under certain conditions. First, the Church employed the expression *divortium a vinculo matrimonii* (divorce from the bonds of matrimony) to designate a marriage as *null and void* because of certain impediments such as (1) a previous *verbal* contract of marriage in words of the present tense, (2) kinship or affinity within the seventh degree, or (3) the spiritual relationship in which, for example, the principals in the sacrament of baptism were supposed to stand. As stated above, the man and woman who had stood sponsors to a child were held by the Church to become spiritually kin by that act and therefore they could not marry. Secondly, canon law permitted *divortium a mensa et thoro* (divorce from board and bed) on three grounds: (1) adultery, (2) heresy or apostasy, (3) cruelty. In such instances the Church granted a *separation order*, permitting husband and wife to live apart. With respect to *divortium a vinculo* there can be little doubt that the powerful and the well-to-do frequently resorted to it as a means of terminating an unsatisfactory marriage and that the doors to fraud were thrown wide open. In this connection Howard writes: "Before the Reformation the voidance of alleged false wedlock on the ground of pre-contract or forbidden degrees of affinity, spiritual relationship, consanguinity, or on some other canonical pretext, had become an intolerable scandal." [1] "Spouses who had quarreled," says a historian of English law, "began to investigate their pedigrees and were unlucky if they could discover no '*impedimentum dirimens*' or cause which would have prevented the contraction of a valid marriage." [2] Apparently money would accomplish much in the ecclesiastical courts of the later Middle Ages. In his work on *The Family* Thwing characterizes the annulment of marriages as "a flourishing business of the mediæval Church," and adds: "No exercise of its power yielded more money, or caused more scandal."

[1] *Op. cit.*, Vol. II, p. 59.
[2] Pollock and Maitland, *History of English Law*, Vol. II, p. 391, footnote 1.

In addition to granting *annulments* of marriages contracted by an infringement of the marriage prohibitions of canon law, the Roman curia granted *dispensations* to marry or to remain in the married state in cases where these prohibitions had also been disregarded. The papal registers contain numerous allusions to these dispensations granted usually to persons of power and wealth who could pay for the privilege. Thus in 1361 Prince Edward, son of Edward III, received from the Roman curia a dispensation permitting his marriage to Joan Countess of Kent to whom he was related not only by consanguinity but by "spiritual affinity," since he had been godfather to her son by a former marriage. The dispensation was granted on condition that the prince found two chapels and endow them with twenty marks yearly. A similar instance was that of Henry VIII who married Catherine of Aragon, the widow of his deceased brother Arthur. Such a union was prohibited by the Church. However, a dispensation permitting the marriage was obtained from the papal curia. Years later, when Henry VIII had become tired of Catherine and was casting amorous eyes on Anne Boleyn, he applied to Pope Clement VII for an annulment of his marriage on the ground that it was invalid from the beginning. The Pope, it may be said, after a long period of indecision, refused to grant the annulment. The refusal, however, was not announced until the impatient Henry had induced Archbishop Cranmer to declare his marriage with Catherine null and void. Later he induced a compliant Parliament to pass the Act of Supremacy (1534) which made the king — not the Pope — the head of the English church. Abram states that in 1357 fifty men and as many women received dispensations to remain in marriages contracted within the fourth degree of relationship. Furthermore, in 1413 the Pope granted his nuncio power to permit one hundred persons related in the third degree, or the third and fourth to remain in marriages so contracted and to declare their children legitimate.[1] It can hardly be doubted that consider-

[1] Abram, A., *English Life and Manners in the Later Middle Ages*, pp. 119-121.

able sums were exacted for these permissions, highly valued as they were by their recipients.

The Homes of Early Days. — Tacitus' famous account of the life of the Germans of the first century, so often quoted above, briefly describes their homes and mode of living. Every one, he says, "surrounds his house with a vacant space, either by way of security against fire, or through ignorance of the art of building. For indeed, they are unacquainted with the use of mortar and tiles; and for every purpose employ rude, unshapen timber fashioned with no regard to pleasing the eye. . . . They also dig subterraneous caves, and cover them over with a great quantity of dung. These they use as winter retreats and granaries, for they preserve a moderate temperature : and upon an invasion, when the open country is plundered, these recesses remain unviolated, either because the enemy is ignorant of them, or because he will not trouble himself with the search." In these rude homes dwelt our Teutonic ancestors, wearing but one garment called by Tacitus the *sagum*. This seems to have been a short square mantle made of some rough shaggy material or of the skins of animals. The dress of the women was very similar to that of the men, except, according to Tacitus, "that they more frequently wear linen which they stain with purple ; and do not lengthen their upper garment into sleeves, but leave exposed the whole arm, and part of the breast." [1]

In the Anglo-Saxon era in England, every freeholder, on obtaining an allotment of land, surrounded his possessions with a mound of earth and dug a ditch around the whole. Inside the earthen wall was an open space called the yard (*geard*) within which stood the rude buildings which made up the *ham* or home of the Anglo-Saxon. The main building was called the *heal* (hall). Here the householder dispensed hospitality to

[1] Tacitus, *Germania* (Oxford trans.), pp. 306–308.

all honest men who came to his doors, and here his friends and retainers slept at night, on the straw-strewn floor. In the hall the well-to-do thane entertained his friends at his generous board, and his lady served wine to her lord's guests. Even an Anglo-Saxon queen frequently left her raised seat beside the king to pass the wine-cup among his trusty followers. In the hall or courtyard, the lord and his lady dispensed clothing and loaves to the poor, hence the name *hlaf-ord* (loaf-owner) and *hlaf-dig* (loaf-giver), from which terms come our names "lord" and "lady." Thus the word "lady" in its origin was bound up with the gracious charity, which, in those early days, was regarded as the special duty of the well-born woman and her noblest grace. Separate chambers were built outside the hall to accommodate the women of the family. Each small building was connected with the hall and was called a *bur*, whence comes our expression of the "ladies' bower." Among the poorer classes the homes were rough and the bed-chambers were few or none until, in the words of Wright, "we arrive at the simple room in which the inmates had board and lodging together, with a mere hedge for its enclosure, the prototype of our ordinary cottage and garden." [1] Anglo-Saxon houses remained much the same in structure and arrangement until the end of the Saxon period. None had an upper story, but consisted only of the ground floor. Country houses were built on high ground, offering a wide prospect in all directions; and thus they afforded the protection so much needed in those warlike days.

The Home as a Center of Industry. — Quite as truly as in primitive Palestine, Greece and Rome, the home of the early Middle Ages was the heart of the industrial life of the community. The rude Teuton tilled his fields, hunted wild animals, made weapons and crude implements and went to war. When peace prevailed, he lay about the house or caroused with his chosen companions. His wife, on the other hand, was

[1] Wright, *History of Domestic Manners in England during the Middle Ages,* p. 11.

engaged in a wide variety of productive occupations. In the words of Tacitus : "All the bravest of the warriors, committing the care of the house, the family affairs, *and the lands*, to the women, old men, and weaker part of the domestics, stupefy themselves in inaction. . . ." The quotation is of peculiar interest as showing that even agriculture, in the first Christian centuries, was carried on by the Teutonic women. Furthermore, the whole clothing industry, with its numerous skilled processes, was likewise entirely in the hands of the women. Archbishop Theodore of Canterbury, in his *Pœnitentiale* so often referred to, forbids Anglo-Saxon women to employ themselves on Sunday in such occupations as shearing sheep, carding wool, beating flax, washing garments, weaving, spinning or sewing. Although this indicates only a portion of the activities of the busy housewife of the period, it shows that in the seventh century the textile industry, woolen as well as linen, was wholly carried on by the wives and daughters of the family. Such was the case prior to the twelfth century when weaving became a skilled craft in the hands of men. But even then the preparatory work, the wool-combing, spinning, drawing out of the yarn and winding remained in the hands of women.[1] In the same way all the activities connected with the preparation of food and drink were home industries directed by the housewives. Women were the cooks, the brewers, the bakers in these early days. Later in the Middle Ages, as craft gilds grew up, men tried to take over in part the brewing and baking that had so long been carried on in the homes. But even then women were not wholly excluded from these incorporated industries, as the town records in the Rhine cities and in Frankfort-on-Main abundantly prove.[2] Nor did the work of women end here. When candles succeeded rush-lights, chandlery developed as a domestic industry — another occupation for the busy *hausfrau*. Soap-making was likewise in the hands of housewives; and it is highly probable that before

[1] See Bücher, Karl, *Die Frauenfrage in Mittelalter,* p. 15.
[2] *Ibid.,* p. 19.

tanning of skins became a male industry the processes were carried on in the home in part, at least, by women.

A favorite occupation of women of rank throughout the Middle Ages was embroidery. So skilled in this art did Anglo-Saxon women become that the finest embroidery and needlework in Europe was known in the eleventh century as "English Work." Bishop Aldhelm, in a quaint eighth-century work in praise of virginity, complains of the vanity of Anglo-Saxon women who "sought to arrange delicately their waving locks, curled artificially by the curling-iron, with their cheeks dyed red with stibium." Apparently these arts of allurement, so common in our own day, have an ancient history. But the worthy bishop is on less solid ground when he reproves women for changing the natural color of fleeces to red and purple — a transformation which appears wholly for the better. The complaint is of interest, however, as showing that women understood the art of dyeing wool at an early period. Tacitus mentions the practice as common among the German women in the first Christian century.

HOME NURTURE AND TRAINING IN THE MIDDLE AGES

When a child was born in the early centuries of the Middle Ages, the father, as head of the household, decided whether the tiny infant should be reared. As we have seen, infanticide and child exposure were not uncommon at this time, owing to the hard conditions of existence. In spite of the steady opposition of the Church, which decreed severe and long-continued penances for such offenses, destitute parents killed or exposed their infants in times of warfare or of scarcity of food. Even so late as the eleventh century the inhabitants of Schleswig occasionally cast unwelcome children into the sea, although these were probably isolated cases.[1] This cruel custom bore more severely on girl babies than on boys, since the latter were relied upon to continue the family name and to be the hope

[1] Boesch, *Kinderleben in der deutschen Vergangenheit*, p. 12.

of the parents in their old age. In the countries of North Germany and Scandinavia, if a child were sprinkled with water and given a name, or if its lips were smeared with honey, it could no longer be killed or exposed. Little by little the custom of child exposure yielded to civilization, and as the position of women improved, their instincts of love and pity had increasing weight in determining the fate of the child they had borne. In the quaint old city of Nuremberg during the Middle Ages, provision was made for poor women about to become mothers, perhaps with a view to preventing infanticide or abortion. Midwives, who had almost wholly in their own hands the bringing of children into the world, were enjoined to make ready a bed and all necessary things for the confinement of poor women and to attend them as long as was necessary. Every year they were to present their account to the city exchequer and receive compensation for their outlay.[1]

In North Germany, Iceland and Scandinavia the new-born child was laid on the floor at the feet of its father, who then decided whether or not it should be allowed to live. If the decision were favorable, the little one was handed over to the midwives to be bathed and probably swaddled, *i.e.*, wrapped tightly with cloths from head to feet. It was then sprinkled and given a name by the father. The nurses and midwives of these early days were saturated with superstitions and practiced all manner of strange traditional rites which were believed to help the little stranger on the strenuous path of life that lay ahead of it. Sometimes a fresh egg, the symbol of fruitfulness, was laid in the baby's bath; or a coin was placed there to insure to the little one ample means in its later life. Again, after its bath, the new-born child was laid close against the left side of its mother in the belief that she would draw from it all sickness and protect it thus from child-pains, leprosy and the falling-sickness. Against these and many other superstitious practices, kept alive by ignorant midwives, municipal ordinances were occasionally directed. For example, an ordinance

[1] Boesch, *op cit.*, p. 11.

of Gotha, as late as the seventeenth century, after enjoining midwives to be God-fearing and lead Christly lives, continues: "On the contrary all superstition and misuse of God's name and word . . . such as use of written characters, drawings, gestures, and making the cross, amputation of the navel-string with certain questions and answers, . . . sprinkling before or after the bath, and such-like are forbidden, not alone to themselves, but also if they observe such unchristly and blamable practices in other people they shall dissuade them earnestly from the same and also report every case to the priest or magistrate." [1]

Very early in its life the infant was admitted to the sacrament of baptism, which apparently grew to be a costly affair in the later Middle Ages, so much so that it became necessary to regulate the expense by municipal ordinance. A Nuremberg law of the fourteenth century forbade the decoration of baptismal robes with gold, silver or pearls under penalty of a fine of two florins. Not more than twelve guests were permitted to attend the baptism and not more than three of these should later be entertained at the home of the parents. Even the entertainment was limited by the ordinance to spice-cake and wine. Not content with lessening the expense of baptism for the parents, the law cut down the christening gifts of dower money, made by god-parents and friends, to 32 Pfennigs. [2]

In the early centuries of the Christian era, the boys of the Teutonic and Anglo-Saxon peoples grew up naked and dirty in the rude homes of their parents. Their training consisted largely in running, jumping, learning the use of spear and javelin, training in the sword-dance and later in hunting and fighting. A *wergild* was set upon the boys of some Teutonic tribes at eight years of age. At twelve, as we have seen, the Anglo-Saxon boy was freed from the control of father or guardian so far as his estate was concerned. Likewise when the German youth was fifteen years of age he was commonly

---

[1] Boesch, *op. cit.*, pp. 18, 19.
[2] *Ibid.*, p. 28.

regarded as old enough to bear arms. After these had been conferred upon him, in the midst of the assembly of his people, either by the chief, his father or some member of the "kin," the boy was then admitted to the rights and duties of a freeman. From this time he was responsible for his acts before the law in his own person.

Not much can be said concerning the intellectual training of children during the early Middle Ages. Such education was distinctly the exception and not the rule, save for those children who were dedicated by their parents to the monastic life. In the time of the good king Alfred (9th century), began the custom of placing English children in the houses of prominent nobles and princes to be educated. Yet the brothers of Alfred could neither read nor write, and this was true of most other nobly born children of the time. Such weak and unmanly arts were left to monks and a few women. Later, the Anglo-Saxon youths were sent to Normandy to be taught riding, hunting, fighting, grooming horses and serving at table in the Norman castles. This was in the eleventh century, when feudalism was reshaping social customs and was beginning to hold up ideals of obedience and service as the qualities of a true knight.

In the homes of the early Middle Ages, then, such training as the boys received was largely physical and moral, although simple religious instruction was doubtless given in coöperation with the Church. The age was rude and half barbarous, and education reflected the low stage of civilization then attained by the peoples of Western Europe.

THE LATER MIDDLE AGES; CHANGES IN FAMILY LAW AND CUSTOM

Growing Power of the Church over Marriage and Divorce. — It will be remembered that, in the tenth and eleventh centuries, the Christian Church sought to add sanctity to marriage by insisting that a priest take part in the nuptial ceremony

before the door of the church, and that subsequently a bride
mass be performed within the church, followed by the benediction of the priest upon the newly married pair. After the
twelfth century "self-gifta," or the giving of the woman to the
man by herself alone or by some guardian chosen by herself,
became a common custom. At this point the Church intervened and brought marriage more completely under its own
control. So long as the father or a near relative, acting as
guardian, handed over the bride to the groom the clergy did
not interfere with their natural right. But when any third
person, chosen by the bride herself, could perform this important act in marriage, the Christian priesthood took this
function into their own hands. They went further and
threatened with the awful penalty of excommunication the
layman who would give a woman in marriage. Thus from the
thirteenth century on the marriage rituals of *continental*
Europe show that the clergy are the important factors in the
ceremony. It is the priest and not the parent or chosen guardian who gives the woman to the man with the solemn words in
the Latin tongue: "I join you in the name of the Father, the
Son and the Holy Ghost, Amen." [1] Such, however, was not
the custom in England. The individualistic Anglo-Saxon has
maintained his right to give his own daughter in marriage
down to the present day, as is shown by the Anglican marriage
service in which the clergyman says: "Who giveth this
woman to this man?"

Clandestine Marriages. — Doubtless the motive of the
Church in taking such action was to impress upon the contracting parties the seriousness and solemnity of marriage
as one of the seven sacraments of the Church. This doctrine,
taught long before, was first formally promulgated in 1164
in the famous theological work of Peter the Lombard called
the *Sentences*. But the Church was probably moved to take
marriage into her own hands for another reason. As early as
the ninth century Christianity had come into conflict with the

[1] Howard, Vol. I, pp. 309–312.

rooted idea of the Germanic peoples that marriage is a *civil contract* — not a religious rite. As we have seen, this idea was particularly strong in England, although it was influential on the Continent as well. While the Church steadily sought to extend its control over marriage, some persons resented its action and insisted on a private lay ceremony, which was often clandestine in character. The custom of the time permitted a man and woman to take each other for husband and wife in words of the present tense, *e.g.*, "I *take* thee to be my wedded wife. . . ." In this lay and private contract may be found the source of the "common law" marriage of England and America. Sometimes this simple ceremony took place before witnesses, sometimes in the absence of any other parties. Clandestine marriages of the latter kind became so frequent from the thirteenth to the sixteenth century as to constitute well-nigh a public scandal, since they not infrequently led to grave social wrongs. A man thus married could and did easily throw off the responsibilities he had assumed at marriage, and in consequence his wife and children might become public charges. Yet the Church was loath to pronounce such unions invalid, since such action would stamp the unfortunate offspring as illegitimate. Hence the canonical laws on marriage, as formulated by Peter the Lombard, tended to make a clear distinction between *legal* and *valid* marriages. A marriage contracted without the knowledge of the Church was pronounced *illegal* although not *invalid*. Such marriages were visited with ecclesiastical penalties in the form of severe penance; but they were not declared null and void, nor were the parties compelled to separate. After the Norman Conquest numerous canons forbade private marriages and prescribed penalties for the priest who performed them. In 1215, at the Fourth Lateran Council, Pope Innocent III attempted to stem the flood of clandestine marriages by requiring the publication of banns in all Christian countries. Yet, if a man and woman were contracted in words of the present tense (*per verba præsenti*) the Church continued to hold them as man and wife. This meant that a mere private verbal contract to marry, if in the form "I *take* thee to be my wedded wife," etc., was sustained by canon law against a subsequent marriage performed with due publicity by an officiating priest. In taking this ground the Church paved the way for serious abuses which were not remedied until the sixteenth century.

Effects of Feudalism upon Marriage and the Family. — When the feudal system was thoroughly established, Western Europe was divided into fiefs or landed estates, large and small, which were held on condition of military service rendered some overlord in return for his protection of the lands and persons of the holders. The lesser lords held their lands of some more powerful noble to whom they owed allegiance and well-defined services. Finally the most powerful of the nobility held their own lands as fiefs of the King, whose vassals they were. Thus was developed a landed aristocracy which assumed almost sovereign powers over their immediate vassals.

The effects of this social system upon marriage laws and family customs were profound and far-reaching.

Status and Property Rights of Women. — It will be recalled that, before the feudal system became established, women had been conceded considerable property rights. On the Continent the Teutonic woman had entire control of her *gerade* or personal property given her by her family at marriage. She could even alienate it without her husband's consent, and if it took the form of a considerable sum of money, she might be economically independent. The wife also owned her morning-gift and separate earnings. Whether she *controlled* these during her husband's lifetime is a disputed point. Probably not, although mandates have come down to us wherein a wife gives her husband authority to transact business for her.[1] This seems to point to the wife's personal control of her own property. The German widow, at any rate, had the independent management of her morning-gift for life. Among the

[1] Buckstaff, *Woman's Property Rights in Anglo-Saxon and Anglo-Norman Law*, p. 236.

Anglo-Saxons the wife who bore children became co-possessor of the family property with her husband. The latter could not alienate her property; and, since she was by law the absolute owner of her morning-gift, or, if none were granted at the marriage, of an undivided portion of her husband's property, she appears as a consenting party in sales of land or personal property made by him. On the death of her husband the Anglo-Saxon widow was entitled both to the ownership and control of her property by gift or inheritance, and to her morning-gift. Also toward the close of the Anglo-Saxon period, a widow was freed from guardianship save in the conduct of a legal case and apparently sometimes pleaded her own cause before the courts. A century before the Norman Conquest in England a widow named Wynflæd appeared before the court in person and pleaded her own case, producing as witnesses not only loyal thanes, but women whose testimony was accepted as valid before the law.[1]

All this was changed, however, under the feudal system which gradually curtailed the property rights of women and lowered their status. Fortunately there has come down to us a description of the laws and customs of England in the reign of Henry II (1154–1189), which has been ascribed to the great Anglo-Norman lawyer Richard Glanvill. This interesting *Tractate* is of enormous value since it outlines in important features the legal practice in England almost to modern times. The document shows that the morning-gift of Anglo-Saxon days had by this time given place to the Norman "dower" or the life use of one third of the husband's real estate *at marriage*, without regard to his later accumulations or losses. The law of Glanvill prescribed that this proportion might not be increased *even by agreement between husband and wife*. Nor might the husband give his dwelling-house to his wife as dower, since that belonged to his heir. Here we may plainly trace the influence of the ideas of primogeniture and entail which have governed the disposal of landed property in England down to

[1] Young, "Anglo-Saxon Family Law," in *Essays in Anglo-Saxon Law*, p. 182.

our own time. In addition to her privilege of dower the wife was permitted a *life use* of one third of her husband's personal property. But the Anglo-Norman wife had no control over her dower during the lifetime of her husband, nor could she in any way interfere with his management of it. So complete was her subordination that, even if her husband should sell the lands composing her dower, she could claim nothing after his death if it could be proved against her that she opposed him at the time of the sale. Nor did her disabilities end here. After her husband's death the widow must go through a complicated process at law to obtain her dower, and if her husband's heirs were disposed to dispute her claim, she must find a champion who would uphold her rights in open combat. Woe betide the unfortunate lady who was not charming enough to find a champion ! Her property rights must have suffered sorely in a world so completely "man-made." In two respects, however, the laws of Glanvill concerning dower were softened at a later period. (1) Under Henry III, in 1217, a widow was permitted to receive as dower one third of all the real estate of which her husband was possessed *at his death*. (2) In the reign of Edward IV a husband might, if he chose, endow his wife with the whole of his real estate for life. Apparently this privilege was very rarely used.[1]

With respect to the inheritance of estates the English woman in feudal times was placed at a further disadvantage. Under the Anglo-Saxon régime daughters might inherit equally with sons, there being no law to prevent this. But with the Norman kings came new customs. Glanvill writes concerning inheritance by women : "If anyone has a son and heir, and besides him a daughter or daughters, *the son succeeds to the whole;* . . . because in general it is true that a woman never takes part in an inheritance with a male, unless a special exception to this exist in some particular city by the custom of that city." [2] In the feudal period, also, there grew up the Roman

[1] Buckstaff, *op. cit.*, p. 260.
[2] *Ibid.*, p. 254. Italics mine.

custom whereby the parents of a girl gave her a dowry at her marriage. This property belonged to the husband so long as the marriage lasted, and he had a life interest in it if his wife died before him. At the death of her husband, however, a widow was entitled to the life use of both her dowry (*maritagium*) and her dower.

The legal status of the woman under feudalism seems also to have been somewhat lowered. To quote from Glanvill: "Husband and wife were one person and that person was the husband." This meant, of course, that the woman was bound wholly by her husband's will and was represented by him in the courts (since she was not a "person" in a legal sense). "While she was in the power of her husband," writes Glanvill, "she was not able to contradict his will in anything and so was not able against his will to look out for her own rights." [1] This grim injustice of feudal family law in England has been characterized by an eminent French writer as having "the harshness of the primitive barbaric codes." [2]

With feudalism came a further limitation of the power of English women. A widow was no longer permitted to be the legal guardian of her own children — a right that had been granted to her under early Saxon law. The orphaned child of large inheritance usually came under the guardianship of his overlord, who sometimes profited richly by "farming out" the care of the child to scheming persons who desired to marry the young heir to a daughter or son of their family. If the orphan were an only daughter, and hence an heiress, the overlord was very careful to assert his right to marry her to a man of his own selection or to one of whose loyalty he was thoroughly assured. So with the widow. She must obtain the consent of her liege lord to a second marriage under penalty of forfeiting her dower; and more often than not the overlord of a rich widow made a profitable bargain with the knight or squire who sought her hand and the management of her es-

[1] Buckstaff, *op. cit.*, pp. 252–253.
[2] Laboulaye, *Recherches sur la condition des femmes*, p. 276.

tates. By the opening of the twelfth century the extortions of the overlord with respect to the wards and widows under his control called forth a species of charter from Henry I. In this interesting document the King declared : "And if any one of my barons and men wish to give in marriage his daughter, or sister, or granddaughter, or kinswoman, let him talk to me about it ! But I will neither take anything from him for this license nor will I forbid him to give her, unless he should intend to unite her with my enemy. And if, my baron or other man being dead, his daughter remain his heir, I will give her with her land by the advice of my barons. And if, the husband being dead, his wife survive and be without children, she shall have her dower and marriage, and I will not give her to a husband, except according to her will." In closing, the King exhorts his barons to "forbear similarly towards the sons or daughters or wives of their men." [1]

The causes of the feudal disabilities just described are not far to seek. As the military tenure of land became common, the rights of women correspondingly decreased because feudalism valued the services of a man in fighting strength far more highly than the services of a woman within the home. Then, too, a suitor for the hand of some noble damsel often performed feudal services for his bride's father in order to obtain her dowry, and quite naturally such a suitor felt that he had earned certain rights in her property. Finally, it should be remembered that if a woman were permitted to hold large estates the overlord would feel by no means certain of receiving his feudal dues in military service. To quote from Mrs. Putnam's interesting study of *The Lady*, the lands of a mediæval knight were held "from his overlord on condition of the payment of rental in the form of military service. Every acre of ground was valued in terms of fighting men and only the knight in person could be sure of rallying the quota and producing them when required. If the knight died, in harness or in his bed, and left a widow with young chil-

[1] Wright, *Womankind in All Ages of Western Europe*, pp. 100, 101.

dren or a daughter as his sole heir, there was a good chance that the rent would not be paid. The overlord had a right, in view of his interests in the matter, to see that a fief should not be without a master; in other words, to marry as soon as might be the widow or the daughter of the deceased to some stout knight who was willing to take the woman for the sake of the fief. . . . In fact, it could be said of the lady as truly as of the serf that she 'went with the land.' She knew this full well herself. In the romance of *Girars de Viane* the Duchess of Bourgoyne came to the king, saying: 'My husband is dead, but of what avail is mourning? Give me a strong man to my husband, for I am sore pressed to defend my land!' " [1]

Home Life in the Feudal Castle. — It must not be supposed that women under feudalism were always miserable and oppressed. Such was doubtless far from being the case. Nothing is more common in history than the cheerful acceptance by men and women alike of economic and social disabilities if these have long been customary and unchallenged. Then, too, it must be remembered that in the later centuries of feudalism the rude races of Western Europe were gradually taking on the customs and ideas of civilized people. With the decline in frequency of robber raids and devastating warfare, more opportunity was furnished the knights and barons of feudal times to improve their manners in the presence of women, and to gain some appreciation for the gentler human qualities that tend to flourish in times of peace. This development in civilization was wholly favorable to the position of women in the family and was furthered by life in the feudal castle. The rude home of Anglo-Saxon days gave way, after the Norman invasion, to the fortress-castle of feudal times. Within this almost impregnable retreat the knight and his lady passed their days in an isolation so complete that it must often have driven the baron to take part in some robber foray or questionable adventure from sheer inactivity and boredom. But this very isolation of the

[1] Putnam, *The Lady*, pp. 116–117.

family members tended to draw them together in a closer sympathy. "Never, in any other form of society," writes Guizot, "has a family, reduced to its most simple expression, husband, wife and children, been found so closely drawn together, pressed one against the other, separated from all other powerful and rival relations. . . . Now whenever man is placed in a certain position, the part of his moral nature which corresponds to that position is favorably developed in him. Is he obliged to live habitually in the bosom of his family, with his wife and children, the ideas and sentiments in harmony with this fact cannot fail to obtain a great empire over him. So it happened in feudal society." [1] But this is not the whole story. When the lord of the castle went forth with his retainers in quest of booty or in defense of his rights, his lady was left in sole charge of his fief. She was its manager in time of peace and its defender against attack. Such a situation of power and dignity must have had a potent influence in the development of the mind and character of the high-born women of the Middle Ages. Just as in the period of the Roman conquests the responsible positions into which Roman matrons were thrust in the absence of their husbands tended to develop in them a sense of personal dignity and worth, so did similar conditions call forth like sentiments in the feudal lady. This enhanced self-esteem, when combined with real efficiency, must have contributed much toward elevating the position of women in the eyes of men. Then, too, women became heirs to vast estates in default of male issue. Indeed female owners of rich fiefs — single women and widows — were not uncommon ; and their position was one of relative freedom and power.

In the thirteenth and fourteenth centuries the status of nobly born women had greatly improved. Ladies who had been richly dowered at their marriage with lands and vassals became, at the death of their husbands, fairly independent agents. Such women, if allowed to remain unmarried,

[1] *Histoire de la civilization en France*, tome III, pp. 343–346.

might be owners of castles and manors and as such might assume the rights and obligations of knights toward their overlords. As we have seen, the wife's position in the feudal castle had steadily become more honorable as sentiments and manners had improved. The very word "courtesy" refers to the manners prevailing in the court or family of the lord and lady. Outside the manor house and castle a very different code of conduct toward women was common for many centuries. Wright, in his study of *Womankind*, quotes a stanza from an ancient poem of the thirteenth century in which some troubadour ascribes the origin of courtesy to the influence of women.

> "There is reason enough why
> We ought to hold women dear;
> For we see happen very little
> Courtesy, except through women.
> Well know I that for the love of ladies
> The very clowns become courteous." [1]

Education of Pages and Daimoiselles. — Out of feudalism arose the curious custom by which the sons and daughters of lesser knights were sent to the castles of famous lords and churchmen to be educated. The lord of the castle took charge of the boys, who received a thorough training. First as pages, they were taught obedience and loyal service by the performance of certain humble tasks such as waiting on table, serving the ladies and caring for the horses and armor of the overlord. With this went education in gentle manners, such as would be pleasing to ladies, and in skillful riding. At the age of fourteen the page became a squire and for seven years more was trained in the arts of war and in personal attendance on his lord both at home and on the field of battle. When the youthful squire had been thoroughly imbued with the ideals of chivalry — loyalty to his church, his lord and his lady — he might, by acts of prowess, attain the coveted distinction of knighthood. For the knight of the Middle Ages was not born to this honor, but achieved it.

[1] Wright, *Womankind in All Ages of Western Europe*, p. 161.

While the boys of the castle were thus being trained in manly pursuits and ideals, the girls were receiving the education deemed suitable for them at the hands of the lady of the castle. All the long day they sat in certain rooms of the castle, under the eye of the lady, learning how to spin and weave, to make clothing, to embroider girdles and garments, sometimes with marvelous pictorial scenes, and above all to weave the wonderful tapestries of the feudal period. In the late afternoon or early evening they repaired to the quaint conventional gardens surrounding the castle, where they were joined by the pages and squires. Very demure were these damsels of the thirteenth century, if we may judge by the illustrated MSS. which have come down to us. Rather rigid manuals of etiquette for ladies began to be written about this time. One of the earliest French codes was entitled *Le Chastoiement des Dames*.[1] It exhorted young maidens to be modest in the presence of men, not to talk too much, to walk erect and not too fast lest they outstrip their companions, and above all not to turn to right or left when they walked abroad, or to let men kiss them. Such exhortations lead us to suspect that the very proper "daimoiselles" of the medieval castle were, after all, much like the girls of the present day.

It is highly probable that most of these young women received some education in reading, writing and in the French language. But even if they were not so taught, the troubadours kept them well-informed concerning the literature of their day — the love-songs, romances and epics which extolled the charm of ladies and the prowess of knights. Moreover, well-born women were trained as nurses and leeches throughout the Middle Ages. The young "daimoiselle" was very early schooled not to shrink from blood. She learned to bandage wounds, even at times to set bones, to prepare medicinal draughts from herbs, and "to succour the men on

---

[1] Written by Robert de Blois in the second third of the thirteenth century. See Hentsch, *De la Litterature didactique du moyen age s'addressant spécialement aux femmes*, pp. 75–80.

whose lives her life depended." The romances of the period teem with references to women's skill in nursing and healing, to their knowledge of soothing ointments and herbs. Medical recipes have been handed down from the Middle Ages and testify to the importance of women as the physicians of the household.

Influence of Chivalry upon Family Life in the Castles. — In the twelfth century, as we have seen, grew up that form of social discipline known as chivalry, which furnishes so rich a fund of material to the romancers of a later and more prosaic age. At its best chivalry gave to the rude nobles of the Middle Ages much-needed ideals of loyalty to Church and liege-lord, prowess in behalf of the weak, and idealistic love and service of their chosen lady. To show courage and endurance of an almost superhuman order in the eyes of the maiden of his heart became the supreme ideal of many a lusty knight, and, it may truly be added, the "open sesame" to the affections of many a fair "daimoiselle." Indeed, one nobly born English maid boldly declared that she would wed no man who was not "handsome, courteous and accomplished, and the most valiant of his body in all Christendom." Her guardian thereupon proclaimed a tournament, with the damsel and her estates as the rich reward of the victor.

Much time was spent by the ladies of the castle in weaving girdles and ribbons to adorn the helmets of their chosen knights. Sometimes a maid of high degree condescended to lead her champion's horse by the bridle into the lists, where he proclaimed himself the true servant of love and beauty. Thus there grew up in those centuries of bloodshed and plunder, of oppression of the weak by the strong, the sentiment of romantic love. Rare indeed in pagan civilizations, almost unknown at the dawn of the Middle Ages, it was destined to spread over the whole of Christendom and to prove a great civilizing influence. For, when the lady comes to set a spiritual price upon her love and favor, when the knight willingly pays that price in brave devotion and courteous service, then love has risen from a purely sensual plane and has become an affair of the heart and the mind. In Provence, the home of poetry and romance, the ideal of romantic love was born; but it was rapidly carried over France and the rest of feudal Europe by the troubadours and minnesingers of the age. As early as 1160 a troubadour from the South sang of the great emotion "which was coming to add beauty to the world." In the words of Tennyson:

> "For indeed I know
> Of no more subtle passion under heaven,
> Than is the maiden passion for a maid;
> Not only to keep down the base in man,
> But teach high thought and amiable words,
> And courtliness and the desire of fame
> And love of truth and all that makes a man."

In time love-making bade fair to become the most important business of knights and ladies; and the ability to write verses in praise of one's lady was the most highly prized accomplishment of the time. Jongleurs and troubadours were welcome guests in every castle and manor house, and often addressed their ardent yet conventional songs to the lady of the castle herself. In the twelfth and thirteenth centuries scholasticism was at its height and the organization of knowledge in accordance with the logic of Aristotle was the prevailing intellectual ideal. It is not surprising, then, to learn that formal codes of love were speedily drawn up for the use of all sighing lovers. Mrs. Putnam quotes from one of these works:

"Every lover is wont to grow pale at sight of the beloved."

"Virtue alone makes one worthy of love."

"Every action of the lover ends in thoughts of the beloved."

"The true lover cares for nothing save what he deems pleasant to the beloved." [1]

There are many pages of such declarations, followed by minute precepts concerning the manner and address of the lover.

[1] *The Lady*, p. 142.

Absurd as all this may seem to the twentieth-century mind, let us not ignore the tremendous significance of the chivalric movement in planting in the souls of men a respect and consideration for womanhood, a willingness to serve women and some appreciation of the profound gulf between ideal love and brute lust.

So much for the brighter side of chivalry. That it has a darker aspect cannot be gainsaid. In those days marriage did "not mean the union of two souls but of two fiefs." Married women, unhappy and lonely, finding little congeniality or companionship in the society of their husbands, claimed the right to love. Marriage, arranged by their parents, was a duty; love was a free gift and a joy. The former secured to the man a housekeeper; to the woman an assured social position; and to both the promise of offspring to maintain the family name and inherit the estates. But love implied a spiritual union, and its favors were the reward of service, the crown of true devotion. Often, however, this idealistic philosophy of affection must have given place to mere passing fancy or uncontrolled passion. Husbands were supposed to close their eyes to the amours of their wives and seek their true love in some lady to whom they owed no irksome marriage duty.

A curious account of the devotion of a medieval knight of the thirteenth century to a flint-hearted lady is found in the verses of one Ulrich von Lichtenstein. This Austrian noble, in his quaint poem *Frauendienst*,[1] describes his years of service of a noble lady, already married. For reasons not given, this service carries him to Rome as a pilgrim and to Venice in the guise of a queen. Apparently the knight is really engaged in a series of aimless adventures which end in his visiting his lady in the garb of a leper. He sits at the castle gate by day and receives food from the hands of the lady's maidservants. At last his prayer is heeded and he is lifted by means of a bed coverlet to the oriel window of his lady's chamber. This he

[1] Service of Women.

gladly enters and finds his beloved seated upon a bed and surrounded by her maids.   But his hopes are dashed to earth
when the lady meets his prayer for her love with the words:
"Nay, your courage may not aspire so far that I should lay
you here by my side. . . . My lord and master shall live
ever free from fear lest I should love another man than he;
for (even though I feared it not for God's honour and mine
own), yet my lord would keep close watch over me; . . ."
That Ulrich's love was not free from self-seeking appears in
his reply.   Turning to his aunt, who had served as go-between
in the affair, he complains: "How shall this be?   If I get no
profit of my coming, then shall I be crestfallen; . . ."   Crestfallen he is, indeed, before his adventure is done, for his lady
plays a sorry trick upon her amorous knight.   Having persuaded him to consent to be lowered from the window on the
condition that she hold his hand, she then offers to kiss him.
In the words of Ulrich, "I was so overjoyed that I let go her
hand: swift then was my downward journey; and had God
not been with me, I had lightly broken my neck."   Sometime
later Ulrich casts off this heartless lady and consoles himself
with a more complaisant love.[1]

Doubtless the fair "daimoiselles" of the castle as well as
the mistress were the inspirers of many romantic poems and
ardent love verses.   Life in the medieval castle admitted of
little privacy and encouraged extreme intimacy between the
sexes.   The couch of my lord and lady was placed in the main
hall, separated only by curtains from this public assembling
place.   Pages and squires slept in one upper room and
"daimoiselles" in another; and visiting in bedrooms was a
common custom.   In an atmosphere supercharged with sex-
feeling, with the loose song of the troubadour or the example
of friends to weaken her defenses, many a girl must have suc-
cumbed to the seduction of the youth with whom she was daily
brought into close contact.   "Feudal society," says Wright,
"was polished and brilliant but impure."   He might have

[1] Coulton, *A Mediæval Garner*, pp. 303-402.

added "insincere"! For when love-making was reduced to codes and when the romantic verses of troubadours and minnesingers became conventionalized, then artificiality more and more vitiated the love affairs of knight and lady. The movement had become self-conscious, subject to detailed precepts and hence lacking in sincerity and genuineness. Yet, before it gave way to a new order, chivalry had accomplished much in giving men and women a vision of the meaning and worth of romantic love. As the centuries passed this love came to be more often joined with marriage, not opposed to it.

POSITION OF WOMEN IN THE LATER MIDDLE AGES

In the literature of the later centuries of the Middle Ages a conflict of ideas about the nature and usefulness of women is clearly apparent. As Eileen Power has pointed out,[1] there were three distinct groups holding views about women in opposition at many points. First was the ecclesiastical group of monks and priests, who, under the influence of asceticism, denounced woman as the instrument of the devil, a being basically evil and grossly inferior to man. So bitter were these denunciations of the clergy against women, that Chaucer's Wife of Bath was led to remark:

> "For trusteth well, it is an impossible
> That any clerk [2] will speak good of wives, . . ."

On the other hand, chivalry, as described above, tended to idealize women and to glorify courtly or romantic love. The good knight worshiped God in heaven and his lady on earth, and eagerly listened to the romances and songs of the troubadours exalting the graces and virtues of women.

Among the most spiritual of these were the lays of Walther von de Vogelweide, a German minstrel of the twelfth century. In one of his poems, called *Love and Dream*, he writes:

[1] See her article on "The Position of Women" in Crump, G. C., and Jacob, E. F., *The Legacy of the Middle Ages* (Oxford, Clarendon Press, 1927).
[2] Meaning 'cleric.'

"'Take Lady this garland': thus spake I to a maid in fair attire: 'then will you grace the dance with these bright flowers in your hair.' . . . She took that I offered her, even as a child that is honoured; her cheeks flushed red, as a rose in a bed of lilies; then her bright eyes were ashamed, yet she sweetly bowed in greeting to me. This was my guerdon; if I had more reward, that I keep to mine own heart. . . . Methought I had never greater bliss than this content of mind. The blossoms from the trees fell all the while around us on the grass; lo! then must I laugh aloud for joy. Yet, even while I was so merry and so rich in my dream, then the day dawned and I must needs awake." [1]

A third group was composed of the plain men of the middle and laboring classes who, while not hesitating to assert the superior authority of the husband, yet granted to hard-working and reasonably docile wives a considerable measure of "rough and ready equality." Countrywomen living with their husbands in humble cottages on small farm holdings worked side by side with the men in the fields, doing all of the rough work except plowing and even acting as sheep shearers and thatchers' assistants. [2] In the towns the women were busy from dawn till after dark in carrying on their household industries and even a variety of trades. Under such conditions it was inevitable that wives, whose labors were indispensable to the maintenance of the family, should have won some degree of respect and equality of status from their husbands. Yet, in theory at least, the subordination of women to men was vigorously taught. In the fourteenth century the Italian Del Lungo, in his work entitled *Women of Florence*, upholds this view in his "commandments" to women:

"The seventh commandment is that thou shalt not do any great thing of thine own accord without the consent of thy

---

[1] From Coulton, G. G., *Life in the Middle Ages* (1930). Four volumes in one. Vol. III, p. 15. Source extracts selected, translated and annotated by Coulton. Quoted by permission.

[2] See Power, Eileen, *op. cit.*, pp. 411–412.

husband, however good reason there seem to be unto thee for doing it : and take care thou dost on no account say to him, 'My advice is better than thine,' even though truly it were better, for by so doing thou couldst easily drive him into great anger against thee and great hatred."

Truly this advice would seem to have been wise, since husbands stirred by "great anger" were quite capable of inflicting permanent injury on their wives, as in the tale told by Geoffrey de la Tour Landry for the instruction of his daughters. In this tale a wife is described as answering "her husband before strangers like a rampe (*i.e.*, virago) with great villainous words, dispraising him and setting him at nought; . . ." Finally her husband, "angry of her governance, smote her with his fist down to the earth; and then with his foot he struck her in the visage and broke her nose, and all her life after she had her nose crooked, . . . And this she had for her evil and great language, that she was wont to say to her husband. And therefore the wife ought to suffer and let the husband have the words, and to be master, for that is her worship; . . ." [1]

During the fourteenth and fifteenth centuries were composed those tales for audiences of different social classes called the *fabliaux*. These stories, written by the *trouvères*, constitute, on the whole, a collection of anti-feminist writings, which at their worst were, in the words of a critic, "incredibly base and nasty." A good example of this sort of literature is *The Fifteen Joys of Marriage*, a bitter diatribe against women, which is ascribed to Antoine de la Sale (1388–1422) and was probably written for the middle class of artisans and traders. Each of the "joys" of marriage is described in a separate tale, setting forth the greed, vanity, deceitfulness, disloyalty and lustfulness of women, in the hope, perhaps, of warning single men to keep out of the "osier trap" of matrimony.[2] It was

---

[1] Coulton, G. G., *Life in the Middle Ages* (1930), Vol. III, p. 23. Translated from the "Book of the Knight of the Tower," c. 1371.

[2] See the translation made by Richard Aldington (Dutton, 1926).

not until Christine of Pisa (1363–1431) took up her pen in defense of her sex and wrote *La Cité des Dames* that any serious attempt was made to reply to the misogynists of the Middle Ages and to set forth the virtues, the talents and the useful accomplishments of women.

Home Life of the Common People under Feudalism. — Hitherto we have spoken chiefly of the family life of lords and ladies — a life much more favorable to the growth of refinement of feelings and manners than that of their humbler vassals. Yet it is the working masses of the people that are the chief prop of any nation and form the most numerous part of its population. These plain folk were divided in the later Middle Ages into three classes: (1) the trading class, which lived in the rapidly growing towns; (2) the yeomen, or free farmers; (3) the serfs, who were bound to the soil, and who owed clearly defined services in labor to their overlord. The last two classes lived in the country districts; and, whereas the serfs were often badly off, the yeomen owned their small farms and sometimes became so prosperous that poor knights sought their daughters in marriage as a means of repairing their fallen fortunes. The traders and handicraftsmen constituted the burgher or free citizen class of the towns and cities. By their own efforts they had passed through the training stages of apprentice and journeyman, had made a "masterpiece" in their craft and, if they had sufficient means, had paid the high fee which admitted them to full membership in their particular industrial gild. Then they received the proud title of "Master" and their wives that of "mistress," from which terms have sprung our modern democratic titles "Mr." and "Mrs."

A wide chasm intervened between the burgher class and the society of the castle or manor. Although traders and skilled craftsmen represented an intelligent third estate and some of them were becoming well-to-do, if not wealthy, yet the speech of the men and women of this class was extremely coarse and their manners were almost wholly lacking in refinement. So much is made plain by the popular literature of the time. These folk tales and verses are invaluable for the light they throw on the life of the common people out of which they sprang. Sorry is the showing made by the middle-class wives of the fourteenth century, who are depicted as poorly educated, ill-tempered and gross in speech and manners. The men are likewise coarse and tyrannical in their treatment of their wives. Apparently the women were left much to themselves and were expected to remain at home immersed in household duties and in the endless task of spinning. By the fourteenth century the spinning-wheel had been invented, as is made plain by the illustrations of the period; but its use was confined to the well-to-do. Hence most thread and yarn were spun with the ancient hand spindle. Now this work could be carried on in groups as well as singly; so it is not surprising to learn that women took to "gadding about" and meeting with their neighbors for gossip, not infrequently in the taverns of the town. To this social dissipation their husbands often objected and enforced their prohibitions with smart blows. For the laws of the age permitted any husband to beat his wife into submission so long as he broke no bones nor destroyed an eye! Wright describes a scene in a French farce of the fourteenth century in which a group of husbands suddenly appear in a tavern where their wives have assembled. They try to drive the women home with angry words and when these fail they resort to blows. In a rage the wives resist and the scene ends in a general scuffle.

But although popular literature reveals the gulf that exists between the coarse-mannered burgher or yeoman family, and the more refined society of the lord's court, yet there are evidences that already this gap was being bridged at not a few points. As the burghers gained in wealth they grew in power and influence and were able to wrest valuable rights and privileges from king and noble. They began to build substantial houses in the important trading towns; they traveled and became intelligent observers of men and affairs in other lands. Also they showed a disposition to send their daughters to convents to be educated and to dress both wives and daughters with a richness rivaling that of the ladies of the castle. Books treating of good manners, called " courtesy books," began to be written in England from about 1430 on, although they had appeared in Italy and France more than a century before. These evidences of increasing wealth and refinement did not escape the notice of some of the impoverished knights of the period who had squandered their substance. Not a few of these wasteful gentlemen were driven to seek alliances with the daughters of wealthy burghers, trading their title and social position for the rich dowry of their brides. Needless to say such unions, entered into with contempt by the man and with discomfort and humiliation by the woman, were rarely happy. Yet they served in some measure to break down the rigid barriers between classes in medieval times and gradually to acquaint the middle class with those more refined sentiments and manners which had come to flower in the feudal castles.

FAMILY NURTURE AND TRAINING IN THE LAST CENTURIES OF THE MIDDLE AGES

At the close of the medieval era parents understood little more of the principles of child hygiene and household sanitation than they had known a thousand years before. In consequence, the mortality rate among infants and young children was appallingly high. Women were expected to be fruitful during their entire fertile period, with no attempt to "space" children as in modern times. It was not uncommon for a woman to bear fifteen or more children, although only three or four would ever grow to maturity. In the words of Dean Inge, "a melancholy procession of cradles and coffins" succeeded each other in most fifteenth-century homes; and the death of infants was piously ascribed to the will of God.

Family discipline remained severe, sometimes even harsh and cruel, and children were brought up to regard their parents with awe. Fathers and mothers no doubt believed that the frequent use of the rod was necessary to enforce that instant obedience and almost servile respect of parents that the age demanded; and the church taught in and out of season the old maxim, " spare the rod and spoil the child." The didactic books of manners and morals which became popular during the fifteenth century enjoin children to rise early, wash and dress and then seek out their parents to kneel and humbly ask their blessing. It is told of Sir Thomas More, Lord High Chancellor of England a century later, that he never entered his court in the morning without first making his way to the more modest court of his father to beseech his blessing. Many well-brought-up children were taken to mass every morning before breakfast and after their breakfast were required to stand reverently beside the table while grace was said, making the sign of the cross. Well-bred children might not sit in the presence of their parents without permission and addressed them in letters as "Right worshipful" mother, or father, as the case might be.

In feudal times the English custom of sending children, both boys and girls, away from home to be trained in the homes of others was firmly established. An Italian who accompanied a special mission from Venice to England in 1496–1497 was unpleasantly impressed by this practice and describes it as follows:

"The want of affection in the English is strongly manifested towards their children; for after having kept them at home till they arrive at the age of 7 or 9 years at the utmost, they put them out, both males and females, to hard service in the houses of other people, binding them generally for another 7 or 9 years. And these are called apprentices, and during that time they perform all the most menial offices; and few are born who are exempted from this fate, for every one, however rich he may be, sends away his children into the houses of others, whilst he, in return, receives those of strangers into his own. And on inquiring their reason for this severity, they answered that they did it in order that their children might learn better manners. But I, for my part, believe that they do it because they like to enjoy all their comforts themselves, and that they are better served by strangers than they would be by their own children." He adds that the children "never return, for the girls are settled by their patrons, and the boys make the best marriages they can, and, assisted, by their patrons, not by their fathers, they also open house and strive diligently to make some fortune for themselves ; . . ." [1]

Possibly this Italian visitor to England tended to exaggerate the frequency of the English custom of sending children away from home for training in the houses of strangers. Yet there is a solid basis of fact underneath his criticism. The middle and poorer industrial classes did very generally apprentice their children to others to learn useful trades, and the nobility likewise often sent their boys and girls to the castles of great lords to be trained in gentle manners and taught the arts of war and of courtly life. Apparently mothers and daughters sometimes tired of each other's society and the mother used every effort to get her daughter "placed" in some outside family. Thus Margaret Paston, a member of a respectable family of English farming "squires," writes her son Sir John Paston in 1469, urging him to "purvey" for his sister "to be with my Lady of Oxford, or with my Lady of Bedford, or in some other wurshepfull place, wher as ye thynk best, . . . for we be eyther of us werye (weary) of other." [2] Doubtless Margaret Paston hoped that by placing her children in the homes of powerful lords or rich patrons their chances of material advancement and of making a good (*i.e.*, profitable) marriage were considerably enhanced. Agnes Paston's second

---

[1] Sneyd, C. A., ed., *A Relation of the Island of England* (London, printed for the Camden Society, 1847), pp. 24, 25.

[2] *Paston Letters*, 1422–1509 (Edinburgh, 1910), Vol. II, Letter 601.

son John Paston III was placed in the home of the Duke of Norfolk and her daughter Elizabeth was put to work in another household.[1]

Not rarely this apprenticing of children must have entailed for them overwork, lack of affection and loneliness. Poor little Dorothy Plumpton, one of these placed-out daughters, wrote her father "diverse messages and writings," urging him to let her come home, to which no reply was made. The girl finally writes her indifferent parent : "Wherefore it is thought in these parts . . . that you have little favour unto me; the which errour you may now quench, if it will like you to be so good and kind a father unto me." [2]

The marriages of children were still arranged by their parents (if not by patrons), and mercenary considerations played the chief part in marital arrangements. Stern old Agnes Paston made every effort to marry her young daughter Elizabeth to a rich widower of fifty named Stephen Scrope, who, by his own account, was disfigured in consequence of a long illness. To overcome the natural distaste of her daughter for this marriage the mother beat her once or twice a week for months and her head was "broken, in two or three places." Finally the poor girl yielded to her mother's will; but fortunately the plan fell through for some reason not known. However, for ten years Elizabeth remained in her home, the wretched victim of her mother's sharp tongue, and apparently quite unwanted, until her marriage with Robert Poynings was at last arranged and she was off her scheming mother's hands.[3]

Occasionally reference to a love match appears in the Paston correspondence, as in the case of Margery Paston, who fell in love with the chief bailiff of the Paston estate, a young man named Richard Calle. Terrible were the

---

[1] See Bennett, H. S., *The Pastons and their England* (Cambridge University Press, 1922), pp. 78-85.

[2] *Plumpton Correspondence*, p. 202. Quoted in Bennett, *The Pastons and their England*, p. 85.

[3] See *Paston Letters*, Vol. I, Letters 71, 185, 196. See also Bennett, *op. cit.*, pp. 31-33.

family scenes when Margery at last summoned up the courage to inform her parents that she had betrothed herself to a suitor held to be so far below her in social station. Finally her parents asked the Bishop of Norwich to examine the girl and learn from her if she had in truth formally pledged herself to marry the young man. For in the Middle Ages a formal betrothal was held to be as binding as a marriage. After the Bishop had questioned Margery, who bravely stood to her guns and admitted that she had plighted her troth in due form, she returned to her home only to find its doors closed against her by her mother's order. For some time Margery and her suitor stayed under religious guardianship at a nunnery in Blackborough until the family opposition had sufficiently weakened to permit of their marriage.

Progress and Retardation in the Middle Ages. — This brief survey of marriage and family life during the thousand years of the Middle Ages may serve to make clear to the student that real progress had been achieved in civilizing human relationships. Largely owing to the influence of Christianity, purchase marriage in its grossest form has been done away with; divorce has been forbidden by the Church; the relations between husbands and wives have become somewhat more friendly, brightened, here and there, by a love marriage; and parents in general have come to accept a definite responsibility for the religious and moral and even, sometimes, the intellectual education of their children. But it would be easy to overestimate the advances made by the family during the medieval period. Marriages were arranged for by parents on a monetary basis, with little consideration for the wishes of their offspring; children were regarded pretty generally as the property of their parents to be browbeaten and disposed of as seemed good to them; nowhere were boys and girls regarded as individuals with personal rights to be respected; the patriarchal family was as firmly intrenched as ever and the husband and father might be a domestic tyrant if he would, with the full protection of the law. Furthermore, the complete control of marriage and divorce by the Christian Church, although it unquestionably operated to increase the respect of the medieval barbarians for matrimony, yet was an ironclad regulation, taking little account of circumstances and bearing hard upon individuals. The age of regard for personal freedom and respect for individuality had not yet dawned.

SELECTED READINGS

SOURCES

Aldington, Richard (trans.). *The Fifteen Joys of Marriage* (ascribed to Antoine de la Sale, c. 1388–1462), Broadway Translations, 1926.

Coulton, G. G. (trans. and comp.). *Life in the Middle Ages*, 4 Vols. in one, 1930, Vol. I, pp. 216, 225–226; Vol. III, pp. 15, 114–115, 119.

——. *The Mediæval Garner*, London, Constable and Co., Ltd., 1910, pp. 383–502.

Furnivall, F. J. *Child Marriages, Divorces and Ratifications*, Early English Text Society, 1897, pp. 56–85.

——. *The Babees Book*, Early English Text Society, N. Trübner and Co., 1868, No. 32, pp. vii–xxii, lxiv–lxvi, 4–15.

Haddan, A. W., and Stubbs, Wm. *Councils and Ecclesiastical Documents*, Oxford, 1869–1878, *Pænitentiale of Theodore*, Vol. III, 173–213.

Paston Letters, 1422–1509, John Gairdner, ed., Edinburgh, 1910.

Sneyd, Charlotte A., ed. *A Relation of the Island of England*, London, Camden Society Publication, 1847.

Surtees Society Publications, Vol. LXIII.

Tacitus, Cornelius. *Germania.*

Thatcher, O. J., and McNeal, E. H. *Source Book for Mediæval History*, Scribner, 1907, pp. 549–562, 592–602.

Thorpe, B. *Ancient Laws and Institutes of England*, Folio, London, 1840, Vol. I, pp. 11, 22–23, 123, 254–257.

SECONDARY WORKS

Abbot Gasquet (Rev. Francis Aidan). *Christian Family Life in Pre-Reformation Days*, Educational Briefs, No. 17, Phila., 1907.

Abram, A. *English Life and Manners in the Later Middle Ages*, London, G. Routledge and Sons, N. Y., Dutton, 1913.

Bennett, H. S. *The Pastons and their England*, Cambridge University Press, 1922, Chs. III–VII.

Boesch, Hans. "Kinderleben in der deutschen Vergangenheit," in *Monographien zur deutschen Kulturgeschichte*, Leipsic, 1900, pp. 6–40.

Bücher, Karl. *Industrial Evolution*, S. M. Wickett (trans.), 1912, pp. 102–133.

——. *Die Frauenfrage im Mittelalter*, Tubingen, H. Laupp'sche, Buchhandlung, 1882, pp. 13 ff.

Buckstaff, Florence G. "Married Women's Property in Anglo-Saxon and Anglo-Norman Law," in *Annals of American Academy of Political and Social Science*, Vol. IV, 1893.

Chrisman, Oscar. *The Historical Child*, Boston, Badger, 1920, Ch. XI.

Crump, G. C., and Jacob, E. F. *The Legacy of the Middle Ages*, Oxford, 1927, Ch. VII, "The Position of Women," by Eileen Power.

Davis, Wm. S. *Life on a Mediæval Barony*, N. Y., Harper, 1923, pp. 72–112.

Encyclopedia of Religion and Ethics, "Teutonic Family," Vol. V, pp. 749–754.

Esmein, A. *Le Mariage en droit canonique*, Paris, 1891, 2 Vols., Vol. I, pp. 63–92; Vol. II, pp. 159 ff.

Green, Mrs. A. S. *Town Life in the Fifteenth Century*, Macmillan, 1907, 2 Vols. in one, Vol. I, Ch. I; Vol. II, Chs. I–IV.

Gummere, F. B. *Germanic Origins*, Scribner, 1892, Chs. III–VI.

Howard, George E. *History of Matrimonial Institutions*, University of Chicago Press, 1904, Vol. I, Chs. VI–VIII.

Jarrett, Bede. *Social Theories of the Middle Ages*, Boston, 1926, pp. 50–57, Ch. III.

Jeaffreson, J. C. *Brides and Bridals*, Hurst, 1782, Vol. II, pp. 299–325.

Lacroiz, P. *Historie de la vie privée*, Lacour et Cie, 1852, Vol. II, pp. 1–60.

Lecky, W. E. H. *History of European Morals from Augustus to Charlemagne*, N. Y., Appleton and Co., 1879, Vol. II, pp. 340 ff.

McAnnally, D. R. "About the Wedding Ring," in *Popular Science Monthly*, 1887, Vol. XXXII, pp. 71–76.

Phillips, M., and Tomkinson, W. S. *English Women in Life and Letters*, Oxford, 1926, Chs. I, II, III, VII.

Pollock, Sir F., and Maitland, F. W. *The History of English Law*, Little, 1895, Vol. II.

Putnam, Emily. *The Lady*, pp. 106–145, Sturgis and Walton, 1910.

Reich, Emil. *Woman through the Ages*, London, Methuen and Co., 1908, Vol. I, pp. 170–199.

Salzman, L. F. *English Life in the Middle Ages*, London, Oxford University Press, 1926, Chs. I, II.

Schuster, E. J. *The Wife in Ancient and Modern Times*, London, Williams and Norgate, 1911, Ch. VIII.

Smith, and Cheetham, A. *Dictionary of Christian Antiquities*, 2 Vols., 1875–1880, article by Ludlow on "Arrhæ," Vol. I, pp. 142–144.

Thrupp, John. *The Anglo-Saxon Home*, London, 1862, pp. 25–116.

Weinhold, Karl. *Die deutschen Frauen in dem Mittelalter*, Vienna, 1882, 2 Vols.

Wright, Thomas. *The Homes of Other Days*, pp. 22–113; *Domestic Manners and Sentiments in England during the Middle Ages* (same work appearing under both titles), London, Chapman and Hall, 1862; N. Y., Appleton and Co., 1871, Chs. II, III, VII, VIII, XI, XII, XX.

Wright, Thomas. *Womankind in Western Europe from the Earliest Times to the Seventeenth Century*, London, 1869.

Young, Ernest. "Anglo-Saxon Family Law," in *Essays in Anglo-Saxon Law*, ed. by H. Adams, Macmillan, 1876, Essay IV.

CHAPTER VII

THE FAMILY DURING THE RENAISSANCE

General Nature of the Renaissance. — The term "Renaissance" has been frequently criticized by contemporary historians, since it suggests a sudden outburst of creative energy, a rapid change in the interests, social, political, economic and intellectual, of the European nations. Such a view is manifestly incorrect. Throughout the entire course of the Middle Ages the barbaric peoples of Western Europe were slowly learning the principles which govern civilized societies — respect for property and law, consideration for the weak, and some regard for the finer, spiritual values of life. Very gradually the virile Lombards, Franks and Teutons, as well as the inhabitants of central and southern Italy, who were the pioneers of the new order, were educated by Church and State and the daily demands of economic and social life to the point where they may be said to have "caught up" with the civilizations of Greece and Rome. First in Italy, then in the northern countries, came an expansion of industry and trade, an influx of wealth, and with these the opportunities for leisure and the cultivation of mind and taste which commonly follow upon the solution of the more urgent economic problems of life. Hand in hand with economic development went the establishment of stronger central governments — national and, in Italy, municipal. These governments sought in some measure to curb the lawlessness of the nobility intrenched in castle and manor, to develop the resources of the country, to strengthen the respect for law and order, and to protect the burghers or free citizens in their remarkable development of the trade and manufactures of the country. All these influences had been silently at work for centuries, and the Renaissance merely marks the beginning of the harvest which we are still gathering. Thus the intellectual and æsthetic awakening of the fifteenth and sixteenth centuries was the outcome of many coöperating forces, all tending to open the eyes of men to the wonder and complexity and interest of human nature and human life. "Humanism," or the study of the pursuits and activities proper to mankind, as the literatures of Greece and Rome revealed them, was the absorbing interest of the times. With such study there went a heightening of the sense of personal power and worth, a flowering of the spirit of individualism which revealed itself in a freedom of thinking and of living unheard of in an earlier and cruder age.

EFFECT OF THE MOVEMENT UPON THE STATUS OF WOMEN

Social Effects: Freer Social Life of the Courts. — Such a movement of intellectual and social emancipation could not leave the homes and the women untouched. So we are not surprised to learn that in some respects the condition of the women of the Renaissance was markedly improved, while in others it remained practically unchanged until later influences had completed the work of emancipation. Certain it is that in France and Italy, and to a less extent in Germany and England, married women of the ruling class were permitted a far greater degree of freedom in social intercourse than was countenanced in the Middle Ages. The delightful accounts of Castiglione, the famous author of *The Book of the Courtier*, written in the sixteenth century, reveal an ease, refinement and freedom in the social life of the Italian courts. Society in the castles and palaces of the princes of Italy and France was becoming cultured and brilliant, and was distinguished by the important rôle assigned to the women. They participated fully in witty or learned conversation; they set the standards in manners and morals; they were frequently as well educated in the classics and as familiar with the highly spiced romances of the period as the men. Nobles and princes pledged their devoted service to the fair ladies of the court and sought to meet their ideals of what is suitable and pleasing in conduct and speech. The tales of Boccaccio [1] vividly portray the free social relations of men and women of noble birth and reveal a license in speech not sanctioned by cultivated society today. Indeed the period is noteworthy for its curious blending of the gross with the refined in conversation and manners. Castiglione and Boccaccio in Italy and Margaret of France [2] paint in glowing colors these Renaissance "salons" in the courts of the ruling dukes and princes. Conversation was characterized by the quick stroke and parry of repartee and wit, and at times was overloaded with literary allusion.

Something of the liberty accorded to married women was extended to the marriageable girls of southern countries. In most of the cities of Italy they were not immured so closely in convent or home as had been the case during the century preceding. At thirteen or fourteen years of age, when their education was thought to have been completed, French girls of noble family were brought out into the world as in modern times. This was accomplished in two ways: either the damsel was sent to be lady-in-waiting to some woman of princely rank who kept a "school of manners" at her court, or she was launched into society at her mother's side. Old-fashioned folk and the more serious-minded men, such as Vives, Spanish scholar and tutor to the Princess Mary of England, were horrified at such laxness and insisted that girls be shut away from all social influences until their marriage. Such had been the custom in the "good old times" of their youth. But the tide in France and Italy was strongly setting against such

---

[1] *The Decameron.*

[2] Sister of Francis I, King of France, a brilliant light among the intellectual women of France and author of a series of tales called the *Heptameron* which are modeled after the *Decameron* of Boccaccio.

strictness; and only Venice shut up its girls within convent walls, safely hidden from the eyes of men, until duly qualified suitors should carry away these nunlike maidens to adorn their homes.

In the northern countries of Germany and England the brilliant court circles of Italy and France were largely wanting. These nations were far slower in appropriating the elegancies and refinements of social life. The courts of Henry VIII and Edward VI showed few of the graces, intellectual and social, of the ducal courts of Mantua, Ferrara, Milan and Florence. Even in the golden days of great Elizabeth grossness of speech and manners was very general. And among the burgher or citizen class, not alone of England but of all countries, the refining influences of courtly speech and courtesy toward women very slowly filtered down. Yet we are told that as early as the fifteenth century English traders and artisans felt a growing sense of self-respect and dignity which tended to stir within them some aspiration for polite manners. From 1430 onward one *Book of Courtesy* after another appeared in England, for the use of gentlefolk and commoners alike. Clearly "manners" was becoming "a subject of serious anxiety," for might not the prosperous burgher enter the ranks of the gentleman by the judicious marriage of his son or daughter? [1] Some of these early manuals of etiquette have been collected and edited. A study of one of them, *The Young Children's Book*,[2] published about 1500, reveals clearly the need of such timely admonitions concerning manners at table and elsewhere. Children serving as pages at the tables of the nobility, or in their father's castle, are warned not to spit over or on the table, nor to throw bones on the floor. Another work of slightly earlier date called *The Babees Book* (1475) urges boys not to scratch themselves at table, not to stuff their food into a full mouth or pick their teeth with their knives. They are enjoined also not to dip their meat in the

---

[1] See Green, *Town Life of the Fifteenth Century*, Vol. II, Ch. I.
[2] Furnivall, *The Babees Book*, p. 17.

common salt-cellar, or put their knives in their mouths, or leave the table without washing their hands.[1] All these manuals reveal a growing regard for the decencies of life, a consideration for other people, which promises much for the gradual refining of life in the home as in the court.

Platonism and Platonic Love. — A study of the social changes wrought by the Renaissance would be incomplete without some mention of the profound influence of the study of Plato upon the prevailing conceptions of love between man and woman. The platonic doctrine that love aspires toward the beautiful, and by the stepping-stones of earthly loveliness is led toward that eternal and perfect beauty and goodness which is God Himself, found eager followers among the more refined spirits of the age. Even Cardinal Bembo espoused the doctrine and gave to it a marvelous impetus by his dignified plea for a more spiritual love between the sexes, untainted by carnal desire. By the end of the fifteenth century we are told that "every man of polish and refinement had selected a lady and become her servant." [2] Women, especially, were profoundly attracted by the new doctrine. Married at an early age, as all of them were, to men commonly quite unknown to them, many young women who had become mothers at sixteen remained ignorant of love. Neither their hearts nor their minds had been won by the husbands and masters whom they respectfully addressed as "Sir," while they signed their wifely letters your "wife and subject" or "your humble, obedient handmaid and friend." To such women, disillusioned and hungry of heart, the theory of celestial love, free from all fleshly dross, made a powerfully moving appeal. Margaret of France, and Elizabetta, Duchess of Urbino, with many other noble ladies, became leaders in the cult of spiritual love. De Maulde calls these women "unhappy dilettanti of love " [3]

---

[1] Furnivall, *The Babees Book*, pp. 4 ff.; see also "Stans Puer ad Mensam," *ibid.*, pp. 27-33.
[2] Boulting, *Women in Italy*, p. 27.   [3] *The Women of the Renaissance*, p. 186.

who strove with sincere earnestness to pass from earthly passion to a union of mind and soul with the beloved.

Yet, although some women, like the noble Vittoria Colonna, friend of Michelangelo, passed through the ordeal of platonic love with unscorched garments, there were others who paid the price of playing with fire. The literature of the period reveals great laxness in morals no less than ideals of purity and love. Doubtless platonism appealed less to men than to women, and its doctrines in many instances were utilized by the ambitious and the empty-headed as a means of pushing themselves forward in the world by gaining the good will of court ladies. Then, too, there must have been a goodly number of avowed platonists among men who found the doctrine of celestial love too ethereal for their complete acceptance. Such half-hearted devotees would warmly subscribe to the words of a young noble at the court of Margaret of France:

"Madam, when our mistresses stand on their dignity in halls and assemblies, seated at their ease as our judges, we are on our knees before them; we lead them out to dance with fear and trembling; we serve them so sedulously as to anticipate their requests; we seem to be so fearful of offending them and so desirous of doing them service that those who see us have pity on us, and very often esteem us more simple than foolish. . . . But when we are by ourselves, and love alone doth mark our looks, we know right well that they are women and we are men, and then the name of liege lady is converted into sweetheart, and the name of servitor into lover." [1]

So the courtly service of love was soon degraded from a romantic cult into a fashionable pastime. In the sixteenth century there arose Platonic Academies, which were in many respects nothing but courts of love. "Vanity strutted there and the devotees of love, in suitable Court-dress, exchanged Petrarchistic wailings before admiring princesses and their maids of honour at the palace." [2]

[1] *Heptameron*, Tale 40, and "Prologue" of first day; quoted in De Maulde, *op. cit.*, p. 351.   [2] Boulting, *op. cit.*, p. 33.

The resemblance that platonism bears to the earlier movement of the twelfth and thirteenth centuries, in which chivalrous love was exalted into a philosophy of life and codified into a legal system, is clearly apparent. Both movements originated in idealistic feeling that prompted its subjects to cultivate the more spiritual phases of love. Both degenerated into an artificiality in many cases insincere and fantastic. But it should not be overlooked that platonism, like its forerunner, did create within the souls of the more noble-minded men and women a realization of the true nature of ideal affection. Little by little men and women, here and there, came to see that there was really no necessary antagonism between love and marriage; that, although marriage might be, for the majority, a contract of a social and economic nature, into which love did not enter, yet for a few more fortunate spirits it might be the consummation of a pure, romantic affection and thus the crown of life. Castiglione voices this feeling when he makes the Magnifico say: "If my Court Lady be unmarried and must love, I wish her to love some one whom she can marry; nor shall I account it an errour if she shows him some sign of love. . . ." [1] This was an advanced position for a fifteenth century writer to take, one not at all in accord with the prevailing idea that love and marriage were incompatible. The actual situation is bluntly described by Boccaccio. "Everyone will concede," says this rare teller of tales, "that he has not a wife to his mind, but one that fortune has bestowed." For many generations the popular proverbs about women reflected the low esteem in which they were held by all but the most enlightened. It was an old saying in Bologna that "Woman is paradise for the body, purgatory for the soul, hell for the purse"; [2] and this proverb fairly reflected the feeling of the mass of men concerning the wives and mothers of the race. Yet the Court poets who sang the beauty and purity of women, who praised their gifts of mind and soul, not only stimulated

[1] *The Courtier* (1901), p. 225.
[2] Quoted in Boulting, *op. cit.*, p. 35.

some noble ladies to make themselves worthy of this high praise, but actually did accomplish something to elevate the conception of womanhood. So the seeds were sown in Italy which slowly ripened to the harvest of the nineteenth century.

Effects of the Renaissance upon the Legal Status of Women. Dowry, Dower and Property Rights. — If the social position of the more favored women was raised during the Renaissance, if they were educated and held in higher esteem, it yet remains true that little advancement was made in freeing them from the financial and legal disabilities of the Middle Ages. Very generally girls were regarded as eligible mates in proportion to the size of the dowry they could bring their husbands. Haggling by the parents over the essential matter of dowry was as open and unashamed as in any business transaction of the day. In Italy, at least, the wife's dowry was conveyed to the home of the husband immediately after the marriage ceremony had been performed, and a receipt was thereupon given for it. The management and profits of the dowry belonged exclusively to the husband, who quite often employed it as capital in increasing his business. He was required by law, however, to provide for the restoration of the dowry to his wife in case of divorce or his own death. In the latter event the dowry was held by the wife *in trust only* for her children. In Italy the wife's dowry seems to have been fairly well protected. The husband who squandered this property might be legally sued and required to restore not only the original amount but sometimes a threefold sum. On the other hand, the custom of setting aside a definite portion of the husband's property for the life use of his widow gained no foothold in Italy. In France and England, however, the law required that one third of the husband's real and personal property should descend to the wife after his death. This represents the "dower" of common law. At the beginning of the sixteenth century in England, however, the earlier custom of granting the wife one third of the husband's *personal* property had fallen into disuse in many parts of the country. This meant that in the larger portion

of England a testator was no longer bound to leave his widow
and children any share of his movable goods and chattels, but
might bequeath all his personal property to whomever he
wished.[1]

In England a married woman possessed absolutely no property at her own disposal. In one respect only was the rigor
of this law at all relaxed. If property were left to a *trustee* in
trust for a married woman and designed for "her sole and
separate use, equity [2] would recognize this trust, and prevent
the husband from dealing with the property in a manner detrimental to the wife's interest." When the property was held
by a trustee for the wife's benefit, although not given to her
for her sole and separate use, equity *"was bound to follow the
law and allow the husband to claim it for his own; yet it would
not assist him in the claim, unless he agreed to make an adequate provision for her out of the fund."*[3] Even the personal
effects, clothing jewels, money, furniture, etc., which the
wife owned before marriage or which were bequeathed to her
afterwards, became the absolute property of her husband.
However, the bed, apparel and ornaments of a widow, known
as her "paraphernalia," were restored to her *if her husband had
not sold them during his lifetime.*

From these provisions and others, which denied the wife
the right of contract and suit and the right to bequeath
property by will without the consent of her husband, it is
evident that the legal personality of the English wife was
almost wholly merged in that of her husband. Nor was this
condition peculiar to England. In Italy, although girls were
declared of age at fourteen they could transact no legal business
without the assent of both father and husband, or of their
trustees. Women in many Italian states were also deprived of
the right to enter a lawsuit in their own names or to appear in

---

[1] Cleveland, *Woman under the English Law*, p. 173.
[2] Equity is a system of law designed to supplement and correct common law,
especially where the latter seems rigorous and unjust.
[3] Cleveland, *op. cit.*, p. 108.   Italics mine.

person at the trial. The justification for this widespread attitude must be sought in history. During the lawless centuries of the Middle Ages, when brute fighting strength was a valuable asset in the defense of property and personal rights, women were in real need of the protection which fathers, brothers and husbands could afford them. In such periods the qualities of women as peace-lovers, home-makers and dispensers of charity always tend to be rated far below their real social value when contrasted with physical force. So women came to be regarded as weak dependents upon father or husband; and the laws and customs respecting women naturally reflected popular sentiment. Both Protestant and Catholic canon law recognized the husband's property in his wife, her legal subjection to him and his absolute control over her property.

The persistence of medieval ideas and customs concerning the subjection and the duties of women into the freer period of the Renaissance is clearly brought out in literature. In the well-known tale of *Paolo and Francesca*, the middle-aged husband Giovanni kills his beloved young brother Paolo when he surprises him in the chamber of his girl-wife Francesca, whom he also kills. Public opinion appears to have sustained the husband in the exercise of his ancient rights. Again, in Shakespeare's comedy *The Taming of the Shrew* the playwright puts into the mouth of the shrewish Katherine, now thoroughly tamed by her husband's method of starvation, the prevalent theory of the age regarding women. Katherine is addressing two other young wives who show signs of rebelling against their husband's commands :

> "I am ashamed that women are so simple
> To offer war where they should kneel for peace,
> Or seek for rule, supremacy and sway,
> Where they are bound to serve, love, and obey.
>
> . . . .
>
> "Come, come, you froward and unable worms!
> My mind hath been as big as one of yours,
> My heart as great; my reason, haply, more,
> To bandy word for word and frown for frown;

But now I see our lances are but straws;
Our strength as weak, our weakness past compare, —
That seeming to be most, which we indeed least are.
Then vail your stomachs, for it is no boot,
And place your hands below your husband's foot:"[1]

THE CHURCH IN ITS RELATION TO MARRIAGE

The various streams of the Renaissance movement in Germany rather speedily combined in one vigorous current of religious revolt called the Protestant Reformation. Luther in Germany, Calvin in France and Switzerland and John Knox in Scotland sounded the trumpet of revolt and led the masses of the people in their attack upon the abuses that had grown up within the church. The result was apparently inevitable — a complete breaking away from the Mother Church and the establishment of several Protestant sects instead of the former unified body of Christians. From the sixteenth century onward "the Church" is a term which may apply to the Roman Catholic communion, or to the growing body of Lutherans in Germany, of Calvinists in Switzerland, Holland and Scotland or of Anglicans in England, where the break with the Roman Church was more gradual than in Germany and was accomplished without an open revolt on the part of the English people.

The Roman Church and the Family. — In the previous chapter [2] reference was made to the fact that the Church, in taking the stand that betrothals in words of the present tense (*per verba præsenti*) constituted valid although not legal marriage, had prepared some very perplexing problems for itself. In the twelfth century Peter the Lombard had declared [3] that spousals (*sponsalia*) *per verba præsenti* (*i.e.*, in words of the present tense, as "I *take* thee," etc.) constituted a valid and binding marriage, whereas *sponsalia per verba de futuro* (*i.e.*, in words of the future tense, as "I *will take* thee," etc.) had no

---

[1] Act V, Scene II.
[2] See pp. 223–224.
[3] In his *Sentences*, Book IV.

such binding power. This famous Schoolman is, then, largely responsible for the fact that the Church was caught in a mesh of verbal distinctions which had deplorable results. Men and women (or boys and girls) who contracted unions in words of the present tense were held to be as indissolubly bound together as if the marriage had occurred within the church before witnesses, had been duly recorded and had been consummated by physical union. Of course a marriage thus loosely contracted, with witnesses few or none, could be easily disavowed. Dishonorable men had no difficulty in finding persons to declare in the proper ecclesiastical court that they had never really espoused the woman, but had only formed an illicit relationship with her. Clandestine marriage increased in frequency from the twelfth century onward. Such unions were common in Holland, Portugal and Italy, as well as in Germany and England. "So severe," writes Howard, "were the provisions of Swiss legislation to check this evil, toward the close of the Middle Ages, that even the innocent were deterred from appealing to the courts to enforce their matrimonial rights." [1] Endless difficulties arose with respect to abandoned wives and children, and the Bishops' courts of the fifteenth and the first half of the sixteenth century were kept busy adjudicating such matrimonial cases. A further difficulty was created by the fact that the difference between the present and the future tense is not sharply defined in everyday speech either in German or English. Martin Luther, with his wonted bluntness and energy, has pointed out this fact : "They [2] have played a regular fool's game," he writes, "with their *verbis de præsenti vel futuro*. With it they have torn apart many marriages which were valid according to their own law, and those which were not valid they have bound up. . . . Indeed I should not myself know how a churl [3] would or could betroth himself *de futuro* in the German tongue, for the way one be-

---

[1] Howard, *History of Matrimonial Institutions*, Vol. I, p. 346.
[2] The authorities of the Roman Church.
[3] A countryman.

troths himself means *per verba præsenti*, and surely a clown knows nothing of such nimble grammar as the difference between *accipio* and *accipiam;* [1] therefore he proceeds according to our way of speech and says; 'I will have thee,' 'I will take thee,' 'thou shalt be mine.' Thereupon 'yes' is said at once without more ado." [2]

At the Council of Trent in the middle of the sixteenth century the Roman Church cut the Gordian knot of this perplexing problem in one clean stroke. This famous Council decreed that, whereas all marriages previously contracted by mere verbal consent of the parties and without parental sanction should be held valid, thenceforward all marriages not celebrated in the presence of a priest and two or three witnesses should be null and void. By this decree the Roman Church freed itself from the evils of clandestine marriages and took a decisive forward stride toward making marriage a public concern. Indeed a step toward publicity had been taken as early as 1215, when Pope Innocent III required that the banns of marriage be three times published in the Church before the ceremony was performed. But this decree was not rigidly enforced, although the marriage rituals of the Renaissance period all contain careful directions for asking and publishing banns. The Council of Trent, while decreeing that publication of banns be everywhere enforced, did not take the further step of making such publication essential to a valid marriage. Hence the nobility had little difficulty in obtaining a license from the bishop, dispensing with the obligation of publishing their marriage banns.[3]

With respect to divorce, the Roman Church maintained the position which it had held during the later centuries of the Middle Ages. Since marriage was a mystical sacrament ordained of God, it was an indissoluble union. Only in cases

---

[1] *Accipio* — I take; *accipiam* — I will take.
[2] Luther, "Von Ehesachen," in his *Werke* XIII, p. 102; quoted in Howard, *op. cit.*, Vol. I, p. 341.
[3] See Howard, *op. cit.*, p. 361.

where the contracted parties were within the numerous forbidden degrees of kinship or were "spiritually related" could a *divortium a vinculo* be granted. This was in reality not a divorce but an *annulment* of a union held by the Church never to have really existed. Furthermore, in cases where adultery, desertion, impotency or extreme cruelty could be proven, the ecclesiastical courts granted the plaintiff a *divortium a mensa et thoro* which was only a legal separation. It has been pointed out in a previous chapter that during the Middle Ages annulments of disappointing marriages could be obtained by persons of wealth and influence without great difficulty. It is true that Henry VIII was unable to secure such a dissolution of his marriage with Catherine of Aragon; yet his sister Margaret Tudor was markedly successful in her "matrimonial adventures." Not only did she obtain papal sanction for her marriage with James IV, to whom she was related within the forbidden degrees, but she secured a divorce from her second husband on the trumped-up plea that James IV had lived for three years after the battle of Flodden Field and so was alive at the time of her second marriage.[1] But from the time of the Reformation to the present the Roman Church has enforced its view of the indissoluble character of a true marriage with great consistency.

Attitude of the Anglican Church toward Clandestine Marriages. — The Established Church of England unfortunately took no such sensible stand against clandestine marriages *per verba præsenti* as had the Roman Catholic Church. Hence England suffered from all the evils attendant on such marriages until the middle of the eighteenth century. Interesting evidence of the binding character of mere verbal contracts in words of the present tense is furnished in a rare old English book, *Of Spousals*, published in 1686. In this quaint work the author declares that in his own day spousals *de præsenti* were everywhere valid :

"But that woman, and that man, which have contracted

[1] See Howard, *op. cit.*, Vol. II, p. 58.

Spousals *de præsenti:* as, (I do take thee to my Wife) and (I do take thee to my Husband) cannot by any agreement dissolve these Spousals but are reputed for very Husband and Wife . . .; and therefore if either of them should in fact proceed to solemnize matrimony with any other person, consummating the same by Carnal Copulation, and Procreation of Children, This Matrimony is to be dissolved as unlawful, the Parties marrying to be punished as Adulterers, and their Issue in danger of Bastardy." [1]

Further evidence of the evils resulting from these loose verbal contracts is furnished by Furnivall in a valuable work on *Child Marriages, Divorces and Ratifications.* The evidence consists of depositions made in trials before the Bishop's court and the Mayor's court in Chester 1561–1566. This collection abounds in illustrations of the frequency of marriages *per verba præsenti,* especially among the common people. It also shows how numerous were the cases that were brought before the Bishop's court, either for the dissolution of such unions or for their enforcement when husband or wife refused to acknowledge the marriage. [2]

As early as 1540 Henry VIII had attempted to right this evil by a statute which was unfortunately repealed in the reign of Edward VI. Of this statute Swinburne writes as follows : "Worthily, therefore, was that Branch of the Statute of noble King Henry the Eighth, establishing (That marriages contracted and solemnized in the Face of the Church, and consummate with bodily knowledge, or fruit of Child or Children, should be judged and taken for lawful and indissoluble, notwithstanding any Precontract of Matrimony, not yet consummate with bodily knowledge, etc.) worthily, I say, and upon good ground was this Branch of that Statute (established by the Father) repealed and made void by his gracious Son King Edward the Sixth, for Spousals *de præsenti* though not consummate, be in truth and substance very Matrimony and

[1] Swinburne, *Of Spousals* (ed. 1686), p. 13.
[2] Early English Text Society (1897), Vol. 118, pp. 56–85.

therefore perpetually indissoluble except for Adultery. . . ."
Yet, in spite of the binding character of such contracts, the
writer goes on to say that Spousals "*de præsenti* be destitute
of many legal effects wherewith Marriage solemnized doth
abound. . . ." [1] These effects in civil law were, briefly, that
such a contract, not followed by a religious marriage, cost a
woman her right of dower in her husband's lands and rendered
her children illegitimate. With respect to the latter point,
however, the law of the English Church was not in harmony
with that of the State, as Swinburne makes clear:

"Concerning their issue, true it is, that by the Canon Law,
the same is lawful; But by the Laws of this Realm their Issue
is not lawful, though the Father and the Mother should afterwards celebrate Marriage in the Face of the Church. Likewise
concerning Lands by the Canon Law, the foresaid Issue may
inherit the same, . . . But it is otherwise by the Laws of this
Realm, for as the Issue is not legitimated by subsequent Marriage, no more can he inherit his Father's Land; . . ." [2]

Now, since Church law in England rested upon the sanction
of the State, it was the statutes of the realm that were followed
in all cases where disagreement arose. Hence many English
children were rendered bastards, whose parents were held to be
bound together by a verbal contract well-nigh as firmly as if
their marriage had been duly solemnized by a clergyman. Nor
could these children be made legitimate by the marriage of
their parents after their birth. Clearly the canon law was
more just in this regard than the civil statutes. In Scotland
the ruling of the church in respect to this matter was followed
as it is at the present time. Hence the subsequent marriage of
parents in Scotland legitimatized their children born out of
wedlock.

Not only did the Anglican Church hold two persons contracted in words of the present tense to be married, but the
ecclesiastical laws could force the parties thus contracted to

---

[1] *Op. cit.*, pp. 14, 15.
[2] *Ibid.*, p. 223.

solemnize the marriage. Should one of the parties refuse so to do, "he or she so refusing may for his Contumacy or disobedience therein, be Excommunicated : . . ." If after forty days, the party still remained obdurate, the Ordinary [1] might crave "the aid of the Secular Power, Whereupon a Writ *de Excommunicatio Capiendo*, is to be directed to the Sheriff, for the apprehension of the Body of the same Party Excommunicated ; who being apprehended by virtue thereof, is to be kept in Prison, without Bail or Maniprise, until he or she have humbled themselves and obeyed the Monition of the Ordinary, . . ." [2]   This being done, and the Church being satisfied, the Ordinary is to absolve the party and secure his release.

Views of Luther and the Protestant Reformers concerning Marriage. — It is clear enough that the English Church did not greatly change the *form* of marriage as a result of the Reformation, and such was the case in Germany. But a profound change of view was accomplished throughout the Protestant world with respect to the *nature* of marriage. No longer was it regarded as a mystical sacrament, but rather as a civil contract necessary to society and blessed of God. Luther is not always clear on this point, for he goes so far as to speak of marriage as a "most spiritual" status, "ordained and founded" by God himself. In the view of the great German reformer, marriage and the family constitute the very foundation stones of human society which would "fall to pieces" without them. Yet this profound reverence for the married state did not preclude Luther from viewing it as a "temporal business" with which the church should not interfere, but rather should "leave to each City and state its own usages and customs in this regard." [3]   On the whole Luther is distinctly favorable to the view that marriage is a *civil* matter to be regulated and perhaps celebrated by state authorities ; hence, as Howard has pointed

---

[1] A bishop or his deputy acting as an ecclesiastical judge.

[2] Swinburne, *op. cit.*, pp. 231–232.

[3] Luther, *Preface to the Short Catechism* (1529) ; quoted in Howard, *History of Matrimonial Institutions*, Vol. I, p. 387.

out, he must be regarded as the most influential agency in bringing about civil marriage.[1] Doubtless Luther was moved to take this ground by his belief that great evils grew out of Church jurisdiction in marriage, the most flagrant being the abuses connected with the enforced celibacy of priests. Also he held, like many others in his day, that ecclesiastical jurisdiction had produced the whole intolerable burden and perplexity of clandestine marriages, since it was the ruling of a Churchman that had elevated contracts *per verba præsenti* into valid matrimony. Because he clearly saw that the clergy were not true to their vows of celibacy and that many "lived in concubinage in return for a yearly tax paid to the bishop,"[2] Luther took the radical step of declaring the right of the clergy to marry — a right that he claimed to be based alike upon nature and the ·Scriptures. Not only did he preach this doctrine, but in 1525 he boldly acted upon it by marrying Katherine von Bora, a nun escaped from the Cistercian convent of Nimbschen. Little by little, as his followers recovered from the first shock produced by his action, they tended to accept the theory of the right of priests to marry. Somewhat later this came to be the view in England, where, in 1548, the obstacles to the marriage of the clergy were removed by statute law, even though the act declared that "it were most to be wished that they would willingly endeavour themselves to a perpetual chastity."[3] The statute was repealed, however, in the reign of Catholic Mary (1553–1558), and was not reënacted under Elizabeth, who had great distaste for the theory of a married clergy. A letter written by a married clergyman to the Archbishop of Canterbury in 1559 throws light on the unhappy position in which many married priests found themselves at this time. "The Queen's Majesty will wink at it [*i.e.*, the statute above referred to] but not stablish it by law,

---

[1] Luther, *Preface to the Short Catechism* (1529); quoted in Howard, *History of Matrimonial Institutions*, Vol. I, p. 388.

[2] For this whole discussion see Howard, *op. cit.*, Vol. I, pp. 386–389.

[3] Statutes at Large, Vol. II, p. 283.

which is nothing else but to bastard our children." [1]   It was not until 1603 that the statute of Edward VI was reënacted by James I in response to a petition addressed to him by numerous Puritans.

An important reform accomplished by the Protestant Revolt, not only in Germany but in all Protestant lands, was the sweeping away of many of the impediments to marriage established by the Roman Church of the Middle Ages.   Quite generally it was agreed that all barriers due to so-called "spiritual kinship" should be broken down and that persons should be permitted to marry within the third degree of consanguinity.   Unfortunately, both Germany and England tended to find impediments to marriage in the ancient Levitical law; [2] and this led, in England, to those acrimonious controversies over the right to marry a deceased wife's sister which have been unhappily handed down to the present time.   Moreover, despite the more liberal views of Luther on this matter, Protestants in all lands at first followed the ruling of the Mother Church, which positively forbade marriages between Christians and non-Christians.   Such unions were called "mixed marriages"; and German literature concerning marriage abounds in bitter discussions of the disadvantages attending such unions.

SPREAD OF CIVIL MARRIAGE

In consequence of Luther's insistence on marriage as a civil contract, the Protestant states gradually assumed authority over marriage, thus depriving the church of the power it had exercised since the tenth century.   Nevertheless marriages were celebrated solely by the church for a generation or more after Luther's death.   Indeed, although Luther did not insist on church marriage, he preferred it and wrote a model church ceremony.   Gradually, however, popular acceptance of the

---

[1] Howard, *op. cit.*, Vol. I, p. 396.
[2] Leviticus, XVIII, 6–19.

theory that marriage is a civil matter led to celebrations of marriage by civil officials as well as by the clergy in both Holland and Germany. England, on the contrary, clung to ecclesiastical marriage until well into the nineteenth century, with the sole exception of the period from 1653 to 1658 when Cromwell was Lord Protector of England. Shortly after Cromwell's accession to power a Civil Marriage Act was enacted by Parliament in 1653. This act prohibited ecclesiastical marriage and prescribed an obligatory civil celebration before a justice of the peace. To prevent unlawful unions the law prescribed that banns should be published three times in the church or an announcement of intention to marry should be posted in the market place. The magistrate who officiated at a marriage was required to demand a certificate declaring that publication had been duly made, as well as proof of the consent of parents to the union if the couple were under twenty-one years of age. In accordance with Puritan ideas, the marriage ceremony was stripped of all so-called "papistical" symbolism and the use of the ring was sternly prohibited. The ceremony consisted simply of the publicly expressed consent of the couple to take each other as husband and wife "in the presence of God the Searcher of all Hearts" and before the assembled witnesses. The justice then pronounced the couple to be man and wife.

Not only did the Cromwellian law delegate all authority over the celebration of marriage to the civil authorities but it provided that all "matters and controversies touching contracts and marriages" were to be referred to the justice of the peace or to such officials as the "parliament shall hereafter appoint." It is significant that the English Dissenters were apparently as opposed to divorce as was the Roman church, for no provision for trial of divorce cases was made under the Protectorate. One positive benefit conferred by the Civil Marriage Act should be mentioned here, *viz.*, that during this brief period a far more careful registration of marriages was made than had been previously practiced. Other benefits consist in the blow struck by the act against clandestine marriages and in the conferring of authority over marriage to the State. But these advances were short-lived, since, after the Restoration of Charles II in 1660, the Act was repealed. In the Puritan colonies of Plymouth and Massachusetts Bay, however, influenced as they were by the views of Luther and Calvin concerning the " temporal " nature of marriage, civil celebration of marriages, customary from the founding of the colonies, was made obligatory by law in Massachusetts Bay from 1646 to 1686. Similar laws provided for civil marriage in the colonies of Connecticut, New Haven and Rhode Island.

BETROTHAL AND MARRIAGE

Prevailing Customs. — As in the Middle Ages, marriage was preceded during the Renaissance by the solemn contract of betrothal. The student of the period is particularly impressed by four current ideas and customs with respect to espousals and marriage: (1) The popular sentiment concerning the character of marriage; (2) the predominant part played by the parents in arranging the marriage; (3) the early age at which betrothal and marriage ceremonies were performed; (4) the view of betrothal as a binding contract second only to marriage in its indissolubility. Concerning the first it may be said that there was little advance over the later Middle Ages in the mercenary character of marriage. It was still looked upon as a convenient social arrangement for securing the birth of legitimate children and advancing the social or financial status of the contracting parties. Not only was romantic love usually unassociated with marriage, since the bride and groom quite commonly had no acquaintance previous to their betrothal, but it was a general belief that the two had nothing in common. "Marriage," wrote Margaret of France in the sixteenth century, "is not a perfect state; let us be satisfied with wisely accepting it for what it is, a makeshift, but reputable." [1]

[1] *Heptameron*, Tale 40, quoted in De Maulde, *op. cit.*, p. 49.

A social writer has further described the marriage of the Renaissance age as "a business partnership, a grave material union of interests, rank and social responsibilities, sanctified by the close personal association of the partners. . . . To mingle with it love, the absolute, great enthusiasm of heart or intellect, was to lay up for oneself disasters, or at least certain disappointment." [1] Such was the prevalent view of the marriage relation in all the countries of Western Europe during and long after the Renaissance period. It is not surprising, then, to read the following contemporary account of a court marriage in England so late as the seventeenth century.

"On Thursday was a marriage at Court betwixt Lord Mandeville's eldest son and Susan Hill, a kinswoman of the Lord Marquis.[2] They were married by the Lord Keeper in the King's Bed-chamber, who took great joy in it, and blessed the Bride with one of his shoes. The principal motive of this Match, besides fair words and promises, was the paying back of £10,000 or security for it, of that sum the Lord President [Lord Mandeville, the groom's father] lent when he was made Lord Treasurer; and some say the Lord Marquis ties his own land for £5000 more; and withal he [*i.e.*, the groom] is to have a table of ten dishes and bouche [3] at Court (as they call it), which began the day of the Marriage, till some better place fall to his lot. Indeed he had need of some amends, having forsaken a Match of £25,000 certain with the Lady Craven's daughter, that was designed and reserved for him." [4]

So these two pawns, the young Mandeville and the girl relative of the Duke of Buckingham, are married to make good a debt owed the groom's father; and the young man receives the condolences of his friends for giving up a better marriage bargain. Only among the poorer classes, who dance on the village greens and frolic together in holiday seasons, is there

[1] De Maulde, *op. cit.*, pp. 22, 23.
[2] Later Duke of Buckingham, favorite of James I.
[3] *Bouche* means victuals, eating, living.
[4] Nichols, *The Progresses . . . of King James I* (collected from MSS. and rare papers), Vol. IV, p. 805.

any free choice in marriage.   And even here it is in some degree restricted by financial considerations and parental authority.

The second noteworthy fact concerning Renaissance marriages is the controlling part taken by the parents in all the arrangements.   There was general agreement that young girls, and, perhaps to a somewhat less degree, young men, must be prudent and not insist on marrying to please themselves if they would escape the penalties of such outrageous folly.   Marriage was a serious affair to be discreetly, not to say shrewdly, arranged by the parents and relatives of those concerned.   Not only did all men hold this view, but it seems to have been the expressed opinion of some of the most able women of the time, such as Margaret of Valois and Anne of France, eldest daughter of Louis XI.   The future husband of Lady Jane Grey, a girl of sixteen, was presented to her by her parents with not a word of warning, and she was informed that their commands concerning him would be duly communicated to her.   Very rarely did a girl rebel against the matrimonial plans of her parents. Yet in 1579 Margherita Gonzaga, who had been married at sixteen to Ercole II of Ferrara, an elderly man, twice widowed, wrote to her father concerning her sister's contemplated marriage : "Having heard that a marriage is being arranged between La Polisena and Gian Francesco Mainoldo, I am anxious to write four words to your highness, and I earnestly implore you not to allow her to be married against her will.   Your highness will recollect very well that when I was at Mantua and was asked if I believed she would be content, I replied that the Gonzaga knew how to endure what might be insupportable to others." [1]

The docility shown by most girls in respect to their marriage arrangements was doubtless due in some measure to the severity of home discipline.   But it must not be forgotten that with the decline of monastic fervor and the closing of many convents in England and Germany, the only career open to women was marriage.   Not to marry meant complete social failure, and a

[1] Quoted in Boulting, *Women in Italy*, p. 58.

galling dependence upon one's family for the whole of one's days. No wonder most young women shuddered at the thought of such a life and gladly chose the lesser evil.

The third custom which strikes the student of this period with peculiar force is that of child betrothals and marriages. Among powerful families, desirous of enhancing their social and political prestige, or of increasing their wealth, such contracts were very common. Children of high rank were sometimes betrothed by their relatives before they had left the cradle. Occasionally go-betweens were employed by noble Italian families to inform the relatives of a girl child of the most eligible young men in the marriage market and to negotiate the betrothal. Such betrothals often occurred when the girl was only three or four years old. The talented poetess Vittoria Colonna was betrothed to the Marquis of Pescara at this age, although the marriage did not take place until she was seventeen. This was rather unusual, as betrothals in Italy were often followed by marriage when the girl was twelve years old, this being the legal, marriageable age in most countries of Europe. In vain did physicians of the period point out that for the sake of the health of the wife and the vigor of the offspring, the consummation of marriage should be deferred until girls had reached their sixteenth year. Most parents were anxious to get their girls off their hands early in life, for it was regarded as mildly disgraceful to have a daughter unmarried or unbetrothed at sixteen or seventeen. Furthermore, since the girl's whole function in life was held to be wifehood and motherhood, and since most of her days would be spent in the home of her husband, parents rather sensibly held the opinion that a girl should go to her future home while she was in the plastic and impressionable age, before habits of thought and conduct had become definitely formed, so that she could not so easily be shaped to her husband's will. And be it remembered that quite often the husband was not of the same age as his girl bride. Young men demanded a period of freedom before thrusting their heads into the noose of matrimony. Thus it came about that men of thirty-five were betrothed to girls of fourteen, after their wild oats had been gayly sown.   At times, however, boys as well as girls were betrothed in their early childhood.

In a valuable work on *Child-Marriages . . . in the Diocese of Chester*, 1561–1566 A.D.,[1] Furnivall has collected depositions in trials conducted in the Bishop's court and entries from the Mayor's books, concerning betrothals and marriages in the English town of Chester.   These all go to show that in England, as in Italy and France, children were betrothed and married by their parents when mere infants.   Thus we find the case of one Elizabeth Hulse, married at four years of age to George Hulse, aged eleven, and seeking a divorce in the Bishop's court on the ground that "she could never fansie or cast favour to hym, nor never will do ; . . ."   The children were married in the chapel of Knotisford and on the girl being asked how she, a mere infant, knew of this fact, "she sais she knowis not, but bie the sayenge of her father & mother, forther, she sais, she was married to hym biecause her frendes thought she shuld have had a lyvinge bie hym ; . . ."   This unfortunate marriage was never consummated, since both parties proved obstinately reluctant to carry out the contract ; and it was probably annulled by the ecclesiastical court.   A similar case was that of Roland Dutton, married to Margaret Stanley when he was nine years of age and she but five.   As was customary the two children lived apart after the marriage until the age of puberty. When the time approached for the consummation of the union, the boy declared "that he would refuse to take the said Margaret to his wief ; and that he would not consent to the said marriage which was solempnized in his minoritie. . . ." Apparently in England, in the sixteenth century, children dared to assert their will against that of their parents when it came to marriage with an unpromising mate.   But these cases were doubtless exceptions to the general custom of meek compliance.   Quite often the court was appealed to for ratification

[1] Early English Text Society (1897), Vol. 118.

of a child marriage when the parties had attained a "ripe" age and desired to live together as husband and wife. Such a case is that of John Starkie and Alice Dutton, married four years previous to the action for ratification, at ten years of age, and now prepared to assume the duties of man and wife![1]

The fourth custom that impresses the student of the Renaissance period is the binding character of the betrothal contract. This, of course, was a heritage from the Middle Ages when betrothal was regarded as a form of marriage and the unchastity of the engaged girl was punished as severely as adultery. Espousal or betrothal was a ceremonious contract, broken only with difficulty and with some loss of prestige. In Italy, among the nobility, the bride-elect was quite often not seen by the young man until the day of the signing of the betrothal contract. Venetian girls, clad in white or peacock blue, with their hair hanging loose, were led into the room where were gathered their family and friends, the unknown suitor and the notary public. Dutifully the girl knelt before her parents to receive their blessing. Then followed the signing of the contract with due formality, after which it was taken by the notary to be published in the Palace of the Doges. Yet, in the sixteenth century, betrothals were more frequently annulled in Italy than in the Middle Ages — an index of the growing spirit of individualism. In Germany, however, Luther exercised all his powerful influence in favor of the customary view that betrothal is a contract no less solemn and indissoluble than that of marriage.

In Elizabethan England the popular mind seems to have been in some doubt concerning the parental practice of giving children in marriage against their will. Pamphlets were printed from time to time in which the pros and cons of parents' rights in this matter were vigorously debated. Davis refers to one such pamphlet in which the question was raised : Has not a father the right to bestow a child at will since "children are the goods of the parents"? A reply is flung

[1] Furnivall, *op. cit.*, p. 42.

back in another pamphlet : "Not so, children are not obliged to obey parents if forced into wedlock out of sordid motives; and to match a lively young woman unwillingly with 'an infirm and decrepit person' is most unwise and a great occasion for incontinency." The case is cited of a young woman forced to marry a rich old widower named Page. After the marriage the girl fell in love with a steward named Strawbridge and the two lovers, with the aid of two servants, strangled the old husband in his bed. The wife and the servants all fell under suspicion, were tried and hanged. Apparently this tragedy aroused strong popular feeling, for a ballad reciting the tale was hawked about which ended with this apt couplet :

> "Lord!   Give all parents wisdom to foresee,
> The match is marred where minds do not agree." [1]

The Marriage Ceremony. — Among the patrician classes, especially in Italy, where ceremonial was dearly loved, the rite of matrimony was performed with elaborate splendor. In the words of De Maulde : "The opening scene was as imposing and brilliant as the subsequent years of married life were to prove sombre and colourless." [2]   In gorgeous procession the bride and groom walked from their homes to the door of the church where the brilliant party was met by the priest.   Standing in the porch the priest put to the parties the momentous question : "Wilt thou have this woman to be thy wedded wife . . . ?" and "Wilt thou have this man . . . ?"   When the "I will" had been duly uttered, the couple were sprinkled with lustral water, after which the wedding procession wound through the nave to the altar rail, where the bridal mass was sung and the benediction pronounced. Then followed feasts and pageants, concerts, dramatic performances and dances, lasting for days together.   Brilliant pictures of the wedding festivities in Italian cities are painted

---

[1] See Davis, Wm. Stearns, *Life in Elizabethan Days*, p. 100.
[2] *The Women of the Renaissance*, p. 37.

by contemporary writers. We read of triumphal arches, decorated façades of palaces, lavish banquets with gold plate and ruinously costly decorations, the performance of dramas and musical fêtes, and the reading of poems written for the happy occasion by renowned literary lights.

As we have seen, not all marriages during the Renaissance were ecclesiastical and ceremonious. Until the Council of Trent (1545–1563) pronounced such unions null and void, it was not uncommon for a man and woman to marry themselves, in the presence of a notary and one or two witnesses, by simply holding hands and pronouncing the words "I take thee to be my wedded wife" and "I take thee to be my wedded husband." In Italy one witness to such a marriage was deemed sufficient if he were a priest, a magistrate or a notary since these men had the necessary skill to attest the validity of the marriage in writing. Indeed a promise and an exchange of rings constituted a marriage in Italy and elsewhere, although the absence of witnesses made it easy for the man thus married to abandon his wife if he chose.[1]

Many curious and uncouth wedding customs prevailed among the humbler folk during this period. In the more remote parts of Italy the bride kept up a plaintive wailing before her marriage, which is thought by some writers to be a survival of marriage by capture. Another quaint Italian survival, perhaps of purchase marriage, was the *serraglio*. When the bride was on her way to the church she was stopped by a band of young men, one of whom presented her with a bouquet, and received from her a ring in return, after which the bridal party proceeded to the church. At the wedding feast which followed, the recipient of the ring returned it in another floral offering to the bride ; whereupon the bridegroom was forced to ransom it with a sum of money which the young man and his companions spent in feasting and revels. De Maulde gives a realistic picture of French wedding festivities among the country people. "In the rural parts of France

[1] Boulting, *Woman in Italy*, pp. 68–72.

the company only rose from the table to sit down again, or to dance under the elms. Deep drinking, love, quarrels, broad jests, strange customs, such for instance as the *jus primæ noctis*,[1] or the drinking match, traditional with the country lads, — all this developed a boisterous gaiety. The bridegroom alone groaned under it, for among the middle and lower classes it was the correct thing to invite to one's wedding as big a crowd as possible. . . . When night came he had not even the right of taking his rest; ordeals of every kind lay in wait for him; and in the morning he was bound to go on laughing, to receive more visits, and profess himself the happiest fellow in the world." [2] One is perhaps permitted to wonder whether his lot was worse than that of his bride, shrinking from the rude songs and coarse pranks so popular at the time. For in those days, when primitive impulses and customs were not held in check by refined feeling, the bride and groom were put to bed by their friends to an accompaniment of practical jokes and full-flavored jests which must have caused many a sensitive soul to recoil in disgust. The wedding customs of the present day, sometimes not overrefined, are the lineal descendants of these coarser practices of Renaissance times.

HUSBAND AND WIFE

Authority of the Husband. — After the wedding festivities were fairly over, and husband and wife settled down to the daily routine of married life, the young bride had ample opportunity to discover that her path was by no means strewn with roses. A French writer of the sixteenth century thus describes what should be the attitude of a woman to her husband: "To pay honour, reverence and respect to her husband,

---

[1] A medieval custom which gave to the overlord the right to lie with the bride of any of his vassals on the wedding night. Sociologists are not agreed concerning the frequency or the prevalence of this practice.

[2] *Op. cit.*, pp. 38–39.

as to her master and sovereign lord . . . obedience in all things just and lawful, adapting herself and bending to the habits and disposition of her husband, like the useful mirror which faithfully reflects the face, having no private purpose, love or thought ; . . . she must be in all and through all with the husband . . . wash his feet, keep his house." [1] Nowhere can be found a more satisfactory statement of the relations of husband and wife during the centuries when the patriarchal family idea was paramount in Europe. The power of the husband to enforce obedience to his will by threats, blows and confinement to the house, was rarely questioned at this time. "Woman, good or bad, needs the stick" was an ancient and honorable saying in Tuscany ; and its observance was general throughout Western Europe. Only when the wife sustained severe bodily injuries did the law rather reluctantly intervene. Even Petrarch favored the occasional chastisement of wives ; nor did he perceive any more clearly than his contemporaries the startling incongruity between the courtly service of women and the practice of wife beating.

When they reflected upon the matter at all, men asserted themselves to be the superiors of women in all respects and therefore entitled to hold them in dutiful subjection. In *The Book of the Courtier* Castiglione makes the lord Gaspar say that "every woman universally desires to be a man" since man is "far more perfect than woman." Whereupon the Magnifico Giuliano replies : "The poor creatures do not desire to be men in order to be perfect, but in order to have liberty and to escape that dominion over them which man has arrogated to himself by his own authority." [2] As the discussion of women's weaknesses and virtues gayly proceeds among the courtiers, the lord Gaspar suggests that there are probably many husbands who "hourly wish for death" because of the "torment of their wives."

[1] Charron, "La Sagesse," quoted in Finot, *The Problem of the Sexes*, p. 86.
[2] *Op. cit.*, p. 185. Trans. from the Italian by Leonard E. Opdycke.

"'And what pain,' replied the Magnifico, 'can wives give their husbands that is as incurable as are those that husbands give their wives? — who if not for love, at least for fear are submissive to their husbands?'

"'Certain it is,' retorted my lord Gaspar, 'that the little good they sometimes do proceeds from fear, since there are few in the world who in their secret hearts do not hate their husbands.'"

Again the gallant Magnifico took issue with this hostile critic of women, and asserted that "wives nearly always love their husbands more than husbands love their wives . . ." and this in spite of the fact that many women known to him "suffer in this world the pains that are said to be in hell." [1]

Sometimes these unhappy women fled from their homes to escape unbearable ill usage at the hands of their husbands, only to be returned by their own fathers or brothers, "as a result of the appalling free-masonry between men."

Affection between Husband and Wife. — Yet it must not be supposed that hatred or indifference were the only feelings that animated husband and wife in the fifteenth and sixteenth centuries. The affection existing between some married pairs has come down to us in history. Who questions the love of Sir Thomas More, of Luther and of a score of lesser men for their wives, who generously returned this affection? The family relatives who selected the partners of their sons and daughters sometimes chose more wisely than could the young people themselves. An Italian husband, Giovanni Rucellai by name, wrote of his deceased wife that "she was a very dear lady to me and a good housewife and mother, preserved to me long, for she lived fifty-five years and departed this life Ap. 24, 1418, and this I account the greatest loss I ever suffered or ever could have." A century later Isabella Guicciardini wrote to her absent husband : "Realize what my condition is, always remembering that I cannot see you. . . . Do you think I am so happy, with two little maids, sometimes

[1] *Op. cit.*, p. 193.   Trans. from the Italian by Leonard E. Opdycke.

seeing folk and chattering, but mostly writing and praying and chaffering and keeping my accounts?" [1] The love of Margaret of Navarre for her faithless husband, Henri D'Albret, has been often related. And it may truly be said that whatever pain he may have caused her during her lifetime, he yet nourished a spark of genuine affection for his brilliant wife and sincerely mourned her death. A quaint chronicler of the day thus describes his grief : "What shall we say of the King, bereft of his Margaret? No longer did he run a strong course. He seemed as one swaying from side to side, wretched and ill at ease, like those, who, unaccustomed to the sea, cross from one vessel to another, trying to avoid falling into the water. So this poor prince strayed hither and thither." [2]

Some husbands and wives got along happily and comfortably, even with mild affection, by seeing little of each other. In such marriages undue strain was avoided by infrequent meetings. The woman did her duty as wife and mother when called upon to perform it. At other times she tasted the joys of a free being, — free to study, to manage her household and children as she saw fit, to mingle in the social life of the court and the castle. Meanwhile her spouse likewise enjoyed his liberty, sailing the seas, going to war, engaging in affairs of state and quite often enlisting in the chivalrous service of some fair feminine platonist as he moved from court to court. The wives of Italian tradesmen, too, enjoyed some freedom, since their husbands were often absent for months at a time carrying on their business in foreign cities. Such women, however, were usually closely watched by their husbands' relatives, who, in accordance with ancient custom in Italy, dwelt in the same neighborhood, as a family group, and kept a sharp lookout on the conduct of this otherwise unguarded wife. It is possible that English wives had greater liberty at this time than those on the Continent. A Dutchman writing in the sixteenth century comments thus on the liberty of Englishwomen :

[1] Quoted in Boulting, *op. cit.*, p. 100.
[2] Olhagaray, *Histoire de Bearn et de Foix.*

"Wives are not kept so strictly as they are in Spain or elsewhere. Nor are they shut up, but they have the free management of the house or housekeeping, after the fashion of those of the Netherlands and others their neighbors. They go to market to buy what they like best to eat. They are well-dressed, fond of taking it easy, and commonly leave the care of household matters and drudgery to their servants. . . . In all banquets and feasts they are shown the greatest honour. . . . All the rest of their time they employ in walking and riding, in playing at cards or otherwise in visiting their friends and keeping company, conversing with their equals (whom they term gossips) and their neighbors, and making merry with them at child-births, christenings, churchings and funerals; and all this with the permission of their husbands, as such is the custom. Although the husbands often recommend to them the pains, industry and care of the German or Dutch women, who do what the men ought to do both in the house and the shops, for which services in England men are employed, nevertheless the women usually persist in retaining their customs. This is why England is called the paradise of married women. The girls who are not yet married are kept much more rigorously and strictly than in the Low Countries."[1]

Unfaithfulness in Marriage. — During the Renaissance, as at the present time, the double standard of morals prevailed. Even then, however, fair-minded men here and there questioned its justice as most men and women question it today. On the whole, however, the unfaithfulness of the husband to the marriage bond was lightly regarded and mildly punished, while adultery on the part of the wife sometimes met with death — at least within the circle of the Italian courts. Castiglione has cleverly expressed the argument of the ages in support of a double moral standard and has met this argument with a cogent reasoning hard to refute. My lord Gaspar states the affirmative position in the following words:

[1] Quoted in Hill, *Women in English Life*, Vol. I, pp. 115–116.

"Therefore . . . it is wisely ordained that women are allowed to fail in all other things without blame, to the end that they may be able to devote all their strength to keeping themselves in this one virtue of chastity; without which their children would be uncertain, and that tie would be dissolved which binds the whole world by blood and by the natural love of each man for what he has produced."

To which the Magnifico pertinently replies:

"But tell me why it is not ordained that loose living is as disgraceful a thing in men as in women, seeing that if men are by nature more virtuous and of greater worth,[1] they could all the more easily practice this virtue of continence also; and their children would be neither more nor less certain, for although women were unchaste, they could of themselves . . . in no wise bear children, provided men were continent and did not take part in women's unchastity. But if you will say the truth, even you know that we men have of our own authority arrogated to ourselves a license, whereby we insist that the same sins are in us very trivial and sometimes praiseworthy, and in women cannot be sufficiently punished, unless by shameful death, or perpetual infamy at least."[2]

In Southern lands, in Italy and France, the immoralities of the husband were more open, although probably not more frequent, than in England and Germany. Francis I, king of France, publicly remarked that the man who lived without a mistress was a "nincompoop"; and it is certain that term could never have been applied to him. The custom of buying slave girls, Circassians, Tartars and Russians, in the markets of Venice was quite common during the Renaissance. The dignified Cosimo de' Medici, patron of scholars and artists, was not above owning a beautiful Circassian slave girl, who served as his mistress and who became the mother of his bastard son Carlo de' Medici. The wealthy burghers in Italy were as

---

[1] Lord Gaspar had just contended for the greater virtue, strength and perfection of men.

[2] *The Book of the Courtier*, p. 206.

frequent offenders as the nobility in respect to keeping slave concubines or mistresses. Ostensibly these girls were employed in well-to-do middle-class families as nurses and domestic servants, but usually they were completely at the disposal of their masters. Much ill feeling was no doubt caused in families by these illicit unions; and yet few Italian women would have dreamed of making this offense a cause for separation. If a woman had a comfortable home and a reasonably kind husband, why should she complain? Indeed the attitude of many good wives of the period toward their husbands' illegitimate children seems to the modern student of history surprisingly generous. Quite frequently they received these little ones into the family and brought them up with their own children. The illegitimate son of Cosimo de' Medici was reared in his own family. The noble Elizabetta, Duchess of Urbino, brought up her illegitimate niece; Bianca Maria Visconti took charge of her illegitimate granddaughter, Caterina Sforza, until the child's father married again, when his new wife accepted and reared her with her own little ones. This same Caterina paid her debt of generosity when she brought up her husband's illegitimate child with her own offspring.

Occasionally penalties were visited upon adultery even when committed by men. In parts of northern Italy an adulterer was condemned to lose an eye, besides paying a heavy fine, if any one chose to bring him to judgment. In other parts of Italy both the man guilty of rape and the adulterer were fined. Then, too, women of means and influence in all Christian countries could obtain legal separation from an unfaithful husband through the ecclesiastical courts; but such relief seems to have been rarely resorted to in the South, though it was fairly common in England among the well-to-do.

But were wives always faithful to their husbands, however erring these might be? Apparently not. It is not strange that, married when very young to men unknown to them, ardent women yielded to temptation and fell passionately in love. In the courts of France and Italy a degenerate platonism emphasized the importance and the joys of love; and the whole subject of sex relations was freely and continually discussed. In an atmosphere surcharged with sentiment not a few young wives forgot their marriage vows. Sometimes the husbands, themselves unfaithful, shut their eyes to the errors of their wives so long as they acted with some discretion. But the stern old law of Rome, repeated in the law of the Lombards, permitted a husband to put his adulterous wife to death if surprised in the act. At one time or another the wives of the proud Dukes of Ferrara, Mantua and Milan paid with their lives for the crime of adultery.

It is noteworthy that a commission appointed by Henry VIII made an elaborate report on the *Reformation of Ecclesiastical Laws*. In this report the radical suggestion was made that divorces *a vinculo* (giving the right of remarriage) be granted for adultery, malicious desertion and mortal enmities; and that divorces *a mensa et thoro* (from bed and board), which were legal separations giving no right to marry again, be abolished.[1] But England was not ready for this radical step, and legal separation granted by an ecclesiastical court remained for many years the only mode of divorce in cases of adultery.

THE HOMES OF THE RENAISSANCE

Improvements in Architecture and Furnishings. — With the growth of industry and commerce and with the resulting increase in wealth there went a marked improvement in the homes of the upper and middle classes, both in architecture and furnishings. The desire for more beautiful and comfortable homes was first felt in Italy long before the northern countries had outgrown their taste for the uncomfortable castles and manor-houses of the late Middle Ages. One of the most splendid of the Italian palaces was that of Urbino,

[1] Cleveland, *Woman under the English Law*, p. 226.

built by Duke Federico di Montefeltro in the fifteenth century. Castiglione thus describes it :

"Among his other praiseworthy deeds, he built on the rugged site of Urbino a palace regarded by many as the most beautiful to be found in all Italy ; and he so well furnished it with everything suitable that it seemed not a palace but a city in the form of a palace ; and not merely with what is ordinarily used, such as silver vases, hangings of richest cloth of gold and silk, and other similar things, — but for ornament he added countless antique statues in marble and bronze, pictures most choice, and musical instruments of every sort, nor would he admit anything there that was not very rare and excellent. Then at very great cost he collected a goodly number of most excellent books in Greek, Latin and Hebrew, all of which he adorned with gold and silver, esteeming this to be the chiefest excellence of his great palace." [1]

Such a passage is valuable not only as giving the reader a peep into the luxurious homes of Renaissance princes, but also as serving to illustrate the rapid development of æsthetic and intellectual taste during the period. What noble of the Middle Ages would have spent his gold in pictures, statues and rare books in foreign tongues to beautify his castle and enrich his mind? Feudal days were past now and the homes of nobles no longer housed a company of retainers and fed them in the great bare halls. Instead there was an appalling number of trained and paid servants attached to every important household. One lady of Ferrara in the sixteenth century boasted a personal staff of four secretaries, a chief lady and seven maids of honor, six maids of the bedchamber, doctors, equerries and other servants to the number of nearly two hundred. Surrounded by this small army of attendants, the Renaissance lady of France and Italy lived amid costly and beautiful surroundings. The delicately carved furniture, stiff and uncomfortable though it doubtless was, the splendid plate and glass, the elaborately decorated beds with lace covers,

[1] *The Book of the Courtier*, p. 9.

silken hangings, and gold fringe, as unhealthful as they were elegant, the tapestries and hangings of stamped leather, the walls painted in the wonderful frescoes of great artists — all these were evidences of the luxury of princely homes.

But there is a darker side to this glowing picture. The lack of sanitary arrangements in these splendid palaces would shock to the core of his being the modern man of the middle class. The windows were still innocent of glass and wind and rain were kept out by oiled linen, often torn and dirty. The crowd of elegant pages of the court of Ferrara were provided with but one comb and one copper wash basin among them, with which to make their toilets. Indeed, the ducal family were not above using pewter dishes, when not entertaining prominent guests, and ordinarily ate simple food. Everywhere sumptuousness rubbed elbows with dirt and discomfort.

The houses of the English nobility during the reigns of Henry VIII, Edward VI, Mary and Elizabeth were gradually made over into comfortable and even luxurious dwellings. In a *History of Leicestershire* [1] a writer of the sixteenth century describes the homes of the great nobles and the numerous staff of servants kept to manage them. As the English nobility emerged from the semi-barbarity of medieval life in castles and manors, they found it necessary to hold in check their household staffs by a code of minute domestic regulations governing all the servants from the steward to the pot-boy. Frequently the households of dukes and earls were conducted with something of the splendor and formality of the English court. Lofty Gothic dining rooms took the place of the bare eating halls of the medieval castle. Chapels were built in connection with every great house and choral services were held there daily until long after the Reformation. Richly carved ceilings, Flanders tapestries and armorial bearings were found everywhere, intertwined with family proverbs and devices. Privacy, almost unknown in the

---

[1] Nichols, *op. cit.*, Vol. III, p. 681.

medieval castle, was now dearly prized. The lord and lady
no longer slept in the hall of the castle; but each had a lofty
chamber, with the sleeping rooms of attendant squires, pages
and gentlewomen close at hand. Family portraits hung on
the walls and armchairs began to take the place of uncomfortable stools.

Yet in England, as in Italy, conditions existed in the homes
of the nobility that would be deemed intolerable by families
of modest means today. Although a few plaited mats and
rugs from Turkey might be found in the castles of noblemen,
yet in most homes, even up to the king's palace, the floors
were covered with rushes gathered in the early spring and
expected to do service for an entire year. During the spring
and summer season this natural carpet was not unpleasant;
but in winter, after months of droppings of grease, ale, dirt
and all sorts of rubbish had sifted through the floor covering,
the case was quite different. Multitudes of vermin bred in
the rushes and even climbed the walls into tapestries and
hangings. Before the next March brought a new supply of
rushes and a cleaning out of the old, fastidious gentlemen and
ladies found the odor almost insupportable and carried about
with them a scent-ball to be held daintily to the nose. Wax
and tallow candles lighted the rooms of the gentry, but, as
they were somewhat costly, ordinary rooms were still lighted
by candles of rushes dipped in evil-smelling kitchen fat.

The homes of the prosperous middle class in the English
towns showed improvements not unlike those of the nobility.
As early as the fifteenth century the merchants of Bristol and
other towns began building fine houses three stories in height,
some of the more pretentious ones having a tower in which
treasures of silver plate were securely stored. Underground
were great cellars with groined roofs where wine and ale were
kept. The ground-floor commonly was used as a warehouse or
shop where the merchant or master craftsman plied his trade.
Above were the living-rooms and bedchambers of the family,
sometimes with a fine hall built out in the rear, having a lofty

roof of carved timber. Wealthy burghers emulated the nobility in hanging their walls with tapestries. But few, if any,
of these middle-class homes could boast a library; for these
traders were practical materialists as yet, with little interest in
the things of the mind.[1]

It is evident that the improvement in the architecture and
furnishings of English homes did not always commend itself
to conservative natures with a bent for looking back to "the
good old times." In a *Description of England in Shakespere's
Youth*, Harrison writes thus gloomily of the changes that had
taken place:

"And yet see the change, for when our houses were builded
of willow, then had we oken men; but now that our houses are
come to be made of oke, our men are not onlie become willow
but a great manie through a Persian delicacie crept in among
us, altogether of straw, which is a sore alteration. . . . Now
have we manie chimnies, and yet our tenderlings complaine
of rheumes, catarhs and poses. Then had we none but rere-
dosses and our heads did never ake. For as the smoke in those
daies was supposed to be a sufficient hardning for the timber of
the house; so it was reputed a far better medicine to keepe the
goodman and his familie from the quack or pose, wherewith as
then verie few were oft acquainted."

One is permitted to wonder what this dissatisfied gentleman
would have thought of the household improvements other than
chimneys which were introduced a generation later, — such
innovations as glass for windows instead of oiled paper or linen,
mattresses in lieu of straw pallets, and feather pillows instead
of the hollowed log of earlier times. Yet conveniences were
scarce in those days, and even in nobles' houses the introduction of a few unexpected guests meant that the host might have
to give up his own toilet accessories, since there were not
enough to go around! Erasmus ascribed the frequency of the
plague in England "partly to the incommodious form and bad
exposition of the houses, to the filthiness of the streets and

[1] Cf. Green, *Town Life in the Fifteenth Century*, Vol. II, p. 84.

to the sluttishness within doors. The floors," says he, "are commonly of clay, strewed with rushes, under which lies unmolested an ancient collection of beer, grease, fragments, excrements . . . and everything that is nasty." [1]

Home Industries. — Although the development of the gilds in the late Middle Ages tended to put men in control of industries previously carried on solely by women, yet there was much productive labor still remaining for the busy housewives to do. Even great ladies found their time fully occupied in directing the work of their large retinues of servants, in keeping careful accounts of household supplies and expenditures, in making conserves and brewing medicines from herbs carefully stored in the herb room of every household. All food such as butter, cheese, bread, ale and wine was carefully measured and weighed before being given to the servants; and noble ladies frequently attended to this work themselves. Caterina Sforza, wife of the Duke of Milan, was reputed to be an excellent housekeeper, and during her lifetime made a large and valuable collection of recipes.

The wives of nobles of large estates not only had household duties to perform, but, in the absence of their lords, they kept buildings in repair, supervised the labor on the land and replenished the stores. Henry Percy, Earl of Northumberland, declares that "in this state of England wifes commonly have a greater sway in all our affairs than in other nations Germany excepted." [2]   In the morning hours the lady devoted much time to distilling drinks. In a quaint work on *The English Housewife*, written in the seventeenth century, the writer mentions *twenty-two* distilled drinks from mint, hyssop, thistle, dill, and other herbs too various to mention.

But if noble ladies were busy in directing servants and making drinks and confections, what shall be said of the wives of yeomen and tradesmen? Certain it is that they were astir with the dawn in summer, and at five on dark winter mornings.

---

[1] Quoted in Furnivall, *The Babees Book*, p. lxvi.
[2] *Archæologia*, Vol. XXVII, pp. 339–340.

The prosperity of the whole family was felt to be in large measure in the keeping of the prudent housewife. English rhymes expressed this feeling in the jingle:

> "For husbandry weepeth
> Where huswifery sleepeth
> And hardly he creepeth
> Up ladder to thrift." [1]

So the *Hausfrau* in Germany and the "good wife" in England carried on a variety of domestic industries such as curing meats, brewing ale, dipping candles, making soap, baking bread and doing all the family cooking. A modern writer describes in detail the process of bread-making: "The bake-house with its bolting house and sieves attached, its 'troughs to lay Leven in,' its moulding tables, its brake for kneading or 'dough sheet' for treading the dough, and its large brick oven, was the heart of the culinary department." [2] If the goodwife made white bread, she ground the coarse meal upon "block stones" in good old primitive fashion, bolted it through fine bolting cloth and thus carried out all the processes from the beginning.

The author of the *English Housewife* says of the art of malt-making that the "office belongeth particularly to the Housewife; and though we have many excellent men-malsters, yet it is properly the work and care of women, for it is a house-work and done altogether within doors where generally lyeth her charge; . . ."

But these were only a part of her activities. When the food and drink were prepared, the housewife turned to her spinning-wheel, ever at hand; or she heckled hemp and flax, carded wool and scoured and bleached yarn. When the woolen or linen cloth was spun, woven, cleansed and sometimes dyed, she made it up into garments for the family. The weaving of the cloth was quite often done outside the household at this time by village weavers employing in their own homes a limited number

---

[1] Tusser, *A Book of Huswifery* (ed. 1812), p. 236.
[2] Markham, *The English Housewife* (ed. 1683), pp. 185–186.

of apprentices and journeymen. When the material, duly woven, had been returned, it was customary in some well-to-do-families to send it to the village tailor to be made up, or to employ the tailor at home. Increase of wealth and luxury were causing some country people to be dissatisfied with the old home-made products and to sigh for the more elegant goods made by craftsmen in the larger cities. These skilled artisans were taking over some of the industrial processes formerly belonging to the housewife. Caps and gloves, hosiery, shoes and girdles were quite commonly manufactured by master workmen in highly specialized trades which were organized into gilds. Card-makers, combers, clothiers, weavers, fullers and dyers all plied their separate trades and had their gild organizations from which women, with the exception of widows of gild members, were generally excluded.

Home Nurture and Education. — As in the Middle Ages, midwives were very largely employed in the delicate office of bringing children into the world. Only in specially serious cases were men physicians summoned to lend their aid. A curious Renaissance custom, handed on from earlier times, decreed that the Italian mother should receive the congratulations of her friends shortly after the birth of a child. Hence there was often a stream of visitors pouring in and out of the "lying-in-chamber," felicitating the parents and admiring the infant. Frequently gifts were presented to mother and child in these days. Families were very large, and the strain upon the woman, who began her duty of child-bearing at a ruthlessly early age, must have broken her health in many instances. Quite commonly a girl-wife became a mother at sixteen, as did the young Marchioness of Este, who proudly announced to the citizens of Modena in 1499 that "this 25 Mar. at the tenth hour by the ineffable grace of God, we gave daylight to two lusty female twins." But children born of girl-wives and boy-husbands were not always "lusty." The rate of infant mortality was terribly high in this age when medicine, antisepsis and sanitation were in their infancy. Apparently girl babies received but a scant welcome, especially in powerful families, where boys were universally desired. It is related of Isabella, the beautiful and talented Marchioness of Este, that she put aside a gilded cradle, prepared for a boy, when a female child was born to her. On this melancholy occasion Lorenzo de' Medici actually wrote a letter of condolence to the disappointed father.[1]

Midwives took charge of mother and child for some days after the birth. Quite often they were ignorant and superstitious women whose skill, so far as they had any, was gained through much practice unenlightened by sound theory. A quaint book for the benefit of German midwives was published by one Rueff, about 1580. He gives the following advice to these women concerning the care of their tender charges:

> "Now mark with diligence what I say to you,
> The child shall bathe every day,
> With lukewarm water, and soon
> After the bath thou shalt anoint it
> With oil of roses to make it healthy.
> Thou shalt also, at the same time,
> Stretch its limbs up and down
> Until it can stretch itself.
> Thou mayst also delicately bend them for him
> While they are still so tender
> According to thy pleasure, as thou wilt
> By which means they will be well-formed.
> Likewise mayst thou also carefully shape
> The ears of the child while they are still soft,
> The nose in order that the outline
> May be clear and smooth." [2]

Rueff also recommends the practice, not yet wholly forgotten, of hanging red corals around the neck and arms of children. "This strengthens the child," says Rueff, "and makes it happy and virtuous." The medieval custom of swaddling children was still prevalent in all the countries of Europe. The wrappings were commonly retained until the child was nearly a year old; and one wonders why such treat-

---

[1] Boulting, *op. cit.*, p. 165.
[2] Boesch, *Kinderleben in der deutschen Vergangenheit*, p. 17.

ment, still quite general in the south of Europe, did not result in the child's losing the use of his arms and legs.

Because of the Catholic doctrine that unbaptized infants lost all share in the joys of heaven and were condemned to the pains of hell, great care was taken that the baptism of the child should take place at the earliest possible day. Well-to-do families sought to make a baptismal ceremony a sumptuous and expensive affair. In Venice the infant of noble birth was taken to the church in pompous procession, carried under a canopy or in a gilded chair. Splendid baptisteries were built in many churches where gathered the parents, godparents and friends of the child in their richest silks and brocades. Costly presents to the parents as well as the infant candidate for baptism were expected of every god parent, and the expense this custom entailed upon them was so great that sumptuary laws were passed in Italy and Germany to regulate the practice. Likewise the banquets furnished by parents to the baptismal party were lavish in the extreme. In Magdeburg in 1583 all entertainment at the baptism of a child was abolished by law, with the exception of a simple meal to the midwives.[1]

Although it was the general custom during the Renaissance for mothers to nurse their infants, yet this practice was by no means universal. Despite the protests of physicians and learned men the women of the well-to-do classes tended to shirk their duty in this respect and to turn their children over to wet-nurses. An Italian moralist of the fifteenth century declaimed hotly against the custom, declaring that mothers deserved the hate of their children who put them "to the slavish breasts of Tartars and Saracens and the women of other animal and outlandish folk." Even if the mother suckled her children, foreign-born slave nurses were employed by most prosperous Italian families to care for them during childhood. Frequently the children were sent to foster-nurses in the country, where they remained until they had passed the more

[1] Boesch, *Kinderleben in der deutschen Vergangenheit*, p. 28.

troublesome stages of infancy and early childhood. This custom was more general in France and Italy than in England, where the nurse, selected with some care, commonly entered the family and took charge of the children until they were fully grown. Quite commonly her position in the family was dignified and responsible, and she often won the affectionate esteem of her foster children. An instance of this is furnished by Shakespeare's talkative nurse in *Romeo and Juliet*, who was a real foster-mother to her charge whom she dearly loved. Readers of Shakespeare will recall her affectionate words:

> "God mark thee to his grace!
> Thou wast the prettiest babe that e'er I nursed;
> And I might live to see thee married once,
> I have my wish." [1]

Home Training. — During the Renaissance, as in all ages, the early training and education of children was confided to the mother, even where nurses were employed. She it was who formed the speech of the child with loving care, as she formed its manners and morals and gave it the earliest instruction in religion. A writer of the period pays tribute to the mothers of Ferrara who "possess a truly admirable quality; they train their children so well in courtesy, manners and the show of breeding that all the ladies of all other lands might copy them." Numerous works appeared in the fifteenth and sixteenth centuries admonishing parents to the utmost diligence in the upbringing of their children, especially with regard to their religious and moral training. Both Catholics and Protestants vied with each other in exalting the importance of family education, and in urging parents to a fuller appreciation of the responsibilities of parenthood. In 1498 appeared in Germany the *Seelenführer*, or *Soul's Guide*, a handbook of instruction with much good advice addressed to fathers and mothers. The author declared with earnestness that all Christian instruction should begin in the family.

"Let parents, therefore, be admonished to see that their

[1] *Romeo and Juliet*, Act I, Sc. III.

children grow up in Christian fear and reverence, and that their home be their first school and their first Church.   Christian mother, when thou holdest thy child, which is God's own image, on thy knee, make the sign of the holy cross on his forehead, on his lips and on his heart, and as soon as he can lisp teach him to say his prayers.   Take him betimes to confession, and instruct him in all that is needful to make him confess rightly.   Fathers and mothers should set their children a good example, taking them to mass, vespers, and sermons on Sundays and saints' days as often as possible." [1]

A catechism by Diedrich Coelde, which was published about the same time, exhorts parents to teach their children the Lord's Prayer, the Apostles' Creed, and the Ave Maria. Morning and evening they should bless their little ones, then make them kneel to God in thanksgiving.   Children should be taught to say "Benedicite" and "Gratias" before and after meals, to eat and drink with moderation, and to behave modestly in the streets.   Parents are warned that most of the sin in the world is the result of bad training in the home; and hence they are urged to be strict in discipline and not to spare the rod.

With somewhat broader outlook Luther writes on family instruction.   Recognizing, as he did, "three hierarchies, established of God" — the State, the Church and the family — he taught that the family was the basis of the other two.   From the Fourth Commandment it is obvious that God attaches great importance to obedience to parents.   "Where this is not the case, you will find neither good manners nor a good government. . . ."   Family government is the basis of all other government.   "For where obedience is not maintained at the fireside, no power on earth can insure . . . the blessings of a good government; . . .   If now the root is corrupt, it is in vain that you look for a sound tree or for good fruit." [2]   Rever-

---

[1] Quoted in Janssen, *History of the German People*, Vol. I, p. 31.
[2] *Exposition of Exodus*, 20 : 12, quoted in Barnard, *German Teachers and Educators*, p. 131.

encing, as he did, the married state, as well as that of parenthood, Luther writes with enthusiasm of them both. "The parental estate God has especially honored above all estates that are beneath Him, so that he not only commands us to love our parents, but also *to honor* them." Parents should appreciate profoundly the responsibility resting upon them, "to train up their offspring for society and the Church. . . ." "Let every one know, therefore, that above all things it is his duty (or otherwise he will lose the divine favor) to bring up his children in the fear and knowledge of God; and if they have talents, to have them instructed and trained in a liberal education that men may be able to have their aid in government and in whatever is necessary." To bad or neglected home training Luther attributes most of the social evils of his time. Hence he earnestly declares : "No one should become a father unless he is able to instruct his children in the Ten Commandments and in the Gospel, so that he may bring up true Christians. But many enter the state of holy matrimony who cannot say the Lord's Prayer, and knowing nothing themselves, they are utterly incompetent to instruct their children." At least once a week the father, as head of the family, should examine his children in the Ten Commandments, the Creed and the Lord's Prayer. On rising in the morning and retiring at night children should repeat these foundation principles of Christianity, and neither food nor drink should be given them until they have fulfilled this important duty.[1]

Doubtless there was much more formal religious training given to children in the sixteenth century than now. Religion played a more prominent part in the lives of individuals and of families in those days than in this more secular-minded age. Well-nigh every noble house had its chapel, where the family assembled daily to hear priest or chaplain read the mass or the service of the reformed sects.

Discipline was severe in those days, and the parent was warned by the Church itself against neglecting the rod. Al-

[1] Cf. Painter, *Luther on Education*, Ch. VI.

though there is evidence that gentler methods were beginning to prevail in Italy, such was not the case in the Northern countries.   Children knelt daily to receive parents' blessing, addressed them in formal terms of great respect, as "Sir" and "Madam," and were rarely permitted to sit in their presence. Even when fully grown, English girls in Edward VI's time were required to stand at the side of the room when visitors were present, unless the mother relented and gave them a cushion to kneel on.   For small offenses these young ladies were freely chastised with the large fans carried by their mothers — even before company ! [1]   Much evidence exists that severe home discipline was not only the practice but the accepted theory of the age.   Vives, the Spanish Renaissance scholar, and tutor of the Princess Mary,[2] urges mothers, while loving their children, to "hide their love, lest the children take boldness thereupon to do what they list.   Nor let not love stop her to punish her children for their vices, and to strengthen their bodies and wits with sad [*i.e.*, wise] bringing up." [3] Usually parents needed no urging to severity, and contemporary letters and accounts dealing with the discipline of children are painful reading to people of the present age, when regard for the individuality and self-respect of the child has perhaps gone too far.

In his quaint work, *The Scholemaster*, Roger Ascham, once tutor to the Princess Elizabeth, tells us of the upbringing of the gentle Lady Jane Grey as described by herself :

"One of the greatest benefits that God ever gave me is that he sent me so sharpe and severe Parents, and so jentle a scholemaster.   For when I am in presence either of father or mother, whether I speake, kepe silence, sit, stand, or go, eate, drinke, be merie or sad, by sewying, plaiyng, dauncing, or doing anie thing els, I must do it, as it were in soch weight, mesure, and

---

[1] Howard, *Lady Jane Grey and Her Times*, p. 110.

[2] Eldest daughter of Henry VIII.

[3] *Vives*, "Of the Instruction of a Christian Woman" (1523); edited by Foster Watson (London, 1912), pp. 128–129.

number, even as perfitelie as God made the world, or els I am so sharply taunted, so cruellie threatened, yea presentlie sometymes, with pinches, nippes, and bobbes, and other waies which I will not name for the honor I beare them, so without measure misordered that I think myself in hell till tyme cum that I must go to M. Elmer, who teacheth me so jentlie, so pleasantlie, with soch faire allurements to learning, that I thinke all the tyme nothing whiles I am with him. And when I am called from him, I fall on weeping." [1]

Intellectual Education. —With the Renaissance the intellectual growth of preceding ages came to fruition. Everywhere the boys, and often the girls, of prominent families were carefully instructed in the classical learning of the time. The revival of intellectual education came first to Italy, then penetrated the countries north of the Alps. England and Germany were among the last nations to be affected by the new culture. About 1500, Richard Pace describes a conversation at an English dinner table concerning the education of children. One man had just announced his intention of finding a good teacher for his children when another "burst out furiously with these words: 'Why do you talk nonsense, friend?' he said; 'A curse on these stupid letters; all learned men are beggars: . . . I swear by God's body I'd rather that my son should hang than study letters. For it becomes the sons of gentlemen to blow the horn nicely (apte), to hunt skilfully, and elegantly carry and train a hawk. But the study of letters should be left to the sons of rustics.'" [2]

Fortunately for the future of England, however, this medieval notion was not shared by many of the gentlemen of the day. Boys of noble families were carefully educated by tutors at home, not only in the Greek and Latin classics, but in music, "writinge, plaienge att weapons, castinge of accomptes." Quite often they were sent abroad with their

[1] *Op. cit.*, ed. by John E. B. Mayor (1911), p. 97.
[2] Prefatory Letter to Colet in Pace's *De Fructu;* quoted in Furnivall, *The Babees Book*, p. viii.

tutors to travel and become acquainted with the languages and institutions of other countries — especially France. The medieval custom whereby boys were sent away from home to the houses of prominent nobles and statesmen to be educated had by no means died out in sixteenth-century England. In 1511 the household of the Earl of Northumberland contained several "Yong Gentlemen at their Fryndes fynding," *i.e.*, supported by their relatives in order that they might learn letters, manners and warfare in the earl's castle and later be advanced to important posts at court or elsewhere. More than a half a century later the Earl of Essex sent his son to be educated, partly in the household of Lord Burleigh, and partly in that of the Earl of Sussex. In a letter to the former he states his purpose in the education of his boy to be — "so that he might . . . reverence your Lordship for your Wisdome and Gravyty . . ." and "frame himself to the Example of my Lord of Sussex in all the Actions of his Life, tending either to the Warres, or to the Institution of a Nobleman, . . ." [1]

The Renaissance brought not only a more liberal education to the sons of nobility and gentlemen, but it extended the benefits of culture to their daughters also. That quickened sense of the worth and possibilities of human personality, so characteristic of this age, opened the eyes of many parents to the capacities and talents of their girls and resulted in securing for them an education in the classical languages and literatures no whit inferior to that bestowed upon the boys. Many are the eulogies of learned women furnished by the literature of the time. Castiglione wrote of his ideal Court Lady, "I wish this Lady to have knowledge of letters, music, painting, and to know how to dance and make merry; . . ." [2] This view was apparently shared by many parents, not alone in Italy, but in France and England. A modern writer describing this education tells us: "Little girls sucked in Latin with their mother's milk; . . . they were given a tutor at an age when

---

[1] *Murdin's State Papers*, pp. 301–302, quoted in *The Babees Book*, p. xv.
[2] *The Book of the Courtier*, p. 180.

they ought to have been learning nothing but how to walk; at seven they were expected to be able to maintain a conversation, and at thirteen to have finished their studies and be ripe for matrimony." [1] The author refers here chiefly to French and Italian girls, who mature early; yet the statement needs little modification to apply to the girls of Northern lands. At the age of thirteen we are told that Mary Stuart made a public address in Latin; and at fifteen the ill-fated Lady Jane Grey was well versed in four languages and read Plato in Greek with appreciation. Quite commonly tutors were engaged to teach girls in their homes. Occasionally sisters and brothers were educated together by the same male teachers. This seems to have been a common practice at the courts of Italian despots. Caterina Sforza was instructed with her brothers and so were the daughters of the Grand Duke Cosimo de' Medici and the Duke of Mantua.

But it must not be supposed that all of the girls' reading was of a severely classical sort. The tales of Boccaccio and French romances modeled after them were eagerly read by French and Italian maidens and must have done woeful harm to moral standards by driving home to the minds of these young maids the dubious conviction that love should not be sought in marriage but rather outside its bonds.

In this brief account of the Renaissance education of boys and girls not a word has been said of the intellectual training of the common people. The reason is not far to seek, since such education hardly existed. The majority of women, at least, were very little affected by the revival of culture taking place during the fifteenth and sixteenth centuries. The wives of the respectable burghers of Germany, England, France and Italy were almost wholly illiterate in many instances, and were not at all ashamed of their ignorance, since no one looked upon it as discreditable. Their training was in household duties, and can be said to have been both varied and thorough. No girl was held to be ready for matrimony

[1] De Maulde, *The Women of the Renaissance*, pp. 91, 92.

who could not spin and weave, make and mend clothing, cook and brew, and tend the sick. Even the daughters of the highest nobility received some of this training. Vives is but expressing the accepted opinion of his age when he exhorts the mother of a carefully educated girl that "she shall, beside the learning of the book, instruct [her] also with women's crafts; as to handle wool and flax, to spin, to weave, to sew, to rule and over-see an house." [1]

Contrast between Home Education in the Renaissance and at the Present Time. — Cursory as is this study of home training and education during the Renaissance, perhaps it will serve to make clear how vastly more important was the rôle played by the family then than now. The units of society in the sixteenth century were families — not individuals as at present. The parents passed much more time at home than is possible for fathers and mothers in this age of factories, workshops, offices and clubs; and their personal responsibility for the religious, moral and industrial training of their children was pressed upon their attention by precept and example. The contrast presented by the exclusively home education of the Renaissance girl and the almost completely *extra*-home-training of the modern girl, is a striking one. At present the well-educated American girl spends most of her time between seven and twenty-one in activities and interests outside the family circle; and, at the end of her formal education, she may have had no instruction whatever in the duties of wife and mother. Today the State, as a super-parent, protects the right of *all* children to schooling, at least up to the age of fourteen, and compels parents to send their children to school. In Renaissance days discipline was harsh, sometimes to the point of actual cruelty, yet the State very rarely curtailed the authority of parents over their children, as it most certainly would do in similar cases occurring at the present time. Clearly, this encroachment of

[1] "Of the Instruction of a Christian Woman," in Foster Watson, ed., *Vives and the Renaissance Education of Women*, p. 123.

the government upon ancient family rights had then scarcely begun. The spirit of individualism, the respect for personal rights has so developed since the eighteenth century, that not only does public opinion condemn the severe punishments of that earlier age, but the State actively intervenes to protect the child, wherever necessary, from its own parents. All these changes and many others mark the revolution that has been silently effected in the power and influence of the family since the sixteenth century.

SELECTED READINGS

SOURCES

Castiglione, B. *The Book of the Courtier*, Scribner, 1901, pp. 171–194, 205–209, 218–227.

Eby, Frederic (ed.). *Early Protestant Educators*, N. Y. and London, McGraw-Hill Book Co., 1931, pp. 22–34.

Furnivall, F. J. *Child Marriages in the Diocese of Chester*, Early English Text Society, Vol. 118, pp. xxix, xxxv, xliii–liii, 56–71, 184–202.

Furnivall, F. J. *The Babees Book*, Early English Text Society, Vol. 32.

Harrison, Wm. "Description of England in Shakspere's Youth," in *Holinshed's Chronicles*, New Shakspere Society, 1877, Vol. I.

Knox, John. *First Blast against the Monstrous Regiment of Women*, English Scholar's Library, ed. by Edw. Arber, London, 1878, Part II, pp. 11–53.

Tusser, Thomas. *Five Hundred Points of Good Husbandry* (together with a *Book of Huswifery*), Wm. Mayor, ed., 1812, pp. 240–279.

Vives, J. L. "Of the Instruction of a Christian Woman," in Foster Watson, ed., *Vives and the Renaissance Education of Women*, N. Y., Longman's, Green and Co., 1912.

Withington, Lothrop (ed.). *Elizabethan England*, by Wm. Harrison, London, Walter Scott Pub. Co., no date, Chs. VII–IX.

SECONDARY WORKS

Boulting, Wm. *Woman in Italy from the Introduction of the Chivalrous Service of Love to the Appearance of the Professional Actress*, London, Methuen and Co., Ltd., 1910, Part I, Ch. I, Part II, Chs. I–VIII.

Cannon, M. A. *The Education of Women during the Renaissance,* Washington, Catholic Education Press, 1916.

Cleveland, Arthur R. *Woman under the English Law,* London, Hurst and Blackett, 1896, pp. 169–236.

Crane, T. T. *Italian Social Customs of the Sixteenth Century,* Cornell Studies in English, Yale University Press, 1920.

Davis, W. S. *Life in Elizabethan Days,* N. Y., Harper and Bros., 1930, pp. 39–47, 91–103.

Del Lungo, Isidoro. *Women of Florence,* N. Y., Doubleday Page, 1908, Ch. IV.

De Maulde, Renée la Claviere. *The Women of the Renaissance,* trans. by Geo. H. Ely, London, Swan, Sonnenschein, and Co., 1900, Book I, Chs. I–IV; Book II, Chs. II–IV.

Hare, Christopher. *The Most Illustrious Ladies of the Italian Renaissance,* N. Y. and London, Harper and Bros., 1911, pp. 3–43, 105–134.

Howard, Geo. E. *History of Matrimonial Institutions,* Chicago, University of Chicago Press, 1904, Vol. I, Ch. IX.

Howard, Geo. *Lady Jane Grey and Her Times,* London, 1822, pp. 86–96, 109–124, 153–163.

Hill, Georgiana. *Women in English Life,* London, Richard Bentley and Son, 1896, Vol. I, Period II, pp. 113–144.

Lanciani, Rudolfo. *The Golden Days of the Renaissance in Rome,* pp. 195–205.

McQuoid, Percy. *Shakespeare's England: an Account of the Life and Manners of His Age,* Oxford, Clarendon Press, 1916, Vol. II, Ch. XX.

Painter, F. N. V. *Luther on Education,* Philadelphia, Lutheran Publishing Society, 2nd ed., 1889, Ch. VI.

Phillips, M., and Tomkinson, W. S. *English Women in Life and Letters,* Oxford University Press, 1927, pp. 31–40, 94–98.

Putnam, Emily. *The Lady,* N. Y. and London, G. P. Putnam's Sons, 1910, pp. 158–210.

Reich, Emil. *Woman through the Ages,* London, Methuen and Co., 1908, Vol. I, pp. 157–169, 227–272; Vol. II, Ch. I.

Tickner, F. W. *Women in English Economic History,* N. Y., E. P. Dutton and Co.; London and Toronto, J. M. Dent and Sons, Ltd., 1923, Part II, Chs. V, VI, VII.

CHAPTER VIII

THE ENGLISH FAMILY IN THE SEVENTEENTH AND EIGHTEENTH CENTURIES

Social Classes in England in the Seventeenth Century. — Although the decay of the feudal system had the effect of weakening, in some degree, the barriers between the various social classes in England, yet these obstacles were by no means removed in the seventeenth century. On the contrary society was sharply marked off into grades, each jealously maintaining the precise degree of prestige that belonged to it and shutting its doors to most applicants for admission from other and lower social ranks. In those days it was exceedingly difficult for any man to pass from the life station in which he was born to any higher one. The plowman, the independent farmer, the artisan seldom, by any chance, rose from their humble stations to that of the gentleman. Occasionally a man of great talent made his mark in literature or the church and was granted a half-grudging admission to the ranks of the well-born. But these climbers were the rare exceptions. Not only was it next to impossible for any man to raise his social class, but it was exceedingly difficult for the laboring man even to change his place of abode and his kind of labor. Once apprenticed to learn a trade, that trade and no other he was expected to practice. Moreover, the artisan or plowman was forced by the English laws of settlement to ply his industry in the town or parish where he was born or trained. This economic inflexibility and its unfortunate effects upon the working-classes did not escape the more observant members of the English Government. We are told that towards the close of the seventeenth century "an attempt was made by the Commons to bring about some relaxation of the laws of settlement, in the full knowledge and avowal of the fact that such restraints created paupers, by preventing the people from seeking and from obtaining employment where the need of it existed, and by insisting upon their starving on the parochial pittance in places where it was an utter impossibility for capital to support labour." [1] But the state wholly failed to remedy the evil, which continued for many years after the seventeenth century.

At this time the English people were roughly divided into the following classes: [2] (1) the aristocracy and gentry, consisting in the year 1688 of about 16,600 families, having an aggregate income of about £6,000,000 a year derived from their landed estates. It has been calculated that of the 154,000 persons composing these families, above 80,000 were servants attached to the great households. Below the landed aristocracy were (2) the "freeholders of the better sort," numbering 40,000 and having an income of about £3,500,000 or £91 a year to each family. Every freeholder is assumed to have had two servants in his family, making 80,000 dependents in this class. Next came (3) the class of lesser freeholders or yeomen, numbering about 120,000 and maintaining (on estimate) about 60,000 dependents in their households. The total income of this class is estimated at £6,500,000 or about £55 per year to each family. These three classes, comprising nearly 176,000 families, and deriving their income almost wholly from the land, constituted about one fifth of the entire population of England. There should further be noted (4) the professional class, consisting of those nobles and gentry in the civil service, the army and the navy, together with lawyers, clergy and physicians; (5) the trading or merchant class; (6) the artisans and day-laborers. Among these

---

[1] See *8 and 9 Wm. III*, cap. 3; Sydney, *Social Life in England*, p. 141.
[2] See King, Gregory, *Scheme of the Income and Expense of the Several Families in England* (1688), quoted in Sydney, *op. cit.*, pp. 136 ff.

last should be included that miserable class of apprentices who were too often treated little better than slaves by the masters to whom they were bound for seven years by the Act of Apprentices of Elizabeth's reign (1562). It will be seen that, whereas the first three classes derived their income from the land, the last three were supported by their own labor in one form or another. These latter classes constituted about four fifths of the English population in 1688.

The Household Membership: Family and Servants. — It must not be forgotten that in the seventeenth century a man's family included not only his wife and children, but all his servants and retainers, from the chaplain who conducted services daily in the chapel of the great house down to the humblest kitchen wench. In those days the master and mistress of a retinue of attendants held themselves personally responsible for the moral and physical well-being of every servant; and, although they ruled their household literally with the rod, disciplining children and servants alike, yet they admitted their dependents to a degree of familiar intercourse that it would be hard to find today. The servants of a noble family were most frequently drawn from the neighboring respectable tenantry and were treated, not as hirelings, but as humbler members of the household, whose interests were identified with those of their employers. Indeed the name "servant" was applied indiscriminately in the seventeenth century to any one who served another, thus including the young gentleman who waited at his lord's table, and the young lady who served in the chamber of a peeress. Of this conception of service Bishop Heber writes: "There was then no supposed humiliation in affairs which are now accounted menial, but which the peer received as a matter of course from the 'gentlemen of his household,' and which were paid to the knights or gentlemen by domestics chosen in the families of their own most trusted tenants; whilst in the humbler ranks of middle life it was the uniform and recognized duty of the wife to wait on her husband, the child on his parents, the youngest of the family on his elder brothers and sisters." [1]

It was part of the busy life of most English gentlewomen personally to superintend the work of every member of the family if not to share in it. Only in the great households of wealthy peers did the steward take over the duties of supervision and training of servants which had always been the province of the housewife. The Earl of Cork had so enormous a retinue of household servants that he prepared a set of rules governing such matters as their work, their behavior, and the tables at which they should eat. For be it remembered that rules of precedence, determined by fine distinctions in social station and the grade of service performed, were as important and binding in the servants' quarters as in the apartments of their employers. With a view to the health of their souls, the Earl provided that all servants except officers "shall meet every morning before dinner and every night after supper at Prayers." The steward was empowered to examine and dismiss "any subordinate servant of ye whole Familie"; and he was enjoined to know all the women servants under "ye degree of Chamber-maydes" by name and not to change them often except for due cause. Separate tables were provided for the steward and "ye gents" and for the "Wayter" and other gentlemen; and "ye longe Table" in "ye Hall" was to accommodate all the lesser servants. [2] In many families the servants were called to family prayers daily and were examined by their mistresses every Sunday after church with the laudable intent of discovering what spiritual nutriment they had received from the sermon and how much they knew of the catechism and the Bible. We are told that Mrs. Walker, the pious wife of an English clergyman, taught her servants to read a chapter from the Bible every day, and as soon as

---

[1] Quoted in *Barnard's Journal*, article on "English Home Life and Education," Vol. 26, p. 379.

[2] See Bradley, *The English Housewife in the Seventeenth and Eighteenth Centuries*, p. 132.

one of the group had learned to read intelligently, she presented him or her with a Bible. At the hour of family prayer the whole household gathered together, including the farm laborers; and if any man was paid by the piece, his loss was made up to him. On Sundays this worthy lady walked to church attended by her entire family, children and servants, and in the evening all were assembled again for religious instruction.[1] In the *Memoir* of Mary Rich, Countess of Warwick, we read: "Nov. 13, 1668. After dinner I spent the whole afternoon in examining and exhorting my servants to prepare themselves to receive the sacrament. I was enabled to speak with much seriousness and affection to them, and I did much endeavour to bring them to a seriousness in the matter of their souls."

In consequence of the personal interest in their welfare shown by master and mistress, and despite cuffings and beatings, the servants of the seventeenth century showed a devotion to the family and its interests in happy contrast to the indifference of their successors of the present day. Indeed the "domestic servant question" may be said to have been practically unknown in the country districts of England until after the Restoration of Charles II. Servants followed the heads of the family abroad in times of civil war and exile, and were frequently remembered in the wills of those they had so loyally served. Such bequests must have been especially acceptable in those days when the wages of servants varied from 30 shillings to £6 per annum!

THE POSITION OF WOMEN IN THE SEVENTEENTH AND
EIGHTEENTH CENTURIES

Statutes Affecting Women. — During the seventeenth and eighteenth centuries the English family remained patriarchal in type. Throughout this long period the law did little or nothing to free the woman from her subordinate position in

[1] *Barnard's Journal*, Vol. 26, pp. 380–382.

the family. Yet a few statutes were enacted which were of direct interest to women. Two of these concerned the wardship of heiresses. In those days there still existed the ancient feudal custom of "court wardships" by which minor heirs of large estates became, on the death of the father, wards of the king. Now the ruler, having no personal interest in these children, frequently granted some relation who applied for the privilege and paid well for it, the right to bring up the young heir and arrange for his or her marriage at the proper time. Otherwise the girl or boy remained a ward of the court. This meant that the child's education was quite likely to be superficial, if it were not entirely neglected. Furthermore, a royal ward might be disposed of in marriage by the king as he saw fit. A case in point is that of Mary Blacknall and her sister, who were left by the death of their father heiresses to a large property and at once became court wards. In the *Verney Papers* we learn that four of their maternal relatives "procured from the court of wards a lease of their lands, with the custody of their persons during their minorities, and the right of bestowing them in marriage, by payment of a fine of 2,000£ half of which was paid down, and a bond given for the remainder." The object of this arrangement was to secure to the young ladies a careful education and the power of choosing a husband on attaining a proper age. The 2000£ was just so much money which it was deemed by their relatives worth while to pay out of their fortunes in order to release them from the oppressive power exercised over infant heiresses by the court of wards for the benefit of the crown. Later the older sister died and little Mary Blacknall at eleven years of age became sole heiress. Then it was that the temptation to marry her among themselves led three of the guardians to plan her marriage to the son of one of their number — a Mr. Libb. However, the fourth guardian, Mr. Wiseman, defeated the scheme by appealing to the court of wards, which at once made out an order restraining the other guardians from such action. Two years later the little girl was *offered* to Sir

Edmund Verney for his son, the father binding himself to pay the remaining 1000£ to the court. It is agreeable to learn that Mr. Wiseman gave his consent to this commercial arrangement only when it had been agreed that his ward should not be forced to the marriage against her will. In 1629 the girl was married to Ralph Verney, while still under fourteen. The young couple, however, did not live together for several years. Ralph Verney returned to Oxford to finish his studies, and only then returned home to claim his bride, who had meanwhile been living with his mother and learning the arts of housekeeping. Apparently this marriage, arranged in a purely business-like spirit, turned out to be a singularly happy one.[1]

But all court wardships did not end so fortunately. The king's need of funds led to outrageous misuse of his prerogatives with respect to royal wards and provoked sharp resentment from the English nobility. On the restoration of Charles II in 1660 action was immediately taken to abolish military tenure of lands with the rights of wardship and marriage which had belonged to such tenure since the feudal system began. The same Act of Parliament provided that a father might appoint a guardian by will to serve until his child should attain the age of twenty-one years. It will be noted that the mother is not mentioned in this Act, the reason being that she had no rights of guardianship in her children, and therefore could not appoint a guardian by will. Apparently, however, a mother might be permitted the right of co-guardianship with the nearest male relative, for, in his *Autobiography*, Lord Herbert of Cherbury relates that, after his father's death, his mother desired her brother, Sir Francis Newport, "to haste to London to obtain his (Lord Herbert's) wardship for his and her own use joyntly, which he obtained." [2]

In 1670–1671 an act was passed concerning the disposal of the property of a married man or woman who died intestate. In such cases the wife received half her husband's property for

[1] *Verney Papers* (Camden Society Pub.), Vol. 56, pp. 145–146.
[2] *Op. cit.* (ed. 1771), p. 35.

life if there were no offspring, and one third if children were born to them. If a married woman died intestate, her whole estate was enjoyed by her husband during his lifetime.[1]

So late as 1663 the age-long right of a husband to inflict bodily chastisement upon his wife was upheld by the courts. In the case of Bradley *versus* Wife the English court "refused to bind the husband over to keep the peace, at the suit of his wife, unless it could be proved that her life was in danger, 'because by law he has power of castigation.'"[2] It is significant of a marked change of sentiment in this regard, however, that eleven years later, when Lady Leigh proved ill-treatment against her husband in the courts, Lord Chief Justice Hale gave it as his opinion that the "moderate castigation" mentioned in the legal register "was not meant of beating, but only of admonition and confinement to the house . . . and decided that a husband had no right to chastise his wife with personal correction."[3] From that time on it is possible that the only punishment a husband could *legally* inflict upon his wife was confinement to the house.[4] But let it not be supposed that wife beating ceased in England after the judgment of the Chief Justice was pronounced. As is well known, the custom has persisted among the less enlightened classes down to the present time, since English law grants an abused wife no right to bring suit against her husband for assault and battery.

Legal Position of Women. — The status of married women in England in the last quarter of the eighteenth century is so ably discussed by a historian of that period that it seems well to quote at length from his book.[5] First he carefully details the privileges of a married woman. These consist chiefly

---

[1] Chapman, *The Status of Women under English Law*, p. 34; *Statutes of the Realm*, 22–23, Ch. II, c. 10, sec. 6.

[2] Cleveland, *Women under the English Law*, pp. 221–222.

[3] *Ibid.*, p. 222.

[4] See below, p. 316, on this point.

[5] Alexander, *The History of Women* (London, 3d ed., 1782), Vol. II, pp. 488–511.

in her exemption from imprisonment for debt; her right to proper maintenance by the husband so long as she lives with him, or, in case of cruel treatment, her privilege of separate maintenance; her further right to demand security for the good behavior of the husband in case of gross ill-usage, and to sue for restitution of conjugal rights if she were deserted by him. A husband, although vested with power over all the goods and chattels of his wife, may not devise by will the ornaments and jewels which she is accustomed to wear, "though it has been held that he may, if he pleases, dispose of them in his lifetime." Since husband and wife are one and the husband the legal person, he "is liable to answer all such actions at law as were attached against his wife at the time of their marriage, and also to pay all the debts she had contracted previous to that period. . . . A wife may purchase an estate, and if the husband does not enter his dissent before the conveyance, he shall be considered as having given such consent, and the conveyance be good and valid. A wife who is accustomed to trade may sell goods in open market; and such goods a husband by virtue of his authority over her, shall not have any power to reclaim." [1]

The writer then goes on to describe a further privilege sometimes extended to the English wife in the form of a marriage settlement. These "settlements" became very popular in the eighteenth century as a means whereby a wife might escape complete financial dependence on her husband. In the words of Alexander: "It is no uncommon thing, in the present times, for the matrimonial bargain to be made so, as that the wife shall retain the sole and absolute power of enjoying and disposing of her own fortune, in the same manner as if she were not married; *by which inequitable bargain, the husband is debarred from enjoying any of the rights of matrimony, except the person of his wife.*" [2] Such generous marriage settlements, however, were probably the exception rather than the rule, since most

[1] Alexander, *The History of Women*, Vol. II, pp. 488–495.
[2] *Ibid.*, p. 496. Italics mine.

men disapproved as cordially as the worthy Mr. Alexander of so "inequitable a bargain." Yet it became customary among the well-to-do for the future husband to allow his bride a fixed annual sum for her separate use. Also it was a common practice for the man to settle upon his wife a specified amount of land and money which constituted her "jointure" as it was called. This property, like the dower of common law, which it was designed to replace, was strictly reserved for the use of the wife after her husband's death, and could not be touched by his creditors. Thus, by means of jointure or dower, the wife was provided for in the event of her widowhood.

So much for the privileges of a British wife in the year of our Lord 1782. What was her position in other respects? Let us turn again to Alexander.

"In Britain, we allow a woman to sway our sceptre, but by law and custom we debar her from every other government but that of her own family, as if there were not a public employment between that of superintending the kingdom, and the affairs of her own kitchen, which could be managed by the genius and capacity of woman. We neither allow women to officiate at our altars, to debate in our councils, nor to fight for us in the field; we suffer them not to be members of our senate, to practise any of the learned professions, nor to concern themselves much with our trades and occupations. We exercise nearly a perpetual guardianship over them, both in their virgin and their married state, and she who, having laid a husband in the grave, enjoys an independent fortune, is almost the only woman among us who can be called free. Thus excluded from every thing which can give them consequence, they derive the greater part of the power which they enjoy, from their charms; and these, when joined to sensibility, often fully compensate, in this respect, for all the disadvantages they are laid under by law and custom.

"As the possession of property is one of the most valuable of all political blessings, and generally carries the possession of power and authority along with it; one of the most peculiar disadvantages in the condition of our women is, their being postponed to all males in the succession to the inheritance of landed estates, and generally allowed much smaller shares than the men, even of money and effects of their fathers and ancestors, when this money or those effects are given them in the lifetime of their parents, or devised to them by will; for otherwise, that is, if the father dies intestate, they share equally with sons in all personal property. When an estate, in default of male heirs, descends to the daughters, the common custom of England is, that the eldest shall not, in the same manner as an eldest son, inherit the whole, but all the daughters shall have an equal share in it."

.   .   .   .

"But besides these laws, which for the most part operate so as to hinder the fair sex from getting possession of any considerable property, the laws of marriage again divest them of such property as they really are in possession of. By marriage all the goods and chattels which belong to the woman become vested in the husband, and he has the same power over them as she had while they were her sole and absolute property. When the wife, however, is possessed of real estate in land, the power which the husband acquires over it is not so extensive, he only gains the right to the rents and profits arising out of it during the continuance of the marriage; but if a living child is born to him, though it should die in a very short time, he becomes, in that case, tenant for life, by the courtesy of the country. If there happens to be no child, then at the demise of the wife the estate goes to her heirs at law. But the property of her goods and chattels devolves upon the husband, who has the sole and absolute power of disposing of them according to his pleasure.

"Every married woman is considered as a minor, and cannot do any deed which affects her real or personal property, without the consent of her husband; if she does any such deed, it is not valid and the husband may claim the property of what she disposed of, as if no such disposal had been made. As a married woman cannot dispose of her property while living, so neither does the law give her that power at her death. In the statute of wills she is expressly prohibited from devising land, and even from bequeathing goods and chattels without the leave of her husband, because all such goods and chattels are, without any limitation, his sole and absolute property; whether they were such as the wife brought along with her at the marriage, *or such as she acquired by her labour and industry afterward.*" [1]

. . . .

"If a husband and wife are jointly possessed of houses and lands which are settled upon the survivor, if the husband destroys himself his wife shall not have the half that belonged to him; it becomes the property of the crown, as a compensation for the loss of a subject. When a husband and wife agree to live separate, and the husband covenants to give her so much a year; if at any time he offers to be reconciled and to take her home, upon her refusal, he shall not any longer be obliged to pay her a separate maintenance. If a legacy be paid to a married woman who lives separate from her husband, the husband may file a bill in chancery to oblige the person who paid it to his wife to pay it again to him with interest."

. . . . . .

"The power which a husband has over the person of his wife, does not seem perfectly settled by the laws of this country, it is nevertheless certain, that she is not to go abroad, nor to leave his house and family without his approbation; but what coercive methods he may make use of to restrain her from so doing, or whether he may proceed any farther than to admonition and denying her money, seems a point not altogether agreed upon.

"When a wife is injured in her person or property, so limited is her power, that she cannot bring an action for redress with-

---

[1] Italics mine.

out the consent and approbation of her husband, nor in any way but in his name. If, however, such husband has abjured the realm, or is banished from it, he is considered as dead in law, and his wife in that case may sue for redress in her own name and authority. . . . When a widow is endowed of certain lands and tenements, and sells them, the heir at law may not only recover them of the purchaser, but also refuse to restore them back to the widow, or to pay her any dower in their stead. By the laws of England, a father only is empowered to exercise a rightful authority over his children; no power is conferred on the mother, only so far as to oblige these children to consider her as a person entitled to duty and a reverential regard." [1]

A review of this formidable array of deprivations and restrictions laid upon married women shows that the vast majority are concerned with the ownership and disposal of property. Clearly in these respects the hands of a British wife were firmly tied. Such arrangements point to the fact that *marriage and patriarchal family organization were designed in large measure for the protection of private property, and for its control and inheritance by males.* Other ends were doubtless served by these institutions, but the economic purpose was fundamental from the dawn of history to the latter half of the nineteenth century.

THE IDEAL OF WOMANHOOD IN ENGLAND

The Seventeenth Century Ideal. — Despite the numerous limitations with which the life of a married woman in England was hedged around, and the subordinate position occupied by her in family and State, yet it would be a mistake to assume that women were held in low esteem throughout the whole of this period. When the conditions of social life in the early seventeenth century are taken into consideration, the ideal of womanhood at that time seems fairly high. To be sure, that

[1] Alexander, *The History of Women* (London, 3d ed., 1782), Vol. II, pp. 505–513.

ideal might be summed up in the words "a virtuous housewife," and the feminine "vertues" most highly extolled were
beyond question discreetness, modesty and humility; yet the
conception was worthy as far as it went.   In his quaint book
The English Gentlewoman, published in 1641, Brathwaite has
happily expressed the feminine ideal of his age.

"For shee loves without any pointed pretences to be really
vertuous, without any popular applause to be affably gracious,
without any glorious gloss to be sincerely zealous.   Her Education hath so enabled her as shee can converse with you of all
places, deliver her judgment conceivingly of most persons, and
discourse most delightfully of all fashions.   Shee hath been
so well schooled in the Discipline of this *Age*, as shee onely
desires to reteine in memory that *forme* which is least affected
but most comely; to consort with such as may improve her
Knowledge and *Practise* of goodnesse by their company; . . .
Diligent you shall ever find her in her imployments, serious in
her advice, temperate in her Discourse, discreet in her answers.
. . . Take upon her to instruct others, she will not, such is
her Humility; albeit, every moving posture which comes from
her may be a line of direction unto others to follow her. . . .
However, she might boast of *Descent*, her desire is to raise
it by *Desert*. Shee holds, no family can be truly *Generous*,
unlesse it be nobly vertuous. Her *life* must express the line
from which she came." [1]   And again; "Shee distates none
more than those busie housewives, who are ever running into
discourse of others families, but forget their own.   Neither
holds shee it sufficient to bee onely an Housekeeper; or
Snayle-like to bee still under roofe; shee partakes therefore
of the Pismere in providing, of the Sareptan widow in disposing; holding ever an absent providence better than an im-
provident presence. . . .   She conceives no small delight in
educating the young and unexperienced Damsels of your
sexe; wherein she reteines an excellent faculty and facility." [2]

[1] *Op. cit.*, opening pages of dedication to Anne, Countess of Pembroke.
[2] *Ibid.*, Address to the Reader.

It will be noted that the author of this ideal picture does not omit all mention of the intellectual training of his perfect gentlewoman. Her education is to enable her to "converse with you of all places, deliver her judgment conceivingly of most persons, and discourse most delightfully of all fashions" (*i.e.*, customs). Yet there can be little doubt that the intellectual impulse of the Renaissance had largely spent itself in the seventeenth century. In consequence it is probable that neither men nor women were as thoroughly educated as they had been in preceding generations. It is true that gentlemen's sons very generally studied the classics at home with tutors or in the great Public Schools of England; but their training became largely conventional as the respect for learning grew less deep and less sincere. Certain it is that neither Puritan nor Cavalier set great store on the thorough education of girls. The Puritan was averse to it because he harked back to the conception of the early Church Fathers of woman as the cause of the original sin, therefore a creature to be kept under strict government. The Cavalier was more indifferent than hostile, partly because woman was tending to become for him a plaything whose sex was her most alluring charm, and partly because custom had almost wholly restricted women's education to domestic management.

After the Restoration of Charles II in 1660 a change came over the spirit of English society, at least among the wealthy and high born. Men and women became infected with the feverish gayety and low moral ideals of the Court and abandoned the quiet of their country estates for the excitements of fashionable life in London. Quite often fashionable women were as frivolous, and in some instances as vicious, as the men. Of the change that had taken place in social life and ideals Sir John Evelyn wrote with some feeling at the close of the seventeenth century :

"Thus you see, young sparks, how the stile and method of wooing is quite changed . . . since the days of our forefathers (of unhappy memory, simple and plain men as they were), who courted and chose their wives for their modesty, frugality, keeping at home, good housewifery, and other æconomical virtues then in reputation; and when the young damsels were taught all these in the country and at their parents houses, the portion they brought was more in virtue than money, and she was a richer match than one who could have brought a million and nothing else to commend her. . . . The virgins and young ladies of that golden age . . . put their hands to the spindle, nor disdain'd they the needle; were obsequious and helpful to their parents, instructed in the managery of the family, and gave presages of making excellent wives. Nor then did they read so many romances, see so many plays, and smutty farces; set up for visits, and have their days of audience, and idle pass-time. . . . Their retirements were devout and religious books, and their recreations in the distillatory, and knowledge of plants and their virtues, for the comfort of their poor neighbors and use of the family, which wholesome plain dyet and kitchen physick preserved in perfect health." [1]

The Ideal Woman of the Eighteenth Century. — When every allowance has been made for the human tendency to look back to the "good old times" of one's youth and to disapprove of the social innovations introduced in one's old age, Sir John Evelyn's account still remains substantially correct. A profound alteration for the worse had come over the social life of his time; nor did the tone of morality improve in the eighteenth century, which is rightly known as the most artificial and perhaps heartless epoch in English history. In the *Spectator* (1712) Addison satirizes the empty life of the fashionable lady of the time in the following extract from *Clarinda's Journal:*

"Wednesday. From Eight to Ten. Drank two Dishes of Chocolate in Bed, and fell asleep after 'em.

"From Ten to Eleven. Eat a Slice of Bread and Butter, drank a dish of Bohea, read the *Spectator.*

[1] "Mundus Muliebris," in *Literary Remains* (ed. 1834), pp. 700–702.

"From Eleven to One. At my Toilet, try'd a new Head.[1] Gave orders for Veney [2] to be combed and washed. *Mem.* I look best in Blue.

"From One till Half an Hour after Two. Drove to the Change. Cheapened a couple of Fans.

"Till Four. At Dinner. *Mem.* Mr. Frost passed by in his new Liveries.

"From Four till Six. Dressed, paid a visit to old Lady Blithe and her Sister, *having heard they were gone out of Town that Day.*

"From Six to Eleven, At Basset.[3] *Mem.* Never sit again upon the Ace of Diamond." [4]

It can hardly be expected that the ideal of womanhood would be high at a time when social life was frivolous and coarse. On the contrary, that ideal may truthfully be said to have reached its lowest ebb. The writings of the time abound in references to the "fair sex" and bear eloquent testimony to the eighteenth century Englishman's conception of woman's character and functions. The emphasis laid on "female delicacy" and "sensibility," the insistence upon woman's dependence on man as constituting her supreme charm, the universal tendency to place the highest value upon qualities peculiar to sex, all conspire to make these works almost nauseous reading. A few quotations will bring this feminine ideal more clearly before the reader. In his oft-quoted *Legacy to his Daughters*, Dr. Gregory writes:

"One of the chief beauties in a female character is that modest reserve, that retiring delicacy which avoids the public eye, and is disconcerted even at the gaze of admiration. . . . When a girl ceases to blush she has lost the most powerful charm of beauty. That extreme sensibility which it indicates, may be a weakness and incumbrance in our sex, as I have too

---

[1] Headdress.
[2] Venus, her lap-dog.
[3] A gambling game of cards.
[4] *Spectator*, No. 323.

often felt, but in yours it is peculiarly engaging." [1]   Apparently Dr. Gregory's ideal woman is never for one moment to be wholly spontaneous, but must constantly hold in mind the disturbing fact that "female delicacy" may be easily marred. Thus he warns his daughters in dancing never to allow themselves "to be so far transported with mirth as to forget the delicacy of [their] sex. Many a girl, dancing in the gaiety and innocence of her heart, is thought to discover a spirit she little dreams of." [2]

Perhaps one of the best expressions of the dominant conception of womanhood in the eighteenth century is that of Lord Kames:

"A man says what he knows; a woman what is agreeable; knowledge is necessary to the former; taste is sufficient to the latter.   A man who does his duty can brave censure; a woman's conduct ought to be exemplary, in order to be esteemed by all.   The least doubt of her chastity deprives her of every comfort in the matrimonial state. *In the education of females accordingly, no motive has greater influence than the thought of what people will say of them.*" The mother must take account of this, and very early teach her little daughter submission to the will of those in authority over her.   "This is essential to the female sex, forever subjected to the authority of a single person, or to the opinion of all." [3]   When the girl has been made duly "tractable" she should then be taught that to "make a good husband is but one branch of a man's duty; but it is the chief duty of a woman to make a good wife."   "Woman, destined to be obedient, ought to be disciplined early to bear wrongs, without murmuring.   This is a hard lesson; and yet it is necessary even for their own sake; sullenness or peevishness may alienate the husband; but tend not to sooth his roughness, nor to moderate his impetuosity. Heaven made women insinuating, but not in order to be cross:

[1] *Op. cit.* (ed. 1784), pp. 35–36.
[2] *Ibid.*, p. 68.
[3] *Loose Hints upon Education* (ed. 1781), pp. 135–137.   Italics mine.

it made them feeble, not in order to be imperious: it gave a sweet voice, not in order to scold: . . . it did not give them beauty, in order to disfigure it by anger." [1]

In one of his well-known letters to his son, Lord Chesterfield etches sharply the prevailing conception of women held by English gentlemen of fashion about the middle of the eighteenth century.

"Women . . . are only children of a larger growth; they have an entertaining tattle and sometimes wit, but for solid reasoning good-sense, I never knew in my life one that had it, or who reasoned or acted consequentially for four-and-twenty hours together. . . . A man of sense only trifles with them, plays with them, humors and flatters them, as he does with a sprightly, forward child; but he neither consults them about nor trusts them with serious matters, though he often makes them believe that he does both, which is the thing in the world that they are proud of; for they love mightily to be dabbling in business — which, by the way, they always spoil — and being justly distrustful that men in general look upon them in a trifling light, they almost adore that man who talks more seriously to them, and who seems to consult and trust them: I say, who seems; for weak men really do, but wise ones only seem to do it." [2]

It never seems to have occurred to this caustic critic of women that their shallow education had much to do with the lack of "reasoning good-sense" which he had observed in certain members of the sex.

Foreigners visiting England in the eighteenth century comment on the low state of sexual morality. Thus Archenholz writes that it was estimated in his day that London alone harbored 50,000 prostitutes, not counting the "mistresses" kept by many men of wealth. This widely prevalent vice was hushed up as much as possible by the "taboo" long ago

---

[1] *Loose Hints upon Education* (ed. 1781), pp. 228–229.

[2] *The Best Letters of Lord Chesterfield*, edited by Edw. G. Johnson (9th edition), pp. 91–92.

set upon discussion or even recognition of its existence. Women, especially, were expected to go about with eyes and ears firmly closed. Now and then fathers instructed their daughters that when married they should feign ignorance of the immoral lives of their husbands. In 1700 the Marquis of Halifax, an honorable man, embodies this counsel in his *Advice to a Daughter*: "First then, you are to consider, you live in a time which hath rendered some kind of Frailties so habitual that they lay claim to large grains of allowance." A woman should regard herself as recompensed for the strict virtue required of her by holding the honor of the family in her keeping. "This being so, remember, That next to the danger of committing the fault yourself, the greatest is that of seeing it in your Husband. Do not seem to look or hear that way. . . ."

The foregoing panegyrics on the ideal "female" character were of course written by men and glorify those elements of passive docility, gentleness, and clinging dependence which have always appealed to the masculine sex. But it is a little discouraging to find that the literary women of the period — such writers as Hannah More and Letitia Barbauld — uphold much the same ideal of womanhood. Not gifted with the far-sighted vision that would enable them to glimpse the widening opportunities in the fields of education and of employment soon to be laid open to women, they still maintain that the home is the only sphere possible to their sex. Even while urging that women should receive a more thorough and practical education than is given them in the boarding schools of the period, Hannah More appeals to "men of sense" not to oppose "the improvement of the other sex, as they themselves will be sure to be gainers by it; the enlargement of the female understanding being the most likely means to put an end to those cavils and contentions for equality which female smatterers so anxiously maintain." [1]

Yet protestants against these cramping doctrines were

[1] *Strictures on the Modern System of Female Education*, p. 14.

not lacking even among the women. Toward the close of the seventeenth century appeared a ringing *Essay* by Mrs. Bathsua Makin, urging that competent schools for girls be erected and prophesying that if women were intelligently educated, men would speedily be ashamed of their ignorance. Later were published the protests of Mary Astell,[1] sharply criticizing the injustices in the marriage relation, the false ideal and the shallow education of women.

The French Revolution and Mary Wollstonecraft. — But the age was not ready for these mildly advanced doctrines, and so the eighteenth century drew toward its close with no apparent change in the ideas and practices respecting women. Then came the revolt of the American Colonies, closely followed by the Revolution in France; and England was thereupon invaded by strange and alarming theories of liberty, equality and human brotherhood. The uprising of the French people against king and privileged aristocracy, the attacks directed against the Church as repressive of all freedom of thinking, the almost frenzied assertion of fundamental human rights, common to all — these were bound to make themselves felt in the most conservative English circles. The letters of Horace Walpole to Hannah More are replete with accounts of the horrors being enacted across the Channel, and are aflame with indignation against the outrages committed — an indignation which took small account of the oppressions that had provoked them. Even the women of the day read of the new social philosophy which served as the gospel of the French people in their revolt, and which was producing restless discontent among the laboring class in England. Most of them, like their husbands and fathers, were terrified by its doctrines and turned from them with strong aversion. For these educated women belonged to the aristocratic class from which the ranks of the conservative Tories were regularly recruited. In the words of a modern writer: "They had been brought

[1] *Some Reflections upon Marriage* (4th ed., 1730); *An Essay in Defense of the Female Sex* (1696); *A Serious Proposal to the Ladies* . . . (1694).

up in the settled conviction that it was their duty to labour among the poor, and they could not understand the fierce cry of the poor for power to labour for themselves." [1] Nor did they understand any better the profound influence that these new theories of democracy were bound to exert upon the education and life of their own sex.

But one woman clearly saw the broader implications of this democratic upheaval, even as she saw and resented the flimsy education and superficial lives of the titled ladies of her day. Aglow with the vision and hope of a new order in which all women — wives and mothers as well as maidens — should play a nobler part than was possible to them under the limitations of the eighteenth century, Mary Wollstonecraft wrote her *Vindication of the Rights of Women*. Ill-organized and abounding in needless repetitions as the work doubtless is, it yet was the most stirring and significant contribution to feminist literature that had appeared among any people. A comparison of Mary Wollstonecraft's fervid appeal published in 1792 with the works of Mary Astell, written a century before, reveal how far the former had progressed beyond the relatively conservative position of her predecessor. The *Vindication of the Rights of Women* might be said to take as its thesis this ringing statement: "It is time to effect a revolution in female manners — time to restore to them their lost dignity — and make them, as a part of the human species, labor, by reforming themselves, to reform the world." [2] Let women fill their heads with sound knowledge and their days with wise employments, and their "virtue" will pretty well take care of itself, says this eighteenth-century feminist. It has more than once been pointed out that Mary Wollstonecraft's fearless attack on the eighteenth-century custom of emphasizing the sex qualities of women at the expense of their intellectual gifts did much

---

[1] Blaese, *The Emancipation of Englishwomen*, p. 76.
[2] *Op. cit.*, in *The Humboldt Library of Popular Science Literature*, Vol. XV, p. 60.

to bring about the author's condemnation by the preachers of "female delicacy." For she sought to show in the plainest language that so long as both men and women were agreed to concentrate their attention on the sexual character of women, society would steadily deteriorate in morals. "This desire of being always women, is the very consciousness that degrades the sex." The power women should seek is not a gross physical influence over men but a control of their own natures by means of a trained reason.[1] Therefore every woman should have such education as will "exercise the understanding and form the heart — or, in other words, . . . enable the individual to attain such habits of virtue as will render it independent. In fact, it is a farce to call any being virtuous whose virtues do not result from the exercise of its own reason." [2]

One of the most radical and fervent doctrines of the writer's creed is her belief in the right of every woman to be regarded as an *individual* with peculiar capacities of her own worthy of respect and development. Therefore the end of women's exertions should be "to unfold their own faculties, and acquire the dignity of conscious virtues." [3] And, again, speaking of women's need of economic independence, she writes: "The being who discharges the duties of its station is independent, and speaking of women at large, their first duty is to themselves as rational creatures, and the next in point of importance, as citizens, is that which includes so many, of a mother." [4] Even if a woman's duties are limited to managing her family, educating her children and assisting her neighbors, she cannot properly discharge these duties if she lacks, "individually, the protection of civil laws; she must not be dependent on her husband's bounty for her subsistence

---

[1] *Op. cit.*, in *The Humboldt Library of Popular Science Literature*, Vol. XV, p. 76.
[2] *Ibid.*, p. 38.
[3] *Ibid.*, p. 42.
[4] *Ibid.*, p. 153.

during his life or support after his death; for how can a being be generous who has nothing of its own? or virtuous who is not free? " [1] Mary Wollstonecraft is, perhaps, the first woman of her time to perceive the dignity and independence which would accrue to women from opening to them the world of labor and permitting them to earn their own living. "How many women," she bitterly exclaims, ". . . waste life away, the prey of discontent, who might have practised as physicians, regulated a farm, managed a shop, and stood erect, supported by their own industry, instead of hanging their heads surcharged with the dew of sensibility. . . . How much more respectable is the woman who earns her own bread by fulfilling any duty, than the most accomplished beauty!" [2] These were brave words to be uttered in the England of the eighteenth century!

Unfortunately it cannot be said that the clarion tones of this new declaration of independence made a favorable impression upon the English mind, for this was too busily engaged in horrified repudiation of the principles of the French Revolution and in the attempt to prevent these disturbing theories from upsetting the equilibrium of the masses of the English working people. Mary Wollstonecraft was subjected to a storm of criticism and disapproval from her countrymen and was promptly dubbed a "hyena in petticoats." The removal of the legal, economic and educational disabilities of women was destined to be the work of the nineteenth century.

MARRIAGE IN THE SEVENTEENTH AND EIGHTEENTH CENTURIES

Persistence of the Idea of Marriage as an Economic Contract. — As might be expected, little change was effected during this period in the conception of marriage as fundamentally a

---

[1] *Op. cit.*, in *The Humboldt Library of Popular Science Literature*, Vol. XV, pp. 153–154.

[2] *Ibid.*, p. 156.

contract to secure social and economic benefits — a contract arranged in most cases by the parents. "The girls of the seventeenth century enjoyed but a brief spring-time. With dawning womanhood, while they were yet in the schoolroom, in some cases even in the nursery, careful parents were already considering the choice of a husband." [1] Poor Ralph Verney, who was guardian of his five orphaned sisters, had many anxious years of matrimonial negotiations before the last girl was successfully married off. His difficulties were enormously increased by the fact that his deceased father, Sir Edmund Verney, had left a marriage portion for only one of his daughters. Very open and unashamed was the bargaining, and many were the demands on Ralph's slender property before he had the profound satisfaction of giving away the last sister at the marriage altar. [2]

Early marriages were the rule throughout the seventeenth century. Thus Lady Mary Villiers was a widow at nine; Mary Blacknall was married to Ralph Verney at thirteen; and Herbert of Cherbury was married at fifteen to his cousin Mary, who was twenty-one. This latter match was quite frankly arranged by the parents and guardians, so that the young lady could inherit the property of her father, Sir William Herbert of St. Gillian's, who made his daughter's inheritance conditional upon her marrying a man whose surname was Herbert. [3] Yet here and there were parents, even in the seventeenth century, who deliberately permitted to their daughters freedom of choice in marriage. The fair Lady Dorothy Sidney was sensibly left to choose her own husband and so likewise was the Puritan maid, Lucy Apsley. Even where the marriage was contracted for by the parents the right of veto remained with the girl and the youth, although few young persons probably dared to use it.

Occasionally a certain idealism may be found coloring the

[1] Godfrey, Elizabeth, *Home Life under the Stuarts*, p. 113.
[2] See *Verney Memoirs*, Vol. I, Ch. XXVII.
[3] *Autobiography of Edward, Lord Herbert of Cherbury* (ed. 1771), p. 36.

conception of marriage in the seventeenth century — not that this has been wholly lacking since the Renaissance, but that now it is becoming more apparent. Toward the middle of the century an English gentleman, writing to felicitate Master Hugh Penry upon the latter's marriage with his sister, says: ". . . I heartily congratulate this marriage, and pray that a blessing may descend upon it from that place where all marriages are made which is from Heaven, the fountain of all felicitie. . . ." [1] This same idealistic gentleman, replying to a friend who has urged him to marry, writes:

"'Tis the custom of som (and 'tis a common custome) to choose Wives by the weight, that is, by their wealth. . . . The late Earl of Salisbury gives a caveat for this, That beuty without a dowry . . . is as a gilded shell without a kernel; therefore he warns his son to be sure to have something with his Wife, and his reason is, *Because nothing can be bought in the Market without money.* Indeed 'tis very fitting that he or she should have wherewith to support both according to their quality. . . . But he who hath enough of his own to maintain a Wife, and marrieth only for money, discovereth a poor sordid disposition." [2]

Half a century later Mary Astell denounces the prevailing customs whereby wives are chosen for their dowries, not for their characters. "In a word," she declares, "when we have reckon'd up how many look no further than the making of their Fortune, as they call it; who don't so much as propose to themselves any Satisfaction in the Woman to whom they plight their Faith, seeking only to be Masters of her Estate, that so they may have Money enough to indulge all their irregular Appetites; who think they are as good as can be expected, if they are but, according to the fashionable term *Civil Husbands;* . . . when to these you have added such as marry without any thought at all, further than that it is the custom of the World, what others have done before them, that

---

[1] Howell, James, *Familiar Letters* (ed. 1645), Section 2, p. 33.
[2] *Ibid.*, pp. 89–90.

the Family must be kept up, the antient Race preserved, and therefore their kind Parents and Guardians choose as they think convenient, without ever consulting the Young one's Inclinations, who must be satisfied, or pretend so, at least, upon Pain of their Displeasure, and that heavy Consequence of it, Forfeiture of their Estate : These set aside, I fear there will be but a small Remainder to marry out of better Considerations. . . ." [1]

But such ideas and practices were deeply rooted in the past, and it is not surprising that matters had not greatly improved by the middle of the eighteenth century. Steele in the *Guardian* deplores the mistake made by parents who "make love for their children, and without any manner of regard to the season of life, and the respective interests of their progeny, judge of their future happiness by the rules of commerce." [2] Yet the occasional references in eighteenth century literature to free choice on the part of fashionable ladies, who are hard put to it to select one among their lovers [3] show that parental prerogative in the matter of arranging marriages was gradually being undermined. Writing in 1796 to his daughters Dr. Gregory says of free choice in marriage :

"If I live to that age when you shall be capable to judge for yourselves, and do not strangely alter my sentiments I shall act towards you in a very different manner from what most parents do. My opinion has always been, that when that period arrives, the parential (*sic*) authority ceases. . . . If you did not chuse to follow my advice, I should not on that account cease to love you as my children." [4]

Disinclination of Men for Marriage. — Certainly the young people of the eighteenth century had larger opportunities to meet and know each other than were permitted them in previous periods. They visited in their homes, and mingled freely

---

[1] *Some Reflections upon Marriage* (ed. 1730), pp. 35–36.
[2] *Op. cit.*, No. 73.
[3] Steele, *The Tatler*, No. 258.
[4] *Legacy to His Daughters*, pp. 125–126.

in the dancing academies so popular at the time. Yet a
marked disinclination on the part of young men to marry
became very noticeable in the reign of Queen Anne. "The
whole literature of the day," says Ashton, "speaks of the tendency of young men to avoid the trammels of matrimony." [1]
The author is inclined to lay this reluctance at the door of the
new custom of marriage settlements whereby a generous
jointure was secured to the bride on the death of her husband
and "pin-money" was allowed her during his lifetime. If the
pin-money were large enough, a wife might be made economically independent of her husband; hence the custom was very
unpopular in Queen Anne's day, and even later. Steele, in
The Tender Husband, represents two fathers as wrangling over
this vexed matter. One of them, Sir Harry Gubbin, exclaims:

"Look y', Mr. Tipkin, the main Article with me is that
Foundation of Wives Rebellion, — that cursed Pin Money —
Five Hundred Pounds *per annum* Pin Money.

"*Tipkin*. The word Pin Money, Sir Harry, is a term —

"*Sir H*. It is a Term, Brother, we never had in our Family,
nor ever will. Make her Jointure in Widowhood accordingly
large, but Four Hundred Pounds a Year is enough to give no
account of."

Marriage Customs. *Clandestine Marriages.* — Although
clandestine marriages had been common enough in the seventeenth century, their frequency had so increased in the
eighteenth as to constitute a grave scandal. As early as the
reign of William III (1689–1702) an Act had been passed which
sought to enforce the law requiring a five-shilling duty on
marriage licenses and imposing a fine of £100 on any person
who married couples without a license. Yet the law seems to
have been easily evaded. At this time certain chapels in
London were exempted from the visitation and control of the
Bishop. Of these "lawless Churches" as they were called,
St. James's near Aldgate and Holy Trinity attained an unsavory notoriety as places where any unmarried couple of legal

[1] Ashton, *Social Life in the Reign of Queen Anne*, p. 25.

age could be united in matrimony with no preliminary formalities or embarrassing questions asked. Occasionally the rector of one of these churches fell into the clutches of the ecclesiastical authorities and was suspended from office for a few years. But as soon as he was reinstated he returned to the profitable business of marrying without license or banns.[1]

But the greatest scandal in this respect grew out of the irregular marriages performed in the prisons of the Fleet and the Queen's Bench. Early in the reign of Anne, clergymen imprisoned in the Fleet for debt began their infamous trade of marrying whatever couples presented themselves, without requiring either banns or license. These impecunious gentlemen boldly advertised their willingness to unite all comers in matrimony for a small sum. An illicit register was kept to record these marriages as early as 1674. The records show that an unprincipled clergyman named John Gaynam plied a brisk and lucrative marriage business in the Fleet between the years 1709 and 1740; and there were numerous other ordained ministers who also turned a pretty penny in the same unlawful trade. In the Queen's Bench prison matters were even worse, for there laymen officiated as well as clergymen. So great did the scandal become, that in 1712 a Marriage Act was passed (10 Anne, cap. 19) renewing the penalty of £100 attached to the performance of an illegal marriage and giving half the penalty to the informer. The Act also imposed an extra duty of five shillings on every marriage license or certificate, while it provided that "if any gaoler or keeper of any prison shall be privy to or knowingly permit, any marriage to be solemnized in his said prison, before publication of banns, or license obtained as aforesaid, he shall for every such offence forfeit the sum of one hundred pounds. . . ."[2]

The Hardwicke Act. — Unfortunately this Act of Anne seems to have been practically inoperative from the first, and Fleet

---

[1] See Ashton, *op. cit.*, p. 29.

[2] *Ibid.*, pp. 27–32. See also Howard's exhaustive account of Fleet marriages in his *History of Matrimonial Institutions*, Vol. I, pp. 435–460.

marriages continued to be performed until 1753, when the Hardwicke Act was passed.[1]   By the terms of this law, which was hotly contested in the Commons, all marriages, save those of Jews, Quakers and members of the royal family, were to be celebrated only after publication of banns or securing of a license, and only during the hours from eight to twelve in the morning (the canonical hours), in an Anglican Church or chapel, and before an Anglican clergyman. "To solemnize marriage in any other manner or in any other place or without banns, except by special license of the archbishop, is punished with fourteen years' transportation, and the marriage is declared void."[2]   To secure the publicity so urgently necessary, the act provided that at least two witnesses must be present at the marriage and registers must be accurately kept by the clergy. Such registers might not be falsified or destroyed under pain of death. In case of the marriage of minors by license, failure to obtain the parents' consent rendered the marriage void. Imperfect as it was, this Act marked a long stride forward in the regulation of marriage by the State, in contradistinction to the Church, and in the abolition of clandestine unions.

Private Marriages. — Even when couples did not seek to evade the law, private marriages seem to have been very popular in the age of Queen Anne. Doubtless this mode of tying the matrimonial knot was favored because the chief parties could thus avoid the noisy and expensive festivities that accompanied a public marriage in eighteenth century England. In his valuable study of English life at this time M. Misson describes these "incognito" marriages as follows:

"The Bridegroom . . . and the Bride . . . conducted by their Father and Mother, or by those that serve them in their room, and accompany'd by two Bride men and two Bride maids, go early in the morning with a Licence in their Pocket and call up Mr. Curate and his Clerk, tell him their Business,

---

[1] Act of 26 George II, c. 33.
[2] Howard, *op. cit.*, p. 458.

are marry'd with a low Voice, and the Doors shut; tip the Minister a Guinea and the Clerk a Crown; steal softly out, one one way, and t'other another, either on Foot or in Coaches; go different Ways to some Tavern at a Distance from their own Lodgings, or to the House of some trusty Friend, there have a good Dinner and return Home at Night as quietly as Lambs. If the Drums and Fiddles have had notice of it they will be sure to be with them by Day break, making a horrible Racket, till they have got the Pence, and, which is worst of all, the whole Murder will come out." [1] The writer goes on to describe in plain language the rude sports in which the bridesmaids and groomsmen indulged at the expense of the newly married pair, who doubtless were thoroughly out of patience before they were at last left in peace.

Doubtless marriage was made very easy for every one of legal age during this period. Until the passage of the Hardwicke Act in 1753 any boy of fourteen and girl of twelve who desired to escape parental discipline and lead a "free" life might be indissolubly joined in the bonds of matrimony without their parents' consent and at little expense. Ashton quotes the advertisement of a Hampstead chapel which advertisement was designed to fill the coffers of the chapel at the expense of unthinking couples: "As there are many weddings at Sion Chapel, Hampstead, five Shillings only is required for all the Church fees of any Couple that are married there, provided they bring with them a license or Certificate, according to the Act of Parliament." A little later, in 1716, the chapel generously offered to marry all persons applying there without any fee whatever, provided they should "have their wedding dinner in the gardens." [2] The law requiring that banns be proclaimed three times in church before the marriage was celebrated had become thoroughly unpopular and was frequently evaded by securing a license. Misson says concerning the

---

[1] Misson's *Memoirs and Observations in His Travels over England* (trans. by Ozells, 1719), quoted in Ashton, *op. cit.*, pp. 32–33.

[2] Ashton, *op. cit.*, p. 31.

custom of banns that "very few are willing to have their Affairs declar'd to all the World in a publick Place, when for a Guinea they may do it *Snug*, and without Noise; and my good Friends the Clergy, who find their Accounts in it are not very zealous to prevent it."

THE HOMES OF THE SEVENTEENTH AND EIGHTEENTH CENTURIES

Architecture and Furnishings. — The homes of the nobility and gentlefolk of England in the seventeenth century must have been in many respects delightful dwelling places, full of sober beauty and charm. The revolution in domestic architecture that began during the reign of Henry VIII was carried much further during the reign of Elizabeth. While the prevailing desire for privacy did not lead to the abandonment of the great hall of the mansion, it did develop private apartments such as the parlor, the withdrawing room and lofty bed-chambers. The dirty rushes which strewed the floors in Henry VIII's day gave place in the seventeenth century to floor coverings of leather or to Indian and Persian carpets. The influence of the great architect, Inigo Jones, who came to England early in the seventeenth century with Anne of Denmark, was wholly to encourage the Englishman's desire for privacy in his home and for furnishings which expressed his personal taste. Under the Stuart kings the houses of the great nobles improved vastly both in comfort and elegance. Yet, with all their paneled walls, elaborate carving, hangings of silk, velvet or tapestry, glass painted in heraldic designs and costly foreign furniture, these homes were not so essentially English as the less pretentious manor-houses, built of timbered oak, and boasting myriad windows with leaded panes. The country homes of the well-to-do in Stuart days were quite commonly self-supporting, capable of provisioning themselves with very little assistance from the outside world of industry. Each had its slaughter-house and brewery, its malt-house and sometimes its mill for grinding the grain raised on the estate. Even laundries had been added to most houses, for the family washing was now very generally done at home. Surrounding the house were spacious grounds traversed by paths which ran between stiff rows of clipped yew trees. One of these paths brought the sauntering visitor to the fish-ponds, stocked with carp; another led to the herb garden behind its low hedge, where lavender, rosemary and thyme were carefully tended by the housewife.

To Sir John Evelyn we are indebted for a delightful description of the furnishings of a manor-house in the closing years of the Stuarts:

"They had cupboards of ancient useful plate, whole chests of fine Holland sheets, (white as the driven snow) and fragrant of rose and lavender, for the bed; and the sturdy oaken bedstead, and furniture of the home, lasted one whole century; the shovel-board, and other long tables, both in hall and parlor, were as fixed as the freehold; nothing was movable save joynt-stools, the black jacks, silver tankards and bowls. . . .

"Things of use were natural, plain and wholesome; nothing was superfluous, nothing necessary wanting: . . ." [1]

Another description of a seventeenth-century home is found in Howell's *Familiar Letters*. The writer pictures it as "so virtuous and regular a House as any I believe in the Land both for æconomical government, and the choice company, for I never saw yet such a dainty race of children in all my life together, I never saw yet such an orderly and punctual attendance of servants, nor a great House so neatly kept. . . . The kitchen and gutters and other offices of noise and drudgery are at the fag end, there's a back gate for beggars and the meaner sort of swains to come in at. The stables butt upon the Park, which for a chearfull rising ground, for groves and browsings for the Deer, for rivulets of water may compare with any for its bignes in the whole land; it is opposite to the front of the great House, whence from the Gallerie one may see much of the game

---

[1] "Mundus Muliebris," in *Literary Remains* (ed. 1834), pp. 700–701.

when they are a hunting. Now for the gardning and costly choice flowers, for ponds, for stately large walks green and gravelly, for orchards and choice fruits of all sorts, there are few the like in England : . . ." [1]

Contrast this charming picture with that presented by the homes of the poorer peasantry, described by a modern historian as almost uninhabitable. "One chimney, one unglazed window, a roof thatched with straw, and four bare walls, afforded shelter from the summer's heat and the winter's cold, but that was all. Of comforts there were none. The cottage had no flooring, save that which was furnished by nature. . . . The mud walls were rarely covered with any coat of plastering; there was no ceiling under the straw roof, and when the hovel contained any other chamber, it was accessible only by means of a ladder or by a post indented with notches for the reception of the feet in climbing up to it. The doors and windows never closed sufficiently to exclude the rain or the snow, and in rainy weather puddles were scattered over the inequalities in the mud floor. Nor were the furniture and domestic utensils comparable in any respect with those which the households of the humblest cottagers are now found to contain." [2] Even in these days of marked inequality in the living conditions of rich and poor, it is questionable whether our tenement dwellers, ever sink to such a state of abject wretchedness and discomfort as characterized the peasantry in England during and after the seventeenth century. The children born into these homes were reared in ignorance and squalor, suffered, in the fen lands, from ague and frequently died of plague or smallpox in the absence of capable medical assistance. The parish doctors of those days were apt to be quacks, whose scanty knowledge was too often the product of a dubious experience.

In the reign of Queen Anne (1702–1714) the architecture of English houses underwent some changes which resulted in the red brick villas of many gables and a somewhat motley design

---

[1] *Op. cit.* (1645), Part II, p. 9.

[2] Sydney, *Social Life in England*, pp. 146–147.

that are commonly called "Queen Anne" houses. A recent writer is bold enough to assert that the so-called Queen Anne style "never had any existence at all except in the brains of modern æsthetics and china maniacs." [1] Be that it as may, it is certain that comfort and convenience in the interior planning of these houses were subordinated to the graceful proportion of the exterior. On the other hand the furniture of the period is marked by simplicity and elegance, as well as by an admirable adaptation of each piece to the end it was designed to serve.

During the early part of the Georgian period (until 1750), the classical designs of an Italian architect, Andreas Palladio by name, determined the style of English architecture. Although these homes were no doubt very fine and stately, it is questionable whether Italian villas were properly at home in the somewhat gray and inclement environment of England. Undoubtedly the Georgian homes built in the country were more comfortable and convenient than many of the city houses. These solid, spacious dwellings are thus happily described: "We all know the mellow brick Georgian houses with their stone facings and their spreading cedar trees about them. . . . The large square rooms could comfortably accommodate the hooped petticoat. . . . The front door is always in the center and is often surmounted by a graceful pediment. On either side are large sashed windows, the tiled roof slopes sharply up behind the parapet, and the chimneys are clustered at the four corners. We know that behind each of these houses is a large and charming garden, full of sweet-scented, old-fashioned flowers. . . ." [2]

The Economy of the English Household. — Within these country homes of the Stuart and Georgian periods the busy housewife plied her various tasks and entertained her friends with lavish hospitality. Less proficient than the elegant belles of London and Bath in the arts of the toilette and of killing

[1] Bradley, *The English Housewife*, pp. 267–268.
[2] *Ibid.*, p. 194.

time, these English wives and mothers were highly skilled in a bewildering variety of household industries. A picture of the ideal home maker of the early seventeenth century is drawn in Brathwaite's *English Gentlewoman:*

"Her household she makes her commonweale; wherein not any from the highest to the lowest of her feminine government, but knowes their peculiar office and employment; to which they addresse themselves (so highly they honour her they serve) with more love than feare. She becomes Promoter, I meane of no office to wrong her Countrey, but the tender care of a mother in behalfe of her well-educated progeny; . . . Markets shee seldom visits, nor any place of freer concourse; for she findes when her eyes are abroad, her thoughts are estrang'd from home." [1]

In such quaint language the author embodies the belief of the age that household duties should engross the entire interests and activities of every good wife and mother. Her home should be in very truth her world. Little marvel it is that even today some women are narrow individualists in tastes and employments, and are rarely moved to extend their active helpfulness to social movements for the betterment of mankind beyond the walls of their home. The ideal is too deeply rooted, the custom too firmly established to be easily modified or transformed.

The most valuable source of our knowledge of the industries carried on in an English household during the seventeenth century is probably the curious old work on *The English Housewife* written by Gervase Markham. However, this is only one of a large number of similar publications which served a valuable educational purpose. After descanting upon the moral virtues of a wife and her obligation to be temperate and modest "in her behaviour and carriage toward her Husband" even when "mishaps, or the misgovernment of his will may induce her to contrary thoughts," the writer plunges at once into his principal theme and describes in illuminating detail the duties

[1] *Op. cit.* (ed. 1641), p. 398.

of the housewife in the various departments of household economy. First and foremost among her "vertues" he places the "preservation and care of the family touching their health and soundness of body. . . ." To this end the housewife must know "how to administer any wholsom receipts or medicines . . . as well to prevent the first occasion of sickness as to take away the effects and evil of the same, when it hath made seizure on the body." To be sure Markham concedes that the "depth and secrets of this most excellent Art of Physick, are far beyond the capacity of the most skilful woman, as lodging only in the brest of learned Professors, . . ." yet this fact does not deter him from enumerating a host of minor ills which beset mankind, each with its appropriate remedy. Dandelion, poppy-seed, sorrel, lettuce, "Spinage," elder-leaves, featherfew, yarrow and "tansie" are only a few of the plants and herbs whose virtues the good housewife must know how to convert into medicinal draughts for the healing of her household.[1] No wonder the herb garden was so important a feature of the English homes of the period! Indeed some women attained great skill both in "physick" and surgery. The wife of Col. Hutchinson relates in her *Memoirs* that she attended the wounded of both sides during the siege of Nottingham.

Next in importance Markham places the art of cookery, going so far as to say that "she that is utterly ignorant therein, may not by Laws of strict Justice challenge the freedom of Marriage, because indeed she can then but perform half her vow; for she may live and obey, but she cannot cherish, serve and keep with that true duty which is ever expected." [2] Space is wanting to detail the multifarious household labors that are involved in the culinary art. It must suffice to mention that knowledge of herbs for seasoning, of the "compounding of Sallets" (salads), of fricasseeing, making of puddings, boiling, stewing and roasting meats, preparing of various sauces, making pastry, concocting marmalades, jellies, pastes and all kinds

[1] *Op. cit.* (9th ed., 1683), pp. 4–48.
[2] *Ibid.*, p. 49.

of conserves, baking "bisket bread" and plain bread, this and much more practical knowledge must be possessed by her who aspired to the proud title of skillful housewife. Some space is given by Markham to the important tasks connected with "Ordering of Banquets" both "great Feasts" and "humble" ones. Truly the quantity and variety of meats, fish, "sallets," fricassees and "Quelquechoses" figuring in a so-called "humble feast" seems overwhelming to the modern reader. For Markham declares that the meal should include "no less than two and thirty dishes which is as much as can conveniently stand on one Table, and in one mess; . . ."[1] And the English housewife must have prepared or supervised the preparation of every dish![2]

An entire chapter is given up in Markham's book to "Distillations and Their Vertues." The housewife is advised to obtain some good stills either of tin or "sweet earth" " and in them she shall distill all sorts of waters meet for the health of her Household. . . ." There follows a formidable list of these medicinal waters, such as angelica, sage water, rosemary water, saxifrage water and water distilled from bean-flowers, strawberries, vine leaves, goats' milk, asses' milk, lilies and calves' feet, which last is best "for the smoothing of the skin, and keeping the face delicate and amiable. . . ."[3] Having distilled medicines and lotions, the busy homeworker may then turn her attention to preparing the various perfumes and sweet salves so highly valued in the seventeenth century, and to the "election, preserving, and curing of all sorts of wines, because they be usual charges under her hands, and by the least neglect must turn the Husband to much loss. . . ."[4]

"Our English Housewife, after her knowledge of preserving and feeding her Family, must learn also, how, out of her own endeavors, she ought to cloathe them outwardly and inwardly

[1] *Op. cit.* (9th ed., 1683), p. 101.
[2] *Ibid.*, pp. 49–101.
[3] *Ibid.*, p. 101.
[4] *Ibid.*, pp. 112–113.

. . . the first consisting of Woollen cloth and the latter of linnen." [1] To this end "it is the office of a Husbandman at the shearing of his sheep to bestow upon the House-Wife such a competent proportion of Wooll, as shall be convenient for the cloathing of his Family. . . ." After receiving the raw wool the housewife is instructed to separate that portion she intends to "spin white" from that she intends to "put into colours." She is taught with great detail how to dye the wool, oil it, card it, and spin it "upon great wool-wheels. . . ." Then comes the careful division of the wool into parts for the warp and the "weft" respectively before it is "delivered up into the hands of the Weaver"; for, be it remembered that in the seventeenth century, most of the weaving of fabrics was done outside the household.

Having prepared her wool, the housewife may next turn her attention to the making of linen cloth. And here opens up a wide range of activities in the right performance of which she receives full instructions. She must know where best to sow the hemp and flax seed, and how to weed, "pull" and moisten the plants when they are above the ground. Much skill is required in first watering and then drying the hemp or flax. Next it must be twice "swingled" or beaten with a "Swingle-tree dagger," after which the heckling may begin. This of course consists in combing the hemp first with a coarse wide-toothed instrument, then with "a good straight Heckle made purposely for Hemp. . . ." The heckle used for flax must be "much finer and straighter" than that for hemp, but the process is the same. Then follows the spinning, reeling, scouring and "whitning" of the hempen and linen yarn, which is finally wound into balls ready for the weaver. But when the woven cloth is returned, it must be again scoured and whitened before it is made up into household linen and garments. [2]

Lest the housewife find time hanging heavily on her hands she is further introduced to the mysteries of butter and cheese

[1] *Op. cit.* (9th ed., 1683), p. 122.
[2] *Ibid.*, Bk. 2, Chs. V, VI.

making, the care of the dairy and even the rearing of calves. Then, too, it is important that she know how to prepare malt from which "is made the Drink by which the Household is nourished and sustained. . . ." This is a many-sided industry in itself and leads directly to the allied art of brewing. Ale and beer were then the most popular drinks of Englishmen, and minute are the directions for the skillful preparation of these national beverages.[1]

It has seemed worth while to outline in some detail the household industries of the seventeenth century that the reader may appreciate what an invaluable producer the English housewife assuredly was. In these days, when most of the complicated processes named above have been entirely removed from the home, women of narrow education and interests, who can afford to keep a servant or two, must frequently find time hang heavily on their hands. The idle "lady" is largely a phenomenon of modern times, due in part to the increase and dissemination of wealth consequent upon the industrial Revolution, in part to the transformation of industry from the domestic to the factory system, and in part to the pride taken by successful men in maintaining their wives in an indolent luxury which is supposed to enhance their charms. Even so early as the latter part of the seventeenth century this parasitic type of idle, pleasure-loving woman was emerging and being shaped by a variety of circumstances. But it was during the eighteenth and nineteenth centuries that she became gradually perfected as a type.

Home Nurture and Education. — How important a part was played by English homes during this period in the nurture and training of children? A numerous offspring was the rule in these days, yet relatively few children were reared. If the literature of the time is to be believed, the child mortality was truly appalling when compared with our modern age. In her delightful *Memoirs*, Ann, Lady Fanshawe, mentions fourteen children born alive to her, between the years 1645–

[1] *Op. cit.* (9th ed., 1683), Bk. 2, Chs. VII, IX.

1665, of whom only two lived to grow up![1] Seven of these little ones died in infancy, and there can be little doubt that the ignorance of child hygiene and diet prevalent among mothers and physicians at this time was chiefly responsible for this harvest of death. In a recent study of *The Infant Welfare Movement in the Eighteenth Century* Ernest Caulfield has collected some startling statistics of the causes of infant deaths in London about 1741. He estimates that 75 per cent of all children christened were dead before they had reached five years of age. Certain Englishmen, as Thomas Coram and George Armstrong, horrified by this holocaust of babies, urgently advocated that mothers nurse their own infants and clothe them comfortably. Doctors were exhorted not to leave obstetrics and infant health to "old women" but to concern themselves far more actively in these fields of their profession, so long neglected.

In the seventeenth century the swaddling of babies was no longer practiced in England, so English infants, at least, were freed from those cramping bands that provoked the indignant protests of Rousseau in the *Émile*. But it is probable that the infant of wealthy parents received less of the mother's personal care than in the previous periods. The nurse became an important figure in the well-to-do households of the time and exercised a control over the children, both boys and girls, which was all but supreme. Although this nursery government of the boy ceased when he was seven years of age and went away to school, it frequently continued in the case of the girl until she was married. The nurse it was that taught her small charges the fascinating rhymes now gathered together in *Mother Goose*. "Old King Cole," "Tom the Piper's Son" and the "Robin Hood" songs were childhood favorites then as now. Also children looked to their nurse to recount those charming fairy tales that were old even in the seventeenth century — such tales as "Puss in Boots," "Cinderella," "Sleeping Beauty" and "Bluebeard." The games of English children at this

[1] *Memoirs of Ann, Lady Fanshawe* (ed. 1907).

time were probably more varied than ours of to-day. There can be little doubt that in the absence of our wealth of expensive toys, which are more or less exact reproductions of their complicated originals, the playthings of English children made far larger demands on their imagination and resourcefulness than do ours. The games of small boys and girls of that day were often imitations of the various industries they saw going on about them. In these they were assisted by the delightful resources of an English country house of the Stuart period. The shed of the harness maker, the blacksmith's forge and the fascinating shop of the carpenter, all could be found on the premises, and must have been unfailing sources of profitable amusement.[1]

Family discipline continued to be severe in the seventeenth century, although even then signs were not lacking that a milder order of control was creeping in. Yet the rod and strict confinement on bread and water were still freely used; and we are told that Elizabeth Tanfield, first Lady Falkland, never addressed her harsh and autocratic mother save on her knees![2] In the *Verney Memoirs* we read a pathetic letter in which the grandmother of Ralph Verney's little boy, who was not yet three years old, urges her son not to have the child forcibly "strudgeled" and to allow no one but his tutor to whip him. But this was perhaps an exceptional case. Gentler relations were fortunately coming to prevail between parents and children; and these were greatly furthered by the individualistic movement of the eighteenth century, especially in France. Very slowly ideas concerning the personal rights of children began to influence English society and resulted in modern legislation for the protection of children, and in an enlightened public opinion in favor of rational and kindly methods of discipline.

While still in the nursery, English children laid the foundations of their education under the guidance of nurse and

[1] See Godfrey, *English Children in the Olden Time*, pp. 62–63.
[2] Godfrey, *Home Life under the Stuarts*, p. 9.

mother. At two years of age, they must learn the alphabet, and for this purpose much use was made of wooden blocks with the letters printed on them — an invention of Sir Hugh Plat in the late sixteenth century. Having mastered the rudiments of learning, the child was promoted to study of the "hornbook," the original primer of our forefathers. This quaint invention usually consisted of a piece of board on which were printed the letters of the alphabet in large and small type, the Lord's prayer and, in Catholic countries, the "Hail Mary." Over the printed matter was fastened a piece of horn to protect it. From these humble beginnings of knowledge the child advanced to reading of the primer. One of the earliest was Coote's *The English Schoole Master*, published in 1636. At an early age, also, children were taught to count and to perform simple reckoning by the aid of the abacus, which was found in well-nigh every English nursery until the end of the eighteenth century.

These simple tasks, together with religious instruction and learning of the catechism — Anglican or Westminster — constituted the bulk of nursery education. But the little boys of the period had a tremendous advantage over the girls, since they were free to play out-of-doors when their tasks were done; whereas the girls must train their tiny fingers to make the samplers of fine canvas worked in delicate cross-stitch, so highly prized at the time. One cannot but pity these small maidens thus early condemned to "keep the house" and strain eyes and nerves over intricate work too often in advance of their undeveloped powers of coördination and control. A few of these marvelous samplers have been handed down to modern times; and one wonders whether the pious and dutiful sentiments painfully worked thereon really expressed the thoughts and feelings of the young needlewomen. Even when the daily "stint" on her sampler was done, the little girl could not escape into the out-of-doors. Mother or nurse was at hand to teach her to "sew a seam" with the painstaking care that evokes admiration and wonder in this more impatient and hurried generation.

After nursery days were past, the education of boys and likewise of girls (so far as they received any) was frequently intrusted to a private tutor.   Quite commonly tutors in French, in playing on lute and virginals, and in dancing, were engaged to instruct girls of the well-to-do classes in their homes, while their brothers were wrestling with the intricacies of Latin and Greek grammar in preparation for public school and University. We are told that Colonel Hutchinson personally supervised the education of his sons and daughters even while employing numerous carefully chosen tutors for them.   But complaints were not lacking at this time of the carelessness of parents in selecting their sons' teachers.   Thus Peacham, writing in 1634, says: "It is not commonly seene, that the most gentlemen will give better wages, and deale more bountifully with a fellow who can but teach a dogge, or reclaime an hawke, than upon an honest, learned and well-qualified man to bring up their children!" [1]

Nor were matters improved in the eighteenth century. DeFoe expends much biting sarcasm in attacking the English custom of entailing estates in favor of the eldest son.   With his future thus provided for, the education of the heir was intrusted to inferior tutors; and the younger sons, who must shift for themselves, were carefully educated for the professions or government service.   DeFoe declares that the difference between a liberal education "and the meer old woman literature of a nurse and a tutor" is clearly demonstrated in English families, "where the bright and the dull, . . . the man of sence and learning and the blockhead is as often to be disscern'd where one is untaught and good for nothing because he is to have the estate, and the other is polish'd and educated because he is to make his fortune; . . ." [2]   To defects of ignorance and lack of training, DeFoe attributes the fact that many English landowners "are also in but very indifferent condicion as to family circumstances, and many even of the greatest estates are overwhelm'd in debt. . . ." [3]

---

[1] *Compleat Gentleman*, p. 31.
[2] *Compleat English Gentleman* (ed. 1730), p. 68.   [3] *Ibid.*, pp. 104–105.

But carelessness, or niggardliness, in the choice of household tutors was not the only charge brought against eighteenth century parents. The literature of the period fairly bristles with references to the neglect of their maternal duties by fashionable ladies. Thus DeFoe writes : "It is indeed too true that this wealthy age is so entirely given up to pleasure, and it prevails so much among the ladyes as well as among the men, that it grows a little unfashionable for the mothers to give themselves any trouble with their children, after they have 'em, but to order their dress and make them fine and to make a show of them upon occasion. 'Tis below a lady of quallity to trouble her selfe in the nursery, as 'tis below the gentleman of quallity to trouble himselfe with a library." [1]

Not only were the girl children of society-loving mothers confined to the nursery under the care of servants, but when their nursery education was ended they were quite commonly sent to fashionable boarding schools where they were taught a mere smattering of French, music, needlework, and dancing, which last was a highly valued art. Even the training of the growing girl in household management and the arts of cooking was apt to be neglected in favor of elegant and often useless needlework and "accomplishments." Whereas girls in the seventeenth century were carefully instructed by their mothers in "the preparation of whatever required more art or curiosity for the closet or the parlor, as preserving, drawing spirits in an alembic or cold still, pastry, angelots, and other cream cheese . . ." and were trained in all forms of useful needlework, city girls in the eighteenth century were not uncommonly sent to the schools of professional pastry cooks to get a smattering of this homely knowledge and skill. Ashton mentions these schools and quotes from the advertisement of a famous one in Lincoln's Inn Fields which claimed to teach "all Sorts of Pastry and Cookery, Dutch hollow works, and Butter Works. . . ." [2] In his play, *The Tender Husband*, Steele

[1] *Ibid.*, p. 71.
[2] *Social Life in the Reign of Queen Anne*, p. 24.

represents an aunt as upbraiding her niece for her ignorance of domestic arts. The aunt informs the girl that her mother "spent her time in better Learning than ever you did. Not in reading of Fights and Battels of Dwarfs and Giants; but in writing out receipts for Broths, Possets, Caudles and Surfeit Waters as became a good Country Gentlewoman." Yet no doubt the country homes, at least, continued to give girls a careful training in household management.

But, if the education of their daughters in domestic affairs was neglected by some fashionable mothers, they never over-looked the training of their girls in social graces and in the supremely important art of getting a husband. On this point Hughes has expressed his sentiments in the *Spectator:* "The general mistake among us in the educating our children is, that in our daughters we take care of their persons, and neglect their minds; in our sons we are so intent upon adorning their minds that we wholly neglect their bodies. . . . When a girl is safely brought from her nurse, before she is capable of form-ing one simple notion of any thing in life, she is delivered to the hands of her dancing-master; and with a collar round her neck, the pretty wild thing is taught a fantastical gravity of behaviour, and forced to a particular way of holding her head, heaving her breast, and moving with her whole body; and all this under pain of never having a husband, if she steps, looks or moves awry. This gives the young lady wonderful workings of imagination, what is to pass between her and this husband, that she is every moment told of and for whom she seems to be educated." [1] One is tempted to ask why, indeed, should not a girl's home education have been directed solely to one end? Since getting a husband was the goal of existence for nine tenths of the women of England, since failure in this respect meant lamentable failure in life at a time when opportunities for single women to attain honorable financial independence were conspicuously wanting, surely few women would hesitate to exercise all their charms to capture a mate rather than sit

[1] Chalmers' *British Essayists*, "The Spectator," Vol. VII, pp. 25–26.

at the fireside of reluctant relatives in the rôle of unwelcome old maids ! In those days to be an "old maid" was nothing short of a tragedy ; for it meant that a woman, no matter how comfortably fixed in life, would lead an empty existence, barren of purpose and large interests, and irrevocably stamped with the crushing mark of the unsuccessful.

With her inimitable satiric humor Jane Austen describes in *Pride and Prejudice* the deep satisfaction of every member of the Lucas family when the oldest daughter, Charlotte, becomes engaged to Mr. Collins, an unattractive bore who had but a week previously offered his heart and hand to Charlotte's best friend. Everyone is delighted. Sir William and Lady Lucas rejoice at marrying off an aging daughter of twenty-seven. The younger sisters are happy at the prospect of being introduced to society sooner than they had dared to hope, since they had been held back to enhance Charlotte's "prospects." The brothers congratulate themselves that their sister will not fall back on them for support after her parents' death. Charlotte herself was "tolerably composed." Although she was well aware that Mr. Collins was "neither sensible nor agreeable; [that] his society was irksome, and his attachment to her must be imaginary," yet she had at long last captured a husband. "Without thinking highly either of men or of matrimony, marriage had always been her object ; it was the only honourable provision for well-educated young women of small fortune, and however uncertain of giving happiness, must be their *pleasantest preservative from want.*" [1]

This vivid picture of the plight of all single women at this time, not only in England but elsewhere, was painted early in the nineteenth century when the knell of the old order was already sounding. Economic and social conditions, together with a false conception of woman and her functions, were responsible for the situation in which women found themselves. It required both an economic and social upheaval to modify

[1] *Op. cit.*, Everyman's Library (1906), pp. 105–106. Italics mine.

the prevalent ideas about women and to transform their social
status and education.

SELECTED READINGS
SOURCES

Addison, Joseph.   *The Spectator*, Nos. 33, 53, 66, 92, 157.

———.   *The Guardian*, No. 155.

Alexander, Wm.   *History of Woman*, Philadelphia, J. H. Dobelbower,
    1796, 2 Vols., Vol. I, pp. 332, 461, 501–506; Vol. II, pp. 1, 112, 502–
    511.

Astell, Mary.   *Some Reflections upon Marriage*, London, Wm. Parker,
    4th ed., 1730, pp. 1–55.

———.   *An Essay in Defense of the Female Sex*, London, A. Roper and
    E. Wilkinson, 1696, pp. 5, 14, 23, 32–33, 48–49.

Bennett, John.   *Strictures on Female Education*, Philadelphia, W. Spots-
    wood and H. & P. Rice, 1793, pp. 44–45, 81–124, 133–139, 144–152.

Brathwaite, Richard.   *The English Gentleman and the English Gentle-
    woman*, London, John Dawson, 1641, Dedication and pp. 397–400.

DeFoe, Daniel.   *The Compleat English Gentleman*, ed. by K. D. Bülbring
    from the author's MSS., London, 1890, pp. 68–180, 247–255.

Edgeworth, Maria.   *Practical Education*, N. Y., Brown and Stansbury,
    1801, Ch. XX.

Evelyn, Sir John.   *Literary Remains: Mundus Muliebris*, Wm. Upcott,
    ed., London, 1834, pp. 699–713.

Fanshawe, Anne (Harrison).   *Memoirs of Ann, Lady Fanshawe*, N. Y.,
    John Lane Co., 1907.

Godwin, Mrs. Mary W.   *Thoughts on the Education of Daughters*, London,
    J. Johnson, 1787.

Gregory, Dr. John.   *A Father's Legacy to his Daughters*, London, 1784,
    pp. 18–19, 31–52, 68, 120–137.

Hayley, Wm.   *A Philosophical, Historical, and Moral Essay on Old
    Maids*, London, T. Cadwell, 1785, 3 Vols., Vol. I, pp. 7–19.

Howell, James.   *Familiar Letters*, Aberdeen, 1753 (10th ed.).

Kames, Henry Home.   *Loose Hints upon Education*, Edinburgh, Bell,
    Robinson, and Murray, 1782, pp. 8–12, 133–136, 222–229.

Markham, Gervase.   *The English Housewife*, London, H. Sawbridge,
    1683, entire.

More, Hannah.   *Essays on Various Subjects, Principally Designed for
    Young Ladies*, Philadelphia, Young, Stewart and McCulloch, 1786.

———. *Strictures on the Modern System of Female Education*, N. Y., E. Duyckisick, 1813, Vol. I, pp. 64–70, 105–115, Ch. VII; Vol. II, pp. 14–31, 172–178.

Steele, Richard. *The Tatler*, Nos. 61, 141, 185, 201, 248.

———. *The Guardian*, Nos. 73, 172.

Swinburne, Henry. *Of Spousals*, London, D. Brown, 1711.

Tusser, Thomas. *A Book of Huswifery* (together with *Five Hundred Points of Good Husbandry*), London, Lackington, Allen, and Co., 1812.

Verney, Frances Parthenope. *Memoirs of the Verney Family during the 17th Century*, 2 Vols., N. Y., Longmans, Green and Co., 1925.

"Verney Papers," in *Camden Society Publications*, 1853, Vol. 56, pp. 145–169.

Wollstonecraft, Mary. *Vindication of the Rights of Women* (1792). Reprinted in *Humboldt Library of Science*, XV, pp. 37–45, 75–83.

SECONDARY WORKS

Ashton, John. *Eighteenth Century Waifs*, London, Hurst and Blackett, 1887, pp. 17–30.

———. *Social Life in the Reign of Queen Anne*, Chatto and Windus, 1882, Chs. I–III, V, VIII.

———. *The Dawn of the Nineteenth Century in England*, London, T. F. Unwin, 1916, Chs. XXXIII, XXXIV.

Ballard, Geo. *Memoirs of British Ladies*, London, T. Evans, 1775, pp. 204–224, 264–266.

Bradley, Rose M. *The English Housewife in the 17th and 18th Centuries*, London, E. Arnold, 1912.

Chapman, Annie B. and Mary W. *The Status of Women under the English Law*, N. Y., E. P. Dutton and Co., 1909; see Acts 1492–1832.

Clark, Alice. *Working Life of Women in the Seventeenth Century*, N. Y., E. P. Dutton and Co., 1919, Chs. V, VI.

Cleveland, Arthur R. *Women under the English Law*, London, Hurst and Blackett, 1896, pp. 169–236.

Godfrey, Elizabeth (pseud.). *Home Life under the Stuarts*, N. Y., E. P. Dutton and Co., 1904, Chs. I, II, VII–IX, XII, XIV–XVI.

———. *English Children in the Olden Time*, London, Methuen and Co., 1907, Chs. I–III, IV–VI, XI, XIII.

Hill, Georgiana. *Women in English Life*, London, R. Bentley and Sons, 1896, Vol. I, 145–192, 307–350.

Howard, G. E. *History of Matrimonial Institutions*, University of Chicago Press, 1904, Vol. I, Ch. II; Vol. II, pp. 85–109.

Phillips, M., and Tomkinson, W. S. *English Women in Life and Letters*, New York, Oxford University Press, 1927, Chs. II, III, IV.

Reich, Emil. *Women through the Ages*, London, Methuen and Co., 1908, Vol. II, pp. 39–67.

Sydney, Wm. Conner. *Social Life in England from the Restoration to the Revolution, 1660–1690*. N. Y., Macmillan and Co., 1892, pp. 159–163.

Tickner, F. W. *Women in English Economic History*, London and Toronto, J. M. Dent and Sons, 1923, Chs. VI–VIII.

CHAPTER IX

THE FAMILY IN THE AMERICAN COLONIES

The Early Settlements. — In the early years of the seventeenth century began the first stream of emigration from the mother-country in England to the untried shores of America. Political and economic as well as religious reasons were responsible for the first colonization of the New World; although the first two motives operated more largely in the founding of Virginia and the latter in the settlement of the first New England colonies. Much has been written of the courage that burned high in the hearts of the men who left their native land to plant new homes in an inhospitable wilderness. Literature acquaints us in great detail with the cruel hardships these men endured, with their strenuous daily toil in building houses and raising crops, with their constant anxiety concerning their Indian neighbors and their brave defense of homes and families against the merciless onslaughts of the savages. But until recent years comparatively little tribute has been paid to the unflinching loyalty and courage of the wives and mothers of these pathfinders. Nor has it been clearly recognized that the crushing hardships, the enervating disappointments, which always accompany the colonization of a virgin wilderness, would have been impossible of endurance had not the women lent their invaluable aid to the work of making homes. That the English colonization of America was successfully carried out only with the help of a small band of women is stated by a modern historian to be "one of the best authenticated facts in the history of America's infancy." [1] He cites as evidence the unsatisfactory conditions that prevailed in

[1] J. A. Bruce in *Woman in the Making of America* (1912), p. 3.

the first Virginia colony so long as the men labored on without wives or homes. Discontent and restlessness were rife and were about to break forth in open rebellion when the Virginia Company in England came under the direction of a wise and far-sighted man, Sir Edwin Sandys, who clearly saw that the disaffection of the colonists was chiefly caused by their loveless lives and their homeless state. The Records of the Virginia Company [1] contain his blunt and sensible advice to his colleagues: "We must find them wives, in order that they may feel at home in Virginia." And with no unnecessary delay wives were indeed found for these eager settlers — young, honest, hard-working girls, who left the mother-country for the new land of their adoption with the wistful hope that it might provide them with good husbands and good homes. These courageous maids, ninety in number, were received with the utmost enthusiasm and were eagerly besieged by the lonely colonists who desired them in marriage. Only a man who could demonstrate his ability to support a wife and who could afford to pay the passage money of his chosen one, amounting to one hundred and twenty pounds of leaf tobacco, was granted the privilege of securing a bride from among this bevy of English maids. Moreover, it was stipulated that he must win the consent of the young woman, which was in no way to be forced. In such primitive fashion was the Virginia colony furnished with wives and mothers. The effect upon the discontented settlers was speedy and beneficent. In the quaint words of the chronicler, men then "sett down satysfied" in the homes they had founded; and they no more sighed for the comforts of Old England.

Not only was the spirit of colonial wives undaunted by danger and suffering, but their helpfulness was of the most practical and energetic sort. New England women helped their husbands in the task of building their first rude log homes and later they set to work to furnish them. This was accomplished largely through their own efforts, eked out by

[1] Vol. I, p. 269.

the household treasures brought from England.   The wives
of the first Pennsylvania settlers assisted in digging the caves
in the high banks of the Delaware that served as their first
homes.   In the records of the Quaker family of Hard we may
read of Elizabeth Hard's share in building such a home.   The
account is written by her niece :

"All that came wanted a Dwelling and hastened to provide
one.   As they lovingly helped each other, the Women even
set themselves to work that they had not been used to before;
for few of the first settlers were of the Laborous Class, and help
of that source was scarce.   My good Aunt thought it expedient
to help her Husband at the end of the saw, and to fetch all
such Water to make such kind of Mortar, as they then had to
build their chimney.   At one time being overwearied there-
with, her Husband desired her to forbear, saying, 'thou had
better, my dear, think of dinner'; . . ." Unfortunately the
poor lady lacked all wherewithal for a meal and walked away
in discouragement, quietly weeping as she went.   But she soon
bravely reminded herself that she now had the priceless gift
of liberty of conscience for which she long had prayed; so,
dropping on her knees, she begged God for forgiveness and
help.   The narrative goes on to tell us that scarcely had she
risen and started to seek food when the cat appeared with
"a fine large Rabbit, which she thankfully received and
dressed as an English hare.   When her Husband came to
dinner, being informed of the particulars, they both wept
with reverential Joy, and Eat their Meal, which was thus
seasonably provided for them, in singleness of heart." [1]   It is
gratifying to learn that later, when this same Hard family,
together with their relatives, the Morrises, became well-to-do
and owned rich family plate, some of it was engraved with
the design of the provident cat bringing the rabbit in her
teeth.

Severe as were the sufferings in the Middle Colonies they
were not so cruel as those endured by the settlers on the bleak

[1] Quoted in Wharton, A. H., *Colonial Days and Dames*, pp. 68, 69.

coast of New England. We read in *Winthrop's Journal*[1] of the loss of precious cattle and swine through the attacks of wolves; of the bitter cold which froze feet and fingers, of the outbreak of scurvy, and of the scarcity of even the coarse Indian corn which was the staple article of food among the colonists for several years. In the course of a few years, however, more substantial and comfortable homes took the place of the log huts hastily built as temporary shelters from the bitter cold. About 1650 Johnson, in his *Wonderworking Providence of Zion's Saviour in New England*, quaintly describes Boston as "a City-like Towne . . . crowded on the Sea-banks and wharfed out with great industry and cost, the buildings beautifull and large, some fairely set forth with Brick, Tile, Stone, and Slate, and orderly placed with comly streets, whose continuall enlargement presages some sumptuous City. . . ."[2] No doubt this enthusiastic Puritan's account is somewhat biased by his praiseworthy desire to glorify the "wonder-working Providence" whom he so devoutly worshiped. Apparently many of these early houses were of wood, fairly spacious and comfortable, the forerunners in architectural design of the typical colonial dwellings of a later period. Little by little, as the first hand-to-hand conflicts with an inhospitable Nature were crowned with success, life became something more than a struggle for bare existence. Gradually a few comforts crept into the homes of the settlers scattered along the coasts from the Carolinas to Massachusetts, and these home comforts increased as the years passed by. In the plantation homes of the South, in the neat Dutch houses of Manhattan, and in the colonial dwellings of New England, various types of family life were developed. But in all was the true spirit of the home. These newer generations were American born and felt no such heartsick longing for the mother-country as must have frequently troubled their parents. Their traditions, their hopes, their purposes were

[1] Edition of 1908, Vol. I, pp. 58, 68, 105.
[2] *Op. cit.*, edited by Jameson (1910), p. 71.

bound up with the new land that they were so hopefully and energetically developing.

THE STATUS OF WOMEN IN COLONIAL DAYS

Establishment of English Common Law. — It is not to be expected that the English colonists of America would all at once change their customary ideas and practices with respect to womankind. These men, Cavaliers and Puritans alike, had been reared amid authoritative traditions of the intellectual, social and legal inferiority of women; and these traditions they naturally brought with them to the land of their adoption. English private law became the "common law" of the colonies with a few changes that will be noted later. The details of this system of private law have been given in the preceding chapter. Therefore it is necessary only to recall that married women were controlled, both in person and in property, by their husbands, whom they were bound to serve and obey. They were in legal phrase *sub potestate viri* — under the power of the husband — and be it remembered that the husband held the purse-strings. Only in case an allowance strictly for their personal use were settled upon women at marriage were they relieved from a condition of complete financial dependence. Even the clothing and ornaments of a married woman belonged to the husband during his lifetime and might be disposed of as he saw fit; whereas her chattels, or property in money and movables of any sort, became his absolute property, as did also the wife's earnings. Likewise the husband was the sole guardian of the offspring of the marriage, and he alone could determine important questions concerning the education, religious training, preparation for life-work and marriage of his boys and girls.

The status of married women according to the English common law is thus described by Mr. Justice Blackstone, writing late in the eighteenth century:

"By marriage the husband and wife are one person in law;

that is, the very being or legal existence of the woman is suspended during the marriage, or at least is incorporated and consolidated into that of her husband. . . . Upon this principle of a union of person in husband and wife depend almost all the legal rights, duties and disabilities that either of them acquire by the marriage. . . . For this reason a man cannot grant anything to his wife, or enter into covenant with her; for the grant would be to suppose her separate existence, and to covenant with her would be only to covenant with himself; and therefore it is also generally true that all compacts made between husband and wife when single are voided by the inter-marriage." [1]

Yet it should be noted that, despite her loss of legal personality, a wife might inherit property from some third person, although the husband at once assumed its control and enjoyed its profits as long as the marriage continued. Only if her husband died before her was his widow granted the management of her property. At the death of the wife the husband lost his interest in her landed estate except in case a living child was born of the marriage. In such an event, even if the child were not living at the time of the wife's death, the husband became vested with an estate in her lands for the remainder of his life. This is technically called his "estate by the courtesy of England" or merely his "courtesy estate." This English custom became thoroughly established among the colonies in America.

But the husband of colonial times had certain disabilities as well as advantages growing out of the marriage relation. He must maintain his wife in accordance with his means, whether or not she brought him property at marriage. To be sure, the American colonists were as shrewd bargainers with respect to marriage contracts as were their English forefathers; and they took good care to see that a dowry, big or little, went with the woman of their choice. Indeed, the higgling of the Puritan Judge Sewall over matters of dowry and settlement

---

[1] Blackstone's *Commentaries*.

with the three fair widows whom he successively sought in marriage, makes interesting reading. The bargaining is quite open and unashamed on both sides.[1] Yet it must be remembered that if the advantage went against the husband he was required by law properly to support his wife and was held liable not only for her necessary debts contracted after marriage but for any unpaid debts for which she was liable before the marriage. This provision of English law led to the crude and curious custom of "smock-marriages" in some of the colonies — a practice imported from the mother-country. It was held by certain of the more ignorant men and women of the time that if a widow were married in her smock without other clothing and without head-gear her husband would be exempt from paying her anti-nuptial debts. We are glad to learn that many of these marriages took place in the evening, thus saving some shreds of the bride's modesty. Alice Morse Earle in her delightful book, *Customs and Fashions in Old New England*, has collected some interesting instances of "smock-marriages." Certain it is that they were not confined to New England. As late as 1748 a certain Mr. Hahn, traveling in Pennsylvania, relates that a bridegroom in that colony went to meet his widow-bride on the highroad and announced in the presence of several witnesses that the clothing he considerately threw over her scantily clad person was only lent for the wedding festivity.[2]

Not only was the right of a woman to proper maintenance by her husband secured to her by the common law, but her dower rights in her husband's lands were likewise carefully protected throughout the colonies. With this end in view the law required that the husband obtain the concurrence of his wife in the sale or alienation of any considerable portion of his landed estate.

So much for the wife's property rights. The colonists seem

[1] See Sewall's *Diary* (Massachusetts Historical Society, Boston, 1882), Vol. III, pp. 269–274; also pp. 302–303.

[2] Earle, *op. cit.*, pp. 78–79.

also to have taken some steps to protect the person of a married woman from assault or libel. In most of the American colonies a man was not permitted to beat his wife — a luxury which he had long enjoyed in Old England — nor could he even belabor her with his tongue too freely. Doubtless many married men in colonial times were guilty of both offenses, but their wives might bring action against them at any time. In his history of *Haverhill*, Chase mentions the case of a man who, when summoned for beating his wife, boldly claimed his right so to do on the ground that she was his "servant and slave." But this was by no means the theory of his fellow citizens, as the offender no doubt discovered to his cost. Indeed, throughout the New England colonies, the charge of extreme cruelty was sufficient if established to secure for the wife a legal separation, although not often a complete divorce unless accompanied by infidelity. In the southern colonies, however, where the Church of England was established, and where, in consequence, marital cases if brought to court at all must be tried in ecclesiastical courts, no provision seems to have been made during colonial times to free a woman from the tyranny of a cruel husband.[1]

But if the wife's rights in respect to abuse, corporal and verbal, were duly protected, so also were the husband's. Everywhere in the colonies a "curst and shrewish tongue" exposed a married woman to the hateful penalty of stocks, pillory or ducking-stool. Indeed this last-named instrument for the punishment of scolding wives seems not to have disappeared in a few states until early in the nineteenth century.

Right of Women to Hold Lands. — In the New England colonies little encouragement was given to independent women (*i.e*, single women and widows) to take up and develop lands. Mistress Deborah Moody, who purchased large tracts of land near Swampscott, Massachusetts, was not very cordially received by the colonial authorities and soon removed to the

---

[1] See Howard, *Hist. of Mat. Inst.*, Vol. II, pp. 34–37, for Mass. Bay Colony; and for the Southern Colonies, pp. 366–376.

Dutch colony of New Netherlands. Yet the town authorities of Boston were scrupulous in including women when they made allotments of land to families according to their numbers; and the town of Salem granted "maid-lotts" to single women in the early days of settlement. The practice, however, came under the disapproval of Governor Endicott, who advised that it be abandoned, thus avoiding "all precedents and evil events of granting lotts unto single maidens not disposed of." [1]

The southern and middle colonies were more hospitable to independent women settlers. Haddonfield, New Jersey, was settled by a young woman, Elizabeth Haddon by name, who came alone to the colony when she was only nineteen years old, and managed her father's extensive lands with remarkable business judgment. Another courageous woman was the widow Mary Tewee, who took up an enormous tract of land in Pennsylvania which she cleared and cultivated. But the most remarkable case of the kind is that of Mistress Margaret Brent, who, with her scarcely less capable sister Mary, emigrated from England to the Maryland colony in 1638. The two sisters took up land, built manor houses and became active in a variety of business affairs. When Leonard Calvert, Governor of the colony and brother of the Proprietary, Lord Baltimore, died in 1647 he appointed Margaret Brent as his sole executrix — a truly surprising step to take in those days! The lady seems to have distinguished herself not only in business but in the public affairs of the colony. We read that when the small army, which had served the government in certain troubles and had remained unpaid, was on the verge of mutiny Mistress Brent took matters into her own capable hands. With no authority she sold cattle belonging to the Proprietary and paid off the angry men. Apparently Lord Baltimore wrote a tart letter of protest to this "meddling" dame, for the Assembly gallantly intervened in her behalf. In a joint letter they said:

[1] Earle, *Colonial Dames and Goodwives*, pp. 50-51.

"As for Mrs. Brent's undertaking and meddling with your Lordship's estate here . . . we do verily believe and in conscience report that it was better, for the colony's safety at that time, in her hands than in any man's else in the whole province after your brother's death." [1]

After reading this account we are not surprised to learn that this same dauntless lady in 1648 boldly entered the Assembly and, in the words of the record, "requested to have vote in the House for herself and voyce allsoe, for that on the last Court 3rd January it was ordered that the said Mrs. Brent was to be looked upon and received as his Lordship's Attorney." It is not difficult to imagine the dismay and disapproval that filled the masculine breasts of the members of the Assembly at this unheard-of request from a woman. Very promptly they put America's first advocate of woman's suffrage in her place, for the record reads: "The Governor deny'd that s'd Mrs. Brent should have any vote in the house. And the s'd Mrs. Brent protested against all proceedings in this present Assembly unless she may be present and have vote as afores'd." [2]

Attitude toward Women in the Colonies. — In the southern colonies, especially in Virginia, the scarcity of women during the early days of settlement caused them to be held in high esteem and to be eagerly sought in marriage. Although the common law of England had been thoroughly established throughout these colonies, with all its disabilities respecting women, there sprang up and flourished in the plantation homes of the South a spirit of chivalrous courtesy and regard for women. This attitude had early characterized the finer type of English Cavalier — the type which was in part responsible for the founding of the great plantations of the South.

The spirit is exemplified in the words of Governor Spotswood of Virginia, spoken to his friend Colonel Byrd on the occasion of the latter's visit to the Governor's house "Germanna" on

[1] Bruce, *Women in the Making of America*, pp. 26–27.
[2] Quoted in Earle, *Colonial Dames and Goodwives*, pp. 47–48.

the edge of the wilderness. To this frontier settlement the Governor had brought his gently bred wife, who cheerfully and bravely accepted her isolated life. Of her the Governor said, when his friend rallied him on his husbandly devotion, "that whoever brings a poor gentlewoman into so solitary a place from all her friends and acquaintances, would be ungrateful not to use her with all possible tenderness." [1] And, on the whole, the wives of the Southern planters received a degree of tender consideration not so generously bestowed on those of the middle and New England colonies. Not that the women of the North were not loved and respected, for they surely were. But love in stern New England was somewhat rigidly controlled and its open manifestations were on the whole discouraged. Then, too, the Puritans, as we have seen, cordially embraced the view of the ancient Hebrews, of Paul and of the Early Christian Fathers, that women were an inferior order of beings to be wisely held in control by their lawful husbands and masters. If a descendant of the Massachusetts Puritans could, in the year of our Lord 1876, write as follows of women's sphere, what must have been the rooted conviction of his ancestors?

"The ordinary occupations of the female sex are necessarily of a kind which must ever prevent it from partaking of the action of life. However keenly women may think or feel, there is seldom an occasion when the sphere of their exertions can with propriety be extended much beyond the domestic hearth or the social circle." [2]

Now, since the "social circle" in Puritan New England was highly restricted until after the first quarter of the eighteenth century, it is safe to assume that Puritan women's lives were almost wholly bounded by the interests of home, with the weekly visit to the meeting-house on Sunday and the "Lecture" on Thursday. But even their liberty to attend

[1] Wharton, *Colonial Days and Dames*, pp. 86–87.
[2] Adams, Charles Francis, "Memoir of Mrs. Adams" in his *Familiar Letters of John Adams and his Wife Abigail Adams* (Cambridge, 1876), p. xxii.

religious meetings became a subject of controversy in the Providence colony, where an order had been passed that no man should be molested for his conscience. Governor Winthrop relates that a certain man, Verin by name, refused to permit his wife to go to the meeting held by Roger Williams "so oft as she was called for." Whereupon certain men of the colony would have summoned this husband for censure. "But," relates Winthrop, "there stood up one Arnold . . . and withstood it, telling them that, when he consented to that order, he never intended it should extend to the breach of any ordinance of God, such as the subjection of wives to their husbands, etc., and gave divers solid reasons against it." [1] No wonder married women in these days signed their letters "Your faythfull and obedient wife"; and, when they ventured to offer advice to their husbands, were pretty likely to follow it up, as did sweet Dame Winthrop, with words like these: " . . . but I shall allways submit to what you shal thinke fit."

MARRIAGE LAWS AND CUSTOMS IN THE COLONIES

Prevailing Ideas of Marriage and Family Government. — Throughout the colonies marriage was held in high esteem, not only as a means of perpetuating an honored family name but also because large families were necessary to people the vast stretches of the new country. In New England, and to a much less degree in the middle colonies, marriage was looked upon as a civil contract, the ceremonies of which could be conducted by a civil officer. In the southern colonies, however, and during the eighteenth century, this was true of Maryland also, the English idea of marriage as a sacrament to be performed solely by a clergyman of the Church of England very generally prevailed.

The patriarchal form of family organization prevailed in all the colonies; but the belief in the sacredness and importance of family government was even more deeply rooted

---

[1] *Journal*, p. 155.

among the Puritans than among their fellow colonists in the South. This was largely due to the fact that the Puritans derived most of their ideas of government — both State and family — from the Mosaic laws set forth in Deuteronomy and Leviticus. Thus we find the Puritans justifying the autocratic power of the household head by reference to the similar power held by the patriarch in ancient Israel who ruled his family as a monarch. Nor did the stern settlers of New England hesitate to embody the grim prescriptions of the Hebraic law in their codes. Thus the early laws of Massachusetts Bay, as well as of Connecticut and New Haven, provided that the obstinate and unruly child should meet with the penalty of death. The law of the Connecticut colony reads:

"If a man have a stubborn and rebellious son of sufficient years and understanding, *viz.:* sixteen years of age, which will not obey the voice of his father or the voice of his mother, and that when they have chastened him will not hearken unto them, then may his father and mother, being his natural parents, lay hold on him and bring him to the magistrates assembled in court, and testify unto them that their son is stubborn and rebellious . . . such a son shall be put to death. Deut. xxi, 20, 21." The same penalty was prescribed for the child or children who should "curse or smite their natural father and mother." [1]

It is gratifying to learn, however, that no record exists of the actual carrying out of the provisions of these laws in a single instance. But so much cannot be said of another law, likewise taken from the Hebrew code. So high was the esteem in which pure family life was held by the Puritans that they did not shrink from prescribing the death penalty for adultery with a "married or espoused wife." Only in Rhode Island and Plymouth was the law softened to severe flogging. In Plymouth was added the penalty of wearing the scarlet letter *A* upon the breast until death released the offender. Although the colonial magistrates appear to have shrunk from exacting

[1] Trumbull, *Blue Laws True and False* (1876), pp. 69-70.

the full penalty prescribed by law, yet the records of the Massachusetts Bay colony show that two persons were executed for adultery in 1644 and a third execution is mentioned by Cotton Mather in his *Magnalia Christi*.[1] It is a noteworthy fact that no distinction of sex was made in the Puritan laws concerning adultery. Man and woman suffered alike, in striking contrast to the Mosaic law that limited the penalty to the adulteress only.

Social Disapproval of Single Blessedness. — Holding such views of the sacredness of the family and the importance of firm household government, it is not surprising to learn that the Puritan colonists looked askance upon bachelors and "antient maids" especially if these unyoked individuals sought to live independent lives. It was very generally believed that every unmarried person should be connected with some respected family which would be responsible for his morals and for his obedience of the laws of State and Church. In colonial Hartford "the selfish luxury of solitary living" was taxed twenty shillings a week;[2] in colonial Pennsylvania (1766) unmarried men sometimes paid double taxes; and in the New Haven colony it was enacted in 1656 "That no single person of either sex do hence forward board, diet, sojourn, or be permitted so to do, or to have lodging; or house room within any of the plantations of this jurisdiction, but either in some allowed relation, or in some approved family licensed thereunto, by the court, or by a magistrate . . . ; the governor of which family, so licensed, shal as he may conveniently, duly observe the course, carriage and behaviour, of every such person, whether he, or she walk diligently in a constant lawful imployment, attending both family duties, and the publick worship of God, and keeping good order day and night, or otherwise."[3]

Similar ordinances were passed by the colonies of Massa-

[1] Howard, *op. cit.*, Vol. II, p. 170.
[2] *Ibid.*, p. 153.
[3] Trumbull, *Blue Laws*, p. 258.

chusetts Bay and Plymouth. The latter settlement enacted that "henceforth noe single person be suffered to live by himselfe or in any family but such as the selectmen of the Towne shall approve of; . . ." Offenders were to be "sumoned to the Court to be proceeded with as the matter shall require." [1] Apparently these laws were enforced for we read that in 1762 "Thomas Henshaw and Thomas Hall, singlemen, being convicted of living from under family government, . . . are ordered forthwith to submit themselves" to such government "and to appear at the next court and bring with them certificate thereof." [2] Clearly a single man in colonial New England gained his freedom with marriage, not lost it as has sometimes been ironically supposed. Indeed "'Incurridgement' to wedlock was given bachelors in many towns by the assignment to them upon marriage of home-lots to build upon. In Medford there was a so-called Bachelor's Row, which had been thus assigned." [3]

One is tempted to speculate concerning the feelings of these earnest Puritans, so seriously engaged in bringing single youths and maids under the discipline of family government, could they come to life and behold the freedom accorded bachelors and unmarried girls at the present time. Certain it is that they would cordially disapprove not only the independence granted these shirkers of family responsibilities, but also the number of single women, young and old, in modern society. In Boston all such "antient maids," we are told, were regarded as "such a curse as nothing can exceed it, and look'd on as a Dismal Spectacle. . . ." Yet the writer of this statement, an English visitor to New England, does not hesitate to pay his respects to one of these luckless virgins who, although "now about Twenty Six years (the Age which they call a *Thornback*) yet . . . never disguises her self by the Gayetys

[1] *Plymouth Colonial Records*, Vol. XI, p. 223; quoted in Howard, Vol. II, p. 154.

[2] *MSS. Records of County Court for Middlesex*, Vol. III, p. 21; quoted in Howard, Vol. II, p. 155.

[3] Earle, *Customs and Fashions in Old New England*, p. 37.

of a Youthful Dress, and talks as little as she thinks of Love:
. . . The two great vertues essential to the Virgin-State,
are Modesty and Obedience; and these are so remarkable
in her, as if she was made of nothing else. . . . Her Looks,
her Speech, her whole behaviour are so very chaste, that but
once going to kiss her, I thought she'd ha' blush'd to Death."
Just tribute having been paid to the modesty of this "old
(or Superannuated) Maid" of twenty-six, the quaint chronicler
then eulogizes her "Matchless Obedience" to her parents
which "extends itself to all things that are either Good or
Indifferent, and has no Clause of Exception but only where
the Command is unlawfull." With admiration he relates that
he has "known her Scruple to go to Roxbury [not a Mile from
Boston] without her Father's Consent." Such docility furnishes the writer with opportunity to descant upon the sacred
power of the parent over his offspring, a right "so undoubted,
that we find God himself gives way to it and will not suffer the
most Holy Pretence, no, not that of a Vow to Invade it, as we
see in *Numb*. 10." [1] Apparently the views of the Englishman
and the Puritan colonists in respect to the autocratic power
wielded by the household head were entirely harmonious.

Courtship Customs. — Throughout the colonies there prevailed the English custom that the approval of parents should
be secured before courtship began. Great importance was
attached to this formality in the New England colonies where
numerous laws concerning courtship were passed from time
to time. In the first code of Connecticut we read that "no
person whatsoever, male or female, not being at his or her own
dispose, or that remaineth under the government of parents,
masters or guardians, or such like, shall either make, or give
entertainment to, any motion or suit in way of marriage,
without the knowledge and consent of those they stand in such
relation to, under the severe censure of the court in case of
delinquency, not attending this order; nor shall any third

[1] Dunton, *Letters from New England*, in Publications of the Prince Society
(Boston, 1867), pp. 99–101.

person or persons intermeddle in making motion to any such, without the knowledge and consent of those under whose government they are, under the same penalty." [1] The law of the New Haven colony is in similar strain prohibiting any "indeavor to inveagle, or draw the affections of any maide, or maide-servant . . . without the consent of father, master, guardian, governor . . . or (in the absence of such) of the nearest magistrate, whether it be by speech, writing, message, company-keeping, unnecessary familiarity, disorderly night meetings, sinful dalliance, gifts, or any other way . . ." under penalty of forty shillings for the first offense. [2] Truly the young men of colonial New England were compelled to walk circumspectly in love as in all else ! Yet there seems to have been considerable freedom allowed young people in cases where the parents approved of their association. John Dunton, the English traveler, from whose letter regarding old maids I have already quoted, once took a long horseback journey with a fair damsel who rode a pillion behind him. And this in the seventeenth century in Puritan Massachusetts ! Yet there is evidence that such freedom was not approved by the magistrates. A statute of Massachusetts declares in unmistakable terms against this "loose and sinful custom of going or riding from town to town, — . . . oftimes men and women together upon pretence of going to lectures, but it appears . . . much to drink and revel in ordinaries and taverns. . . ." For the prevention of such merrymakings it was ordered "that all single persons who merely for their pleasure take such journeys . . . shall be reputed and accounted riotous and unsober persons, and of ill behavior . . . and shall be committed to prison for ten days, or pay a fine of forty shillings for each offence," unless they are able to "give bonds and sufficient sureties for good behavior in twenty pounds." [3] Thenceforth,

[1] Trumbull, *Blue Laws*, pp. 106–107.
[2] *Ibid.*, p. 242.
[3] Whitmore, *Colonial Laws of Mass.* (1672–1686), pp. 236–237; quoted in Howard, Vol. II, p. 154.

it would appear, the young man in Massachusetts who desired to take his chosen maid a-riding must first give proper guarantee of decorous conduct ! Yet these strict Puritan standards had clearly broken down in the eighteenth century. Mrs. Earle cites one Captain Geolet who made a trip through New England about 1750 and had much to say of " ' Turtle Frolicks ' and country dances with young ladies of refinement and good station in life." [1] Curiously enough the custom of chaperonage seems to have been non-existent ; for young men escorted girls to dancing parties and accompanied them home afterwards with no older person in attendance.

From the *Diary* of Judge Samuel Sewall, the reader gets many a gleam of light upon colonial courtship customs in New England. The Judge's daughter Mary was sought in marriage by one Mr. Gerrish, whose father, a minister, wrote in due form to obtain Mr. Sewall's consent to his son's waiting upon the young lady. This being granted, the Judge invited the young man to his house and noted in his diary the progress of the courtship. Apparently Mr. Gerrish was anxious to proceed with all decorum, for the Judge records : "He asked me . . . whether it were best to frequent my House before his father came to Town. . . ." Having received permission, the would-be lover made a serious misstep; for on the Friday appointed for his call the Judge notes in his diary : "In the evening S. Gerrish comes not ; we expected him, Mary dress'd herself; it was a painfull disgracefull disapointment." Yet, "painfull" as the occurrence doubtless was, it seems not to have cost the young man his chances; for a later item reads : "S. Gerrish comes. Tells Mary except Satterday and Lord's-day nights intends to wait on her every night; unless some extraordinary thing hapen." Courtships in those days were not expected to drag along, but to be got over with decent haste and not too much sentiment. Such was the case with Mary Sewall's wooing, for six months later we read : "Midweek, Augt 24. In the evening Mr. Pemberton marrys Mr.

[1] *Colonial Dames and Goodwives*, p. 201.

Samuel Gerrish and my daughter Mary: He began with Prayer, and Mr. Gerrish the Bridegroom's father concluded: . . ." [1]

Another daughter of Judge Sewall, Betty by name, was a shy, nervous girl who fled from the approach of lovers. In consequence her shrewd old father, intent on his daughter's making a good match, was disappointed in his matrimonial schemes more than once. He records under date of January, 1698/9, that "Capt. Tuthill comes to speak with Betty, who hid herself all alone in the coach for several hours till he was gone, so that we sought at several houses, till at last came in of her self, and look'd very wild." Poor, shy Betty! At last she summoned courage to send her unwelcome suitor away on the ground that she "was willing to know her own mind better." [2] But her troubles were not over, for a few months later another wooer appeared in the shape of one Mr. Grove Hirst. The first mention of this gentleman is found in a statement in the Judge's *Diary* under date of September 28, 1699. Upon returning from a short journey he records: "Find my family in health, only disturb'd at Betty's denying Mr. Hirst. . . . The Lord sanctify Mercyes and Afflictions." A month later we read: "Mr. Wm. Hirst comes and thanks my wife and me for our Kindness to his Son in giving him the Liberty of our house. Seems to do it in way of taking leave." [3] But apparently this suitor was not so easily discouraged as the Captain, for a year later the Judge inserts this brief item in his journal: "Octr 17th. 1700 . . . Mr. Grove Hirst and Elizabeth Sewall are married by Mr. Cotton Mather. . . . Sung the 128 Psal. I set York Tune not intending it. In the New Parlor." [4] So timorous Betty at last was married off and the old Judge had the satisfaction of seeing one more daughter well "set up in life." The records of this courtship are of especial interest

---

[1] Sewall's *Diary* (Massachusetts Historical Society, 1879), Vol. VI; *Sewall Papers*, Vol. II, pp. 250–251, 268.
[2] *Ibid.*, Vol. V, pp. 491–492.
[3] *Ibid.*, Vol. V, pp. 502–503.
[4] *Ibid.*, Vol. VI, p. 24.

as showing that considerable freedom was allowed Puritan girls to reject the advances of unwelcome lovers, even when they were heartily approved by the parents.   Disappointed as Judge Sewall clearly was at Betty's repeated denial of her suitors, yet it seems never to have occurred to him to force his daughter's consent.

The Mercenary Character of Marriage. — If the courtship of the Sewall girls reveals the cautious methods by which Puritan suitors secured the consent of parents to their advances, as well as the independence of Puritan maids in making up their minds to marry, the wooing of numerous fair widows by Judge Sewall himself makes humorously evident the mercenary aspect of marriage in all the colonies, as in the mother-country.   Less than four months after his wife's death we find the Judge writing : "This morning wondering in my mind whether to live a Single or a Married Life ; . . ."   But he does not "wonder" long ; for he soon decides to wait upon the Widow Denison whose husband has but just departed this life, leaving his will to be "proven" by the Judge himself.   Lest this seem indecent haste, it should be remembered that widows were not long permitted to remain in single blessedness in any of the American colonies.   Life was hard in early colonial days and it was felt by men and women alike that its difficulties could best be faced in partnership.   Then, too, widows were held in high regard in all the colonies.   Even in Revolutionary days we are told that "the reign of widows was absolute" ; and the statement is supported by reference to the early love affairs of Washington, Jefferson and Madison, all of whom were profoundly influenced by "the characteristic glamour which hung around every widow." [1] This "glamour," to be sure, was largely practical in character.   Most widows had the life use of property left to them by their deceased husbands.   Moreover they were well trained and experienced in domestic economy — not amateurs like girls of seventeen.

The courtship of the Widow Denison, however, appears

[1] Earle, *Colonial Dames*, pp. 30–36.

not to have proceeded smoothly. It would seem that this lady was ill-disposed to give up the comfortable provision made for her in her husband's will for the less generous allowance the Judge was willing to make her. Thus we read: "Ask'd her what I should allow her; she not speaking; I told her I was willing to give her Two (Hundred?) and Fifty pounds per anum during her life, if it should please God to take me out of the world before her. She answer'd she had better keep as she was than give a Certainty for an uncertainty; She should pay dear for dwelling at Boston. I desired her to make proposals but she made none. I had Thoughts of a Publishment [1] next Thorsday the 6th. But now I seem far from it. May God, who has the pity of a Father, Direct and help me!" [2] A few weeks later the Judge, thoroughly disheartened, decides "that it seem'd to be a direction in Providence not to proceed any further; . . ." and he so informs the fair widow. Thereupon courtship and higgling over money matters cease for a time — but not for long. Soon we find the Judge courting — and winning — the Widow Tilly. Unfortunately, however, his second wife died less than a year after the marriage, and the luckless widower was once more thrown upon the matrimonial market.

This time the Judge's choice speedily lights upon the Widow Winthrop. But the lady meets his advances with the objection that she "could not leave her house, children, neighbours, business. I told her she might do som Good to help and suport me." [3] Mistress Winthrop, however, is not easily convinced that she will benefit herself by marrying again. Nor does she hesitate to tell her aged suitor that he is in need of "a Wigg," and, further, that his "Coach must be set on Wheels, and not by Rusting." [4] Undismayed by these plain hints, the Judge patiently pursues his courtship under discouraging difficulties

[1] The law required that the intention to marry be thrice published in town meeting or "public lecture."

[2] Earle, *Colonial Dames*, p. 202.

[3] *Ibid.*, p. 267.

[4] *Ibid.*, p. 270.

and finally gets down to a discussion of marriage settlements. "Told her I had an Antipathy against those that would pretend to give themselves; but nothing of their Estate. I would give a proportion of my Estate with my self. And I supos'd she would do so. As to a Perriwig, My best and greatest Friend, I could not possibly find a greater, began to find me with hair before I was born, and had continued to do so ever since; and I could not find in my heart to go to another." [1] A little later the Judge records: "Spoke of giving her a Hundred pounds per anum if I dy'd before her. Ask'd her what sum she would give me, if she should dy first? Said I would give her time to Consider of it. She said she heard as if I had given all to my children by Deeds of Gift. I told her 'twas a mistake, Point-Judith was mine &c. That in England I own'd, my Father's desire was that it should go to my eldest Son; 'twas 20 £ per anum; she thought 'twas forty. I think when I seem'd to excuse pressing this, she seem'd to think 'twas best to speak of it; a long winter was coming on." [2] Clearly this New England widow could look out for her own interests even against so shrewd a bargainer as the Judge. We may infer, also, that she did not regard her elderly wooer as a "good match"; for she finally told him very positively that "she could not Change her Condition." During his last call upon Mistress Winthrop both the widow and her parlor must have had a chilling effect upon the Judge, since he records that "The Fire was come to one short Brand besides the Block, which Brand was set up in end; at last it fell to pieces and no Recruit was made." [3] So, thoroughly discouraged, the old man takes his leave, and that, apparently, "for good."

But a few months later this persistent suitor is found writing to the Widow Gibbs proposing marriage — under definite conditions. His financial proposition, which figures prominently in the letter, is as follows: "For your children, or some

---

[1] Earle, *Colonial Dames*, p. 272.
[2] *Ibid.*, p. 274.
[3] *Ibid.*, p. 275.

in their behalf, to give Bond to indemnify me from all debts contracted by you before the Marriage ; and from all matters respecting the Administration. This, I told you [in a previous letter] I peremptorily insisted on. I was to secure you Forty pounds per anum during the term of your natural Life in case of your Survival." [1] Despite the dictatorial tone of this "love letter" and its distinctly bargaining flavor, the Widow Gibbs seems to have been reasonably satisfied with her suitor, for their banns were published a few days later. Let us hope the lady never knew how much lower she was rated by the Judge than was the Widow Denison of earlier days ! The provision for the latter, it will be remembered, was 250 pounds yearly; whereas the final object of the Judge's calculating affections was fain to be content with a beggarly income of 40 pounds in case she survived her husband.

But mercenary marriage was not confined to the New England Colonies. Social and economic considerations likewise determined marriages among the planters of Virginia and the Carolinas. Eighteenth century marriage notices in South Carolina frequently mentioned "a large fortune" as one of the qualifications of the bride-to-be. Calhoun states that a common form of marriage notice in this colony was : "So-and-so to Miss ——, a most amiable young lady with £10,000 to her fortune." [2] Nor was the mercenary character of marriage less evident in the middle colonies, where bargaining about dowry and dower was as common as elsewhere. We are told that in New York the Dutch women were as shrewd pre-marital traders as the men, hence they were saved from getting the worst of the deal as often happened in the other colonies. Occasionally young men would advertise in the colonial newspapers of the eighteenth century their willingness to marry any woman well endowed with worldly goods.

Bundling. — It is hardly possible to discuss courtship customs in colonial days without reference to the crude practice

[1] *Ibid.*, p. 303.
[2] *Social History of the American Family*, Vol. I, p. 255.

of "bundling" which seems to have been most prevalent in rural settlements along the Connecticut Valley and on Cape Cod. In his *Knickerbocker's History of New York*, however, Irving refers to this custom as having spread among the Dutch girls of New Netherlands. He attributes the practice to the Yankee settlers in the colony, of whom he writes: "Among other hideous customs, they attempted to introduce among them that of *bundling*, which the Dutch lasses of the Netherlands, with that eager passion for novelty and foreign fashions natural to their sex, seemed very well inclined to follow, but that their mothers, being more experienced in the world, and better acquainted with men and things, strenuously discountenanced all such outlandish innovations." [1] It is at least questionable, however, whether this rude practice was not brought over to the new land by the Dutch settlers themselves from Holland, where a similar custom had long existed in the country districts. An account of the character and extent of the practice may be found in Howard's valuable *History of Matrimonial Institutions* [2] and a fuller treatment is given by Stiles in his book *Bundling in Its Origin, Progress and Decline* (Albany, 1871).

Bundling was limited to the poorer classes, who were forced to a rigid economy in the matter of firewood and candles. As many of the early homes consisted of only one room, a young man courting a girl was permitted by her parents to lie with her (without either of the pair undressing) after the family had gone to bed. In this way the suitor was able to pursue his courtship in reasonable comfort after the fire had died down. Surprisingly enough this custom seems to have led to fewer sexual offenses than might be expected, although public opinion never gave it general sanction. Nevertheless our forefathers in Massachusetts and Connecticut, especially in the impoverished class, appear to have tolerated it without much disturbance of mind. Charles Francis Adams has found

[1] *Op. cit.* ("Geoffrey Crayon" edition), p. 217.
[2] Vol. II, pp. 181–188.

evidence of the survival of bundling in eastern Massachusetts until after the Revolutionary War.

Growing Freedom of Social Life an Aid to Courtship. — As the eighteenth century advanced, social intercourse became freer and more pleasure-loving. Even in New England the harsh Puritan spirit was gradually becoming softened. An English traveler in New England gives us a glimpse of one approved method of courtship in Boston : "On the South," he writes, "there is a small but pleasant common, where the gallants, a little before sunset, walk with their Marmalet-Madams till the nine o'clock bell rings them home to their respective habitations." Daily life in the colonies followed a very different schedule of hours than at present. Rising was earlier and so, indeed, was going to bed. Calhoun relates[1] that at the end of the seventeenth century young ladies in South Carolina received their beaus about three o'clock and expected them to depart by six, since the family retired not long after seven in winter and eight in summer. This custom may, however, have been confined to folk of modest means and Puritan traditions.

An English visitor in Boston in 1740 thus describes the social life of the gentry at that time :

"For their amusements, every afternoon, after drinking tea, the gentlemen and ladies walk the Mall. From there they go to one another's houses to spend the evening, that is, those who are not disposed to attend the evening lecture. This they may do, if they please, six nights out of seven, the year round . . . . The government is in the hands of the Dissenters, who do not allow theatres or music houses. But although plays and such entertainments are not held here, the people don't seem to be dispirited or to mope for want of them. For both the ladies and gentlemen dress and appear as gay, usually, as courtiers in England on a coronation day or birthday. And the ladies here visit, drink tea, and do everything else in the height of fashion. They neglect the affairs of

[1] *Social History of the American Family*, Vol. I, p. 257.

their families with as good a grace as the finest ladies in London."

In the southern and middle colonies society became really gay during the eighteenth century and manners were characterized by much freedom. But it should be remembered that coarseness and lack of restraint were characteristic of eighteenth century manners in Europe, especially in England, and the colonies were merely adopting standards and practices which prevailed in the mother-country. A certain "Lucinda," known as the "Young Lady of Virginia," has left us a lively record of social customs and manners in the colony of her birth during the eighteenth century. She writes her friend Polly Brant:

"The Gentlemen dined to-day at Mr. Marionbirds. We have supped and the gentlemen are not returned yet. Lucy and myself are in a peck of trouble for fear they should return drunk. Sister has had our bed moved in her room. Just as we were undress'd and going to bed the Gentlemen arrived, and we had to scamper. Both tipsy! . . . Hannah and myself were going to take a long walk this evening but were prevented by the two Horrid Mortals, Mr. Pinkard and Mr. Washington, who seized and kissed me a dozen times in spite of all the resistance I could make. They really think, now they are married, they are prevaliged to do anything. . . ." [1]

In a society so gayly careless of conventions we may well believe that ample opportunities were afforded colonial youths and maidens to know each other and to carry on those preliminary skirmishings that sometimes lead to serious courtship. Southern girls were doubtless "sad coquettes in their youth . . . although they look so demure in their portraits, and proved such exemplary wives and mothers in later years. Duels and despairing lovers seem scarcely to have ruffled the serenity of their lovely countenances, or to have made their hearts beat faster under their stiff bodices." [2]

[1] *Journal of a Young Lady of Virginia*, 1782 (ed. of 1871), p. 15.
[2] Wharton, *Colonial Days and Dames*, pp. 197-198.

Precontract. — Very generally in the New England colonies the ancient custom of formal, public betrothal was carefully preserved and even regulated by statute. In Plymouth the "couple — having the consent of the parents or guardians, in the case of two minors — made before two witnesses a solemn *promise of marriage in due time*, the ceremony having the formality of the magisterial wedding then in vogue." [1] In Massachusetts, New Hampshire and Connecticut, also, the customary ceremony of pre-contract was celebrated with much formality, although in Massachusetts it was not established by law. A Connecticut statute of 1640 reads : "It is ordered by the authority of this court, that whosoever intends to join themselves in marriage covenant shall cause their *purpose of contract* to be published in some public place and at some public meeting . . . at the least eight days before they enter into such contract whereby they engage themselves each to other, and that they shall forbear to join in marriage covenant at least eight days after the said contract." [2]

But this Puritan custom of public betrothal seems not to have been favorable to morality. In the first place the "betrothed woman was put, both by law and social custom, one step above the woman who was not betrothed, and one step below the woman who was married. This was so as respects the civil and criminal law." [3] The natural outcome was that couples thus solemnly betrothed regarded themselves as half married and not infrequently lived as husband and wife before the marriage ceremony had been performed. Indeed it has been maintained that precontract "must be held responsible for a very large share of the sexual misconduct revealed in the judicial records. Before the general court of Plymouth the cases of uncleanness after contract and before marriage are very numerous. . . . Members of some of the most illustrious

[1] Goodwin, *The Pilgrim Republic*, p. 600. Italics mine.

[2] Trumbull, *Blue Laws*, p. 106. Italics mine.

[3] Shirley, "Early Jurisprudence of New Hampshire," *Proclamation of New Hampshire Historical Society* (1876–1884), p. 308; quoted in Howard, Vol. II, p. 180.

families of New England were guilty of indiscretions in this regard." [1] Doubtless the colonial authorities were largely to blame for this state of affairs. By elevating the ceremony of betrothal into a public affair, announcement of which must be published eight days beforehand, the Puritan fathers in effect placed a premium upon illegal sex relations after precontract and before marriage. The authorities, indeed, although they punished such social offenses with fines or whipping, yet reduced this punishment "in general one half, or less than one half what it would have been had there been no betrothment." [2] Naturally, in the eyes of young offenders, the lesser punishment indicated a lessening of the offense, and sexual intercourse between betrothal and marriage was quite often the outcome. Nevertheless, despite the manifest evils which resulted from attaching legal significance to the ceremony of precontract, the custom and the law alike persisted at least up to the middle of the eighteenth century.

Colonial Marriage Laws. — Very generally, in the American colonies laws were passed providing that (1) due notice should be given of the intention of marriage; (2) clear evidence of parental consent should be furnished; (3) the marriage should be celebrated by certain persons duly recognized by law; (4) the records of all marriages should be kept by town or county clerk or registrar.

Banns, Publication and License. — In all the colonies from New Hampshire to Georgia provision was made that the banns of the marriage should be read three times in some public place. In Virginia banns were published on "three severall Sundays or holydays in the time of devyne service in the parish churches where the sayd persons dwell accordinge to the booke of common prayer. . . ." [3] And such was the custom in the Carolinas and Georgia where the Church of England had at least

---

[1] Howard, *op. cit.*, Vol. II, p. 186.
[2] Shirley, *op. cit.*, p. 308; quoted in Howard, Vol. II, p. 180.
[3] Act of 1631; quoted in Cook, "Marriage Celebration in the Colonies," *Atlantic Monthly* (1888), Vol. 61, p. 355.

nominally been established. But in these southern colonies
the parties intending marriage were also privileged to obtain
a license from the Governor, or, later, from the county court,
instead of publishing banns. This privilege was welcomed by
the more sensitive members of the community, who shrank
with distaste from the publicity associated with the publishing
of banns.

The middle colonies varied somewhat in their laws regulating the announcement of intention to marry. In Maryland,
like her sister colonies to the South, either banns or license were
demanded : whereas in Pennsylvania the parties were required
to affix "their intention of marriage on the court or meeting-
house door of the county wherein they dwell, one month before
the solemnizing thereof " and to prove their "clearness of all
other engagements" by a certificate secured from some
reputable persons.[1] Thus, owing to Quaker influences, Pennsylvania required no banns nor did it apparently adopt the
custom of granting a license. New Jersey, also, required
that a notice of the proposed marriage be posted for two weeks
in some public place or that banns be three times proclaimed
in church. Later, after the colony was united with New York,
power was granted to the Governor to issue licenses. In New
York, likewise, after England had obtained control of the
colony in 1664, the English custom of banns or license was
established by the so-called "Duke's laws." This legal code
clearly states that any marriage celebrated without banns or
license or without minister or magistrate is void.[2] The provision is noteworthy as one of the very few of its kind to be
found in the body of colonial laws. Most of the other colonies
were apparently content to punish infringement of the marriage laws concerning publicity with fines or other penalties,
without going to the length of declaring marriages not properly
published or celebrated as null and void.

Throughout the New England colonies laws were enacted re-

[1] Act of 1683; quoted in Cook, *op. cit.*, p. 358.
[2] Cook, *op. cit.*, p. 360.

quiring banns or the posting of a notice of intention to marry in some public place. Rhode Island, in its code of 1647, provided that "No contract or agreement between a Man and a Woman to owne each other as Man and Wife shall be owned from henceforth as a lawful marriage . . . but such as are in the first place, with the parents, then orderly published in two severall meetings of the Townsmen." [1] The New Haven colony laws also provided "That no persons shal be either contracted or joyned in marriage before the intention of the parties proceeding therein, hath been three times published, at some time of public lecture, or town meeting in the town, or towns where the parties, or either of them do dwel . . . ; or be set up in meeting upon some post of their meeting house door, in publick view, there to stand so as it may be easily read by the space of fourteen daies; . . ." [2] Similar laws were enacted in Plymouth, Massachusetts and New Hampshire; and each code provided that no one "under the covert of parents" should marry without their consent.

The Celebration of Marriage. — The colonies were as circumspect in their regulation of the celebration of marriage as they were in respect to its publication. In the southern colonies, where the Episcopacy was sooner or later established, the tendency was very strong to restrict the performance of the marriage ceremony to clergymen of the Church of England. In 1661–1662 a Virginia law provided that "noe marriage be solemnized nor reputed valid in law but such as is made by the ministers according to the laws of England." [3] For more than a hundred years thereafter (and indeed this had been the custom since the settlement of the colony) no lay magistrate or dissenting clergyman could join parties in marriage in the colony of Virginia. But in 1780 and again in 1784, after the Revolutionary War, acts were passed providing, under certain conditions, that it should be "lawful for any ordained minister

---

[1] Act quoted in Cook, *op. cit.*, p. 352.
[2] Trumbull, *Blue Laws*, p. 242.
[3] Cook, *op. cit.*, pp. 353–354.

of the gospel . . . to celebrate the rites of matrimony according to the forms and customs of the church to which he belongs. . . ." This concession marks the spirit of toleration that was becoming characteristic of all the colonies at this time. It was followed by another concession to the lay spirit in the Act of 1784 which granted to the courts in the remote frontier districts of Virginia the power to nominate certain "sober and discreet laymen" to celebrate marriage in those places where no clergyman could be found, according to the forms and customs of the Church of which these appointees were members. Thus Virginia, by the close of the eighteenth century, had at least partially abandoned the principle of ecclesiastical marriage and had sanctioned that of lay celebration under clearly defined conditions.

The history of the laws regulating marriage in the other southern colonies is similar to that of Virginia. In all the Church of England was somewhat loosely established and its laws requiring marriage by a clergyman of that church were nominally enforced. But as early as 1728 the Carolinas sanctioned the performance of the marriage ceremony by "any lawful magistrate" *in the absence* of a clergyman of the Church of England, or with his expressed consent. A further step toward toleration was taken in 1766 when Presbyterian ministers were singled out from other dissenters and permitted to solemnize marriage "in their usual and accustomed manner." This paved the way for the Act of 1778, passed during the stress of the Revolution and authorizing all "regular ministers of the gospel, of every denomination . . . and all justices of the peace in this State, . . . to solemnize the rites of matrimony, according to the rites and ceremonies of their respective churches." A similar Act was passed in Georgia in 1785.

Only in Maryland was a different course pursued. Starting, under Catholic rule, with a policy of complete toleration and recognition of either religious or civil marriage as legal, this colony became the seat of a bitter struggle for supremacy between the adherents of the Church of England on the one hand and the Catholics and Quakers on the other. By the end of the seventeenth century the advocates of episcopacy had won. Soon after assuming control, they passed the Act of 1717 which provided that all members of the Church of England desiring marriage should "apply themselves to a minister for the contracting thereof. . . ." But unfortunately the authorities were not content to stop here. Imbued with the idea that only a marriage celebrated by a duly ordained minister of the gospel is legal, the law-givers enacted in 1777 that no marriage should henceforth be celebrated in Maryland "unless by ministers of the Church of England, ministers dissenting from that Church, or Romish priests, appointed or ordained to the rites and ceremonies of their respective churches. . . ." The Quakers only were permitted the privilege of lay celebration. It is an interesting fact that this law has been made part of the present Maryland code. Thus this state is the only one in the Union which has failed to sanction the celebration of marriage by a civil magistrate.[1]

In the middle colonies, where no church party gained exclusive control, religious toleration and the lay celebration of marriage had no such hard-fought battles to wage. From its foundation by William Penn, the colony of Pennsylvania proclaimed a policy of complete religious toleration. In accordance with this principle, marriages which were solemnized by any form of religious society were recognized as both valid and legal. It has sometimes been charged against the Quakers that they tended to repudiate marriage or at best to celebrate it in a loose and irregular way. Nothing could be more untrue to the facts. The Society of Friends indeed permitted its members to take each other in marriage on the ground that marriage is "God's joining not man's." But it was carefully

---

[1] For this whole discussion see Howard, *op. cit.*, Vol. II, pp. 228–263, and pp. 353–357. Also see Hening's *Statutes*, Vol. I, pp. 156–158, 181–183, 332, 433; Vol. II, pp. 49–51; Vol. III, pp. 441–442.

stipulated that this ceremony should take place in "Publick Meeting" in the presence of at least twelve witnesses, after due publication had been made. A later statute required that one of the twelve witnesses demanded by the previous law should be a justice of the peace. It is clear that the Pennsylvania Quakers held marriage in great esteem and took pains to surround it with due safeguards of publicity and registration.[1]

In East and West New Jersey the law of 1668 permitted the celebration of marriage by an "approved minister or justice of the peace within this province," thus sanctioning civil marriage from the beginning. But toward the close of the seventeenth century New Jersey was united with New York in one royal province. Thereafter an attempt was made to enforce the matrimonial laws of the Church of England upon the people. But the attempt was not crowned with success. By the Act of 1719 it was made lawful for "any religious society in the province to join together in the holy bonds of matrimony such persons as are of the said society. . . ." Apparently, then, justices of the peace lost the right to celebrate marriage at this time, although the power seems to have been later restored; for an Act of the General Assembly of 1752 forbids ministers, *justices* or others to join persons in marriage without banns or license under penalty of a fine of £200.[2] In 1795 it was clearly enacted that "every justice of the peace of this State, and every stated and ordained minister of the gospel . . . is authorized and empowered to solemnize marriages."[3]

Under Dutch rule marriages in New Netherlands were required to be celebrated by a minister of the Dutch Reformed faith. But the "Duke's laws," promulgated for his colony of New York in 1664, after providing for publication of banns, public posting of intention to marry or securing a license from

[1] Howard, Vol. II, pp. 315-324.
[2] *Ibid.*, p. 313, footnote.
[3] Cook, *op. cit.*, p. 359.

the Governor, declare that "it shall be lawful for any minister or for any Justice of the Peace to join the parties in Marriage, Provided that the said partys do purge themselves by Oath before the Minister or Justice that they are not under the bonds of Matrimony to any other person." The Duke's laws were reënacted in 1684 and were changed in no important particular before the Revolution.

In the New England colonies the course of affairs was somewhat unusual. From the beginning of their history as colonizers there existed among the Puritans a strong distrust of all ecclesiastical forms sanctioned or enforced by the Church of England. This suspicion, amounting to active dislike, was extended to the ecclesiastical celebration of marriage. At the outset the Puritan colonists stoutly proclaimed the principle of Luther and Cromwell that marriage is a civil contract and should therefore be celebrated by a civil officer, duly empowered by law. Very generally the New England law and custom required that marriage be celebrated before a justice of the peace or other magistrate and did not sanction celebration by the minister of any faith. Indeed Governor Winthrop relates that on the occasion of a "great marriage . . . solemnized at Boston" the bridegroom procured the pastor of his home church in Hingham to preach. "But the magistrates," writes the Governor, "hearing of it, sent to him to forbear." One of the reasons assigned was that "we were not willing to bring in the English custom of ministers performing the solemnity of marriage, which sermons at such times might induce. . . ." [1] Yet for sixteen years no law was passed in Massachusetts enforcing the prevailing custom of civil marriage, lest such a statute be "repugnant to the laws of England." But in 1646 the colonists of Massachusetts Bay enacted that "no person whatsoever in this jurisdiction shall join any persons together in marriage, but the magistrate, or such other as the General Court or Court of Assistants shall authorize in such place where no magistrate is near." Similar

[1] Winthrop's *Journal* (1908), Vol. II, p. 330.

statutes were enacted in New Haven, Connecticut and Rhode Island.[1]

Toward the close of the seventeenth century, however, when the colonists' fear of ecclesiastical domination had greatly lessened, their hostility to ecclesiastical marriage rites also declined. Therefore no strong opposition was made to the order of council issued in 1686 by Dudley, as president of New England, authorizing ministers as well as justices of the peace "to consummate marriages, after three several times publication or license from the president or deputy." [2] Four days after Dudley had received his commission the "first marriage with prayer-book and ring" was celebrated in Boston and no doubt some zealous Puritans were scandalized thereby. But gradually such opposition died down in all the colonies save Rhode Island, which refused to clergymen the right to solemnize marriage until 1733. Shortly after securing their charters the other New England colonies enacted laws empowering ministers of all denominations to perform the rites of matrimony.

No prescribed ritual for marriage existed in the New England colonies in early times. The ceremony was usually performed at the home of the bride and we may be sure that prayer, exhortation and psalm-singing played a prominent part. But it was not long before a discreetly decorous merrymaking followed the wedding ceremony and in the latter part of the eighteenth century marriages were made the occasion for much gay revelry in New England. Even Judge Sewall does not condemn the "Cake and Sack-Posset" which seemed invariably to follow the psalm-singing and prayers in weddings of his own day.[3]

Registration of Marriages. — Very generally in the colonies provision was made for the proper registration of marriages.

---

[1] Cook, *op. cit.*, p. 351; also Whitmore, *Colonial Laws of Massachusetts* (1660–1672), p. 172.

[2] Quoted in Howard, Vol. II, p. 135.

[3] See Sewall's *Diary*, Vol. VI, pp. 403–404; Vol. VII, p. 253.

In New England the town clerk or clerk of the writs was charged with the duty of keeping a register of marriages as well as of births and deaths. In Plymouth the clerk was allowed "thripence apece for each particular person soe registered." [1] Moreover, the parties to the marriage were required to report it to the clerk within one month under penalty of a fine of three shillings, half of which went to the clerk if he had entered a complaint of neglect. By the code of 1647, failure to publish and register a marriage in Rhode Island brought upon the offending bridegroom a fine of five pounds paid to the parents of the maid. All the accessories also each forfeited five pounds, half of which was turned over to the bride's parents. It has been pointed out by the historian that an effective system of registration was thus established in colonial Rhode Island "such as recent legislation has attempted to revive." [2]

Throughout the southern colonies provision for the registration of marriages was also carefully made. In Virginia the minister of every parish was required to keep a record of all solemnized weddings and to make an annual return to the quarter court on the first of June. In North Carolina in 1715 the Governor was empowered to choose from among three freeholders nominated by the inhabitants one man to be register of deeds; and until there was a clerk of the parish church in that district this official was to keep a record of betrothals and marriages. In 1696 Georgia and South Carolina likewise required that every man hereafter married in those colonies should record his marriage in the register's office within thirty days after celebration or else forfeit "one royall" for neglect. Furthermore, at the time of registration he must produce a certificate under the hand of minister or magistrate, attested by six witnesses of the ceremony. [3] Simi-

---

[1] Howard, Vol. II, p. 144.

[2] Arnold, *History of Rhode Island*, Vol. I, p. 208; quoted in Howard, Vol. II, p. 148.

[3] Howard, Vol. II, p. 260.

lar provisions were made in the middle colonies. By the Duke of York's laws "The Minister or Town Clerk of every parish shall well and truly and plainly" record all births, marriages and deaths in his district "in a Book to be provided by the Church-warden for that purpose." If the master of a family or person concerned failed to report the marriage within one month, he should pay a fine of five shillings.[1] Likewise the laws agreed upon in England for the governing of Pennsylvania provided that a certificate of marriage "under the hands of parents and witnesses shall be brought to the proper register of that county and shall be registered in his office." [2]

Summary. — A review of colonial legislation with respect to marriage gives clear evidence that the first settlers made every attempt to safeguard the institution of matrimony and to prevent thoughtless persons from entering into the contract carelessly and without due formality. Parental consent, given to the town or county clerk personally or in writing, was everywhere required; due notice of the marriage by banns or posting or, in default of banns, by license from the Governor, was demanded in all the colonies; the solemnization of marriage was regulated by law; and, finally, registration of the marriage in town or county clerk's office, or, in colonies where the Church of England was established, by the parish clerk, was a universal requirement. In none of the colonies was "self-marriage" (incorrectly called common-law marriage) in which the parties took each other for husband or wife without the presence of magistrate or clergyman sanctioned by law. Even in Pennsylvania the law of 1693 required that one of the twelve witnesses to the Quaker ceremony of marriage should be a justice of the peace. In all the other colonies marriage by magistrate or clergyman, or (in the frontier districts of Virginia) by a layman licensed by the courts was inflexibly demanded by law. Yet there can be little doubt

---

[1] *Colonial Laws of New York*, Vol. I, p. 19; quoted in Howard, Vol. II, p. 288.

[2] "Laws Agreed upon in England," in Linn, *Charter and Laws*, p. 101; quoted in Howard, Vol. II, p. 318.

that "self-marriage," contrary to legal provisions, did occur from time to time throughout the colonies. In such cases, except where the law expressly declared the marriage void,[1] the offenders were liable to punishment for contracting an *illegal* marriage, but their union was not declared *invalid*. Thus the old medieval distinction between marriages contracted contrary to law and those which were null and void from the beginning [2] seems to have crept into colonial legislative practice. Even in the colonies where illegal marriages were also declared invalid the statute was probably itself invalid because not in accordance with the laws of England.[3]

DIVORCE IN THE COLONIES

New England Laws and Practices. — Colonial laws and practices with respect to (1) absolute divorce and (2) separation from bed and board, show marked differences. In New England, where the idea of civil marriage was so deeply rooted, it is not surprising to learn that civil divorce was likewise sanctioned and provided for. In his interesting *History of Massachusetts*, Governor Hutchinson, who was presiding officer in the divorce court for many years, makes the following statement concerning the colonial lawgivers: "In matters of divorce they left the rules of the canon law out of the question. . . . I never heard of a separation, under the first charter,[4] *a mensa et thoro*. . . . In general what would have been cause for such a separation in the spiritual courts, was sufficient, with them, for a divorce *a vinculo*. Female adultery was never doubted to have been sufficient cause; but male adultery, after some debate and consultation with the elders, was judged not sufficient. Desertion a year or two, when there was evidence of a determined design not to return,

---

[1] As in New York, until 1684, Virginia (by the Act of 1661–1662) and probably Rhode Island.

[2] Because they were within prohibited degrees of consanguinity.

[3] See Howard, Vol. II, pp. 232 and 287.

[4] 1630–1692.

was always good cause; so was cruel usage of the husband." [1]

During the early colonial period the authority to grant divorces in Massachusetts resided in the Court of Assistants, which held its sittings twice yearly. By the *Acts and Resolves* of November 3, 1692, entire jurisdiction over matrimony and divorce was conferred upon the Governor and Council. A later Act of 1696 empowered these authorities to assign the woman, if the innocent party, a reasonable portion of her husband's estate "not exceeding one-third part thereof" as alimony.[2] Howard has prepared some valuable tables setting forth the salient facts in cases of divorce and annulment brought before the Court of Assistants during the periods 1639–1692, 1739–1760 and 1760–1786. A study of these tables brings some interesting facts to light. Forty cases of divorce or annulment were brought before the Court during the first period mentioned above. Of these, four were suits for annulment and the marriages were declared void. In two instances the causes assigned for annulment were bigamy and in two others "affinity," *i.e.*, marriage within the prohibited degrees. In one of these latter cases a man had married his brother's wife; in the other the man had married an uncle's widow — both unions being forbidden in the code of Leviticus and also in Puritan law. Twenty-eight of the forty divorce suits were brought by women. It is noteworthy that the Court apparently regarded the adultery of the husband as insufficient cause for granting a divorce to the wife, since in only one instance was the decree of dissolution of marriage issued on the sole ground of adultery. And even this decree was reversed on appeal. But adultery, accompanied by desertion or cruelty, or desertion, aggravated by remarriage or refusal to provide, was in every instance accounted just cause for dissolving the marriage. During the period 1739–1760 only three decrees for absolute divorces were issued, together

[1] *Op. cit.*, Vol. I.
[2] *Acts and Resolves*, Vol. I, p. 209.

with two decrees of separation. But in the third period, 1760–1786, the number of divorces, separations and annulments of marriage greatly increased. Ninety-six petitions were presented to the Governor and Council, and in seventy-six cases absolute divorces were granted. In thirty-seven instances, where decrees of dissolution were issued, the husband was the plaintiff and the charge against his wife was adultery. The wife's charges were again, as in the former period, adultery accompanied by cruelty, desertion or failure to provide. In only one case, where the wife was plaintiff, that of Rosanna *v.* Wm. Scott, was the marriage dissolved on the sole ground of adultery. Decrees of separation were issued in favor of the wife in ten instances, commonly on the ground of cruelty or desertion and failure to provide.

This analysis makes clear several important facts: (1) The New England colonists did not hesitate to go counter to English law and practice in regarding the dissolution of marriage as a civil function and in endowing the legislative body with full rights in respect to such dissolutions. (2) Although far more generous treatment was accorded wives, in respect to divorce or separation, than was conceded in the other colonies, yet discrimination in favor of men very generally existed. The husband could and did obtain divorce on the ground of adultery only whereas in the vast majority of cases the wife could not. (3) The practice of granting separations on the grounds of cruelty, desertion or failure to provide became more frequent during the late colonial period than it had previously been. (4) The privilege of remarriage was granted to a woman in case the husband had been absent four or five years and his whereabouts was unknown.

Connecticut colony was unique in intrusting its divorce cases almost wholly to the courts of law. Of divorce law and practice in Connecticut Howard writes: "Perhaps in none of the other colonies was so liberal, and on the whole so wisely conservative, a policy adopted. . . . Separation from bed and board was rejected. . . . Reasonable and fairly liberal causes of divorce *a vinculo* were clearly specified; husband and wife were treated with even justice; and although legislative divorce, always liable to abuse, was permitted, the greater part of litigation seems always to have been intrusted to the regular courts. In short, Connecticut, in all the more essential respects, anticipated the present policy of civilized nations by nearly two hundred years." [1]

Divorce in the Southern and Middle Colonies. — In the southern colonies, where the Church of England was established, English law and custom with respect to divorce and separation were very generally followed. Now in seventeenth century England, it will be remembered, the ecclesiastical courts still had jurisdiction in such matters. Absolute divorce was not granted by these courts, and separation from bed and board was permitted only on the grounds of adultery and cruelty. But the colonists of Virginia and the Carolinas showed no desire to set up the English ecclesiastical court in the country of their adoption. Indeed, this tribunal was never established; nor was any other court given jurisdiction in respect to the dissolution of marriage. The result was that no divorces or legal separations were granted in the southern colonies throughout the colonial period. "Their statute books are entirely silent on the subject of divorce jurisdiction." [2] Of course parties might and did separate by mutual consent; and in Virginia, at least, the county courts received and granted petitions for alimony from parties thus separated. Now, since no statute empowered the courts to take action in petitions for alimony, we are forced to believe that the authority was assumed without legal sanction because of the exigencies of the situation.

In the middle colonies, also, a highly conservative policy in regard to divorce was very general. New Netherland, to be sure, influenced by the doctrines of the Protestant reformers, occasionally granted a petition for absolute divorce or for sepa-

[1] *Op. cit.*, Vol. II, pp. 353–354.
[2] Howard, Vol. II, p. 367.

ration. But when this Dutch colony passed under the rule of England the English law concerning separation was adopted. However, here, again, as in the southern colonies, no ecclesiastical court having jurisdiction in cases of adultery and cruelty was ever established. Hence neither divorces *a vinculo* or *a mensa et thoro* were granted in New York during the colonial period, except in a few isolated cases, occurring previous to 1689, when the Governor of New York seems to have arbitrarily assumed the power to grant divorces.[1] Similarly in Pennsylvania, although the code of 1682 recognized absolute divorce on the ground of adultery, yet no tribunal was empowered to grant such divorce. There are, however, two instances of absolute divorces granted by the colonial legislature in Pennsylvania. The first decree was issued by the council in 1769 and was sustained; but a later decree of 1772 was declared void by the English king in the following year.[2]

In conclusion it may be said that the strong contrasts between the procedure of New England respecting divorce and that of the middle and southern colonies seems largely based upon (1) religious differences and (2) the relatively non-interfering policy of England with regard to her subjects in the colonies of New England. The theory of marriage as a civil contract, which could be made binding by a civil magistrate and therefore could be dissolved by a civil court, was fundamental in the doctrine of Lutherans and Calvinists alike. The English Church had not assented to it; and therefore, wherever this Church gained even doubtful primacy in the colonies, the narrow tenets of the Anglican communion respecting marriage and divorce were made binding. It is interesting to note, however, that even in cavalier Virginia, where the Church of England was most firmly established, the colonists were unwilling to set up the English ecclesiastical court. To that extent they refused to go; apparently sharing, in some degree,

[1] See Howard, *op. cit.*, Vol. II, pp. 383–384.
[2] *Ibid.*, p. 387.

the New England distrust of the jurisdiction of the Anglican church. Doubtless, the independent and aggressive spirit of the New England colonists, their strong and prompt resentment of any encroachment upon their chartered privileges, was in part responsible for the fact that their institution of civil divorce was not declared void by the English government, as being directly contrary to the law of the mother country.

HOMES AND HOME LIFE IN COLONIAL DAYS

Houses and House Furnishings. — In New England the rude log cabins of the first settlers soon gave place to more commodious and comfortable homes, some built of brick and stone and some of wood. About the middle of the seventeenth century the houses were built of oak with great stone chimneys and sometimes had an overhanging second story to afford better defense in case of an attack by Indians. "Lean-to" houses in which the second story sloped down to the first in the rear were quite popular. Weeden thus describes their interiors: "This class of houses had four main rooms, the larger ones often twenty feet square, on one floor. On the ground was a parlor, or 'great' room, for company; a bedroom; a kitchen, the main assembling place of the family; and a milk and cheese pantry." [1] But let it not be supposed that all classes were thus comfortably and spaciously housed. The laboring class and small farmers of this period were well content to live in one-storied houses of two rooms — a kitchen and a family bedroom. In the country districts log huts had by no means disappeared in 1650; and even the deep pits lined and roofed with boards, so often used by settlers in a new country, could occasionally be found. During the latter half of the seventeenth century, however, New England houses showed considerable improvement. Most of the better class of houses boasted a second story projecting a foot or so beyond the first. Sometimes they were gabled on the front, thus

[1] *Economic and Social History of New England*, p. 214.

allowing for bedrooms in the attic. The windows were diamond paned, with the glass cased in lead, and frequently swung
outward on hinges. The house of a well-to-do Hartford merchant is described as having a parlor, hall, "spaceroom" and
kitchen on the first floor, with second-floor chambers above
each room and another chamber in the garret.[1] Yet, despite
the increased spaciousness of colonial homes in New England
the household must have been sadly crowded. An old manu-
script of 1675 states that the average family comprised 9.02
persons, including the servants. It was not uncommon for a
New England wife to bear twenty children, although, because
of the enormous child mortality, few lived to maturity. Judge
Sewall had fourteen children, seven sons and seven daughters;
yet, in his old age, only four were living. No wonder that
"trundle-beds" were set up in every bedroom!

During the eighteenth century, especially in the latter half,
were built those charming colonial houses of which too few
remain in New England. One has only to visit such New
England towns as Litchfield, Connecticut, Concord and Salem,
Massachusetts, and Portsmouth, New Hampshire, to see these
simple, yet pleasing homes, painted white, with green blinds,
and often with beautiful colonial doorways.

In the southern colonies the early rude shelters likewise gave
place to comfortable abodes. Writing about 1705 Beverley
says of Williamsburg homes : "The private dwellings are . . .
very much improved, several gentlemen there having built
themselves large brick houses of many rooms on a floor; but
they don't covet to make them lofty, having extent of ground
to build upon; and now and then they are visited by high
winds, which would incommode a towering fabric. They love
to have large rooms, that they may be cool in summer. Of late
they have made their stories much higher than formerly, and
their windows larger, and sashed with crystal glass; adorning
their apartments with rich furniture.

"All their drudgery of cooking, washing, daries, &c., are

[1] Weeden, *op. cit.*, p. 284.

performed in offices apart from the dwelling houses, which by this means are kept more cool and sweet." [1]

Thus early was the delightful plantation home of the South, in its essential features, established on Virginia soil. Of these homes Mrs. Wharton writes: "Later, there arose upon the banks of the James, the Potomac and the Chesapeake, stately mansions surrounded by plantations that rivalled the parks of old England — Shirley, Brandon, Westover, Gunston Hall, the home of the Masons, Flower de Hundred, Wyanoke, the Hermitage, Wye House — names synonymous with generous living, hospitality, and all the charms with which refined womanhood adorns a home." [2]

Most of the ordinary dwelling-houses, however, were small and covered with shingles of pine or cypress wood. Beverley seems inclined to complain somewhat bitterly of the "ill-husbandry" of the Virginia colonists in the matter of furnishing their homes. Thus he writes "that though their country be overrun with wood, yet they have all their wooden-ware from England; their cabinets, chairs, tables, stools, chests, boxes . . . and all other things, even so much as their bowls and birchen brooms, to the eternal reproach of their laziness." [3]

As one goes farther south into the Carolinas, the dignified brick mansion, modeled after the manor-house of England, gives place to houses with white pillars and porches, in imitation of Italian villas. Located on green points of land thrust out into the rivers, these southern plantation homes boasted gardens laid out in formal Italian style, with paths edged with box and approached through avenues bordered by tulip trees. The lawns were sown with the silvery grass seed widely used in England. As for the furnishing of these homes, it was in the handsome, solid style of the English Georgian mansion.

In the middle colonies no single type of home architecture seems to have developed if we except the Dutch houses in New

---

[1] *History of Virginia* (reprint in 1855 of 2nd ed. of 1722), p. 235.
[2] *Colonial Days and Dames*, p. 81.
[3] *Op. cit.*, p. 239.

Netherland, which were, of course, highly typical, in some respects, of that cleanly and thrifty people.   Irving humorously
describes the homes in the town of New Amsterdam, later New
York.

"The houses of the higher class were generally constructed
of wood, excepting the gable end which was of small, black and
yellow Dutch bricks, and always faced on the street, as our
ancestors, like their descendants, were very much given to
outward show, and were noted for putting the best leg foremost. The house was always furnished with abundance of
large doors and small windows on every floor, the date of its
erection was curiously designated by iron figures on the front,
and on the top of the roof was perched a fierce little weather-
cock, to let the family into the important secret which way
the wind blew.

"In those good days of simplicity and sunshine, a passion
for cleanliness was the leading principle in domestic economy,
and the universal test of an able housewife — a character
which formed the utmost ambition of our unenlightened grand-
mothers. . . .   The whole house was constantly in a state
of inundation, under the discipline of mops and brooms and
scrubbing brushes. . . .

"The grand parlor was the sanctum sanctorum, where the
passion for cleaning was indulged without control.   In this
sacred apartment no one was permitted to enter, excepting
the mistress and her confidential maid, who visited it, once a
week, for the purpose of giving it a thorough cleaning, and
putting things to rights — always taking the precaution of
leaving their shoes at the door, and entering devoutly on their
stocking-feet." [1]

Life was simple and homely in all the colonies, especially in
the North where the kitchen was very generally the family
living-room, not only because it was the cosiest room in the
house, but also because it was the warmest.   Its great fireplace
and enormous brick oven served to warm at least half the

[1] *Knickerbocker's History of New York*, pp. 182–183.

kitchen, whereas in the stiff and uninviting parlor the atmosphere in winter was frigid enough only a few feet from the hearth fire. In the farm-houses of New England, home life centered around the hospitable kitchen fireplace until well into the nineteenth century. Whittier has painted in attractive outlines the happy evenings passed beside the blazing logs of the hearth-fire — a picture which might easily apply to colonial New England of a century before. Another description, this time of Dutch home life around the kitchen hearth, is furnished by Irving. He says: "As to the family, they always entered in at the gate, and most generally lived in the kitchen. To have seen a numerous house-hold assembled around the fire, one would have imagined that he was transported back to those happy days of primeval simplicity, which float before our imaginations like golden visions. The fireplaces were of truly patriarchal magnitude, where the whole family, old and young, master and servant, black and white, nay, even the very cat and dog, enjoyed a community of privilege, and had each a right to a corner. Here the old burgher would sit in perfect silence, puffing his pipe . . .; the goede vrouw, on the opposite side, would employ herself diligently in spinning yarn or knitting stockings. The young folks would crowd around the hearth, listening with breathless attention to some old crone of a negro, who was the oracle of the family, and who, perched like a raven in a corner of a chimney, would croak forth for a long winter afternoon a string of incredible stories about New England witches — grisly ghosts, horses without heads — and hair-breadth escapes, and bloody encounters among the Indians." [1]

Furniture was plain and rather meager in the seventeenth century, save in the homes of the leading colonists. Although "Turkey Carpettes" are frequently mentioned in inventories of the seventeenth century, the term refers to table-covers. The floors were very generally uncovered, although sometimes they were sanded. "Forms" or benches and stools of various

[1] *Op. cit.*, p. 184.

heights were commonly used for seats. Chairs were less numerous; yet an inventory of the furnishings of Governor Eaton's home in New Haven, taken in 1657, shows that his living-room or "hall" boasted no less than six of these useful articles of furniture.[1] Very stiff and hard were most of these chairs, although their wooden seats were sometimes covered with cushions. Not until late in the seventeenth century did chairs with cane seats appear; and about the same time the easy-chair came into use. Every inventory of the period mentions at least one chest. These were commonly made of oak, cedar and cypress and sometimes had drawers. They were designed to hold most of the family clothing as well as table and bed linen. Pendulum clocks were comparatively rare until the eighteenth century, the colonial housewife being content to mark time indoors by means of an hour-glass or a water-clock. It is said that John Davenport of New Haven who died in 1760 owned the first clock.[2] Candles of the fragrant bayberry were extensively used long before tallow became plentiful. Mrs. Earle describes a primitive kind of lamp used in New England called "Betty lamps." "They were a shallow receptacle, usually of pewter, iron or brass, circular or oval in shape, and occasionally triangular, . . . with a projecting nose an inch or two long. When in use they were filled with tallow or grease, and a wick or piece of twisted rag was placed so that the lighted end could hang on the nose."

As to table furnishings in the seventeenth century, the inventories make plain that most of our colonial forefathers used napkins generously but were lacking both in the quantity and quality of their tableware. In an age when forks were rare even in England it is not surprising to learn that few colonists were blessed with them until the latter half of the century and even then they were far from common, as the inventories of the household furnishings show.[3] It is said that Governor

[1] Earle, *Customs and Fashions in Old New England*, p. 108.
[2] *Ibid.*, p. 125.
[3] Weeden, *Economic and Social History of New England*, p. 292.

Winthrop probably had the first fork ever brought to the new country. In 1633 he received a letter from one E. Howes, saying that the latter had sent him a "case containing an Irish skeayne or knife, a bodekyn and a forke *for the useful application of which I leave to your discretion*." But early in the eighteenth century forks apparently became common. Judge Sewall in 1718 makes careful note of a gift to the Widow Denison of two cases each containing a knife and fork. Very little earthenware, and of course no china or porcelain, was to be found in the colonies in the early days. Instead, wooden platters and trenchers were very common, as well as pewter dishes which were always kept bright and shining. Of the wooden trenchers (frequently nothing but square blocks of wood whittled by hand) we are told that Harvard College purchased them by the gross for the use of students.

In the rigorous climate of the New World the colonists felt the need of warm and generous fires. Probably the fireplaces of many colonial homes were "the largest ever built in any land." Some were ten feet or more in depth and broad enough to hold the huge logs in common use. On each side of the comfort-bringing hearth were placed home-made benches, with backs high enough to protect the family members from the bitter chill felt outside the warmed circle. Very early in colonial times fire sets, consisting of a pair of andirons, tongs and a long-handled fire shovel, were in general use. These were made of brass, copper, iron or steel and ranged in design from very simple styles to elaborately wrought pieces, adorned with dog's heads or grotesque figures. In Salem, Massachusetts, may be seen very fine examples of colonial hearths designed by McIntyre, who followed the style of the famous decorator Adam. The mantelpieces above these fireplaces are remarkable for the simple beauty and harmony of their contour. After 1745 the Franklin stove, invented by Benjamin Franklin, tended to supplant in favor the open fireplace. Although making no æsthetic pretensions, these stoves gave out far more heat than did the log hearth-fire.

Charming old chairs, bureaus, secretaries, chests and sofas of Chippendale, Sheraton and Adam design adorned the colonial homes of the Revolutionary period; and four-poster beds, of English model, with hangings of chintz or hand-embroidered linen to shut out cold draughts, were widely used. In England, whence well-to-do colonists imported their furniture, mahogany was employed for making beds until after 1720. The English furniture craftsman, Chippendale, designed beautiful four-poster mahogany beds with elaborately carved footboards and sidepieces. Few of these made their way to colonial America, however, and, indeed, they were not common in England.

In the homes of the wealthier colonists, candlesticks began to be supplemented by truly magnificent chandeliers in the latter part of the eighteenth century. One of the finest specimens of such may still be seen in the old Warner house in Portsmouth, New Hampshire. China ware, of beautiful coloring and great variety of design, began to displace wood and pewter during the eighteenth century. Delft ware, made in Holland, Lowestoft china of English make decorated with rose garlands, Crown Derby, Wedgwood, and luster ware filled the china cupboards of prosperous colonists and were the pride of housewives. Yet the use of pewter for household purposes continued through the eighteenth and into the early nineteenth century. American silverware of simple design and solid weight first began to be made by one John Hull, who was born in Massachusetts in 1624 and amassed a considerable fortune as a silversmith. But soon Hull had several rivals in his craft; and in the next century his products were quite outshone in workmanship by those of Paul Revere of historic fame. Curiously enough silversmiths did not set up their craft in New York until the middle of the eighteenth century, when one George Ridont came to the colony from London and practiced his trade. The silver sugar-bowls, pitchers and spoons, the creamers and teapots of colonial times have been carefully preserved in some families and handed down for many generations.[1]

Domestic Industry in Colonial Times. — We may be certain that the well-trained English housewives of the seventeenth century, who joined their husbands in establishing new homes in the strange land of America, did not leave their housewifely knowledge and skill behind them. After the first problem of immediate shelter had been met, the settlers turned their energies to developing a permanent food supply. Fortunately, the soil of the new country proved favorable to the production of most of the grains and fruits of England and the "lean years" which followed the landing of the colonists gave place before long to comparative plenty. In his quaint *Wonder-Working Providence of Zion's Saviour in New England*, Johnson writes in 1647 that "the Lord . . . hath blest his people's provision, and satisfied her poor with bread, in a very little space, everything in the country proved a staple commodity, wheat, rye, oats, peas, barley, beef, pork, butter, cheese . . .; and those who were formerly forced to fetch most of the bread they eat, and beer they drink, a hundred leagues by Sea, are through the blessing of the Lord so encreased, that they have not only fed their elder Sisters, Virginia, Barbados, and many of the Summer Islands that were prefer'd before her for fruitfulness, but also the Grandmother of us all, even the firtil Isle of Great Britain. . . ." [2] Of necessity the food of the colonists was changed somewhat from that of England to meet the new conditions. Indian corn or "guinney wheat" soon became a staple article of diet, which the colonial housewives from Virginia to Massachusetts ground in stone mortars (later in hand-mills called "querns") and prepared in a variety of ways. Writing in 1705, Beverley says of the Virginians: "The bread in gentlemen's houses is generally made of wheat, but some rather choose the pone,

[1] For the entire subject of colonial household furnishings, see Northend, Mary H., *Colonial Homes and their Furnishings*.

[2] *Op. cit.* (ed. 1910), pp. 246–247.

which is the bread made of Indian meal. Many of the poorer sort of people so little regard the English grain, that though they might have it with the least trouble in the world yet they don't mind to sow the ground, because they won't be at the trouble of making a fence particularly for it." [1]

Doubtless the colonists learned from the Indians how to transform the "dainty Indian maize" growing in their fields into such dishes as Indian pudding, hasty-pudding, corn-pone, hominy and samp. They learned, too, how to prepare delectable "sukguttahhash" (succotash) from beans and corn. Kitchen-gardens soon were attached to most homes and furnished a varied supply of vegetables and fruits. Cattle at first were scarce, so that fresh meat was a great luxury for many years. But fish, clams and oysters were abundant and wild turkeys and game proved plentiful and delicious until the hunters' guns drove them away from the settlements. Apparently little malt was made at home in the early days, so the housewife was relieved of one elaborate and tedious task — at least for a time. Beverley tells us that most Virginia housewives brewed their beer with malt "which they have from England, though barley grows there very well; but for want of the convenience of malt-houses, the inhabitants take no care to sow it." A little later he explains that the expense of building a "malt house and brew house too . . . can never be expected from a single family; . . ." [2] Yet in 1708 Judge Sewall makes this entry in his *Diary:* "Nov. 15, 16. Our Malt-House by the Mill-Crick is raised."

The domestic arts of pie and tart making as well as preserving were all revived by the colonial housewives. Writing in 1671, a New England author says that the "Quinces, Cherries and Damsins [3] set the Dames a-work. Marmalet & Preserved Damsins is to be met with in every house." [4]

---

[1] *History of Virginia*, p. 237.
[2] *Ibid.*, p. 261.
[3] Damson plums.
[4] Quoted in Earle, *Customs and Fashions*, p. 155.

Another household task which did not fall to the lot of all housewives, at least in New England, was the baking of bread. Johnson mentions "Bakers" among those men who "have left the husbandmen to follow the Plow and Cart, and they their trades; . . ." [1] These bakers and their bakeshops were carefully regulated by law in most of the New England settlements. In the New Haven colony laws of 1643 it is ordered that "every person within this jurisdiction, who shall bake bread for sale, shall have a distinct mark for his bread, and keep the true assizes thereafter expressed and appointed." The statute then provides in detail for the weight of loaves of various prices fixed by law. [2]

But the industries connected with the production and preparation of food and drink were but a small part of a goodwife's duties in colonial times. The task of furnishing the house with the means of light on the long winter evenings was in her hands. Although the "Betty lamps" previously described came into use quite early, yet most housewives depended on candlelight. The making of candles of tallow or bayberries was an important household industry which required several days' work in the preparation of the tallow, making of wicks, and tedious dipping of each candle in turn. Some favored housewives were the owners of candle molds which reduced the labor of candle-making surely one half.

Of course the industries of carding, spinning, weaving and making of housespun garments, as well as table-linen and bed-linen, were relegated wholly to the goodwives of colonial times. Yet, in the early days when hemp and flax were scarce, the spinning-wheel and the domestic loom must have been little used. So serious did this lack become that, in 1640, the Massachusetts General Court directed the towns to inquire what seeds were necessary for the growth of flax and "what men and women are skilful in the braking, spinning

[1] *Wonder-Working Providence*, p. 248.
[2] Trumbull, *Blue Laws*, pp. 193-194.

and weaving . . . that course may be taken for teaching the boyes and girls in all towns the spinning of the yarne." [1] A few months later a bounty of 3*d*. in a shilling for linen, woolen or cotton cloth was provided by the court on condition that the two former be spun of "wool or linen grown here." Unfortunately this bounty was withdrawn shortly after. Connecticut also took similar action in the same year.

In 1656 the Massachusetts Court "fearing that it will not be so easy to import cloths as it was in past years, thereby necessitating more home manufacture," directed the selectmen in every town to encourage the women, girls and boys to spin and weave. Each family was to be assessed for one or more spinners or for a fractional part. Every person so assessed was required to "spin for 33 weeks every yeare, a pound per weeke of lining cotton or wooling and so proportionably for halfe or quarter spinners under the penalty of 12*d*. for every pound short." To encourage wool, hemp and flax production the act provided that the common lands be cleared for sheep and that hemp and flax seeds be carefully saved and sown. [2] Soon the fulling of cloth quite largely passed out of the household to the fulling-mills, the first of which in Massachusetts was licensed as early as 1655. [3] Spinning was, however, almost entirely a home industry during the colonial period. Not so with weaving. Most families had looms of their own, but quite early weaving became, as in England, an industry carried on in large part by craftsmen. Johnson mentions weavers as plying their trade in Massachusetts as early as 1647. [4]

In the South the silk industry engrossed the attention of women as well as men, and steps were taken by Virginia in 1661 to encourage it. Beverley states that "prizes were appointed for the makers of the best pieces of linen cloth, and

[1] *Mass. Col. Rec.*, Vol. I, p. 294.
[2] *Ibid.*, Vol. III, p. 396.
[3] Weeden, *op. cit.*, p. 200.
[4] *Op. cit.*, p. 248.

a reward of fifty pounds of tobacco was given for each pound of silk. All persons were enjoined to plant mulberry trees, for the food of the silkworm, according to the number of acres of land they held." It is pleasant to record that several southern women were successful in the raising of silkworms and the manufacture of silk. Notable among these was Elizabeth Lucas Pinckney who, in 1755, "carried with her to England enough rich silk fabric, which she had raised and spun and woven herself in the vicinity of Charlestown, to make three fine silk gowns, one of which was presented to the Princess Dowager of Wales, and another to Lord Chesterfield." [1] The third is still in the possession of the family. As in New England, so in Virginia, the Assembly was early concerned about the decline of domestic cloth manufacture, and shortly after the accession of Charles II this body caused "looms and workhouses to be set up in the several counties, at the county charge. They renewed the rewards of silk, and put great penalties upon every neglect of making flax and hemp." [2] Apparently these early statutes of Virginia did not accomplish all that the framers hoped, for Beverley states in 1705 that Virginians "have all their clothing of all sorts from England; as linen, woollen, silk, hats and leather. Yet flax and hemp grow nowhere in the world better than there. Their sheep yield good increase, and bear good fleeces; but they sheer them only to cool them." [3] No doubt, the tobacco industry in Virginia tended to swamp all others that might profitably have been carried on.

Certain it is that in most of the colonies the spinning wheel of the housewife and her girls was rarely idle, and the loom was often in use where the professional weaver had not established himself. The members of the family, including the servants, or "hired help," as they were called in New England, were numerous indeed and all must be clothed. When the

---

[1] Earle, *Colonial Dames and Goodwives*, p. 83.
[2] Beverley, *op. cit.*, p. 58.
[3] *Ibid.*, p. 239.

busy goodwife was not spinning or carding or weaving, she was sitting by the evening fire knitting stockings or swiftly plying her needle, an implement "far more useful than the pen, and almost as powerful as the sword, in those days of early home-making." Mrs. Wharton cites Thomas Nelson Page's charming reference to a Virginia housewife who, when her husband complained of the gate being broken, playfully replied, "Well my dear, if I could sew it with my needle and thread, I would mend it for you." Many of the able men who were the first framers of our constitutional government were not ashamed to wear the clothing made in their own homes by the busy fingers of their wives. In 1776 Abigail Adams writes to her husband in Philadelphia: "I feel concerned lest your clothes go to rags, having nobody to take any care of you in your long absence; . . . I have a suit of homespun for you whenever you return." [1]

In 1778 one Christopher Marshall, a well-do-do Philadelphia Quaker, left in his diary, the *Remembrances*, an eloquent tribute to his wife's tireless industry in their home. To do justice to her services, he tells us, "would take up most of my time, for this genuine reason, how that from early in the morning till late at night she is constantly employed in the affairs of the family, which for some months has been very large; for beside the addition to our family in the house [is] a constant resort of comers and goers which seldom go away with dry lips and hungry bellies. This calls for her constant attendance, not only to provide but also to attend at getting prepared in the kitchen, baking our own bread and pies, meat, &c., but also on the table. Her cleanliness about the house, her attendance in the orchard, cutting and drying apples of which several bushels have been procured, add to which her making of cider without tools, for the constant drink of the family, her seeing all our washing done, and her fine clothes and my shirts, the which are all smoothed by her; add to this, her making of twenty large cheeses, and that from one cow, and daily

[1] *Familiar Letters*, p. 182.

using with milk and cream, besides her sewing, knitting &c."[1]

A vivid contrast has recently been drawn between the "Priscilla" of colonial days and the "Priscilla" of modern times with respect to the value of each as a producer of home necessities. So priceless were the services of the former maiden that she might well have been justified in taking the initiative and saying to John Alden: "John, I know you love me and I love you. Let us marry and I will help you make our home. As soon as you have built the house, with the help of our neighbors, I will furnish it. I will take the raw wool you supply me with and spin, weave and fashion it into warm blankets and homespun clothing for us both and I will knit all your worsted stockings. Then, too, I will sow hemp and flax seed, and make the fibres of the plants into linen sheets, napkins and cloths for our beds and table. I will take charge of all the work of lighting our home and will prepare the food that you bring to me from the farm and garden."[2] Surely the John Alden of colonial days was no economic loser in this experiment of marriage and setting up a new home. On the other hand one should not criticize too severely the "John" of present times who hesitates long before taking unto himself the luxury of a wife who knows little or nothing of the skilled art of homemaking.

The Colonial Home as a Training School of the Young. *Early Nurture.* — In all the colonies children were warmly welcomed and, as we have seen, families were very large. Not only was a numerous offspring a fulfillment of the divine command to "be fruitful and multiply" but children were most valuable aids to their parents in the struggle for a comfortable livelihood. We are told that Sir William Phipps, first royal Governor of Massachusetts (1692–1695), was one of twenty-

---

[1] *Extracts from the Diary of Christopher Marshall*, 1774–1781 (Albany, 1877), pp. 57–58.

[2] Mrs. Carrie Chapman Catt in a lecture given under the auspices of the Columbia University Institute of Arts and Sciences.

six children, all born of the same mother; and it is well known that Benjamin Franklin was one of a family of seventeen. Yet, as we have seen, child mortality was very high in those days when little was known of the hygienic care of infants and when homes were far from warm and comfortable in the coldest days of winter. Mrs. Earle writes: "There lies open before me an old leather-bound Bible with the record of my great-grandfather's family. He had sixteen children. When the first child was a year and a half old the second child was born. The baby was but four days old when the older child died. Five times did that mother's heart bear a similar cruel loss when she had a baby in her arms; therefore when she had been nine years married she had one living child, and five little graves bore record of her sorrow."[1] Only two children of the Puritan divine, Cotton Mather, survived their famous father — and so the record goes. No wonder women were expected to be fruitful as an important part of their life work!

The colonial baby was likely to be ushered into the world by a midwife, who was assisted by several nurses. A spirit of kindly helpfulness prompted busy housewives in the colonies to proffer their services to a neighbor who was about to become a mother. These friendly helpers did much of the housework during the confinement of the mother and assisted in caring for the new-born infant. Judge Sewall's *Diary* abounds in references to the midwives, nurses and women who attended his wife on the numerous occasions when their help was needed. He refers, also, to the custom, doubtless handed down from the Middle Ages, of entertaining these women with a plentiful dinner. In 1694, after the birth of his daughter Sarah the Judge makes this entry: "Women din'd with rost Beef and minc'd Pyes, good cheese and Tarts."[2]   Again, on January 16, 1702, he writes: "My Wife Treats her Midwife and Women: Had a good Dinner, Boil'd Pork, Beef, Fowls; very

---

[1] *Child Life in Colonial Days*, p. 5.
[2] *Op. cit.* (Massachusetts Historical Society), Vol. V, p. 394.

good Rost Beef, Turkey-Pye, Tarts." He carefully names the *seventeen* women who partook of this bounteous spread and adds: "Comfortable, moderat wether: and with a good fire in the Stove warm'd the Room."[1]

Unfortunately there was not always a stove to warm the room, and many a baby, at least in the middle and New England colonies, must have shivered in its cradle whenever it was not placed near the fireplace. In those days babies' little shirts were made of linen, and even the warmth of the homespun blankets in which they were wrapped could not wholly counteract the chilling effect of such garments. Then, too, helpless infants were taken to church to be christened very early in their earthly careers. At least in Massachusetts few days were allowed to pass after the birth of a child before it was brought before the minister with a view to outwitting "the old deluder Satan." Again it is Judge Sewall who furnishes us with testimony of the ruthlessness with which babies were carried out into the bitter cold of a New England winter and into the damp chill of the meeting-house to be christened. Under date of Feb. 6, 168$\frac{6}{7}$ he writes of his week-old child: "Between 3 and 4 P.M., Mr. Willard baptiseth my Son, whom I named Stephen. Day was Lowring after the storm, but not freezing. Child shrunk at the water but cry'd not." Apparently poor little Stephen, despite his Stoic control, did not survive his chilly welcome into the world, for a few months later his father records that this "dear Son Stephen is carried to the Tomb. . . ."

Family Discipline. — As might be expected, the colonists brought with them to the new world the ideas of family discipline that prevailed in seventeenth century England. Everywhere children were trained to render respect and obedience to parents, and their childish offenses were punished with severity as the best means of driving out "the old Adam." In a work on *Children and Their Education* written by John Robinson, the beloved pastor of the Pilgrim flock in Holland,

[1] *Op. cit.* (Massachusetts Historical Society), Vol. VI, p. 51.

the common belief in the inherent evil of child nature is set forth. "Surely," he declares, "there is in all children (though not alike) a stubbernes and stoutnes of minde arising from naturall pride which must in the first place be broken and beaten down that so the foundation of their education being layd in humilitie and tractablenes other virtues may in their turn be built thereon." Certain it is that the process of breaking down the child's stubborn will began early in most families and was conducted with thoroughness. Yet, for all his Puritan sternness, Judge Sewall makes very few references to the punishment of his children. Once he records chastising his little son Joseph who "threw a knop of Brass and hit his Sister Betty on the forehead so as to make it bleed and swell; upon which, and for his playing at Prayer-time and eating when Return Thanks, I whip'd him pretty smartly." [1] Little sinful, four-year old Joseph! His attempt to hide from his father "behind the head of the cradle" served forcibly to remind the latter of "Adam's carriage" after he had eaten the forbidden fruit and thus brought sin into the world! It is pleasant to know that Cotton Mather heartily disapproved of the "slavish way of education carried on with raving and kicking and scourging, in schools as well as in families. . . ." His son testifies of him that "He would never come to give the child a blow, except in case of obstinacy, or something very criminal. To be chased for a while out of his presence he would make to be looked upon as the sorest punishment in his family."

Religious Training in the Family. — It is a truism to state that religion played a far more prominent part in the lives of the American colonists than in those of their descendants. In the southern and middle colonies children were carefully educated in the catechism of the Church of England and were very early familiarized with its ritual. Likewise the Society of Friends enjoined upon all parents the painstaking education of their offspring in the principles of morality and religion

[1] *Diary*, Vol. I, p. 369.

accepted by them. But it was in New England that religious training was most severe and, it may truthfully be added — gloomy. Family prayers were almost universal, and the daily reading of the Bible by parents and children was never overlooked in most families. Judge Sewall writes in 1689: "It falls to my Daughter Elizabeth's Share to read the 24 of Isaiah which she doth with many Tears not being very well, and the Contents of the Chapter, and Sympathy with her draw Tears from me also." Poor Betty Sewall! Her fear of death and punishment for sin was never far from her sensitive mind during her whole lifetime. Her father records a few months later that when he reached his home in the evening his wife told him that Betty had been dejected and sorrowful all day. A "little after dinner she burst out into an amazing cry, which caus'd all the family to cry too." Her mother's questioning at last revealed the cause — "she was afraid she should goe to Hell, her Sins were not pardon'd." The Judge adds: "She was first wounded by my reading a Sermon of Mr. Norton's, about the 5th. of January. Text Jno, 7.34. Ye shall seek me and shall not find me. And those words in the Sermon, Jno. 8.21. Ye shall seek me and shall die in your sins, ran in her mind, and terrified her greatly." [1] One cannot refrain from thinking that the childhood years of many sensitive children besides Betty Sewall were darkly overshadowed by the Puritan doctrines of original sin, predestination and election, and the punishments of a fiery, material hell, so faithfully taught them by parents who sought to perform their utmost duty. Even boys were profoundly affected at times by the theological instruction they received at home. Judge Sewall tells us how he tried to arouse his son Sam to the "need he had to prepare for Death," but is forced to record that he "seem'd not much to mind, eating an Aple." Later, however, when the boy was saying the Lord's Prayer, "he burst out into a bitter Cry and said he was afraid he should die. I pray'd with him," writes the father, "and read Scrip-

[1] *Diary*, Vol. I, pp. 419–420.

tures comforting against death, as 'O death, where is thy sting,' etc." [1]

Apparently the religious instruction given in the home did not always prove satisfying to parents. In 1657 a Puritan divine writes a friend: "Do your children and family grow more godly? Much ado have I with my own family; hard to get a servant that is glad of catechising or family duties. . . . Even the children of the godly here and elsewhere make woful proof. . . ."

In the better class of families the manners of children were carefully looked after. Little books of etiquette were written and widely circulated during the eighteenth century. Mrs. Earle has reproduced the title-page of one of these courtesy books published in London in 1701. It was called *The School of Manners* and contained unbending rules of behavior for children "at Church, at Home, at Table, in Company, in Discourse, at School, abroad, and among Boys." Another such manual of behavior, published just before the Revolution, was called *A Pretty Little Pocket Book*. In this work children were exhorted never to speak unless spoken to, never to sit down at table until grace had been said, never to take salt from the common dish except with a clean knife, and never to throw bones under the table !

Following the custom in England, some parents did not permit their children to sit at table with them, but required them to stand through the whole meal. Of this practice Mrs. Earle writes : "Sometimes they [the children] had a standing place and plate or trencher; at other boards they stood behind the grown folk and took whatever food was handed them. This must have been in families of low social standing and meagre house-furnishings. In many homes they eat or stood at a side-table and trencher in hand, ran over to the great table for their supplies." [2]

Notwithstanding the care and pains spent by most Puritan parents upon the moral and religious training of their children,

[1] *Op. cit.*, Vol. I, pp. 308–309.   [2] *Child Life in Colonial Days*, pp. 216–217.

the lawmakers of Massachusetts Bay and later of Connecticut conceived it to be an important part of their business to have oversight of the young, whether these were under family government or not. A Massachusetts Act of 1642 empowered the selectmen of every town "to take account from time to time of all parents and masters, and of the children, especially of their ability to read and understand principles of religion and the capital laws of their country, and to impose fines upon such as shall refuse to render such account to them when they shall be required. . . ." In 1654 it was ordered that "Magistrates have authority to whip divers children and servants who behave themselves disrespectfully, disobediently and disorderly toward their parents, masters and governors."

Such interference with the rights of parents seemed perfectly just and natural to our Puritan forefathers. And indeed the tendency in this and other countries has for many years been in the direction of State control of the rearing and education of children. Our statutes compelling the attendance of children at school and limiting the power of parents to chastise or abuse their offspring are encroachments upon parental privilege no less marked, although more humane, than those of Puritan New England.

Industrial Training in the Home. — Not many idle hours or happy playtimes fell to the lot of children in the northern colonies, at least in early times. Life was too strenuous in this new land and the struggle to wrest a livelihood from the wilderness too intense not to react upon the children. Moreover, Isaac Watts' oft-quoted lines regarding Satan's skill in finding mischief "for idle hands to do" were more popular in the eighteenth century than now. Boys and girls were very early put to work both in and out of doors, although the tasks in farm and garden fell more largely to the share of boys. Yet the labor of children was not sharply divided according to sex. Boys were taught to weave garters and suspenders on the small tape-looms found in almost every family, while girls took part in the spring sowing on the farm and shared with their brothers the task of weeding flax fields and vegetable gardens. We have seen how the governments of Virginia and the New England colonies sought to encourage the raising of wool and flax. Flax manufacture was a complicated industry involving, we are told, about twenty different operations. Half of these could be carried on by children who learned to hetchel flax, comb wool, skein yarn, wind spools with newly spun thread, and even fasten the warp threads to the frame of the loom. Tiny girls of six or seven began the task which was to be theirs through life — the spinning of flax and later of cotton. For this a small hand distaff was often used which was called a "rock." Some children became very dexterous in making smooth, well-twisted thread with this simple appliance. The Massachusetts law of 1642 enjoined it upon the selectmen to see that even the boys and girls who tended cattle . . . "be set to some other employment withal as spinning upon the rock, knitting, weaving tape, &c. . . ."

In Virginia and other colonies where silk raising became a craze at one time or another, boys and girls were frequently set to work picking mulberry leaves from the trees which were kept low by pruning. The care of silkworms was held to be fit work for children, and it was commonly said that two boys "if their hands be not sleeping in their pockets," could care for six ounces of seed from hatching till within two weeks of spinning, when "three or four more helps, women and children being as proper as men," were needed to feed, cleanse, air and dry the worms.[1]

In addition to tasks of cooking, sewing, spinning and weaving, girls in the colonies must learn to make samplers, not only that they might become expert needlewomen, but also in order to learn their letters. Mrs. Earle describes the eighteenth-century sampler as "a needlework hornbook, containing the alphabet, a verse indicative of good morals or industry, or a sentence from the representations of impossible

[1] Earle, *Child Life in Colonial Days*, p. 310.

birds, beasts, flowers, trees, or human beings." [1] Dutiful and virtuous were the sentiments stitched by childish fingers into the canvas of their samplers; and one wonders what were the inner feelings of the little needlewomen, pining to be out of doors, as they embroidered such verses as the following:

> "Next unto God, dear Parents, I address
> Myself to you in humble Thankfulness.
> For all your Care and Charge on me bestow'd,
> The means of learning unto me allowed.
> Go on! I pray, and let me still Pursue
> Such Golden Arts the Vulgar never knew."

Probably most boys and girls in colonial days received their industrial training in the home from their own parents. However, in poor families, girls as well as boys, were apprenticed when very young. The colonial laws made early provision for binding out orphans and the children of indigent parents with suitable persons who would care for their morals and teach them various industries. The girl's indenture, however, unlike that of the boy, did not stipulate that she was to be taught a specific trade; hence she probably received a general training in spinning, weaving and household tasks. In Boston in 1720 a "Spinning School House" was established which owed its origin to the public spirit of a philanthropist who later turned over the equipment to the city "for the education of the children of the poor." Later the city itself organized several spinning schools where orphans and neglected children were taught to be skilled spinners. We are told that the girls sometimes plied their tasks on Boston Common surrounded, at first, by an admiring audience of townspeople. [2] Virginia, also, in the Act of 1646 empowered the county commissioners to send two children from each county "at the age of eight or seven years at the least . . ." to James City . . . "to be employed in the public flax houses under such master and mistress as shall be there appointed in carding, knitting

---

[1] Earle, *Child Life in Colonial Days*, p. 328.
[2] Abbott, Edith, *Women in Industry*, p. 21.

and spinning." The commissioners were enjoined to "have caution not to take up any children but from such parents who by reason of their poverty are disabled to maintain and educate them." [1]

Intellectual Education. — As we have seen, scant attention was given to the intellectual education of girls throughout the American colonies. Boarding-schools and private day and evening schools were established after 1725, but they offered instruction chiefly in reading, writing, keeping of accounts and a smattering of music, with dancing and embroidery taught by special teachers. Such was the education of English girls in the eighteenth century; and the English idea of superficial "accomplishments" as constituting the sole necessary education for "females" crossed the seas to the colonies. Here and there a girl received serious intellectual training at the hands of a cultivated father who refused to accept the ideal of "female education" almost universal in colonial days. But ordinarily girls in the northern colonies were sent to dame schools to learn to read, sew, spin and knit — the reading not always being followed by training in writing. Therefore many colonial women were forced to "make their mark" whenever their signature was required, as deeds and documents of colonial times abundantly prove. In the New England colonies, at least in Massachusetts, girls were permitted to attend the town elementary schools only at hours when the boys were not using the building, *i.e.*, early in the morning and late in the afternoon. Even this grudging privilege was restricted to the summer months and was promptly withdrawn at the approach of winter on the ground of regard for "female health." Boys, however, seem to have attended the New England town schools pretty generally and those who intended to enter Harvard or Yale were prepared in the town grammar schools established by law in the colonies of Massachusetts and Connecticut.

---

[1] Clews, Elsie, *Educational Legislation . . . of the Colonial Governments* (New York, 1899), p. 356; Hening, *Statutes*, Vol. I, pp. 336–337.

Apparently, then, the colonial family restricted its education of the young very largely to moral, religious and industrial training, relegating such intellectual education as was deemed fitting to the dame school, the town, church or private school, and, in the southern colonies, to tutors brought in from the mother-country. Even Judge Sewall in his voluminous *Diary* makes no mention of giving intellectual instruction to any of his numerous offspring. Occasionally such home instruction was given, however, but it was certainly unusual.

The Plantation Family of the South. — In the southern colonies a type of home life developed, which was peculiar to that region, and deserves special consideration. Unlike the Puritan homes built in towns or villages, the colonial "mansion" of the southern planter was set in wide acres of tobacco, cotton or rice fields. These plantation homes, established in a virgin wilderness by men of English stock and strong English feeling, were the nurseries of a type of man and woman peculiar to the South and differing in many respects from their stern and more democratic Puritan cousins of the New England colonies. A fortunate combination of fertile soil, mild climate and valuable indigenous products, such as tobacco and cotton, made of these southern settlers, in whom the land-owning instinct was already strong, an agricultural class, reproducing many of the aristocratic customs and characteristics of their English forefathers. Along the rivers of Virginia and the Carolinas large plantations were established, vast tracts of land were cultivated and the products shipped by natural waterways to the coast. The institution of slavery was doubtless of the greatest assistance to the settlers in maintaining manor-houses similar to those of the landed gentry of England. Early in the seventeenth century a Dutch ship brought the first cargo of slaves from Africa to Virginia and thereafter for many generations English, Dutch and New England traders kept the southern landholders amply supplied with negro slave workers. This condition, in the words of Thomas

Nelson Page, "emphasized class distinction and created a system of castes, making the social system of Virginia as strongly aristocratic as that of England." [1]

Just as the southern planter sought to reproduce the manorial estate of the English gentleman in the wilds of America, so he transplanted the English Church to his new abode. Likewise he adopted the English system of primogeniture and entail, carefully seeing to it that his house and lands descended to his eldest son or his nearest male heir.

Several contemporary descriptions have come down to us of colonial plantation homes. In his valuable *Journal* Philip Fithian describes a year of residence in 1773–1774 as tutor in the house of Mr. Robert Carter of Virginia, and draws a vivid pen picture of his surroundings. The mansion stood on the "high, craggy banks of the River Nominy" and was known as Nomini Hall. Around it were wide stretches of fertile land worked by negro slaves. The house, our journalist tells us, "is built with Brick, but the bricks have been covered with strong lime Mortar; so that the building is now perfectly white. It is seventy-six Feet long from East to West; and forty-four wide from North to South, two Stories high; . . ." On the ground floor, in addition to dining-rooms and a study, was "a Ball-Room thirty Feet long." At equal distances from the corners of the main house stood four other buildings — the school-house (for the children of the family only), the stable, the coach-house and the work-house where the family washing was done. In the triangle made by the wash-house, stable and coach-house were placed the "Kitchen, a well built House as large as the School-House; Bake-House; Dairy; Store-House and several other small Houses : all which stand due West, and at a small distance from the Great House, and form a little handsome Street." Not far away stood the planter's mill and granary where the wheat and corn from his fertile acres were ground and stored. To the east of the mansion were "two Rows of tall, flourishing, beautiful Poplars . . . [which]

[1] *The Old South* (New York, 1900), p. 104.

form an extremely pleasant avenue, and at the Road, through them, the House appears most romantic, at the same time that it does truly elegant." [1]

So much for the plantation home at its best — and many such charming residences there were, scattered through the southern colonies on the wooded heights overlooking quiet rivers. But the estates of some planters, especially near the western frontiers, were far from being either so pretentious or so comfortable. Indeed, as the traveler proceeded into the interior, the stone houses gave place to wooden ones, the extensive farms to smaller holdings, the numerous retinue of slaves to half a dozen or so, until the typical log shelter of the frontiersman was reached, standing like a faithful scout at the outposts of civilization.

What was the character of the life on the great estates near the coast? In the first place every plantation of any size was well-nigh an economic unit, producing almost all the food and drink needed for its own consumption as well as some of the materials for clothing, although much of the latter was imported from England. It was an important industrial establishment, carrying on agriculture, milling, gardening, horse-raising and dairying. Within doors the lady of the mansion was probably the busiest member. Hers was the duty of overseeing the labors of a horde of household slaves, and of feeding, clothing and caring for the health of every negro worker on the estate. On her devolved the careful oversight of all supplies, locking them up from thieving fingers and giving them out when needed. She must not only know how to spin, weave and fashion garments for scores of men, women and children — her own family and the families of her slaves — but she must train ignorant, undisciplined and child-like beings to perform a wide variety of household tasks with industry and skill. All this required enormous executive ability and almost infinite patience, firmness and tact. Thomas Nelson Page has

[1] Fithian, *Journal and Letters*, 1767–1774 (Princeton, 1900), pp. 128–131.

paid enthusiastic tribute to the wife and mother of the southern plantation.

"She was the necessary and invariable functionary, the keystone of the domestic economy which bound all the rest of the structure and gave it its strength and beauty. From early morn till morn again the most important and delicate concerns of the plantation were her charge and care. . . . From superintending the setting of the turkeys to fighting a pestilence, there was nothing that was not her work. She was mistress, manager, doctor, nurse, counsellor, seamstress, teacher, housekeeper, slave, all at once. She was at the beck and call of every one, especially of her husband, to whom she was 'guide, philosopher and friend.'" [1]

In addition to this rather overwhelming catalogue of duties the southern matron was expected to maintain the lavish hospitality so dear to the hearts of all colonists of the South. "Little excuse," says one writer, "was needed to bring people together where every one was social, and where the great honor was to be the host." And so it is not surprising to find Fithian's *Journal* fairly bristling with references to social doings — to dancing parties where the minuet was performed with stateliness and charm, to dinners, excursions on horseback and by boat, house-warmings and card parties. The hostess who entertained at a dance well knew that most of her guests must be accommodated for a night or two, since distances were great, and all must be entertained at her generous table. Literally the lady of the southern plantation kept open house where all her friends were welcome at all times.

Such a laborious life must have proved onerous if not exhausting to many a southern housewife. No wonder that Thomas Nelson Page stops in the middle of a panegyric in honor of Virginia matrons to record that the lady was "often delicate in frame, and of a nervous organization so sensitive as perhaps to be a great sufferer; . . ." [2]

[1] *Social Life in Old Virginia*, pp. 37–38.
[2] *Ibid.*, pp. 35–36.

Home Training and Education. — In these charming plantation homes boys and girls were educated in the ideals of their fathers and grandfathers before them. They developed, through association and training, the same delicate breeding, the same aristocratic ideas, the same high-spirited and narrow devotion to their established social structure that were conspicuous in their forbears. As we have seen, most of these southern plantation children were taught by tutors in their own homes until the girls were sixteen or thereabouts and the boys fitted for higher study. Then the sisters entered happily into the round of social gayeties that enlivened colonial life in the South while their brothers were sent to William and Mary College or, more probably, to Oxford or Cambridge in the mother country. Thence these young men returned, more in love than ever with the life of the landed aristocracy, to perpetuate unchanged the social and economic system in which they held so favored a position. Such a life as they led was not stimulating to intellectual research or to social reconstruction. It was too agreeable, too well oiled by the labor of an enslaved class, to challenge their highest intellectual powers. In the words of Professor Trent, himself a southern gentleman :

"Southerners lived a life which, though simple and picturesque, was nevertheless calculated to repress many of the best faculties and powers of our nature. It was a life affording few opportunities to talents that did not lie in certain beaten grooves. It was a life gaining its intellectual nourishment, just as it did its material comforts, largely from abroad, — a life that choked all thought and investigation that did not tend to conserve existing institutions and opinions, a life that rendered originality scarcely possible except under the guise of eccentricity." [1]

[1] *William Gilmore Simms* (1899), p. 37.

SELECTED READINGS

SOURCES

Adams, Charles Francis, Jr., ed. *Familiar Letters of John Adams and His Wife Abigail Adams,* N. Y., Hurd and Houghton, 1876.

Beverley, Robert. *The History of Virginia,* reprinted from the second revised edition, London, 1722, pp. 54, 58, 231–232, 235–239, 262–264. Richmond, Va., J. W. Randolph, 1855.

Dunton, John. *Letters from New England,* Boston, Publications, The Prince Society, 1867, Vol. 4, pp. 67–73.

Fithian, Philip. *Journal and Letters,* 1767–1774, The University Library, 1900, pp. 50, 51, 56–57, 62–66, 75, 87, 103, 109.

Johnson, Edward. *Johnson's Wonder-Working Providence, 1628–1651,* ed. by J. Franklin Jameson, 1910, pp. 71, 246–247.

Kemble, Frances Anne. *Journal of a Residence on a Georgian Plantation in 1838–1839,* N. Y., Harper and Bros., 1864.

Sewall, Samuel. *Diary,* 1674–1729, 3 Vols., Collection of Massachusetts Historical Society, Boston, 1878–1882, 5th series, Vols. 5–7.

Trumbull, James Hammond. *True Blue Laws of Connecticut and New Haven,* Hartford, Conn., American Publishing Co., 1876, pp. 60, 69–70, 78–79, 87, 104, 106–107, 123–124, 150–152, 156, 159, 216–219, 241–243, 261, 279.

Winthrop, John. *Winthrop's Journal, 1630–1640,* Scribner, 1908, Vol. I, pp. 120, 266–268, 285–287; Vol. II, 43–44, 161–163, 225, 330.

SECONDARY WORKS

Adams, Charles Francis, Jr. *Some Phases of Sexual Morality in Colonial New England,* reprinted from the Proceedings of the Massachusetts Historical Society, Cambridge, J. Wilson and Son, 1891.

Andrews, C. M. *Colonial Folkways,* Yale University Press, 1921, Vol. 9, Chs. III, VII.

Brooks, Henry Mason, comp. *The Olden Time Series: The Days of the Spinning Wheel in New England,* 6 Vols., Boston, Ticknor and Co., 1886, Vol. 2.

Bruce, Henry A. *Woman in the Making of America,* Boston, Little, Brown and Co., 1912.

Cook, Frank G. "Marriage Celebration in the Colonies" in *Atlantic Monthly,* LXI, 1888, pp. 350 ff.

Crawford, Mary C. *Social Life in Old New England*, Boston, Little, Brown and Co., 1914, Chs. V, VI.

Earle, Alice Morse. *Child Life in Colonial Days*, N. Y., London, Macmillan, 1889.

——. *Colonial Dames and Good Wives*, Boston and N. Y., Houghton Mifflin and Co., 1895.

——. *Colonial Days in Old New York*, N. Y., Scribner, 1896.

——. *Customs and Fashions in Old New England*, N. Y., Scribner, 1893.

——. *Home Life in Colonial Days*, N. Y., Macmillan, 1898.

——. *Margaret Winthrop*, N. Y., Scribner, 1895, Chs. I–III, VI, pp. 174–180.

Goodwin, John A. *The Pilgrim Republic*, Boston, Ticknor and Co., 1888.

Howard, George E. *History of Matrimonial Institutions*, 3 Vols., University of Chicago Press, Callaghan and Co., 1904, Vol. II.

Irving, Washington. *Knickerbocker's History of New York*, 2 Vols., N. Y., G. P. Putnam's Sons, 1894, Book III, Chs. III, IV, VII.

Lawrence, Henry W. *The Not-Quite Puritans*, Boston, Little, Brown and Co., 1928, Chs. III–IX.

Page, Thomas Nelson. *Social Life in Old Virginia*, N. Y., Scribner, 1898.

Putnam, Emily. *The Lady*, N. Y., Sturgis and Walton Co., 1910, pp. 282–323.

Ravenel, H. A. *Eliza Pinckney*, N. Y., Scribner, 1896.

Weeden, Wm. Babcock. *Economic and Social History of New England, 1620–1789*, 2 Vols., Boston and N. Y., Houghton Mifflin and Co., 1890, pp. 170, 191–198, 200, 212–219, 227–230, 291–310, 388–399, 413, 428.

Wharton, Anne H. *Colonial Days and Dames*, Philadelphia, J. B. Lippincott, 1895.

Winsor, Juston, ed. *The Memorial History of Boston, 1630–1880*, 4 Vols., Boston, J. R. Osgood and Co., 1880–1881, Vol. I, 229–231, 303–304, 483–497, 512–518; Vol. II, 450–462, 479–480, 485.

CHAPTER X

THE ENGLISH FAMILY IN THE NINETEENTH AND TWENTIETH CENTURIES

The Industrial Revolution in England. — Until after the middle of the eighteenth century industry was almost wholly organized around the family. Writing about 1725, Daniel DeFoe describes the domestic system of cloth industry as he saw it during the course of a leisurely journey through England.[1] He writes of seeing most of the cottages in the north filled with "lusty fellows," some working at the loom, some at the dye-vat, still others dressing the cloth. Women and children, the latter as young as four years of age, were busily at work carding and spinning. The cloth, " Kersie or Shalloon," manufactured by such simple domestic implements as the single-thread spinning wheel, the hand loom (requiring two men to throw the shuttle back and forth) and the wooden combing card for combing out wool and flax by hand, was sold in the neighboring towns by the master.

Such was the simple cottage system of industry, which, after the middle of the eighteenth century, was doomed to disappear as inadequate to meet the changing needs and demands of a new age. The epoch-making geographical discoveries of the sixteenth century were followed by the colonization of the New World in the seventeenth and eighteenth centuries. Thus new markets were opened to European merchants and a powerful stimulus given to overseas commerce. But the expansion of the world known to Europeans and the resultant expansion of commerce were not accom-

---

[1] *A Tour Thru' the Whole Island of Great Britain* (4th edition, 1748), Vol. III, pp. 137-139.

panied by an equal growth in the quantity of manufactured products. Limited to a small output by the nature of the hand instruments in use, the English workers could not keep up with the colonial demand for woolen and linen cloths. Then began in England a remarkable era of inventions. In 1767 James Hargreaves, a weaver by trade, invented the spinning jenny which, on the turning of a wheel, drove eight spindles at once. The next year Arkwright invented a roller machine for spinning which was driven by water power. Quick to see the possibilities of his new invention, Arkwright established the first factories in England in which were installed power machines for spinning. In 1779 one Crompton invented a contrivance known as a "mule" which could spin much finer thread than Arkwright's roller machine.

Spinning could now be done by water-power machines far more expeditiously than could weaving by hand. The urgent need for a loom worked by mechanical means to keep pace with the increased output of yarns and thread stimulated the inventive capacity of an English clergyman named Cartwright, who, in 1787, gave to the world the first power loom. It proved almost as immediate a success as Crompton's spinning "mule," and in a quarter of a century twenty-four hundred power looms had been set up in England.

A tremendous forward movement in the direction of substituting machines for man-power was taken when James Watt invented a single-acting steam engine in 1769 and in 1782 patented a double-acting steam engine. Two years later he invented the first steam carriage to be run on ordinary highways. It was not until 1813, however, that a locomotive for service on a railroad track was constructed, and not until 1814 that Stephenson built a locomotive resembling those in use at present. Seven years earlier Robert Fulton, an American, had built and operated the first practical steamboat.

Development of the Factory System. — As a result of the invention of power machinery, great factories sprang up in those districts of England given over to textile manufacturing. In them were gathered the handworkers of the outlying country who speedily learned that they could no longer compete with machine-made goods. Gradually, and not without much distress and bitterness, the industrial system of England was completely transformed. One by one the cottages that had been the centers of home industry were abandoned; and apprentices and masters alike sought the rapidly growing towns and cities where factories were built and expensive machinery installed. This influx of working population led to the erection of cheap and ugly houses in the neighborhood of the factories. Built close together, without even a tiny patch of ground that could serve as a garden, these working-men's homes were the forerunners of the unsightly tenements and slums of our modern cities. No longer was the worker an independent agent; on the contrary he became wholly dependent on the capitalist who owned the factory and its machinery and who was thus in a position to fix both the wages and the working hours of his employees. After ages of industrial history extending from ancient to modern times, during which the family had been the unit of industry, the household group was at last displaced by the crowded factory with its underpaid body of workers.

Effects of the Industrial Revolution on the Home. — Needless to say the industrial revolution wrought a profound and fundamental change in the family life of the small workman in England. Instead of plying his trade in his own home, surrounded by his wife, his children and his apprentices, whose work he directed, he betook himself at the shriek of the whistle to the factory, where he labored with his fellows in crowded, unwholesome rooms until the evening. Instead of carrying through a piece of work to its end and thus experiencing the satisfaction that comes to the worker from the finished product, he carried on one simple mechanical process from morn till night, which, as division of labor became more and more minute, was but a small portion of the work necessary to a completed product. Absent from home the entire day, his influence over his children was necessarily weakened and he became distinctly less powerful a force in shaping the life and ideas of his family.

But this was not the sole effect of the industrial revolution upon family life in England. Except in a few industries where bodily strength was essential, the new machinery was so easily operated that, little by little women and children were drawn into the busy life of the factories. Not only was their labor as effective as that of the men but they could be hired far more cheaply. Before the middle of the nineteenth century the wives and children of workingmen were actually taking the places of husbands and fathers in the mills. Thus Gibbins writes:

"A curious inversion of the proper order of things was seen in the domestic economy of the victims of the cheap labor system, for women and girls were superseding men in manu- facturing labour, and, in consequence, their husbands had often to attend, in a shiftless, slovenly fashion, to those house- hold duties which mothers and daughters hard at work in the factories were unable to fulfil. Worse still, mothers and fathers in some cases lived upon the killing labour of their little children, by letting them out to hire to manufacturers who found them cheaper than their parents." [1]

In the half century from 1841 to 1891 the number of women in the textile factories of England increased 221 per cent, whereas the increase of men during this period was only 53 per cent.[2]

It can hardly be doubted that the efforts of women in Eng- land to increase the family income by laboring in the factories not infrequently resulted in lessening the earning power of husbands and fathers. But this was not the only harmful effect of their entrance into the field of labor. Whole families in many of the English mill towns were employed all day in

[1] Gibbins, *Industry in England*, p. 392.
[2] Robinson and Beard, *The Development of Modern Europe*, Vol. II, p. 48.

the factories, from little children four or five years of age to the mother and father. Indeed, the English system of employment was known as the "family system." Grave abuses grew out of this condition. Homes were ill kept, meals were hastily prepared and unappetizing and the foundation was laid for those hard drinking habits of the English laboring class so frequently pointed out and deplored by social writers during the nineteenth century. Furthermore family discipline was gradually undermined and the old English traditions of the duty of parents with respect to the moral and religious training of their children were well-nigh forgotten. The children themselves, employed from their earliest years in feeding and tending machines in the textile factories, grew up in the densest ignorance and in moral darkness. Before two decades of the nineteenth century had passed, the English nation began to awake to the tremendous social evils bred by such family conditions. Then was initiated that long course of factory legislation which was ultimately to free England of the most harmful forms of child labor. It is interesting to note that steps toward this reform had many years before been taken by the socialist Robert Owen in his mills at New Lanark, Scotland.

But injurious as were the first unregulated effects of machine industry and factory labor upon family life, this is only part of the story. The change from the domestic system of production to the factory system had far-reaching and beneficial consequences on the lives of women. In the first place women employed in factories earned their own living and contributed to the support of the family. Although the economic independence of employed women in all grades of paid service received no legal recognition in England until 1870, and thus married women for nearly a century after the industrial revolution were still regarded as financial dependents whose personal property was owned and administered by the husband, yet the fact that women could and did earn their own living was bound to bring about a change in public opinion in course of time. And with the change in popular sentiment regarding the right of wives to own the wages they had earned and to administer the property they possessed at marriage, went a drastic revision of the married women's property laws that had made financial dependents of wives since feudal times. But this is not all. The industrial revolution brought leisure to busy housewives of the middle class who had been engaged from morning to night in a round of productive employments of the utmost importance to the well-being of the family members. No longer must the spinning wheel hum for long hours of every day, or the housewife devote her energies to weaving cloth, making garments, table and bed linens, dipping candles, brewing ale and preparing butter and cheese. Little by little these industries were taken out of the home into manufacturing plants and married women outside the ranks of wealth were endowed with leisure for the first time in social history — leisure which might be spent in self-improvement.

Changes in the Economic, Legal and Social Status of Women. — The deep-moving forces at work to bring about the emancipation of wives were not wholly economic in origin. Theories of liberty, equality of rights and brotherhood began to take shape in France and in the English colonies of America that were destined to work profound changes in the lives of men and later of women also in all western lands. The political revolutions in America and France, in the closing decades of the eighteenth century, were signs of a growing spirit of democracy, a quickened perception of the nature and extent of human rights, which was bound in course of time to transform the institutions of all countries. In England, the land where ideas and customs "mellow down from precedent to precedent," the enlargement of the rights and opportunities of the common man came gradually and without violence, after England's richest colonies had been lost. Little by little, first in the new American Republic and later in the mother country, the ideal of manhood suffrage was realized; and the benefits of free public education were extended to all classes.

To Englishmen first came the liberation that was later to be extended to women. This, of course, was wholly natural. Men were still almost universally regarded as the dominant sex — masters in private as in public life by the gifts of nature and education. Therefore political freedom, educational advantage and the right to organize in order to uphold their economic rights were first awarded to them. But the strong current of democratic feeling could not fail to draw the women into its forward movement as the generations passed. It is the purpose of the following discussion very briefly to trace the course of events leading to the emancipation of women in England.

Extension of Property Rights. — Up to the year 1857 the English law took no steps to remedy the hard position of married women with respect to their property disabilities. But in that year an Act was passed partially to protect the property of a deserted wife. The Act provided that at any time after her desertion a woman might apply to a police magistrate for a protection order. The order once granted, any property that she had acquired *after her desertion*, either by her own labor or by gift or bequest, became protected and belonged to her as completely as if she were a single woman.[1] In 1861 this Act was followed by another designed to protect the property rights of a woman whose husband had been convicted of a serious assault upon her person.[2] The Act of 1861 granted to a wife thus assaulted the right to obtain a magistrate's order exempting her from liability to cohabit with her husband and placing her in the position of a single woman with respect to her property.

Obviously these Acts were of benefit only to wives who had

---

[1] Chitty, *Statutes at Large*, Vol. VIII, pp. 855–869; 20 and 21 Vict., c. 85.

[2] It will be remembered that as early as 1674 Chief Justice Hale had rendered the opinion that a husband had no right to inflict personal chastisement upon his wife.

been deserted or abused. Yet, for many years liberal minded Englishmen had regarded the private law of England as needlessly harsh in respect to the property rights of all married women. Appeal after appeal for its amendment had been made to Parliament by both men and women with little effect. But in 1870 a Married Woman's Property Act was passed which applied equally to all married women. The provisions of this Act may be briefly summarized:

1. All the earnings and savings bank deposits of a married woman were her sole and absolute property.

2. The rents and profits (only) of all landed property belonging to her were to be her own. The husband however was still privileged to administer this estate.

3. All personal property coming to a married woman not in excess of £200 was to be her own.

4. Any married woman or woman about to be married having £20 or more invested in certain specified banks might have this sum transferred upon the books to her name as her separate property.

5. Every married woman was allowed to insure her own or her husband's life for her separate use.[1]

Radical as this legislation was doubtless held to be in its own day, it proved unsatisfactory after a short time. Clearly an Act which left the management of a married woman's real estate and the ownership of all personal property above the value of £200 to her husband would not be permanently satisfying. Therefore in 1882 England took the final step in the emancipation of her wives and mothers from the property restrictions under which they had labored since the Norman Conquest. The Married Woman's Property Act of 1882 gave to every woman married on or subsequent to January 1st, 1883, the absolute ownership of all property belonging to her at the time of the marriage or coming to her afterwards, including earnings and property acquired by skill or labor. As a result of this Act, a married woman in England

---

[1] 33 and 34 Victoria, c. 93; Chitty's *Statutes*, Vol. VIII, pp. 709–712.

can now hold and dispose of real and personal property as freely as a single woman and without the intervention of a trustee. Her husband has no legal rights over her property. Moreover, the Act of 1882 permitted a woman to enter suit, to contract, or to bring criminal action in her own name and without her husband's consent, with respect to all property belonging to her *before marriage*. Thus, after many centuries, the English woman came to be recognized as a "person" in the eyes of the law. With her emancipation went the partial freeing of the husband from his ancient liabilities as to (1) his wife's ante-nuptial debts, and (2) any civil wrongs (torts) committed by her.

While granting to a married woman almost full property rights, the Act of 1882 rendered her liable to support a pauper husband out of her separate estate, as well as to maintain her children and grandchildren in a manner suitable to her station so long as the husband was unable to meet his responsibility in the matter.[1]

Although the property disabilities of married women in England have almost wholly disappeared from the statute-books, there remains the law of primogeniture which even now discriminates against the elder daughter in favor of the younger son in the inheritance of landed estates. It is doubtful whether this ancient custom, grounded in the feudal system, will easily yield to the pressure of public opinion and the attacks of progressive women against its apparent injustice. Many fair-minded persons are in favor of its continuance on the ground that, with equal division of estates, the vast landed properties of England would be divided, subdivided and alienated by sale. This would mean changing proprietors and a weakening of the tie between landlord and tenant. But these arguments hardly seem satisfactory to the thoughtful student of twentieth-century institutions. Even among the English lower middle class, which so long has regarded with pride its landed aristocracy, the retention of great

[1] 45 and 46 Victoria, c. 75; see Chitty's *Statutes*, Vol. VIII, pp. 713 ff.

estates in the little isle of England in the hands of a small group of proprietors is beoming unpopular. It would seem as if the drastic system of land and inheritance taxes, leveled through the initiative of Chancellor Lloyd George against wealthy English landowners, must in time bring about a more equitable distribution of land among a far larger number of individuals. This would mean an increase in the detached homesteads of England, and might also result in inheritance of a fair portion of the family estates by daughters.

Extension of Educational Opportunities to Englishwomen. — Little by little, during the first decades of the nineteenth century the views of Englishmen regarding women were undergoing a silent transformation. Woman, who had so long been regarded as the handmaid and dependent of man, was being forced by economic pressure into the field of labor. The poorer women entered the factories; their middle-class sisters, some years later, were driven to take up the only employment deemed not degrading for a gentlewoman — the work of teaching. Before many years economic independence, replacing as it did the old enervating dependence upon husband or relations, caused some women to discover and develop strong personalities. No longer was a Mary Wollstonecraft alone in declaring that women were individuals with minds and characters worthy of broad and thorough training. Large numbers of women were demanding wider intellectual opportunities and asserting their right to think for themselves. The intellectual achievements of Mary Somerville, Harriet Martineau, George Eliot and the Brontë sisters did much to inspire those women of the second half of the nineteenth century who enthusiastically labored to improve the educational opportunities of women. With sure insight these leaders of a new movement perceived the intimate relation between freeing the minds of their sex and improving their social and economic status. In consequence they threw themselves heart and soul into the cause of the more thorough education of women. One stronghold after another was won until in the present year (1933) a large number of excellent secondary schools exist to prepare young women for education in English universities. No institution of higher learning is closed to them, and only the ancient university of Cambridge still refuses to admit women to degrees and full privileges.[1]

The effect of the higher education of English women in developing their initiative and individuality can hardly be over-estimated. Largely owing to the intelligent and organized efforts of women, aided by a growing body of enlightened Englishmen, social legislation has been passed in England that has vastly improved the status of women in the home as well as in the world of affairs. These reforms in English domestic relations laws deserve detailed consideration.

RECENT REFORMS OF DOMESTIC RELATIONS LAWS

Laws regarding the Marriage Relation. — Subject to the consent of both parents if living together, if not, of the parent responsible for the child, boys may marry at fourteen years and girls at twelve — the old common law ages. It has been proposed, however, to raise the age of consent to marriage to sixteen years and to declare a marriage under that age absolutely void. Such a proposal passed the House of Lords in recent years but failed to be approved by the Commons.

In case of a marriage in church the ceremony is usually preceded by a publication of banns in the parish or parishes in which the parties reside. But, in accordance with the *Marriage Act* of 1836, a Registrar's certificate, duly posted for twenty-one days in the office of the Registrar of the district in which the church is located, is equivalent to publication of banns. In case of a marriage outside of church, the marriage may be by certificate of the Registrar as above, or by license from the Registrar, for which a considerable extra charge is made. The Archbishop of Canterbury is also empowered to grant a special license, permitting a marriage

[1] Cambridge grants so-called "titular" degrees to women.

to be celebrated in any place without publication of banns. Such licenses are rare.

After marriage the duty rests upon both spouses (unless separated judicially or by agreement) to live and cohabit with each other. If either partner refuses to cohabit and lives apart from the other against his will, a petition for "restitution of conjugal rights" may be made by the innocent party to the court, which will then order the offending party to return to cohabitation. For many years the law of England enforced the penalty of imprisonment against the partner refusing to obey the court order. But public opinion was slowly changing in respect to this question and the change is reflected in the *Matrimonial Causes Act* of 1884. By the terms of this act, refusal to comply with an order for restitution of conjugal rights does not result in imprisonment but rather is deemed by law to amount to desertion without reasonable cause. If the husband is the deserter, he may be compelled to make periodical maintenance payments to the wife; similarly, the court has discretionary power to order part of a wife's property or earnings to be paid over for the benefit of husband and children. As may be imagined, English law did not readily abandon the ancient idea that a husband has a proprietary interest in his wife's person and services. The case of Jackson *vs.* Jackson, brought before the courts in 1891, will illustrate the point. In this instance the wife left her husband's home and refused to return; whereupon the husband petitioned for the usual court order for restitution of conjugal rights, which was duly issued. The wife refused to obey the order and the husband, exercising what he no doubt held to be his time-honored rights, seized his wife on her way to church and imprisoned her in his home. The wife's friends applied for a writ of habeas corpus and carried the case to the courts. A long legal battle followed in which feeling ran high; but the case was finally settled in favor of the wife. Since 1891, then, a husband in England cannot compel his wife to live and cohabit with him. Of course the wife, also, is denied the right to use compulsion against her husband.

Married Women's Property Acts. — Reference has already been made to the Acts of 1870 and 1882 which fundamentally altered the economic and legal position of married women in England. Every woman married on or after the 1st of January, 1883, now holds as her separate estate all property belonging to her, whether acquired before or after marriage, and may dispose by will or otherwise of such property as freely as if she were a single woman (*feme sole*). Women married *prior* to January 1st, 1883, however, may control only such property as may have accrued to them after that date. Thus, even now, the old English common law permits the husband to manage his wife's pre-marital property and enjoy the income thereof if his marriage occurred before the Married Women's Property Act of 1882 went into effect. Despite the independence of most married women with respect to their property, it still remains true that certain property "is subject to restraint on anticipation." [1] This means that if a gift of property is made to a married woman which is subject to "restraint on anticipation," she may not dispose of the capital or anticipate the income before it actually falls due; and property so restrained cannot be made liable for her debts unless by court order the restraint is removed.

Another recent law of England affects the inheritance rights of husband or wife in the estate of the other. Under the old common law a widow had the right to dower, or the life use of a third part of her husband's freehold property. Similarly the husband had the right of a life tenancy in the real estate of his deceased wife which was inheritable by her children. These rights of dower and curtesy have been completely swept away by the *Administration of Estates Act* of 1925 which went into effect on January 1st, 1926. At the present time a husband in England has the right to exclude his wife and children after his death from any share in his

[1] See Crofts, *Women under English Law*, p. 35.

property (except in the case of entailed estates); and the wife has a similar freedom. The Act of 1925 also has altered the older laws regarding inheritance by husband or wife of the property of an intestate spouse. Husband and wife now inherit equally in case of intestacy. The survivor inherits absolutely the personal effects of the intestate and the sum of £1000. Also he or she has a life interest in one half of the remainder of the estate ; and, if there is no issue of the marriage who reaches the age of 21, a life interest in the other half of the remainder. If there are no relations of the intestate nearer than second cousins, the survivor inherits the whole of the remainder of the estate absolutely.[1]

STATE INTERVENTION IN THE CONTROL OF PARENTAL RIGHTS AND PRIVILEGES

Nothing is more noteworthy in the social legislation of England during the last century than the number of Acts of Parliament directly affecting the custody and control of children by their parents. Up to 1839 the English Government had scarcely questioned the well-nigh absolute power of parents over their offspring. In only two special cases had parental rights been curtailed. During the reign of George II a statute was enacted designed to prevent the children of criminals and vagrants from being drawn into the evil ways of their parents. This act provided that the children of men or women convicted of criminal offenses should be taken from their parents and apprenticed to honest persons to learn a trade. A further attempt to limit the guardianship rights of unfit parents was made during the same reign. The law in this instance declared that an infant possessed of property so as to fall under the jurisdiction of the Court of Chancery might be taken away from parents grossly unfit to rear it and be placed in the custody of some person nominated by the court. It will be noted that in both instances where the law interfered with the time-

[1] Crofts, *op. cit.*, p. 38.

honored rights of English parents, the incapacity of those parents to bring up children had been abundantly demonstrated.[1]

Before the middle of the nineteenth century popular sentiment in regard to the inviolable character of the father's rights of guardianship had begun to change. This change was reflected in English legislation. As early as 1839 an Act was passed amending the law with respect to the custody of minor children. The Act provided that upon petition of a mother whose children were in the exclusive custody of the father, or of a guardian appointed by him, a Judge in Equity might make an order allowing the mother to visit her children at specified times. In case the children were under seven years of age they might even be delivered over to the custody of the mother. But it was expressly declared that no mother guilty of adultery was to benefit by the act.[2] Strictly limited as were the privileges granted to mothers by the Act of 1839, this law at least made it possible for women separated from their husbands and for mothers whose children had been taken from them by the arbitrary act of the father to see their offspring on stated occasions and even to care for them until they had reached the age of seven.

In the following year, 1840, an Act was passed empowering the court to take any child, whether possessed of property or not, out of the control of a parent or guardian convicted of crime and to place him in charge of suitable guardians selected by the Court.[3]

Mothers' Rights of Guardianship. — With the exception of the special cases mentioned above, mothers in England had no rights of guardianship of their children, according to common law, until 1886. In that year the *Guardianship of Infants Act* was passed by Parliament which granted to a mother equal rights in the custody and care of her children with any guardian

---

[1] Cleveland, *Women under the English Law*, pp. 200 and 211.
[2] 2 and 3 Victoria, c. 54; summarized in Cleveland, *op. cit.*, p. 270.
[3] *Ibid.*, pp. 270–271.

appointed by the father to act after his death. In the appointment of guardians by a court account was to be taken of her wishes as well as of the father's. If the father died without appointing a guardian, or was incapacitated, the mother might appoint a guardian and she might also select one to act jointly with the father after her death.

It will be seen that the law of 1886 by no means gave an English mother equal rights of guardianship of her children with the father. During the father's lifetime the mother had generally no rights against him with respect to the custody and control of the child. This meant that the father had sole power to settle matters of discipline, schooling, medical care, religious education and choice of a vocation of his children. Under the *Custody of Children Act* of 1891 the court was empowered "to refuse to give the custody of a child to a parent who had been grossly unmindful of his duties"; and under other statutes the court could deprive parents of children whom they had ill-treated. In the case of a girl under sixteen years, whose parents had encouraged her seduction or prostitution the court could also remove the girl from the parents' custody. No further important legal change with respect to guardianship of children was made until the end of the first quarter of the twentieth century. The Act of 1925, however, made a fundamental change in at least the *principle* on which questions relating to the custody and rearing of children are to be decided by the courts. In the preamble of the act it is declared that "Parliament by the Sex Disqualification (Removal) Act, 1919, and various other enactments, has sought to establish equality in law between the sexes, and it is expedient that this principle should obtain with respect to the guardianship of infants and the rights and responsibilities conferred thereby." The court then goes on to lay down the further principle that in any court proceeding where the custody, upbringing, administration of property or application of the income of property of a minor child is in question, the court, in deciding the question, "shall regard the welfare of the infant as the first and paramount consideration, and shall not take into consideration whether from any other point of view the claim of the father, or any right at common law possessed by the father, in respect of such custody, upbringing, administration or application is superior to that of the mother, or the claim of the mother is superior to that of the father." The act further provides that the mother shall have the same power to apply to the court as is possessed by the father.[1]

At the present time, then, the father has a prior right by common law to the guardianship of his children; but if a question arises with respect to the manner in which he exercises that right and the question is carried to the court that body will decide it without reference to the father's ancient right but only with regard to the well-being of the child.

Illegitimacy Laws. — The old common law of England was merciless in its denial of rights to a child born out of wedlock. Such a child was called a "bastard" or *filius nullius* — nobody's child — a term that accurately described his legal status. Common law recognized no *legal* relationship between a father and his illegitimate child, nor, indeed, between the mother and her offspring. Unlike the legal systems of Europe, English law refused to allow a bastard child to be legitimized by the marriage of his parents after his birth, although canon law recognized such legitimation. Because no legal relationship was held to exist between a bastard and his parents, the illegitimate child had no rights of inheritance from either father or mother. However, common law granted to the mother the custody of her child. In 1576, during the reign of Queen Elizabeth, a law was enacted compelling the father to contribute to the support of his illegitimate child if his identity could be established.

No important change was made in England's illegitimacy laws until recent times. In 1918 the old Elizabethan law requiring support of the child by the father was amended and improved, but no fundamental change was made in it. In

[1] Crofts, *op. cit.*, p. 49.

1926, however, a *Legitimacy Act* was passed which reflected a marked alteration in popular sentiment regarding the illegitimate child and his rights of inheritance. By the provisions of the act, which came into effect on January 1st, 1927, the legitimation of a child by the marriage of his parents after his birth is clearly recognized, except in cases where either parent was married to a third person at the time of his birth. Moreover a legitimated person may now inherit most kinds of property. Where property is entailed, however, and its inheritance depends on relative seniority, the legitimated child may be compelled to yield to a younger son, since he ranks as if he had been born on the day he was legitimated. The Act of 1926 further provides that an illegitimate child may succeed to his mother's (not his father's) property, provided she died intestate and left no legitimate descendants. Similarly a mother may inherit from an illegitimate child who dies intestate.[1]

Judicial Separation and Divorce. — Among the English Dissenters of the sixteenth century, more liberal ideas concerning divorce than those of Roman canon law were occasionally upheld.[2] Yet despite the impassioned pleas of the poet Milton for greater freedom of divorce, England retained, with scant changes, the divorce practices sanctioned by the canon law well into the nineteenth century. In the words of Howard: "It is a striking illustration of the completeness with which in social questions the English mind was dominated by theological modes of thought that no change in the law of divorce was effected until the present century. Yet there was crying need of reform. The rigid tightening of the bonds of wedlock seems to have produced its natural fruit. Immorality grew apace. The lot of the married woman became harder even than before the Reformation."[3] During the eighteenth and first half of the nineteenth century a conflict arose between

---

[1] Crofts, *op. cit.*, pp. 57–60.
[2] See Howard, *History of Matrimonial Institutions*, Vol. II, pp. 73–92.
[3] Howard, *op. cit.*, Vol. II, p. 92.

the spiritual courts that, strictly speaking, alone had the right to grant divorce, and the temporal courts that occasionally took cognizance of divorce cases when these involved questions of dower.   Even in the closing years of the seventeenth century attempts were made by persons of influence to break their marital chains by a special act of Parliament.   But such relief was reserved for the wealthy and powerful and a decree was granted only after convincing evidence of the flagrant infidelity of the guilty party.   In 1798 the House of Lords limited even this privilege by requiring that "all bills of divorce shall be preceded by a sentence of separation *a mensa*, issuing out of the ecclesiastical court; . . ." [1]   By this act the spiritual court was given large powers to hinder the aggrieved party from resorting to Parliament at all.   Only in case of adultery could an ecclesiastical court be prevailed upon to issue a separation order; it resolutely refused to grant such relief for malicious desertion unless this were accompanied by cruelty.   Therefore divorces *a vinculo* secured by parliamentary action were rare; probably not more than two hundred were granted for the century and a half during which Parliament took divorce under its jurisdiction.   Of these, only three or four were granted to women, even when their wrongs were proven beyond a doubt. [2]

But by the middle of the nineteenth century even conservative Englishmen were no longer firmly convinced that marriage was an indissoluble bond and were in favor of more liberal legislation.   In 1857, despite the most bitter opposition from the Church party, jurisdiction in matrimonial cases was entirely removed from the spiritual courts and placed in the hands of a new civil "Court for Divorce and Matrimonial Causes."   But, unfortunately, the *Matrimonial Causes Act* of 1857 perpetuated the same inequality of rights in respect to divorce as had previous legislation and practice.   While granting to a husband the right of absolute divorce

[1] Howard, *op. cit.*, Vol. II, p. 104.
[2] *Ibid.*, p. 106.

on account of the adultery of the wife, the law granted to the woman the same relief only if the husband's adultery were aggravated by cruelty, or malicious desertion for two years and upwards. Moreover, the injured husband might unite with his petition for divorce a claim for damages against his wife's paramour; whereas no such privilege was permitted the aggrieved wife. The damages thus recovered might be "applied by the court for the benefit of the children of the marriage or for the maintenance of the wife." [1]

Even in that period there were not lacking Englishmen who hotly opposed the passage of the law on the ground of its gross injustice to women. Gladstone earnestly attacked it; and the attorney-general who introduced the bill declared that if the measure "were thrown aside and the whole law of marriage and divorce made the subject of an inquiry, I should be the last man to limit the field of discussion or to refuse to consider a state of law which inflicts injustice upon women most wrongfully and without cause, and which may be considered approbrious and wicked; . . ." [2] Doubtless the attorney-general salved his conscience by the further statement that the "present bill need not be the end-all of legislation upon the subject." Nevertheless the Act of 1857 determined English divorce practice for many years.

The law prescribes that a sentence of divorce must always be a decree *nisi;* only after a period of six months can it be made absolute. [3] Either party to the divorce may marry again; but in order to conciliate the Anglican clergy the Act provides that no clergyman of the "United Church of England and Ireland" may be compelled to solemnize the marriage of a divorced person, although he cannot legally prevent a clergyman of the same communion from using his church or chapel for such a purpose. The fact that the remarriage of divorced

---

[1] *Statutes at Large*, Vol. XCVII, p. 537; 20 and 21 Victoria, c. 85.

[2] Howard, *op. cit.*, p. 111.

[3] In Scotland, on the contrary, a decree of absolute divorce becomes effective immediately.

persons was legal in civil law but illegal in the ecclesiastical law of England has led to acrimonious debates and bitter conflicts of authority. About twenty-five years ago the Bishop of London forbade his chancellor to issue marriage licenses without the Bishop's consent, although the chancellor was well within his legal rights in granting such licenses without consulting his superior. In cases where a clergyman of the Established Church has refused to remarry divorced persons, an appeal has sometimes been made to the courts, which invariably have censured the clergyman for refusing to obey the law of the land. Yet the conflict goes on and neither side has yielded ground.

The law of 1857 provided further for a *judicial separation* granted to either husband or wife on the ground of adultery, cruelty or two years' desertion. After such separation order was granted, the wife had all the rights of a single woman with respect to the control of her property and the power to contract and sue.

Finally, provision was made for a third method of terminating the marriage relation by means of a "magisterial separation." A woman deserted by her husband might apply to a local magistrate instead of the divorce court in London for an order to protect her property and earnings from being seized by her husband or his creditors. This measure, enacted prior to the laws of 1870 and 1882 that freed a wife's earnings and property from her husband's control, must have brought genuine relief to a deserted wife. The wife has been further protected by the *Matrimonial Causes Act* of 1878 which attempts to shield her from the assaults of a brutal husband. By the terms of this Act, in case of aggravated assault upon the wife endangering life or health, she may obtain from the magistrate a "separation order" freeing her from the obligation to live with her husband, placing the children of the union in her custody, and forcing the husband to pay her such weekly alimony as appears to the court to be just.[1] Such a

---

[1] 41 and 42 Victoria, c. 19; Chitty's *Statutes*, Vol. VIII, pp. 880–881.

"magisterial separation" has all the effects of a judicial separation and can be more easily and expeditiously obtained. Thus its relief is frequently sought by women in the humbler walks of life. It is a surprising fact that a woman brutally beaten cannot even now bring action for damages against her husband in the English courts. Her only recourse is a separation order.

It will readily be seen that the Act of 1857, while granting judicial separations for the causes of adultery, cruelty or desertion and seeking to protect a deserted or abused wife from the greed or brutality of her husband, hedged around *absolute* divorce with difficulties and limited it to the one cause of adultery. The mere fact that an absolute divorce could be obtained only at considerable expense from the "High Court" sitting in London put its benefits wholly out of the reach of the poor and rendered the law inequitable. In 1909 King Edward VII appointed a Royal Commission on Divorce and Matrimonial Causes to investigate thoroughly the whole difficult problem of divorce in England. Three years later, after diligent inquiry and the examination of 246 witnesses, the Commission published both a majority and a minority report. The majority report, signed by the Chairman, Lord Gorell, together with all the Commissioners save three, took the following liberal positions: 1. Absolute divorce should be granted for six causes: (*a*) adultery, (*b*) desertion for three years and upward, (*c*) cruelty, (*d*) incurable insanity, after five years' confinement, (*e*) habitual drunkenness, found incurable three years after a first order of separation, and (*f*) imprisonment under a commuted death sentence. 2. Facilities should be given for hearing divorce cases in courts throughout the country in instances where the joint income of husband and wife does not exceed £300 and property £250. 3. Power should be given to the courts to declare marriages null and void in cases of (*a*) unsound mind, (*b*) epilepsy and recurrent insanity, (*c*) specific disease, (*d*) when a woman is in a condition which renders marriage a fraud upon the husband, (*e*) in

case of wilful refusal to perform the duties of marriage.
4. The Commission further recommended that divorce reports
should not be published until the conclusion of the case, and
that judges should hear divorce cases without a jury.

Quite as significant as the sweeping changes in the proposed
law extending the grounds of divorce is the fact that a large
majority of the Commission were earnestly in favor of equalizing the rights of husband and wife in respect to obtaining
divorce. In this connection the Report declares: "The
social and economic position of women has greatly changed
in the last hundred and even in the last fifty years. . . . In
our opinion it is impossible to maintain a different standard
of morality in the marriage relation without creating the
impression that justice is denied to women, an impression
that must tend to lower the respect in which the marriage
law is held by women." [1]

The minority report, presented by three members, of whom
the Archbishop of York was one, strongly objected to the
positions taken by the majority as based on "purely empiri-
cal" evidence with "not even the semblance of finality."
It urgently maintained that divorce legislation should be
grounded on the bed rock of changeless principle, not on the
shifting sands of "present expediency." With this preamble
the minority submitted proposals that may be summarized
as follows:

1. There should be equality of the sexes.

2. The grounds of divorce should emphatically *not* be extended.

3. There should be local divorce courts with facilities to
the poor, but not on so large a scale as recommended by the
majority.

4. Marriages should be rendered null on the grounds set
forth in the majority report (see above).

5. The publication of divorce reports should be limited.

[1] Digest of Commission's Report in Magazine Section of *New York Times*,
Sunday, Nov. 24, 1912.

6. A man should be presumed dead after a continuous absence of seven years with no communication.

A minority of the Commission, then, favored a continuance of the existing situation which rendered it impossible for either partner in the marriage relation to obtain an absolute divorce on the grounds of cruelty (no matter how continuous or extreme), of habitual drunkenness, of desertion or of hopeless insanity. These gentlemen, in effect, recorded their conviction that any marriage relation stopping short of adultery is to be preferred to a liberal divorce policy which might open the way to frequent divorces obtained on easy grounds by mutual consent of the parties.

It is an interesting fact that the leading newspapers and journals of England sided with the minority report. The *Manchester Guardian*, an excellent Liberal paper, held up the United States as an awful example of the effects of loosening the marriage bond. It declared that even if there is a popular demand in England for more liberal divorce laws, "it would be impossible to accept solutions of the problem which would strike a deadly blow at the purity and stability of family life . . . and approximate the English law of divorce to that which obtains in the United States of the American Union, where the percentage of dissolution is forty-three times what it is in England and Wales." In this connection it might be pertinent to inquire whether the low rate in England necessarily indicated that domestic life in that country was happier or more successful than here. Even a very moderate loosening of the rigid restrictions upon divorce in England and Wales in recent times has resulted in a prompt increase in the number of divorces, which reveals much discord and misery in family life now smoldering just beneath the surface.

Despite the majority opinion of the Divorce Commission of 1909, advocating several causes of divorce, Parliament was unwilling to change the existing divorce law until 1923. The *Matrimonial Causes Act* of 1923 took a modest step forward in that it established complete equality between the sexes with regard to grounds of divorce. Either party to a marriage may now obtain an absolute divorce on proof of adultery on the part of the other. If the petitioner is successful, the court pronounces a decree *nisi*, which is an order that the marriage be dissolved after six months from the date of the order unless sufficient cause is shown why the decree should not be made absolute. An official called the "King's Proctor," or any private individual, may intervene during the six months in order to prove adultery of the petitioner, collusion or any other bar to the divorce. If no such intervention is made, the plaintiff may petition the court to make the decree absolute, a petition which is thereupon granted. The decree absolute leaves both parties free to remarry.

Prior to the *Matrimonial Causes Act* of 1923, it was customary for a wife whose husband was guilty of both adultery and desertion to apply to the court for an order of restitution of conjugal rights. Before the order was issued by the court the wife must first have written a conciliatory appeal to her husband asking him to return to their home and resume cohabitation; and she must have satisfied the court that she had sent this appeal. Now that husband and wife have been put on a plane of equality with respect to divorce, petitions for restitution are rarely presented except as a preliminary to a suit for judicial separation based on desertion.

In addition to equalizing the causes for divorce, the *Matrimonial Causes Act* of 1923 also extended jurisdiction over divorce to the Court of Assizes, thus lessening the costs of divorce to the poor. Prior to the Act petitioners for divorce were compelled to appeal to the High Court in London. If the petitioner lived at some distance from the city, the costs of coming to the superior court and paying the expenses of self and witnesses were prohibitive for persons of small income. Now the costs of divorce action have been greatly diminished and in consequence the number of divorces annually in England has been sharply increased. In 1928 the total number of decrees *nisi* made absolute was 4,018, and in 1929 a provisional list of cases in the Michaelmas term of the courts showed an increase of more than 400 over that of the preceding year. A prominent English divorce authority has said that 80 per cent of the annual divorces are undefended; and in only 2 per cent of the cases are husbands required to pay alimony.[1]

Liberalization of the rigid English divorce laws will be sought in the session of Parliament that opens November 7, 1933. A bill providing for a marked increase in the legal causes of divorce is reported to have won the support of many influential members of the House of Commons. Under the proposed bill the grounds for divorce will include: adultery, desertion for three years, grave physical and mental cruelty, incurable insanity, habitual drug taking or drunkenness and imprisonment on a commuted death sentence.

In addition to absolute divorces *judicial separations* with no right of remarriage are granted by the court on the grounds of adultery, desertion without just cause for two years or noncompliance with a decree for restitution of conjugal rights, which last, since the Act of 1884, is regarded as equivalent to desertion. A successful suit for separation, of course, gives neither party the right to remarry.

In addition to judicial separations granted by a divorce court, English law, as stated above, has conferred upon magistrates the power to grant *separation orders* with maintenance to complaining wives. By the terms of a series of Acts passed between 1895 and 1925 a Court of Summary Jurisdiction may grant a separation order to a wife whose husband has been convicted of a serious assault on her person, of persistent cruelty to her or her children, of desertion, of wilful neglect of wife or children, of habitual drunkenness or drug addiction, of forcing his wife to cohabit with him while he is suffering from a venereal disease of which he has knowledge, or, finally, of compelling his wife to adopt the life of a prostitute.[2]

[1] *New York Times*, Nov. 1, 1929.
[2] See Crofts, *op. cit.*, p. 29.

In any of the cases cited above, the court may make an order permitting a wife to live separately from her husband and requiring the husband to pay her a weekly sum not in excess of £2 for her maintenance, with 10 shillings additional for each child under the age of sixteen. The wife, also, may, in the discretion of the court, be given the custody of the children.

A married man may also apply for a separation order if his wife is habitually a drunkard or drug-taker, or has persistently been guilty of cruelty to his children. In such a case the husband, even though he be the innocent party, must pay for the maintenance of the wife. Such separation orders may be obtained at the small cost of two shillings, and thousands of couples annually are separated by this method.

It is significant, as evidence of the deep-rooted conservatism of England with regard to all issues related to marriage, that such serious injuries to the marital relation as habitual drunkenness or drug-taking, gross physical cruelty, or driving a wife to prostitution are not legally held to be causes for granting absolute divorce.

On issuing a decree of dissolution of marriage in favor of the wife the divorce court may order the husband to provide maintenance for the wife. This may take the form of payment of a lump sum, or of periodic payments. If an annual payment is ordered by the court the amount is usually not in excess of one third of the joint incomes of husband and wife. A guilty wife is not entitled to maintenance. In suits for divorce, judicial separation or nullity, the court may provide for the custody, maintenance and education of the children of the marriage.

Void and Voidable Marriages. — A marriage is held to be void *ab initio* in cases where either of the parties is already married, where the parties are within certain forbidden degrees of relationship, where, by reason of insanity or some other cause, there is absence of consent on the part of either party, or where the necessary legal formalities have not been complied with. In such cases it is not necessary to apply to the court for a decree of nullity, unless the facts are in doubt. If one of the parties to a marriage is incapable of consummating it, however, the marriage is not void but *voidable*, that is, it becomes void only after a decree of nullity has been pronounced by the court.

Summary. — When the student of social institutions passes in review the profound changes in domestic relations laws and in the character of family life which have occurred in England during the past century and a third, he is impressed by the steady trends in the direction of freeing wives and children from arbitrary patriarchal authority; of granting economic independence to married women; of opening ever-larger opportunities for education and vocations to all women; and of bringing marital and family affairs increasingly under the authority of the State. As for children it may truly be said that during the last half century or more the State has constituted itself a super-parent to protect the rights of the young to health, kindly treatment, maintenance and education.

SELECTED READINGS

Adams, Elizabeth. "The Higher Education of Women," in Monroe, Paul, *Cyclopedia of Education*, N. Y., Macmillan, 1911–1919, Vol. V, pp. 801 ff.

Blease, W. Lyon. *The Emancipation of English Women*, new ed., London, David Nutt, 1913, Chs. III, IV, V.

Chitty, Joseph. *Statutes at Large*, London, Sweet, n. d., Vol. VIII, pp. 709–713, 855–869, 880–881.

Cleveland, Arthur R. *Women under the English Law*, London, Hurst and Blackett, 1896, pp. 169–182, 201–207, 211–217, 226–228, 235–236.

Crofts, Maud I. *Women under English Law*, London, Butterworth and Co., 1928, Chs. II, III.

DeFoe, Daniel. *A Tour through the Whole Island of Great Britain*, 4th ed., London, 1748, Vol. III, pp. 137–139.

Emery, G. F. *The Law Relating to Husband and Wife*, London, Effingham Wilson, 1929, entire.

Gibbins, Henry D. *Industry in England, Historical Outlines*, 6th ed., N. Y., Scribner, 1914, pp. 391–406.

Howard, Geo. E.   *History of Matrimonial Institutions*, University of Chicago Press, Callaghan and Co., 1904, Vol. II, pp. 73–120; Vol. III, pp. 28–100.

Hutchins, B. L., and Harrison, A.   *A History of Factory Legislation*, 2d ed., London, King and Son, 1911, Chs. II, IV, VI, X.

Mill, John Stuart.   *Of the Subjection of Women*, London, Longmans, Green, and Co., 1869.

Robinson, J. H., and Beard, C. A.   *Development of Modern Europe*, 2 Vols., N. Y., Ginn and Co., 1929, Vol. I, pp. 244–245, 446–454.

Strachey, Ray.   *The Cause; a Short History of the Women's Movement in Great Britain*, London, G. Bell and Sons, 1928, Chs. I–III, VII–IX, XIII.

Wallis-Chapman, A. B. and Mary.   *The Status of Women under the English Law*, passim, N. Y. and London, E. P. Dutton and Co., 1909.

CHAPTER XI

CHANGES IN THE AMERICAN FAMILY, *Roles* DURING THE NINETEENTH AND TWENTIETH CENTURIES 75

After the Revolutionary War was ended in 1781, the new states of America began their independent life under disheartening conditions of impoverishment and depletion of energy. Thousands of families had lost sons in the war and had been plunged into penury. Sectionalism and disunity threatened the integrity of the new republic and distrust of centralized government was a widespread sentiment. Yet the nineteenth century soon to dawn was destined to be an era of dramatic expansion, of the conquest of a continent both territorially and industrially and of a complete transformation of the family.

When the nineteenth century opened, the American family was a closely knit institution, holding its members together by economic, legal and religious bonds, as well as by those of affection and authority. Still patriarchal in type, the family was governed by the husband and father, whose power over wife and children was not yet challenged. Law, religion and public opinion united in support of father-power; and unquestionably this centralization of authority in the father was a factor in maintaining family solidarity. Yet the knell of the patriarchal family was sounding even in the early decades of the new century. Powerful social forces were at work sapping the ancient props of father-power and reducing it to shadowy proportions. Paramount among these forces were (1) the extension of the frontier farther and farther into the wilderness of the West; (2) the rapid development of machine industry; (3) the powerful influence of liberalism and democratic ideas; (4) the weakening of dogmatic religion. Each of these social influences deserves brief consideration with reference to its effects upon the unity of family life.

SOCIAL INFLUENCES AFFECTING THE AMERICAN FAMILY

Influence of the Pioneer Movement upon the Family. — Momentous in its consequences for the patriarchal family was the pioneering movement that set in shortly after the Revolutionary War and resulted in extending the frontier first to the Appalachians, then to the Mississippi, later to the lofty barrier of the Rocky Mountains and finally, with resistless pressure, to the Pacific Ocean. By the eighteen-thirties western emigration had become a powerful current, deepened and widened by the ruthless exploitation of labor in the industrial East. The army of adventurous pioneers was made up of men eager to improve the conditions of life for themselves and their families, fired with hope that the unconquered regions of the frontier would open up to them the gates of freedom and opportunity. As James Truslow Adams has so convincingly shown,[1] this "American dream," cherished by hardy pioneers, has had far-reaching influence in shaping the attitudes, ideals and social philosophy of the American people. This spectacular march of thousands of men and women, uprooted from their homes in the East, to the rude frontier, there to subdue forests and convert the virgin wilderness into fruitful farms and pasture lands, was almost without parallel in history. Commenting in the 1830's upon this mighty social movement, the French traveler DeTocqueville writes:

"No event can be compared with this continuous removal of the human race, except perhaps those irruptions which caused the fall of the Roman Empire. . . . Then, every newcomer brought with him destruction and death; now, each one brings the elements of prosperity and life."[2]

---

[1] *The Epic of America*, passim.

[2] *Democracy in America* (English ed., 1898), Vol. I, pp. 374-375.

Space forbids consideration of the hardships suffered by the pioneers and their loyal wives in establishing new homes. To physical sufferings must be added the injustices they endured at the hands of land speculators. After building his home and improving the land, many a pioneer was outbid at the public land sales by the agents of greedy Eastern capitalists and lost the farm, cleared and cultivated with almost superhuman effort. Not until 1862 did the Government make any serious effort to protect the pioneersman and his family. In that year was enacted the Homestead Bill which granted 160 acres of free land to every settler who built a homestead and improved the land. Yet even then the settlers' homes and acres seem not to have been fully protected from land speculators. Calhoun cites Ely as stating that entire communities of hard-working settlers were pauperized by the greed of corrupt land sharks.[1]

Such an immense emigration of peoples from the settled communities of the East to the western wilderness could not fail to have far-reaching effects upon the family. In the first place a powerful blow was struck at family solidarity. Households in the East lost some of their best blood — sons with initiative, determination and ability. At times only the middle-aged and the elderly were left in the family homestead. Estates, small and large, were divided by will among sons and daughters scattered over the frontier, and frequently property was sold and broken up. Often not even the homestead was left to serve as a gathering place and unifying center for the widely dispersed members of the family. Inevitably, also, the "great family," or clan of relatives, united by blood and by common traditions and interests, was greatly weakened by the pioneering movement and at present survives only here and there in the more quiet byways of American life.

Economic Changes. — Quite as important in its influence upon the patriarchal family was the development and spread

[1] For this whole subject see Calhoun, *Social History of the American Family*, Vol. II, pp. 167–170.

of machine industry which, after 1820, steadily supplanted the age-old domestic system of production. As early as 1834 the Frenchman Chevalier expressed his astonishment at the rapid growth of factories and of "pasteboard" towns around their smoke-stacks. Writing of Lowell, Massachusetts, he comments on the fact that nearly five thousand young women from seventeen to twenty-four years of age, the daughters of farmers, were employed in the new textile factories, "remote from their families, and under their own control." Such a separation of girls from parental authority seemed to him an astounding situation, which, he truly remarks, "would be difficult to conceive of" in France.[1]

It is not hard to understand how factory industry and the financial independence of sons and daughters employed in the new mills would inevitably act as a solvent of the ties binding the patriarchal family together. Sent out into the world from humble homes to make their own way, the girls from the farms of New England and New York soon learned to rely upon their own efforts for support. With the loosening of the economic ties that held them in dependence upon the father went the strengthening of the feeling of personal independence. Thus early were laid the foundation stones of the economic self-reliance of American women. For when women had once demonstrated to the satisfaction of men that they could earn their own living, the movement to free all women, especially wives, from the proprietary and legal disabilities laid upon them by the domestic codes of the Middle Ages grew apace. Nor is this the whole story. The very general employment of women in factories made it possible for spinsters, widows and orphaned children to be self-supporting and thus freed from a humiliating dependence upon relatives. So the way was paved for a complete transformation of public opinion regarding the duty of the head of a family to support all his dependent "female" relatives, no matter how serious

---

[1] Chevalier, Michael, *Society, Manners and Politics in the United States* (trans. from the 3rd Paris ed., Boston, Weeks, Jordan and Co., 1839).

a drain this might entail upon his resources. Gradually there developed during the nineteenth century a popular sentiment in favor of the extra-domestic employment of women who would otherwise be dependents upon the bounty of relatives, until, at the close of the century, it was taken for granted that all self-respecting women without means would go to work and pay their own way.

But the influx of women into gainful employment was not accomplished without a barrage of criticism from those conservatives who saw clearly enough that such financial independence would tend to loosen the bonds that held women narrowly to the circle of the home. Writing in 1855, Margaret Fuller Ossoli, literary daughter of New England, comments on the strictures, very prevalent in her day, against the exodus of women from their "proper" domestic sphere and points out that a large proportion of women could not remain at home if they would. She writes:

"Thousands and scores of thousands in this country, no less than in Europe, are obliged to maintain themselves alone. Far greater numbers divide with their husbands the care of earning a support for the family." [1]

Spread of Democratic Ideas. — Scarcely less powerful as a solvent of family attitudes and habits was the popular acceptance of democratic ideas. Under the impact of the theory that all men are created free and equal and should have equality of opportunity to achieve a satisfying life, the English custom of primogeniture and entail was overthrown in the new states of America. After the Revolutionary War a few old families with large estates, such as the Livingstones, the Carrolls and the Calverts, attempted to found manors on the English plan and hold their property intact by entailing it in favor of the first-born son. But democratic public opinion would have none of this practice; and one by one the states abolished entail in their new constitutions. Hence it came

[1] *Women in the Nineteenth Century* (Boston, John P. Jewett and Co., 1855), p. 219.

about that in most instances a man's property was equally divided by will among his children. This democratic practice had certain weighty social consequences. In the first place the more or less equal division of property operated to scatter family estates and in time to weaken family ties. History makes plain that the unbroken existence through generations of a family homestead and family lands has acted as a strong bond holding the family members together and deepening family sentiment. Moreover, the equal division of a father's property among his children had the obvious consequence of placing sons and daughters on a plane of economic equality and allowing no special privileges to any.

No doubt, as DeTocqueville points out, the spread of democratic ideas in America tended to bridge the ancient gulf between the law-giving father and his children. "In a democratic family," writes DeTocqueville, "the father exercises no other power than that which is granted to the affection and experience of age; his orders would perhaps be disobeyed, but his advice is for the most part authoritative." [1] Probably DeTocqueville's familiarity with the autocratic authority exercised in his time by the average French father may have disposed him to over-emphasize the freer spirit of the American home. Yet, unquestionably, the patriarchal family of an earlier epoch was being gradually reshaped, under the impact of democratic principles, into the freer family of the twentieth century, composed of individuals whose rights are guaranteed by law and custom. In DeTocqueville's eyes this individual freedom within the family was particularly conspicuous in the case of unmarried daughters. Commenting on this phenomenon he writes:

"Long before an American girl arrives at the marriageable age, her emancipation from maternal control begins: she has scarcely ceased to be a child, when she already thinks for herself, speaks with freedom, and acts on her own impulse." [2]

[1] *Democracy in America* (Century Co., 1898), Vol. II, p. 241.   [2] *Ibid.*, p. 241.

The same was true in the case of the American boy. Little by little the father's authority was relaxed as the youth entered adolescence and began to earn his own living. Indeed DeTocqueville remarked that in America there appeared to be no adolescent period in the strict sense of the term: "at the close of boyhood the man appears, and begins to trace out his own path."

Position of Wives Uninfluenced by Democratic Ideas. — It is a curious and striking fact that application of the new theories of personal right, freedom and opportunity, was restricted for many decades to the children of the family. Prior to the Civil War wives were subordinated to their husbands in most states and were given no control of the property they brought in marriage. Their lives were dedicated almost exclusively to the service of husband and children and to the careful management of the home. It followed that the interests of American wives were in general confined to family, church and neighborhood affairs, and their contacts with important social movements, much more their participation in them, were drastically limited. This narrowness of life and of outlook did not escape the keen eyes of DeTocqueville, who declared that in America "the independence of woman is irrecoverably lost in the bonds of matrimony." The young daughter "makes her father's home an abode of freedom and of pleasure; the wife lives in the home of her husband as if it were a cloister." Very shrewdly he opined that the restricted lives of American matrons were due to the "religious opinions" and the "trading habits" of a "puritanical people"; — the "religious opinions" being derived from Biblical doctrines concerning the subordination of wives, and the "trading habits" being responsible for the desire of men to receive full value in services from the wife they must support.

The Weakening of the Religious Tie. — Another influence at work to weaken family ties was the decline of the power of religion over the thinking and the habits of the American people. As late as 1855 Philip Schaff, in a book written with the desire to explain America to Germany, declared that "the custom of family devotion" and "the strict observance of the Sabbath" were almost universal.[1] Yet powerful influences were at work even then to loosen the grip of dogmatic religion and lift the shadow of Puritanism under which men and women had lived for more than two centuries. The spread of tolerance and knowledge through public education; the enormous expansion of science, together with the widening dissemination of the scientific spirit; the titanic growth of machine industry, with its concomitant development of worldly interests and the desire to amass wealth — all these tendencies sapped at the roots of religious belief and brought about a decrease of religious observances in the family circle. Little by little grace at meals, daily Bible reading and family prayers morning and evening were discontinued and thus one more bond holding the family together was loosened.

THE WOMAN'S RIGHTS MOVEMENT

It was not possible that the individualistic movement of the eighteenth and nineteenth centuries, with its clear expression in democratic principles, could be permanently confined in its effects to men. Early in the nineteenth century began that slow change in public opinion regarding the economic status and legal rights of married women that resulted in a gradual revision of the domestic relations laws of the various states. Connecticut led the way in 1809 by granting to wives the right to dispose by will of such of their property as the husband could not legally claim. At the opening of the Civil War at least seven other states had followed the lead of Connecticut and six more had taken the more important step of according to wives the legal right to own and manage property belonging to them by gift or bequest.[2]

---

[1] *America* (Scribner, 1855), p. 91.
[2] See Wilson, *Legal and Political Status of Women in the United States*, passim.

But the movement for the emancipation of wives was tardy in its inception and even more belated in its realization. In 1845 the American writer Edward Mansfield attributed the denial of legal personality to married women to the Scriptural saying that a man shall "cleave unto his wife and they twain shall be one flesh." Upon this assumption of the essential oneness of husband and wife the disabilities and duties of the wife were grounded. With entire frankness Mansfield declares that the husband "has the sole right to the remedies for legal wrongs committed against [the wife's] person. [His] control over the person of his wife is so complete that he may claim her society altogether, — that he may maintain suits for injuries to her person; — that she cannot sue alone; that she cannot execute a deed or valid conveyance, without the concurrence of her husband. In most respects she loses the power of personal independence, and altogether that of separate action in legal matters." [1]

Add to this description of the husband's rights the following important details, and a valid picture will be sketched of the disabilities of the American wife in the middle of the nineteenth century. At marriage the woman "loses the entire personal control over her property as long as the marriage continues. . . . The personal property of the wife, as such, in her own right, such as money, goods, animals and movables of all descriptions, vests at marriage, immediately and absolutely, in the husband. He can dispose of them, as he pleases, and, on his death, they go to his representative, as being entirely his property. [Although a husband does not acquire an absolute title in his wife's lands, he] enters by marriage into possession of his wife's real estate, has the power to manage it, and finally, the entire use and profit of it." [2]

It was this denial of legal personality and property rights to wives that was the primary source of the "woman's rights

---

[1] *The Legal Rights, Liabilities and Duties of American Women* (John P. Jewett and Co., 1845), pp. 270–273.

[2] *Ibid.*

movement " in America : the demand for political emancipation of women was chiefly motivated by the ardent desire to free American wives from their status of subordination and financial dependence. Space forbids any but the briefest account of this constructive effort, organized and led by American women with the assistance of a handful of generous-hearted men. Beginning in the eighteen-forties, the woman movement set before itself three supreme goals : to free the persons and property of married women from the absolute control of their husbands and to secure legal personality to wives; to open to all women opportunities for a sound and liberal higher education; and to secure to women full political rights. Prominent among the leaders of the crusade was Lucy Stone, a young woman of Massachusetts, who was one of the early graduates of Oberlin College in 1847. On the occasion of her marriage to Henry Blackwell, a man of markedly liberal opinions, a marriage contract was signed by the pair which contained the following courageous and forward-looking statements :

"While we acknowledge our mutual affection, by publicly assuming the sacred relationship of husband and wife, yet, in justice to ourselves and to a great principle, we deem it our duty to declare, that this act on our part implies no sanction of, or promise of voluntary obedience to, such of the present laws of marriage as refuse to recognize the wife as an independent rational being, while they confer upon the husband an injurious and unnatural superiority, investing him with legal powers which no honorable man would exercise, and which no man should possess. . . . We believe that personal independence and equal human rights can never be forfeited, except for crime; that marriage should be an equal and permanent partnership, and so recognized by law; that, until it is recognized, married partners should provide against the radical injustice of present laws, by every means in their power." [1]

[1] Published in the *Boston Traveler* and the *New York Tribune*, May 4, 1855.

Unquestionably the "woman movement" in America accomplished much in educating public opinion to an acceptance of marriage as an equal partnership and to a gradual revision of the laws that bore most unjustly upon women. Yet the battle for equality of rights and opportunities had by no means been won at the close of the nineteenth century. Writing in 1892, Matilda Gage brought a sharp indictment against a majority of the states of the Union for retaining on their statute books laws that gave the husband the custody of his wife's person and the father sole guardianship rights over his children; that gave the control of all the wife's property into the hands of her husband and bestowed upon him "the absolute right to her labor and all products of her industry," including her wages. Indignantly the writer concludes with the words: "That woman is an individual with the right to her own separate existence has not yet permeated the thought of church, state or society." [1]

The Higher Education of American Women. — As in England so in the American democracy the improvement in the status of women — especially of married women — has been synchronous with their higher education. In colonial days, as we have seen, the education of girls other than in household duties was not seriously considered. Even as late as 1788 the town of Northampton, Massachusetts, now the seat of Smith College, voted to be at no expense for the education of girls. And Boston, home of New England culture, in 1790 admitted girls to its public schools only in the summer months. Not until 1822 were girls in Boston freely admitted to the common schools.[2]

Yet, after the Revolutionary War, public opinion began to change with regard to the education of girls. Not only were they admitted to the summer district schools but many towns made provision for their attendance at the boys' winter schools at hours when the boys were not using the

[1] *Woman, Church and State* (2d ed., 1893), p. 329.
[2] Johnson, *Old-Time Schools and Schoolbooks*, p. 139.

buildings. But such education as the girls received was shallow enough, consisting merely of reading, writing, spelling, sewing, knitting and making elaborate samplers. As for higher education many young women received none at all. Others attended boarding schools, where imperfectly educated teachers dispensed doubtful accomplishments. In an earnest address made to the legislature of New York, in 1819 in behalf of the establishment of "a seminary for females," Mrs. Emma Willard urged that the elevation of the minds and characters of women would be a benefit to the entire community. "As evidence that this statement does not exaggerate the female influence in society," she writes, "our sex need but be considered, in the single relation of mothers. In this character, we have charge of the whole mass of individuals, who are to compose the succeeding generation ; during that period of youth, when the pliant mind takes any direction, to which it is steadily guided by a forming hand. How important a power is given by this charge ! Yet, little do many of my sex know how, either to appreciate or improve it."

Owing to the efforts of a little band of devoted women, ably led by Catherine Beecher, Emma Willard and Mary Lyon, the earliest advanced academies and seminaries for girls were founded. Most advanced of these was Mt. Holyoke Seminary, opened in 1837 as a result of the splendid campaign of Mary Lyon carried on through the length and breadth of Massachusetts. In 1855 was chartered Elmira College offering a collegiate course of study to young women. After the Civil War followed Vassar, chartered in 1861, but not opened until 1865, Wellesley, chartered as a Seminary in 1870 but empowered to grant degrees in 1877, Smith College chartered in 1871, and Bryn Mawr chartered in 1880. Meanwhile certain men's colleges, notably in the Middle West, threw open their hospitable doors to women. Oberlin admitted women from its foundation in 1833 and the University of Michigan followed its example in 1870. Since that time most of the institutions for higher learning in the United States have either admitted women to their courses and degrees or have established a woman's college in connection with the University. Of the latter type are Barnard College of Columbia University and Radcliffe College affiliated with Harvard.

Thanks to this vast extension of their educational privileges, accompanied, as it was, by the removal from the statute books of most of the hampering economic and legal restrictions of the past, American women have developed intelligent and vigorous personalities. No longer confined to home, church and neighborhood, they are taking an active part in movements for social betterment, from the support of public housing for the city's low paid workers, and the improvement of sanitary conditions in factories and slums, to the enactment of minimum wage laws and unemployment insurance. With every year that passes, more women are coming to see that their interests cannot wisely be confined to their own homes but must expand to include the homes of the entire community. If signs do not fail, the campaign to secure wholesome family life and decent home surroundings for all sorts and conditions of men and women will more and more challenge the attention and receive the intelligent coöperation of American womanhood.

A SURVEY OF DOMESTIC RELATIONS LAWS AT PRESENT

As stated above, a dozen or more states had taken action prior to the Civil War granting to wives the right to dispose of certain property by will or even, in a few instances, to own and control property. After the four years' conflict was at an end, the movement for the emancipation of wives from the disabilities of English common law proceeded more rapidly. Yet progress has always been impeded by the fact that, in the forty-eight commonwealths of the American Union, new ideas are not received and acted upon with equal speed. Unlike England, which can enact a progressive law, such as the Married Women's Property Act, and put it into immediate operation throughout the country, the United States must wait for one backward state after another to enact laws freeing married women from feudal disabilities. Therefore the states of this nation present no united front of advanced legislation as do certain other countries. Although in a majority of the commonwealths the status of married women is nearly equal to that of their husbands, a surprising number of medieval laws still remain on the statute books.

Married Women's Property Laws. — In only twenty-two states has a married woman unrestricted rights of contract, as if unmarried. The limitations of that right are various in the remaining twenty-six states, ranging from the restriction in several states that a wife may not convey real estate unless the husband join in the conveyance,[1] to the blanket regulation in Texas that a wife has practically no right to contract without the consent of her husband. In Florida a married woman who desires to contract as freely as a *feme sole* must secure a court decree granting her unrestricted right of contract. In Georgia a married woman is not permitted to become surety for any person; while in Pennsylvania she may not act as indorser, guarantor or surety for another.[2]

So much for contractual rights. What is the situation with respect to other property rights of married women? In thirty-one states husband and wife have an equal interest in the other's real estate; in seventeen states they have not. For example, in Alabama a husband, whose wife dies intestate leaving a separate estate, receives one half of the personal property and the use of *all* the real estate for life; whereas if a married man dies, leaving a solvent estate, his widow is entitled only to one half his lands if there are no lineal descendants. If there are such descendants, she receives only one third, which is also the proportion she receives if the estate is insolvent. Furthermore, if the widow's separate estate amounts to more than this dower right, she receives

---

[1] In several states a similar restriction is laid upon the husband.

[2] See *A Survey of the Legal Status of Women in the Forty-Eight States* (pub. by the National League of Women Voters, March, 1930), pp. 9–19.

nothing at all. Again, in the states of Nevada and New Mexico, where the system of community property prevails, at the death of the wife the husband takes all the community property, although at the husband's death the wife takes only one half. On the other hand, in three states — Michigan, Montana, and Utah — the wife has the right of dower but the husband has no corresponding right.

The system of "community property," which is found in the Southwest and the far West, needs brief explanation. There are eight community states, namely, Louisiana, Texas, Arizona, New Mexico, Nevada, Idaho, California and Washington. These states are among those carved out of vast territories originally owned by Spain, and in this region the law of community property generally prevailed. By the terms of the present law all property owned by husband and wife before marriage belongs to his or her separate estate, as does all property acquired by gift or devise after marriage. But property acquired after marriage *by the joint efforts of husband and wife* is held to be community property and is owned jointly by the couple. But here the rub comes; for, although the property is owned in common, the husband alone has the right to control it and receive the proceeds. Thus, if husband and wife own and manage together any gainful enterprise, the husband receives, administers and invests the financial returns. In five of the community states, moreover, a wife's earnings are held to be community property and by law pass into the control of the husband. Only if the wife be separated from her husband, or if he deserts her or becomes insane can she enjoy the fruits of her own labor in Arizona, California, Louisiana, New Mexico and Washington. In Nevada a wife may control her wages only when the husband has allowed her to appropriate them to her own use, in which case they are deemed a gift from him to her.[1] It will be seen that such a practice might easily work hardship upon the wife; and such, in fact, is sometimes the case. Not long ago, in the

[1] *A Survey of the Legal Status of American Women* (ed. 1930), p.129.

state of California, a married woman who for years had supported herself and an idle husband by working in a café was denied by the courts the right to hold and manage her earnings, since these were community property and hence under the control of her husband. In consequence the woman was forced either to continue turning over her wages to her husband, who allowed her a niggardly sum for her support, or to separate from him.

Outside the community-property states, the wife has been granted by law full ownership and control of her earnings in all states save Georgia, where the husband may still take his wife's wages unless the pair have permanently separated. Another relic of feudal law is found in Florida, where the husband controls his wife's separate estate unless she has been empowered by a court decree to take charge of her own estate. In Louisiana, likewise, a wife may control only that portion of her property which was not included in her dowry. The separate property of the Louisiana wife is divided into the dotal and the paraphernal. The dotal property is that which the wife brings to the husband to assist him in meeting the expenses of the marriage establishment and corresponds to the dowry of olden times. The paraphernal property includes all forms of property owned by the wife which do not constitute a part of the dotal property. Apparently the custom of granting a dowry to a girl at marriage is rapidly becoming obsolete in Louisiana, hence dotal property is very rare.

With regard to the matter of inheritance of a deceased child's estate, forty-five states grant the parents equal rights. In Arkansas and Virginia, however, the father is given the preference. In Tennessee *inherited* real estate passes to the parent of the same blood as that through which the inheritance came — clearly an attempt to preserve family lands within the family. American commonwealths have proved more willing to grant mothers equal rights of inheritance with fathers in the property of a deceased child than to permit mothers to share equally with the father in the earnings of their minor children. In only thirty states is this right granted to mothers. Probably the discrimination is based upon the fact that the law makes the father primarily liable for the support of his children.

Guardianship Laws. — In thirty-nine states the old laws giving to fathers sole rights of guardianship of their children have been wiped off the statute books and the parents have been endowed with equal rights. In eight states — Alabama, Georgia, Kentucky, Louisiana, North Carolina, Oklahoma, Texas and Vermont — the father's rights are supreme. Another relic of medieval law is found in the Georgia statute permitting a father to will away from the mother the custody of her child without her consent. In ten other states the father may by testament dispose of the custody of a child to someone other than the mother, if he secures his wife's consent. These states are Arizona, New Mexico, California, Idaho, North Dakota, South Dakota, Utah, Oklahoma, North Carolina and New Jersey. In the remaining thirty-seven states the father may not dispose of his child's custody to someone other than the mother with or without the mother's consent.

Marriage Laws. — *Common law marriages* have lingered on in the United States long after they had been eradicated in Europe. At present these informal unions have been abolished by law in sixteen states and in eight other states they are not recognized, although no statute has been enacted abolishing them. In the remaining twenty-four states — exactly half — common-law marriages are still valid, a situation that bears mute witness to the strength of custom and the inertia of lawmakers.

A tendency has been evident in this country for the last two decades to require a *health certificate* of one or both parties before a marriage license is issued. Such a law has been enacted in eleven states; and in New York, the twelfth state legislating on the matter, the parties applying for a license must each sign and verify a statement concerning freedom from venereal disease. In nine states there is a legal provision prohibiting the marriage of the venereally diseased, although no measures have been taken to enforce the law. With regard to the effectiveness of these laws in realizing their purpose it may be said that they probably accomplish relatively little because the physicians who grant the certificates commonly make only superficial examinations to discover the presence of venereal disease. Thorough tests like the Wassermann are lengthy and expensive, and the fees received by physicians in the majority of cases do not, in their judgment, warrant them in making these searching tests. Even in the state of Wisconsin, where the law requires the man to be examined for any venereal disease within fifteen days prior to applying for a marriage license, and to file a physician's certificate stating that he is free from venereal disease "as nearly as can be determined by thorough examination and by tests when necessary," surveys of the operation of the law reveal that it is sometimes carelessly administered by physicians whose fees are small. Nevertheless these legal provisions represent a distinct advance beyond the neglect of this important matter shown by the remaining twenty-six states, in which no laws whatever have been enacted.

Great variety of legislation regarding the *marriage ages* of men and women exists in the forty-eight states. It should, perhaps, be explained that these laws refer to three different sets of conditions : (1) the ages below which no boy or girl may marry ; (2) the ages at which they may marry *with the parents' consent;* (3) the ages at which men and women may marry *without the parents' consent.* In eleven states the laws require that both men and women must be twenty-one years of age before they may marry without parental consent ; in thirty-two states, men of twenty-one and women of eighteen may marry without the consent of parents ; in four states both men and women may marry without parental consent at eighteen years of age.

With the formal consent of parents or guardian, girls may be married at sixteen years and boys at eighteen in sixteen states; while in five states girls may marry at fifteen and boys at eighteen with consent. In three states, Alabama, Georgia and Arkansas, boys of seventeen and girls of fourteen are permitted to marry with parental consent. In two states, Connecticut and Pennsylvania, boys and girls may both marry at sixteen provided parents are willing. In seven states boys may marry at sixteen and girls at fourteen with parental consent. These states are Iowa, Kentucky, North Carolina, Texas, Utah, New York and Vermont. The state of New Hampshire lowers even these ages, for the law permits a boy to marry at fourteen and a girl at thirteen with parental consent. Finally, in eleven other states — Colorado, Florida, Idaho, Louisiana, Maine, Maryland, Mississippi, New Jersey, Rhode Island, Tennessee and Virginia — the old common law ages of marriage are still recognized, fourteen years for boys and twelve for girls if parents or guardians consent. This condition of child marriage, permitted in at least nineteen states, with parental consent, is evidence of the powerful influence of tradition, not alone on our legislators but on the popular mind. Such laws, framed in the Middle Ages, should long ago have disappeared from the statute books of enlightened states. Mary Richmond and Fred Hall, who made an investigation of child marriages in America in 1924, tell us that although census returns do not give age at marriage, the 1920 census shows that 12,834 girls, recorded as married, were 15 years old at the time the census was taken and 5,554 others were under 15, giving a total of 18,388 girls still under 16 who had married at 15 or younger. With the aid of four census reports made between 1890 and 1920, and the help of actuarial life tables, the authors estimate that approximately 343,000 women and girls, living in the United States at the time the study was made, began their married lives as children during the previous 36 years.[1] That young girls of fourteen and fifteen are physically and mentally mature enough to take up

[1] Richmond and Hall, *Child Marriages* (1925), pp. 56–57.

the serious responsibilities of marriage is a wholly unwarranted assumption and laws permitting children so to do are a social stupidity.

DIVORCE LEGISLATION IN THE UNITED STATES

The discussion in a previous chapter of divorce regulations in the American colonies will make plain that our forefathers, at least in the North, adopted a rather tolerant attitude toward this question as compared with the mother-country. During the nineteenth century the whole trend of divorce legislation in the various states has been in the direction of multiplying the causes for which the marriage bond may be dissolved. Thus Massachusetts in the statute of 1786 recognized only two causes for divorce — adultery and impotency. Today this state recognizes seven causes. As late as 1848 Virginia granted absolute divorce only for adultery; at present she also has placed seven causes upon her statute-books. In 1795, the states of the Northwest Territory, from which many of the North Central States were carved, recognized only three grounds for divorce.[1] Today, Ohio recognizes ten causes, Indiana seven, and Illinois nine.[2] Moreover, in state after state of the Union, first in the North, then much later in the South, jurisdiction in divorce cases was transferred from the legislative bodies to the courts. In the New England States this reform was accomplished shortly after the Revolution, except in Connecticut where, even in early colonial times, the courts had entire jurisdiction. But in the South progress was much more tardy. It was nearly fifty years after the Revolutionary War before Virginia and Maryland granted the courts even partial jurisdiction. Not until 1851 was the Assembly in both these states deprived of all authority in divorce trials, although Maryland had given her courts jurisdiction in 1842 and Virginia in 1827.[3]

[1] Howard, *op. cit.*, Vol. III, pp. 5, 10, 114–120.
[2] *A Survey of the Legal Status of Women* (ed. 1930).
[3] *Ibid.*, p. 31.

As the nineteenth century progressed, the different states concerned themselves with various questions involved in the granting of divorces. (1) Shall the parties in a divorce be permitted to remarry, or shall the guilty party be restrained? (2) What provisions shall be made concerning residence in the states where the divorce is sought and due notice to the defendant in order to prevent clandestine divorce? (3) What regulations shall be framed with respect to (*a*) alimony, (*b*) the control of property and (*c*) the custody of children in cases where divorce is granted? The conclusions reached regarding these important matters can be summed up only very briefly: With regard to remarriage of the parties to a divorce the statutes of the states vary greatly. In New England, remarriage is generally permitted, although Massachusetts requires that a period of two years elapse before the guilty party may marry again.[1] In New York, on the contrary, a state which limits the causes of divorce to adultery, the guilty party may not marry within the commonwealth during the lifetime of the wife. An exception to this law is allowed where the defendant convicted of adultery offers proof to the court which rendered the judgment that he has led an exemplary life for five years after the decree was made absolute. The effect of this law is largely nullified by the fact that a marriage solemnized in another state is recognized as legal in New York; therefore the guilty party has only to make a short trip to a neighboring state if he desires to remarry. In all the southern states severe restrictions on remarriage after divorce existed until after the middle of the nineteenth century. Later these laws were modified, and in the states of Tennessee, West Virginia, Missouri, Texas, New Mexico and Arizona were removed. In striking similarity to the law of the ancient Hebrews is the regulation in Louisiana [2] that when divorce is granted for adultery the guilty party is forever forbidden to marry his or her accom-

---

[1] General Laws of Massachusetts (1932), Ch. 208, Sec. 21.
[2] Revised Civil Code of Louisiana (1925), Article 161.

plice. Very generally the western states permit remarriage with some restrictions.

In all the states of the Union a period of residence either before or after marriage is required of one of the parties. This period varies from six weeks in Nevada to five years in Massachusetts. In the latter instance, however, if both parties were inhabitants of Massachusetts at the time of the marriage and the libellant has lived in the state for three years preceding the filing of the libel the time may be cut to three years.[1] Whereas Nevada has gained an unsavory notoriety because of the short term of residence required of the plaintiff and the ease with which a divorce can be obtained, Massachusetts refuses a divorce to any plaintiff who clearly has moved to the state for that purpose. In this matter, as in our whole body of divorce legislation, the utmost disharmony prevails. Each commonwealth has gone its own way without regard to its neighbors. In nearly all of the states, however, the statutes require that due notice of the pending divorce suit be given the defendant.

With regard to alimony, distribution of property and the custody of children, the regulations of the various states show greater unanimity. Very generally temporary alimony is required of the husband for the support of wife and minor children pending judgment in a divorce suit. The courts also are empowered to grant the wife, if she be the plaintiff in a successful suit, such part of the real and personal estate of her husband as seems just. Furthermore, after judgment has been rendered in her favor, the wife is entitled to immediate possession of her own personal and real estate. On the other hand she is not entitled to dower except in a few states as, *e.g.*, Missouri, where the wife, if she obtains the divorce, is regarded as in the position of a widow. On the other hand, if the husband be the libellant and win his suit the divorced wife is deprived of dower.[2] In the New England States, also,

---

[1] General Laws of Massachusetts (1932), Vol. II, Sec. 5.
[2] Revised statutes of Missouri (1929), Sec. 331.

a wife is entitled to dower if the cause of the divorce be the husband's infidelity or sentence to penal servitude, or if the husband die before a decree *nisi* granted the wife has become absolute.[1]

The practice of granting alimony to the innocent party in a divorce suit appears to be on the decline. Unfortunately the Census Bureau has ceased to furnish statistics concerning alimony since 1922. The census report on *Marriage and Divorce* for that year showed that in 1916 alimony was granted in 15.3 per cent of divorces — in 4.7 per cent of the cases where the husband was libellant and in 20.1 per cent of those in which the wife was libellant. In 1922 — six years later — the total percentage of divorces in which alimony was granted had fallen to 14.7. It would be interesting to know whether the percentage has further declined during the last decade; but the Census Bureau has no figures on the subject. One fact seems clearly apparent — that the percentage of divorce cases in which alimony is granted by the court is much smaller than popular opinion has been inclined to believe. This condition may, perhaps, be partly explained by the ever-increasing numbers of married women in gainful employment.

Summary. — When the student surveys with a wide sweep the changes in the American family that took place during the nineteenth century and compares the home of 1833 with that of 1933, he cannot fail to realize that the family has undergone a basic transformation. The patriarchal household ruled by the father has all but disappeared. Wives and mothers have not only achieved political emancipation but a considerable degree of economic independence. The higher education of women has individualized them, as it long ago individualized their brothers; hence women, married and single, are discovering ever-widening social interests and are actively participating in well-nigh every social movement to secure the public good. Children, likewise, have been freed from too harsh parental discipline and are regarded in

[1] See General Laws of Massachusetts (1932), Sec. 27.

most enlightened homes as individuals, like their parents, with personalities to be respected. The State has intervened to protect the fundamental rights of children to humane treatment, to education and to freedom from exploitation, at least until the completion of the fourteenth year. The family at its best has become democratic in form, a free association of persons bound together by ties of affection, comradeship and mutual help, in which the rights of each member are respected and the future of the individual is not sacrificed, as so often was the case in the past, to the strength and solidarity of the family.

SELECTED READINGS

A Survey of the Legal Status of Women in the Forty-Eight States, National League of Women Voters, Washington, D. C., March, 1930.

Adams, Elizabeth. "The Higher Education of Women," in Monroe, Paul, *Cyclopedia of Education*, N. Y., Macmillan, Vol. V, pp. 801 ff.

Calhoun, Arthur. *Social History of the American Family*, Cleveland, Arthur H. Clark Co., 1918, Vols. II, III.

Carlier, Auguste. *Marriage in the United States*, Boston, 1837.

Chevalier, Michael. *Society, Manners and Politics in the United States*, trans. from 3rd Paris ed., Boston, Weeks, Jordan and Co., 1839.

DeTocqueville, Alexis. *Democracy in America*, N. Y., The Century Co., 1898, Vol. II.

Gage, Matilda. *Woman, Church and State*, N. Y, The Truth Seeker Co., 1893.

Goodsell, Willystine. "The American Family in the Nineteenth Century," in *Annals of the American Academy of Political and Social Science*, Vol. 160, March, 1932, pp. 13–22.

Graves, Mrs. A. J. *Woman in America*, Harper, 1858.

Howard, Geo. E. *A History of Matrimonial Institutions*, University of Chicago Press, 1902, Vol. II, pp. 73–120; Vol. III, pp. 5, 10, 31, 82, 114–120.

Mansfield, Edward. *The Legal Rights, Liabilities and Duties of American Women*, Salem, John P. Jewett and Co., 1845, pp. 270–273.

Ossoli, Margaret Fuller. *Woman in the Nineteenth Century*, Boston, John P. Jewett and Co., 1855.

Wilson, Jennie. *Legal and Political Status of Women in the United States*, passim, 1912.

CHAPTER XII

PROBLEMS OF THE TWENTIETH CENTURY FAMILY

Evidences of the Maladjustment of the Modern Family to Social Conditions. The Instability of the Family. — Perhaps the characteristic of the twentieth-century family that most sharply challenges the attention of the student of family history is its instability. It is a far cry from the closely knit, highly unified family organizations of the ancient Romans or the Middle-Age Teutons to the more loosely organized household of modern times wherein each member tends to claim independence as an individual with a personality to be developed and respected. Nowadays, at least in America, homesteads with surrounding lands, held in the same family for generations and serving to strengthen the family bond are rare indeed. No family head holds all the property, real and personal, of its members in his own control; nor does he represent his wife and children before the law, paying their fines for civil offenses. The father is no longer the religious head of his family, offering prayers and sacrifices to household gods whose supreme function it is to maintain the unity of the family and its estates. At present it is rather rare for a single will to impose itself upon every member of the family and secure unquestioning obedience to its dictates by the exercise of physical force backed by the authority of the State. Instead, the modern household not infrequently presents the phenomenon of a group of clashing wills, an association of highly individualized persons, each asserting his rights and maintaining his privileges with greater or less success. The family unity of modern times — and many homes today exemplify this unity in strength and beauty — is more a spiritual oneness of mutual love and consideration, of common interests and goals than a unity secured by centering all authority in one head. Obviously the individualistic spirit has undermined and in part superseded the autocratic; and although the gain to humanity has been priceless, the advance has not been made without some loss. The family of the twentieth century is markedly unstable; it would seem that in some instances it has paid for the independence of its members the costly price of its very existence or its existence in a changed and incomplete form.

The social literature of the age abounds in references to this instability of the modern family and foretells its extinction, at least in its present form. We are told that monogamic marriage is doomed; that it was based wholly upon economic foundations, *i.e.*, upon the desire of men to transmit property intact through legitimate issue, thus securing the perpetuation of the family name and lands. With the break-up of the economic, religious and legal bonds that once made of the monogamic family a strongly cemented unit, we are assured that looser and less permanent forms of associations will in all probability take its place. Writers in this strain point to certain conditions in modern family life as evidence of the truth of their contention. They call attention to the wide prevalence of divorce, the increase of family desertion, the effect of modern industry in disintegrating the family and the inroads of individualism. All these conditions merit careful consideration.

The Problem of Divorce. — At present the United States stands first among civilized lands in the number of divorces granted annually by its courts. As early as 1885 more marriages were dissolved in this country than in all the rest of the Christian world combined, the figures being as follows: United States, 23,472; Christian Europe, 20,131.[1] Quite as startling is the fact of the rapid increase in divorce in the United States during the past few decades. For example, in the

[1] Ellwood, *Sociology and Modern Social Problems*, p. 114.

ten years from 1890 to 1900 the number of divorces obtained increased 66.6 per cent over the preceding decade, whereas the population increased only 20.7 per cent. During the thirty-year period 1900–1930 the number of divorces granted increased by leaps and bounds, both absolutely and in relation to population growth. In 1900 the courts granted 55,751 divorces, an increase of 8.4 per cent over the preceding year. In 1906 the number of divorces was 72,062, an increase of six per cent over the preceding year; ten years later the number had risen to 112,036. Then came a break in the annual census reports on marriage and divorce, probably due to the war and its aftermath. In 1923 the number of divorces had risen to 165,096, a total which is nearly 200 per cent greater than that of 1900 and ten per cent in excess of the preceding year. Seven years later, in 1930, the number of divorces granted had risen to the disturbing total of 191,591; but in 1931, the last year for which census statistics are available, this figure had fallen to 183,664, a loss of 4.1 per cent over 1930. This loss may probably be explained by the financial stringency caused by the depression. However, the number of marriages also fell in 1931 by about 66,000, so that the ratio of divorces to marriages was the highest in the history of the country — 17.3 divorces to every 100 marriages, or one divorce to every 5.7 marriages.[1]

If the "only fair method for comparing divorce rates" be, as Cahen maintains,[2] the divorces per thousand of the married population, it may be said that in 1931 the rate was 3.46 divorces per one thousand of the married people in this country.[3] Cahen estimates that in the period from 1867 to 1929 population increased about 300 per cent, marriages about

---

[1] This last ratio does not, of course, mean that out of every 5.7 marriages performed in 1931 one ended in divorce; the ratio merely represents the proportion of divorces granted to marriages celebrated in that year. Figures taken from *Marriage and Divorce* (1931), p. 10.

[2] *Statistical Analysis of American Divorce* (Columbia University Press, 1932), p. 19.

[3] Census Report on *Marriage and Divorce* (1931), p. 15.

400 per cent and divorces about 2000 per cent.[1]   This means, of course, that in a period of 62 years the rate increase of divorce was approximately five times greater than that of the married population.   Although some writers are inclined to believe that the divorce rate in the United States will reach a saturation point before many years, there are no signs at present that this point is being approached.   Based on the country's married population, the percentage of divorces has advanced since 1912 at the rate of 30 per cent a decade.[2]   Yet in a majority of the states in 1931 there was a definite decrease in the percentage of divorces as compared with 1930, a decrease ranging from 26.4 per cent in Mississippi to 1.7 per cent in Minnesota.[3]   However, as previously suggested, this decline is probably due to the economic and financial chaos of the preceding years.   Cahen estimates that if divorces continue to increase at the same rate as in the period 1922–1929, by the year 1965 the majority of American marriages (51 per cent) would end in divorce.[4]   Such estimates should not, of course, be understood as facts, but as calculations depending upon many obscure factors for their realization.   It is quite possible that, if the movement to educate youth for marriage gains headway, there may be a marked fall in divorce rates before many years.

Most divorces in the United States are granted for three causes — cruelty, desertion and adultery; only a small proportion are granted for such grounds as failure to provide and drunkenness.   In 1931 the census report shows that 42.4 per cent of the total divorces (182,203) were granted for cruelty, 27.9 per cent for desertion and 7.5 per cent for adultery. Only 1.5 per cent were granted for drunkenness and 4.1 per cent for "neglect to provide."   If full and intimate knowledge of the facts of these divorce cases were available, it would

[1] Census Report on *Marriage and Divorce* (1931), p. 21.
[2] Cahen, *op. cit.*, p. 23.
[3] *Marriage and Divorce*, p. 11.
[4] *Op. cit.*, p. 30.

probably appear that the percentage of cases where marital unfaithfulness was the true cause of the divorce should be sharply increased. Women, in particular, prefer to assign almost any cause than that of adultery in seeking a divorce because of the unsavory notoriety attending the trial of such cases. Of the divorces granted to husbands in 1931 the cause was desertion in 41.9 per cent of the cases; whereas of the divorces granted to wives only 22.7 per cent were for the cause of desertion. By far the greater percentage (45.1) of divorces received by wives was granted for the cause of "cruelty," an elastic term under which may be brought many causes of marital strife and unhappiness. It has long been known by divorce court judges that *the true reasons for the wreckage of marriages are often not the legal causes that are aired in court.* Rather are they those frictions, uncongenialities and active dislikes growing out of incompatibility of temperaments and tastes. If public opinion remains favorable to easy divorce, it is a serious question whether there would not be distinct social gain in wiping legal causes for divorce off the statute books and granting a severance of the marriage relation to every couple who convince the judge or referee *in camera* that no hope remains of effecting a mutual reconciliation between them.

Apparently the most dangerous years of married life are the first five. During that period 43.3 per cent of all divorces granted in 1931 were obtained. Over 4 per cent of divorces in that year were granted to couples who had been married less than a year and 8.3 per cent to those married three years. On the other hand a high percentage of divorces in a five-year period (16.6) was granted to married pairs who had lived together ten to fourteen years. Slightly over 10 per cent of the divorces of 1931 were granted to couples who had been married more than twenty years! Obviously long periods of marital life spent together are no guarantee of the permanence of marriage.[1]

[1] Census Report on *Marriage and Divorce* (1931), p. 27.

Contrary, perhaps, to popular belief, relatively few divorce cases are contested by the partner against whom charges are brought. In 1931 only 13.9 per cent of divorces was contested and in 1928 only 11.7 per cent. Wives refuse to contest about as frequently as husbands, whatever the charge may be. Such a situation clearly points to mutual unhappiness and dissatisfaction with the marriage.

It has long been a matter of knowledge that the existence of children in a family acts as a deterrent to divorce and, conversely, that a majority of divorces is granted to couples who are childless. In 1931 no children were reported in 57 per cent of divorces, children were reported in 38 per cent and in 4.9 per cent no report was made concerning children. Surprisingly enough, fathers are less likely to bring action for divorce in families where there are children than are mothers. In 1931 no children were reported in 63.6 per cent of the divorces granted to husbands; whereas in those granted to the wife only 54.5 per cent reported no children. Perhaps this disparity may be explained by the fact that a man with dependent children, especially if they were very young, would find greater difficulty in nurturing and educating them than would a woman, and therefore would be more reluctant to institute divorce proceedings.

For many years a large proportion of divorces has been granted to wives, who, apparently, find marriage a more unsatisfying and unhappy relationship than do men. As early as the period 1887–1896 the wife received 65.8 per cent of all divorces granted; and the proportion has steadily risen until in 1931 the wife was granted 72.8 per cent of the divorces and the husband only 27.2 per cent.[1]

On the basis of census figures for 1928, Cahen has worked out diagrams showing the chances of divorce in marriages where there are children and where there are not. He states that about 18 per cent of all marriages end in divorce; and quotes Lotka's calculation that about 17 per cent of American

[1] Census Report (1931), pp. 17 and 32.

marriages are sterile. On the basis of these figures Cahen estimates that 71 per cent of childless marriages will end in divorce and only 8 per cent of marriages with children.[1] It must be remembered that these figures refer only to the year 1928 and cannot be regarded as true in general.[2] Unquestionably, however, there is a striking negative correlation between the birth rate and the divorce rate, as Ogburn has shown [3] with respect to 170 American cities. When the age of the wife is held constant, the correlation is −0.54, showing that those cities with high percentages of divorces also have low birth rates per 1000 married women between the ages of 15 and 25 — the most fruitful years.

Since the alleged legal causes of divorce are in most instances not the real ones, it would be interesting to know what were the true reasons impelling over 183,000 married couples to seek divorce in 1931. Cahen has brought together the chief causes assigned by eight investigators — judges and officials connected with Bureaus of Domestic Relations — who have come in contact with thousands of divorce cases. It is a very striking fact that not one of these men agrees with any other as to the outstanding causal factors in divorce. The causes given (to mention but a few) range from feeble-mindedness, poverty and physical mismating, to female independence, hasty marriages, uncontrolled temper and faulty education. Such marked disagreement among those investigators close to the conditions suggests that the true causes of divorce are obscure and intertwined and, as Professor Lichtenberger has indicated, are "produced by dynamic changes in modern civilization." [4] These far-reaching changes are economic,

---

[1] *Op. cit.*, pp. 113–114.

[2] The percentage of divorces granted to childless couples in 1928 was 56.6. By adding to this figure the percentage of couples *not reporting as to children*, Cahen obtained the percentage of 63 for childless couples, on which his estimate is based.

[3] Groves and Ogburn, *American Marriage and Family Relationships* (1928), p. 376.

[4] *Divorce, a Social Interpretation* (1931), p. 258.

political, social, ethical and religious. Taken together they have not only transformed the family in functions and in the relationships of its members, but have profoundly altered basic conceptions of marriage and the attitudes of husband and wife to each other and to family life. Divorce but expresses the maladjustment of spouses to the new material and spiritual conditions.

However beneficial divorce may be as a means of ending intolerable marital relationships, it can hardly be questioned that the legal severance of marriage is itself not rarely a source of unhappiness and maladjustment both to married pairs and to children. Like a surgical operation, divorce may put an end to serious evils but leave in its wake obscure ills that are slow in clearing up. Far better than the dubious cure of divorce is that intelligent prevention which prepares young persons for marriage by laying frankly and fully before them the problems and difficulties in that relationship and showing ways of avoiding these pitfalls that others have tried with success.

FAMILY DESERTION AS A PROBLEM

Further evidence of the unstable character of the contemporary family is furnished by the large numbers of cases of family desertion. No complete and reliable data regarding this phenomenon have, apparently, been compiled, and social investigators are therefore compelled to fall back upon estimates. In 1928 the National Desertion Bureau sent questionnaires to a large number of urban organizations for Family Welfare, Child Care and Legal Aid. The question was asked: "Is family desertion a vexing problem in your community?" Out of 145 replies, 134 were affirmative. Among 93 cities sending returns, desertion rates ranged from 28 to 203 per 100,000 population. The fact that the smaller cities showed the larger desertion rates was explained in the Report of the Desertion Committee as probably due to the fact that the welfare organizations in large cities deal with only a part of the desertion problem. It was the considered judgment of the Committee that the ratio for the smaller cities more closely represented the true ratio for all cities than did that of the large centers. The Report went on to estimate the probable number of desertions in the United States in 1920, on the basis of 100 desertions per 100,000 population, as not far from 50,000.[1] This estimate is admittedly a guess, and the fact that so little exact knowledge exists with regard to desertion in America suggests the need for a large number of painstaking studies of family desertion in our cities such as Professor Mowrer has made in the city of Chicago. Mowrer found that in 1919 there were 2311 desertions in Chicago or a ratio of 90 to 100,000 of the population.[2] By dividing the city into areas, he further discovered that there were 13 communities in which there were neither divorces nor desertions in that year. Such a situation, as Professor Mowrer points out, clearly indicates the need for "a complete knowledge of the cultural characteristics of each area or community" in order to interpret the data.[3]

Probably the most illuminating general treatment of family desertion is contained in Joanna Colcord's study of *Broken Homes*, published fourteen years ago. In discussing the causes of desertion, the author warns us to be wary of accepting "blanket theories," such as economic pressure, bad housekeeping and sexual incompatibility. While these factors no doubt are elements in the problem, Miss Colcord declares that "there is no one cause or group of causes underlying breakdowns in family morale."[4] However, the author cites the report of a court of domestic relations which had made an analysis of over 1500 cases of family desertion, compiling a

---

[1] Report of the National Desertion Committee Compiled from Questionnaires (1928). Mimeographed material cited by Cahen, *Statistical Analysis of American Divorce*, pp. 16–17.

[2] *Family Disorganization*, p. 118.

[3] *Ibid.*, p. 122.

[4] *Op. cit.*, p. 21.

list of 25 causes and then calculating the percentage of cases due to each. Summarizing these causes under five heads, Colcord presents them as follows : [1]

		Percentage
1.	Distinct sex factors	39.03
2.	Alcohol and narcotic drugs	37.00
3.	Temperamental traits	15.40
4.	Economic issues	6.27
5.	Mental and physical troubles	2.30

Like divorce, desertion is a symptom of deep-seated difficulties in marriage and the family situation, to which there are probably many contributory factors. For many years state and municipal laws have been revised in the direction of making desertion and non-support of dependent children a criminal offense. New York City has enacted an ordinance making the abandonment of minor children in destitute circumstances a felony, and several states have passed similar laws. These laws have probably acted to some extent as a deterrent to family desertion by creating in the minds of would-be deserters a wholesome respect for the law and in encouraging wives to stand up for their legal rights. Yet the desertion rate has remained remarkably stable over a considerable period. Some social workers believe that during the last few years the rate has been definitely increasing. It should be clearly understood that legal measures will no more serve as a panacea for desertion than for divorce. According to Miss Colcord social workers are now abandoning their earlier disciplinary measures in desertion cases and are seeking to discover the obscure, perhaps multiple, causes of family abandonment. Only in the last resort do they take cases into court, after painstaking case methods have failed. This change of treatment has its source in the belief that the result of court action is definitely to snuff out any small spark of marital affection that might have been rekindled and have served to bring about a reconciliation. [2]

[1] *Family Disorganization*, p. 22.   [2] *Ibid.*, p. 53.

In the previous discussion family desertion among the poor, who are brought to the attention of social agencies because of need, has been chiefly considered. But it must not be forgotten that among more privileged groups desertion is one of the most frequent causes of divorce. For example, in 1931, the percentage of divorces granted for desertion was 27.9 — over one fourth of the total. It is generally believed by court officials and social investigators, however, that many of these cases are collusive, both husband and wife agreeing to the desertion in order to furnish legal cause for the severance of a marriage that seems no longer endurable. This deliberate attempt to manufacture legal cases for the severance of marriage is one further argument against the retention of statutory grounds of divorce. Not only do they frequently fail to represent the true reasons for seeking divorce but they are productive of deceit and fraud.

FAMILY DISINTEGRATION DUE TO INDUSTRIAL CONDITIONS

Divorce and desertion are not the only conditions undermining the solidarity of the American family. The entire industrial situation undoubtedly contributes to the same end. In the words of a modern social writer:

"Certain aspects of our industrialism, such as the labor of women and children in factories, the growth of cities, and the loss of the home through the slum and the tenement, the higher standards of living and comfort, and the resulting higher age of marriage — all of these have had, to a certain extent at least, a disastrous effect upon the family." [1]

Features of Contemporary Industry. — During the nineteenth century hand labor was in large measure supplanted by machines and in consequence production was enormously increased. With the constant improvement of machinery has also gone a more and more minute specialization of industrial processes, so that laborers, gathered by thousands in

[1] Ellwood, *Sociology and Modern Social Problems*, p. 136.

huge factories, perform simple, repetitive machine tasks for eight or nine hours a day.   Moreover, the machine age is even now being transformed into the "age of power," when enormous and intricate machinery is operated by electrical energy with, apparently, an ever-decreasing need of human labor. Unquestionably the constantly augmented use of power to operate complex machines with uncanny effectiveness is creating serious problems of man-labor distribution and of unemployment.

Another characteristic of contemporary industry is the *growth of great industrial corporations* and the corresponding decline of small manufacturing concerns.   In these vast corporations the single laborer is lost and becomes but a cog in a machine.   Little concern is felt by the owners and industrial engineers of huge plants for the worker so remote from the orbit of their daily lives.   Even less concern is felt for the employee as a member of a family.   The *impersonality* of modern industry is complete from this aspect.   Years ago Samuel Dike pointed out that the "ultimate atom" of industry is the individual.   "In the market of wages the family is the accident of the laborer rather than his essential." [1]

Modern industry is further characterized by a marked *inequality in the distribution of wealth and income*.   Of course this is no new social phenomenon, but the disparity is particularly glaring in the present age.   Enormous accumulations of wealth in the hands of the leaders of industry and finance are in striking contrast to the meager wages and even impoverishment of a considerable proportion of wage-earners. A few figures will make this abundantly clear.   Willford I. King has estimated that in the year 1928 the realized income (total book income) drawn by entrepreneurs and other property owners was $38,296,000,000 in current dollars.   If the purchasing power of the dollar in 1913 be taken as the index, the realized income becomes $24,055,000,000.   The total realized income of the United States in 1928 is estimated as

[1] " Problems of the Family," in *Century Magazine*, XXXIX, pp. 392–393.

89,419,000,000 in current dollars. Therefore it may be seen that the relatively small group of property owners received not far from one half of the national income — 42.8 per cent in 1928. What was the amount received by employees in the form of total wages, salaries, pensions and compensation for injuries? This total King estimates as $51,123,000,000 or 57.2 per cent of the entire realized national income. In purchasing power, using the dollar of 1913 as index, this amount shrinks to $29,967,000,000. If salaries, pensions and compensation for injuries be eliminated and *wages* alone be considered, the total is $18,895,000,000 in terms of the 1913 dollar. But these total amounts perhaps mean little. What were the *average annual earnings of wage workers*, taking account of unemployment? In 1927 King estimates that wage to be $1205 in current dollars, but in terms of the purchasing power of the 1913 dollar it falls to $705.[1] It will readily be seen that if this last figure represented the entire family income of a married worker in 1927 it would have been totally inadequate to maintain the family at the level rather vaguely termed "the American standard of living," *i.e.*, the health and comfort level. But it should be understood that the wages of the chief supporter of the family are often perforce supplemented by those of his wife and older children.

The unequal distribution of national income will be made plainer, perhaps, by the following figures, taken by the well-known economist Stuart Chase, from the latest available Federal income tax returns covering the year 1927. Mr. Chase shows that 41,000,000 workers out of 45,000,000 employed persons in the country made no income report to the Government because their incomes averaged $1500 — an amount too low to be taxed. This means that in 1927 over 90 per cent of workers were exempt from the Federal tax because of small incomes. And this in one of the peak years of our so-called

[1] King, W. J. (assisted by Lillian Epstein), *The National Income and Its Purchasing Power* (N. Y., National Bureau of Economic Research, Inc., 1930), pp. 94, 108, 112, 122, 124, 130, 136, 146, 152.

American prosperity! But this is not all. More than 10,000 persons in that year reported incomes of from $100,000 to $1,000,000; 273 persons reported incomes of from $1,000,000 to $5,000,000; and 10 persons in this democracy admitted to incomes of more than $5,000,000 a year! When interpreted, these figures mean that less than ten per cent of the income receivers of the country secured more than 25 per cent of the income; and *less than one per cent of American income receivers secured 12 per cent of the entire national income.*[1]

In addition to the features of present-day industry discussed above, there should be mentioned the important fact of the *urbanization of life* primarily due to the massing of human beings around factories. It has been said that modern industry "is almost equivalent to 'city life,' because the great industry, the factory system, builds cities around the chimneys of steam engines and electric plants." Whether city life is favorable to the well-being and unity of the family is an important question at the present time which can only be mentioned here.

Finally it may be pointed out that *unemployment* is a permanent feature of industry today — not a rare phenomenon to be found only in periods of economic depression. In a brief for State Unemployment Systems issued by the People's Lobby in 1930 the average minimum percentage of unemployment among non-agricultural wage and salary earners is given for seven years — 1921 through 1927. In 1921, a year of depression, 15.3 per cent, or about 4,270,000 workers, were estimated to be unemployed. For four years of the seven the number of jobless was over 2,000,000 and in only two years of the period did the total fall below 1,750,000. It should be kept in mind that these figures can at best be no more than estimates, based on incomplete data, because the United States has not yet fully established a national system of unemployment bureaus in which accurate statistics of the

---

[1] Chase, Stuart, *Poor Old Competition* (pamphlet published by the League for Industrial Democracy, 112 East 19th Street, New York City, 1932), p 7.

number of men and women out of work may be found. If, however, these estimates be accepted as even approximately correct, they are far from reassuring when viewed in the light of our much vaunted American prosperity. But what shall be said of unemployment during the current depression, already well along in its fifth year? As a result of an incomplete survey made in 1930 by the United States Census Bureau the number of persons out of work and looking for a job is reported as 2,429,062, or five per cent of all gainful workers. If to this number be added "persons having jobs but on lay-off without pay" — surely an unemployed group — the total rises to 3,187,647, not including workers on part-time jobs. Since 1930 this number has risen rapidly and the army of the jobless has been variously estimated by the American Federation of Labor and by social investigators as between 12,000,000 and 15,000,000 workers in the year 1933. Such a situation is nothing short of a national tragedy. It indicates such grave and fundamental defects in our industrial organization as seriously to raise the question in thoughtful minds whether so inefficient an economic system, based on production for individual profit, can survive this period of economic chaos and human misery for which it is in large measure responsible.

Influence of Industrialism upon the Family. — The sketch given above of the salient features of modern industrialism has perhaps served to suggest certain of its effects on family life. It may be said that the low wages paid very generally to unskilled and semi-skilled workers have, obviously, a very direct effect on the standard of living and the quality of family life which they may enjoy. Low wages, accompanied by economic insecurity, the bugbear of a large proportion of laborers, are responsible for poverty; and the partial failure of industry properly to protect its workers from dangerous machines and unhealthful working conditions is responsible for industrial accidents and diseases, taking a heavy toll from the chief wage-earner. All these conditions react upon the family. Poverty is directly related to *bad housing* and to the ugly, unsanitary slums of our modern cities. In the city of New York are still standing tenement buildings that were condemned in 1901 by the Tenement House Commission as unfit for human habitation, and they still serve as dwellings for families of the lowest income groups. Dark, ill-smelling, unsanitary, with "dumb-bell courts" and rooms wholly lacking in light and air, save such as reaches them from an outside room, these tenement "homes" are a disgrace to our civilization. Nor is New York City the only populous center to tolerate such conditions. Surveys made in Philadelphia, in the "steel cities" of Homestead and Pittsburgh, in Cincinnati, Chicago, Washington and places farther west disclose housing conditions nearly, if not wholly, as bad as those of New York. What sort of family life will be developed in such homes and what kind of citizens will be reared in them? That prostitution, illegitimacy, juvenile delinquency and crime are correlated with impoverished slum homes, together with vicious neighborhoods, is a well-established fact. The marvel is that so much of decent, self-sacrificing, affectionate family life does exist in these outrageous dwellings.

When the father's wage is insufficient to support his family, even at the "minimum health and decency level," the wife and mother goes to work to supplement the family income. The census of 1930 reports a large increase in the number of married women employed since 1920. In the latter year a total of 1,920,281 married women were in gainful occupations; in 1930 this total had risen to 3,071,302, an increase of 1,151,-021, or 60 per cent. Such a phenomenal gain in the army of married women workers is evidence of the severe economic pressure to which the families of wage-earners are subjected. Not by any methods of intelligent marketing and management can the father's wage be stretched to cover the essential needs of a family with two or three children.

In the five-year period 1915–1920 numerous budget estimates of the minimum cost of living for a family of two adults and three children, inaccurately called the "typical" family, were prepared in various localities of the United States. One such estimate was made by Professor Ogburn in January, 1920, for the bituminous mining towns. Using as a standard the "health and decency" level of living which is next higher to the "minimum subsistence" level, Ogburn estimated that the minimum annual cost for a family of five, with three children under fourteen years, was $2243.94. In November, 1920, the Labor Bureau, Inc., of New York City made a similar budget study in behalf of unions in the printing trades. For a working man's family of five this estimate of the minimum cost of support at the "health and decency" level was $2632.68.[1] These carefully estimated budgets, which eliminate nearly every item except those essential to health and decency, are in startling contrast to the average annual earnings of wage workers in all industries in 1920, which are calculated by W. I. King to be $1273.[2] Wages fall short of budget estimates by $970 in the case of Ogburn's budget and by $1359 in the case of the Labor Bureau estimate. Of course two facts must be kept steadily in mind in interpreting these data. First, there is no "typical" American family of five members. Investigations show that one fourth to one third of laboring men are single. Moreover, Paul Douglas found [3] that only 17.7 per cent of 11,156 married workers had three children under fourteen years. On the other hand 11.2 per cent had four children and 4.8 per cent had five or more. This means that 16 per cent of workers had from four to more than five dependent children, and 17.7 had exactly three, making a total of 33.7 per cent of 11,156 families that had three or more dependent children under fourteen years. The second point to be kept in mind is that *wage averages give no accurate picture of the actual family income contributed by a particular wage-earner.* In some families the father's wage would be more

---

[1] *Family Budgets of American Wage Earners* (National Industrial Conference Board), p. 37.

[2] *The National Income and Its Purchasing Power*, p. 146.

[3] *Wages and the Family*, p. 35.

than adequate to support the family; in others it would fall below even the low average annual wage by several hundred dollars.

That married women's wages play an important part in keeping the family level of living up to the so-called "American standard" is shown by studies made by the Women's Bureau of the United States Department of Labor. Investigations made in four cities in 1920 disclosed that of 14,551 married women workers reporting, 10.6 per cent were the sole bread-winners of the family, 78 per cent were one of two bread-winners and 11.4 per cent were one of three breadwinners in the family group.[1]   In a study of 541 families in Manchester, N. H., it was discovered that a proportionate share of the family income was earned by 19.7 per cent of wives and mothers who were wage-earners. Although the earnings of these women were small, they "were by no means of inconsiderable value to the family."[2]

Of the 405 women (mothers, wives and daughters) who contributed all their earnings to the family income, wives and mothers constituted 16.1 per cent of the group earning $12 to $13 a week and 42.5 per cent of the group earning $17.50 and under $20 a week.[3]

Needless to say, problems of household management and child welfare are created when mothers are employed all day outside the home. Studies made by the Children's Bureau in Manchester and New Bedford show a much higher percentage of infant mortality in those families where the mother works outside the home almost up to the period of confinement and also in families where she returns to employment as soon as possible after the child's birth.[4]   Although the high infant

---

[1] *What the Wage-Earning Woman Contributes to Family Support*, Bulletin of the Women's Bureau, No. 75, Table 11, p. 14.

[2] *The Share of Wage-Earning Women in Family Support*, Bulletin of the Women's Bureau, No. 30, pp. 12–13.   [3] *Ibid.*, p. 57.

[4] See *Infant Mortality.   Results of a Field Study in New Bedford, Massachusetts.*   Publications of the Children's Bureau, No. 68, p. 42.   Also see a similar study made in Manchester, N. H., Bureau Publications, No. 20.

mortality rates disclosed in these studies were in part due to the extra-domestic employment of mothers, poverty and ignorance were also important factors. A high infant mortality existed in families of low income, where the foreign-born mothers were ignorant of the elementary principles of child hygiene, *even when these mothers were not employed outside the home.* In both the Manchester and the New Bedford studies a high correlation existed between the wages of fathers and infant mortality. When the chief breadwinner's earnings fell below $450, the infant mortality rate in Manchester rose to the shocking figure of 242.9 — almost one infant death to every four births ! [1]

On the other hand when the father's wage reached even the low figures of $850 to $1049, the death rate of babies fell to 125, being almost cut in half. In the highest wage-group of $1250 or over, the infant mortality rate sank to 58.3. Similar conditions were discovered in New Bedford. [2]

Another problem associated with the extra-domestic employment of mothers is that of providing proper care and guidance for young children, to say nothing of older ones. In the Women's Bureau study of employed women in four cities in 1920, cited above, it was found that 4466 breadwinning mothers had children under five years of age, 1561 more had children five and six years old at home, while another group of 1134 mothers had children of five and six who were in school. [3]

What is the outlook for babies and toddlers when the mother starts out at an early hour for the day's work in factory or laundry? Some receive sporadic care from older children in the interval between school sessions and after school. Occasionally several working women employ a neighbor to care for a group of their young children. If an older relative, mother or aunt, is living with the family, she takes charge of the children. Once in a while a mother will leave a small baby at home,

[1] *Op. cit.*, p. 49.
[2] *Op. cit.*, p. 41.
[3] Women's Bureau Bulletin, No. 75, p. 17.

with dangerous articles put out of its reach and with a nursing bottle tied round its neck ! Such desperate measures reveal the extent of our social indifference and negligence toward working mothers and their difficulties. In most sections where wage-earners live, there is a quite insufficient number of day nurseries where these babies and toddling children could be properly cared for. Katherine Anthony, in her investigation of 370 working mothers, living in the middle western section of New York City, discovered that only two day nurseries had been established in that populous area and these could accommodate only 120 children. Yet there were 221 children below school age belonging to these employed mothers.[1] In a society where men willing to work are not paid a living family wage, thus forcing their wives to eke out the family income by wage-earning, it would seem that society could at least make ample provision for the intelligent care and guidance of young children in day nurseries. In Russia and France laws have been enacted compelling factory owners to furnish and equip nurseries in the factory buildings, to which mothers may repair twice a day to nurse their babies. Each nursery is provided with a care-taker of small children. Such an enlightened policy might well be imitated in America.

PROBLEMS CREATED BY LIBERALISM AND INDIVIDUALISM

In eighteenth-century France was centered that great libertarian movement whose purpose was to free the bodies and minds of men from the cramping restrictions that were the relics of medieval authoritarianism. Not only did European liberalism seek to strike from mankind political and economic fetters but to set free the minds of men from the prison-house of outworn intellectual, religious and ethical systems. At first this deep-moving libertarian impulse was confined to men; but as time wore on, women likewise were profoundly affected by it. Impelled by its dynamic stimulus, women have

[1] *Mothers Who Must Earn*, p. 151.

struggled and won through to economic, legal and political independence and have been granted full opportunities for higher education — liberal and professional.

Such a transformation in the lives of women, opening as it does to their eyes the infinite variety and interest of the world and challenging them to embark upon unknown seas of discovery and endeavor side by side with men, obviously could not take place without profound reactions upon marriage and the home. Higher education has revealed women to themselves *as individuals,* endowed with tastes, talents and capacities for growth that cannot attain fulfillment merely in the conscientious performance of domestic duties.

Individualism and Marriage. — Some educated women today, although by no means all, are discovering that marriage in its present customary form closes to them the doors of opportunity for congenial work and personal development and, if they have no independent means, places them in a position of humiliating financial dependence upon their husbands. Women who have followed stimulating and interesting careers before marriage and have tasted the joys of economic independence may find wedlock in truth what long ago the Englishwoman Mona Caird termed it — a "trap." [1] Although many persons are loath to believe it, not a few wives and mothers find domestic pursuits and the exacting care of young children positively distasteful. This is not to say that these women are selfish and unloving; merely that they are individuals who, however deeply they may love husband and children, find their most satisfying and developing work outside the home. Such women become restless and discontented if held closely to domestic employments; and their sense of frustration may express itself in ways prejudicial to the atmosphere of the home and harmful to sensitive children. Here is a very real problem growing out of marriage and family life at present; and it cannot be solved by ignoring its existence or by directing sharp criticism at dissatisfied wives. Fortunately for the harmony

[1] See *The Morality of Marriage,* pp. 98–137.

and success of family life, by no means all women fail to find a rewarding outlet for their talents in household tasks and child-care. It is probable that at present a majority of educated women discover in the problems of home-making and child-rearing a full and satisfying career.

The trend toward individualism in modern life is probably in no small measure responsible for another problem — that of the *marriage rate*. Although the census returns show an almost unbroken increase in the number of marriages for every year since 1887, yet during the last decade there have been five years in which the number of marriages fell below that of the preceding year. The rather sharp declines in 1930 and 1931 are readily explainable by the economic depression with its heavy toll of unemployment; but it is not so easy to account for the fall in marriages in the prosperous years of 1924, 1927 and 1928. However, it is possible that these decreases, in no case large, may be due to temporary causes.

The real problem is concerned, not with the national rate of marriage, but with the percentage of marriages among college women graduates. These percentages have been generally low — much lower than those for women in general. For example, studies made by Sprague show that only 53 per cent of Vassar graduates of the classes 1867–1892 were married in 1915 — twenty-three years and more after graduation; and the alumnæ of the early classes at Wellesley make an even poorer showing twenty-six years and more after leaving college.[1] Similar gloomy figures are revealed by an investigation published in 1918 by the *Journal of the Association of Collegiate Alumnæ*. The colleges investigated included eight eastern women's colleges together with Cornell, and returns were received from 16,739 alumnæ. Only 39.1 per cent of these women were married in 1914. However, if all alumnæ of the classes succeeding 1900 were omitted, the percentage rose to 51. It is interesting to note that in recent years evidence is piling up of a higher marriage rate among college

[1] *Journal of Heredity* (April, 1915).

women. The alumnæ registers of practically all the eastern
women's colleges show a gradually rising percentage of
married graduates. In the case of Smith College the *Alumnæ
Census* of 1931 shows that, of 7689 alumnæ reporting, 60 per
cent were married. If the graduates of the last ten classes
were eliminated, the percentage rose to 66. Gratifying as this
increase of marriages among college women may be, however,
the proportion of these women who marry still remains distinctly lower than that of women of comparable ages in the
country at large. The Federal census returns for 1930 are not
yet complete at this writing but those for 1920 show that, of
the comparable age-group, 25–34 years, 76.5 per cent of women
in the United States were married; and of the age-group,
35–44 years, 80.3 per cent were married.

Is the low rate of marriage among college women (and to a
less degree among college men) a social loss? Even when every
allowance is made for the valuable services rendered by unmarried graduates as teachers, physicians, scientists, social
workers and, indeed, in almost every field of social importance,
it would seem that the loss to society is real. These college
women, sifted again and again in the long years of their
education, represent real intellectual ability and probably
other gifts as well. By all the laws of heredity, at least a
portion of their talents should be inherited by their children.
But even if the transmission of intellectual gifts from parents
to offspring appears at times not to conform wholly to Men-
delian laws, the *social heredity* of the children of college women
is in most instances superior to that afforded by mothers of
inferior education. College-bred mothers not only have the
broader interests and knowledge that are the fruit of liberal
education but they would naturally tend to surround their
children with cultural influences, forming their tastes and
interests according to relatively high standards.

The causes of the small proportion of marriages of college
women are many and various. There is a powerful trend
among graduates in the direction of seeking paid employment

and this may have an unfavorable effect upon marriage in several ways.   In the first place young persons who leave home to take up work in cities where they have few if any acquaintances are frequently shut off from social contacts with congenial individuals of the opposite sex.   This social isolation of educated young women, earning their living in large cities where neighborliness is all but unknown, is a genuine obstacle to marriage as Paul Popenoe has pointed out more than once.[1]   Then, too, young women who achieve success in an occupation well suited to their abilities and challenging their interest think twice before giving up financial and personal independence, as well as absorbing work, to marry and take up domestic duties, together with the responsibility of making the husband's limited income support two or more.   Another reason for the low marriage rate among college women is no doubt to be found in the high ideals of love and the marriage relationship many of them cherish, as well as the exacting standards they hold with regard to men they are willing to marry.   Probably, also, these women are quite astute enough to know that the men who desire them in marriage by no means think of them as *individuals* in the same sense as men, with ideas and abilities worthy of respect and consideration.   Too many men today (as always) regard women almost solely as potential wives and mothers, not as developed persons whose ideas and practical proposals on important issues are worthy of serious consideration.   Finally, it must be remembered that it takes two to make a marriage and the onus of responsibility for low marriage rates cannot be laid wholly on women's shoulders.   A considerable proportion of young men discover that bachelor life can be made very comfortable as well as very free in modern cities.   Even under the changed conditions of modern life young women accept in general the convention that the man must take the initiative in asking a mate.   Therefore, it is not surprising to hear college women, reproached by eugenists and social writers for their low ratio of marriages,

[1] See *Jour. of Social Hygiene* (April, 1932), pp. 218–224 .

indignantly replying: "The authors of such articles do not suggest — I have never seen one that did — that a woman cannot marry alone nor even produce children by herself."

The Problem of the Birth Rate and Birth Control. — Regard for the individual and his right to a full and satisfying life has played a considerable rôle in the declining birth rates so conspicuous in every advanced country in the world. It is precisely in the most civilized nations, where respect for personality has developed farthest and an intelligent foresight into the consequences of impulsive action is encouraged, that the birth rates are most depressed. In the United States the birth rate [1] remained fairly high up to 1915. In that year the rate for the registration area [2] was 25.1. During the next ten years the birth rate fell steadily until in 1925 it was 21.5. In 1932 the rate had fallen to the low level of 17.3 — a decline of 4.2 in seven years. The rural birth rate has always been markedly higher than the urban but the disparity between the two is decreasing. In 1932 the birth rate in American cities was 16.3 and in rural areas 18.3.[3]

Even sharper have been the declines in the birth rate in certain countries of Europe. In the year 1929 the rate in England and Wales had fallen to 16.3 and in 1933 it had reached a record low of 14.4.[4] Other European countries with markedly depressed provisional birth rates are shown on page 506.[5]

With a very few exceptions it is precisely the countries least advanced in an economic sense and most backward (up to very recent times) in bringing education within the reach of the mass of the population that have the highest birth rates. Economic retardation and popular unenlightenment are the chief

---

[1] The birth rate represents the number of births per 1000 of the population.

[2] *New York Times*, Jan. 25, 1934.

[3] Bureau of the Census, *Provisional Figures for Live Births* . . . (1932).

[4] *New York Times*, Jan. 25, 1934.

[5] Figures furnished by the courtesy of Louis I. Dublin, statistician of the Metropolitan Life Ins. Co.

sources of high birth rates.   The rates for the selected countries
are as follows : [1]

COUNTRY	BIRTH RATE	YEAR
Sweden	14.5	1932
France	17.3	1932
Germany	15.1 [2]	1932
Switzerland	16.8	1932
Norway	16.7	1931
Denmark	18.0	1932
Belgium	17.5	1932

COUNTRY	BIRTH RATE	YEAR
Russia	44.4	1927
Portugal	34.2	1925
Roumania	34.1	1927
Japan	32.2	1931
Spain	28.3	1932
Italy	25.2	1929

The birth rate in Italy has been falling gradually but with
much steadiness for two decades (save in the war period 1916–
1919), and this despite a determined crusade waged by the
Italian government in recent years to increase the number of
births in that impoverished country.   A falling birth rate is in
opposition to the Fascist philosophy of a powerful state, well
equipped with man-power to be used in times of war.   Therefore a few years ago the government offered a bonus of from
200 to 400 lire ($10.50–$21.00 when the dollar was at par) to
each family having *eighteen* children.   Later the necessary
number of offspring was reduced to twelve and more recently

[1] Registrar-General's Statistical Review of England and Wales.   London,
1931.   Foreign Rates, p. 118.   Russia's birth rate was secured from the *New
York Times*, February 22, 1931, the rates for Japan and Spain through the
courtesy of the Metropolitan Life Insurance Co.
[2] Exclusive of the Saar region.

to ten. Names of families writing to the authorities to claim the bonus are published in the daily newspapers as a mark of honor.[1] On December 20, 1933, ninety-two "champion mothers," who have borne 1288 children (an average of 14 apiece), made a visit to Rome at the expense of the state to celebrate "Mothers and Infants Day," one of Italy's most important national holidays. In the capital city they were accorded the honor of a reception by Mussolini himself. It is an ironically amusing fact that the expense of transporting these poor, working-class mothers and entertaining them in Rome was met out of funds raised by means of a bachelors' tax on all young men over twenty-five who remain unmarried.[2] It is pertinent to ask whether the government efforts are crowned with success — are births increasing in Italy? Despite the privileges and honors accorded to parents with very large families the Italian birth rate had fallen to 23.8 in 1932 — a loss of nearly 3 points in four years.

The low French birth rate has likewise aroused the concern of the government and brought about the enactment in 1921 of drastic laws against the sale of birth control literature or the dissemination of any information concerning the prevention of conception. Even the *favorable discussion* of birth control has been made illegal! For many years France has had a practically stable population. In 1930 there was an excess of births over deaths of 19,000; whereas in 1931 there was an excess of deaths of 34,679.[3] It is highly probable that this stabilized population has been one of the important factors in the relative prosperity of the French people during the prolonged period of economic depression through which the world is passing. The full force of this depression was not felt in France much before 1933.

When considering the lowered birth rates in Europe and America it is well to keep carefully in mind the fact that national death rates have likewise been falling. This means that

---

[1] *Birth Control Review*, Feb. 1929.   [2] *New York Times*, Dec. 21, 1933.
[3] *New York Times*, July 26, 1931.

the rate of natural increase of the population [1] has not fallen
so sharply as has the birth rate.   For example, England and
Wales, with a birth rate in 1929 of 16.3 and a death rate of
13.4, had a rate of population increase of 2.9 per 1000 or 290 per
100,000.   In 1933 both the birth rate and death rate had fallen
and the natural increase was 2.1.   England and Wales, then,
still have a growing population and so has Scotland ; but it is
to be expected that Great Britain, like France, will reach a
stabilized population in the near future.   So, likewise, with the
United States.   In 1932 the birth rate for the 44 states and the
District of Columbia, included in the birth registration area,
was 17.3 and the mortality rate in the death registration area
was 10.9, which means that this country had a rate of natural
increase in 1932 of 6.4 or 640 per 100,000 people.[2]   This
represents a fairly large annual population increment.   But
it should be understood that the United States has not a
"balanced" population, in other words, one in which the persons of fertile age are in the standard ratio to other elements.
Owing to an enormous immigration to this country of young
men and women accustomed to the large families of eastern,
south-eastern and central Europe, the population has been
thrown out of balance and the natural increase is greater than
it would have been without immigration.   According to the
estimate of Louis Dublin, if allowance be made for the large
proportion of women of fruitful age in the United States, the
population approached stabilization in 1930.   Owing to the
fact that Congress has enacted a series of statutes since 1921
which have drastically curbed immigration to this country, the
population unbalance will probably be rectified before many
years have passed.   The United States will then join France,

[1] This represents the difference between the birth rate and the death
rate.

[2] The birth and death registration areas include those states which keep
careful registers of births and deaths.   The birth registration area includes
about 94.7 per cent of the national population and the death registration area
approximately 96.3.   Figures are taken from the census reports of 1931 and 1932,
the statistics for the latter year being provisional.

Great Britain, Sweden and other countries which have reached practically stabilized populations.

Is this to be regretted? In the opinion of many thoughtful students of population problems a stable population is a boon and not a curse. Professor East has estimated on the basis of all available data that the population of the world doubled in the one century from 1800 to 1900.[1] At this rate there would be "standing-room only" on the earth in a few centuries. Moreover the food resources of our planet are definitely limited and even with progress in the reclamation and improvement of arable land these resources cannot be stretched to feed billions more people. Population crowding and inadequate food resources are the fertile causes of extreme poverty, malnutrition, disease, famine and pestilence. Nature removes the surplus populations of China and India by cruel means; and although Japan, by the application of Western science, has been able to prevent the most spectacular and terrible consequences of a high birth rate and a surplus population in a small insular country, yet millions of Japanese farmers and laborers are eking out a bare existence today at a dangerously low level. During the prolonged economic crisis of the last four and one half years, with its accompanying unemployment and widespread distress, there can be no question that the constantly falling birth rates in many countries have prevented in considerable measure even more acute and general suffering. From these briefly sketched points of view, then, low birth rates have been a wholly beneficent influence.

But the crux of the birth rate problem lies not so much in decreasing populations as in *the differential birth rate*. In other words, the lowest birth rates are found among the most educated and gifted groups, and, conversely, the highest rates exist among the impoverished and poorly educated millions of unskilled and semi-skilled labor. A recent English study of the number of births per 1000 married males under 55 years disclosed that births among dock laborers were 231, among

[1] *Mankind at the Crossroads* (1923), pp. 66–67.

510 A History of Marriage and the Family

earthenware makers were 181 and among costers and hawkers
were 175. On the other hand, the births per 1000 among
physicians were 103, among clergymen of the Anglican Church
101 and among solicitors (lawyers) 100. American statistics
are no more reassuring. Recent data show that about 60 per
cent of Smith College alumnæ were married in 1931 and there
were 1.61 children per married alumna.[1] Of 4008 alumnæ of
Barnard College, 46.9 per cent were married in 1930. If the
graduates who had been out of college ten years or less were
eliminated the percentage rises to 56. The average number of
children per marriage, including graduates up to 1929, is only
1.2.[2] At Vassar the percentage of married alumnæ had risen
in 1931 from 53.2 for the classes 1892 to 1896 to 72.5 for the
classes 1912–1916. Also the average number of children per
marriage had risen from 1.9 for the classes 1892 to 2.2 for the
classes of 1907 to 1911.[3] Obviously the alumnæ of our
eastern women's colleges are not reproducing themselves, even
when allowance is made for the fact that not all families
included were completed. A similar situation is disclosed in
Cattell's investigation of 643 men of science. Of the men who
were married in this group and whose families were complete
the average number of children was 2.25.[4] Ross and Baber's
study of middle class completed families disclosed that, when
infertile families were included, the number of children was
2.81 per marriage.[5] Statisticians hold that, taking into consideration existing marriage and death rates, 3.7 children per
married couple are needed to reproduce the parents.

If the views of psychologists and eugenicists be accepted
that a great preponderance of mental ability is found in the
professional and higher business classes the fact that educated

[1] Smith College Quarterly, July, 1931, p. 408.
[2] Barnard Alumnae Register, 1930.
[3] Vassar Alumnae Quarterly, May, 1931.
[4] "Families of American Men of Science," Scientific Monthly, Vol. IV, March,
1917, pp. 254–255.
[5] "Changes in the Size of American Families in One Generation," University
of Wisconsin Studies in the Social Sciences, No. 10, 1924.

and gifted men and women are not reproducing themselves is a fact of grave social significance. In the words of Professor Cattell, with reference to American men of science and their small families, "The loss to the welfare of the nation and the world from the supression of the social traditions and the germ-plasm [of these gifted men] is incalculable. Until democratic society learns that services for society must be paid for by society and that the two most important services are scientific research and the bearing and rearing of children, the universities, on which three fourths of our scientific men depend for support, have great responsibilities." [1] Clearly Professor Cattell believes that larger families among talented and highly educated men and women are of such great social value that society should make it financially possible for such married individuals to have sufficient offspring at least to ensure that the parental strains will not die out. Eugenicists are even now interested in the question as to whether family allowances might not well be paid to families of healthy stock and high mental and social qualities to make more certain the continuance of those stocks. Before embarking on such a policy thoughtful consideration might well be given to certain questions that intrude themselves. First, have we yet developed any accurate measure of the *innate* ability of the working classes, handicapped as they are by low incomes, poor housing, often in slum neighborhoods, and sometimes by positive malnutrition? Terman, in his studies of "genius" in California school children, found 20.4 per cent of highly gifted children among the wage-earning group. Is it not probable that *if the environmental conditions had not been weighted against this class* it would have made a better showing? *Intelligence tests still test unequals.* Secondly, society surely finds other qualities valuable besides high intellectual ability, — such traits as regard for the common good, mutual helpfulness, willingness to coöperate, and common honesty, which have not markedly distinguished the influential business class in the past as the

[1] *Op. cit.*, p. 257.

revelations concerning the conduct of big industries, banking and the stock exchanges, published during the last four years, have made plain. Thirdly, is enough known of heredity confidently to infer that the child of a college graduate or even of a man of science will be a superior citizen to the child of a skilled mechanic? These and other considerations should give us pause before embarking on a policy of paying family allowances to the educated class to the exclusion of the poor and under-privileged.

Birth Control. — It is generally agreed that the most important cause of the declining birth rate is the practice of contraception among the intelligent and informed social classes. Hitherto the laws enacted in many lands, *e.g.*, England and the United States, have retarded the fall of the birth rate. In this country a Federal obscenity act was passed in 1873, owing to the influence of Anthony Comstock, founder of the Society for the Suppression of Vice, which included under the category of "obscene" all devices designed to prevent conception and all literature which described these contraceptives and advised concerning their use. This act of Congress prohibited the circulation through the mails of contraceptive material and literature thereon and a later act applied the prohibition to all common carriers. The states of the Union have very generally followed the lead of the Federal government in laying some prohibition upon the sale, advertisement or transportation of contraceptive literature and devices. But so beneficial to individuals and families has been the practice of birth control, making possible, as it does, the 'spacing' of children in the interest of the mother's health, as well as the limitation of the family to the purchasing power of its income, that it has proved impossible to prevent the dissemination of birth control information from reaching large numbers of people. Birth Control Leagues have been organized in this and other countries to educate public opinion in behalf of contraception, to bring about the repeal of the anti-birth control laws, and to establish clinics wherein scientific advice on prevenception can be given patients. In the United States 144 of these clinics have been established in the last few years,[1] operating ostensibly within state laws that have been considerably relaxed. No great prophetic insight is required to foresee the time, in both Great Britain and America, when the laws now operating to prevent the dissemination of birth control information, as well as the sale of tested devices, will be wiped off the statute books and will give place to competently staffed clinics, where every citizen may learn to limit his family in accordance with the dictates of health, family budgets and child welfare.

The Question of Sterilization. — Within the last twenty-five years society has gradually awakened to a more adequate realization of the enormous social costs involved in permitting unrestricted propagation among the congenitally feeble-minded, epileptics and the hereditary insane. The Reports of the Bureau of the Census, as well as the Reports on Mental Patients in State Hospitals and Reports on the Feeble-Minded and Epileptics in State Institutions,[2] for the years 1923, 1926, 1927 and 1928 all show an alarming increase in the number of such patients in institutions. In the year 1880 the number of mental patients in State Hospitals per 100,000 of the population was 63.7. In 1910 this number had risen to 173; and in 1930 to 236.1 — an increase of 36.4 per cent in twenty years, and of 270 per cent in fifty years! The ever-increasing number of feeble-minded and epileptics in state institutions is likewise far from reassuring. In 1922 these patients numbered 39.9 per 100,000 population; in 1929 the ratio had risen to 53.2, an increase of 33.3 per cent in five years.[3] Doubtless part of this alarming growth in numbers may be explained by the increasing tendency to commit the feeble-minded and insane to institutional care, but this will hardly account for the enormous increases recorded. Hardly less disturbing to

---

[1] See *Birth Control Review*, Dec. 1933, p. 3.

[2] These are published by the United States Dept. of Commerce.

[3] See *Birth Control Review*, April, 1933, pp. 94, 95, where the figures are conveniently assembled.

students of society are the ever-mounting costs of maintaining these social inadequates in public institutions. The total expense of maintenance in state hospitals for mental patients rose from $75,154,424 in 1922 to $105,733,982 in 1930; while the cost in state institutions for the feeble-minded and epileptics mounted from $18,114,177 in 1922 to $23,812,303 in 1928.[1]

In view of these facts it is not surprising that the theory has gained ground among intelligent people that society should take steps to prevent propagation among the obviously unfit. Segregation of the feeble-minded, epileptic and mentally diseased has been tried out in America to a greater extent than in any other country. But such a method is hopelessly inadequate to prevent multiplication of the socially unfit, since it is quite impossible to segregate all of them. Therefore, the policy of sterilization, with the primary purpose of race improvement, has been gaining adherents in this country for a generation past. The first sterilization law was passed by the legislature of Indiana in 1907; and since that time sixty-three different laws have been enacted in the United States. At the present writing twenty-six states have operative sterilization laws; four states — New York, New Jersey, North Carolina and Nevada — have enacted statutes which are not now in force; and the remaining eighteen states have taken no action regarding sterilization.[2] The laws of the twenty-six states which have legislated in some instances provide for sterilization of hardened criminals and the venereally diseased as well as of mental defectives.

It was not to be expected that such drastic legislation would pass unchallenged. Cases have been carried to the supreme courts of eighteen states. In nine instances the state sterilization laws have been declared unconstitutional on the ground that they infringe the Fourteenth Amendment of the Federal

---

[1] See *Birth Control Review*, April, 1933, pp. 94, 95, where the figures are conveniently assembled.

[2] E. A. Whitney, M.D. "Selective Sterilization," in *Birth Control Review*, April, 1933, p. 35.

Constitution in that they deny "due process of law" and "equal protection of the laws" to all people; and, further, because the surgical operation is "a cruel and unusual punishment" which violates the respective state constitutions. On the other hand, in nine instances the acts have been upheld by state courts as constitutional. In 1927 the Federal Supreme Court held unequivocally in the Buck *vs.* Bell case that the Virginia law, authorizing the sterilization of mental defectives and other unfit persons, *under careful safeguards*, is not a violation of the Fourteenth Amendment of the Constitution. Since that famous decision was rendered several new sterilization laws have been enacted and the supreme courts of Kansas and Idaho have upheld the legality of their state laws.

Since the Indiana law was enacted in 1907, 16,066 sterilization operations have been legally performed in the United States up to January 1, 1933. The state having the largest total of sterilizations is California with a record of 8504. In this state the rights of the individual are carefully safeguarded. After a competent State Board of Eugenics has declared that a mental defective (or other socially unfit person) in a state institution should be sterilized, a copy of the order must be sent to the legal guardian or known next of kin of the patient. By law the order must set forth the grounds on which sterilization is recommended and give notification that the patient or his representative has the right to appeal to the courts. If no relative or guardian is known, notice and copies must be sent to the Public Defender of the county from which the patient was committed and it shall be his duty to protect the interests of the patient. If no Public Defender exists in the said county the Board must ask a Judge of the Superior Court to appoint a guardian for this purpose. If the relative, legal guardian, Public Defender or court-appointed guardian shall consent in writing to the operation as ordered by the Board, the operation shall take place at such time as the superintendent of the institution in charge of the patient shall designate. The right of the patient or his representative to select a competent physician of his own choice and at his own expense is also safeguarded. If no such choice is made the operation is performed by a member of the medical staff of the institution to which the patient has been committed.

The enlightened law of California was not drawn until an extended study of sterilization laws and court decisions in other states had been made and not until many consultations with medical superintendents of state institutions in California had been held. This careful procedure is in striking contrast with the arbitrary law recently enacted in Germany under National-Socialist rule. By the terms of this act 1700 "hereditary health courts" are to be set up throughout the country, consisting of one judge and two physicians. Physicians must report to these courts all cases which come to their attention of persons suffering from the nine diseases confidently designated in the law as "hereditary." In addition all patients in state institutions afflicted with these diseases will become subject to sterilization. It is estimated that 400,000 persons, about equally divided between men and women, will undergo sterilization operations after January 1, 1934, when the law went into effect. The only limitation upon the arbitrary character of the law is the provision that a patient sentenced to sterilization may appeal to a "supreme hereditary health court," of which twenty-seven have been set up throughout the nation. From the judgment of this higher court there is no appeal. The individual must arrange for his own sterilization or be sterilized by force. The estimated cost of the 400,000 operations will be borne by the government insurance system and the German authorities hold that the expense will be negligible when compared with the enormous cost to the nation of caring for its social incompetents.[1] A sterilization bill, much less drastic in character is at present (March, 1934) under consideration by the British Parliament. Sweden, also, a country which has long provided for voluntary sterilization, is at present considering a compulsory law.

[1] See *New York Times*, Dec. 21, 1933.

PROBLEMS OF FAMILY RELATIONSHIPS

In an age of intense competitive effort like our own, characterized as it is by hurry, pressure and nervous tension, as well as by the breakdown of old beliefs and standards of action, it would be surprising if the family did not feel the full impact of these conditions. The relationships of the members of the family to each other are profoundly affected by the social milieu, not alone with respect to the economic, legal, educational, religious and social setting of life but with regard to the dominant ideas, modes of conduct and ideals of action that prevail in society. The family has been described as "a unit of interacting individuals," and the responses of its members to each other are conditioned not only by what goes on within the family but by what goes on outside. Each member is in reciprocal relationship with every other — husband with wife, mother and father with children, brothers and sisters with each other — and this interplay of personalities is made more complex in the degree in which the family has wide and vital contacts with the community.

In the past, when the family was patriarchal in character and the father a domestic monarch, there was little room for the opposition of points of view, the clashing of wills and interests that so frequently occurs in the contemporary family. Today the family approaches a democracy in type, wherein each member is recognized as an individual before the law whose rights are guaranteed against injustice, cruelty and exploitation. No doubt the family in olden times was more unified, since it expressed the will of one member — the father. It was also more simple in its personal relationships. But this relative unity and simplicity were purchased at the expense of the free development, the self-respecting independence of every family member except the husband and father. At present, our democratic family life has lost both stability and simplicity; but in it each member may grow into more complete realization of his personality.

Husband and Wife Relationships. — It can hardly be questioned that the relations of husband and wife could be made more harmonious if certain facts and conditions making for disharmony were better understood by the man and woman who start out to found a new family. To be forewarned of these possible difficulties is, in the case of intelligent persons, to be forearmed against them. What, then, are some of the more serious obstacles to the happy and successful interplay of the personalities of husband and wife within the family?

Needless to say, the most critical period of the new relationship of husband and wife is in its beginning. Both man and woman are trying to reorganize their personal lives and adjust them to a new set of circumstances, filled with emotional possibilities. In spite of all the love and good will the spouses may bring to their enterprise, harmonious adjustment can hardly be achieved without some clashing of opposed interests, desires and attitudes. No family, not even the most successful, escapes a minimum of conflict. Happy marriage is the *achievement* of two young persons who are willing to face realities and to effect working compromises; it is not tossed into their laps by the gods.

Among the difficulties that may be met in early married life which should be faced with intelligent understanding and good will, a few seem of outstanding significance. First, there is the danger that the daily intimacy of married life, in which every act and idea is shared, and in which there is little room for privacy, may prove irksome to one partner or to both. Husband and wife each needs a certain amount of independent life, a current of new experiences, not necessarily shared by the other, in order that he or she may have fresh interests and outlooks to bring back into their common life.

Mental hygienists and psychiatrists have recently pointed out another serious stumbling block to happy marital relationships, namely, the impulse of one mate to *look up to* or (more or less unconsciously) *look down upon* the other. The woman who begins her married life by an exaggerated admiration for her mate, a constant tendency to look up to him, will probably seek to build her personal life wholly around her husband, making all her thoughts, life interests, purposes and plans center in him. In consequence she will fail to grow into a strong and integrated personality, broad-minded, alert to the varied challenges of social life, and above all independent. So wholly may she identify her interests and her actions with those of her husband that he may tire of and even resent this self-subordination, this constant identification of his wife's life with his own. On the other hand, one spouse (more often the husband) may begin marital life with a feeling of superiority to his mate, a sense of his importance within the family as the income provider, of his wider and more realistic contacts with life outside the home — in a word he may tend to look down upon his wife. If the woman is intelligent, with a developed personality and tastes and interests of her own, this superior attitude of her husband will sooner or later become a fruitful source of friction.

A grave difficulty in the way of happy marital relationships is often found in the demand that marriage shall be an intensified romantic courtship. Wives are much more likely to make this mistake than husbands. The woman has enjoyed her courtship immensely; she has liked being the center of attention and eagerly pursued for her favors. Yet if she cannot face reality, if she cannot turn her back upon romantic glamour and accept a new relationship, intimate, deep and tender, but involving responsibilities and challenging self-control, she reveals herself as emotionally immature. She is holding on to an adolescent relationship instead of growing up to a new one demanding greater maturity of feeling and understanding of the demands life makes upon adults.

But there is another aspect of this question. However desirable it may be for a man and woman to pass on from the rosy yet somewhat unreal glamour of courtship to the deeper intimacy and responsibilities of marriage, it is not well that one spouse should "flatten out" and settle down into a tame routine, in which is no beauty, no adventure, no stimulating joy. This mistake is more likely to be made by the man than the woman and it may easily destroy satisfying relationships in marriage.

Another problem that will probably grow increasingly important as the years pass, is created by the desire of the wife to be gainfully employed outside the family. This desire may be motivated by the wish to add to the family income or by the longing to exercise her talents in a more stimulating field than is offered by domestic employments. But the wife's hope is often opposed to a fixed pattern of ideas formed in the husband's mind in his youth and which might be labeled "The man should support his wife" pattern. This dominating idea may be reënforced by a feeling of active dislike of his wife's financial independence, and by carking jealousy of her success if it be too pronounced. Instances where the wife has achieved a degree of financial success and social recognition not equaled by her husband are not altogether rare even now. Unquestionably, here is a fruitful source of conflict in personal relationships, and it can only be met by fair-minded consideration on the part of husband and wife of all aspects of the case and the attempt to reach a compromise satisfactory to both if possible.

Psychiatrists today have much to say of certain "mind sets" or mental patterns which exercise a very real effect upon the actions and reactions of the members of a family group. Among these so-called "mental mechanisms" might be mentioned certain personal habits and mannerisms of which one person may be quite unconscious but which serve as a constant, daily irritant to the other. Habits of snuffling, tapping, eating soup noisily, mannerisms of language or conduct or dress, may prove rasping to the souls of others, and, although minor sources of family friction, may prove in the end very disturbing to successful relationships. To these mental patterns may be added forms of thinking, judging and emotional response that a man or woman may never have noticed in his mate before marriage but which serve as constant sources of irritation in the revealing intimacy of marriage. Sometimes frank discussions of these unconscious habits help one spouse or the other to become aware of them and to attempt to modify or eliminate them.

Then, too, there are emotional complexes which, if firmly fixed in the personality of one or both partners, may cause endless harm in the interplay of personalities. One or the other partner may enter marriage the victim of deeply engrained fears — fear of sex relationships, fear of pregnancy, fear of being inadequate to the demands of marriage. Or the emotional complex may take the form of a haunting feeling of inferiority, a sense that one is incapable of meeting the challenges and strains of life, that one compares unfavorably with one's mate, and, indeed, with most other people as well. A person crippled by persistent feelings of inferiority fears and resents the most well-meant criticism, is constantly on the lookout for slights, and is always trying to say or do something to win admiration from others and thus allay the ever-present sense of being inadequate and inferior. It is not difficult to comprehend how such a "mental mechanism" might interfere at every point with happy family relationships. The origin of the complex goes back probably to circumstances in early childhood or youth; the feeling was not detected and wisely dealt with by parents and teachers in time to prevent its becoming a fixed mind set.

Another emotional habit which strikes at the very roots of successful family life is jealousy. Like feelings of inferiority, this trait was probably acquired in childhood and was not wisely treated before it became deeply fixed in the personality. Jealousy is generally regarded as one of the meanest of all human traits and one of the most destructive of marital relationships. All of us have seen painful displays of this emotional habit which may show itself in husband or wife, brothers or sisters, without regard to sex. Like romantic day-dreaming after marriage, jealousy is an example of emotional immaturity. The man who sulks because his wife receives marked attentions at a dinner-party, the woman who cannot bear to see her husband enjoy talking with another woman, simply have not grown up emotionally. Their emotional development was arrested at the level of the child or the adolescent; and only if they can be led to perceive and admit this fact and to make a brave fight to weaken the hold of this emotional habit is there much hope that happy relationships may be established within the family.

Among the many mental complexes that disturb husband and wife relationships, none is more menacing than the so-called "parent-fixation." The term is, of course, applied to a fixed trait of dependency upon one or the other parent to whom the offspring is deeply and sometimes exclusively devoted. In the case of the husband his love of his mother may interfere with normal hetero-sexual love and, indeed, may render it forever impossible. The person afflicted with a mother-fixation — and this trait is more commonly found in men than in women — is always seeking comfort, sympathy and active help from his mother in meeting the hard spots of life. He cannot face reality and overcome difficulties because he has never been trained to do so. He is forever comparing his wife with his mother to the disadvantage of the former. The woman linked to such a man soon finds she has married a dependent weakling, who takes all his worries and defeats to his sympathizing mother and who is forever trying to change his wife into the beloved image of his mother. Needless to say, the mother is probably chiefly responsible for the dependency of her son by her failure to help him conquer difficulties in his boyhood. She is likewise responsible for his exclusive devotion to her, by reason of the fact that she showed too fond and possessive a love of her son in his boyhood years and claimed too much of his time and affection. In marriages where one member has a mother-fixation, harmonious relationships are fatally handicapped. Only when the dependent member has been led to face this trait, to acknowledge it and to struggle against its habitual manifestations whenever they appear is there much hope of happy family life.

Family finances may be the fountain-head of grave difficulties between husband and wife. If one mate tends to be extravagant while the other is cautious and thrifty, this situation may easily eventuate in bitter charges of miserliness on the one side and of selfish squandering on the other, until daily life is punctuated with these acrid recriminations and marital happiness flies out of the window. No marriage should ever be entered upon without the fullest and frankest discussion of questions of family financing, with honest admissions on the part of one or both fiancés of faults of extravagance or undue frugality. An engaged couple would do well to agree upon some method of income-apportionment between husband and wife long before the wedding day, and also firmly resolve to keep a careful family budget.

These are only a few of the obstacles in the way of successful husband and wife relationships that must be taken into consideration when young people fall in love and start out on that honorable and difficult enterprise of founding a family. Young men and women should have these stumbling-blocks called to their attention and explained both in their origin and consequences. Only by letting in the light into hitherto dark places of personality and family life can this generation hope to improve the personal relationships of family members and thus increase their happiness and content.

Parent-Child Relationships. — The day has passed when intelligent parents take it for granted that biological parenthood carries with it the wisdom and skill to bring up children successfully. The constant increase in scientific knowledge about physical and mental growth of children, their behavior problems and possible "complexes," together with the steady decline of belief in parental instinct as an infallible guide in the upbringing of the young, have been responsible for such a movement for parent education as the world has never seen before. Psychology teaches and parents are coming to believe that the emotional patterns of the adult are laid down early in the life of the child and therefore the experiences and relationships in the home in the first six years of life may make or mar the small boy or girl on whom the parents' hopes are fixed.

Only a few of the ways in which well-meaning parents may spoil their relationships with their children and, even more regrettably, mar the developing characters of their offspring can be briefly considered here. Parents who are absorbed in each other to such an extent that they forget the "mothering" and cuddling that their children — all children — need may awake some day to a realization that they have a "difficult" child in the home, jealous, sullen and resentful. On the other hand, too possessive and absorbing a love for a child on the part of a parent — usually the mother — will create family difficulties of a different sort. The husband and father may develop a lively jealousy of his child if he is made to feel after its birth — as not rarely he is — that the advent of the baby has drastically altered his intimate relationship with his wife, that he no longer holds first place in her affections but has been relegated to a subordinate position. But this is not all. The wealth of love the mother pours upon her child may be accompanied by a hungry possessiveness and an anxious desire to spare him every unhappy and difficult experience in life that may result in implanting in the child a "mother-fixation." Such a complex may forever prevent his developing into a free, self-reliant personality or "falling in love" in a normal, natural way. These emotionally possessive mothers (less often fathers) encourage a favorite child to bring all his little difficulties to them to be resolved and so implant in the child's nature the seeds of dependence and inability to cope with reality that in the years to come will permanently undermine his character. Occasionally the relationship of father and daughter may take on the same character with the same deplorable results. The personality of the child in such instances has been "devoured" by the doting parent.

As Professor Groves has so convincingly shown, some parents fail to grow up emotionally and visit upon their luckless children the infantile expressions of feeling which they have never learned to control. In the words of Groves: "The parent who is himself a child storms and bosses, praises extravagantly, and in the same measure scolds, teases, hugs, spanks, and ignores his offspring in whirlwind pace, until the only thing the youngster is sure of is he never knows what is coming next, but that there will be plenty of it." [1] Needless to say such emotional infantilism does not furnish the soil for happy parent-child relationships grounded in mutual affection, respect and confidence.

Among the most deep-seated of our human impulses is the desire to make an impression on others, to command attention and hold the center of the stage. Sensible persons learn fairly early in life to curb this impulse to "exhibitionism," but this does not hold true of young children, who will go to great lengths to center the interest of adults — especially parents — on themselves. If such a tendency is not understood and given wise treatment by parents, a child may go far toward destroying peace and harmony in the home.

A case in point [2] is that of a small boy about three years old who had developed the habit of throwing himself on the floor and indulging in a temper tantrum whenever his wishes were crossed in the slightest respect. Any adult who has seen a child in such a temper, kicking, screaming at the top of his lungs and finally holding his breath until he grows purple in the face, will comprehend the alarm felt by the parents of this human mite. Although they tried to refrain from yielding to the child's demands until he resorted to holding his breath, they capitulated at that point and gave the boy what he wanted. Finally, in sheer desperation, the unhappy parents took their son to a nursery school and explained the situation, saying that the child was spoiling their home. The father, an

---

[1] *The Drifting Home*, p. 157.
[2] Told the writer by the manager of a large nursery school.

army officer, told the head teacher that he had spanked the boy to cure him of tantrums until he " didn't dare spank him any more." Properly shocked, the teacher explained that the father's method was probably the worst he could have used and suggested that the child be placed in the nursery school. The parents gladly consented and the small son was brought to the school the next day. At first he was quiet and a little shy, but was finally drawn into the activity of a group of his own age. It was not long before something went wrong and the child threw himself on the floor, screaming and kicking. Quietly the teacher withdrew the children to another part of the room and the play went on. No one looked at the raging boy on the floor and when he played his last card and held his breath until his face turned a purplish red, even then no one seemed interested or concerned. The teacher knew well that no child will hold his breath to the point of suffocation. After a considerable time, during which the boy made all the noise he could, he gradually calmed down and finally turned on his side and watched the children building a railroad. Soon the teacher drifted over to him and quietly asked if he would like to help. Hesitant at first, the boy finally joined the group and played quite happily. There were several more tantrums during the next few weeks, but they ceased when the child became convinced that he could not draw attention to himself that way. His was a clear case of exhibitionism; he would bear even severe spankings to have the alarmed attention of his parents centered on himself. The problem was explained to the relieved father and mother and it was suggested to them that, while they should not yield to the child during a tantrum, they might well give him more of their affection and companionship in his happy moments. Following this advice, the parents established a friendly comradeship with their small son whose temper-tantrums finally almost ceased.

Another question confronting parents is that of avoiding all well-founded causes of jealousy in children. An only child who has received all the care and affection of his parents should not be confronted with a "new" baby without careful preparation. A wise mother will tell the child of the expected advent of a baby brother or sister and try to enlist his interest in the newcomer and stir his desire to help and protect the helpless family member. Parents have been known actually to try to arouse a child's jealousy of a new baby for their own amusement. This is literally playing with fire, for jealousy, once implanted, is hard to uproot and may easily become a permanent trait of character taking ugly forms. For the same reason parents should carefully avoid showing favoritism toward one child in the family. The records of psychiatrists abound in instances of the harmful effects of this parental error, especially on the unfavored child, who may easily develop an inferiority complex to trouble his relations with his fellows as long as he lives.

This brief discussion of some of the difficulties met by parents in establishing happy relationships of trust and affection with their children is manifestly quite incomplete. Volumes could be written on this theme — and have been. But a few of the more common pitfalls have been indicated. These should not be unduly discouraging and alarming to those who may be parents in the future. Parent education is open to almost everyone today, and a generous seasoning of this stored wisdom with common-sense and humor adds greatly to its flavor and nutritive effects.

FREEDOM IN LOVE

The last twenty-five years have seen the formulation of a new theory of sexual and love relations — the outgrowth of the philosophy of individual freedom. The exponents of this view are perhaps more often than not thoughtful and educated persons who believe that the monogamic family, the ideal of western Christendom, is an outworn institution whose maintenance does more harm than good. These writers draw upon the historic mistakes and failures of monogamy to furnish

evidence for their position.   They show that *true* monogamy
has existed only in a fraction of marriages, since many men and
a few women in all ages have been unfaithful to their marriage
vows.   Furthermore, they produce concrete evidence that the
monogamic family has suppressed the rights and freedom of
individuals, especially of wives and children.   Pointing out
that one of the chief supports of monogamy has been economic,
they claim that this institution has repeatedly sacrificed the
happiness of sons and daughters to the maintenance or extension of the family estates.   They further maintain that the
ideal of pre-marital chastity, consistently held up by Christianity, although never satisfactorily enforced upon men, defeats its own end of a life-long union in marriage, since the lack
of sexual experience before wedlock is one of the chief causes
of marital unhappiness and divorce.

On the positive side these advocates of freedom in sex and
love relations declare that such freedom is the right of the
individual;   that suppression of all sexual impulses until persons are economically able to marry in the later twenties or
early thirties inflicts positive harm on young men and women,
being responsible for nervous tensions, maladjustment to life
and serious psychopathic conditions.   They claim that sexual
freedom would add to the joy of living, would decrease the
terrible possessiveness of sexual love as shown in marriages
past and present and would make it possible for young persons,
after sufficient experience in sex relations, to choose mates to
whom they were really adapted in temperament and, perhaps,
to enjoy those mates for many years, if not for life.

Like many exponents of a new way of life, the greatest
strength of this school of thinkers lies in indicating the weakness and defects of the older system.   It cannot be denied that
the charges brought against the monogamic family have been
true in the past and are true to a much less extent at present.
But the critics of monogamy overlook certain important
facts in regard to this long-lived institution.   In the first place
they ignore or minimize the fact that this type of family is a

product of social conditions and needs, that it has a very ancient history and that it tends to supplant, all over the civilized world, the polygamic family. With no intention of using the fallacious argument that because an institution is old it must therefore be useful, the writer would point out that so universal an institution as the monogamic family would not have survived so many millenniums, and would not have the strength it reveals at present if it did not meet certain deep human and social needs. Sexual desire is only one of the props of the family and possibly one of the less significant. Certain powerful impulses in human nature are inextricably intertwined with sexual love in most men and women. Such are the longing to make a home with one's mate, to rest on his or her affection and understanding, to enjoy mutual comradeship and, in most cases, to have children to link spouses more intimately together in the joys and responsibilities of parenthood. These impulses, although perhaps not so urgent and demanding as the sexual drive, are rooted deep in the natures of men and women and furnish solid support for the monogamic family. Under a régime of sexual freedom they would probably remain unsatisfied.

Another weakness in the position of the advocates of freedom in sex love is their very general failure to realize the essential services which the monogamic family has rendered to society. First of all it has furnished a stable abiding place for men and women to which they might return after the struggle and tension of the market-place, reasonably assured of finding understanding sympathy, affection and active helpfulness. Then, too, the family with all its faults has been and is immeasurably the best nursery and school for young children. Psychologists and mental hygienists alike tell us that childhood needs above all a sense of security, permanence and affection. This abiding sense the family furnishes in most instances — and it is indispensable to the normal development of the young. If sex relationships ever came to be looked upon as temporary, children would be the chief sufferers.

Uprooted from one home after another, expected to adjust to a new "parent" — father or mother — every few years or less, their condition would indeed be tragic.

But the attacks of individualism on the monogamic family probably need not be taken too seriously. Like religion, government and law, this age-old institution will survive the wholesome shocks it has received and emerge, it is to be hoped, in modified and more satisfying form. Already there are signs that young women are moving away from theories (and, in some instances, practices) of sexual individualism to a belief in the desirability of permanent marriage, homes that endure and children upon whom the interests and plans of parents may focus. Having swung far toward undisciplined freedom, the pendulum appears to be swinging back toward a modified form of mid-Victorianism. Ample evidence exists in the statements of young college women to the effect that marriage, home-making and children are experiences that they sincerely desire and do not intend to lose.

Although prophecy in these years of breath-taking social change is dangerous, it may not be too hazardous to venture the prediction that the monogamic family will live on into the future, despite its serious difficulties and its baffling problems of personal adjustment and will prove more satisfying to its members than it has been in past generations. Probably the last vestiges of father-power will disappear; women will much more generally continue in gainful employment after marriage, contributing their share to the family income; children, while assured of the heart-whole affection and concern of both parents, will spend more time with children of their own age in nurseries and nursery-schools — private and public — under the care of experts; and the family, having relinquished almost all of its ancient responsibilities, save the guidance of the young, will be held together chiefly by the strong ties of love, comradeship, respect for the personalities of its members and mutual helpfulness.

SELECTED READINGS

Cahen, Alfred. *Statistical Analysis of American Divorce*, Columbia University Press, 1932.

Caird, Mona. *The Morality of Marriage*, London, Geo. Redway, 1897, pp. 115–127, 138–156.

Calhoun, Arthur W. *A Social History of the American Family*, Arthur H. Clark Co., Cleveland, 1919, Vol. III, Ch. XIV.

Colcord, Joanna. *Broken Homes*, N. Y., Russell Sage Foundation, 1919.

Goodsell, Willystine. *Problems of the Family*, N. Y., The Century Co., 1928, Chs. VII–XII, XVI–XXIV.

Groves, E. R. *The Drifting Home*, Boston, Houghton Mifflin Co., 1926, Chs. IV, IX.

——. *The American Family*, Chicago and New York, Lippincott, 1934.

Groves, E. R. and Gladys. *Parents and Children*, Phila., Lippincott, 1928.

Groves, E. R., and Ogburn, W. F. *American Marriage and Family Relationships*, N. Y., Holt, 1928.

Key, Ellen. *Love and Marriage*, N. Y., Putnam, 1911, Chs. II, III.

Keyserling, Herman. *The Book of Marriage*, N. Y., Harcourt, Brace and Co., 1926, pp. 3–49.

Lichtenberger, J. P. *Divorce, a Social Interpretation*, N. Y. and London, McGraw Hill, 1931.

Lindsey, Benjamin B. *Revolt of Modern Youth*, N. Y., Boni and Liveright, 1925.

Lindsey, Benjamin B., and Wainwright, Evans. *Companionate Marriage*, N. Y., Boni and Liveright, 1927, Chs. VII, VIII, IX.

Lippman, Walter. *A Preface to Morals*, N. Y., Macmillan, 1929, Ch. XIV.

Richardson, F. H., M.D. *Parenthood and the Newer Psychology*, N. Y., Putnam, 1926, Chs. I, IV, VI, X.

Sapir, Edward. "What Is the Family Still Good For?" *American Mercury*, February, 1930, pp. 145–151.

Waters, Miriam. *Youth in Conflict*, N. Y., Republic Publishing Co., 1925, Chs. I, II, XIII.

——. *Parents on Probation*, N. Y., New Republic, Inc., 1927, Chs. I–V.

CHAPTER XIII

SOCIAL AID IN FAMILY CONSERVATION

THE CONTEMPORARY TREND TOWARD SOCIAL AID TO FAMILIES

During the last forty or fifty years it has been driven home to the minds of social workers and students of society that the family as an institution is not functioning successfully under the conditions of modern life. Our present economic system presses hard upon low paid laborers and even "white collar" workers, rendering it difficult for them to preserve the security and stability of their families. The entrance of married women into the field of gainful employment, whether of necessity or by choice, has tended in some instances to undermine parental authority, to create behavior problems in children and to encourage juvenile delinquency. Our modern pleasure philosophy, together with the current emphasis on freedom, independence, conservation of personal rights, have bred difficult problems of family relationships and even family preservation in many homes. The new light shed by child psychology, mental hygiene and psychiatry on the nature of the child and the basic importance of family guidance in the first years of life have brought home to at least some parents a deep realization of their need of education in fulfilling the responsibilities of parenthood. With the partial breakdown of ancient religious and moral beliefs and loyalties, the family not rarely finds itself adrift, without chart or compass, in a rapidly changing society that has abandoned many of the old standards of life and has as yet set up no new ones which command general allegiance.

For these and many other reasons the modern family is unstable, ill adjusted and in need of aid and support from the outside. So important to the state is this basic institution of society, serving, as it does, as the nursery and school of every new generation, that governments and social agencies have at last abandoned their ancient policy of leaving the family to shift for itself, and have awakened to its crucial need of various forms of social assistance. Some of the more influential modes of social aid in the interest of family conservation will be briefly considered in this chapter.

Forms of Economic Aid. — One of the most basic forms of family assistance is economic in character. Clearly the family cannot carry on successfully (if at all) without an income that assures at least the essentials of subsistence to its members. This assurance probably a million families have not had even in "prosperous" times; and in a period of economic collapse like the present nearly ten million families have felt the cruel effects of unemployment, with its stoppage of income and its accompanying anxiety, malnutrition, weakening of personal and family morale and, in many instances, family breakdown.

What have governments done to relieve the family of crushing economic pressure threatening its very existence? As yet it may frankly be admitted that little has been accomplished relative to the need. To be sure some American states have enacted *minimum wage laws*, and the Federal government has included such laws in most of the industrial codes, newly adopted under the NRA. But these agreements fix minimum wages at amounts varying between $11 and $15 in the case of unskilled or semi-skilled labor. Clearly little or no account is taken of family necessities in fixing wages under the codes. Moreover, these minimum wages tend to become rather generally maximum wages in low-paid industries. Laws have also been enacted in many European countries, and later in some states of America, providing for *workmen's compensation, old age pensions*, and, outside of the United States, for *unemployment insurance*. These enactments have aided in steering the family ship over the dangerous rapids caused by industrial accidents and sickness as well as by loss of steady employment. The United States, which embarked on its prolonged period of economic slump with a fixed belief that unemployment insurance was a "dole," breaking down personal initiative and self-respect, has been slowly changing its attitude during four years of undisguised charity in the form of "hand-outs" of food, clothing and money. In countries like Great Britain and Germany, where unemployment insurance is firmly established, a large proportion of the workers who receive this assistance have contributed to the insurance fund which helps to support them and their families. Therefore, it may truly be said that the "dole," in its real meaning, has flourished chiefly in our own country during the past few years of widespread economic distress. At present signs are not lacking that America has learned its lesson and that one state after another will enact statutes providing for some form of compulsory unemployment insurance in the near future. Wisconsin led the way in enacting such a law in 1932 and reports favorable to the passage of such laws have been made to the legislatures of several states by commissions appointed to study the question.

Sickness and Maternity Insurance. — Beginning in 1883 when a national sickness insurance law was passed in Germany, one European country after another has enacted laws providing for compulsory or voluntary insurance of workers against sickness. Up to 1930 the countries which had placed such legislation on the statute books included Austria-Hungary, Denmark, Belgium, Great Britain, the Netherlands, Russia, Roumania, Sweden, Switzerland, Jugo-Slavia, Czechoslovakia, Luxemburg, Greece and France. In certain countries, as Germany, Great Britain and Austria, sickness insurance is a *compulsory* measure; in other countries, as Belgium and Denmark, it is *voluntary*. The funds in many cases are provided by contributions from employers and employed; in other instances by employers, employees and the State. State grants to insurance funds are made in Great Britain, Denmark, Norway, Sweden and certain cantons of Switzerland.[1]

Significant as a sign of the heightened concern of modern states for the welfare of the family is the inclusion of *maternity insurance* in most systems of national sickness insurance. In Italy and Spain,[2] laws providing for maternity insurance were enacted without provision for national sickness insurance. The benefits included under maternity insurance vary in different countries. By the terms of France's recently enacted social insurance law,[3] an insured working woman or the wife of an insured man is entitled to the same *medical aid*, during pregnancy and for six months after childbirth, as is provided for the sick. This includes treatment by a physician, medicine, therapeutical appliances, hospital care and surgical care. In addition a *cash benefit* amounting to a fixed proportion of her weekly wage is paid the mother for six weeks before and after childbirth on condition that she give up her regular employment. Furthermore, a woman who nurses her child is entitled to a *nursing benefit*, varying from 50 to 150 francs a month and payable for a period of nine months. Finally, if the mother is incapacitated for work by pregnancy additional benefits will be paid for children under the age of 16 who are not employed. This enlightened law has been framed after a study of maternity benefit systems in other European countries and reflects the active concern of France since the World War to conserve the family and increase the national birth rate.

Maternity and Infant Welfare Legislation in the United States. — In the United States no national or state system of maternity insurance has been established. A step in that direction was taken in 1921 when "An Act for the Promotion of the Welfare and Hygiene of Maternity and Infancy" passed the Federal Congress. By the terms of the act (1) Federal

---

[1] H. J. Harris, "Maternity Benefit Systems in Certain Foreign Countries," Bureau Publications No. 57, 1919, U. S. Children's Bureau.

[2] By an act passed March 22, 1929.

[3] Passed in April, 1928, and put into effect in amended form, July 1, 1930.

financial aid would be furnished to states complying with certain conditions laid down in the law; (2) such moneys were to be applied to the reduction of maternal and infant mortality and to the protection of the health of mothers and infants; (3) the United States Children's Bureau was empowered to administer the act; (4) the states of the Union were vested with complete authority to initiate and administer their own plans to realize the ends of the Federal act, subject only to the approval of the Federal Board of Maternity and Infant Hygiene in Washington.   The act further provided that, beginning June 30, 1923, a Federal appropriation of $1,240,000 would be granted annually to the states *for five years*.   Of this amount $240,000 annually was to be granted outright and equally apportioned among the states; $240,000 additional was to be apportioned among those states that matched dollar for dollar the Federal allotment; and $710,000 was to be apportioned among the states on the basis of population if matched by an equal state appropriation.   To secure the benefits of the law the states should act through their legislatures by (1) formally accepting the provisions of the Federal act; (2) designating and setting up a state agency to carry out the purposes of the act and to submit detailed plans for realizing those ends to the Federal Board of Maternity and Infant Hygiene.   State agencies were further required to make such reports to the Children's Bureau concerning their operations and expenditures under the act as the Bureau might require.

By June 30, 1923, the legislatures of all the states had convened and forty commonwealths had accepted the provisions of the law, commonly known as the Sheppard-Towner Act. By 1927 forty-five states of the Union and the Territory of Hawaii had accepted the terms of the act and had appointed state agencies to carry out its provisions.[1]   So beneficial were the results of the Federal law that, at the close of the five-year period, ending in June, 1927, the life of the act was extended to

[1] *The Promotion of the Welfare and Hygiene of Maternity and Infancy*, Children's Bureau Publication, No. 194, p. 1, Washington, 1928.

June 30, 1929, when the law was repealed. It may be asked why so far-sighted and beneficent an act was ever rescinded. The answer appears to be that the United States is still a highly individualistic nation, fearful of laws and policies that have any tincture of so-called "socialism," and especially distrustful of legislation which would encroach on the ancient "privilege" of the family to struggle against heavy odds of poverty and sickness alone and unassisted.

Varied and valuable were the benefits conferred by the Sheppard-Towner Act prior to its repeal. They included circulation of literature on infant and pre-natal care; holding of conferences throughout the country; instruction of mothers in hygiene and nutrition; progress in the education of midwives (who deliver many foreign-born and negro women); better pre-natal care of mothers and post-natal care of both mothers and infants; the education of the public as to the possibilities and importance of public-health work for mothers and babies; the establishment of *permanent* pre-natal and child-health centers; and, best of all perhaps, a reduction of the national infant mortality rate[1] from 76 in 1922 to 65 in 1927 — a saving of 11,000 babies out of every 1,000,000 born. In 1932 this rate had fallen to 57.9. Less encouraging was the fall of the maternal mortality rate [2] which, for the United States, is one of the highest among civilized countries. However, this rate fell from 66.4 in 1922 to 64.7 in 1927.[3]

Mothers' Pensions and Mothers' Aid. — The movement in behalf of granting public funds to widowed mothers with dependent offspring marks a reaction of the public mind against the institutional care of young children. In America and a few other countries there has developed a growing conviction that even a doubtfully good home administered by a decent, affectionate mother is a better place to nurture children than a

---

[1] Deaths of infants under one year of age per 1000 live births in the birth-registration area.

[2] Deaths of mothers from childbirth or its after effects per 10,000 live births in the birth-registration area.

[3] See Children's Bureau Publication, No. 194, pp. 8–33.

public institution where life is regimented and the young may be deprived of all personal affection and understanding. This belief is reënforced by the testimony of physicians, psychologists and social workers, all to the effect that young children need nurturing love and the individual care and interest of a mother. The records of child asylums show a high mortality among babies and young children because of the absence of the motherly affection they so deeply need. In consequence, several countries have adopted systems of granting public funds to mothers in broken families who will remain at home and care for their children.

In the United States, the White House Conference called by President Roosevelt in 1909 to consider problems arising out of the care of dependent children led to the passage in 1911 of the first law for the payment of state funds to needy mothers in the state of Missouri. The act was at first limited in application because of a clause restricting its provisions to large population centers but the limitation was subsequently removed. Illinois was the first state to enact a state-wide "funds to parents" law in July, 1911. During the next fifteen years forty-two states, together with the Territories of Alaska and Hawaii, had fallen in line with similar legislation and in 1931 only two states — Georgia and South Carolina — had failed to enact laws providing state aid for needy mothers with dependent children.[1]

At first this form of public aid was called "widows' pensions" and was restricted in its application largely to widows by the laws of many states. But the constant tendency has been to broaden the scope of the acts by amendments and new legislation to include among the mothers eligible for assistance those whose husbands have deserted or are imprisoned, incapacitated (physically or mentally) or divorced. Thus an increasing number of families have benefited from the provisions of the state laws. By June 30, 1931, the laws of only two states restricted aid to widows, hence this type of family assistance is now generally known as "Mothers' Aid." In only ten states,

[1] *Mothers' Aid, 1931*, Bureau Publication No. 220, pp. 2–3.

however, may aid be granted to "any needy mother," married or single, although the laws of 10 other states are almost as liberal. Even expectant mothers are eligible for aid in 7 states and unmarried mothers have been made eligible by the laws of Michigan, Nebraska and Tennessee. Moreover, in 18 states the laws provide that the aid may be granted to persons other than the mothers, usually the guardian or other person standing in place of a parent.

In most states the laws provide that grants may be paid until the child is exempt from school attendance which means until he is 16 years of age in the majority of cases. But in 4 states and one city (St. Louis) the aid ceases when a child has reached 14 years. The *amount* of the grant varies in the different states. At first the general practice was to fix a definite sum as payable for each dependent child but that method was proved by experience to be a faulty one. It has come to be recognized that a policy of leaving the amount of the grant to the judgment of the agency administering the law has very distinct advantages. Yet only 11 states and the District of Columbia have included this flexible provision in their laws. Most states specify the maximum grant that may be paid monthly or weekly; and very generally the law provides a larger grant to the first child than to additional children. Taking a family of three children as a basis for comparison of the maximum monthly grants that may be given in the 33 states which limit aid to a definite amount per child, it is found that the sums range from $60 to $70 in 4 states down to $20 to $29 in 7 states. It will readily be seen that the latter amount is quite inadequate for the proper support of three young children and this statement holds true of the majority of limited state grants. In consequence, the chief purpose of mothers' aid laws — to provide sufficient income so that the mother may give up gainful employment and make a good home for her children — is partially defeated. In many instances, as the agency records show, mothers are forced to supplement grants in aid by working outside the home two or three days in every week.

During the year ending June 30, 1931, the amount spent for mothers' aid in 44 states and the District of Columbia was $33,885,487.36. The number of families aided per 10,000 of the population ranged from 24 in Wisconsin to 2 in North Carolina and 1 in Maryland. Obviously this wide variation cannot be accounted for by differences in necessity. It is probable that the need of family aid is not greatest in the states where the largest number of families receive assistance but in those less fortunate states where there is not much wealth and where the income level of the majority of the population is low. In these states (as well as in a few prosperous commonwealths like Pennsylvania) there are long lists of eligible families waiting for assistance.[1]

Outside the United States mothers' pensions are granted in Great Britain, certain Canadian provinces, New Zealand and Denmark. While the laws providing for mothers' allowances in Canada are flexible and the amount of the grants is determined by family need, the Danish and New Zealand acts definitely fix the amounts to be paid and limit the aid to widows. In 1925 Great Britain enacted a widows', orphans' and old-age contributory law which provided for the grant of weekly allowances to widows (or widowers) with dependent children and to orphans. The pensions are payable to the widow of a man insured under the National Health Insurance Act who had paid 104 contributions prior to his death after January 1, 1926, when the act went into effect. Grants are also made to the children of an insured man and to orphans who have lost both parents and are the offspring of an insured man or woman. The amounts of the pensions paid are ten shillings weekly [2] to widows, five shillings for the eldest child and three shillings for each additional child. Orphans and children removed from the mothers' custody receive seven shillings six pence (about $1.90 weekly) until they have reached fourteen and one half

---

[1] For the whole question of mothers' aid see the Children's Bureau Publication, No. 220, 1931.

[2] About $2.54 in terms of the present exchange.

years of age, or sixteen years if they are in regular attendance at a day school.

The funds to provide for these pensions are obtained by (1) compulsory weekly contributions from employed men and women and (2) contributions from the British treasury of £4,000,000 annually for the period of ten years. It will readily be seen that Great Britain is contributing more generously to widows' pensions *proportionately to her population*,[1] than are the states of the American Union, despite our richer resources.

Although the British Commonwealth of Australia has developed no system of mothers' pensions, a law of 1912 provides for a grant of £5 to be paid to all mothers, *married or unmarried*, who are residents of Australia and who give birth to a living child. In presenting the bill the prime minister declared that great care had been taken to avoid any stigma of charity attaching to the grant. He further stated that in his judgment it "is the duty of the community, and especially the duty of a national parliament, to protect every possible life." Such a measure is justified as "a provision for the safety of the State." The law provides that only one allowance will be paid for each confinement. In 1916–1917 the claims for payment of the state grant numbered 132,866 and the expense to the Australian Government was (in American money) $3,221,793. Students of the operation of this unique law declare that many well-to-do families fail to claim the grant. When compared with the benefits which accrue to a working-class mother in certain European countries before and after confinement, including medical, surgical and hospital care, maternity benefit payments and nursing benefits it is very doubtful that Australia's scheme of a lump payment at childbirth furnishes equal advantages.

The System of Family Allowances.— After the World War, when deprivation and misery were very general in working-

---

[1] The population of the British Isles is about 45,000,000; of the United States about 126,000,000.

class families, much interest was aroused in a few countries, notably Great Britain, France and Australia, in a proposed policy of paying a "living wage," or family wage, to workers. The unfavorable reaction of the constant struggle against poverty on the productivity of workers began to be recognized by large-scale employers. This fact, together with a growing realization of the falling national birth rates, drove some employers "to allow the question of the human needs of workers and their families to intrude itself into discussions about wages." Out of these discussions there emerged the two concepts of a "living wage" and of a "normal family." This typical family was regarded as one of five members, a father, mother and three children; and a "living wage" was conceived as one which would support in decency such a "standard family."

No sooner had these ideas been formulated, however, when investigations undertaken in Great Britain, France and the United States disclosed that there was no such thing as a "normal" or "standard" family. An investigation made in five industrial towns of England, supplemented by facts from the British Census reports for seven other cities and towns, brought to light the fact that of 13,475 workers only 8.8 per cent had three dependent children. To be sure it was discovered that 9.9 per cent of the workers had *more* than three children; but on the other hand 27 per cent were found to be bachelors or widowers with no dependent children and nearly 25 per cent were married men with no children or no dependent child below fourteen.[1] Similarly an extended investigation made by a group of Parisian manufacturers in 1919 disclosed that the "standard family" was characteristic of only 6.4 per cent of the married workers, although these constituted 63 per cent of all workers.[2]

---

[1] See Rathbone, *The Disinherited Family: A Plea for the Endowment of the Family* (London, 1924), pp. 17–18.

[2] Douglas, Paul, *Wages and the Family*, University of Chicago Press, 1925, pp. 32–33.

In the United States an investigation of the size of workers' families was made by the United States Department of Labor which showed that of 11,156 such families only 17.7 per cent could be classified as "standard," *i.e.*, having three dependent children. Somewhat more than two thirds of the families had less than three children and 16 per cent had more than three.[1] Furthermore, all three of the investigations cited brought to light the fact that many workers' families lacked wives and mothers. It was the revelation of these conditions that led Eleanor Rathbone to declare that if every one of the 8,360,000 adult male workers in England were paid a "standard family" wage "provision would be made for 3 million phantom wives, and for over 16 million phantom children in the families containing less than three children, while on the other hand, in families containing more than three children, those in excess of that number, over $1\frac{1}{4}$ million in all, would still remain unprovided for." [2] A further quietus to discussions of a "normal family" wage system, which should be national in scope, was furnished by Australia. In 1919 the government appointed a commission to determine the basic wage necessary to support a family of five under the prevailing cost of living. The commission reported in 1920 that such a basic wage, allowing for "reasonable standards of comfort," would be £5 17s. per week in Sydney and £5 6s. 2d in Brisbane. Thereupon the prime minister called upon the statistician of the commonwealth, Mr. Knibbs, to render a judgment on the feasibility of paying such basic wages to every adult male employee. Mr. Knibbs' reply was far from encouraging. He declared that it was out of the question to pay this wage to every worker, since the entire produced wealth of the country, including the portion which went to employers in the shape of profit, if divided equally among employees would not yield the necessary weekly amount.[3] Thus the incipient movement in support of

---

[1] Douglas, *op. cit.*, pp. 34–37.
[2] Rathbone, *op. cit.*, p. 20.
[3] *Ibid.*, p. 178.

a "standard family" wage payable to every worker was definitely halted.

But this does not mean that no progress has been made in the direction of paying married workingmen according to the size of their families. Quite the contrary is true. France was the first country to demonstrate that the problem of paying workingmen according to the number of their dependent children may be solved in another way, without necessarily action by the government. This method consists in the collection of a fund by employers themselves from which allowances are paid to their married employees according to the number of children under a specified age. The movement was initiated in 1916 by M. Romanet, managing director of large iron works in Grenoble, France. Convinced by an investigation of the households of several employees that the financial situation in families with young children involved real hardship and deprivation, M. Romanet induced the owner of the industry to try the novel experiment of paying *family allowances* (*allocations familiales*) to workingmen with children under thirteen.

Soon the experiment aroused interest among employers and employees in other metal industries in the district and was finally adopted by the owners. To avoid discrimination against married men M. Romanet hit upon the plan of inducing employers to pool the cost of family allowances and form a general compensation fund (*caisse de compensation*). According to this scheme the expense of the family allowances is divided among all coöperating employers in proportion to the total number of their employees or according to their wages bill. Since May, 1918, when the enlarged plan was initiated, compensation funds have been set up in a wide variety of industries throughout France. At the end of the year 1924 there had been organized 159 compensation funds, comprising almost 10,000 business organizations, and paying 900 million francs, annually, to 3,000,000 wage-earners' families.[1]

[1] *Monthly Notes*, Jan. 1925. Family Endowment Society, 50 Romney St., London S. W. 1.

In Belgium and Austria systems of family allowances have likewise been set up since 1920. So far has the practice gone in Belgium that family allowances were made generally applicable to workers by a law enacted in August, 1930. Four types of funds are meeting the costs of these allowances for the support of children, *viz.*, funds created by royal decree, auxiliary public funds, funds initiated by employers and, finally, the national compensation fund. Allowances are paid for the support of children until they are fourteen years old, or until sixteen if they continue their education. So liberal is the law that it provides for foster children, illegitimates recognized by their parents and children in the care of relatives.[1] A continuous interchange of experiences has gone on between France and Belgium since the family allowance system was adopted in those countries. Therefore, the example of Belgium was followed in France when a national compulsory system of family allowances was provided for by a law of March 11, 1932. The workers benefiting under the act include manual and non-manual workers in industry, commerce, agriculture and the liberal professions. The amount of the allowance to be paid for each dependent child will be determined for each department of France by ministerial decree. The cost of the allowances will be met by levying payments upon every employer of manual or non-manual workers, these contributions to be pooled in a compensation fund.[2]

In New South Wales, Australia, where a basic wage system has been put into effect, allowances (called "endowments") are paid for every child *after the first one*, when the family income, *i.e.*, the combined wage of man, wife and employed children, falls below a stipulated amount. The basic wage is calculated for a man, wife and one child and was fixed by Parliament in December, 1929, at £4. 2s. 6d. for an adult male

[1] Georges Heyman, *La généralisation des allocations familiales en Belgique*, Louvain, 1931.

[2] For a summary of the French law see *Monthly Labor Review*, Washington, D. C., April, 1932, p. 796.

worker. If workers have more than one child the younger children are provided for according to the terms of a Family Endowment Act which came into effect in New South Wales in July, 1927. Endowments are paid *to the mother* at the rate of five shillings a week for each dependent child under fourteen, unless the total family income equals the amount of the basic wage plus the weekly endowment payments. Certain residential requirements must be met by mother and child and endowments are not paid to the children of foreigners unless they were born in New South Wales. The Family Endowment Act requires employers to make quarterly payments into a fund at the rate of 1 per cent of their total wages bill.[1]

In New Zealand, likewise, an act passed in 1926 provided for payments to workers' families of two shillings weekly for each child under fifteen *after the second child*. Payments are restricted to families whose income does not exceed £4 per week and are paid from the state treasury — not from an employers' contributory fund.

Legislation providing for state or nation-wide systems of child endowment reveals the growing concern of governments with the family and their recognition of the fact that, under the present industrial system, workers' families are called upon to endure real hardships, too often undermining the health, security and happiness of the family members.

LEGAL PROTECTION OF THE FAMILY

Since the middle of the nineteenth century nations have shown an increasing concern for the welfare of the family and a growing disposition to enact legislation safe-guarding marriage, protecting the rights of wives and children, penalizing family deserters and regulating divorce. In preceding chapters [2] the

---

[1] See article by George Anderson on "Wage Rates and the Standard of Living," in *Annals of the American Academy of Political and Social Science*, Nov. 1931, pp. 166–175.

[2] Chapters X and XI.

progress of this legislation in Great Britain and th
States has been briefly indicated.   Probably these tw
speaking countries, together with the British Comm
of Canada, New Zealand and Australia, have gone farther than
any other states in freeing married women from property
restrictions and from patriarchal power, while they have
granted to them larger rights in the guardianship of children[1]
and equal rights with respect to divorce.   In these and other
countries, also, laws have been enacted to protect children
against parental cruelty and exploitation, to guarantee
to them at least a minimum of education, of vocational
guidance, of playground space and of protection from vice
and crime.

Revision of Marriage Laws in the United States. — Marriage
laws have been progressively revised in this country with the
object of eliminating hasty and unwise marriages.   The age at
which young people may marry without parental consent has
been raised in many states.   For example, in at least eleven
states both the man and the woman must be twenty-one years
of age before they may marry without consent of parent or
guardian.   On the other hand, in thirty-seven states girls of
eighteen may marry without parental consent; and boys in
four states may marry at the same age without consent.
Furthermore, in ten states of the Union, incredible as it may
seem, children may marry at the common-law ages of twelve
for girls and fourteen for boys, provided the consent of parents
or guardian is secured.   Clearly much remains to be done by
way of legislation to prevent the marriage of immature young
persons with or without parental consent.   Education of public
opinion against too youthful marriages is much needed.   At
present the American public lends little active support to legal
restrictions upon marriage.

This failure of the public to initiate and support reforms
in marriage laws is shown by the fact that twenty-four states
still permit so-called "common-law marriages" in which the

[1] Entire equality of rights in many — not all — American states.

parties take each other for husband and wife without witnesses or written record.[1] Occasionally the unhappy consequences of such marriages are blazoned forth in the public press, where one may read of the appeals of "common-law widows" to the courts to be awarded a portion of the estate of their deceased partners who had neglected to provide for them.

A forward step in marriage legislation has been taken by several American states which require that an interval of five days (usually) intervene between application for the marriage license and its grant. Such a requirement has no doubt prevented many a hasty and ill-advised marriage but the great majority of states are slow to take action in this matter. Again, at least eleven states attempt to protect the parties to a marriage by requiring applicants to secure a health certificate before the license is issued. In nine other states there is some legal provision against the marriage of the venereally diseased.[2] But these health safeguards are often either inadequate or carelessly carried out. The cost in time and money of a searching examination to determine the existence of venereal disease is so considerable that many physicians grant the certificate to a person of modest means after a cursory examination. In other instances, where laws forbid the marriage of epileptics and the feeble-minded, the license clerk is permitted to accept the mere statement of the applicants that they are free of these defects. In New York State each of the applicants for a marriage license must make an affidavit that he (or she) has not to his knowledge been infected with a venereal disease; or, if so infected within five years, that tests have shown that he is now free of it. No certificate of a physician is required — only the statement. Such enforcement of futile laws designed to protect the parties to a marriage is a travesty. No wonder a student of marriage legislation in this country has

[1] Under a bill signed by Governor Lehman, May 2, 1933, New York State will not recognize common-law marriages contracted in the future.

[2] *Survey of the Legal Status of Women in the Forty-Eight States*, National League of Women Voters, 1930.

recently written: "In other words candidates establish their own qualifications for marriage." [1]

Divorce Legislation. — In most modern nations marriage is ideally conceived as a lifelong union entered into by mutual choice and sustained by affection and comradeship. Unfortunately, however, marriages do break up, not only for the legal causes of desertion, cruelty, adultery, etc., but because of deep-seated incompatibilities that finally destroy mutual affection and harmonious companionship. Here the law steps in. Not only does it establish the legal procedure through which a dissolution of the marriage may be secured but it sets up the valid grounds on which the divorce may be granted. Although these legal causes may seem generous indeed [2] in the eyes of peoples living under codes that deny divorce for any reason save adultery, *e.g.*, Great Britain, or refuse it for any cause whatever, as certain Catholic countries, yet safeguards have been thrown around divorce procedure in recent decades which are designed in part to prevent hasty or one-sided divorce. For example, some state codes have lengthened the period of residence required before action for divorce may be instituted if the libellant is not a citizen of the state. Again more careful provision has been made for giving notice to the defendant of the divorce action and protecting his (or her) interests by the appointment of counsel if he does not contest the suit. And be it remembered that a high proportion of divorce cases are not contested.

Striking exceptions to the trend toward lengthening the residence period for non-citizens of a state before divorce proceedings may be instituted are furnished by the states of Arkansas, Idaho and Nevada. The last-named commonwealth, which long had a residence requirement of six months, reduced the period in 1927 to three months in the hope of

---

[1] On this whole subject see Fred S. Hall, "Marriage and the Law," in *Annals of the American Academy of Political and Social Science*, Vol. 160, March, 1932, pp. 110–115.

[2] The state of New Hampshire has eleven legal grounds for divorce.

attracting more divorce "business" to the state. In 1931 Arkansas reduced her residence period to three months and Idaho followed suit the next month. Not to be outdone Nevada promptly responded by lowering her residence requirement to six weeks. In consequence, this state has continued to be the Mecca of unhappily married couples whose longing for release it has successfully commercialized. But, in the opinion of Lichtenberger,[1] this competition for revenue from divorce actions will not spread to other states since it does not meet with popular approval.

Because of the confusion caused by the multiplicity of divorce laws in the forty-eight states, especially since a divorce obtained in one state is not necessarily valid in another, movements in behalf of a uniform nation-wide divorce code were initiated early in the twentieth century. These bore fruit in the drawing up of a uniform law prepared by a committee of the Congress of Governors which met in Washington in 1906. This law was later adopted by the Congress and presented to the legislatures of the several states. But only three states have ever placed the law on their statute books. Apparently public opinion is either indifferent to such legislation or is doubtful of its value. Interest in the law flagged until the General Federation of Women's Clubs took up the matter and attempted to secure a uniform divorce law by means of an amendment to the Federal Constitution, giving power to the Congress to frame uniform marriage and divorce laws for the states of the Union. In 1923 Senator Capper introduced a Uniform Divorce Bill in Congress, preceded by the introduction of a joint resolution proposing a Constitutional amendment as outlined above. But despite the vigorous efforts of the sponsors of the measure it failed of passage. The opponents of the bill pointed out that its provisions encroached upon the powers definitely conferred upon the states by the framers of the Constitution; that a uniform law, if at all liberal, would

[1] See his contribution on "Divorce Legislation" to the *Annals of the American Academy of Political and Social Science*, March, 1932, pp. 116-123.

arouse bitter opposition in states allowing only one or two causes for divorce or none at all, as in the case of South Carolina. Perhaps the most searching criticism of a uniform law was made by Elizabeth Cady Stanton in 1894 when she pointed out that such a law would stifle experimentation in the various states in better forms of divorce legislation.

Among all socially-minded people who desire the well-being of both the individual and society the mounting tide of divorce is a matter of serious concern and regret. But the method of stemming this tide is another question and a difficult one. So long as marriages rest on free consent, not on social and legal coercion, so long as men and women continue to believe that a true marriage is grounded in mutual love and respect, not on force, so long will divorces continue to mount. It has been pointed out over and over again that divorce is a symptom of profound maladjustment and unhappiness within marriage — that the marriage in any spiritual sense has already been destroyed before the divorce is sought. Why not focus our attention on the alleviation of the social conditions that make happy marriages difficult of achievement? Why not, above all, give young people all the enlightenment that psychology, mental hygiene and the biological sciences can furnish to help them to form standards of successful marriage and to recognize many of the obstacles to the realization of those standards? To attack the effect and not the causes of a social evil is unintelligent. Divorces will not be lessened much nor will the misery they cause be alleviated by restrictive legislation. But much may be done by righting economic conditions reacting harmfully on the family; even more by educating youth to appreciate the enhancement of life that comes through a happy marriage, and to understand the ways in which it may be lost.

EDUCATIONAL AID TO THE FAMILY

In the past when the family conformed to a fixed pattern, consistent with the social conditions and governing ideas of a relatively unchanging society, the need for educational aid from organizations outside the home was not felt. To be sure the church gave instructions from time to time about the upbringing of youth in piety and morals, but that was the extent of the educational assistance rendered the family with regard to its specific tasks. But in these years of bewilderingly swift social change, when well-nigh every institution of society is undergoing alteration and every standard and custom of life is being sharply challenged in the light of fresh knowledge, the need of the family for educational guidance has been made abundantly manifest.

The social response to this need has been gradual but varied. In the case of the growing child in the home parents are being enlightened concerning methods of child guidance free from the harsh authoritarianism of the past. Their eyes are being opened to the importance of sex education, of the guidance of the boy and girl in making moral choices and reflecting on the consequences of acting in this way or that, of developing sound attitudes toward economic life — the sources and use of money. The family will always be the most significant educational institution of society, for here are shaped the child's ruling ideas, habits, attitudes toward others and toward current social practices that may (and do) govern the whole of life. In the home, under wise or unwise parents, the child forms his first conceptions of the meaning of marriage and the relationships of family members to each other and to social groups outside.

Nevertheless family education, good or bad, needs to be supplemented by the school. Therefore, in the last few decades schools have added to their traditional curriculum courses in household economy. The course of study is also being constantly enriched by courses in child psychology and training, definitely directed toward parenthood. Likewise sociological subject-matter, treating of the historical evolution of the family and its indispensable functions in social life, is more and more being included in the curricula of high schools and colleges. Dr. Leona Vincent of the Merrill-Palmer nursery school reports that in 1929 there were classes in pre-parental education "in hundreds of schools ranging from the sixth grade through work of graduate rank in colleges and universities in almost every state in the Union and in several territories."[1] For example, South Bend, Indiana, is offering ninth-grade students a course "on the baby, preschool child, adolescent child and homemaker." Child-care courses, emphasizing chiefly as yet the physical care and nutrition of children, are being widely introduced in the upper grades of elementary schools. Such a course, prepared by the Minnesota State Board of Health, is used in the seventh grade of some schools. Although it stresses the physical care of the child from infancy to school age, it includes material on habit and character training and the opportunities afforded by the family, the community and the state for promoting child welfare. In some junior high schools, as in New York City, a large hospital doll or a real baby is used for demonstration purposes in the child care courses. In junior high schools in Los Angeles and Oakland, the home economics and child care courses are kept in close touch with the day nurseries in these cities and the students receive practical training and experience in preparing food for the children, caring for their needs and providing recreation for them.[2]

On the college level progress is somewhat slower, although western colleges and universities have been far more hospitable to preparental education than have eastern institutions. A study made in 1927–1928 of the introduction of child care courses in universities and colleges throughout the country disclosed that 93 per cent of the land-grant colleges for white students offered such courses. In addition, 36 per cent of academic colleges and universities and 31 per cent of teachers' colleges and normal schools included child development as part of their home economics offerings. Almost one half of the

---

[1] "Preschool and Parental Education," *Twenty-Eighth Year Book of the National Society for the Study of Education*, 1929, p. 404.

[2] *Ibid.*, pp. 373–385.

courses were definitely designed to train for future parent-hood.[1]

This is a hopeful beginning. Yet it is well to ask ourselves whether courses offered girls (and sometimes boys) between twelve and eighteen years of age will make a sufficiently deep impression and will be soundly scientific enough to be of great service to young persons marrying from six to ten or more years after the subjects have been studied. In a less degree the same question may be asked of college courses. It would seem that the study of family problems by maturer persons before or after marriage, when questions of family relationships, home-management and child nurture are vital and immediate, would have far greater value and practical use than elementary or high school courses can afford. This is not to deny that the preparental courses in elementary and high schools are of worth but to raise the question of *how much* validity and practical value they retain after a considerable period of years.

A wide diversity of educational agencies is tackling the question at the adult end and is giving serious consideration to the needs of young couples who are facing the task of founding stable and happy homes and of educating their young in a society wherein all the old landmarks are disappearing. It has been said that next to social case workers *Protestant ministers* probably receive more calls for help on marriage and family problems than does any other professional group. And within the last few years the churches have responded to the call. Theological schools are offering courses to ministers-in-training designed to inform them about the marital difficulties and family troubles that will probably be brought to their attention in their pastoral work. In some churches clinics have been opened, where the minister or his assistant, together with a few outside available consultants, advise members of their congregations about their domestic problems. In some cases an entire staff, consisting not only of clergymen but also of a full

[1] "Preschool and Parental Education," *Twenty-Eighth Year Book of the National Society for the Study of Education*, 1929, pp. 385-386.

time psychiatric social worker and a large group of experienced consultants, attempt to meet the appeals for help that are constantly coming to them.

Pressure has for years been brought to bear on clergymen to give some preparation for marriage to the young people whom they unite in matrimony. Recently six large Protestant denominations have appointed commissions of investigation on "marriage and divorce" or "marriage and the family" and the Federal Council of the Churches of Christ in America has appointed a "Commission on the Church and Social Service." These commissions have all adopted resolutions to the effect that ministers should be trained to give preparation for marriage and family life to the young persons whom they join in marriage. The General Convention of the Protestant Episcopal Church was the first to respond to these recommendations by adopting a canon in 1931 making it obligatory on the clergy to give instruction to young couples before the wedding ceremony regarding the nature and responsibilities of "holy matrimony." Booklets of instruction are being prepared by church social service departments to help clergymen carry out the recommendations of church conventions and commissions. Some Protestant ministers have become truly wise through experience and have learned how to be most helpful to the couples whom they interview before marriage.

Since 1923 *birth control clinics* have been opened in many states. These agencies at first confined their efforts to giving contraceptive information. Recently, however, their experience of the physical and mental suffering caused married pairs by ignorance of sex hygiene and the nature of marriage has impelled them to expand their instruction to include these subjects. Guidance in marital relationships will probably play an increasingly important part in the services of birth control clinics.[1]

---

[1] See Ralph Bridgman's valuable article on "Guidance for Marriage and Family Life" in *Annals of the American Academy of Political and Social Science*, March, 1932, pp. 144–164.

Valuable guidance in marriage problems is increasingly being afforded by *courts of domestic relations* and by *universities*, through specialists in psychology and psychiatry, family sociology and home economics. Organized guidance services are already offered in a few universities. Passing over these educational opportunities, mention should be made of the significant new tendency toward the establishment of independent *Family Consultation Bureaus*. Public advisory boards for married and betrothed people have been operating in Germany since the first one was established in Dresden in 1911. Rather unfortunately, however, the physicians on these boards give attention chiefly to the biological and hygienic aspects of marriage, ignoring psychological, financial and domestic questions which may be quite as potent factors in destroying marital happiness. More inclusive in the services it renders is the Institute of Family Relations opened in Los Angeles in February, 1930, after two years of preparatory investigation. The staff of the Institute comprises a physician and a social worker, together with consultants representing psychiatry, psychology, social work, religion and many branches of home economics, such as nutrition and budget-making.

The first 1000 cases visiting the Institute came for the following reasons : (1) to secure educational material (35 per cent) ; (2) to seek advice about family maladjustment (25 per cent) ; for premarital information (7 per cent) ; for advice about child welfare (9 per cent) ; for guidance in solving sex problems (7 per cent) ; for help with questions of heredity (5 per cent) ; for legal advice (1 per cent) ; miscellaneous questions (1 per cent). It will be seen that the needs of the modern family, if this group be typical, extend far beyond the requirement of contraceptive information and medical advice.

On the theory that a large number of marital mistakes and failures can be prevented by the right kind of advice and information, a group of agencies in Detroit, assisted by the American Social Hygiene Association, opened the Detroit

Family Relations Bureau early in 1933. Community backing has been generously assured. The services of the Bureau's skilled consultant — a physician — have been requested by neighboring universities and schools and even by the citizens of outlying towns. The topics on which the consultant has most frequently been asked to give enlightenment are "Preparation for Marriage," "Marital Adjustments" and "Psychology of Marriage." The cases that have sought individual advice ranged in age from twelve years to fifty and seemed in the judgment of the consultant "vitally in need of help." Although a few persons "were free from any traceable sex difficulty, . . . the majority presented it as the underlying problem." [1] A similar conclusion has been reached by the staff of the Institute of Family Relations in Los Angeles. Its director, Dr. Paul Popenoe, writes: "The axiom that a sexual maladjustment underlies every instance of marital disharmony has proved approximately true in our own experience." [2] Yet in the face of this real need, relatively few high schools and colleges have worked out carefully planned and integrated programs of sex education.

In addition to the educational services rendered by churches, public schools, universities and family consultation centers, important assistance has been given parents through the study programs arranged by the *parent education movement*. Sixty-one member agencies in this field are coördinated in the National Council of Parent Education. These organizations have done yeoman service in giving parents a sounder understanding of the physical care of children, of child psychology, of behavior problems and of the moral and social guidance of the young. Since 1924 the parent education movement has further concerned itself with research in child development. The interest of the parent education group in a sounder under-

---

[1] Edith Hale Swift, M.D., "Building a Family Consultation Service," *Journal of Social Hygiene*, October, 1933, pp. 367–374.

[2] Paul Popenoe, "A Family Consultation Service," *Journal of Social Hygiene*, June, 1931, p. 313.

standing of child psychology and better methods of child guidance has been one important factor in the founding of the *nursery school.* Not only do the most progressive of these schools assist small toddlers to form hygienic and social habits but they make well-planned efforts to educate parents better to understand the natures and needs of their offspring.

Any consideration, however brief, of the educational assistance given to the modern family would be manifestly incomplete without reference to the significant contributions made by *mental hygiene and psychiatry* to the understanding of human personality — child and adult. These relatively new sciences have shed a flood of revealing light on hitherto dark corners of human nature and have rendered invaluable aid in understanding the sources of anti-social attitudes and conduct in both children and their parents.

SOCIAL AGENCIES SERVING THE FAMILY

The attempt to distinguish with any definiteness between educational and social agencies ministering to family needs is certain to meet with difficulties. Many social organizations include educational services and all educational institutions are agencies of society. Yet if the primary purpose of the two types of organization be accepted as the criterion for classification it may be admitted that a distinction exists between them.

Of great importance in rendering aid to underprivileged families are those social agencies, bearing many names, that are primarily devoted to *social case work* with families. Although these organizations are frequently called upon to give relief to needy households they have recently become mainly concerned with effecting better adjustments of the family members to each other and to social conditions. About the year 1918 a federation of 240 family welfare agencies in different parts of the country was effected under the title of The Family Welfare Association of America. It has been estimated that in 1932 nearly a million families with over four million members were being assisted by welfare associations to make more stable and satisfying adjustments to the hard economic and social conditions surrounding them.[1] The trained professional caseworker today does not tell families what they must do if they wish to receive assistance. Rather, by interviews, she collects and analyzes all the data she can secure about the family difficulties, studies these facts, makes a diagnosis of the case and works out flexible methods of treatment which are wisely revised from time to time. ' These methods involve bringing new and constructive influences into the lives of the family members and eliminating destructive factors that are breaking down morale. By changing environmental conditions, by helping families to make the most of all their resources, by creating in family members a wholesome confidence in themselves, the professional case-worker strives to bring about a satisfactory and permanent adjustment of the family to life. In family case work as now carried on, individual reëducation and guidance play an important rôle and respect for personal freedom and for the individuality of each member of the household has tended to displace the earlier more impersonal executive methods.[2]

The close acquaintance which family case work agencies have perforce made with marital problems and personality maladjustments has impelled them to include guidance in marriage and family relationships in their programs of work. Increasingly, therefore, case-workers are being required to study the social sciences and it is probable that in course of time they will be expected to have some knowledge of mental hygiene, if not of psychiatry. The field of their educational influence, in bringing about family rehabilitation, will unquestionably broaden in the years to come.

[1] See Joanna Colcord, "Remedial Agencies Dealing with the American Family," *Annals of the American Academy of Political and Social Science*, March, 1932, p. 129.
[2] See Bridgman, "Guidance for Marriage and Family Life," *Annals of the American Academy of Political and Social Science*, March, 1932, pp. 145–146.

Among the social agencies extending a helping hand to bewildered parents are the *child guidance clinics*. To these clinics are brought children who present serious behavior problems quite beyond the power of father and mother to solve unaided. The clinic is usually directed by a psychiatrist who is aided by psychologists and psychiatric social workers. In making a study of each child behavior case the experts find it necessary to extend their examinations into the home. Frequently, the child's disturbing conduct is discovered to have its source in parental attitudes and behavior. So generally true is this that psychiatrists do not hesitate to say that most child behavior difficulties are in reality parent behavior problems. Despite the fact that the child guidance clinic represents a relatively new remedial agency, so useful has it proved in aiding parents to understand both their children and themselves better that in 1932 a directory published by the Commonwealth Fund listed nearly seven hundred clinics established throughout the country.

Another social organization whose work has indirectly assisted the family is the *National Recreation Association*. A realization of the importance of play activities in the lives of children has led this Association to crusade for the opening of adequate playground facilities in our crowded, noisy, smoke-infested cities. Under a new Park Commissioner New York City has embarked upon an enthusiastic program for providing attractive, well-equipped municipal play grounds for children mainly in the slum areas of the city. Not only does the Association work for out-door play space for children but it is encouraging parents to provide adequate space and facilities for play at home. Better still it is calling the attention of parents to the importance of playing with their children — a means of strengthening affection and lowering age-barriers between the two generations — and is providing attractive recreation programs for adults and children in their own homes. The family hearth and the big family parlor table with its lamp, around which parents and children used to gather in the evening, may have gone forever, but surely that need not mean that the home is reduced merely to a place for sleeping and eating — a jumping-off point into a whirl of social activities outside.

Protective Agencies Serving Children. — Among the many organizations formed to throw safeguards around children two alone may be considered very briefly here. Some families have deteriorated to the point where children are subjected by their own parents to gross neglect and abuse. When this occurs the *Society for the Prevention of Cruelty to Children* steps in and removes the child from his home to an institution or foster home where he will receive kindly treatment and care. Occasionally, also, families cannot be held together. For various reasons the members of the family must be separated, temporarily or perhaps permanently. In such instances a *child-placing agency* endeavors to provide for the children in a boarding home or a foster home, with a view to their future adoption. Very generally, however, the belief is coming to prevail that the child's own family is much the best place for him to be. Therefore, these agencies try in every way to rebuild the broken family and restore the common life of its members. An interesting trend in some advanced states is in the direction of the assumption by the *state government* of all responsibility for neglected, dependent or delinquent children. Possibly in the future the work of private agencies of child care and protection will be taken entirely over by the American states.

SUMMARY

Space has prevented any but a superficial survey of the many ways in which governments and society, through a multiplicity of organizations, are seeking to increase the stability and well-being of the family. There is ample evidence of a deepening general appreciation of the supreme importance of the services rendered by the family to social life. Together with this appreciation there is developing a better understanding of the serious handicaps under which marriage and family life are carried on in present-day society. These handicaps may be classified as economic, legal, social and educational. It is highly encouraging to students of the family to perceive the breaking down of the old let-alone policy toward the family on the part of organized society and the substitution of a policy of active helpfulness. If basic economic reforms and educational changes are carried forward in an enlightened and humane spirit, the family in the modern state may again become, as in the past, a unified and stable institution. Better than that, it may be the well-spring and nursery of the deepest human joys and satisfactions.

SELECTED READINGS

Abbott, Grace. " The Federal Government in Relation to Maternity and Infancy," *Annals of the American Academy of Political and Social Science,* Sept. 1930, pp. 92–101.

Annals of the American Academy of Political and Social Science. Contributions on " The Modern American Family," Vol. 160, March, 1932. Hall, Fred S., " Marriage and the Law," pp. 110–115. Lichtenberger, J. P., " Divorce Legislation," pp. 116–123. Colcord, Joanna C., "Remedial Agencies Dealing with the American Family," pp. 124–134. Bridgman, Ralph P., " Guidance for Marriage and Family Life," pp. 144–164. Gruenberg, Sidonie M. and Gruenberg, Benjamin C., " Education of Children for Family Life," pp. 205–215. Groves, E. R, " Parent Education," pp. 216–222.

Colcord, Joanna. " Unemployment Insurance in Great Britain," *The Family,* Vol. XII, pp. 85–91.

Douglas, Paul H., *Wages and the Family,* University of Chicago Press, 1925, Chs. II, III.

Goodsell, Willystine. *Problems of the Family,* N. Y., Century Co., 1928, Chs. XI, XII, XXIII, XXIV.

Groves, Ernest R. *The American Family,* Chicago and Phila., Lippincott, 1934. Part IV.

Hall, Fred S. *Medical Certification for Marriage,* N. Y., Russell Sage Foundation, 1925.

Kyrk, Hazel. *Economic Problems of the Family,* N. Y., Harper and Bros., 1933, Ch. XV.

Lichtenberger, J. P. *Divorce, A Social Interpretation,* New York and London, McGraw-Hill Book Co., 1931, Chs. VII, VIII.

Loeb, Sophie I. *Everyman's Child,* N. Y., Century Co., 1920, Chs. I–VIII.

May, Goeffrey. *Marriage Laws and Decisions in the United States,* N. Y., Russell Sage Foundation, 1929.

McCarthy, D. " The Nursery School and the Social Development of the Child," *Journal of Home Economics,* Vol. XXV, pp. 13–18.

National Society for the Scientific Study of Education. Twenty-Eighth Yearbook, 1929, " Day Nurseries," Ch. V., " Maternity and Infant Welfare Centers," Ch. VI.

Popenoe, Paul. " A Family Consultation Service," *Journal of Social Hygiene,* Vol. XVII, No. 6, June, 1931, pp. 309–322.

——. " College Training, Marriage and Parenthood," *Journal of Home Economics,* Vol. XXII, pp. 169–178.

Rathbone, Eleanor. *The Disinherited Family,* London, Edward Arnold and Co., 1924, Ch. VI.

Richmond, Mary, and Hall, F. S. *Marriage and the State,* N. Y., Russell Sage Foundation, 1929.

Spencer, Anna G. *The Family and Its Members,* Phila. and London, Lippincott, 1923, Chs. VIII, XII–XV.

United States Department of Labor, Children's Bureau, Washington, D. C. Harris, H. J., " Maternity Systems in Certain Foreign Countries," Publication No. 57, 1919.

——. Thompson, Laura A., " Laws Relating to Mothers' Pensions in United States, Canada, Denmark and New Zealand," Publication No. 63, 1919.

——. " The Promotion of the Welfare and Hygiene of Maternity and Infancy," Bureau Publication No. 194, 1929.

——. " Mothers' Aid, 1931," Publication No. 220, 1933.

White House Conference on Child Health and Protection. *Education for Home and Family Life,* New York, The Century Co., 1932.

——. *Parent Education, Types, Content, Method,* N. Y., Century Co., 1932.

——. *Nursery Education,* N. Y., Century Co., 1931.

——. *Social Hygiene in Schools,* N. Y., Century Co., 1932.

——. *The Handicapped,* N. Y., Century Co., 1932.

——. *Dependent and Neglected Children,* N. Y., D. Appleton-Century Co., 1933.

INDEX

Maternity insurance, in European countries, 534–5.
Mather, Cotton, mortality among children of, 412; on discipline of children, 414.
Matriarchate, described, 14–15.
Matrilocal residence, 13–14.
Matrimonial Causes Act, 1857, 446–48.
Matrimonial Causes Act, 1878, 448–49.
Matrimonial Causes Act, 1923, 451–53.
Matrimonium justum, 121–22; ceremonial rites of, 123–25.
Matrimonium non justum, 121–22; practically concubinage, 125.
Mattan, gifts to Hebrew bride, 67.
Matthew, Gospel of, on divorce, 71, 180.
Mead, Margaret, on status of primitive women, 28; on infanticide, 38; on status of primitive children, 39; on primitive education, 47.
Medea, Euripides, on women, 95–96.
Medici, Carlo de', son of father's mistress, 283.
Medici, Cosimo de', mistress of, 283.
Medici, Lorenzo de', letter of, to disappointed father, 293.
Medicine, in Middle Ages, 232–33; English housewife and, 341.
Medford, Mass., home lots to new husbands in, 369.
Men: *see* Father; Husband.
Menander, on lives of Greek women, 87.
Menstruation, primitive fear of, 29; theory of moon as cause of, 40.
Mental hygiene and psychiatry, as aids to understanding human personality, 558.
Messiah, expectation of, adds sanctity to marriage, 61.
Metellus Macedonicus, on marriage, 141.
Metronymic system, 12–15; relative status of father and mother under, 25–27; divorce under, 32; Hebrew, 54; among prehistoric Greeks, 82; among Teutons.
Michigan, property rights of women in, 471; University of, coeducational, 468.
Middle Ages, family in, 189–247; changes during, 246–7; explanation of attitude toward women in, 257.
Midwives, in Middle Ages, 219; during Renaissance, 292–93; in colonial America, 412.
Milton, John, on divorce, 445.
Minimum wage laws, 533.
Minnesota, decrease in divorce rate in, 484.
Minnesota State Board of Health, course on child care and nutrition, 553.
Mishna, division of Talmud, 51.
Mississippi, legal age of marriage in, 475; decreased divorce rate in, 484.
Misson, M., on incognito marriages, 334–35; on banns, 335–36.
Missouri, divorce in, 477, 478.
"Mixed marriages," 268.

Mohar, Hebrew purchase price, 67.
Moloch, human sacrifices to, 55.
Monandry, among primitive peoples, 21 and *n. See also* Monogamy.
Monogamy, and theories of pair marriage, 7–9; described, 21; a necessity for majority of Hebrews, 60; disintegration of modern family as doom of, 482; arguments for and against, 527–30.
Montana, property rights of women in, 471.
Montefeltro, Federico di, built Urbino, 286.
Moody, Deborah, as landowner, 362–63.
Moral training, of savage children, 44–46; Hebrew, 77–78; Greek, 108, 109; Roman, 130–32, 151–52; in Middle Ages, 221; during Renaissance, 295–99; in colonial America, 414–16; under factory system, 432.
More, Hannah, on ideal womanhood, 324; on French Revolution, 325.
More, Sir Thomas, childhood of, 243; love of, for wife, 280.
Morning-gift, custom of, described, 201; as wife's property in Middle Ages, 207, 208, 209, 210; changed to, "dower," 225.
Mosaic law, history and records, 51; on child sacrifice, 55; on obedience of children, 55; on ceremonial observances, 56; forbids marriage with brother's wife, 58; recognizes polygyny, 59; on rights of concubines, 59; on valid marriages, 62–63; on betrothal and marriage, 64; on divorce, 70; on circumcision, 77; studied in Jewish schools, 78; Puritan government derived from, 367.
Moses, instructions to, concerning inheritance, 57.
Moses, law of: *see* Mosaic law.
Mother, under metronymic system, 12–15, 25–27; primitive attitude toward functions of, 29; part of, in child training, 45; rights of Hebrew, in divorce, 74; and child training, 77; Greek, training of children, 108, 109; status of, 129–30; attitude toward children of, in Imperial Rome, 150–51; guardianship of children in Christian Rome, 185; Anglo-Saxon, had care of children at father's death, 193; during Renaissance, care of infants by, 294; training of children by, 295–96; in seventeenth and eighteenth century England, no rights of guardianship of child, 311; guardianship rights in nineteenth century, 442–44; increased employment of, 496, 498–500. *See also* Wife.
Mother-name kinship system: *see* Metronymic system.
Mothers' pensions and mothers' aid, in the United States, 537–40; in Great Britain, 540–41; in Canada, Denmark, New Zealand, 540; in Australia, 541.